The Oxford Handbook of
Economic Geography

The Oxford Handbook of

Economic Geography

edited by

Gordon L. Clark, Maryann P. Feldman, and Meric S. Gertler

with the assistance of Kate Williams

UNIVERSITY PRESS

OXFORD
UNIVERSITY PRESS

Great Clarendon Street, Oxford OX2 6DP
OUP is a department of the University of Oxford and furthers the University's aim of excellence in research, scholarship, and education by publishing worldwide in

Oxford New York
Athens Auckland Bangkok Bogotá Buenos Aires
Calcutta Cape Town Chennai Dar es Salaam Delhi Florence Hong Kong
Istanbul Karachi Kuala Lumpur Madrid Melbourne Mexico City Mumbai
Nairobi Paris São Paulo Shanghai Singapore Taipei Tokyo Toronto Warsaw

and associated companies in Berlin Ibadan

Oxford is a trade mark of Oxford University Press

Published in the United States
by Oxford University Press Inc., New York

First published 2000

British Library Cataloguing in Publication Data
Data available

Library of Congress Cataloging in Publication Data
The Oxford handbook of economic geography / edited by Gordon L. Clark, Maryann P. Feldman, and Meric S. Gertler ; with the assistance of Kate Williams.
p. cm.
Includes bibliographical references and index.
1. Economic geography. I. Clark, Gordon L. II. Feldman, Maryann P. III. Gertler, Meric S.

HF1025 .O94 2000 300.9—dc21 00-031353

ISBN 0-19-823410-4

Typeset by Best-set Typesetter Ltd., Hong Kong
Printed in Great Britain by Biddles Ltd.,
Guildford & King's Lynn

For

Noel, Merran, and Lauren
Richard M. Singer
Anita and Len

Editorial Note

Style and spelling throughout the *Handbook* reflect the natural idiom of the international team of contributors. However, English English has been employed in the index.

Preface

Economic geography is a sub-discipline of geography and a growing field of study in economics. It is concerned with the spatial configuration of firms, industries, and nations within the emerging global economy in all its manifestations. Historically, economic geography was preoccupied with the spacing and hierarchical order of settlements, the optimal location for manufacturing and retail activities, and the geographical structure of trade and communication. In this respect, economic geography was firmly anchored in location theory and the methods and techniques of optimization associated with mainstream economic theory. These themes persist in the literature. But they have been overtaken by scholars who have sought to extend the scope and significance of economic geography by reference to some of the most important issues in contemporary economic life including globalization, the growth and decline of regions, innovation, and the restructuring of economic systems.

In economics, economic geography has been heavily influenced by international trade theory. The key ingredients in its revival in economics have included agglomeration economies, increasing returns, and imperfect competition. However, no single unifying theory or approach yet commands the centre of economic geography. There are significant differences between geographers and economists just as there are significant differences amongst geographers and economists. The field is alive with new research and debate about the proper scope and prospects for economic geography. This debate has been joined recently by historians, political scientists, and business theorists from around the world. Economic geography has come to be seen both as a crucial area of innovation in the social sciences and an essential reference point in the debate about the processes of global economic change, innovation, finance, and the future of whole cities and regions over the coming century.

The Oxford Handbook of Economic Geography aims (1) to capture the scope of the field, and its main threads and arguments. Our ambition is (2) to be a key interdisciplinary reference source for this burgeoning field, as well as (3) contributing to the ongoing evolution of the field. In a nutshell, we hope the *Handbook* will (4) serve to define the field in much the same way other handbooks have done for their fields, intersecting with economics, sociology, and institutional and organizational research. The team of editors and contributors combine a wide scope of research strengths and experience internationally recognized in geography and economics as well as in urban studies and planning, business studies, and public policy.

This project is informed by a commitment to three basic building blocks or intellectual pillars. These building blocks are widely shared by geographers and economists though not always articulated or agreed and often contested and disputed. The first pillar is a commitment to recognizing *the diversity of economic life*, including the significance of gender, race, and spatial differentiation in market economies. For many years, economic geographers sought to generalize their findings by assuming regions (or other spatial units of economic analysis) were much the same. They tended to ignore the heterogeneity of places and peoples in a search for universal principles. In recent years, the challenge has been to develop analytical tools that are at once sensitive to differentiation and amenable to a more general understanding of the evolution of the economic landscape. For some analysts, difference and the heterogeneity of the economic landscape demand close, detailed analyses of the particular attributes of certain firms, regions, and industries. For others, particularity has to be balanced against larger economic forces operating at higher spatial scales: there is a tension between the local and the global and between fine-grained case studies and stylized facts.

A second pillar is a commitment to *understanding the processes of change in and across the economic landscape*. Traditional models of location, focused upon the logic of settlement patterns and the structure of trade, assumed a given economic landscape in the context of stable, predictable economic forces. Clearly, economic systems are now subject to global shifts and changes in competitive conditions affecting both the place of a region in the larger economic system and the viability of local systems of production. Of course, there has been debate about the extent of penetration of nations' economic systems by economic forces operating at a number of scales. Understanding the place of London in the world economy is different from understanding the place of Detroit in the North American economy. The challenge is to be sensitive to the interaction between spatial scale and competitiveness in the context of accelerating rates of economic change.

The third pillar is a commitment to understanding the *geographical and institutional organization of economic activity* given marked differences in regions' cultures, institutions, and regulations. Past theories of location have treated the firm, the community, even whole regions and nations as undifferentiated 'black boxes'. While entirely appropriate if the goal is theoretical simplicity, recent research in economic geography across the disciplines aims to make a connection between the theory of the firm (for instance) and its cultural, social, geographical, and institutional contexts. Understanding the different rates of adoption of technology requires not only an appreciation of the nature of the firm, but also the particularities of its locational context, given striking differences between regions with respect to labour, industrial relations, and investment incentives. These building blocks or pillars inform the overall structure of the book and individual chapters. Not all contributors necessarily agree with our points of reference. We do think, however, that each pillar captures a crucial theme evident in the contemporary research in economic geography.

Our intention is to convey a strong sense of the current *debates and points of contention* surrounding each of the topics covered in the book, and to show how these debates have evolved as part of a history of ideas within the field of economic geography. Hence, we asked each author to highlight the most significant competing and complementary perspectives evident within their field of interest. In so doing, our aim is to take the reader right to the frontier of contemporary research, while making clear the connections with past scholarship within and without the disciplines of economics and geography. Rather than simply survey the literature, we also prompted our contributors to make their own arguments, and raise the issues they think vital to the field. We asked contributors to consider the following questions.

1. **What are the questions?** What are the major problems or issues motivating research in this particular field? What is the overriding objective of intellectual endeavour by economic geographers? How does it differ from the approach(es) to the same question as pursued by other social scientists?

2. **How did we get there?** What is the history of ideas in this field? How has intellectual thought evolved? Who have been the most influential thinkers? How have their work, and the intellectual discourse to which they have contributed, shaped this evolution? The intent here is not to provide an exhaustive review so much as a synoptic vision of the field as it has developed in recent times.

3. **What are the contemporary debates?** What are the major competing perspectives on each of the central questions in this field? What are the most significant gaps or 'blind spots'? How is the field likely to develop in the near future, and what are the most promising avenues forward?

In sum, the *Handbook* is a series of themes and arguments written to introduce upper level undergraduates, graduate students, and those new to the field to the crucial issues. We hope it captures the recent development of the field, and we hope it provides a road map to the most interesting themes and arguments relevant to the new millennium.

Gordon L. Clark
Maryann P. Feldman
Meric S. Gertler

Oxford,
September 1999

Acknowledgements

We should first acknowledge the help and encouragement of our colleagues at Oxford University Press. Andrew Lockett, now the publisher at the British Film Institute, encouraged us to begin the project. Over the course of the project, Dominic Byatt eased its progress through the publishing process, helping us to transform an almost impossibly ambitious project into reality. His enthusiasm and the support of the Press have been very important. We should also thank the Press's anonymous referees for their comments and advice; they contributed words of support and points of advice and clarification.

The book was supported by Oxford University. In particular, the resources of the School of Geography have been essential in sustaining the project. Here, we were helped immensely by Pat Woodward's intervention at a crucial stage of the process. As well, Jan Burke has shown, once again, her superb organizational skills. She made the links, and sustained the flow of communications and files between the editors and the contributors. On the face of it, electronic networking ought to make these kinds of global projects routine and easily managed. But as we all know, taming the electronic world requires imagination and persistence.

Having set the book's agenda, established links with our contributors, and having received drafts of papers, the project was realized as a book in collaboration with our editorial manager, Kate Williams. Her clear eyes, her sense of the place of each contribution in the book, and her commitment to the project made all the difference to realizing it in a manner that has made it an enjoyable partnership. For this we are all very grateful. On this point, we would also like to thank our contributors who have supported the project with enthusiasm. When we first cast the *Handbook* as an untried idea, we found many willing to make a commitment to contribute to it. We are very grateful for their vote of confidence. Likewise we are also grateful to our contributors for responding in a timely and patient fashion to our comments, and the many demands of the editorial and production processes.

So, finally, we would like to record our appreciation for the support given to the project by the late Bennett Harrison. He played an important role in the initial stages of the project, suggesting contributors and clarifying the goals of the book. Much has been written of his contributions to economics and geography, by his many friends on both sides of the disciplinary divide. We are saddened by his loss, and hope the book reflects what is possible in terms of collaboration at the intersection of economics and geography.

Contents

The Editors xvii

The Contributors xix

Introduction 1

1 Economic Geography: Transition and Growth 3

Gordon L. Clark, Maryann P. Feldman, and Meric S. Gertler

2 Economic Geography: The Great Half-Century 18

Allen J. Scott

Part I **Conceptual Perspectives**

Section 1 **Mapping the Territory**

3 Where in the World is the 'New Economic Geography'? 49

Paul Krugman

4 Doing Regulation 61

Jamie Peck

Section 2 **Analytical Frameworks**

5 The New Economics of Urban and Regional Growth 83

Edward L. Glaeser

6 Geography or Economics? Conceptions of Space, Time, Interdependence, and Agency 99

Eric Sheppard

Part II Global Economic Integration

Section 3 Investment and Trade

7 The Geography of International Investment 125
Howard J. Shatz and Anthony J. Venables

8 Globalization, Localization, and Trade 146
Michael Storper

Section 4 Development and Underdevelopment

9 Climate, Coastal Proximity, and Development 169
Andrew D. Mellinger, Jeffrey D. Sachs, and John L. Gallup

10 The Great Tablecloth: Bread and Butter Politics, and the Political Economy of Food and Poverty 195
Michael J. Watts

Section 5 Finance Capital

11 The Regulation of International Finance 215
Risto I. Laulajainen

12 Finance and Localities 230
Adam Tickell

Part III Corporate Structure, Strategy, and Location

Section 6 Competition, Location, and Strategy

13 Locations, Clusters, and Company Strategy 253
Michael E. Porter

14 Places and Flows: Situating International Investment 275
Peter Dicken

15 The Globalization of Retail Capital: Themes for Economic Geography 292
Neil Wrigley

Section 7 Remaking the Corporation

16 The Management of Time and Space 317
Erica Schoenberger

17 Corporate Form and Spatial Form 333
David B. Audretsch

Part IV **The Geography of Innovation**

Section 8 **National and Localized Learning**

18 Nation States and Economic Development: from National Systems of Production to National Systems of Knowledge Creation and Learning 353
Bengt-Åke Lundvall and Peter Maskell

19 Location and Innovation: The New Economic Geography of Innovation, Spillovers, and Agglomeration 373
Maryann P. Feldman

20 Restructuring and Innovation in Long-Term Regional Change 395
Cristiano Antonelli

Section 9 **Districts and Regional Innovation Systems**

21 Industrial Districts: The Contributions of Marshall and Beyond 413
Bjørn T. Asheim

22 Innovation Networks, Regions, and Globalization 432
Beat Hotz-Hart

Part V **Localities and Difference**

Section 10 **Labour and Locality**

23 Local Labour Markets: Their Nature, Performance, and Regulation 455
Ronald L. Martin

24 Firms, Workers, and the Geographic Concentration of Economic Activity 477
Gordon H. Hanson

Section 11 **Gender, Race, and Place**

25 Feminists Rethink the Economic: The Economics of Gender/The Gender of Economics 497
Linda McDowell

26 Racial and Economic Segregation in US Metropolitan Areas 518
John F. Kain

Section 12 **Communities, Politics, and Power**

27 Elite Power, Global Forces, and the Political Economy of 'Glocal' Development 541
Erik Swyngedouw

28 Economic Geography in Practice: Local Economic Development Policy 559
Amy K. Glasmeier

Part VI **Global Transformations**

Section 13 **Environment and Regulation**

29 Markets and Environmental Quality 585
R. Kerry Turner

30 Environmental Innovation and Regulation 607
David P. Angel

Section 14 **Trade and Investment Blocs**

31 Spontaneous Integration in Japan and East Asia: Development, Crisis, and Beyond 625
Tetsuo Abo

32 Regional Economic Integration in North America 649
John Holmes

33 The European Union as more than a Triad Market for National Economic Spaces 671
Ash Amin

Part VII **Coda**

34 Pandora's Box? Cultural Geographies of Economies 689
Nigel Thrift

Index 705

The Editors

Gordon L. Clark (gordon.clark@geog.ox.ac.uk) is the Halford Mackinder Professor of Geography and Fellow of the Said Business School at the University of Oxford, and is a Professorial Fellow at St Peter's College, Oxford, UK. He has held appointments at Harvard, Chicago, Carnegie Mellon, and Monash universities and has been an Andrew Mellon Fellow at the National Academy of Sciences (Washington DC). The author of many papers in the field, he has also published books on economic geography and political economy including the recent *Pension Fund Capitalism*, *The Asian NIEs in the Global Economy* (with Won Bae Kim), *Pensions and Corporate Restructuring in American Industry*, *Unions and Communities Under Siege*, and *Regional Dynamics* (with Meric Gertler and John Whiteman). His current research is on pan-European pensions and the evolving single market for financial services.

Maryann P. Feldman (maryann.feldman@jhu.edu) is Research Scientist at the Institute for Policy Studies at the Johns Hopkins University (USA). She is the author of over twenty-five articles on economic geography published in the *American Economic Review*, the *Review of Economics and Statistics*, the *European Economic Review*, and *Industrial and Corporate Change*. Her books include the *Geography of Innovation* and *Innovation Policy for a Knowledge-Based Economy* (with Al Link). Her current research focuses on entrepreneurship and regional development, evolving university–industry relationships, and science and technology policy .

Meric S. Gertler (gertler@.geography.utoronto.ca) is the Goldring Professor of Canadian Studies, Professor of Geography and Planning, and a member of the Centre for International Studies at the University of Toronto, Canada. He has held visiting appointments at Oxford and the University of Wales, Cardiff. His books include *Regional Dynamics* (with Gordon Clark and John Whiteman), *The New Era of Global Competition* (with Daniel Drache), and the forthcoming *Manufacturing Culture*. In addition, he is a founding associate editor of the *Journal of Economic Geography*. His current research focuses on the interregional and international transfer of manufacturing technologies and work practices, regional and national systems of innovation, and economic restructuring in Europe and North America.

Kate Williams (katew@summertown7.u-net.com) is a freelance teacher, writer, and editor living in Oxford, UK. She runs writing programmes at Oxford and Oxford Brookes universities and elsewhere. Her publications include *Study Skills* and *Developing Writing*. She is currently working on *The Postgraduate Student Handbook*.

The Contributors

Tetsuo Abo (abo@main.teikyo-u.ac.jp) is Professor of International Economics and International Management at Teikyo University (Professor Emeritus, University of Tokyo, Japan). He has held appointments at the Free University of Berlin, Florida International University, and Waseda University and has held a fellowship from the American Council of Learned Societies. His books include *Japanese and European Management* (with Shibagaki and Trevor) and *Hybrid Factory* (edited). His current research focuses on global diffusion of Japanese management and production systems and comparison of Western and Japanese industrial technologies.

Ash Amin (Ash.Amin@durham.ac.uk) is Professor of Geography at the University of Durham, UK. He is editor of *Post-Fordism, Globalisation, Institutions and Regional Development* (with Nigel Thrift), *Behind the Myth of European Union* (with John Tomaney), and *Beyond Market and Hierarchy* (with Jerzy Hausner). His current research is on institutional economics, social exclusion, and economic democracy.

David P. Angel (dangel@clarku.edu) is Associate Professor of Geography at Clark University, Worcester, USA. He is also Associate Provost and Dean of Graduate Studies and Research at the university and editor of the journal *Economic Geography*. He is the recipient of numerous grants and awards, including an Abe Fellowship awarded by the Center for Global Partnership in conjunction with the Social Science Research Council and the American Council of Learned Societies. His recent book is *Restructuring for Innovation*. Angel's work examines industrial innovation and the environment, focusing on the promotion of green technology and a 'clean' revolution in Asia.

Cristiano Antonelli (cristiano.antonelli@unito.it) is Professor of Economics at the University of Turin, Italy. He has been a Rockefeller Fellow at MIT, and has held appointments at the OECD, the University of Manchester, and the University of Paris-Dauphine (and other universities). His books include *The Microdynamics of Technological Change*, and the edited *New Information Technology and Industrial Change*. He has published papers in journals such as the *Cambridge Journal of Economics*, the *International Journal of Industrial Organisation*, and *Regional Studies*. His recent work focuses on the economics of innovation and technical change.

Bjørn T. Asheim (b.t.asheim@sgeo.uio.no) is Professor in Human Geography at the Centre for Technology, Innovation, and Culture, the Social Science Faculty, and in the Department of Sociology and Human Geography, University of Oslo, Norway. He is also associated with the STEP-group (Studies in Technology, Innovation, and Economic Policy) in Oslo and is Reader in Economic Geography at the Department of Social and Economic Geography, University of Lund, Sweden. He is the author of many papers on economic and industrial geography including papers on industrial districts and regional innovation systems. Recently, he was guest editor of a special issue of *Regional Studies* on 'Regional Futures' (with Mick Dunford). His current research is on SMEs and innovation policy and regional innovation systems.

David B. Audretsch (daudrets@indiana.edu) is the Ameritech Chair of Economic Development and Director of the Institute for Development Strategies at Indiana University, USA. Previously he was as the Wissenschaftszentrum Berlin für Sozialforschung in Germany. He consults for the US Federal Trade Commission, GAO, ITC, OECD, UN, and EC, as well as private corporations and European governments. He has published many books including *Innovation, Industry Evolution and Employment*. He is the founder and editor of *Small Business Economics: An International Journal*. Audretsch's research focuses on the links between small and medium-sized enterprises, government policy, innovation, economic development, and global competitiveness.

Peter Dicken (P.Dicken@man.ac.uk) is Professor of Geography at the University of Manchester, UK. He has held visiting appointments in the USA, Canada, Australia, Hong Kong, Mexico, and Singapore. In addition to a large number of academic papers, his books include *Global Shift: Transforming the World Economy* (3rd edn.). His major research interests are in global economic change, transnational corporations, foreign direct investment, and economic change in East and South-East Asia.

John Gallup (john_gallup@harvard.edu) is a Research Fellow at the Center for International Development, an Institute Associate at the Harvard Institute for International Development, and a Lecturer in the Department of Economics at Harvard University, USA. His recent research focuses on economic growth and poverty, and the relationship of economic growth to geography.

Edward L. Glaeser (eglaeser@harvard.edu) is Professor of Economics in the Department of Economics at Harvard University, USA, where he teaches the Ph.D. sequence in urban economics. Professor Glaeser is also a Faculty Research

Fellow at the National Bureau of Economic Research, and was both a Sloan Foundation Research Fellow and the John M. Olin Fellow in Law and Economics at the University of Chicago Law School while writing this survey chapter. A co-editor of the *Quarterly Journal of Economics*, he has written many articles on urban and regional economics published in journals such as the *Journal of Political Economy*. His current research focuses on the sources of urban and regional growth and American urban social problems.

Amy K. Glasmeier (akg1@ems.psu.edu) is Professor of Geography and Director of the Center on Trade, Technology, and Economic Growth, Institute for Policy Research and Evaluation, Pennsylvania State University, USA. She is also the John D Whisman Appalachian Scholar for the Appalachian Regional Commission. Glasmeier has published three books on international industrial and economic development including *High Tech America*, *High-Tech Potential: Economic Development in Rural America*, and *From Combines to Computers: Rural Services Development in the Age of Information Technology* and more than 40 scholarly articles. She has testified before the US Congress and the Pennsylvania House of Representatives on issues related to international trade, globalization, economic development, and poverty alleviation.

Gordon H. Hanson (gohanson@umich.edu) is Associate Professor of Economics and International Business at the University of Michigan, USA. Professor Hanson has published numerous papers on international and regional economics in such journals as the *American Economic Review* and the *Quarterly Journal of Economics*. He is an associate editor at the *American Economic Review*, the *Journal of International Economics*, and the *Journal of Economic Geography*, and a Research Associate at the National Bureau of Economic Research. His current research addresses whether increasing returns to scale contribute to the geographic concentration of economic activity and how immigration, international trade, and technological change impact on wages, employment, and industry structure in the USA, Mexico, and Asia.

John Holmes (holmesj@post.queensu.ca) is Professor and Head of Geography and a faculty associate in the School of Industrial Relations at Queen's University in Kingston, Ontario, Canada. His research and teaching interests centre on the political economy of contemporary economic and industrial change in North America. He is the author of numerous journal articles and chapters on economic geography with a particular focus on the automobile industry. His current research is on automobile workers' union strategies in response to continental economic integration and work reorganization, and the restructuring of the North American automotive components industry.

Beat Hotz-Hart (Beat.Hotz@BBT.admin.ch) is Vice-Director of the Swiss Federal Office for Education and Technology (Ministry of Economics) and Professor of Economics at Zürich University, Switzerland. He is author/editor of books on the economy of Switzerland, on technology, innovation, and competitiveness. He has held appointments at the Swiss Federal Institute for Technology and University of Fribourg and has held a three-year National Science Fellowship for advanced researchers. His current activities include the development and implementation of policy in education, technology, and innovation at the Swiss federal level and research on innovation and institutional arrangements, competitiveness, structural adjustment, and economic policy.

John F. Kain (jkain@utdallas.edu) is the Cecil and Ida Green Chair for the Study of Science and Society, Director of the Cecil and Ida Green Center, and Professor of Economics and Political Economy at the University of Texas at Dallas, USA. Previously, he was the Henry Lee Professor of Economics and Professor of Afro-American Studies at Harvard University, where he taught for more than 30 years. His books include (with John R. Meyer and Martin Wohl) *The Urban Transportation Problem*, (with John M. Quigley) *Housing Markets and Racial Discrimination: A Micro-Economic Analysis*, and (with William Apgar, Jr.) *Housing and Neighborhood Dynamics: A Simulation Study*. His current research on Texas public schools is based on the Texas Schools Data Base which includes eight years of linked, micro data for more than 2 million students, their teachers, and the schools they attend.

Paul Krugman (pkrugman@princeton.edu) is Professor of Economics and International Affairs, Woodrow Wilson School, Princeton University, USA. He has also taught at MIT, Yale University, and Stanford University. In addition, he has served on the White House Council of Economic Advisers. He has written or edited many books, including *Geography and Trade*, and more than 200 papers in professional and edited volumes. Krugman is one of the founders of the 'new trade theory' which is about the consequences of increasing returns and imperfect competition for international trade, and international finance. He is also one of the founders of the 'new economic geography'. In 1991, the AEA awarded Krugman the John Bates Clark Medal.

Risto I. Laulajainen (Risto.Laulajainen@geography.gu.se) is Professor of Economic Geography at Göteborg School of Economics and Commercial Law, Sweden. He has held appointments at Helsinki and Tampere, and visiting appointments at Aarhus, Blacksburg, Virginia, and Aichi. His books include *The North Atlantic Sulphur System*, *Spatial Strategies in Retailing*, *Corporate Geography* (with H. A. Stafford), and *Financial Geography*. Current research is on international finance and bulk shipping.

Bengt-Åke Lundvall (bal@business.auc.dk) is Professor of Economics at the Department for Business Studies, Aalborg University, Denmark. He has held visiting appointments at the universities of Sussex, Strasbourg, and Stanford and was deputy director at the OECD Directorate for Science Technology and Industry (1992–5). He is the author and editor of several books including

Product Innovation and User-Producer Interaction, Small Countries facing the Technological Revolution (co-edited with Chris Freeman), and *National Systems of Innovation*. He is now research manager for the research network DRUID (Danish Research Unit for Industrial Dynamics) and project leader for the DISKO project (Danish Innovation System in Comparative perspective). His current research is focused on industrial dynamics and innovation systems, and on the analysis of the learning economy.

Linda McDowell (l.mcdowell@ucl.ac.uk) is Professor of Economic Geography at University College London, UK. She has held posts at a number of British universites, most recently at the London School of Economics, and a visiting position at UCLA. She has published widely in geographical journals and her recent books include *Capital Culture*; *Space, Gender, Knowledge* (with Jo Sharp); and *Gender, Identity and Place*. She is an editor of the *International Journal of Urban and Regional Research*. Her current research is on social exclusion and precarious work.

Ronald L. Martin (rlm1@cam.ac.uk) is University Reader in Economic Geography at the University of Cambridge, UK, and a Fellow of St Catharine's College. He has held visiting professorships at UCLA and the University of Ancona, Italy. He has published 19 books and more than 120 articles. He is currently completing two books on 'Rethinking the British Economy' and 'The New Geography of Work'. He is Honorary Editor of *Transactions of the Institute of British Geographers*, and an editor of the *Cambridge Journal of Economics*, the *Journal of Economic Geography*, and *Géographie, Économie et Société*. His research covers regional development, the geography of labour markets, the geography of money, state intervention, and European economic and monetary integration.

Peter Maskell (Maskell@cbs.dk) is Professor in Regional Economics at Copenhagen Business School and member of the Danish Research Unit on Industrial Dynamics (DRUID), Denmark. He is former chairman of the Danish Social Science Research Council, and member of the European Science Foundation Standing Committee for the Social Sciences. He is the author of several books including *Competitiveness, Localised Learning and Regional Development* (with four Nordic colleagues). His current research is on innovation and inter-organizational co-operation, and on the role of localized capabilities in a globalized economy.

Andrew D. Mellinger (andrew_mellinger@harvard.edu) is a Research Associate at the Center for International Development, Harvard University specializing in the multidisciplinary application of geographic information systems. His areas of research include geography and economic development, landscape ecology, landscape planning, the modelling of urbanization and alternative futures, and comparing road networks in spatial models of ecological change.

Jamie Peck (jpeck@geography.wisc.edu) is Professor of Geography at the University of Wisconsin, Madison, USA. Previously a Professor of Geography at the University of Manchester, he is a co-editor of *Environment & Planning A* and *Antipode*. Publications include *Work-Place: The Social Regulation of Labor Markets* and *Workfare States*. He has been a Harkness Fellow at Johns Hopkins University, and was recently the recipient of a Leverhulme Research Fellowship through which he researched the political economy of welfare reform and workfare in the USA, Canada, and the UK. His research has focused on economic and regulatory restructuring, labour market segmentation, and urban politics.

Michael E. Porter (mporter@hbs.edu) is the C. Roland Christensen Professor of Business Administration at the Harvard Business School, USA and a leading authority on competitive strategy and international competitiveness. Professor Porter is the author of 15 books and over 60 articles. His books include *Competitive Strategy: Techniques for Analyzing Industries and Competitors*, *Competitive Advantage: Creating and Sustaining Superior Performance*, and *The Competitive Advantage of Nations*. Porter also founded The Initiative for a Competitive Inner City in 1994, a private sector initiative formed to catalyse inner-city business development across the USA.

Jeffrey D. Sachs (sachs@harvard.edu) is the Director of the Center for International Development and the Galen L. Stone Professor of International Trade in the Department of Economics, Harvard University, USA. He has honorary degrees from St Gallen University, Switzerland, and Lingnan College, Hong Kong, and the Seidman Award in Political Economy. Professor Sachs has published a large number of articles and books on emerging markets, global competitiveness, economic growth, transition to a market economy, international financial markets, and international macroeconomic policy co-ordination in developing and developed countries. Professor Sachs has been an economic adviser to governments in all parts of the world, and played a central role in Eastern Europe's transition from communism to market economy.

Erica Schoenberger (ericas@jhu.edu) is a Professor in the Department of Geography and Environmental Engineering at Johns Hopkins University, Baltimore, Maryland, USA. She also holds a joint appointment in the Department of Anthropology. Her recent book *The Cultural Crisis of the Firm*, combines her interests in corporate culture and strategy, industrial transformation, technology change, and international investment. Her research focuses on methodology in economic geography as well as industrial and corporate restructuring.

Allen J. Scott (ajscott@ucla.edu) is Professor in the Department of Geography and the Department of Policy Studies at the University of California—Los Angeles, USA. Professor Scott has held appointments at the Universities of

London, Toronto, Hong Kong, and Paris. In 1987–8 he was the holder of a Guggenheim Fellowship and in the winter of 1998–9 he occupied the André Siegfried chair at the Institut D'Études Politiques, Paris. He is also a corresponding Fellow of the British Academy. He is the author of several books on issues of urbanization, regional development, and public policy. His most recent book is *Regions and the World Economy*. His current research is focused on the cultural economy of cities.

Howard J. Shatz (shatz@fas.harvard.edu) is an affiliate of the Center for International Development at Harvard University, USA, and a research associate in the trade section of the Development Research Group at the World Bank. Formerly, he was the Arthur M. Okun Memorial Fellow at The Brookings Institution, USA. His research has focused on the trade behaviour of multinational affiliates, the geographic distribution of direct investment, and the effect of international trade on wages and employment.

Eric Sheppard (shepp001@maroon.tc.umn.edu) is Professor of Geography, and member of the MacArthur Program on International Peace and Cooperation and of the Institute for Social, Economic, and Ecological Sustainability at the University of Minnesota, USA. He has held visiting appointments at the International Institute for Applied Systems Analysis (Austria), University College London, the University of Indonesia, the University of Melbourne, the University of Vienna, and the Economics and Business University of Vienna. He is co-author of *The Capitalist Space Economy* and *A World of Difference: Society, Nature, Development*, and has published many articles on economic geography and regional science. His current research is on the spatial dynamics of competition, the growth dynamics of European cities, international political economy, and environmental policy.

Michael Storper (storper@compuserve.com) is Professor of Regional and International Development in the School of Public Policy at the University of California—Los Angeles, USA, Professor of Social and Human Sciences at the University of Marne-la-Vallée in France, and researcher in the Laboratoire Territoires, Techniques et Sociétés at the École des Ponts et Chaussées in France. His most recent books are *Worlds of Production: The Action Frameworks of the Economy* (with Robert Salais), *The Regional World: Territorial Development in a Global Economy*, and *Latecomers in the Global Economy*. He has been a consultant with the OECD, the European Union, and the Brazilian government.

Erik Swyngedouw (erik.swyngedouw@geog.ox.ac.uk) is University Reader in Economic Geography at the University of Oxford, UK. He is also Official Fellow and Tutor of Geography at St Peter's College. He has held visiting professorships at the Universities of Leuven, Belgium, Seville, Spain, and Thessaloniki, Greece. He is the co-author of *Uneven Regional Development in Belgium* and a book entitled *Towards Global Localisation*. He is currently completing a book entitled *Flows of Power: Water and the Political-Ecology of Urbanisation*. In addition, he co-edited *Regional Policy at the Crossroads: European Perspectives* and *The Urbanisation of Injustice*. Current research projects are focused upon the restructuring of geographical scale. He has a particular research interest in economic restructuring, urban and regional restructuring, and the political ecology of urbanization.

Nigel Thrift (n.j.thrift@bris.ac.uk) is Professor of Geography and Head of Department of the School of Geographical Sciences, University of Bristol, UK. He is author/editor of many books including, most recently, *Mapping the Subject* (co-edited with Steve Pile), *Spatial Formations*, *Money/Space* (with Andrew Leyshon), and *Consumption, Place and Identity* (with D. Miller, P. Jackson, B. Holbrook, and M. Rowlands). He has held appointments at Cambridge, Leeds, ANU, and the University of Wales. His current research is on social and cultural theory, time, and the rise of reflexive economies.

Adam Tickell (a.tickell@soton.ac.uk) is Professor of Geography at the University of Southampton, UK. He has held appointments at Leeds and Manchester Universities and held fellowships from the Economic and Social Research Council and the Canadian High Commission. He has also acted as adviser to a number of policy-making bodies including government departments, the European Parliament, and a number of local authorities in Britain. He has published widely in economic geography, on the restructuring of finance, regulation theory, local governance, and regional development and is the author of a forthcoming book on the culture of finance.

R. Kerry Turner (r.k.turner@uae.ac.uk) is Professor of Environmental Sciences and Director of the Centre for Social and Economic Research on the Global Environment (CSERGE) at the University of East Anglia, Norwich, UK. He has held appointments at Leicester University and University College London and has been visiting professor at the Free University of Amsterdam and the GKSS Research Centre, Geeschalt in Germany. Turner is the author/editor of many books on environmental management and economics including *The Economics of Natural Resources and the Environment* (with D. W. Pearce), *Sustainable Environmental Economics and Management*, and *Elementary Environmental Economics* (with D. W. Pearce and I. Bateman). His current research focuses on wetland economics and management, waste management, coastal zone management, and environmental resources valuation and ethics.

Anthony J. Venables (a.j.venables@lse.ac.uk) is Professor of International Economics at the London School of Economics, co-director of the International Trade Programme of the Centre for Economic Policy Research, UK, and Director of the International Trade section of the World Bank. He has written many papers on international trade and trade policy, and a co-authored book, *The Spatial Economy: Cities, Regions and International Trade* (with M. Fujita and P. Krugman). He is currently researching foreign direct investment, and the interaction between international trade and industrial location.

Michael J. Watts (mwatts@socrates.berkeley.edu) is Chancellor's Professor of Geography and Development Studies and Director of the Institute of International Studies at the University of California, Berkeley, USA. Recent books include *Silent Violence*, *Reworking Modernity*, *Liberation Ecologies* (with R. Peet), and *Globalizing Food* (with D. Goodman). He teaches development studies and political economy, and has worked on rural development, agrarian transformation, and food security in West Africa, India, and Vietnam.

Neil Wrigley (n.wrigley@soton.ac.uk) is Professor of Geography and Head of the Department of Geography at the University of Southampton, UK. He has held appointments at the University of Wales, Cardiff, and the University of Bristol and visiting appointments in the USA, Canada, Australia, and New Zealand. More recently, he was a Senior Research Fellow at St Peter's College, Oxford, and held a UK Economic and Social Research Council Fellowship for work on retailing and regulation. He is the founding co-editor of the *Journal of Economic Geography*, and was previously editor of *Transactions* (Royal Geographical Society). He is the author of many papers and books on the economic geography of the retail industry including *Retailing, Consumption and Capital* (with Michelle Lowe) and the theory of sunk costs (with Gordon Clark). He is currently researching the post-LBO transformation of the US food retail industry for the Leverhulme Trust, and the globalization of retail capital.

Introduction

Chapter 1

Economic Geography: Transition and Growth

Gordon L. Clark, Maryann P. Feldman, and Meric S. Gertler

This volume captures the field of economic geography at a propitious point in time of intellectual transformation and rapid growth.[1] Thirty years ago the field was a quiet backwater in economics, dominated by the analytics of location rather than contemporary theorizing (quite an irony given the history of the discipline; see Thisse and Walliser 1997). Thirty years ago it was a settled area of research in geography, though many of its practitioners were reluctant to acknowledge the spatial implications of the forces of economic change gathering momentum. In economics, the field was preoccupied by theoretical niceties following Alonso's (1964) remarkable synthesis of neoclassical economics with location theory. By contrast, geography had assimilated Berry's (1967) book on market functions and spatial scale, being preoccupied with settlement patterns and the hierarchy of places in national economies. So powerful and so comprehensive were Alonso's and Berry's work that the collective imagination was focused on a world that seemed given—simultaneously conceived and articulated in all its dimensions.

At the dawn of the twenty-first century, the field of economic geography is alive with intellectual argument about issues of profound contemporary relevance (witness Krugman 1991 and Martin and Sunley 1996). It is a field of

[1] This chapter, and the volume, was supported by an initial establishment grant to Gordon Clark from the University of Oxford. Maryann Feldman's research on economic geography has been supported by the National Science Foundation (NSF) (USA), and Meric Gertler's research supported by Social Science and Humanities Research Council (SSHRC) (Canada). We wish to acknowledge the help and encouragement of Dominic Byatt and Amanda Watkins (OUP) and the expert assistance of Jan Burke. We are also grateful for the advice on previous drafts by Kate Williams. None of the above, including our contributors, should be held responsible for the opinions contained herein.

academic enquiry preoccupied with the geographical scope and scale of economies in the context of economic change, the driving forces behind those changes, and the role of localities in global economic transformation. It is a field that encompasses international economics, industry organization, business strategy and innovation (on one side), while being sensitive to the ways in which theoretical perspectives drawn from those traditions are affected and shaped by an appreciation of the persistence of geography (on the other side). *Difference*, *differentiation*, and *heterogeneity* characterize the economic landscape, and are part and parcel of the intellectual agenda motivating the field of economic geography. And yet, notwithstanding the agenda-setting claims made amongst others by Krugman (1991), Fujita *et al.* (1999) in economics, and Scott (1998) and Storper and Salais (1997) in geography, there are no settled recipes for research and no conclusive statements of the proper scope of economic geography.

The Preface of the book flags these issues as significant points of departure for our project. While not all contributors address these issues, and even though the precise meaning of such terms often varies by contributor, it is worth pausing for a moment to explain their significance in more detail. In general, *difference* refers to distinctive geographical patterns of economic performance, measured by indicators such as employment, unemployment, and income. Urban and regional differences in these kinds of indicators have long been a motive force behind research in economic geography. Not only has it been observed that labour market performance varies across the economic landscape within and between nations (see Martin *et al.* 1998), but so too do capital markets, technology and innovation, and many other related asset and factor markets (see e.g. Clark *et al.* 1986). But difference can also refer to social and cultural categorical divisions of the economy, incorporating gender, race, and related signifiers of identity and location (McDowell 1997, 1999).

In recent years, recognition of difference has been joined by a renewed appreciation of the processes of *differentiation*—a realization that difference is actually the product of ongoing economic processes that sustain long-term spatial variation. This is a contentious issue. Persistent difference, produced and reproduced over time, seems to be at odds with conventional neoclassical notions of convergence to a stable equilibrium (Barro and Sala-I-Martin 1995). Whereas some researchers would suggest that persistence is the (unfortunate) result of government policy, others point to scale economies, agglomeration economies, and the virtues and vices of sunk costs (lock-in, commitment, embeddedness, etc.) to explain persistent differentiation. Difference and differentiation characterize large spatially integrated and extensive economies like the USA, and are essential 'variables' in any understanding of the European scene (Smith 1999). For some, difference and differentiation are to be 'solved', for others difference and differentiation are the building bricks for new theories of economic growth and comparative advantage, and for yet others difference and differentiation underpin the intellectual project of economic geography.[2]

We would also like to comment on the significance of *heterogeneity* for economic geography. As social scientists we are accustomed to thinking about economic phenomena through accepted universals like demand, supply, production, and consumption. Whereas some disciplines such as anthropology dispute this practice, being concerned to document the existence of different systems of meaning and related institutions, economic geographers have tended to assume difference and differentiation are the limits to the enterprise. Some of our contributors question this practice, arguing that 'difference within limits' unreasonably narrows the scope of the enterprise to conventional, measured variables. Some of our contributors argue also that 'difference within limits' fails to acknowledge the transformation of modern economies from commodity-manufacturing economies to knowledge-dependent economies.

Reflexive economies are inevitably heterogeneous economies, characterized by information asymmetries, overlapping and disjointed systems of meaning. Therefore, it is important to acknowledge the cultural building blocks of economic geography whether found in gender and racial categories or in the social capital of regions like Silicon Valley (Saxenian 1994). At the same time, it should be acknowledged that we do not subscribe to a radical theory of heterogeneity in economic geography—we do not suppose that rival systems of information and meaning (or systems of governance and market structure) can co-exist without their inter-penetration, juxtaposition, and even competition. But we do suggest that economic geography is now increasingly foregrounding cultural and institutional variables previously thought out of bounds or irrelevant to market performance and innovation (see Gertler 1993, forthcoming; and Cooke and Morgan 1997).

Economists and Geographers

For the editors and contributors to this volume, the intellectual vitality of the field of economic geography is something to celebrate. The field has benefited enormously from new perspectives and methods jostling and competing for recognition in the disciplines underpinning the field. Thus

[2] It should also be acknowledged that difference and differentiation are vital building blocks behind related developments in economic sociology and comparative institutional studies (see the edited volume by Crouch and Streeck 1997). At the same time, it would be unfortunate if emphasis on these concepts caused economic geography or for that matter comparative studies to ignore commonalities of experience between rival systems of governance. See the comments by Susan Strange (1997) on the limits of difference and differentiation for comparative studies.

Allen Scott's opening chapter surveying the history of the field takes us from settled pastures, established methods, and well-defined theories into a veritable new frontier of argument and dissent. At the same time, we are convinced that there are new problems, old issues now filled with great urgency, and questions unresolved—economic geography as elaborated in this volume is a field of research at the heart of the emerging global economy. Where we once might have assumed an ordered structure and spacing of settlements, globalization challenges us to document and explain the spatial scale of economic activity *and* the spatial allocation of economic activity (see e.g. Ellison and Glaeser 1997). Throughout this volume, contributors are focused upon significant problems that are neither settled in space nor settled in theory. We have emerged from the twentieth century into an era of profound economic change, implicating and affected by economic geography.

In contacting potential contributors, we set out our intellectual mandate emphasizing the issues of difference, differentiation, and heterogeneity. Given that background, in the first instance we sought to identify pairs of contributors (economists and geographers) best placed to write on specific topics. Though the structure of the book evolved, each pair was given the probable order of topics, allowing them to know (roughly) what would come before and after their contributions. Rather than ask for a conventional survey of names and themes within each topic, we asked contributors to make the intellectual case for their own view of the matter, recognizing the existence of a paired contributor on the same topic. Not surprisingly, the book is alive with opinion and perspective. At the same time, we have allowed differences of argument and perspective on each topic and between topics to stand unresolved. It did not seem sensible to attempt a grand, ordered, and focused meta-narrative.

Clearly, in such a vibrant field, we have had to select amongst the universe of possible writers and topics. Anyone who has attempted something similar will recognize that the choice of topics and contributors necessarily combines idealism with pragmatism. We sought to include topics and contributors relevant to current problems in economic geography. In doing so, we also were mindful of a variety of constraints: audience, timing, and the available publishing space. Inevitably, important topics and authors have been left out of the picture. For that we apologize, noting, of course, the existence of other complementary undergraduate textbooks (Barnes and Sheppard forthcoming; Bryson *et al.* 1999, and Lee and Wills 1997). No doubt there is a certain arbitrariness in the finished line-up. Nevertheless, we are very fortunate that by virtue of the scope of the book, and by virtue of the reputations of the contributors, we may well have selected the 'new' Alonsos and Berrys of economic geography. As a consequence, this volume captures many of the issues and authors at the forefront of contemporary economic geography, issues and authors that will be debated over the coming decades.

Regions, Nations, and the Global Economy

Historically, the field of economic geography developed around the settlement structure of national economies, reflecting a concern for the optimal and efficient spatial allocation of economic activity whether as a theoretical matter (witness Alonso) or as a set of empirical facts (witness Berry). Assumed was a set of known, ordered, and stable national economic forces. The economic geography of nations was derived from these forces, stepping down to lower spatial scales based upon geographic-specific factor endowments and comparative advantage. Industry production functions were important, markets given, and the costs of transport crucial for the location of industry in relation to markets. The implication for the world economy was plain: it was simply understood to be the product of separate national spaces (economic geography) added up together to create the whole world.

There is no doubt that this logic had a plausible claim on the intellectual imagination. The years immediately after the Great Depression and then World War II were periods of intense political and economic activity aimed at re-establishing national economic order within a system of overlapping but actually quite weak international institutions. Economic management was assumed to be a national matter, and domestic economic regulation was framed around institutions often inherited from the Great Depression. See, for example, Clark (1989) on the origins of the spatial configuration of postwar US labour–management relations. All this is obvious, and surely it is unnecessary to explain further this point. It is, however, important to appreciate that the resulting economic order led in turn to a division of academic labour between macroeconomics being about the patterns and determinants of national economic performance, and economic geography being about the spatial patterns and determinants of activity within those parameters (see Clark *et al.* 1986).

If economic geography was dominated by macroeconomics for much of the postwar period, macroeconomics similarly held sway over international economics. Again the logic was unmistakable. National economies were assumed to be the cornerstone of international trade, being the border at which trade (exchange) was counted and the border defining the interests and processes of trade negotiation. In this world of national borders and influence, regions were sometimes discussed but understood as blocs of nations rather than sub-national units. Indeed, just as macroeconomic policy-makers denied the relevance of internal spatial economic units so national policy-makers denied sub-national industry interests a place in trade negotiation. Even now, the most important multilateral policy-making institutions are dominated by nations, their interests and perspectives, not places. This was taken for granted until trade blocs like the European Union began the process of market integration coupled with a common currency, thereby putting in play (economically and politically) the relevance of national borders. There is now a growing recognition that industries are organized in places and between sets of places rather than being exclusively determined by national spaces (see Feldman 1999).

In designing the book there was an opportunity to redress the inherited academic division of labour by asking our contributors to begin with the global economy and make the connection with economic geography unconstrained by the historical claims of significance maintained by the macroeconomic establishment. In doing so, contributors have had the opportunity to establish connections previously unrecognized, even if precise articulation of those connections remains a vital, disputed arena of research in economic geography. Many market, government, and institutional agents are now interested in the nature and scope of these connections. For instance, the editors discussed this framework with a number of global banking groups concerned to understand the long-term economic geography of Europe given the changing structure of investment portfolios from country-based sets of securities to sector-based securities. In a nutshell the question has become 'Where in Europe will automobiles be produced?' rather than 'What determines the relative economic performance of the German, French, and Italian automobile industries?'

For much of the past two decades national governments have grappled with the elusive issue (and some might say, the illusion) of competitiveness: arguably defined as the enhancement of a jurisdiction's share of global industry market share (see Porter 1990). In this respect, our contributors make two types of connections to economic geography. They suggest that networks and innovation potential are closely related (see Feldman 1994). Economists and geographers separately and together argue that the intensiveness of networks is a necessary condition for competitiveness. In the past, of course, industry performance has been a topic at the heart of microeconomics and allied studies of technological innovation and diffusion. Going beyond that literature, the contributors to economic geography suggest that a deliberate engagement with spatial fixity is necessary, arguing that the spatial structure of networks is a vital ingredient in what is otherwise studied as a microeconomic phenomenon. In essence, economic geography shows that spatial clustering, not just network intensity, is a vital piece of the puzzle (Audretsch and Feldman 1996).

At this point, it should be apparent that economists and geographers approach the global–local split in different ways. Some of the apparent difference can be attributed to inherited skills and expertise; we should not expect otherwise given the acknowledged reputations of our contributors. Some of the apparent difference can also be attributed to the two disciplines' different methodological starting-points. Whether by instinct or training, economists have tended to operate at higher spatial and theoretical levels of abstraction whereas geographers have tended to emphasize the rich texture of contemporary circumstances. Perhaps unfairly, this difference is often characterized in the literature as a disciplinary difference of significance attributed to a priori theorizing in the face of empirically disputed stylized facts (see Clark 1998, and David 1998). In recent years, the methods of economic geography have come under increasing scrutiny, joining a debate about the status and significance of social science methods in general (see e.g., Gibson-Graham 1997).

Even so, there is no obvious template or recipe for research in the field. Just as economic geography has become a wide-ranging field, it could be reasonably argued that different topics and different problems within the field demand different methods. In any event, the stark contrast between economics and geography suggested above tends to fragment upon close scrutiny. For instance, the recent work of geographers such as Webber and Rigby (1997) and Plummer, Haining, and Sheppard (1998) on, respectively, the determinants of postwar economic growth and decline, and the nature and dynamics of spatial price competition, share with many economists formal reasoning and stylized facts. By contrast, economists such as Antonelli (1995) and David, Foray, and Dalle (1998), writing about technological change and economic innovation, rely upon economic geography; they value narrative methods, the pluralism of geography, and the limits of formalism. Given the multidisciplinary nature of the field, we sought ways of respecting these differences by encouraging overlapping contributions around common topics. Otherwise, the temptation is to let economists deal with some issues and geographers other issues, perpetuating an impression that such a division of responsibilities is somehow natural or pre-ordained.

Geographical Scale

One of the imperatives underlying the intellectual transformation and growth of the field has been the decline of the nation-state as the dominant locus of economic activity. By focusing on the decline of the nation-state we do not mean to suggest that it is now somehow irrelevant or profoundly compromised in the face of the twin forces of globalization and localization. Too many commentators have uncritically proclaimed the death of the nation-state for us to reproduce those arguments without a sense of caution and circumspection. After all, there are good reasons to suppose that the nation-state is still very important with respect to questions of comparative advantage. Nation-specific regulatory regimes in areas such as intellectual property, human capital, and finance can all be shown to have far-reaching implications for the global and regional trading potential of firms and industries located within national borders. See, for example, the volume edited by Hopt *et al.* (1998) on national regimes of corporate governance.

Indeed, it could be reasonably argued that nation-states are more important than at any time in the past fifty years as the agents of national economic interests in multilateral institutions and negotiations. If the Bretton Woods agreement could have been thought of as a stable, well-defined framework of some nations' economic interests, that framework has obviously been overtaken by international policy organizations like the OECD (Organization for Economic Cooperation and Development) and the WTO (World Trade Organization). While the re-emergence of economic geography can be argued as being due to the increasing economic significance of sub-national regions and supra-national regions relative to the nation-state, we really mean to suggest that the geographical scale of economic activity and the geographical allocation of economic activity are increasingly open questions of corporate strategy. In this respect, the nation-state may not be the natural home market for firms and industries, nor the necessary scale at which firms and industries are organized. In effect, the twentieth-century bilateral relationship between firms and nations has been undercut by the rapid expansion of global markets (at the highest level), and the apparent focus of corporate management on plant-level efficiency, labour, and productivity (at the lowest level).

Within many larger firms, then, issues of geographical scale dominate corporate strategy. For instance, in the European Union local (national and regional) firms traditionally operated in local commodity markets. But those markets may now be penetrated by firms operating in other national jurisdictions. The spatial reach of firms within European industries is an increasingly important determinant of corporate earnings. In addition, with the advent of the single market, geographical reach may be the single most important determinant of corporate growth potential. At another level, however, competitiveness is arguably also determined by labour productivity and technological change. Some firms have tried to ignore the geography of labour skills and flexibility. Then again, some pan-European firms have decentralized production to sites of value, relying either on local enclaves of productivity or local industry-specific networks of productive value. The single, nationally dominant firm/plant seems to be less likely to succeed in the future. And yet, how firms manage the internal tensions of geographical scale (spatial reach as opposed to spatial dependence) may affect each firm's trajectory.

As we see in this book, there are many academics searching for economic imperatives that could underpin or in some way sustain the vitality of sub-national regions (if not nations). Increasing prospects of capital mobility within supra-regions, whether driven by spatially extensive markets or by new opportunities for market deepening, threaten established patterns of employment. And there is little comfort in claims that corporations must have geographical identities or loyalties. Hyper-mobility based upon advanced electronic communications does appear implausible but so too do arguments in favour of the certainty of geographically embedded inter-firm and intra-firm cultures and relationships (cf. Doremus *et al.* 1998). Notions such as clusters, networks, enclaves, and localized chains of value began with geographers, being a new vocabulary for describing the economic geography of post-Fordism and flexible accumulation. Whether deliberately or not, these notions have become incorporated into national policy-making (witness the recent competitiveness manifesto announced by the UK government) and the development objectives of sub-national regions.

This brings us to the second issue: the spatial allocation of economic activity. To recognize that this issue is hotly contested in theory and practice is to recognize the obvious. For many political interests, shifts in the spatial allocation of economic activity associated with the formation of supra-regions and/or globalization threaten the stability of institutionalized modes of social cooperation. The expansion of firms' spatial reach often carries with it less dependence upon local markets and inherited agreements with political elites. The deepening of firms' dependence upon certain sites of productive value coupled with the emergence of viable switching options often undercuts local bargains with labour while reinforcing competition between sub-national regions for increasingly scarce high-value investment. In the European context, the spatial reallocation of economic activity has tended to undercut nation-state social contracts; in effect, displacing comprehensive agreements relating to the sharing of wealth and power. Whether nation-states can renegotiate social contracts relevant to the new world of globalization and localization remains an open question.

At the root of this issue is the likely long-term map of firms, industries, and regions. Here, we can imagine two scenarios (amongst others). Imagine that firms and their immediate and related industries tend to spatially concentrate, reaping the benefits of agglomeration economies (benefiting firms' cost structures and market competitiveness). This scenario (*A*) is to be found in a wide variety of theorists, from Scott (1988), to Krugman (1991), to Storper and Salais (1997). This is not to say that scenario *A* is their only solution. As they show in this volume, they have extended and developed their arguments to be more sensitive to the counter-forces of agglomeration. One implication from scenario *A* is that an industry landscape of specialization will emerge from a period of restructuring designed to incorporate new options for production and new markets for consumption. By this logic, trade between specialized regions (nations and sub-national) will simultaneously create a supra-regional landscape of employment and wealth. If so, then national political interests will be spatially divided into sub-national coalitions of industry-region interests.

But there are many other theorists who find this scenario implausible; if relevant to the late nineteenth and early to mid-twentieth century (Fordism), it is argued to be less relevant to the twenty-first century. For a strong version of this counter-argument see Rifkin (1995). An alternative scenario (*B*) goes as follows. Imagine that firms can draw upon the benefits of spatial agglomeration (the transactional efficiency of networks, functional specialization, and the spill-over effects of innovation) without being in the same jurisdiction. In effect, imagine that high quality communication networks combined with accessibility over 24-hour cycles allow for rival and related firms in an industry to operate at a distance from one another. We will ignore the issue of the spatial limit of such arrangements for the moment. Also imagine that there are a variety of markets, some large and others small, all of which can be served by single plants or sets of plants. What kind of economic geography is likely to result?

If we deal initially with the landscape of production, over time a heterogeneous industrial map of firms is likely to result. Indeed, we can think of reasons why firms within a given industry may deliberately seek out sites of production characterized by heterogeneity of industry (see Clark 1981). Notice the implication for political elites: they may represent regions wherein there are no dominant or necessarily 'local' firms-industries. In this context, political elites may have very little leverage at any spatial scale. If we reintroduce markets of consumption, two further implications can be identified. First, the tastes and preferences of large markets may dominate small markets, encouraging production firms to concentrate on the former type of market in order to reap economies of scale. Secondly, assuming all markets are accessible, firms may develop mixed strategies of location; larger markets are highly contested, drawing rival producers to locate in ways that facilitate their competitive strategies while smaller markets are less contested, being dominated by either local producers or distant producers that rely upon transport accessibility. Here, spatial agglomeration occurs by virtue of market value, and is reinforced (compared to smaller spatial units) by competitive strategy.

But notice that agglomeration need not be confined to specialized industry-regions. Rather, agglomeration around large markets is a competitive phenomenon, important to all kinds of industries and their firms. At this point, it may be objected that we have introduced markets, and market size, as exogeneous variables. Surely, we should also derive markets, as we have derived regions and the economic allocation of activity. Perhaps, in a larger system of arguments and constraints, this might be possible. Our point here is simply that current and future rounds of corporate restructuring in relation to globalization and localization inherit spatial structure and markets. This is not lost on nations and communities in Europe and North America. Notice also that just because firms tend to locate in large markets, it does not mean that production need be so concentrated. Firms occupy various spaces, and various levels of the spatial hierarchy. A better understanding of the allocation of economic activity requires a better appreciation of the functional and competitive structures of firms in relation to the inherited different systems of places and spaces (unions and labour; see Walker 1999).

Finally, one further complication needs to be introduced. So far, in scenarios *A* and *B*, no mention has been made of the role and significance of finance. A number of our contributors deal with this issue, at a variety of spatial scales. Instead of rehearsing their arguments, let us take the analysis above one step further (as a prelude rather than as an exhaustive assessment). As the spatial reach of firms has grown, so too has the global and supra-regional flow of financial assets. Clearly, there is an important connection between these two phenomena; firms require a broad range of financial services as their reach extends beyond established relationships. At the same time, it has been observed by many that as commodity markets have become spatially integrated at the supra-regional and global scales, the number of financial markets has tended to shrink. In effect, as sub-national regions have claimed firms' interest as sites of production, global financial markets have claimed firms' attention as sites of finance and control. In between, and notwithstanding their control of national currency rates, nation-states have found it difficult to sustain traditional roles (Frankel 1996).

Explanations of financial centralization accompanied by the decentralization of production are not well developed in the economic geography literature (see our contributors and Clark 2000). While many dispute the end-of-geography thesis (including the editors), competition between financial markets has become a vital ingredient in the process of globalization (see Houthakker and Williamson 1996). In fact, competition is increasingly reserved for conflict between the contending global markets, not just national or regional markets. This may not matter, if national systems of banking and finance remain as different as they have been over the past century or so. But the evidence suggests that not only is there competition between global financial markets for the flow of transactions, there is increasing competition between national legal systems of corporate finance for dominance (La Porta *et al.* 1998). The combination, then, puts in play the spatial allocation of economic activity. At this level, national systems may be important ingredients in the allocation of activity. But the fact that a gap has opened up between national financial institutions tied to corporate interests and global financial institutions tied to market intermediation questions the long-term significance of national systems of finance.

This 'gap' is an important issue for the largest global firms. Many have had to establish links in at least two of the three largest markets. For instance, German firms have sought listing on the London and New York stock exchanges as well as Frankfurt. In this respect, there are strong incentives for the largest firms to sever their loyalties to national political and economic coalitions. Indeed, access to global financial markets allows them to extend their spatial reach to the last corners of the global economy while opening up an almost infinite variety of possible sites of production. For these types of firms, finance is a weapon in their armoury, used against less fortunate supra-regional and sub-national regional competitors. At the lowest level of the spatial hierarchy, however, the centralization of financial markets, the decline of regional markets, and the relatively larger distance to finance disables local firms in relation to their higher-tier competitors. Finance is an integral component of the emerging economic landscape of globalization and localization.

Looking Forward

One of the remarkable aspects of the current era is the sense amongst many on the left *and* the right that the nation-state and, by extension all scales of jurisdiction less that the global economy, are redundant. For many of the left, this claim is often associated with an uneasy triumphalism—a self-righteous argument to anyone who will listen that this is the necessary result of unfettered capitalism. Inevitably, they argue, globalization denies the possibility of 'local' solutions to common problems. On the right, globalism is also distrusted, being commonly portrayed as another version of an irresponsive super-state cloaked in the garb of multilateral regulation. For many of our contributors, however, globalization is inevitably rooted in geography. This may or may not be the nation-state. Throughout the book, our contributors argue about the prospects for other 'locations' in the global economy characterized by persistent difference and competitiveness. From globalization to systems of local differentiation and back to the supra-regional organization of trade, our contributors emphasize the spatial embeddedness of these processes. In the main, they eschew the tired rhetoric of old debates seeking new terrain to shadow-box into the next millennium.

This volume is a mandate for further research in the field, not a premature claim of closure on matters of great intellectual importance. In this respect, our intention is that the book should look forward on issues of contemporary relevance rather than looking backwards by reference to the canonical contributions of the past two hundred or so years. In this manner, the pages of the volume are a testament to the fact that the field of economic geography has embraced the economic upheavals of the past twenty years or so. There is little evidence of regret for a passing era, just as there is a strong commitment to making intellectual sense of the new world of economic geography. We intend that the book will be read for the virtues of individual contributions and for the juxtaposition of perspectives and argument. In this way, we have encouraged contributors to set out their own agendas while situating their arguments in the context of broader themes and issues. Consequently, the book is less a dispassionate survey of topics than it is a manifesto for current and future research.

References

ACS, Z. J., AUDRETSCH, D. B., and FELDMAN, M. P. 1994. The recipients of R&D spillovers: firm size and innovation. *Review of Economics and Statistics*, 76: 336–40.

ALONSO, W. 1964. *Location and Land Use*. Cambridge, Mass.: Harvard University Press.

ANTONELLI, C. 1995. *The Economics of Localised Technological Change and Industrial Dynamics*. Boston and Doderecht: Kluwer Academic Publishers.

AUDRETSCH, D. B., and FELDMAN, M. P. 1996. Knowledge spillovers and the geography of innovation and production. *American Economic Review*, 86: 630–40.

BARNES, T., and SHEPPARD, E., eds. forthcoming. *A Companion to Economic Geography*. Oxford: Blackwell.

BARRO, R., and SALA-I-MARTIN, X. 1995. *Economic Growth*. New York: McGraw-Hill.

BERRY, B. J. L. 1967. *Geography of Market Centers and Retail Distribution*. Englewood Cliffs, NJ: Prentice-Hall.

BRYSON, J., HENRY, N., KEEBLE, D., and MARTIN, R. L., eds. 1999. *The Economic Geography Reader*. Chichester and New York: John Wiley.

CLARK, G. L. 1981. The employment relation and spatial division of labor. *Annals, Association of American Geographers*, 71: 412–24.

—— 1989. *Unions and Communities under Siege*. Cambridge: Cambridge University Press.

—— 1998. Stylized facts and close dialogue: methodology in economic geography. *Annals, Association of American Geographers*, 88: 73–87.

—— 2000. *Pension Fund Capitalism*. Oxford: Oxford University Press.

—— GERTLER, M. S., and WHITEMAN, J. 1986. *Regional Dynamics: Studies in Adjustment Theory*. Boston: Allen and Unwin.

COOKE, P., and MORGAN, K. 1997. *The Associational Economy: Firms, Regions, and Innovation*. Oxford: Oxford University Press.

CROUCH, C., and STREECK, W., eds. 1997. *Political Economy of Modern Capitalism: Mapping Convergence and Diversity*. London: Sage.

DAVID, P. A. 1998. Comment on 'The role of geography in development' by Paul Krugman. Mimeo. Oxford: All Souls College.

—— FORAY, D., and DALLE, J.-M. 1998. Marshallian externalities and the emergence and spatial stability of technological enclaves. *Economics of Innovation and New Technology*, 6: 147–82.

DOREMUS, P., KELLER, W., PAULY, L., and REICH, S. 1998. *The Myth of the Global Corporation*. Cambridge: Cambridge University Press.

ELLISON, G., and GLAESER, E. 1997. Geographic concentration of US manufacturing industries: a dart-board approach. *Journal of Political Economy*, 105: 885–97.

FELDMAN, M. P. 1994. *The Geography of Innovation*. Boston: Kluwer.

—— 1999. Empirical studies of innovation and location. *Economics of Innovation and New Technology*, 8: 5–25.

FRANKEL, J. 1996. Exchange rates and the single currency. In *The European Equity Markets: The State of the Union and an Agenda for the Millennium*, ed. B. Steil. London: Royal Institute of International Affairs, 355–99.

FUJITA, M., KRUGMAN, P., and VENABLES, A. J. 1999. *The Spatial Economy: Cities, Regions and International Trade.* Cambridge, Mass.: MIT Press.

GERTLER, M. S. 1993. Implementing advanced manufacturing technologies in mature industrial regions: towards a social model of technology production. *Regional Studies*, 27: 665–80.

—— forthcoming. *Manufacturing Culture.* Oxford: Oxford University Press.

GIBSON-GRAHAM, J. K. 1997. *The End of Capitalism (As We Knew It).* Oxford: Blackwell.

HOPT, K. J., KANDA, H., ROE, M. J., WYMEERSCH, E., and PRIGGE, S., eds. 1998. *Comparative Corporate Governance: The State of the Art and Emerging Research.* Oxford: Oxford University Press.

HOUTHAKKER, H., and WILLIAMSON, P. J. 1996. *The Economics of Financial Markets.* New York: Oxford University Press.

KRUGMAN, P. 1991. *Geography and Trade.* Cambridge, Mass.: MIT Press.

LA PORTA, R., LOPEZ-DE-SILANES, F., SHLEIFER, A., and VISHNY, R. 1998. Law and finance. *Journal of Political Economy*, 106: 1113–55.

LEE, R., and WILLS, J., eds. 1997. *Geographies of Economies.* London: Edward Arnold.

MCDOWELL, L. 1997. *Capital Culture: Gender at Work in the City.* Oxford: Blackwell.

—— 1999. Scales, spaces and gendered differences: a comment on gender cultures. *Geoforum*, 30: 231–3.

MARTIN, R. L., BADDELEY, M., and TYLER, P. 1998. Unemployment disparities: convergence or persistence? *European Urban and Regional Studies*, 3: 195–215.

—— and SUNLEY, P. 1996. Paul Krugman's geographical economics and its implications for regional development theory: a critical assessment. *Economic Geography*, 72: 259–92.

PLUMMER, P., HAINING, R., and SHEPPARD, E. 1998. Spatial pricing in interdependent markets: testing assumptions and modeling price variation: a case study of gasoline retailing in St Cloud, Minnesota. *Environment and Planning A*, 30: 67–84.

PORTER, M. 1990. *The Competitive Advantage of Nations.* New York: Free Press.

RIFKIN, J. 1995. *The End of Work: The Decline of the Global Labor Force and the Dawn of the Post-Market Era.* New York: Tarcher/Putnam.

SAXENIAN, A. 1994. *Regional Advantage: Culture and Competition in Silicon Valley and Route 128.* Cambridge, Mass.: Harvard University Press.

SCOTT, A. 1988. *Metropolis.* Berkeley: University of California Press.

—— 1998. *Regions and the World Economy: The Coming Shape of Global Production, Competition, and Political Order.* Oxford: Oxford University Press.

SMITH, D. 1999. *Will Europe Work?* London: Profile Books.

STORPER, M., and SALAIS, R. 1997. *Worlds of Production.* Cambridge, Mass.: Harvard University Press.

STRANGE, S. 1997. The future of global capitalism: or, will divergence persist forever? In Crouch and Streeck, 1997: 182–91.

THISSE, J.-F., and WALLISER, B. 1997. Is space a neglected topic in mainstream economics? Mimeo. Louvain: Catholic University of Louvain.

THRIFT, N. 1998. Virtual capitalism: the globalisation of business knowledge. In

Virtualism: A New Political Economy, ed. J. Carrier and D. Miller. Oxford: Berg, 161–86.

Walker, R. A. 1999. Putting capital in its place: globalisation and the prospects for labor. *Geoforum*, 30: 263–84.

Webber, M. J., and Rigby, D. L. 1997. *The Golden Age Illusion: Rethinking Postwar Capitalism*. New York: Guilford Press.

Chapter **2**

Economic Geography: The Great Half-Century

Allen J. Scott

Preamble to an Intellectual History of Economic Geography

THE history of economic geography over the second half of the twentieth century is characterized by many twists and turns of substantive focus and sudden changes of theoretical mood. Over time, economic geography has behaved in a manner quite different from that which might be expected of a rationally ordered discipline pursuing some pre-ordained epistemological mission. Its historical course has been notably responsive to changes in external economic conditions, to the unfolding of political events, and to the play of professional ambitions and rivalries. Indeed, like astronomy, petroleum engineering, psychiatry, feminism, or bus driving, economic geography can be seen as a peculiar mix of concepts, methods, cultural conventions, human interests, practices, and empirical concerns that make it fully continuous ontologically with all other concrete social or historical phenomena (cf. Barnes 1974; Barnes *et al.* 1995; Foucault 1969; Latour 1991; Rorty 1979). By the same token, economic geography would seem to offer itself as an especially sensitive (or 'Foucauldian') case of the logic of disciplinary activity compared with, say, physics or chemistry whose highly abstracted and theorized state imbues them with the spurious appearance of ahistorical autonomy. These remarks also imply that any answer to the question 'what are the central problems of economic geography?' is likely to be historically contingent, even if the inertia of tradition and its institutionalization in a system of higher education means that important continuities can be deciphered over time.

My approach emphasizes historical contingency in the sense that I subscribe to the notion that the production of knowledge and the pattern of social life are reflexively intertwined, while at the same time I would also stress that this remark does *not* mean that questions of the logical or empirical validity of knowledge have no meaning. Equally, not all bits and pieces of knowledge, even when we admit their logical and empirical validity, can have equal claim on our attention (Rorty 1979). One of the few general principles that seems to be reasonably evident in this connection is that the concrete questions and problems that society faces at any given historical moment, tend also—in one way or another—to become burning questions and problems for practising social scientists (Mannheim 1952). It must be added, however, that this formulation tells us nothing about the problem of the contextual and positional perspectives that inescapably permeate the work of individual scholars and schools of thought.

Economic geography, then, is constituted as a set of contingent scholarly practices geared to achieving relevant understandings of our world, though not just any understandings. Because it represents a continuous and institutionalized tradition of research activity, economic geography is also identifiable in terms of a series of core intellectual sensibilities and concerns. Despite the fact that many of the theoretical and substantive objectives embodied in this enterprise have been quite unstable over the last half-century, economic geographers (together with an ever-varying array of scholars in adjacent social sciences) have generally and rather insistently focused on questions involving the spatial and locational (or, in another vocabulary, the urban and regional) foundations of economic life, and it is the remarkable collection of insights assembled under these signs that may be designated as 'economic geography'. At the same time, the internal instabilities of the field over the entire postwar period have been accompanied by and intensified by continual disputes over methods, empirical objectives, and theoretical orientations, especially between ascending and waning scholarly fractions (cf. Taylor 1976).

A thorough account of the growth and development of this domain of ideas—one that respects all of the philosophical and theoretical niceties that have come into play as the field has evolved—is obviously beyond the scope of the present chapter. What I shall attempt to provide, rather, is a highly generalized overview of the formation of economic geography since the early 1950s, paying attention to its main intellectual orientations in relation to an ever-changing background of social, political, and professional pressures. Readers seeking more detailed statements about the turbulent history of economic geography, as well as about the discipline of geography as a whole, can find excellent discussions in Barnes (1996), Billinge *et al.* (1982), Claval (1964, 1977), Cloke *et al.* (1991), Fellmann (1986), Holt-Jensen (1988), Johnston (1991), Livingstone (1992), and Peet (1998).

The Metamorphosis

As academic geography emerged in the immediate postwar period it succumbed to one of the most severe identity crises that it has experienced in a perennial history of identity crises. Should geographers continue to hew to the traditional core of the discipline as represented by regional description and synthesis (or as Hartshorne (1939) had formulated the problem, to areal differentiation), in which case they were committed for the most part to idiographic approaches? Or should they, following the programmatic arguments of Schaefer (1953) and McCarty (1954), consider geography as a systematic theory-building discipline eschewing inductive synthesis and pursuing an all-out search for laws of location and spatial order?

If the dominant ideology of the field in the 1940s and 1950s favored the former approach, geography as a whole was also rife with practices that significantly prefigured the latter, and nowhere was this more the case than in those branches of the discipline concerned with economic issues. In both North America and Western Europe, geographers were becoming increasingly preoccupied with efforts to systematize knowledge about practical phenomena such as (1) regional growth and industrial location (e.g. Alexander 1954; George 1958; Harris 1954; Ullman 1958; Wise 1949), (2) patterns of urbanization (e.g. Brush 1953; Dickenson 1947; Harris and Ullman 1945), and (3) flows and interactions through space (e.g. Ajo 1953; Godlund 1956; Hägerstrand 1952). The individuals associated with these efforts (especially the Scandinavians, Ajo, Godlund, and Hägerstrand) can be seen as a sort of vanguard pointing toward theoretical geography as such.

The growing flood of proto-theoretical studies such as these posed rising challenges to the legitimacy of the regional synthetic approach which, as Ackerman (1958) had suggested, was largely unable to produce the kinds of insights that more disaggregative research activity was now routinely delivering. Despite frequent and energetic appeals to disciplinary orthodoxy and tradition (e.g. Hartshorne 1955; Lukermann 1958), the synthesizing idiographic urge in postwar geography was gradually being pushed to the academic sidelines, and by the late 1950s, the path was becoming more open for aggressive affirmation of sub-disciplinary home rule within the field of geography at large, with economic geography backed up by emerging quantitative methodologies leading the way. At least, this was the case in North America and Scandinavia. In Britain, France, and Germany, where disciplinary authority could be more decisively exerted by entrenched academic oligarchies, the path remained for the moment largely blocked.

Spatial Analysis and Regional Science

The long postwar boom in North America and Western Europe brought with it a great expansion of Fordist mass-production industry and the emergence of modern consumer society, though these features were also accompanied by complex and deepening systems of spatial disparities. This was a period, too, in which the Keynesian and welfare-statist policy systems that helped to keep postwar social and economic arrangements on an even keel were gradually brought to a pitch of high and pervasive operation. Concomitantly, cities and regions throughout the developed world were changing and growing in puzzling ways throwing question after question onto the research agendas of academics and onto the dockets of policy-makers (Bailly 1995). Problems of location, spatial development, transportation, and so on had now become of major significance in the sense that they were raised to a new scale of intensity in Fordist economic systems, and were important objectives of governmental action, and by the mid-1950s they were accordingly attracting the attention of increasing numbers of geographers and economists (cf. Friedmann and Alonso 1967).

On the one side, William Garrison and his students in the Department of Geography at Washington University were beginning to press forward in a series of research undertakings focused intently on theoretical and substantive issues of spatial analysis, and they soon came to constitute a sort of pioneer fringe relative to the discipline as a whole. These efforts covered a wide assortment of problems, including industrial location and land-use patterns (Garrison 1959*a*; Garrison and Marble 1957), urbanization and central place systems (Berry and Garrison 1958*a*, 1958*b*), transportation networks (Garrison 1959*b*, 1960), and the spatial dynamics of trade and social interaction (Morrill and Garrison 1960; Nystuen and Dacey 1961). They were also accompanied by loud and increasingly self-confident claims that geography as a whole must become an analytical, law-finding discipline conjoined with quantitative methodologies.

On the other side, Walter Isard and a number of colleagues at the University of Pennsylvania were expressing growing dissatisfaction with economists' approach to the world as a 'wonderland of no spatial dimensions' (Isard 1956: 25), and they were in the process of inventing a new hybrid discipline combining elements of economics with elements of geography (Alonso 1960; Isard 1956; Stevens 1958; Warntz 1959). The central objective of this hybrid *regional science*, as it came to be known, was to rewrite neoclassical competitive equilibrium theory in terms of spatial coordinates so that all demands, supplies, and price variables could be expressed as an explicit function of location. In practice, it was thought, this ambitious theoretical program would eventually come to maturity on the basis of a thoroughgoing reconceptualization of neoclassical economics in terms of Weberian location theory, input-output analysis, and linear programming models of inter-regional exchange (Isard 1957, 1960; Moses 1960).

From their very beginnings, spatial analysis and regional science tended to merge together to form an intellectual amalgam focused on identifying the regularities of the neoclassical space-economy. Spatial analysts and regional scientists, in addition, reached back to an earlier, mainly German, tradition of location theory (e.g. Christaller 1933; Hoover 1937; Lösch 1940; Palander 1935; Von Thünen 1826; Weber 1909) as well as out to a small group of contemporary French economists who were producing highly original work on the theory of growth poles and related regional development ideas (Boudeville 1961; Perroux 1950, 1955; Ponsard 1955, 1958). For the geographers, the association with regional science constituted a critical platform of support, for it offered them a diversity of publication outlets and helped to endow them with a scholarly warrant that greatly strengthened their hand in their continuing and bitter quarrels with traditionalists (Gould 1979). By the early 1960s the battle between the new and the old within the discipline of geography had begun to shift decisively in favor of the new (Burton 1963), at least in North America, and over the next several years quantitative geography (whose main but not exclusive concern was with economic issues) became a sort of commanding orthodoxy, still highly contested to be sure, but now securely in a position of professional leadership.

Over the next decade or so, economic geographers in North America together with their allies in regional science produced a body of writings of exceptional methodological sophistication and intellectual quality on virtually every conceivable aspect of the ways in which space and markets interact to produce patterns of urban and regional development. A significant proportion of these writings was also concerned with establishing policy benchmarks for the guidance of governmental decision-makers and planners, and spatial analysis and regional science (at least in their early incarnations in the 1960s) participated actively in the wider liberal-democratic policy thrust in American academia generally at that time. Two further features of work in economic geography in the 1960s and early 1970s need to be noted. One was the continued steady elaboration of quantitative/mathematical methodologies and languages (e.g. Curry 1970; Dacey 1962; King 1969; Scott 1971; Thomas 1968; Wilson 1970). The other was the swelling mass of philosophical literature that was being produced (e.g. Bunge 1962; Curry 1967; Golledge and Amadeo 1968; Olsson 1970), culminating in the great paeon to positivist philosophy as the essential foundation of geographic scholarship published by Harvey in 1969. This entire effort of research and publication was in high degree driven forward by generous funding from sources such as the Office of Naval Research, the National Institutes of Health, the National Science Foundation, Resources for the Future, as well as from federal and local governmental agencies.

By the mid- to late 1960s, the so-called new geography was beginning to diffuse back to Europe, especially to Britain where, spurred on by the influential publications of Haggett (1965) and Chorley and Haggett (1967), it was already moving into a position of academic importance. In France and Germany where a strong classical geographic tradition remained ensconced in the universities, it was firmly rebuffed. For example, in spite of some scattered attempts to assimilate the new thinking into French geography (cf. Claval 1968; Merlin 1973), it made little headway against a conservative and authoritarian university establishment, though symptomatically (given the Gaullist push to modernize the French economy in the 1960s), spatial analysis and regional science did find a ready home in France among engineers and applied economists (cf. Benko 1998).

In North America, spatial analysis and regional science reached the zenith of their influence some time in the late 1960s and early 1970s (Isserman 1993). Subsequently, as we shall see, they experienced a sharp loss of prestige and persuasiveness, partly for wider political reasons, and partly, as Thisse (1997) has suggested, because of their commitment to forms of economic modeling based on highly restrictive notions of convexity and perfect competition. Quite recently, new life has been breathed into spatial analysis and regional science by Krugman (1991*a*, 1991*b*) who in a certain manner has reinvented this line of inquiry in the guise of geographical economics. Krugman's writings point toward some important new research directions by their insistence on the basic importance of increasing returns effects and imperfect competition in the determination of locational events. A useful critical review of these writings has recently been published by Martin and Sunley (1996), who also pinpoint the strong residual role that the epistemological prepossessions and analytical machinery of microeconomics play in Krugman's geography, and concomitantly, how his work, despite its originality, can perhaps best be seen as a continuation of the tradition of spatial analysis and regional science (see also Dymski 1996). Better yet, we might call it a 'new' regional science.

Brief Interlude I: Behavioral Geography

In conformity with their theoretical roots in neoclassical economics, spatial analysis and regional science explicitly drew on an ontology in which the final irreducible units of society comprise atomized, utility-maximizing, omniscient individuals caught up in competitive markets. Without in any radical sense seeking to oppose this ontological view—in particular, its insistence on the atomized structure of society—a number of economic geographers during the 1960s felt that a more nuanced conception of human motivation and the behavioral environment might offer a more fruitful foundation for scientific investigation.

Already, Gould (1963) had introduced the idea of behavior in relation to uncertainty into economic geography, and in two influential papers, Wolpert (1964, 1965) had begun to question the behavioral axioms embedded in the notion of *homo economicus*. In particular, in his study of farming practices in Southern Sweden, Wolpert (1964) suggested that the spatial structure of the agricultural landscape could not be explained in terms of all-out income-maximizing strategies on the part of farmers; instead, he advanced the claim that economic behavior can be more convincingly analyzed by reference to the notions of bounded rationality and satisficing forms of decision-making.

An ambitious attempt to systematize these themes into a fundamental set of postulates for economic geography was published by Pred in 1967. Pred sought to show that individual decision-makers in any concrete geographic situation can be described in terms of their positions along two continua, one of which is represented by variations in the quantity and quality of information available, the other of which is represented by variations in decision-makers' ability to use that information. As a consequence of the unpredictable position of any given individual in relation to these two continua, locational patterns will almost never be uniquely determinate, according to Pred, but will generally be marked by a strong stochastic element.

Cox and Golledge (1969) introduced the additional concepts of learning and perception into the analytical repertory of behavioral economic geography, and Hägerstrand (1970), concerned that regional science had somehow lost sight of the sentient human being, proposed a novel and in many ways illuminating schema that sought to track the interacting paths of individuals as they moved through the dimensions of time and space. Hägerstrand's ideas, however, had less influence in economic geography than they did in certain other branches of human geography where more humanistic forms of explanation tended to prevail (Gregory 1978). Behavioral geography, as such, became more or less the preserve of a few highly specialized researchers who turned increasingly to experimental psychology for their inspiration. In a highly indicative paper published in 1976, Cullen expressed the by then widely shared view that behavioral geography had ended up in a positivistic blind alley which was every bit as mechanistic as the neoclassical economic geography that it was supposed to supplant.

The Rediscovery of Political Economy

As the 1960s waned, a number of strong new winds started to blow throughout the social sciences in North America. During the second half of the 1960s the Civil Rights Movement and the Vietnam War had engendered a steadily rising political temperature in the United States. Simultaneously, the late 1960s represented the turning-point of both the American Fordist manufacturing system as well as of the Keynesian welfare-statist policy consensus that had held sway over the entire postwar period. By the early 1970s high and persistent rates of unemployment and inflation were becoming stubborn national problems in both North America and Western Europe, and formerly prosperous industries and regions were falling into severe crisis, as represented above all by the near collapse during the 1970s of major manufacturing centers such as the American Midwest, the British Midlands, and the German Ruhr. The insistent methodological individualism of then dominant forms of economic geography was clearly inadequate to the task of dealing with the grand structural forces that seemed to lie behind these developments, and the perception of its inadequacy was reinforced by the critique of capitalism which had now suddenly appeared on the agenda in various branches of the social sciences.

In geography, the most dramatic example of these shifting currents in economic geography is represented by the thinking of David Harvey, whose lengthy positivist statement of 1969 was followed just four years later by a book that opened a window onto a full-blown reinterpretation of geographic questions in terms of Marxian political economy (Harvey 1973). Harvey, along with increasing numbers of other scholars in the field, challenged the self-presumed neutrality of neoclassical spatial analysis and regional science, which they characterized as apologetic technocratic constructions, silently and unselfconsciously serving to mask the structurally determined injustices of capitalism. They repudiated in particular the evacuation of capitalist class relations from the analytical horizon of previous researchers (cf. Blaut 1979; Massey 1979; Peet 1977; Slater 1976). Instead, they now sought to demonstrate how the forces of capitalist accumulation and their associated social structures create and recreate geographic realities in what Soja (1980) called a 'socio-spatial dialectic', and how the conflicts built into these realities are mediated by a state apparatus representing the political condensation of the class tensions in society at large (Dear and Scott 1981). The principal task now was to construct a thoroughgoing historical geography of the capitalist mode of production.

Geographers working within this transformed analytical framework produced a remarkable collection of studies over the 1970s and early 1980s dealing with a wide range of urban and regional predicaments. One important research theme was opened up by anglophone economic geographers together with an allied group of French Marxist urbanists on the logic and dynamics of urban space under capitalism, and the interconnections between land rent, housing provision, and urban planning (Harvey 1985; Lipietz 1974; Massey and Catalano 1978; Preteceille 1973; Roweis and Scott 1978; Topalov 1973; Walker 1981). Another theme that was very much to the fore in this new political-economic approach was concerned with problems of poverty, job loss, deindustrialization, and regional decline (Bluestone and Harrison 1982; Carney 1980; Massey and Meegan 1982; Peet 1975; Rowthorne 1986), and this theme was in turn associated with detailed investigations of regional industrial restructuring and the geography of labor (e.g. Dunford and Perrons 1983; Massey 1984; Soja *et al.* 1983; Walker and Storper 1981). A third important stream of work was devoted to matters of uneven development in capitalism at the regional, national, and international scales (e.g. Forbes 1984; Harvey 1982; Slater 1976; Smith 1984). Much of this latter research also intersected at many different levels with an older and wider tradition of development studies that stressed cumulative causation as a basic mechanism generating patterns of uneven development in capitalism (Hirschman 1958; Myrdal 1957), as well as with a number of concurrent analyses of capitalism as a system of unequal exchange and economic imperialism (Amin 1973; Emmanuel 1969; Frank 1967).

The more orthodox Marxians within this group of economic geographers laid heavy emphasis on the notions of class struggle, the labor theory of value, and structural crisis as the essential foundations of any viable research program. A small group of economic geographers (almost all of them with intellectual roots in the quantitative geography movement) adopted a more heterodox though still distinctly *Marxisant* approach, as expressed in technical analyses of core processes within the capitalist economy and their spatial effects. In its original guise, this tendency mainly involved attempts to derive formal neo-Ricardian or Sraffan models of the spatial structure of capitalist production systems (e.g. Barnes 1984; Scott 1976; Sheppard 1983; Sheppard and Barnes 1990). Later exponents moved on to a variety of related problems concerning the impacts of capital investment, technological change, and the employment relation on locational structures, sometimes from an explicitly disequilibrium perspective (e.g. Clark 1981; Clark *et al.* 1986; Martin 1984; Webber and Rigby 1996).

Even as the appropriation of ideas by geographers from Marxian political economy and related fields was moving into high gear after the mid-1970s, strong dissatisfactions were being voiced about some of the heavy-duty intellectual baggage that had accompanied the transfer. Deep concern was expressed by many geographers about what was felt to be the increasingly structuralist and economistic turn of the discipline. The tocsin bell for structural Marxism was actually rung by a historian (Thompson 1978), but geographers from all parts of the discipline instantly began to relay the message. The result was the publication of a barrage of critical commentaries calling for a geography that was less inclined to interpret spatial forms as unmediated outcomes of the logic of macro-social structures (above all, some ahistorical logic of capital), and that was more open to the force of human intentionality and sensitive to a variety of political experiences and forms of action (Gregory 1981; Thrift 1983). At the same time, wide segments of the discipline were beginning to resonate with the claims of a rising cohort of feminist scholars who were as much concerned with highlighting the role of gender as of class in processes of geographic eventuation (cf. Hanson and Hanson 1980; McDowell and Massey 1984). More generally, structuralist Marxism offered a framework of analysis that was judged insufficiently open-ended and insufficiently alert to the notion of the human subject to accommodate many of the emerging trends that were now coming to be important in the practices of radical activists and in the thinking of the academic left.

Just as these dissenting opinions were being formulated, Giddens (1979, 1984) was putting forth an outline of a theoretical sociology that preserved certain aspects of the notion of structural determination while simultaneosly conjuring up a major role for human agency. It is not possible to compress the intricate and difficult arguments of Giddens into a few lines, but in their barest essentials they pointed to a reconceptualization of the social as a dual domain of over-arching structures and individual practices, where the former are both the medium and the outcome of the latter. Furthermore, a degree of temporal stability of these relations can be expected because historical events are always to some measure concatenated by a recursive logic of social reproduction. This particular view of the macro-dynamics of social life had an enormous influence on human geography generally, and helped significantly to promote a number of new currents in the field.

One segment of the field where Giddens's structure-agency theory had an especially forceful impact was in the ascending localities research program, itself a partial reaction to the spreading neo-conservatism of the 1980s and the concomitant retreat of national governments from Keynesian welfare statism, so that individual regions (i.e. collectivities with specific local interests) were increasingly being left to fend for themselves in the fight to maintain living standards and social services. The problem was especially acute in Britain, where the long-drawn-out crisis induced by the collapse of older industrial communities continued unabated through much of the 1980s.

Brief Interlude II: The Localities Debate

In various publications during the late 1970s and early 1980s, Doreen Massey had blazed an intellectual trail that led resolutely away from grand structural explanations in Marxian economic geography to a more empirically inclined treatment of the space-economy of capitalism (Massey 1979, 1984; Massey and Meegan 1982). Uniqueness and difference had now turned into points of analytic interest rather than mere background noise, and with the affirmation of their investigative significance, any notion of theoretical totalization became correspondingly anathema. Massey's 1984 book on spatial divisions of labor in Britain took seriously the proposition that while both class *and* gender are important in understanding the workings of the space-economy, their concrete effects and political meanings often differ greatly from one area to the next, depending on divergences in underlying geographic and historical circumstances.

This approach met with a sympathetic hearing, above all in Britain, where Giddens's structure-agency theory had become especially influential, and where it was—no doubt in reaction to the perceived excesses of earlier structuralist analyses—increasingly being invoked in studies heavily tilted to the agency side of the formulation. The persuasiveness of the approach was further boosted by the writings of Sayer (1982, 1984) on realist epistemology in economic geography. One of the principal axes of Sayer's reasoning is that although particular kinds of relationships in society may be deemed to be causally necessary, the actual form that they take also depends on the non-necessary contingent circumstances through which they are actually played out. Thus, while we may articulate valid laws about socio-economic processes (such as the tendency for profit rates to equalize across sectors and regions), we cannot expect these laws to be manifest at the empirical level in absolutely uniform regularities because they never actually materialize in *ceteris paribus* form (Sayer 1982). In any case, it was claimed, empirically realized clusters of necessary and contingent relationships are often just as important to the analyst or policy-maker as highly refined abstractions privileging the necessary.

The scene was now set for a spate of research on the economic geography of particular localities stressing the unique and varied ways in which they were responding to both external and internal social pressures. On the one hand, localities were seen as being subject to wider national and international capitalist forces; on the other hand, these forces were also seen as being channeled through complex local contingencies. A large proportion of this research was in practice focused on a continuing concern for the geographic effects of British economic decline and restructuring in the context of Thatcherite policy initiatives which were leaving many localities in an increasingly unprotected position, and one of its roots lies in the studies of job loss and deindustrialization alluded to above. A pioneering paper on the subject was published by Urry in 1981, but it was the collaborative research project on Changing Urban and Regional Systems in the UK (CURS), funded by the Economic and Social Research Program, that constituted the main pole of scientific activity in this regard (Cooke 1989).

The localities research program, as it came to be designated, produced a wealth of detailed inquiries into various case-study areas in Britain, and showed how they were responding in many different ways to the stresses and strains exerted by local, national, and global economic forces. It was also the focus of a brief debate on the problems of concreteness and abstraction in economic geography (cf. Cox and Mair 1989; Duncan and Savage 1989). As Smith (1987) has pointed out, however, localities research quickly assumed the mantle of a rather straightforward descriptive and empirical study program, notwithstanding its own proclamations about the need to hold firmly onto a theoretical anchor. In its twofold embrace of structure-agency theory and realist epistemology, the localities research program had turned for the most part—by default and without any complicity on the part of Giddens or Sayer—into an amalgam of inductive studies of regional economic trends and of commentary on the cut and thrust of local politics. As such, the program was entirely serviceable and sensible, but not especially calculated to give rise to dazzling new insights, and by the early 1990s, it was beginning to fade into the background of economic geography.

A World of Regions

Meanwhile, during the late 1970s to mid-1980s, the attention of a small number of economic geographers on both sides of the Atlantic was being drawn to the resurgence of regional economies in areas that had formerly been peripheral to the main sweep of Fordist manufacturing activities and that were now growing rapidly on the basis of new so-called post-Fordist industries. An important feature of these industries was that they seemed to be marked by relatively high levels of spatial agglomeration, intra-local business networking, innovation, and growth. For the most part, they comprised revivified craft or neo-artisanal sectors in various parts of North America and Europe (Becattini 1979, 1987; Storper and Christopherson 1987), high-technology manufacturing in places like Silicon Valley, Orange County, Route 128, or the London–Bristol axis (Hall *et al.* 1987; Malecki 1980; Markusen *et al.* 1986; Rees and Stafford 1984), and financial and business services in major global cities and other specialized centers (Bailly 1994; Daniels 1979; Pred 1977). Indeed, at the very time when, as already noted, many economic geographers were writing deeply pessimistic accounts about crises in older areas that had been dominated by Fordist manufacturing, a remarkable economic revival was becoming evident in certain other areas that were now developing apace on the basis of post-Fordist industrial growth. A number of different but overlapping research networks or schools of thought, involving geographers, economists, and other social scientists, sprang into being in response to this latter phenomenon. Two of them can be seen as more or less direct responses to economic transformations occurring in their own backyard, so to speak. One of these may be designated the Italian School, as represented primarily by Becattini (1987) and his co-workers at the University of Florence who reactivated the Marshallian idea of the industrial district in an effort to account for the dramatic rise of neo-artisanal manufacturing in Northeast and Central Italy after the 1970s. The other is sometimes referred to as the California School, which in its efforts to account for the peculiarities of the industrial geography of Southern California and the Bay Area put a heavy accent on the role of vertical disintegration, inter-industrial transactional networks, and local labor markets (together with concomitant increasing returns effects), as the main factors underlying the spatial agglomeration displayed by many post-Fordist forms of economic activity (Scott 1986, 1988; Storper and Walker 1989). A third research network was constituted by the more international Groupe de Recherche Européen sur les Milieux Innovateurs (GREMI), an association centered in Paris, but which drew together a diverse group of geographers and economists working on the new regionalism in places like Silicon Valley, the Cité Scientifique to the south of Paris, and the Third Italy; the members of the GREMI network favored the idea that regional growth could best be analyzed in terms of the innovative forces contained in the multiform texture of local economic and social life (cf. Aydalot 1986). The fourth group is represented by the inventors of the concept of flexible specialization (Piore and Sabel 1984), who also drew heavily on the case of Italian neo-artisanal manufacturing as an example of the new organizational-technological paradigm that they maintained was in the process of making its historical appearance.

Piore and Sabel, along with the California School, emphasized the sharpness of the historical divide that seemed to have occurred over the 1970s between Fordist and post-Fordist forms of industrial development in the major capitalist countries. The importance ascribed to this divide was further underpinned by certain appropriations from French regulationist theory, and above all the idea that different historical forms of capitalism can be described in terms of distinctive 'regimes of accumulation' and 'modes of social regulation' (Boyer 1986; Lipietz 1986). Some of the members of the California School proceeded to assimilate the notions of Fordist and post-Fordist forms of economic development into these same terms, and added the further twist that at moments when an industrial divide is being crossed, a 'window of locational opportunity' (Scott and Angel 1987: 884) may briefly open up allowing for large-scale shifts in the spatial pattern of economic activity.

Not surprisingly, in a field as quarrelsome as economic geography, intense debates about the various claims of these different schools of thought were soon raging (Amin and Robins 1990; Gertler 1988; Lovering 1990; Schoenberger 1989). Some of the most vigorous opposition to the new ideas came from Britain where some segments of the laborite left in academia viewed them with deep suspicion as harbingers of a regressive doctrine promoting labor market flexibility and the glorification of the entrepreneur at the expense of workers' rights and welfare (cf. Pollert 1991). The full extent of these debates and the political-*cum*-professional rivalries underlying them defies effective recapitulation in these brief pages. Suffice it to say that one particularly strong line of critical commentary, perhaps best summarized in the statement by Amin and Robins (1990), averred that much of the new work on flexible specialization, post-Fordism, and regional development put too much emphasis on the notion of a sharp historical rupture between Fordist and post-Fordist stages of industrialization, overgeneralized the applicability of the Marshallian model of industrial district formation, romanticized the implications of flexible specialization for labor, and paid insufficient attention to the intensifying influence of oligopolistic multinational corporations. Whatever the merits and demerits of the various arguments arrayed on the different sides of this issue, very little intellectual closure seems actually to have been accomplished. Characteristically, the discussion has simply moved on as the questions themselves have come to be recast in relation to changes in economic and geographic realities.

On the one hand, there has been a marked rise of interest in globalization, an interest growing in part out of an older geographic literature on the international division of labor and the activities of multinational corporations (Dicken 1986; Fröbel *et al.* 1980; Taylor and Thrift 1982). Some researchers have tended to view globalization as a sort of liquefaction process in which capital becomes hypermobile, 'tending to a nomadic existence' (Amin and Robins 1990: 210), and pointing unequivocally to the end of geography (O'Brien 1992). In this view, geographic space is thought of as being constituted by a dynamic system of global flows rather than as a static structure of locations (Castells and Henderson 1987). More recently, there has been a disposition to counter this latter type of formulation by insisting on the stubborn locational rootedness of world capitalism in regional production complexes combined with its continued unevenness of development across the globe (Amin and Thrift 1992; Dicken *et al.* 1997; Lever 1997; Storper 1997; Swyngedouw 1997).

Thus, on the other hand, the topic of the region as a source of competitive advantage in a globalizing economic order has also recently received special attention (e.g. Porter 1990, 1998; Saxenian 1994; Scott 1998). Some of the more important lines of investigation associated with this trend involve attempts to re-write theories of regional development in terms of:

1. the informal cultures, conventions, and untraded interdependencies that sustain (and sometimes hamper) the functioning of localized production systems (e.g. Gertler 1995; McDowell 1997; Peet 1997; Salais and Storper 1993);
2. institutions of social regulation and their effects on regional economic performance and the structuring of local labor markets (e.g. Leborgne and Lipietz 1993; Peck 1996; Peck and Tickell 1994);
3. dynamic learning and innovation processes and the ways in which they shape regional economic change (e.g. Feldman 1994; Malmberg 1997; Simmie 1997).

Much of this research has also been greatly influenced by theoretical notions of evolution, path-dependency, and institutional economics borrowed directly from economists like Arthur (1989), David (1985), Hodgson (1988), and Nelson and Winter (1982).

Economic globalization is now commonly described as an unfinished—indeed incipient—long-term process. Its overall trend is toward mounting levels of functional integration of different national economies; but it is also widely taken to be durably anchored in (and to be responsible for the rise of) a worldwide archipelago of stable regional economies or global city-regions (Veltz 1996, 1997). The new perspectives offered by this convergent set of interests have helped to spark off allied research into such diverse topics as the geography of international finance and money (Clark and O'Connor 1997; Corbridge 1994; Leyshon and Thrift 1995), scales of social regulation from the local through the national and plurinational to the global (Peck and Tickell 1994; Swyngedouw 1997), and, as a corollary, citizenship and democracy (Hirst 1994; Keating 1998), not to mention a new set of debates about the very concept of globalization itself (cf. Agnew and Corbridge 1995; Hirst and Thompson 1996).

The evolving worldwide archipelago of regional economies is a space containing relatively prosperous foci of growth and development, and even a number of erstwhile Third World areas have recently been brought within its ambit, particularly in East and Southeast Asia. Many other parts of the world, however, have clearly been left behind, and these continue to present troubling questions about economic development. There has always been a small group of geographers with an interest in these questions (cf. Brookfield 1975; Corbridge 1986; Forbes 1984; Hecht 1985; Watts 1983), although their writings have never constituted much more than a rather specialized corner of the field. Of late, some of them (together with researchers in affiliated fields) have started to write about the ways in which the wider body of work on regional growth mechanisms cited above might offer some alternative strategic approaches to development in economically backward areas (Aero 1992; Nadvi and Schmitz 1994; Schmitz 1995).

Science, Politics, and Rhetoric

In this discussion, I have tended to treat the main episodes in the postwar history of economic geography as occurring in relatively discrete blocks of historical time. To be sure, each of these episodes can be described in terms of a moment of emergence, a subsequent phase of rapid efflorescence, and a period of decline, where the latter period is often extended over a number of decades. As a consequence, almost all of the episodes identified here continue to leave traces on the work of practicing economic geographers today, just as adherents of this or that tendency whose heyday is long past continue to produce and publish scholarly work right down to the present. The intellectual landscape of economic geography at any given moment in time is therefore best represented as a sort of intellectual palimpsest rather than as a unified front.

Moreover, even as interest in the resurgence of regional economies and the dynamics of globalization remains currently at a high pitch, yet other intellectual preoccupations are starting to be expressed. This is perhaps most clearly evidenced by the increasing influence of cultural geography (and cultural studies more generally) on economic geography, a trend that is no doubt being accentuated as left-liberal attitudes and commitments in academia shift away from a concern with redistributive justice toward issues of identity and selfhood (Sayer 1997). Hence, there is now a rapidly expanding literature that seeks to reproblematize spatial economic phenomena not just as instrumental outcomes, but also as interpretative events that can be best understood in terms of habits and lifestyles, gendered interests, the semiotics of consumption, and so on (e.g. Crang 1997; Crewe and Lowe 1995; McDowell 1997; Thrift and Olds 1996).

From its first emergence after World War II as a conspicuously self-assertive sub-discipline, economic geography has been the scene of a constantly changing parade of theoretical and empirical pursuits combined with virtually ever-present debate and controversy. Economic geography reflects in microcosm the deeply contested and negotiated course which, as Livingstone (1992) has indicated, marks the development of the discipline of geography at large. Barnes (1996) expresses the same idea with his characterization of economic geography as an intellectual terrain fissured by many breaks and dislocations. However, this undoubtedly accurate representation of the history of the sub-discipline should not blind us to the evident continuities that are also an evident element of its temporal structure, and in particular, its resolute concern for spatial and locational processes. One important consequence of this emphasis is that over the last few decades, economic geography has played a major role in countering a widely held view throughout the social sciences that geographic space is of steadily diminishing relevance to the analysis of economic affairs. The findings of economic geographers clearly indicate the opposite. Space becomes not less important but more important with the passage of historical time, not just because it is a domain of strategic resources offering ever more subtle opportunities for economic contestation and differentiation, but also and concomitantly because of its reassertion as a medium of social and political action, that is, as a constantly changing assemblage of territorial interests in the new global economy.

For the same reason, Barnes's proposition that the work of economic geographers represents a system of textual and discursive effects whose essential meaning resides in their status as metaphors strikes me as being rather off-key. Even when one concedes that our knowledge of the world is dependent on concepts created by epistemic and interpretative communities (Sunley 1996), any attempt to depict academic work in economic geography as being in important ways no more than a collection of figures of speech, tends to dissolve away the immensely real substantive issues and purposive human practices that have always been and still are fundamentally at stake in this work. That said, research in economic geography has never proceeded in some serene state of unblinking analytical focus on the world out there. As we have seen, its aims, purposes, and political engagements have been constantly shifting, and each shift has tended to provoke a welter of critique and counter-critique. Much of this proclivity to debate, of course, has served to correct, refine, and clarify ongoing research. Much of it has also been a reflection of the political cross-currents that have swept over the field from time to time. In yet other cases, it has been ignited by the changing fortunes of different professional groups as those whose human capital is sunk in waning problematics engage with those pressing forward with new approaches in the endless struggle to come out on top in the stock-market of ideas.

This state of affairs is only aberrant or irrational in relation to some purely normative epistemology (say, logical positivism or critical rationalism) which treats knowledge as an idealized abstraction rather than as a concrete social phenomenon. In the end, as I intimated at the beginning of this chapter, knowledge and social life are cut from exactly the same cloth of substantive reality. 'Knowing', in the words of Latour (1990: 38) 'is not a disinterested cognitive activity'. This condition of immanence is in part captured by the notion of scientific paradigms and their eventual obsolescence as proposed by Kuhn (1962), but it is perhaps more adequately expressed in a conception of knowledge as an assortment of relatively disconnected (but internally reasoned) fragments, partially formed constellations of ideas and attitudes that are picked up, worked on for a time, then pushed aside again as the tide of social change sweeps along. From this perspective, the goal of theoretical totalization is not so much impossible in principle, or somehow, as postmodernists seem to believe, a necessary misrepresentation of reality, as it is simply pointless and uninteresting (cf. Graham 1988).

I have tried to account for the recent history of economic geography not by reference to how it *ought* to have been or how it *ought* to become according to some a priori theory of knowledge, but rather as an unfolding if internally erratic tradition whose shape and form are irrevocably conditioned by the multiple social realities that it tries to deal with and that circumscribe its modes of operation. The last half-century of economic geographic research has yielded an exceptional harvest of conceptual insights, methodological advances, empirical knowledge, contributions to effective policy-making, and, not least, critical commentary. It is no small tribute to those who have toiled in the vineyard over the last fifty years to say that their efforts have cumulatively transformed economic geography from the small backwater of academia that it once was into the vibrant field of intellectual endeavor that it has now become, and with an impact that resonates increasingly far beyond the discipline of geography itself.

References

Ackerman, E. A. 1958. *Geography as a Fundamental Research Discipline*. Department of Geography, University of Chicago, Research Paper No. 53.

Aero, A. 1992. New pathways to industrialization in Tanzania: theoretical and strategic considerations. *IDS Bulletin*, 23/3: 15–20.

Agnew, J., and Corbridge, S. 1995. *Mastering Space: Hegemony, Territory, and International Political Economy*. London: Routledge.

Ajo, R. 1953. *Contributions to Social Physics: A Program Sketch with Special Regard to National Planning*. Lund Studies in Geography Series B, No. 11. Lund: C. W. K. Gleerup.

Alexander, J. W. 1954. The basic–nonbasic concept of urban economic functions. *Economic Geography*, 30: 246–61.

Alonso, W. 1960. A theory of the urban land market, *Papers and Proceedings of the Regional Science Association*, 6: 149–58.

Amin, A., and Robins, K. 1990. Industrial districts and regional development: limits and possibilities. In *Industrial Districts and Inter-Firm Cooperation in Italy*, ed. F. Pyke, G. Becattini, and W. Sengenberger. Geneva: International Institute for Labour Studies, 185–219.

——and Thrift, N. 1992. Neo-marshallian nodes in global networks. *International Journal of Urban and Regional Research*, 16: 571–87.

Amin, S. 1973. *Le Développement inégal: essai sur les formations sociales du capitalisme périphérique*. Paris: Les Editions de Minuit.

Arthur B. 1989. Competing technologies, increasing returns and lock-in by historical events. *Economic Journal*, 99: 116–31.

Aydalot, P. 1986. *Milieux Innovateurs en Europe*. Paris: Groupe de Recherche Européen sur les Milieux Innovateurs.

Bailly, A. 1994. Evolution des systèmes de production et des localisations des services: vingt-cinq ans au service des services. In *Services et Mutations Urbaines, Questionnements et Perspectives*, ed. J. Bonamy and N. May. Paris: Economica.

——1995. Penser la science régionale. *Revue d'Economie Régionale et Urbaine*, 4: 737–41.

Barnes, B. 1974. *Scientific Knowledge and Sociological Theory*. London: Routledge and Kegan Paul.

——Bloor, D., and Henry, J. 1995. *Scientific Knowledge: A Sociological Analysis*. London: Athlone Press.

Barnes, T. J. 1984. Theories of agricultural rent within the surplus approach. *International Review of Regional Science*, 9: 125–40.

——1996. *Logics of Dislocation: Models, Metaphors, and Meanings of Economic Space*. New York and London: Guilford.

Becattini, G. 1979. Dal settore industriale al distretto industriale: alcune considerazioni sull'unità di indagine dell'economia industriale. *Rivista di Economia e Politica Industriale*, No. 2: 7–21.

Becattini, G. 1987. Introduzione: il distretto industriale marshalliano: cronaca di un ritrovamento. In *Mercato e Forze Locali: Il Distretto Industriale*, ed. G. Becattini. Bologna: Il Mulino, 7–34.

Benko, G. 1998. *La Science régionale*. Paris: Presses Universitaires de France.

Berry, B. J. L., and Garrison, W. L. 1958*a*. Functional bases of the central place hierarchy. *Economic Geography*, 34: 145–54.

—— —— 1958*b*. Recent developments of central place theory. *Papers and Proceedings of the Regional Science Association*, 4: 107–20.

Billinge, M., Gregory, D., and Martin, R., eds. 1982. *Recollections of a Revolution: Geography as Spatial Science*. London: Macmillan.

Blaut, J. M. 1979. The dissenting tradition. *Annals of the Association of American Geographers*, 69: 157–64.

Bluestone, B., and Harrison, B. 1982. *The Deindustrialization of America*. New York: Basic Books.

Boudeville, J. R. 1961. *Les Espaces économiques*. Paris: Presses Universitaires de France.

Boyer, R. 1986. *La Théorie de la régulation: une analyse critique*. Paris: La Découverte.

Brookfield, H. C. 1975. *Interdependent Development*. London: Methuen.

Brush, J. E. 1953. The hierarchy of central places in Southwestern Wisconsin. *Geographical Review*, 43: 380–402.

Bunge, W. 1962. *Theoretical Geography*. Lund Studies in Geography, Series C. Lund: C. W. K. Gleerup.

Burton, I. 1963. The quantitative revolution and economic geography. *Canadian Geographer*, 7: 151–62.

Carney, J. 1980. Regions in crisis: accumulation, regional problems and crisis formation. In *Regions in Crisis: New Perspectives in European Regional Theory*, ed. J. Carney, R. Hudson, and J. Lewis. Beckenham, Kent: Croom Helm, 22–59.

Castells, M., and Henderson, J. 1987. Techno-economic restructuring, socio-political processes and spatial transformation: a global perspective. In *Global Restructuring and Territorial Development*, ed. J. Henderson and M. Castells. London: Sage.

Chorley, R. J., and Haggett, P. J., eds. 1967. *Models in Geography*. London: Methuen.

Christaller, W. 1933. *Die zentralen Orte in Süddeutschland*. Jena: Fischer.

Clark, G. L. 1981. The employment relation and spatial division of labor. *Annals of the Association of American Geographers*, 71: 412–24.

—— Gertler, M. S., and Whiteman, J. 1986. *Regional Dynamics: Studies in Adjustment Theory*. Boston: Allen and Unwin.

—— and O'Connor, K. 1997. The information content of financial products and the spatial structure of the global finance industry. In *Spaces of Power: Reasserting the Power of the Local*, ed. K. R. Cox. New York: Guilford Press, 89–114.

Claval, P. 1964. *Essai sur l'evolution de la géographie humaine*. Cahiers de Géographie de Besançon, No. 12. Paris: Les Belles Lettres.

—— 1968. *Régions, nations, grands espaces: géographie générale des ensembles territoriaux*. Paris: Génin.

—— 1977. *La Nouvelle Géographie*. Paris: Presses Universitaires de France.

Cloke, P., Philo, C., and Sadler, D. 1991. *Approaching Human Geography: An Introduction to Contemporary Theoretical Debates*. New York and London: Guilford.

Cooke, P. 1989. Locality, economic restructuring and world development. In *Localities: The Changing Face of Urban Britain*, ed. P. Cooke. London: Unwin Hyman, 1–44.

Corbridge, S. 1986. *Capitalist World Development: A Critique of Radical Development Theory*. London: Macmillan.

—— 1994. Bretton Woods revisited: hegemony, stability and territory. *Environment and Planning A*, 26: 1829–59.

Cox, K. R., and Golledge, R. G. 1969. Editorial introduction: behavioral models in geography. In *Behavioral Problems in Geography: A Symposium*, ed. K. R. Cox and R. G. Golledge. Evanston, Ill.: Department of Geography, Northwestern University, 1–13.

—— and Mair, A. 1989. Levels of abstraction in locality studies. *Antipode*, 21: 121–32.

Crang, P. 1997. Cultural turns and the (re)constitution of economic geography. In Lee and Wills. 1997: 3–14.

Crewe, L., and Lowe, M. 1995. Gap on the map? Towards a geography of consumption and identity. *Environment and Planning A*, 27: 1877–98.

Cullen, I. G. 1976. Human behavior, regional science and the study of individual behaviour. *Environment and Planning A*, 8: 397–410.

Curry, L. 1967. Quantitative geography. *The Canadian Geographer*, 11: 265–74.

—— 1970. Univariate spatial forecasting. *Economic Geography*, 46: 241–58.

Dacey, M. F. 1962. Analysis of central-place and point patterns by a nearest neighbor method. In *Proceedings of the IGU Symposium in Urban Geography, Lund 1960*, ed. K. Norberg. Lund: C. W. K. Gleerup, 55–76.

Daniels, P. W. 1979. Perspectives on office location research. In *Spatial Patterns of Office Growth and Location*, ed. P. W. Daniels. New York: Wiley, 1–28.

David, P. A. 1985. Understanding the economics of QWERTY. *American Economic Review (Papers and Proceedings)*, 75: 332–7.

Dear, M., and Scott, A. J. 1981. Towards a framework of analysis. In *Urbanization and Urban Planning in Capitalist Society*, ed. M. Dear and A. J. Scott. London: Methuen, 3–18.

Dicken, P. 1986. *Global Shift: Industrial Change in a Turbulent World*. New York: Harper and Row.

—— Peck, J., and Tickell, A. 1997. Unpacking the global. In Lee and Wills 1997: 158–66.

Dickenson, R. E. 1947. *City, Region and Regionalism*. London: Routledge and Kegan Paul.

Duncan, S. S., and Savage, M. 1989. Space, scale and locality, *Antipode*: 21: 179–206.

Dunford, M., and Perrons, D. 1983. *The Arena of Capital*. London: Macmillan.

Dymski, G. A. 1996. On Krugman's model of economic geography. *Geoforum*, 27: 439–52.

Emmanuel, A. 1969. *L'Échange inégal*. Paris: Maspéro.

Feldman, M. P. 1994. *The Geography of Innovation*. Boston: Kluwer Academic.

Fellmann, J. D. 1986. Myth and reality in the origin of American economic geography. *Annals of the Association of American Geographers*, 76: 313–30.

Forbes, D. 1984. *The Geography of Underdevelopment*. London: Croom Helm.

Foucault, M. 1969. *L'Archéologie du Savoir*. Paris: Gallimard.

Frank, A. G. 1967. *Capitalism and Underdevelopment in Latin America*. New York: Monthly Review Press.

Friedmann, J., and Alonso, W., eds. 1967. *Regional Development and Planning: A Reader*. Cambridge, Mass.: The MIT Press.

Fröbel, F., Heinrichs, J., and Kreye, O. 1980. *The New International Division of Labour*. Cambridge: Cambridge University Press.

Garrison, W. L. 1959*a*. Spatial structure of the economy, I. *Annals of the Association of American Geographers*, 49: 232–9.

—— 1959*b*. Spatial structure of the economy, II. *Annals of the Association of American Geographers*, 49: 471–82.

—— 1960. Spatial structure of the economy, III. *Annals of the Association of American Geographers*, 50: 357–73.

—— and Marble, D. F. 1957. The spatial structure of agricultural activities. *Annals of the Association of American Geographers*, 47: 137–44.

George, P. 1958. *Précis de Géographie Economique*. Paris: Presses Universitaires de France.

Gertler, M. 1988. The limits to flexibility: comments on the post-fordist vision of production and its geography. *Transactions of the Institute of British Geographers*, 17: 259–78.

—— 1995. Being there: proximity, organization, and culture in the development and adoption of advanced manufacturing technologies. *Economic Geography*, 71: 1–26.

Giddens, A. 1979. *Central Problems in Social Theory*. London: Macmillan.

—— 1984. *The Constitution of Society: Outline of the Theory of Structuration*. Berkeley and Los Angeles: University of California Press.

Godlund, S. 1956. *Bus Service in Sweden*. Lund Studies in Geography Series B, No. 17. Lund: C. W. K. Gleerup.

Golledge, R. G., and Amedeo, D. 1968. On laws in geography. *Annals of the Association of American Geographers*, 58: 760–74.

Gould, P. 1963. Man against his environment: a game theoretic framework. *Annals of the Association of American Geographers*, 53: 290–7.

—— 1979. Geography 1957–1977: the Augean period. *Annals of the Association of American Geographers*, 69: 139–51.

Graham, J. 1988. Postmodernism and Marxism. *Antipode*, 20: 60–5.

Gregory, D. 1978. *Ideology, Science and Human Geography*. London: Hutchinson.

—— 1981. Human agency and human geography. *Transactions of the Institute of British Geographers*, 6: 1–18.

Haggett, P. 1965. *Locational Analysis in Human Geography*. London: Edward Arnold.

Hägerstrand, T. 1952. *The Propagation of Innovation Waves*. Lund Studies in Geography, Series B, No. 4. Lund: C. W. K. Gleerup.

—— 1970. What about people in regional science? *Papers of the Regional Science Association*, 24: 7–21.

Hall, P., Breheny, M., McQuaid, R., and Hart, D. 1987. *Western Sunrise: The Genesis and Growth of Britain's Major High Tech Corridor*. London: Allen and Unwin.

Hanson, S., and Hanson, P. 1980. Gender and urban activity patterns in Uppsala, Sweden. *Geographical Review*, 70: 291–9.

Harris, C. D. 1954. The market as a factor in the localization of industry. *Annals of the Association of American Geographers*, 44: 315–48.

—— and Ullman, E. L. 1945. The nature of cities. *Annals of the American Academy of Political and Social Science*, 242: 7–17.

Hartshorne, R. 1939. *The Nature of Geography*. Lancaster, Pa.: Association of American Geographers.

—— 1955. Exceptionalism in geography reexamined. *Annals of the Association of American Geographers*, 45: 205–44.

Harvey, D. 1969. *Explanation in Geography*. London: Edward Arnold.

—— 1973. *Social Justice and the City*. London: Edward Arnold.

—— 1982. *The Limits to Capital*. Oxford: Blackwell.

—— 1985. *The Urbanization of Capital*. Baltimore: The Johns Hopkins University Press.

Hecht, S. B. 1985. Environment, development and politics: capital accumulation and the livestock sector in Eastern Amazonia. *World Development*, 13: 663–84.

Hirschman, A. O. 1958. *The Strategy of Economic Development*. New Haven: Yale University Press.

Hirst, P. 1994. *Associative Democracy: New Forms of Social and Economic Governance*. Cambridge: Polity.

—— and Thompson, G. 1996. *Globalisation in Question: The International Economy and the Possibilities of Governance*. Cambridge: Polity.

Hodgson, G. M. 1988. *Economics and Institutions: A Manifesto for a Modern Institutional Economics*. Cambridge: Polity.

Holt-Jensen, A. 1988. *Geography, Its History and Concepts*. London: Harper and Row.

Hoover, E. M. 1937. *Location Theory and the Shoe and Leather Industries*. Cambridge, Mass.: Harvard University Press.

Isard, W. 1956. *Location and Space-Economy*. New York: Wiley.

—— 1957. General interregional equilibrium. *Papers and Proceedings of the Regional Science Association*, 3: 35–60.

—— 1960. *Methods of Regional Analysis: An Introduction to Regional Science*. New York: Wiley.

Isserman, A. 1993. Lost in space? On the history, status and future of regional science. *Review of Regional Studies*, 23: 1–50.

Johnston, R. J. 1991. *Geography and Geographers: Anglo-American Geography since 1945*. 4th edn. London: Edward Arnold.

Keating, M. 1998. *The New Regionalism: Territorial Restructuring and Political Change in Western Europe*. Cheltenham: Edward Elgar.

King, L. J. 1969. *Statistical Analysis in Geography*. Englewood Cliffs, NJ: Prentice-Hall.

Krugman, P. 1991*a*. *Geography and Trade*. Leuven: Leuven University Press.

—— 1991*b*. Increasing returns and economic geography. *Journal of Political Economy*, 99: 483–99.

Kuhn, T. S. 1962. *The Structure of Scientific Revolutions*. Chicago: University of Chicago Press.

Latour, B. 1990. Drawing things together. In *Representation in Scientific Practice*, ed. M. Lynch and S. Woolgar. Cambridge, Mass.: The MIT Press, 19–68.

—— 1991. *Nous n'avons jamais été modernes: essai d'anthropologie symétrique*. Paris: La Découverte.

Leborgne, D., and Lipietz, A. 1993. New technologies and new modes of regulation: some spatial implications. *Environment and Planning D: Society and Space*, 6: 263–80.

Lee, R., and Wills, J., eds. 1997. *Geographies of Economies*. London: Arnold.

Lever, W. F. 1997. Economic globalization and urban dynamics—II. In *Cities, Enterprises and Society on the Eve of the 21st Century*, ed. F. Moulaevt and A. J. Scott. London: Pinter, 33–53.

Leyshon, A., and Thrift, N. 1995. European financial integration: the search for an 'island of monetary stabillity' in the sea of global financial turbulence. In *An Enlarged Europe: Regions in Competition?* ed. S. Hardy, M. Hart, L. Albrechts, and A. Katosz. London: Jessica Kingsley, 109–44.

Lipietz, A. 1974. *Le Tribut Foncier Urbain*. Paris: François Maspéro.

—— 1986. New tendencies in the international division of labour: regimes of accumulation and modes of regulation, In *Production, Work, Territory: The Geographical Anatomy of Industrial Capitalism*, ed. A. J. Scott and M. Storper. London: Allen and Unwin, 16–40.

Livingstone, D. N. 1992. *The Geographical Tradition: Episodes in the History of a Contested Enterprise*. Oxford: Blackwell.

Lösch, A. 1940. *Die räumliche Ordnung der Wirtschaft*. Jena: Fischer.

Lovering, J. 1990. Fordism's unknown successor: a comment on Scott's theory of flexible accumulation and the re-emergence of regional economies. *International Journal of Urban and Regional Research*, 14: 158–71.

Lukermann, F. 1958. Towards a more geographic economic geography. *The Professional Geographer*, 10: 2–10.

McCarty, H. H. 1954. An approach to a theory of economic geography. *Economic Geography*, 30: 95–101.

McDowell, L. 1997. A tale of two cities? Embedded organizations and embodied workers in the City of London. In Lee and Wills 1997: 118–29.

—— and Massey, D. 1984. A woman's place? In *Geography Matters!* ed. D. Massey and J. Allen. Cambridge: Cambridge University Press, 128–47.

Malecki, E. 1980. Corporate organization of R&D and the location of technological activities, *Regional Studies*, 14: 219–34.

Malmberg, A. 1997. Industrial geography: location and learning. *Progress in Human Geography*, 21: 573–82.

Mannheim, K. 1952. *Essays in the Sociology of Knowledge*. Henley-on-Thames: Routledge and Kegan Paul.

Markusen, A., Hall, P., and Glasmeier, A. 1986. *High Tech America: The What, How, Where, and Why of the Sunrise Industries*. Boston: Allen and Unwin.

Martin, R. 1984. Job loss and the regional incidence of redundancy in the current recession: a regional analysis. *Regional Studies*, 18: 445–58.

—— and Sunley, P. 1996. Paul Krugman's geographical economics and its implications for regional development theory: a critical assessment. *Economic Geography*, 72/3: 259–92.

Massey, D. 1979. In what sense a regional problem? *Regional Studies*, 13: 231–41.

—— 1984. *Spatial Divisions of Labour: Social Structures and the Geography of Production*. London: Macmillan.

—— and Catalano, A. 1978. *Capital and Land*. London: Edward Arnold.

—— and Meegan, R. 1982. *Anatomy of Job Loss: The How, Why and Where of Employment Decline*. London: Methuen.

Merlin, P. 1973. *Méthodes quantitatives et espace urbain*. Paris: Masson.

Morrill, R. L., and Garrison, W. L. 1960. Projections of interregional patterns of trade in wheat and flour. *Economic Geography*, 36: 116–26.

Moses, L. N. 1960. A general equilibrium model of production, interregional trade, and location of industry. *Review of Economics and Statistics*, 42: 373–99.

Myrdal, G. 1957. *Economic Theory and Under-Developed Regions*. New York: Harper and Row.

Nadvi, K., and Schmitz, H. 1994. *Industrial Clusters in Less Developed Countries: Review of Experiences and Research Agenda*. Discussion Paper No. 339. Institute of Development Studies, University of Sussex, Brighton.

Nelson, R. R., and Winter, S. G. 1982. *An Evolutionary Theory of Economic Change*. Cambridge, Mass.: Belknap Press.

Nystuen, J. D., and Dacey, M. F. 1961. A graph theory interpretation of nodal regions. *Papers and Proceedings of the Regional Science Association*, 7: 29–42.

O'Brien, R. 1992. *Global Financial Integration: The End of Geography*. London: Pinter.

Olsson, G. 1970. Explanation, prediction, and meaning variance: an assessment of distance interaction models. *Economic Geography*, 46: 223–33.

Palander, T. 1935. *Beiträge zur Standortstheorie*. Uppsala: Almqvist and Wiksells.

Peck, J. 1996. *Work-Place: The Social Regulation of Labor Markets*. New York: Guilford.

—— and Tickell, A. 1994. Searching for a new institutional fix: the after-fordist crisis and the global-local disorder. In *Post-Fordism: A Reader*, ed. A. Amin. Oxford: Blackwell, 280–315.

Peet, R. 1975. Inequality and poverty: a marxist-geographic perspective. *Annals of the Association of American Geographers*, 65: 564–71.

—— 1977. The development of radical geography in the United States, *Progress in Human Geography*, 1: 240–63.

—— 1997. The cultural production of economic forms. In *Geographies of Economies*, ed. R. Lee and J. Wills. London: Arnold, 35–46.

—— 1998. *Modern Geographical Thought*. Oxford: Blackwell.

Perroux, F. 1950. Les espaces économiques. *Économie Appliquée*, 3: 225–44.

—— 1955. La notion de pôle de croissance. *Économie Appliquée*, 8: 307–14.

Piore, M., and Sabel, C. F. 1984. *The Second Industrial Divide: Possibilities for Prosperity*. New York: Basic Books.

Pollert, A. 1991. The orthodoxy of flexibility. In *Farewell to Flexibility?* ed. A. Pollert. Oxford: Blackwell, 3–31.

Ponsard, C. 1955. *Économie et éspace*. Paris: Sedes.

—— 1958. *Histoire des théories économiques spatiales*. Paris: Armand Colin.

Porter, M. 1990. *The Competitive Advantage of Nations*. New York: Free Press.

—— 1998. *On Competition*. Boston: Harvard Business Review.

Pred, A. 1967. *Behavior and Location: Foundations for a Geographic and Dynamic Location Theory*. Lund Studies in Geography Series B, No. 27. Lund: C. W. K. Gleerup.

—— 1977. *City-Systems in Advanced Economies*. New York: Halsted.

Predöhl, A. 1925. Das Standortsproblem in der Wirtschaftstheorie. *Weltwirtschaftsliches Archiv*, 21: 294–321.

Preteceille, E. 1973. *La Production des Grands Ensembles*. Paris: Mouton.

Rees, J., and Stafford, H. 1984. High-technology location and regional development: the theoretical base. In *Technology, Innovation and Regional Economic Development.* Washington: Office of Technology Assessment, 97–107.

Rorty, R. 1979. *Philosophy and the Mirror of Nature.* Princeton: Princeton University Press.

Roweis, S. T., and Scott, A. J. 1978. The urban land question. In *Urbanization and Conflict in Market Societies,* ed. K. Cox. Chicago: Maaroufa, 38–73.

Rowthorne, B. 1986. De-industrialisation in Britain, In *The Geography of De-industrialization,* ed. R. Martin and B. Rowthorne. London: Macmillan, 1–30.

Salais, R., and Storper, M. 1993. *Les Mondes de Production.* Paris: Éditions de l'École des Hautes Études en Sciences Sociales.

Saxenian, A. 1994. *Regional Advantage: Culture and Competition in Silicon Valley and Route 128.* Cambridge, Mass.: Harvard University Press.

Sayer, A. 1982. Explanation in economic geography: abstraction versus generalization. *Progress in Human Geography,* 6: 68–88.

—— 1984. *Method in Social Science: A Realist Approach.* London: Hutchinson.

—— 1997. The dialectic of culture and economy. In Lee and Wills 1997: 16–26.

Schaefer, F. K. 1953. Exceptionalism in geography: a methodological introduction. *Annals of the Association of American Geographers,* 43: 226–49.

Schmitz, H. 1995. Small shoemakers and fordist giants: tale of a supercluster. *World Development,* 23: 9–28.

Schoenberger, E. 1989. Thinking about flexibility: a response to Gertler. *Transactions of the Institute of British Geographers,* 14: 98–108.

Scott, A. J. 1971. *Combinatorial Programming, Spatial Analysis, and Planning.* London: Methuen.

—— 1976. Land use and commodity production. *Regional Science and Urban Economics,* 6: 147–60.

—— 1986. High-technology industry and territorial development: the rise of the Orange County Complex, 1955–1984. *Urban Geography,* 7: 3–45.

—— 1988. *New Industrial Spaces: Flexible Production Organization and Regional Development in North America and Western Europe.* London: Pion.

—— 1998. *Regions and the World Economy: The Coming Shape of Global Production, Competition, and Political Order.* Oxford: Oxford University Press.

—— and Angel, D. P. 1987. The US semiconductor industry: a locational analysis. *Environment and Planning A,* 19: 875–912.

Sheppard, E. S. 1983. Pasinetti, Marx and urban accumulation dynamics. In *Evolving Geographic Structures,* ed. D. Griffith and A. Lea. The Hague, Martinus Nijhoff, 293–322.

Sheppard, E. S., and Barnes, T. J. 1990. *The Capitalist Space Economy: Geographical Analysis after Ricardo, Marx, and Sraffa.* London: Unwin Hyman.

Simmie, J., ed. 1997. *Innovation Networks and Learning Regions?* London: Jessica Kingsley.

Slater, S. 1976. Anglo-Saxon geography and the study of underdevelopment. *Antipode,* 8: 88–93.

Smith, N. 1984. *Uneven Development: Nature, Capital and the Production of Space.* Oxford: Blackwell.

——1987. Danger of the empirical turn: the CURDS initiative. *Antipode*, 19: 59–68.

Soja, E. W. 1980. The socio-spatial dialectic. *Annals of the Association of American Geographers*, 70: 207–25.

——Morales, R., and Wolff, G. 1983. Urban restructuring: an analysis of social and spatial change in Los Angeles. *Economic Geography*, 59: 195–230.

Stevens, B. H. 1958. An interregional linear programming model. *Journal of Regional Science*, 1: 60–98.

Storper, M. 1995. The resurgence of regional economies, ten years later: the region as a nexus of untraded interdependencies. *European Urban and Regional Studies*, 2: 191–221.

——1997. Territories, flows and hierarchies in the global economy. In *Spaces of Globalization: Reasserting the Power of the Local*, ed. K. Cox. New York: Guilford, 19–44.

——and Christopherson, S. 1987. Flexible specialization and regional industrial agglomerations: the case of the US motion-picture industry. *Annals of the Association of American Geographers*, 77: 260–82.

——and Walker, R. 1989. *The Capitalist Imperative: Territory, Technology and Industrial Growth*. Oxford: Blackwell.

Sunley, P. 1996. Context in economic geography: the relevance of pragmatism. *Progress in Human Geography*, 20: 338–55.

Swyngedouw, E. 1997. Neither global nor local: 'glocalization and the politics of scale'. In *Spaces of Globalization: Reasserting the Power of the Local*, ed. K. Cox. New York: Guilford, 137–66.

Taylor, M. J., and Thrift, N. J. 1982. Models of corporate development and the multinational corporation. In *The Geography of Multinationals*, ed. J. Taylor and N. J. Thrift. New York: St Martin's Press, 14–32.

Taylor, P. J. 1976. An interpretation of the quantification debate in British geography. *Transactions of the Institute of British Geographers*, new series, 1: 129–42.

Thisse, J.-F. 1997. L'oubli de l'espace dans la pensée économique. *Région et Développement*, 6: 13–39.

Thomas, E. N. 1968. Maps of residuals from regression. In *Spatial Analysis: A Reader in Statistical Geography*, ed. B. J. L. Berry and D. F. Marble. Englewood Cliffs, NJ: Prentice-Hall, 326–52.

Thompson, E. P. 1978. *The Poverty of Theory and Other Essays*. London: Merlin.

Thrift, N. 1983. On the determination of social action in space and time. *Environment and Planning D: Society and Space*, 1: 23–57.

——and Olds, K. 1996. Refiguring the economic in economic geography. *Progress in Human Geography*, 20: 311–37.

Topalov, C. 1973. *Capital et Propriété Foncière*. Paris: Centre de Sociologie Urbaine.

Ullman, E. L. 1958. Regional development and the geography of concentration. *Papers and Proceedings of the Regional Science Association*, 4: 179–98.

Urry, J. 1981. Localities, regions and social class. *International Journal of Urban and Regional Research*, 5: 455–74.

Veltz, P. 1996. *Mondialisation, Villes et Territoires: L'Économie d'Archipel*. Paris: Presses Universitaires de France.

——1997. The dynamics of production systems, territories and cities. In *Cities*,

Enterprises and Society on the Eve of the 21st Century, ed. F. Moulaert and A. J. Scott. London: Pinter, 78–96.

Von Thünen, J. H. 1826. *Der isolierte Staat in Beziehung auf Landwirtschaft und Nationalökonomie*. Hamburg: F. Perthes.

Walker, R. 1981. A theory of suburbanization: capitalism and the construction of urban space in the United States. In *Urbanization and Urban Planning in Capitalist Society*, ed. M. J. Dear and A. J. Scott. London: Methuen, 383–429.

——and Storper, M. 1981. Capital and industrial location. *Progress in Human Geography*, 5: 473–509.

Warntz, W. 1959. *Toward a Geography of Price*. Philadelphia: University of Pennsylvania Press.

Watts, M. 1983. *Silent Violence: Food, Famine and Peasantry in Northern Nigeria*. Berkeley and Los Angeles: University of California Press.

Webber, M. J., and Rigby, D. L. 1996. *The Golden Age Illusion: Rethinking Postwar Capitalism*. New York: Guilford.

Weber, A. 1909. *Über den Standort der Industrien*. Tubingen: J. C. B. Mohr.

Wilson, A. G. 1970. *Entropy in Urban and Regional Modelling*. London: Pion.

Wise, M. 1949. On the evolution of the jewellery and gun quarters in Birmingham. *Transactions of the Institute of British Geographers*, 15: 57–72.

Wolpert, J. 1964. The decision process in spatial context. *Annals of the Association of American Geographers*, 54: 337–58.

——1965. Behavioral aspects of the decision to migrate. *Papers and Proceedings of the Regional Science Association*, 15: 159–69.

Part I

Conceptual Perspectives

Section 1

Mapping the Territory

Chapter 3

Where in the World is the 'New Economic Geography'?

Paul Krugman

A MAN from Mars—or from the real world—would be surprised to find that economic geography and the theory of international trade are sharply distinct fields, with few intellectual or personal links. Why is the process that puts a bottle of French wine on a Berlin table very different from that which puts California wine on New York tables? True, French workers rarely move to Germany in search of jobs; but then Francophone Swiss are almost as reluctant to move to Zurich. Surely trade and geography ought to be no more than sub-genres of a common literature.

For a combination of technical and historical reasons, however, economic geography and the study of international trade diverged long ago. The standard economic theory of international trade is firmly embedded in the neoclassical tradition—that is, of equilibrium modeling based on the assumption of rational individual behavior. While this tradition need not in principle exclude the possibilities of increasing returns, imperfectly competitive markets, and a crucial role for history, in practice the understandable tendency to follow the line of least mathematical resistance has biased trade theory toward static, perfectly competitive, constant returns stories. Unfortunately, it is not possible to use those stories to address most of the interesting questions in economic geography. So the tradition of international trade theory has sidestepped geographical questions—most modeling imagines a world without transport costs, let alone cities!—while that of geography has sometimes been based on what trade theorists would consider half-worked-out models, and often rejected formalism altogether.

Economics does, however, progress. During the 1980s international trade theory went through a peaceful revolution: the so-called New Trade Theory brought increasing returns, imperfect competition, and multiple equilibria firmly into the mainstream. And though it took a surprisingly long time for the new trade theorists themselves to catch on to the possibilities, *circa* 1990 it became clear that the revolution in trade theory also made it possible to talk about questions of economic geography. The result was what is sometimes called the New Economic Geography.

I am aware that this name can annoy hard-working traditional economic geographers, who feel both that many of the things the 'new' geographers say are old hat, and also that new economic geography ignores almost as much of the reality they study as old trade theory did. But let me reserve a discussion of the new field's limitations for the end of this chapter; the main purpose is to explain what the new geography is, and where in the world of economic analysis it has its proper place.

Goals of the New Economic Geography

At one level everyone understands the economics of metropolitan New York reasonably well. As many histories—for example, Albion (1939)—explain, the city owes its front-rank status to the initial advantages conveyed by a fine natural harbor, the early access to the interior conveyed by the Erie Canal, and the innovations (like regularly scheduled Atlantic crossings) introduced by its merchants in the early nineteenth century. Its importance is now sustained by the advantages conveyed by an existing agglomeration to certain industries, notably finance and communication; even now it is hard to get a better account of how these advantages work than is given by Hoover (1959). And one can understand much of the *internal* structure of the metropolis by thinking in terms of land-use models along the lines pioneered by Alonso (1964).

And yet from the point of view of someone accustomed to the crystalline clarity of international trade theory this level of understanding is quite unsatisfying. You want the discussion of the city's economy to be integrated with an account of the workings of the national (or world) economy as a whole—as an economist would say, you want a *general equilibrium* story, in which it is clear where the money comes from and where it goes. This story should explain both concentration and dispersion—why so many people work in Manhattan, but why so many other people do not. (The long tradition of analysis descending from von Thünen 1826) does an excellent job of explaining the pattern of land use around a city or central business district, but simply assumes the existence of that central focus.) And as far as possible the story should explain the forces of concentration in terms of more fundamental motivations—it should not leave us open to jibes like that of the physicist who said, 'So economists believe that companies agglomerate because of agglomeration economies'.

The goal of the new economic geography, then, is to devise a modeling approach—a story-telling machine—that lets one discuss things like the economics of New York in the context of the whole economy: that is, in general equilibrium. It should allow us to talk simultaneously about the centripetal forces that pull economic activity together, and the centrifugal forces that push it apart—indeed, it should let us tell stories about how the geographical structure of an economy is shaped by the tension between these forces. And it should explain these forces in terms of more fundamental, micro decisions.

This may not sound like such a tall order. But it turns out that for annoyingly technical reasons it is not an easy order to fill. The sorts of stories that might explain agglomeration in terms of micro decisions depend on increasing returns, or at least indivisibilities, at the level of the individual producer. This in turn means that one cannot assume perfect competition; and imperfect competition is notoriously hard to embed in a general-equilibrium story. Transportation costs are also clearly crucial; yet if one wants to have an integrated picture of the economy, this means that the resources used in and income generated by the transportation industry must also be part of the picture. Put one thing on top of another, and it all starts to look too complicated to convey any insights.

But provided one is willing to make some silly but convenient assumptions—assumptions that have also played a role in the new trade theory and the 'new growth theory' that emerged in the second half of the 1980s—things need not be so bad. And that is the strategy employed in the new economic geography.

Games Modelers Play

In our book *The Spatial Economy* (1999), Mashisa Fujita, Tony Venables, and I offer a slogan only an economist could love: 'Dixit–Stiglitz, icebergs, evolution, and the computer'. Yet the slogan captures the essence of the intellectual tricks that we and other new economic geography theorists have used in order to cope with the technical difficulties involved in trying to deal with the subject. Everyone recognizes that these are strategic simplifications, which is to say intellectual cheap tricks; but they do allow us to get past the technical issues and tell stories about the real economics.

'Dixit–Stiglitz' refers to an ingenious analytical model introduced by Avinash Dixit and Joseph Stiglitz more than twenty years ago (Dixit and Stiglitz 1977). What they did was to take an old idea—that of 'monopolistic competition'—and give it a much sharper-edged formulation. Monopolistic competition, in turn, may be described as an attempt to recognize the existence of monopoly power—and the increasing returns that give rise to that power—while sacrificing as little as possible of the simplicity of good old-fashioned supply and demand. Thus firms have market power, and use it; but they are assumed to act in a purely unilateral fashion, never trying to organize cartels or even tacitly collude on prices. Every firm has a monopoly on its own distinctive product; but other firms can introduce products that are (imperfect) substitutes for that product, and the free entry of new firms eliminates any monopoly profits. Telling this story in an uncomplicated fashion requires some funny assumptions both about consumer behavior and about the technology of production; but it has the virtue of producing in the end a picture of an economy in which there are increasing returns, in which markets are imperfect, but in which one need not get into the fascinating but messy issues posed by realistic oligopoly.

'Icebergs' refers to a clever model of transportation introduced by Paul Samuelson (1952) in one of the relatively few papers in traditional trade theory that does put transport costs into the story. Instead of describing an industry that produces transportation services, using capital and labor to get stuff from here to there, Samuelson proposed imagining that goods can be shipped freely—but that part of the shipment 'melts' in transit. Silly, yes: but it sidesteps the need to analyze transportation itself as another industry, and it also turns out to simplify the description of how monopolistic firms set their prices (specifically: it removes the incentive to absorb transport costs, charging a lower f.o.b. price for exports than for domestic sales).

'Evolution' refers to how one thinks about how the economy 'selects' one of several (or many) possible geographical structures. It is typically true of new economic geography models that they have multiple equilibria: that, to put a realistic gloss on it, if somehow Philadelphia rather than New York had become established as the center of the financial industry in 1860, that leadership would be just as self-sustaining today as the one we actually see. It may seem obvious that this means that history determines which of many possible structures actually emerges. But in fact it is not so obvious: what happens if individuals themselves try to forecast the future, and base their decisions on those forecasts? Then one faces the possibility of self-fulfilling prophecies: if most financial firms believed that most other financial firms were about to move to Philadelphia, their belief would be vindicated—but so would a corresponding belief that they would all go to New York, or for that matter Boston. The slogan of evolution in the new economic geography essentially refers to the decision *not* to let the hypothetical players be that forward-looking—to assume that decisions about where to locate are based on current conditions, and therefore to rule out self-fulfilling prophecies. The geography of an economy therefore evolves in a way that reflects history and accident, but not expectations of the future.

Finally, the 'computer' refers to the tendency of new geography theorists to use high-technology numerical examples—the sort of thing that would have been a major undertaking a generation ago, but can now be carried out almost casually on any desktop computer—as an intuition pump, a way to gain a sense of the possibilities implied by the underlying models. It is still possible to learn a great deal from paper-and-pencil analysis, and often the results both of that analysis and of simulations can be given clear intuitive explanations; but both the analysis and the intuition in general are attained on ground first explored with the computer.

Simple examples of how this characteristic method works can be found in a number of places (not only Fujita *et al.* but also Krugman 1991, Puga and Venables 1996, and so on). I will not try to reproduce those examples here. Instead, let us jump straight to the first set of results: the related set of stories about agglomeration and dispersion that has come to be known as the 'core–periphery' model.

Core and Periphery

The simplest stories one might tell in economic geography involve the division of production, or the movement of mobile resources, between two locations. One might, of course, tell such stories based on inherent differences between the locations—in effect, in terms of classical comparative advantage. However, the new economic geography begins with stories that instead ask how the interaction between increasing returns and transport costs might lead to the emergence of a particular geographical structure of production. In the real world, of course, there are rather more than two locations; still, the simplest stories often carry interesting morals.

The first of these stories is an old one: that of the 'home market effect' in international trade (Krugman 1980). Suppose that resources are immobile between two locations; that one of the locations offers a larger market than the other; and that production of some goods is subject to increasing returns to scale. Because of the increasing returns, there is an incentive to concentrate production of each good in only one location; because of the transport costs, other things equal it is more profitable to produce in the location that offers a larger market, and ship to the other. (But the concentration may not be complete: if most other producers are located in the larger market, those who locate in the smaller one may be compensated by reduced competition.) The result, then, is that the location that offers the larger market tends to export those goods subject to increasing returns.

Now suppose that some resources—say, workers—are mobile. If one of the locations offers a larger market, they will have an incentive to move to that location. But the movement of workers itself tends to increase the size of the market wherever they go, decrease it where they come from; so one immediately arrives at the possibility that a small asymmetry between locations, perhaps arising from some small chance event, will prove self-reinforcing. (This idea is not, of course, new: what the core–periphery model offers is, in effect, a more precise formulation of the cumulative process described by Pred (1966).) If not all resources are mobile, however, there will be a countervailing incentive to disperse production to match the geographical distribution of immobile resources. So even the simplest of new economic geography stories—the one told in Krugman (1991)—contains the essential idea that there is a tension between centripetal forces, which foster concentration, and centrifugal forces that oppose it.

This simplest of stories also, it turns out, implies some subtleties that one might have missed in a less carefully worked-out analysis. First, it turns out that the 'backward linkages' that drive the home market effect—the incentive for producers to concentrate where the market is larger—are necessarily supplemented by 'forward linkages', the incentive of workers to be close to the producers of consumer goods. Both backward and forward linkages drive the process of agglomeration, if it occurs.

Secondly, agglomeration need not occur. The qualitative behavior of our imaginary economy depends on whether forward and backward linkages are strong enough to overcome the centrifugal force generated by immobile resources, such as agricultural land. And a small change in the underlying givens—in transportation costs, economies of scale, or the share of the economy's resources that are geographically mobile—can 'tip' the economy, from one in which regions are symmetric and equal to one in which tiny initial advantages cumulate, turning one region into an industrialized core and the other into a deindustrialized periphery. (That is, the dynamics of the model economy are subject to 'bifurcations', points at which their qualitative character suddenly changes.)

Finally, there turns out to be a subtle but important distinction between the conditions under which a core–periphery geography *can* arise and under which it *must* arise. Basically, there is some range of conditions under which an established concentration of industry in one location would be self-sustaining, but under which an equal division of industry will also be stable. At one level this is a technical issue—it means that when doing the algebra of the model, the economist must make separate calculations of the conditions for 'symmetry-breaking' and for 'sustainability'. But it also suggests that the possible evolution of geographical structure in the real world has more complexity to it than one might have supposed. Consider, for example, the future financial geography of Europe. One might notice that the USA has one dominant financial center, and might suppose that with growing integration and the introduction of a common currency the same must eventually be true for Europe; but core–periphery theory tells us that sometimes both a polycentric and a monocentric geography are stable—that while Europe would surely sustain a New-York-style financial capital had one been established, it need not necessarily evolve one starting from its current position.

The core–periphery model, then, provides a basic introductory framework for the new economic geography—a framework that illustrates basic principles, defines basic concepts, and helps form intuition. In that sense it is like the two-by-two models of textbook trade theory. But it is only the beginning of the field.

From Agglomeration to Concentration

The core–periphery model essentially answers the jibe about agglomeration being the result of agglomeration economies by showing how a centripetal tendency can emerge from more micro considerations. Specifically, agglomeration comes from an interaction among increasing returns at the plant level, which motivate individual producers to concentrate their production; transport costs, which make it desirable to locate near the larger market; and factor mobility, which means that as producers move to a location they increase the size of the associated market, making that location still more attractive.

But in practice the concentration of production is greater than that of resources, in the sense that not every agglomeration is an important producer in every industry. There are many cities, but there is only one New York—and only one Detroit, and only one Hollywood. Can new economic geography-type models shed light on such industrial concentration, or must one appeal to other forces not present in the basic approach?

The answer is that while more diffuse, hard-to-model forces like informal diffusion of information surely play an important role in creating and sustaining real-world industrial concentrations, it is also possible with a small modification of the core–periphery approach to shift the focus from agglomeration of resources to geographical concentration of particular industries.

The key is to allow for a vertical structure of production, in which one or more upstream sectors produce inputs for one or more downstream sectors—and in which both upstream and downstream producers are subject to increasing returns and transport costs. As Venables (1996) showed, this immediately means that there are backward and forward linkages that tend to concentrate the upstream and downstream producers in a single location. That is, producers of intermediate goods have an incentive to locate where they have the largest market, which is where the downstream industry is; and producers of final goods have an incentive to locate where their suppliers are, which is where the upstream industry is located.

One can either elaborate or simplify this basic insight. To simplify, one makes the slightly odd assumption that the upstream and downstream industries are really the same—that is, that the same goods are consumed and used as inputs to production of other goods. As shown in Krugman and Venables (1995), this leads to a formal model of industry concentration that is algebraically isomorphic to the core–periphery model, with only a slight reinterpretation of the meanings of the symbols. Thus this simplification highlights the essential similarity between the reasons why population concentrates in particular locations and industries 'choose' particular population concentrations within which to be concentrated themselves.

Alternatively, one can imagine a more realistic input–output structure in which each upstream industry provides inputs to several downstream sectors, and conversely. In that case it becomes possible to talk about what characteristics of the input–output matrix cause industrial clusters to form, and also about the sequence in which regions will industrialize as world markets expand (Puga and Venables 1996).

A shift in focus from agglomeration to industry concentration has the incidental effect of bringing the new economic geography to bear on a traditional issue of international trade theory: the role of external economies in trade. A long tradition, going back to Graham (1923), has considered the possibility that increasing returns at the level of the *industry* (as opposed to the level of the individual plant) can cause otherwise similar countries to specialize in the production of different goods—and also that this process can work to the advantage of some countries at the expense of others (see e.g. Krugman 1987). Many observers have noticed that the motivating examples for such stories, like the Italian advantage in tile production or the British dominance of financial services, tend to involve not just national external economies but specific localizations within countries—a point stressed in modern times by Porter (1990). New economic geography models allow us to revisit this idea with an additional level of insight, because now the external economies are derived rather than assumed, and can therefore be seen to vary in a predictable way as more fundamental parameters of the economy change.

A slightly tongue-in-cheek example is Krugman and Venables (1995), which the authors themselves referred to as 'History of the world, part I'. It shows how a gradual process of growing world trade due to falling transport costs can first cause the world to divide spontaneously and arbitrarily into a high-wage, industrialized 'North' and a low-wage, primary-producing 'South'; then, at a later date, cause the South to rise again at the North's expense. The point is not necessarily that this is a very good story about the actual history of the world economic system; but since stories more or less along these lines have enjoyed considerable popularity over the years, this approach shows how they can be justified by straightforward, dare we say neoclassical, economic models—and also highlights the reasons why the story might *not* work as well as sometimes supposed.

Evolving a Spatial System

Two-location stories are helpful builders of intuition; yet empirical economic geography must cope with a world in which activities are spread across continuous space. Is the new economic geography, like much of traditional trade theory, stuck with 'two-ness' and all the limitations that implies?

The answer is, not necessarily—though there is still quite a difference between what can be formally modeled, or even simulated on a computer, and what one can see on a map.

Perhaps the most appealing, albeit least realistic, approach to the evolution of spatial structure involves applying an idea originally proposed for understanding the process of self-organization in biology by Turing (1952) (yes, *that* Turing). Imagine a 'racetrack' economy—an economy in which activity takes place around the circumference of a circle, and in which goods must be transported along that circumference. And suppose that initially economic activity is nearly uniform across space—what Fujita *et al.* refer to as the Flat Earth. It turns out that if centripetal forces are sufficiently strong, such an economy will gradually evolve a geographical structure in a way that is qualitatively predictable: regularly spaced concentrations of production will start to emerge, with the distance between these concentrations (but not their locations) determined by fundamentals like transportation costs and scale economies. The Turing approach offers as nice an example as one might wish for about how trendy concepts like self-organization might apply in economics, and has a certain charm for those so minded in the way that it makes use of unusual tools for economists, notably Fourier transforms. It even suggests some possibly more general insights. But of course the real world is neither initially flat nor circular, so the approach is in a way no closer to realism than a two-location model.

An alternative, perhaps more directly realistic approach has been followed in a series of papers by Fujita and his students (notably Fujita 1993, Fujita and Mori 1999). The approach starts with a von Thünen 'isolated state': a city, defined as a concentration of manufacturing, surrounded by an agricultural hinterland. (Using the tricks of the new geography trade, it is possible to make this a fully defined equilibrium, in which the existence of the central city is derived from the effects of forward and backward linkages, rather than simply assumed.) Then one gradually increases the population of the economy as a whole. Eventually the outer reaches of the hinterland become sufficiently far from the center that it becomes worthwhile for some manufacturing to 'defect', giving rise to a new city; further population growth gives rise to still more cities; and so on. Key to this approach is the recognition that the attractiveness of any given location for manufacturing can be represented by an index of 'market potential' derived from the underlying economics (Krugman 1993; but the idea of market potential goes back to Harris 1954, and this new work can be regarded as a justification of that approach). The process of change in the economy can then be regarded as involving a sort of coevolution in which market potential determines where economic activity locates, and the shifting location of that activity in turn redraws the map of market potential.

Like the Turing approach, this city-evolution approach ends up suggesting that despite the existence of many possible equilibria, there should be some predictable regularities in spatial structure. Once the number of cities has become sufficiently large, the size of and distance between cities tends to settle down at a roughly constant level determined by the relative strength of centripetal and centrifugal forces, providing some justification for the central-place theory of Lösch (1954). If there are multiple industries that differ in terms of scale economies and/or transport costs, the economy tends to evolve a hierarchical structure reminiscent of Christaller (1933). So this line of work provides a link back to some of the older traditions in location theory and economic geography.

And there is one other payoff to Fujita-type modeling: it offers an interesting viewpoint on the role of *natural* geography in determining economic geography. Anyone who looks even casually at the real geography of economic activity is struck by the important degree of arbitrariness or, at best, historicity involved: New York is New York because of a canal that has not been economically important for 150 years, Silicon Valley as we know it exists because of the vision of one Stanford official two generations ago. Yet rivers and ports surely do matter. Well, in new geography models in which a system of cities evolves, these observations are in effect reconciled. Favorable aspects of a location, such as availability of a good harbor, typically have a 'catalytic' role: they make it likely that, when a new center emerges, it will be there rather than some other location in the general vicinity. But once a new center has become established, it grows through a process of self-reinforcement, and may thus attain a scale at which the initial advantages of the location become unimportant compared with the self-sustaining advantages of the agglomeration itself. In an odd way, natural geography can matter so much precisely because of the self-organizing character of the spatial economy.

How Far Have We Come?

Mainstream economic research tends to be characterized by a boom-bust cycle: when a new set of ideas emerges, there is a wave of excitement as new frontiers of research emerge, followed by a sense of disappointment when the limits of the new ideas become apparent. The new economic geography has certainly followed this pattern. In the first few years economists were excited by the realization that a whole new, important area that had been neglected was now open for systematic thinking—and at least some more traditional geographers had the feeling that at last their field was receiving the attention it deserved. It has become apparent, however, that while new geography models do make it possible for the first time to put spatial considerations into models rigorous enough to become part of the analytical canon, those models are too simple, too stylized to reproduce the real economic geography of the world very well. And to those who are skeptical of formal modeling in any case—a group that includes many geographers—this revelation of the models' limitations may confirm their opinion.

We might note in particular that the new economic geography, like old trade theory, suffers to some extent from the temptation to focus on what is easiest to model rather than on what is probably most important in practice. Long ago Marshall (1890) suggested three main reasons for industrial localization, which in modern terminology we would now describe as backward and forward linkages, thick markets for specialized skills, and technological spillover; the new geography in effect considers only one of these reasons, one that is arguably less important in practice—but easier to formalize—than the others. And of course two-location or one-dimensional models cannot do justice to the geography of a wide, and three-dimensional, world.

Still, there are good reasons why mainstream economics does place a high value on being able to produce tightly specified models—if only to provide the backdrop for less tight, more empirically motivated study. And the new economic geography, while it may be past its first rush of enthusiasm, has ended the long silence of mainstream economics on the whole question of where economic activity takes place and why; now that the conversation has begun, it is sure to continue.

References

Albion, R. 1939. *The Rise of New York Port, 1815–1860.* New York: Charles Scribner's Sons.

Alonso, W. 1964. *Location and Land Use: Toward a General Theory of Land Rent.* Cambridge, Mass.: Harvard University Press.

Christaller, W. 1933. *Die zentrale Orte in Süddeutschland.* Jena: Gustav Fischer.

Dixit, A., and Stiglitz, J. 1977. Monopolistic competition and optimum product diversity. *American Economic Review*, 67: 297–308.

Fujita, M. 1993. Monopolistic competition and urban systems. *European Economic Review*, 37/2–3 (Apr.), 308–15.

——Krugman, P., and Venables, A. 1999. *The Spatial Economy.* Cambridge, Mass.: MIT Press.

Graham, F. D. 1923. Some aspects of protection further considered. *Quarterly Journal of Economics*, 37: 199–227.

——and Mori, T. 1999. On the evolution of hierarchical urban systems. *European Economic Review*, 43 (Feb.), 209–51.

Harris, C. 1954. The market as a factor in the localization of industry in the United States. *Annals of the Association of American Geographers*, 64: 315–48.
Hoover, E. 1959. *Anatomy of a Metropolis*. Cambridge, Mass.: Harvard University Press.
Krugman, P. 1980. Scale economies, product differentiation, and the pattern of trade. *American Economic Review*, 70: 950–9.
—— 1987. The narrow moving band, the Dutch disease, and the competitive consequences of Mrs. Thatcher. *Journal of Development Economics*, 27: 41–55.
—— 1991. Increasing returns and economic geography. *Journal of Political Economy*, 99: 483–99.
—— 1993. First nature, second nature, and metropolitan location. *Journal of Regional Science*, 33: 129–44.
—— and Venables, A. 1995. Globalization and the inequality of nations. *Quarterly Journal of Economics*, 110: 857–80.
Lösch, A. 1954. *The Economics of Location*, English edn. New Haven: Yale University Press. 1st pub. as *Die räumliche Ordnung der Wirtschaft*, 1940.
Marshall, A. 1890. *Principles of Economics*. London: Macmillan.
Porter, M. 1990. *The Competitive Advantage of Nations*. New York: Macmillan.
Pred, A. 1966. *The Spatial Dynamics of U.S. Urban-Industrial Growth, 1800–1914: Interpretive and Theoretical Essays*. Cambridge, Mass.: MIT Press.
Puga, D. 1999. The rise and fall of regional inequalities. *European Economic Review*, 43/2 (Feb.), 303–34.
—— and Venables, A. 1996. The spread of industry: spatial agglomeration and economic development. *Journal of the Japanese and International Economies*, 10: 440–64.
—— —— 1999. Agglomeration and economic development: import substitution vs. trade liberalisation. *Economic Journal*, 109/455 (Apr.), 292–311.
Samuelson, P. 1952. The transfer problem and transport costs. *Economic Journal*, 62: 278–304.
Turing, A. 1952. The chemical basis of morphogenesis. *Philosophical Transactions of the Royal Society of London*, 237: 37–72.
Venables, A. 1996. Equilibrium locations of vertically linked industries. *International Economic Review*, 37: 341–59.
von Thünen, J. 1826. *The Isolated State* (English translation 1966, Oxford: Pergamon).

Chapter **4**

Doing Regulation

Jamie Peck

Introduction

In addition to their rather different ways of seeing the world, economic geographers and geographical economists have different ways of doing things. Economic geographers are more likely to collect their own data, often engage in mid-level theorizing, and are typically sceptical about maximization-equilibrium models and *ceteris paribus* reasoning. More than this, economic geographers generally take it as axiomatic that everything else is *never* equal, that 'the economy' is not an unmediated outcome of universal and trans-historical processes operating across a featureless isotropic plane, but instead functions in a complex, messy, and grounded way in (and through) 'real places'. In contrast to the abstract, orderly, and mathematically regularized world envisaged by orthodox economics, in which synchronic processes and stylized facts hold sway, economic geographers typically confront a world which is more concrete, institutionally cluttered, and—perhaps above all—geographically uneven. By inclination, economic geographers are just as comfortable in finding (local) exceptions to the rule as they are in ratifying some would-be theoretical orthodoxy. All this means that economic geography is, in its very nature, a rather unsettled subdiscipline, where dynamism and invention come as often from destabilizing orthodoxies as from shoring them up. Generally speaking, economic geography also tends to be more self-conscious about both methodological and theoretical issues than is the case in mainstream economics.[1]

[1] Still the best general introduction to methods and methodological debates in economic geography is Massey and Meegan's (1985) *Politics and Method*, which draws out the implicit and explicit methodological assumptions associated with a number of substantive studies of industrial change and restructuring, ranging from the orthodox to the radical. Andrew Sayer's (1992) *Method in Social Science* and Trevor Barnes's (1996) *Logics of Dislocation* explore, from respectively realist and poststructuralist perspectives, the methodological and epistemological foundations of

Notwithstanding the continuing heterogeneity of economic geography, since the mid-1980s there has been a general movement towards various forms of intensive, case-study methodologies, coupled with a 'more qualitative and speculative mode of analysis in the hope of representing the spatial scope and diversity of economic life' (Clark 1998: 74; cf. Hodgson 1988; Dow 1997; Martin 1999). And if there has been a shift in the substantive focus of economic geography over this same period, it has been towards a widespread acceptance that 'institutions matter' in the operation of the economy. Paralleling the rise of 'socioeconomics' more generally, the practice of economic geography has been enriched through engagements with institutionalist and evolutionary economics, economic sociology, international political economy, and the regulation approach. Needless to say, there is no consensus across these fields about *how* institutions matter, and neither is there a single (or even dominant) position on this within economic geography. Nevertheless, there is certainly a widespread concern with processes of social and economic governance, and with the complex roles of 'institutional forms' in mediating, guiding, and sustaining economic development. Jessop (forthcoming: 2) portrays this as an 'integral' conception of the capitalist economy, viewed as an 'operationally autonomous system that is nonetheless socially embedded and somehow needful of complex forms of social regulation'. Certainly, there is an explicit rejection here of the orthodox view of institutions as sources of 'external interference' in an otherwise equilibrating market system. Within the specific domain of economic geography, there has been a shared concern to problematize the roles of regulation, governance, and institutions in the processes of economic development and restructuring, though there remain non-trivial differences around how this should be conceptualized theoretically or operationalized methodologically (see Storper and Scott 1992; Amin and Thrift 1994; Lee and Wills 1997; Sheppard and Barnes forthcoming).[2]

This chapter focuses on some of the ways that economic geographers have been 'doing' regulation, governance, and institutions over the past decade. Necessarily selective, it concentrates on two significant episodes in the recent history of the subdiscipline which in different ways have foregrounded and problematized institutional roles and (dare one say it) functions: first, the debate over economic 'flexibility', which was the dominant one in the early part

contemporary economic geography. Those seeking article-size treatments of these and related issues with specific reference to economic geography should see Sayer (1982), Martin (1994), Pratt (1995), and Clark (1998). More concretely, Schoenberger (1994), Cochrane (1998), and McDowell (1998) have discussed questions of practice and interpretation in intensive, interview-based research in a range of situations.

[2] On the study of institutions and regulation in economic geography, see Moulaert (1996), Moulaert and Swyngedouw (1992), and Peck (1996). For provocative discussions of the reach and range of economic geography, which say a lot about shifting substantive concerns and favoured methods in the subdiscipline, see Sayer (1985) and Thrift and Olds (1996).

of the 1990s, and secondly, the more recent controversies around 'globalization'. Of course, these two episodes do not capture everything that has been happening in the subdiscipline during this time, but they do have a certain heuristic utility in drawing out both distinctive theoretical conceptions and different empirical treatments of how, and how much, 'institutions matter'.

Flexibilism

Geographical economists like Paul Krugman will occasionally dip into economic geography, but for the most part the two subdisciplines are not on the same page, philosophically or methodologically. For Krugman, phrases like 'post-Fordism' are signifiers of politicized, qualitative research: 'if you see that', he explains, 'it means you are dealing with a member of the Derrida-influenced regulation school—deconstructionist geography!' (quoted in Martin 1999: 82). There might of course be a case for deconstructing this statement, but suffice it to say that the roots of the regulation approach lie in (structuralist) political economy, itself somewhat susceptible to poststructuralist critique (see Barnes 1996; Gibson-Graham 1996). Moreover, the regulation approach—with its emphasis on the intertwining of economic and extra-economic factors in the institutionally embedded and socially regularized process of capitalist development—is associated with an open and under-determined stance on the issue of 'post-Fordism' (see Boyer 1990; Tickell and Peck 1995). The approach is not predictive or prescriptive, but works typically through historical analysis to identify institutionally and geographically distinctive modes of economic development, seeking to hold together an appreciation of the generic features of capitalism (such as its appropriation of nature and human labour, its surplus-generating dynamics, its crisis-proneness) with an understanding of its specific (institutional) forms in time and space. Above all, regulationists are concerned with the processes by which capitalist social relations are reproduced, regularized, and 'normalized' through a series of periodized 'regimes of accumulation', the best known of which is 'Fordism'.

The notion of Fordism centres on a series of macroeconomic and macro-institutional articulations between, first, a regime of mass production and mass consumption sustained by relatively stable (and growing) aggregate demand, and secondly, the role of the Keynesian welfare state (KWS) in maintaining full (male) employment, a secure wage, and welfare floor and macroeconomic stability. Empirically, this configuration was most closely associated with the 'Atlantic Fordist' economies of North America and Western Europe during the thirty-year 'long boom' which followed World War II, though in fact a range of nationally specific 'couplings' between Fordist accumulation and Keynesian-welfarist regulation have been identified by regulationists (see Tickell and Peck 1992). Here, conceptual emphasis is placed on these 'structural couplings' between the system of accumulation (a macroeconomically coherent production–distribution–consumption relationship) and the ensemble of state forms, social norms, political practices, and institutional networks which regulationists term the 'mode of social regulation' (MSR). Regulationists emphasize that the MSR should not be reduced to state institutions, but also embraces a series of 'softer' (and often analytically quite intractable) forms of regulation, such as consumption norms, societal expectations, economic habits and conventions, and cultural practices, which together define the social context of the accumulation process. In the postwar era, for example, generalized cultural norms relating to the suburbanized, 'American way of life' played an important role in normalizing the culture economy of Fordism, but this was also a period in which some of the most important regulatory conventions and practices emanated from, or were relayed through, the national state (see Zunz 1998; Steinmetz 1999).

While conceived as Fordism's 'ideal-typical form of state' (Jessop 1994), the specific economic roles of the KWS were not structurally pre-ordained or theoretically necessitated, but instead emerged through historically specific and *politicized* processes of mutual adjustment and co-stabilization on a country-by-country basis. Likewise, the protracted after-Fordist crisis has seen the structures/strategies of the KWS subjected to critique, recomposition, and roll-back (through such means as ideological attacks on 'big government' and state planning, systemic reforms of welfare and labour-market policy, the abandonment of demand management, and so on), such that a range of pluralistic 'governance' regimes and market/pseudo-market 'deregulations' are assuming increased importance in the resultant regulatory vacuum (see Jessop 1999). Structurally, the proliferation of reform strategies and institutional experiments can be linked to an increasingly insistent search for a new 'institutional fix' capable of restoring sustainable growth in the advanced capitalist economies. Part and parcel of this process is the explicit de-legitimation of inherited national-state institutions, and indeed of the national *scale* of regulation itself, as social programming and responsibility is downloaded to the local level while internationalizing economic forces are the object of studied deference.

Regulationists are appropriately reluctant to be drawn into predicting the outcomes of this uncertain and inherently political searching process. For Boyer (forthcoming), it represents an asymmetrical form of 'regime competition' between a range of institutionally specific forms of capitalism—the 'market-led' strategy of the USA and UK, the Japanese path of 'corporatist' regulation, the 'social-democratic' method epitomized by the Scandinavian countries and the 'state-led' approach of France and a number of other continental European states. While it is within the ambit of the regulation approach to provide real-time critiques and diagnoses of this (changing) situation, the outcome is not economically predetermined (or, for that matter, politically guaranteed). So, while the currently prevailing 'rules of the game' at the international level tend to privilege strategies of *short-term flexibility*, which in turn favours the more responsive and market-orientated regimes, this does not mean that such neoliberal models define the 'one best way'. On the contrary, the current rash of neoliberal regulatory experiments should be seen as more of a 'response' than a 'solution' to the conditions of instability and uncertainty at the international scale (conditions which are *themselves* partly a creation of a neoliberalized macro regime). In this respect, neoliberal strategies do not offer the possibility of ameliorating the current crisis; they are in fact 'creatures' of this crisis (Tickell and Peck 1995). But while specific regulatory projects—say, neoliberal workfare experiments—may be contradictory, this does not mean that they will automatically wither. Contradiction, of course, is a characteristic even of 'durable' institutions, like welfare systems, being the source of important institutional dynamics. So, one of the challenges of real-time regulatory analysis is to trace how the logics *and illogics* of emergent institutions are combined and (for regulationists in particular) to explore how they cohere and conflict at the macro level.

The regulationists' understanding of the 'fit' between systems of accumulation and modes of social regulation is, therefore, a complex one. While formally eschewing functionalism, the regulation approach nevertheless permits a kind of 'a posteriori functionalism', specifying as it does through historical analysis the roles of specific institutional forms, codes, and conventions in sustaining (different patterns of) economic growth. Regulationists maintain a consistent methodological position here by insisting that 'institutional forms' are themselves the (under-determined) outcomes of social struggles and political interventions, replete with unintended consequences and rule-changing behavioural adjustments, the full implications and effects of which can only be assessed *ex post*. And because these fortuitous regulatory fixes are, ultimately, '*chance discoveries* made in the course of human struggles' (Lipietz 1987: 15), the process by which MSRs are formed is reducible neither to functionalist responses to the 'needs of capital', nor to conscious action on the part of state technocrats.

This complex and rather slippery conception of institutional forms has proved frustrating for both advocates and critics of the regulation approach. Methodologically, it defines both the means by which particular patterns of capitalist development are sustained and the institutional mechanism by which crisis tendencies are (temporarily) contained. Regulationists do not position institutions over and above the laws of motion of capital, but they do see them playing an important role in normalizing and regularizing particular patterns of development. As Jessop (1992: 50) explains, the underlying dynamics of the capitalist system are seen by regulationists to define the basic tendencies and counter-tendencies, structural contradictions, strategic dilemmas, and overall constraints which inevitably shape modes of regulation, which find provisional, partial and unstable resolution in the latter . . . [MSRs] cannot be properly understood without considering how [they] modify and yet remain subject to the general laws of capital accumulation.

So it is only for heuristic and expository reasons that accumulation and regulation are separated in regulationist accounts. Analytically, they are necessarily and dialectically bound together, but in a wide range of (contingent) ways. The metaphors here tend to be biological rather than mechanical. The MSR should not be visualized as some kind of supportive scaffolding erected around the accumulation process, but instead is implicated in complex and indeterminate ways in the ongoing *reproduction* of this process. As Barnes (1997) observes, regulationists depart from classical Marxism in their insistence that economic reproduction is not the automatic result of some internal logic, but rather stems from the symbiosis that occurs between the accumulation system and the MSR. Here, Barnes explains, other pseudo-biological forces come into play, like chance discovery and the inheritance of acquired characteristics, as regulation and accumulation co-evolve in a non-teleological fashion. No set of institutions can be guaranteed, a priori, to generate growth, but through historical analysis it is possible to reconstruct how certain regimes of accumulation/regulation function as an 'ensemble of regularities [to] secure a general and relatively coherent progression of the accumulation process [allowing] an absorption of, or a temporary delay in the distortions and disequilibria that are born out of the accumulation process itself' (Boyer 1987, translation from Moulaert 1996: 160).

Given these suggestive observations concerning the role of institutions in securing and underpinning growth, it should perhaps come as no surprise that regulationist ideas attracted the interest of post-Fordist speculators. Indeed, the language of regulation theory was in the early 1990s widely appropriated by proponents of flexible specialization—the roots of which lie in institutionalist and transaction-costs economics rather than structural political economy *per se*—even though the theoretical and political tensions between these two modes of analysis are considerable (see Hirst and Zeitlin 1991; Martin 1994). A vulgar rendering of regulation theory was consequently used to shore up speculative post-Fordist assertions, despite the fact that the substantive core of the 'flex-spec' thesis rested on very narrow foundations. The stylized facts of the flex-spec account were derived from a small number of (admittedly vivid) studies of dynamic industries in dynamic regions. Here, there was little or no consideration of the macroeconomic and macro-institutional factors which are given such prominence in the regulationist method, while the prevailing understanding of 'institutional forms' was literal, denuded, and concretist. A caricature of regulation theory was therefore being used to legitimate production-orientated speculation, both narrowing *and foreclosing* the debate around after-Fordist development trajectories (Leborgne and Lipietz 1992; MacLeod 1997).

The dangers inherent in attempting to 'read off' systemic and predictive conclusions from tendentious developments in the production system are only compounded if causal efficacy is subsequently attached to particular institutions. For example, while it may be the case that certain collective services (related to training, marketing, design, etc.) play an important role in underwriting the development of flexibly specialized production systems, this does not mean that the installation of such institutions is sufficient to ensure 'flexible growth'. Real-time analysis of institutional change and regulatory experimentation is a hazardous process, because there is not a predictable, one-to-one correspondence between these extra-economic developments and the course of accumulation and because the process of experimentation is correspondingly multi-directional. Altvater (1992: 22) notes that whereas the 'process of [institutional] destruction is more or less obvious and identifiable, it is much more difficult to deduce the generation of new social forms of regulation [which] can only emerge as the outcome of conflicting tendencies of progressive acts and regressive setbacks'.

While narrow productivism and institutional determinism have no place in the regulationist schema, the regulation approach was nevertheless caught up in the debate around post-Fordism in the early 1990s. According to Graham (1992: 397), post-Fordism was by this time 'on its way to becoming the preeminent narrative of capitalist development', representing a 'zone of rough consensus as well as a locus of disagreement and debate'. Regulationists were, in a sense, on both sides of this debate at the same time, sanctioning certain modes of 'transition thinking', while insisting on exacting analytical standards for the definition of a new regime of accumulation. The tendentious claims of the post-Fordist literature did not come close to satisfying the regulationists' theoretical criteria (for all their use of the jargon), though according to Graham at least the regulationist method was implicated in as far as its concern with crisis-mediating institutional forms gave licence to prescriptive modes of analysis.

In fact, regulation theory offers no guarantees that a successor regime will happen along, just as it rejects the idea that new 'institutional fixes' are the result either of spontaneous forces or political fiat. It differs crucially from long-wave theory in this respect (Kotz 1990). Future trajectories will certainly by shaped by inherited economic and institutional conditions, but there will never be a single path, post-Fordist or otherwise. In this sense, the regulation approach, *qua method*, is not some rigid template for generating binary histories of Fordist pasts/post-Fordist futures. On the contrary, it can be used in an open and reflexive way to interrogate a range of development trajectories, including those—such as Japan—which sit less easily with the stylized history of Atlantic Fordism (see Peck and Miyamachi 1994; Boyer and Yamada forthcoming). More challenging still, perhaps, is to envisage how the regulation approach might be deployed at scales below that of the national state, there being nothing theoretically pre-ordained or fixed, of course, about the scale at which regulatory functions are sited (see Swyngedouw 1997; Jessop 1999; Jessop and Peck 1998; MacLeod and Goodwin 1999).

For some time now, in fact, economic geographers have been exploring the shifting scalar and spatial constitution of regulatory processes, often leading to new taxonomies of economically salient institutional phenomena (see Peck and Tickell 1992; DiGiovanna 1996; Moulaert 1996; Krätke 1999). But of course it is one thing to classify institutions; it is quite another to specify their causal effects and liabilities. This is especially difficult at the local level, where it is often observed that various forms of 'soft' (i.e. non-state) institutions are sometimes argued to exert a more significant influence (Moulaert 1996). While there are no clear methodological guidelines—including in regulation theory—on how to unpack the effects of such 'soft' institutions, there are now some highly suggestive studies of phenomena like 'local production cultures' (see Saxenian 1994; Gertler 1997; Storper 1997) and localized labour-market conventions (see Hanson and Pratt 1995; Herod 1998; McDowell 1999). Such institutional geographies, it has been argued, may in fact exert a powerful influence on regional economic fortunes. For example, Krätke (1999: 683) suggests that a 'region's development is determined not only by its physical resources but also by its "institutional resources" . . . understood as the set of conventions and rules of action prevailing in the economy, which are embedded in the local social structure and show a marked regional differentiation'.

Indeed, the trend seems to be towards 'strong institutionalist' accounts of (local) economic success and failure. While the regulation approach may have given licence to some such searches for coherence and functionality, the determinism that suggests that some institutions are unequivocally 'good for growth' and others 'bad' remains at odds with the original theoretical project of regulationism. Moreover, exhaustive cataloguing of the institutional features of different economic 'systems' is no substitute for demonstrating the (range of) economic effects which are associated with *specific* institutions under *particular* circumstances (cf. Hollingsworth 1997). At worst, this can lead to a 'methodological nationalism' or 'methodological localism' in which explanatory reach is restricted to endogenous institutional attributes, the internal coherence and causal efficacy of which is implied rather than demonstrated.

More promising than those approaches which lay stress on the idiosyncratic institutional 'shells' of different (spatially bounded) economic systems are those which focus on their inter-relations and geographical dynamics. For writers such as Scott (1988, 1998) and Moulaert (1996) the changing institutional landscape both reflects, and presents stimuli for, emerging economic geographies. Scott argues, for example, that a defining characteristic of 'new industrial spaces' is their *distance*—either socially or more often than not geographically—from the (mal)institutionalized and (mal)socialized heartlands of Fordism. New industrial spaces are seen as sites for the production not only of new organizational techniques but also new regulatory norms (such as flexible labour conventions), which are often subsequently reimposed on old industrial regions (see Hudson 1989). In the process, 'new territories are invaded, becoming the social spaces producing new forms of industrial, social, and technical structures, as well as new ideological images. As these are being created, the previously constructed spaces undergo dramatic transformation, trying to adapt to the new requirements' (Moulaert 1996: 161).

Concern with the subtle and complex ways in which institutional geographies are being (re)made has been growing since the mid-1990s, just as the more precocious strains of the post-Fordist/flex-spec literature have begun seriously to wane. In more recent years, the argument that 'institutions matter'—and more specifically that *local* institutions matter—has been framed in terms of the debate on 'globalization'. Indeed, if post-Fordism defined the macro-narrative of the first half of the 1990s, the big-picture issue around which discussion and debate tended to revolve, then globalization seems to have become the macro-narrative of the second half. And again, questions of epistemology and method have been thrown into the mix.

Globalism

The phenomena of internationalization and globalization have been long-standing concerns in economic geography (Dicken 1986), but the more recent rise to prominence of globalization debates across the social sciences has thrown these issues into especially sharp relief. Economic geographers have been particularly exercised by the prevailing conception of globalization in the business literature and in neoliberal political rhetoric, in which the global domain is represented—in close to neoclassical textbook terms—as one of untrammelled, homogenizing and equilibrating market forces. In this hyper-globalized world, transnational corporations call the shots, labour has to learn to be 'realistic' and (globally) competitive, and the national state shrinks to insignificance, both as a unit of analysis and as a political agent. For neoliberal politicians and corporate leaders, this script is an appealing one because it allows the presentation of their (sectional) concerns as systemic, rationalistic, and naturalized interests. It is also associated with a convenient, and typically regressive, form of scale politics, in which the global is the scale of managerial prerogatives and (immutable) economic imperatives, the national is the scale of de- and re-regulatory facilitation/accommodation to these same global 'pressures', while the local is the scale of adaptation, at which market-compatible coping systems are to be constructed not as a shield against globalization but as a way of maximizing its local potential.

In many ways, complementary to the globalization thesis is a parallel narrative concerning new forms of localism and regionalism—based variously on notions of learning networks, reflexive institutional forms, economies of information and association, and so on—which lays stress on the role of local social, institutional, and human capital as key competitive assets on the supply side of the economy (broadly defined). Certainly, there are in political terms both progressive and conservative versions of this localization narrative, just as in analytical terms there are both sophisticated and crude variants of its underlying theoretical premises (for discussion, see Amin and Thrift 1995; Amin 1999). Yet Lovering (1999: 386) insists that there is considerable slippage between these different analytical and normative permutations, contending that the 'dogma that "regions are resurgent" as a result of global transformations implied by the growth of "informational economies" has almost reached the status of an orthodoxy . . . [rather] like the fashion for postfordism which preceded it'.

Methodologically, one of the main challenges presented by the globalization/regionalization thesis, and where there are certainly echoes of post-Fordist debates, is how to obtain a firm conceptual and empirical grasp on a (definitionally) fast-changing situation. While some of the more excitable advocates of the globalization thesis have been guilty of proposing highly exaggerated, selective, and self-serving accounts, some critics are just as guilty of setting up a caricatured argument for the convenience of knocking it down (Amin 1997; Dicken *et al.* 1997). Both Gordon (1988) and Hirst and Thompson (1996), for example, define globalization in ideal-typical terms, as an end-state condition rather than a complex process, before going on to argue that empirically there is nothing especially new and distinctive about the current era. Such accounts tend to emphasize that the magnitude of international trade, for instance, was almost as great prior to World War I as it is today and that contemporary trade flows are structured around 'triadic' trading blocs rather than on a *fully* global basis. These are important contributions to any discussion of globalization, but to (mis)represent this solely in quantitative terms is to miss the point about a whole series of *qualitative* changes which have taken place in TNC strategies and organizational forms, in the structure and orientation of nation-states, in international financial relationships, in cultural forms and flows, and so on (see Amin 1997; Held *et al.* 1999). It is important, in other words, to recognize that some things *have* changed, but to do so without succumbing to the exaggerated narrative of hyper-globalization.

Take the case of the nation-state. Harder versions of the globalization thesis typically have it that the nation-state is withering away, usually in one of two ways. First, the neoliberal variant of this story has it that rolling back the frontiers of the state, through programmes of deregulation, governmental withdrawal, and public-sector austerity, is necessary in order to make space for reinvigorated market forces and an enlarged private economy. Hence,globalization is seen to require a realignment of the boundary between state and market, in favour of the latter. Secondly, a rather more progressive strand of the story has it that regulatory functions and state capacities are not simply being recommodified but are in fact being redistributed between territorial levels or scales. Hence, globalization is associated with the 'hollowing out' of the nation-state, as powers, functions, and roles pass downwards to local and regional bodies, upwards to supranational agencies, and outwards to trans-local and trans-national networks. While both these visions of the nation-state under (implication intended) globalization capture aspects of the contemporary reality, their grasp of institutional, political, and regulatory change is a highly tenuous one. This cannot be reduced to some unidirectional process of deregulation/marketization, nor should it be portrayed as a benign process of zero-sum regulatory redistribution across scales. Rather, what is under way here is a *qualitative reorganization* of the state, involving shifts in its structural form and strategic orientation. Moreover, it is misleading to characterize contemporary state-restructuring trends as a roll-back of the 'state-in-general' when in fact they are being primarily organized around a critique and recomposition of a particular, historically specific form of state, the KWS.

So, as some institutions and regulatory capacities are being rolled back, others are being rolled forward—often, indeed, in the name of 'deregulation' —albeit in radically different forms and with different purposes. Jessop (1999: 384) portrays this as a complex, contradictory, and contested transition between Keynesian-welfarist state forms and (various kinds of) 'Schumpeterian workfare regime', having concluded that the outcomes of the crises and conflicts over the KWS in the 1970s and 1980s 'have not (and never could have) been restricted to simple redistribution or reduction of pregiven functions'. What is at stake here, then, is a process of political and institutional restructuring in state forms, in ways that simultaneously represent responses to and *reconstitutions of* economic pressures, rather than another chapter of the eternal struggle between 'state' and 'market'. 'State' and 'market', of course, are not hermetically sealed and mutually exclusive categories, but are co-constituted and inextricably related (Block 1987; O'Neill 1997). Contrary to the conventional rendering of the state in neoclassical economics as an external, intervening, and interfering force, the state must be seen as inescapably *immanent in* the economy, in a variety of ways—*inter alia*, as a juridical authority, as a regulatory agent, as a source of public employment and consumption demand, as an orchestrator of economic governance regimes, as a producer and validator of economic narratives, as an enforcer of rights and responsibilities.

Of critical importance for the way in which economic policy and regulatory capacities are currently being reorganized, of course, is the role of the nation-state *itself* as an author and disseminator of narratives of economic 'globalization', 'hollowing out', devolution and 'localism', failures of 'big government', and so forth. Jessop observes that the 'geoeconomic narrative concerning "globalization" and its translation into pressures to prioritize "structural competitiveness" on various scales' has been deployed to help

> consolidate a limited but widely accepted set of diagnoses and prescriptions for the economic and political difficulties now confronting nations, regions, and cities and their various economic branches . . . Such narratives lead, inter alia, to the discovery of triad regions, the 'region state', the 'transnational territory', 'entrepreneurial cities', and so forth, as new phenomena and their naturalization on practical, if not normative grounds. (1999: 398)

This does not mean that nothing has changed in terms of the global economic context in which nation-states operate, that economic globalization is just an artifice of neoliberal rhetoric. To be sure, there have been important 'real' and demonstrable changes in the architecture of the global financial system, in the balance and structure of competition between countries, in the global reach of TNCs, in the power and influence of global trade organizations and financial institutions, and so on (see Held *et al.* 1999), such that it is hardly controversial to say that 'state policy *is* becoming more and more driven by external forces' (Amin 1997: 129). Of course, this does not mean that the form and content of state responses is structurally determined, or indeed that it is adequate to conceive of these simply as Pavlovian 'responses' in the first place.

So, as Amin and Thrift (1997: 155) choose to formulate it, 'The relevant practical question . . . is not *whether* globalization allows scope for national or local action, but *what kind* of action is necessary for positive engagement within the global economy'. While neoliberal remedies—based on voluntaristic governance, privatism, and the enforcement of market disciplines and supply-side individualism—may represent the 'response of least resistance' to economic globalization under the current political-economic climate, this is not the only response, even if it may be empirically the most prevalent. Against this current, Amin and Thrift (1995) maintain that it is not only desirable but also feasible to develop locally based, bottom-up *and progressive* economic-governance strategies, building on the associative, networking, and learning capacities of local economies and sustained by a 'thickening' of local institutions. Albeit within a broadly supportive macroeconomic/political framework, Amin and Thrift see real scope for purposeful institution-building at the local level with a view to sustaining and spreading (both socially and geographically) the benefits of economic growth and development. Concrete institutions of economic governance like agencies delivering 'real services' to industry clusters, education and training consortia, producer/consumer co-operatives, social economy initiatives, community development programmes, and even local cultural and civic projects, all have a role in their broadly defined schema, the aim of which is to 'develop and strengthen local institutional networks . . . to provide a region with "voice", with agency, with orchestrating capacities which cannot be reduced to arbitrary statist forms invented by an élite of policy makers on the look-out for a quick fix' (Amin and Thrift 1995: 56). While in part clearly a normative project, this policy programme also stems from an alternative *reading* of the economy, as a composite of

> collective influences which shape individual action and as a diversified and path-dependent entity moulded by inherited cultural and socio-institutional influences. [T]he influences on economic behaviour are quite different from those privileged by the economic orthodoxy (e.g. perfect competition, hedonism, formal rules etc.). Explanatory weight is given to the effects of formal and informal institutions, considered to be socially constructed and subject to slow evolutionary change; to values and rationalities of action ensconced in networks and institutions; to the composition of networks of economic association, especially their role in disseminating information, knowledge, and learning for economic adaptability; and to intermediate institutions between market and state which are relatively purposeful and participatory forms of arrangement. (Amin 1999: 368)

In practical or policy terms, where this leaves individual regions, particularly *lagging* regions, is an open question. And deliberately so for Amin and Thrift (1995: 56), who characterize their contribution as a 'tentative' one, with 'no end-point in the conventional sense'. They are sceptical of imported, off-the-shelf 'solutions' which are lifted 'from the experience of successful regions or some "expert" manual' (Amin 1999: 371), yet rather paradoxically, many of their favoured policy measures are—almost by definition—'informed by the experience of prosperous regions characterized by strong local economic interdependencies' (ibid. 366), such as Emilia-Romagna and Baden Württemburg. There is in fact a persistent risk of circularity in institutionalist accounts, if regional growth is seen to be sustained by those supportive regional institutions which, of course, happen to be located in growth regions (especially when these are the *same* regions privileged in post-Fordist accounts). Conversely, lagging regions are, by implication, cursed with laggard institutions. Institutional co-presence in the same space, of course, does not necessarily mean that (all) the institutions concerned are causally or functionally related to the economic trajectory of that space, or one another. Analytically, this can be seen as a re-run of the post-Fordist argument that everything that happens to be novel and flexible must be part of a systemically coherent, new 'regime'.

In Lovering's (1999) view, arguments around governance and institution-building are intrinsically vulnerable to appropriation by those 'vulgar new regionalists' who are prone to slip clumsily from abstract analysis to crude policy advocacy. The danger, according to Lovering, is that proponents of virtually *all* forms of local institutional reform become 'unwitting agents of the reconstruction of regional governance in Hayekian-liberal terms' (ibid. 391). It is of course a neoliberal conceit that there is an easy-to-assemble kit of readily transferable local governance 'solutions'—usually of a market-orientated nature—to the problems facing lagging cities and regions, despite the manifest failures and manifold silences in this narrowly delimited policy repertoire. Witness, for example, the feeble achievements of the (nevertheless ubiquitous) urban regeneration partnerships, local training initiatives, and booster committees in the UK (see Peck 1995). In fact, these nationally conceived forms of 'centrist localism' produce local impacts that are far more variegated and contingent than their (relatively standardized) design would suggest, often being associated with different economic outcomes and even different functional roles in different locations (see Peck 1998; Imrie and Thomas 1999; Jones 1999).

Again, this highlights the one-to-many correspondence between institutions or policy measures and local (economic) outcomes, which only adds to the hazards of prescriptive policy advocacy. A plausible case might reasonably be made that the loosely structured, permissive, and market-following governance regimes favoured by neoliberals are likely to be rather more dependent on (and indeed submissive to) extant local-economic conditions than progressive alternatives which seek to foster local capacity and developmental potential. Yet to the extent that local associationalist strategies are contingent on either a vibrant private economy or a secure public economy (or both), their deployment is unlikely significantly to counter existing patterns of spatially uneven development. Perhaps the 'regional problem' is more likely to be remade than solved by associationalism.

Aware of these pitfalls, Amin and Thrift's concern is not to impose a single associationalist 'fix' on the regions, but rather to explore configurations of local capacities and macro-level supportive frameworks that permit a plurality of local-level strategies to be developed. Here, the national (and supranational) state has a vital role to play as an agent of what Jessop (forthcoming) calls 'metagovernance' or the 'governance of governance'. As Amin (1997: 376) reminds us, 'in the absence of a conducive macro-economic framework, it seems irresponsible to ask the regions to embark on a long-term and comprehensive overhaul in pursuit of an endogenous pathway to prosperity'. In the rush for governance-based strategies, then, it should not be forgotten that the risk of 'governance failure' is ever-present, even normalized. And neoliberal states, of course, are likely to continue to foster their own form of governance churning as a mode of crisis displacement, rendering through regulatory sleight of hand state and economic failures as failures of local governance.

Such widespread tendencies to fiddle with governance while the economy burns do little or nothing to alter the economic fundamentals of lagging regions, even if they do have more institutions engaged with place-marketing, inward investment promotion, and workforce training than before. While careful probing of the limits and possibilities of local economic governance is clearly an important task, not least in a context in which governance strategies are both empirically prevalent and politically legitimate, there is at least a risk that, as Lovering (1999) puts it, the policy tail begins to wag the analytical dog. More charitably, Jessop draws attention to the

> mutually constitutive links between academic discourse, political practice, and changing economic realities. Academic discovery of networks and governance has coincided with economic changes that make big business and big government ineffective means of economic organization. This confluence may help to explain the widespread fascination with alternative forms of governance, whether rediscovered or newly invented. (1999: 399)

And of course the very methodological act of deeming such phenomena researchable—as the case of business-elite networks shows—tends to lend them status as significant social facts (see Cochrane 1998).

Conclusion

Ever since economic geography's abandonment of neoclassical theory in the 1970s, the subdiscipline has been preoccupied—both conceptually and empirically—with the movements of the 'real economy' over time and space. Necessarily, this has involved dealing with 'institutions' in one way or another, be this in the form of concrete policy measures or, more ambitiously, by way of abstract notions like social/local embeddedness, institutional thickness, and social regulation. Methodologically, economic geographers have generated particular insights into these processes, in part by virtue of their propensity to engage in theoretically informed 'close dialogue' with key actors and participants. While the literature has generated a series of provocative ideas about institutional liabilities, capacities, and tendencies, the very *indeterminacy* of institutional forms, effects, and outcomes means that these are not allowed to acquire the status of deterministic, law-like statements. Because, in realist terms, institutional relations and outcomes are contingent, they cannot be exhaustively theorized in advance and their effects cannot be predicted with certainty.

Correspondingly, economic geographers are rarely prone to make sweeping statements about the anticipated effects of institutions or policy measures. They tend, by inclination, to be suspicious of such predictive, 'big-picture' generalizations. Economic geographers, for example, were quick to prick the bubble of post-Fordist speculation, just as they have been deeply critical of totalizing rhetorics of globalization. Clearly, however, the job of economic geography cannot be just about spoiling the parties started in other disciplines; within the academic division of labour, economic geographers cannot be content simply to be the detail workers, tracking down and documenting local inconsistencies. Perhaps the subdiscipline needs some stylized facts—or at least stylized tendencies—of its own. Now these will not be like the stylized facts of mainstream economics, being more likely to be 'unlaws' than laws, but there is certainly a need for economic geography to codify what it *does* know about economic institutions (and how it found out).

In methodological terms, this (as yet far from complete) task would involve probing institutional liabilities, tendencies, and contradictions under different (local/national) contextual conditions, in order to separate necessary effects from contingent ones. This might involve, for example, rigorous analyses of the same institutions, like training systems or technology-transfer measures, under a range of local economic and political conditions. The corpus of research in economic geography has yet to yield conclusive answers to these questions, but at the very least there are working hypotheses and theoretically informed presuppositions. So, while economic behaviours may be embedded in, and regularized through, institutional forms, it is widely accepted that institutional structures and dynamics are not determined functionally but are relatively autonomous (i.e. they have their own 'laws of motion'). Correspondingly, patterns of economic behaviour are not exclusively determined by institutional rules, and neither can they be predictably manipulated through institutional change. From a geographical perspective, it can therefore be anticipated that institutions will routinely be associated with different (economic) effects in different places; that their forms—and certainly their *effects*—will be difficult to replicate; and that they are unlikely to travel well (see Jessop and Peck 1998; Peck and Theodore 1999). This inescapable spatial indeterminacy in institutional forms, dynamics, and outcomes, coupled with the necessity for extra-economic regulation of 'market systems', means that uneven development and local differentiation will remain fundamental features of the 'real' economy. Hence the persistent insecurity of would-be theoretical and methodological orthodoxies in economic geography. This is the price economic geography pays for its substantive interest in, and methodological concern with, what Massey (1984: 3) appropriately called the 'real world in flux'.

Acknowledgements

Thanks to Ash Amin, Meric Gertler, and Gordon MacLeod for helpful comments on a previous version of this chapter.

References

Altvater, E. 1992. Fordist and post-Fordist international division of labor and monetary regimes. In Storper and Scott 1992: 21–45.

Amin, A. 1997. Placing globalization. *Theory, Culture and Society*, 14: 123–37.

—— 1999. An institutionalist perspective on regional economic development. *International Journal of Urban and Regional Research*, 23: 365–78.

—— and Thrift, N., eds. 1994. *Globalization, Institutions and Regional Development in Europe.* Oxford: Oxford University Press.

—— —— 1995. Institutional issues for the European regions: from markets and plans to socioeconomics and powers of association. *Economy and Society*, 24: 41–66.

——— 1997. Globalization, socio-economics, territoriality. In Lee and Wills 1997: 147–57.

Barnes, T. J. 1996. *Logics of Dislocation: Models, Metaphors and Meanings of Economic Space*. New York: Guilford.

—— 1997. Theories of accumulation and regulation: bringing life back into economic geography. In Lee and Wills 1997: 231–47.

Block, F. 1987. *Revising State Theory: Essays in Politics and Postindustrialism*. Philadelphia: Temple University Press.

Boyer, R. 1990. *The Regulation School: A Critical Introduction*. New York: Columbia University Press.

—— forthcoming. The diversity and future of capitalisms: a 'régulationist' analysis. In *Capitalism in Evolution*, ed. G. Hodgson and N. Yokokawa. London: Edward Elgar.

—— and Yamada, T., eds. forthcoming. *Japanese Capitalism in Crisis*. London: Routledge.

Clark, G. L. 1998. Stylized facts and close dialogue: methodology in economic geography. *Annals of the Association of American Geographers*, 88: 73–87.

Cochrane, A. 1998. Illusions of power: interviewing local elites. *Environment and Planning A*, 30: 2121–32.

Dicken, P. 1986. *Global Shift: Industrial Change in a Turbulent World*. London: Harper and Row.

—— Peck, J., and Tickell, A. 1997. Unpacking the global. In Lee and Wills 1997: 158–66.

DiGiovanna, S. 1996. Industrial districts and regional economic development: a regulation approach. *Regional Studies*, 30: 373–86.

Dow, S. 1997. Mainstream economic methodology. *Cambridge Journal of Economics*, 21: 73–93.

Gertler, M. 1997. The invention of regional culture. In Lee and Wills 1997: 47–58.

Gibson-Graham, J.-K. 1996. *The End of Capitalism (As We Knew It): A Feminist Critique of Political Economy*. Oxford: Blackwell.

Gordon, D. M. 1988. The global economy: new edifice or crumbling foundations? *New Left Review*, 168: 24–64.

Graham, J. 1992. Post-Fordism as politics: the political consequences of narratives on the left. *Society and Space*, 10: 393–410.

Hanson, S., and Pratt, G. 1995. *Gender, Work, and Space*. London: Routledge.

Held, D., McGrew, A., Goldblatt, D., and Perraton, J. 1999. *Global Transformations: Politics, Economics and Culture*. Cambridge: Polity Press.

Herod, A., ed. 1998. *Organizing the Landscape*. Minneapolis: University of Minnesota Press.

Hirst, P., and Thompson, G. 1996. *Globalization in Question: The International Economy and the Possibilities of Governance*. Cambridge: Polity.

—— and Zeitlin, J. 1991. Flexible specialisation versus post-Fordism: theory, evidence and policy implications. *Economy and Society*, 20: 1–56.

Hodgson, G. M. 1988. *Economics and Institutions: A Manifesto for a Modern Institutional Economics*. Cambridge: Polity Press.

Hollingsworth, J. R. 1997. Continuities and changes in social systems of production: the cases of Japan, Germany, and the United States. In *Contemporary Capitalism: The*

Embeddedness of Institutions, ed. J. R. Hollingsworth and R. Boyer. Cambridge: Cambridge University Press, 265–310.

Hudson, R. 1989. Labour market changes and new forms of work in old industrial regions: maybe flexibility for some but not flexible accumulation. *Society and Space*, 7: 5–30.

Imrie, R., and Thomas, H., eds. 1999. *British Urban Policy: An Evaluation of the Urban Development Corporations*. 2nd edn. London: Sage.

Jessop, B. 1992. Fordism and post-Fordism: a critical reformulation. In Storper and Scott 1992: 46–69.

—— 1994. Post-Fordism and the state. In *Post-Fordism: A Reader*, ed. A. Amin. Oxford: Blackwell, 251–79.

—— 1999. Narrating the future of the national economy and the national state? Remarks on remapping regulation and reinventing governance. In Steinmetz 1999: 378–405.

—— forthcoming. The social embeddedness of the economy and its implications for economic governance. In *The Socially Embedded Economy*, ed. F. Adaman and P. Devine. Montreal: Black Rose Books.

—— and Peck, J. 1998. Fast policy/local discipline: the politics of scale and the neoliberal workfare offensive. Paper presented to the annual conference of the Association of American Geographers, Boston, Mass., 25–9 March.

Jones, M. 1999. *New Institutional Spaces: Training and Enterprise Councils and the Remaking of Economic Governance*. London: Jessica Kingsley.

Kotz, M. 1990. A comparative analysis of the theory of regulation and the social structure of accumulation theory. *Science and Society*, 54: 5–28.

Krätke, S. 1999. A regulationist approach to regional studies. *Environment and Planning A*, 31: 683–704.

Leborgne, D., and Lipietz, A. 1992. Conceptual fallacies and open questions on post-Fordism. In M. Storper and A. J. Scott. 1992: 332–48.

Lee, R., and Wills, J., eds. 1997. *Geographies of Economies*. London: Arnold.

Lipietz, A. 1987. *Mirages and Miracles: The Crises of Global Fordism*. London: Verso.

Lovering, J. 1999. Theory led by policy: the inadequacies of the 'new regionalism' (illustrated from the case of Wales). *International Journal of Urban and Regional Research*, 23: 379–95.

McDowell, L. 1998. Elites in the City of London: some methodological considerations. *Environment and Planning A*, 30: 2133–46.

—— 1999. *Gender, Identity and Place*. Minneapolis: University of Minnesota Press.

MacLeod, G. 1997. Globalizing Parisian thought-waves: recent advances in the study of social regulation, politics, discourse and space. *Progress in Human Geography*, 21: 530–53.

—— and Goodwin, M. 1999. Reconstructing an urban and regional political economy: on the state, politics, scale and explanation. *Political Geography*, 18: 697–730.

Martin, R. 1994. Economic theory and human geography. In *Human Geography: Society, Space, and Social Science*, ed. D. Gregory, R. Martin, and G. Smith. Minneapolis: University of Minnesota Press, 21–53.

—— 1999. The new 'geographical turn' in economics: some critical reflections. *Cambridge Journal of Economics*, 23: 65–91.

Massey, D. 1984. *Spatial Divisions of Labour: Social Structures and the Geography of Production.* Basingstoke: Macmillan.
—— and Meegan, R., eds. 1985. *Politics and Method: Contrasting Studies in Industrial Geography.* London: Methuen.
Moulaert, F. 1996. Rediscovering spatial inequality in Europe: building blocks for an appropriate 'regulationist' analytical framework. *Society and Space,* 14: 155–80.
—— and Swyngedouw, E. 1992. Accumulation and organization in computing and communications industries: a regulationist approach. In *Towards Global Localization: The Computing and Telecommunications Industries in Britain and France,* ed. P. Cooke, F. Moulaert, E. Swyngedouw, O. Weinstein, and P. Wells. London: UCL Press, 39–60.
O'Neill, P. M. 1997. Bringing the qualitative state into economic geography. In Lee and Wills 1997: 290–301.
Peck, J. 1995. Moving and shaking: business elites, state localism and urban privatism. *Progress in Human Geography,* 19: 16–46.
—— 1996. *Work-Place: The Social Regulation of Labor Markets.* New York: Guilford.
—— 1998. Geographies of governance: TECs and the neo-liberalisation of 'local interests'. *Space and Polity,* 2: 5–31.
—— and Miyamachi, Y. 1994. Regulating Japan? Regulation theory versus the Japanese experience. *Society and Space,* 12: 639–74.
—— and Theodore, N. 1999. 'Dull Compulsion': political economies of workfare. *Working Paper,* 30. Manchester: International Centre for Labour Studies, Manchester University.
—— and Tickell, A. 1992. Local modes of social regulation? Regulation theory, Thatcherism and uneven development. *Geoforum,* 23: 347–64.
Pratt, A. C. 1995. Putting critical realism to work: the practical implications for geographical research. *Progress in Human Geography,* 19: 61–74.
Saxenian, A. L. 1994. *Regional Advantage: Culture and Competition in Silicon Valley and Route 128.* Cambridge, Mass: Harvard University Press.
Sayer, A. 1982. Explanation in economic geography. *Progress in Human Geography,* 6: 68–88.
—— 1985. Industry and space: a sympathetic critique of radical research. *Society and Space,* 3: 3–29.
—— 1992. *Method in Social Science: A Realist Approach,* 2nd edn. London: Routledge.
Schoenberger, E. 1994. Corporate strategy and corporate strategists: power, identity and knowledge inside the firm. *Environment and Planning A,* 26: 435–51.
Scott, A. J. 1988. *New Industrial Spaces.* London: Pion.
—— 1998. *Regions and the World Economy.* Oxford: Oxford University Press.
Sheppard, E., and Barnes, T., eds. forthcoming. *A Companion to Economic Geography.* Oxford: Blackwell.
Steinmetz, G., ed. 1999. *State/Culture: State Formation after the Cultural Turn.* Ithaca, NY: Cornell University Press.
Storper, M. 1997. *The Regional World: Territorial Development in a Global Economy.* New York: Guilford.
—— and Scott, A. J., eds. 1992. *Pathways to Industrialization and Regional Development.* London: Routledge.

SWYNGEDOUW, E. 1997. Excluding the other: the production of scale and scaled politics. In Lee and Wills 1997: 167–76.

TICKELL, A., and PECK, J. 1992. Accumulation, regulation and the geographies of post-Fordism: missing links in regulationist research. *Progress in Human Geography*, 16: 190–218.

—— —— 1995. Social regulation *after* Fordism: regulation theory, neo-liberalism and the global-local nexus. *Economy and Society*, 24: 357–86.

THRIFT, N. J., and OLDS, K. 1996. Reconfiguring the economic in economic geography. *Progress in Human Geography*, 20: 311–37.

ZUNZ, O. 1998. *Why the American Century?* Chicago: University of Chicago Press.

Section 2

Analytical Frameworks

Chapter **5**

The New Economics of Urban and Regional Growth

Edward L. Glaeser

Introduction

THE location of people and activities determines the nature and quality of our lives. Urban economists and regional scientists share this central conviction about the importance of space. This chapter presents an introduction to recent research by economists on urban and regional growth. While a primary goal of this volume is better coordination between geographers and regional scientists, in this discussion I review only works by economists, excluding the many superb papers by regional scientists in this area.

The new economics of urban and regional growth merges traditional urban economics with the new economic growth theory. The pioneering work in urban and regional growth provided basic methodological insights and an important set of stylized facts about classic urban issues, such as the interdependency between cities and metropolitan areas (Kain and Neidercorn 1963), the role of transport costs (Hoover 1937), and input price differences (Carlton 1983). The new economic growth theory suggests that cities should be understood as centers of idea creation and transmission. If this is so, then cities will grow when they are producing new ideas or when their role as intellectual centers is increasing in importance.

Advances in economic growth theory in the 1980s emphasized the role of technology, intellectual spillovers, and human capital externalities (Romer 1986; Lucas 1988). Knowledge spillovers solved the technical problem in economic theory of reconciling increasing returns (which are generally needed to generate endogenous growth) with competitive markets. This work suggests that if the global economy is endogenously growing (which is hard to deny) and if we believe in truly competitive markets (which is more controversial), then it almost follows that intellectual spillovers are a critical feature of the economic landscape. When economists began to look for intellectual spillovers, cities presented the clearest examples (see Lucas 1988); Jane Jacobs's (1969) anecdotes of technological innovations such as the invention of the bra are among the most vivid examples of intellectual spillovers.

This reasoning generated a mini-renaissance in urban economics and a reappraisal of which agglomeration economies matter. Economists since Alfred Marshall have argued that cities facilitate the flow of ideas. However, most urban research focuses on the role that density plays in reducing transport costs between suppliers and customers (Krugman 1991). However, Dumais *et al.* (1997) show that manufacturing firms in the USA since 1970 have not based their location decisions on the presence of suppliers and customers. Instead, firms locate near other firms that use the same types of workers. As new facts suggest that traditional urban models no longer explain cities and as a new body of theory emphasizes the flows of ideas, a new urban economics is taking place. In this body of research, cities are thought of as informational entities that exist to speed the flow of learning and knowledge. In this review, I examine this new literature on urban and regional growth.

Urban Growth and Agglomeration Economics

The fundamental question of urban economics is why cities exist. Elsewhere (Glaeser 1998), I argue that cities exist to eliminate transport costs for people, goods, and ideas. The urban advantage in eliminating transport costs for goods captures the classic manufacturing cities of the nineteenth century and is formalized in Krugman (1991), but this advantage is decaying over time as transports costs decline and as manufacturing leaves the city.

Models of labor market pooling or the division of labor emphasize the role of cities in facilitating the movement of people. For example, in Marshall's labor market pooling model firms group together because workers want to be able to switch firms if their employer has an idiosyncratic downturn or if the firm—worker match is bad. Indeed, in Dumais *et al.* (1997) the primary variable determining which industries locate near one another is their use of the same type of workers.

Cities also facilitate the flow of ideas between individuals and firms. In dense, urban environments proximity enables workers to acquire human capital by imitating a rich array of role models and learning by seeing. Alternatively, the flow of ideas may increase the rate of technological innovation and may lead dense cities to have a faster rate of new product innovation. If there is a greater variety of new ideas in cities, then these ideas may show up in new firms and better production processes.

This third force predicts that workers and firms will crowd together in dense areas to learn ideas from one another. This force also predicts that areas that are better at producing new ideas will grow more quickly. Cities which produce more ideas will grow because innovators may be temporarily, geographically fixed. According to this view, innovators acquire more ideas in cities and they first implement those ideas in their cities. Eventually, the idea may become old hat and the innovator may move to low cost areas, but at least temporarily the good ideas are implemented in the city. Alternatively, individuals may crowd into cities in the hope of acquiring a new idea. However, this will show up more as a static effect (the overall size of the city) rather than a dynamic effect (the growth of the city).

The Economics of Local Growth

Economic research begins with individual optimization—this is the defining characteristic of economics as a social science. In the urban and regional context, this means that the economic approach to urban growth begins with individuals choosing locations. Most commonly, economists assume that the world can be described by a spatial equilibrium where all individuals live in their preferred locations. Among homogeneous people, a spatial equilibrium implies that people's levels of welfare are constant across space. This assumption about constant utility levels across space underpins most economic work on cities and regions going back to Alonso (1964).

Non-economists tend to find this a little absurd, and indeed few economists take the assumption literally. We assume a spatial equilibrium because sensible alternatives are mind-numbingly complex, and economists cannot perform empirical (or theoretical) work that is not based on a clear model of individual choice. Indeed, macroeconomists in the 1960s and 1970s made predictions without considering individual decision-making; this led to some of the worst mistakes of postwar economic policy.

The concept of a spatial equilibrium is our guide to empirical work. For example, without a spatial equilibrium model, a research might try to measure the effects of city-specific attributes on productivity by examining whether these attributes raise profits or wages or productivity. But in equilibrium, firms will crowd near a city-specific productivity attribute until there are no more profits (and possibly no extra productivity) associated with that location-specific amenity. In equilibrium, there should not be any real differences in wages or profits across space. The empirical importance of this reasoning is that wage or profit (or even productivity) differences across space may not tell us anything about location-specific productivity.

Instead, the existence of a spatial equilibrium means that location-specific productivity effects will produce a greater density of firms and workers, and higher land prices. If a location has a high level of productivity, crowds of firms and workers will come to that place and drive up prices. The following formalization (based on Glaeser *et al.* 1995) formalizes this point. I assume that all firms produce goods with a price, which is fixed and equal to one. All firms have access to an identical constant returns to scale production function $Af(K,L,P) = AK^{\alpha}L^{\beta}P^{\gamma}$ where K is capital, L is labor, and P is the amount of land and where $1 = \alpha + \beta + \gamma$. The national market fixes the prices of capital and labor. The price of land is 'r' and there are $\bar{P}$ total units of land in the city. The wage outside equals w so workers in the city must be paid that as well. In this framework, cities have finite populations only because of the use of land in the production process. In reality, commuting times, pollution, and congestion can also put limits on the growth of cities.

The variable A captures the degree of local productivity and this is our key variable of interest. This variable captures the aspects of the city which are particular to the city. For example, A would include city and time-specific knowledge about techniques of production or the location-specific production amenities. Indeed, our primary interest tends to be estimating the determinants of A and the determinants of changes in A.

We can think of A as having a component which is a function of city-level characteristics and a city-specific component, that is, $A = \bar{A}e^{\Sigma\delta X}$, where X represents city-level characteristics (the level of human capital, the presence of a port), δ represents the coefficients on these characteristics, and $\bar{A}$ represents the base city-level productivity. Solving the model shows $K = A^{\frac{1}{\gamma}}P(\beta/w)^{\frac{\beta}{\gamma}}(\alpha/c)^{\frac{1-\beta}{\gamma}}$, $L = A^{\frac{1}{\gamma}}P(\beta/w)^{\frac{1-\alpha}{\gamma}}(\alpha/c)^{\frac{\alpha}{\gamma}}$ and $r = (1-\alpha-\beta)A^{\frac{\alpha+\beta}{\gamma}}(\beta/w)^{\frac{\beta}{\gamma}}(\alpha/c)^{\frac{\alpha}{\gamma}}$. Thus improvements in location-specific amenities (A) will show up in greater amounts of capital, greater amounts of labor, and higher property values.

In this framework, wages tell us nothing about local productivity. If we assume that workers need to buy land to live or if more crowded cities are less pleasant, then this will no longer be true. As the level of A rises, crowding and land prices will rise and workers will need to be paid more to get them to live in the city. Under those conditions, wages can be used as measures of local productivity (see Glaeser *et al.* 1995; Rappaport 1998). However, wage regressions are difficult to interpret because wages should decrease as cities become more pleasant.

Standard growth regressions tend to focus on the amount of labor (population is usually quite close to labor) in the city rather than capital or land prices, primarily because of data issues. Thus regressions use a version of the formula for L above and transform it so that:

$$Ln\left(\frac{L_{t+1}}{L_t}\right) - \Omega = \frac{1}{\gamma}Ln\left(\frac{A_{t+1}}{A_t}\right)$$

$$= \frac{1}{\gamma}\left[Ln\left(\frac{\bar{A}_{t+1}}{\bar{A}_t}\right) + \sum(\delta_{t+1} - \delta_t)X_t + \sum\delta_{t+1}(X_{t+1} - X_t)\right], \qquad (1)$$

where Ω is a term that is constant across cities. If we assume that city-specific productivity growth is a function of initial characteristics, that is, $Ln\left(\frac{A_{t+1}}{A_t}\right)=\sum \lambda X_t + \varepsilon_t$, then (1) can be rewritten as:

$$(1') \quad Ln\left(\frac{L_{t+1}}{L_t}\right)=\Omega+\frac{1}{\gamma}\sum(\lambda+\delta_{t+1}-\delta_t)X_t+\frac{1}{\gamma}\sum\delta_{t+1}(X_{t+1}-X_t)+\frac{\varepsilon_t}{\gamma}$$

Equation (1′) is the fundamental growth regression. Changes in employment are regressed on a vector of city-specific characteristics.[1] Generally, terms relating to the changes in the X variables are ignored. Formally this requires assuming that changes in the X variables are orthogonal with respect to the initial values. In practice the decision to ignore these terms comes about because of the endogeneity of these change variables. For example, if urban growth is related to increases in the level of human capital which might happen if migrants are more skilled, then controlling for the growth in the level of human capital might completely bias the other coefficients. Rappaport (1998) runs growth regressions with median housing values (as a proxy for land values); these regressions rely on an equality similar to equation (1).

This framework allows us to interpret changes in the labor force in the city and shows that an initial variable can have an effect on the growth of labor in two very distinct ways.

First, a variable may actually increase the growth rate of A. This occurs if the coefficient λ is positive. An example might be that the level of urban diversity leads to more ideas being produced in the city over time and the city becoming a more productive place.

Secondly, a variable might directly determine A and the relationship between that variable and A has become more important over time. This occurs if $\delta_{t+1} > \delta_t$. Thus, there might be a connection between human capital and increases in the level of A, not because human capital causes increases in A but rather because human capital provides a positive productive amenity for firms in each period, and the importance of human capital has risen over time.[2]

These two interpretations are linked with dynamic and static externalities respectively. Dynamic externalities occur when a city-specific feature, such as the level of diversity or the level of human capital, increases the speed with which new ideas are produced and increases the level of growth of productivity

[1] One alternative to the classic growth regression taken by Eaton and Eckstein (1997), (1′), is to follow Quah (1993) and partition the data into subgroups (e.g. cities with less than 50,000 inhabitants, cities with between 50,000 and 60,000) and then estimate a discrete transition model where the probability of moving from one group to another is estimated.

[2] A variable X might also influence population growth if initial levels of X are correlated with changes in X.

in the city. Static externalities occur when a city-specific feature increases city-specific productivity. Thus human capital may increase the level of employment growth without dynamic externalities if the importance of human capital in generating static externalities has risen over time.

Some attempts to relax the spatial equilibrium assumption have occurred. Glaeser *et al.* (1995) examines the possibility that there are costs associated with rapid adjustment to city-specific productivity shocks and suggested a simple way of allowing a slightly more flexible framework. Rappaport (1998) is much more ambitious and considers a full dynamic adjustment pattern where local shocks only work their way through the system over time. In general, slower adjustment tends to make income growth a more plausible dependent variable, as slow adjustment means that shocks to labor demand will increase wages temporarily as the labor supply adjusts. Of course, in these cases the results from looking at employment should move in the same direction as the results using wages or income. Glaeser *et al.* (1995) show that income growth and population growth tend to move together over the past thirty years across cities.

The Unit of Observation

Within the USA, units of observation can be divided into population-based units, which attempt to capture the total number of workers or population within a geographic area, and location-industry units, which capture the number of workers in a particular industry within a particular location. Population units come from the census and include census tracts, cities, counties, metropolitan areas, and states. In principle, most data sets focus on where people live, which is good if we care about consumption amenities but less ideal for measuring the effects of production amenities. Measures of where people work also exist (County Business Patterns or the Economic Census) and these are better for measuring the effect of location-specific productivity. One advantage of using large enough geographic units is that they do a better job of ensuring that people both live and work within their boundaries.

The city has the advantage of being somewhat smaller (which is valuable if we believe that intellectual spillovers are operating in small, dense areas) and being closely tied to the traditional central business district (CBD). Cities are also the natural unit of analysis in cases where politics are an important independent variable. On the negative side, city boundaries are often quite artificial and their small size means that they may be excessively influenced by neighboring political units (i.e. the growth of Cambridge is certainly strongly influenced by the growth of Boston). In principle, some of this correlation across space can be handled by including initial characteristics of the city in question and of neighboring cities.

Alternatively, metropolitan statistical areas (multi-county units generally surrounding a large city) are less artificial geographic units that are meant to include an entire labor market. These multi-county units' main problems are that they may be too large for some purposes and that they change size over time (this is a problem for cities as well, but the changes are generally less extreme). For example, the heterogeneity within a large metropolitan area may be staggeringly large.

To capture increased suburbanization and interconnection, the census bureau has often increased the size of metropolitan statistical areas to include more counties. In that case, the econometrician needs to make a decision about using initial county definitions, or end-point definitions, or allowing the changes to be incorporated in the regressions. In general, initial definitions tend to be the safest procedure. Within metropolitan areas, there is also the debate over whether to use Primary Metropolitan Statistical Areas or Consolidated Metropolitan Statistical Areas (PMSAs or CMSAs), where CMSAs are larger.

A third possible approach is to use counties. These are larger than cities and often parts of metropolitan areas. Counties are natural for studies, which focus on the entire USA. The only problem with county-level regressions is the possible interdependence between counties that are part of the same metropolitan area. States are also a possible unit of analysis for regional analysis (as in Blanchard and Katz 1992), and while the time patterns of states are extremely interesting they are less appropriate for tests of intellectual spillovers since they are so large.

A final possible population unit of analysis is the census tract, which is a tiny sub-city unit of observation (generally between 3,000 and 5,000 inhabitants). These units are interesting for examining determinants of changing demand for neighborhood characteristics. They are less helpful for looking at issues of productivity.

Another approach is to examine city-industries (which may also be metropolitan area-industries or state-industries or county-industries). These are defined as an industry in a particular geographic unit. For example, steel in the Pittsburgh area would be a city-industry. Information on these variables comes from the Economic Census of the US and County Business Patterns. The advantage of looking at city-industries is that we can control for general patterns of industrial growth in the country as a whole quite easily. We can also examine the interaction between industry variables and city variable (i.e. are more human capital-oriented industries attracted to high human capital cities). Glaeser *et al.* (1992) use city-industries, as do Henderson *et al.* (1995) and Glendon (1998).

Within this class, it is also possible to examine variables such as new plant formation. This is a subcomponent of employment growth that may capture the innovation aspects that are particularly important to tests of intellectual spillovers. Dumais *et al.* (1997) examine the determinants of the emergence of new plants. A similar interpretation can be given to the emergence of new products which is examined by Feldman and Audretsch (1999). These can also be thought of as growth regressions with particularly fine-tuned dependent variables. There is a great deal of added precision gained by looking at this type of variable.

As a final comment, it is worthwhile thinking about the relevant time period for growth regressions. Periods of less than ten years tend to have data problems in many cases. Furthermore, there is presumably a non-trivial amount of year to year variation that is not related to growth rates. Even with these high frequency shocks, we can use shorter time periods as long as the econometrician uses area-specific random effects not area-specific fixed effects. Area-specific fixed effects mean that the regression is identifying itself from very high frequency changes which is probably undesirable if the econometrician is hoping the determine the causes of long-term growth.

Facts and Controversies about Urban and Regional Growth

In the last section, I reviewed the methodological issues involved in estimating the determinants of urban growth. In this section, I discuss some basic stylized facts and their interpretation.

Local Human Capital

A significant number of papers confirm the connection between the initial level of human capital in an area and the later growth of that area. Regardless of whether human capital is measured as years of schooling, the percentage with high school degrees, the percentage of college educated, or a measure of education based on the occupational mix, there is a strong, steady connection between growth and initial skills in the area. Glaeser (1994) presents some of the first evidence on this and shows that the connection between skills and growth appears to be getting stronger over time. For example, the connection between initial skills and later growth is stronger over the 1970–90 period than over the 1950–70 period.

Glaeser *et al.* (1995) document this link between human capital and growth more thoroughly using metropolitan areas and find that initial human capital predicts population, employment, and income growth. This work finds that the percentage completing high school appears to be a more powerful variable for the year 1960. Evidence presented by Glaeser (1994) suggests that college education may have become more important in recent years. Rappaport (1998) examines a much larger set of counties and documents that the human capital–growth connection appears to hold with this much larger sample over the post-1970 period. Mody and Wang (1997) show that the connection between human capital and growth even appears in modern China.

In two important essays, Simon and Nardinelli (1996, 1998) examine the connection between human capital and city growth over a much longer time period in the USA and Great Britain. In the USA, they find that a measure of human capital (based on the occupational mix of the cities in 1880) predicts city growth for all subsequent decades. This suggests that long-running historical factors that influence the level of human capital exert a long-standing influence on city growth. The work on urban growth has not yet followed the tendency of the economics profession to focus overwhelmingly on exogenous sources of variation and this will surely be one of the changes in the urban growth literature over the next ten years. However, since the Simon and Nardinelli data relies upon such a long-term measure of human capital, this can be seen as an early attempt to create an instrument for the level of skills in the city. Glendon (1998) confirms their evidence and shows that the primary effect of human capital is not just due to the fact that high human capital cities have high human capital industries which have tended to grow faster over this century.

As suggested by regression (1′) there are two natural interpretations of the connection between human capital and later urban growth. First, the presence of skills in the metropolitan area may increase new idea production and the growth rate of the city-specific productivity level. High skilled people in high skilled industries may come up with more new ideas. Secondly, skills may create a static externality, which has grown more important over time. Rauch (1993) documents the importance of human capital spillovers by showing that nominal wages and housing prices together rise in cities with the average level of human capital (holding the worker's own level of human capital constant). For example, if one learns skills from one's neighbors (as modeled by Glaeser 1998) and if skills have become more valuable over time, then the advantages from being around skilled people may have risen over time. However, some doubt is cast on this explanation since the connection between growth rates and local human capital levels occurs in the middle of the century when the returns to skill apparently fell.

Concentration versus Diversity

Jacobs (1969) argues that new ideas are formed by combining older ideas (see also Weitzman 1998 for a formalization). Cities allow for the mixing of many different industries and occupations. In this cauldron, ideas from different areas get combined and growth occurs. A natural implication of this line of reasoning is that more diverse cities will grow faster than concentrated cities. Alternatively, industrial concentration may be more important. If new ideas are useful only within an industry, then diversity is wasteful. If learning by doing is extremely important for growth, then geographic specialization in a particular form of production may allow the knowledge learned by doing to be used by other forms.

One way to test this hypothesis is to ask whether an initial concentration of the industry later attracts more industry. Initial concentration is measured in two distinct ways. First, initial concentration is measured by the raw employment level of the city-industry. Secondly, initial concentration is measured by the employment level in the city-industry relative to the city size or relative to the size of the industry in the USA. For the second measure, Glaeser *et al.* (1992) use *Share of City Employment in Industry/Share of US Employment in Industry* which captures the degree to which the industry is overconcentrated in the city relative to the industry's concentration in the USA as a whole.

A second test asks whether the level of industrial diversity outside the city-industry in question increases growth. A primitive means of measuring this diversity is to use a four or five industry concentration measure (the share of total city employment involved in the five largest industries). Alternatively (and probably preferably), Henderson *et al.* (1995) use a Herfindahl index across industries.

The connection between initial employment and later employment growth is pretty uniformly negative (Glaeser *et al.* 1992; Henderson *et al.* 1995; Dumais *et al.* 1997). Naturally, this needs to happen if we have a stationary distribution of city-industry employment. However, this indicates that there are limits to the advantages of concentration in fomenting later growth.

Results on concentration and diversity are more mixed. For example, Glaeser *et al.* (1992) find that concentration has negative effects and that diversity is positive. Henderson *et al.* (1995) find that concentration is positive and diversity has no clear effect. However, the negative effect of initial employment in the Henderson *et al.* work is much stronger than the negative effect of raw employment in Glaeser *et al.* (1992). Thus, in some respects the Henderson *et al.* (1992) paper finds even less evidence for the presence of gains from concentration. Miracky (1994) looks at a complete set of industries in the 1970–90 period, and finds few positive or negative benefits of diversity across all specifications. He does find some negative evidence against concentration.[3]

For the moment, the role of concentration and diversity does not seem to have been resolved by the literature. Different time periods and different samples give different results which suggest that there is no universal truth on this topic. My hope is that by investigating the actual hard evidence on innovations, we will be able to assess the relative importance of idea combinations and the role of diversity and concentration.

Cultures of Entrepreneurship

Benjamin Chinitz (1961) argues that the differences between then-successful New York (and then-declining Pittsburgh came about in part because of New

[3] Garcia-Mila and McGuire (1993) also find that industrial mix is important for growth.

York's many small firms and culture of entrepreneurship. Porter (1990) also argues that local competition provides the right incentives for innovation and new ideas. Alternatively, some models suggest that local monopolists invest more in new ideas (since competitors will only steal each other's ideas). A series of urban growth papers have attempted to examine the role of local competition.

The first key question is how to measure competition. A natural measure of the amount of competition is just to measure the number of firms in the city-industry (because of data issues, occasionally plants are substituted for firms). In order to distinguish competition from scale, the number of firms is sometimes divided by the size of the industry in the area (measured by the number of workers or the amount of output). The resulting variable can be interpreted as the number of firms per worker or per unit output, which seems like a natural competition measure. However, this measure is also the inverse of the average firm size so anything that we attribute to competition may actually be a function of smaller firms. Glaeser *et al.* (1992) use the number of firms per worker in the city-industry and then divide this quantity by the number of firms per worker in the industry in the USA as a whole.

The facts about these competition measures are unequivocal. The positive effect of the competition variable is the strongest result in Glaeser *et al.* (1992). Miracky (1994) confirms the remarkable strength of this variable throughout the entire country for the post-1970 period. Every piece of research in this area that I am aware of finds a positive effect of competition on later growth.

While the facts appear to be clear, the interpretation is not. One interpretation of these results is that competition foments intellectual growth. Alternatively, cities that are exogenously growing may have a lot of new plants and firms that are also small. Miracky (1994) suggests that the competition measure captures the place the city-industry has in the industry life cycle (i.e. young growing industries have small firms). Further work will be needed to clarify these issues.

Government and Redistribution

The literature on the connection between government policy and country-level economic growth is vast and has strong conclusions suggesting that government-created distortions can badly hurt growth. The literature on government and local growth is much smaller, which is somewhat appropriate given the small differences in government policies across localities within the USA relative to the differences across countries. There is a literature on industrial location suggesting that pro-business policies (such as right-to-work laws) generally attract firms. The masterpiece of this literature is Holmes (1998) which documents the importance of pro-business policy (e.g. right-to-work laws) in attracting industry using within as well as across state variation. The key insight is that there should be a real shock on the borders of states if policies matter and Holmes finds just such a discontinuity.

The literature connecting growth and policies is much smaller. Glaeser *et al.* (1995) include a large vector of city-level political variables in our growth regressions. We find only two political variables that predict urban growth: the amount of debt per capita of the city in 1960 and spending on sanitation. We interpret the debt effect as the result of reverse causality. Cities expecting large growth borrow because they know that they will be able to repay that borrowing in the future. The sanitation effect is provocative, but hardly an overwhelming stylized fact. Rauch (1995) also shows that the municipal reforms in the early part of this century have little effect on growth.

Rappaport (1998) finds much stronger effects of government policies for the period starting in 1970. His results differ from ours both because of the later time period and because he examines a much larger range of counties. Both the size of government and the extent to which government focuses on redistribution tend to depress later population growth of the region. Vigdor (1998) shows that exogenous reductions in the size of government caused by Proposition $2\frac{1}{2}$ increase the growth of the tax base in particular areas. One explanation for the different sets of results is that transfer policies attract lower human capital people and these people were more negatively associated with city growth during the later time period because the importance of skills had risen.

These results suggest that localities can stymie their own growth with sufficiently negative policies. While local redistribution is probably bad for growth, there is not a clear message about what policies are good for growth. Using the results on human capital from above, it seems likely that policies which will increase the quality of the local human capital will increase the speed of urban growth. This stands as another area of research where we are just beginning to understand the determinants of growth.

A final connection between politics and urban growth is the role of higher levels of governments. While we do not know what policies a city can follow to increase its own growth, we do know that if states and the country as a whole favor particular cities they will grow. Eaton and Eckstein (1997) document the special growth patterns of Paris and Tokyo which are associated with the political factors affecting those cities. Ades and Glaeser (1995) document the political factors, which generate urban primacy across countries. DeLong and Shleifer (1993) show that before the industrial revolution city growth is associated with mercantile, not royal power.

The Convergence Debate

A final critical area of local growth is the debate on whether initial levels of income or population are related negatively to later growth in these variables. Barro and Sala-I-Martin (1991) showed a strong negative correlation between initial income and income growth across states within the USA and across countries. There are many possible interpretations of this finding ranging from slow-moving migration following labor demand shocks to less developed states imitating the technologies of more advanced states. Glaeser *et al.* (1995) show that holding regions constant there is little convergence in income levels across cities between 1960 and 1990.

As argued earlier, population or employment levels are more sensible measures for most local growth regressions than income levels. With population levels there is relatively little evidence of strong convergence at the metropolitan area level. Eaton and Eckstein (1997) show that city population growth in Japan and France follows a parallel pattern where there is neither divergence nor convergence. Glaeser *et al.* (1995) find that within the USA there is some convergence at the city level, but little convergence at the metropolitan area level. It is not surprising that there is more convergence at the city level since limits on land area will tend to bind more tightly for these smaller population units. In a particularly comprehensive study, Beeson *et al.* (1998) show that between 1840 and 1990, population convergence at the county level occurs only for the densest counties. More generally, they find no convergence and even some evidence of divergence.

The pattern where city growth rates are independent of the initial size of the city ties quite closely to the well-known fact of Zipf's law. Zipf's law says that the second largest city is one-half the size of the largest city and the third largest city is one-third the size of the largest city, and so on. Gabaix (1999) shows that Gibrat's law (city growth rates are independent of initial city sizes) implies Zipf's law. Thus, since Zipf's law is one of the most well-documented facts in social science, we should not be surprised that Gibrat's law also appears to hold fairly pervasively.

A final fact that bears on this debate is the stunning persistence of growth rates of population at the state and city level. Blanchard and Katz (1992) show that there is a clear correlation over time in the growth rates of states. Glaeser *et al.* (1995) show the same thing for cities. This fact can be interpreted as evidence for migration responding only slowly to location-specific shocks. Alternatively, it can mean that some places are steadily more productive in producing new ideas and new technologies. In either case, the evidence speaks against a strong form of convergence where gains in one period are offset by relative losses in the next period.

Conclusion

Cities appear to grow faster when they have higher skilled workers and when they have more competitive industrial structures. There is little clear evidence on the role of diversity versus competition. Big cities tend to grow at roughly the same rate as small cities. Big local governments that redistribute highly to the poor tend to reduce local growth. These are useful facts but they do not thoroughly answer the central questions posed at the beginning of this section. The role of human capital supports the role of intellectual spillovers, but there are certainly other interpretations. The other facts are compatible with an idea transmission view of cities, but also with other views.

There are two major avenues for future research. First, we need more attention to be paid to exogenous sources of variation (instrumental variables. All explanatory variables have the problem that they are exogenous and quite potentially correlated with other variables that may truly be driving growth. The second primary avenue for future research is to try and measure the localization of ideas more effectively. Jaffe *et al.* (1993) is the paradigmatic paper in this area which uses patent citations to document that ideas move only slowly over time. Audretsch and Feldmann (1996) also use an innovative data set measuring new product innovations to inform us about idea production in cities. New variables and data sets such as these will be invaluable in understanding the processes that drive urban growth.

References

Ades, A., and Glaeser, E. 1995. Trade and circuses: explaining urban giants. *Quarterly Journal of Economics*, 110/1: 195–258.

Alonso, W. 1964. *Location and Land Use: Toward a General Theory of Land Rent.* Cambridge, Mass.: Harvard University Press.

Audretsch, D. B., and Feldmann, M. P. 1996. Knowledge spillovers and the geography of innovation and production. *American Economic Review*, 86: 630–40.

Barro, R., and Sala-I-Martin, X. 1991. Convergence across states and regions. *Brooking Papers on Economic Activity*, 1.

Beeson, P., DeJong, D., and Troesken, W. Forthcoming. Population growth in U.S. counties, 1840–1990. *Regional Science and Urban Economics.*

Blanchard, O., and Katz, L. 1992. Regional evolutions. *Brookings Papers on Economic Activity*, 1: 1–75.

Carlton, D. 1983. The location and employment choices of new firms: an econometric model with discrete and continuous endogenous variables. *Review of Economics and Statistics*, 65/3: 440–9.

Chinitz, B. 1961. Contrasts in agglomeration: New York and Pittsburgh. *American Economic Review*, 71: 279–89.

DeLong, B., and Shleifer, A. 1993. Princes and merchants: city growth in preindustrial europe. *Journal of Law and Economics*, 36/2: 671–702.

Dumais, G., Ellison, G., and Glaeser, E. 1997. Geographic concentration as a dynamic process. *NBER Working Paper*, No. 6270.

Eaton, J., and Eckstein, Z. 1997. Cities and growth: theory and evidence from France and Japan. *Regional Science and Urban Economics*, 27/4–5: 443–74.

Feldman, M. P., and Audretsch D. B. 1999. Innovation in cities: science-based diversity, specialisation and localised competition. *European Economic Review*, 43: 409–29.

Gabaix, X. 1999. Zipf's law for cities: an explanation. *Quarterly Journal of Economics*, 114/3: 739–68.

Garcia-Mila, T., and McGuire, T. 1993. Industrial mix as a factor in the growth and variability of states' economies. *Regional Science and Urban Economics*, 23/6: 731–48.

Gaspar, J., and Glaeser, E. 1998. Information technology and the future of cities. *Journal of Urban Economics*, 43/1: 136–56.

Glaeser, E. 1994. Cities, information and economic growth. *Cityscape*, 1: 9–48.

—— 1998. Are cities dying? *Journal of Economic Perspectives*, 12/2: 139–60.

—— Kallal, H., Scheinkman, J., and Shleifer, A. 1992. Growth in cities. *Journal of Political Economy*, 100/6: 1126–52.

—— Scheinkman, J., and Shleifer, A. 1995. Economic growth in a cross-section of cities. *Journal of Monetary Economics*, 36/1: 117–43.

Glendon, S. 1998. Urban life cycles. Harvard University mimeograph.

Henderson, J. V., Kuncoro, A., and Turner, M. 1995. Industrial development in cities. *Journal of Political Economy*, 103/5: 1067–90.

Holmes, T. 1998. The effect of state policies on the location of manufacturing: evidence from state borders. *Journal of Political Economy*, 106/4: 667–705.

Hoover, E. 1937. *Location Theory and the Shoe and Leather Industries.* Cambridge, Mass.: Harvard University Press.

Jacobs, J. 1969. *The Economy of Cities.* New York: Random House.

Jaffe, A., Trajtenberg, M., and Henderson, R. 1993. Geographic localization of knowledge spillovers as evidenced by patent citations. *Quarterly Journal of Economics*, 108: 577–98.

Kain, J., and Neidercorn, D. 1963. An econometric model of metropolitan development. *Regional Science Association Papers*, 11.

Krugman, P. 1991. Increasing returns and economic geography. *Journal of Political Economy*, 99: 483–99.

Lucas, R. 1988. On the mechanics of economic development. *Journal of Monetary Economics*, 22: 3–42.

Miracky, W. 1994. Technological spillovers, the product cycle and regional growth. Massachusetts Institute of Technology dissertation.

Mody, A., and Wang, F. 1997. Explaining industrial growth in coastal China: economic reforms . . . and what else? *World Bank Economic Review*, 11/2: 293–325.

Porter, M. 1990. *The Competitive Advantage of Nations.* New York: Free Press.

Quah, D. 1993. Empirical cross-section dynamics in economic growth. *European Economic Review*, 37: 426–34.

Rappaport, J. 1998. Local economic growth. Harvard University mimeograph.

Rauch, J. 1993. Productivity gains from geographic concentration of human capital: evidence from the cities. *Journal of Urban Economics*, 34: 380–400.

—— 1995. Bureaucracy, infrastructure, and economic growth: evidence from U.S. cities during the progressive era. *American Economic Review*, 85/4: 968–79.

Romer, P. 1986. Increasing returns and long run growth. *Journal of Political Economy*, 94: 1002–37.

Simon, C., and Nardinelli, C. 1996. The talk of the town: human capital, information and the growth of English Cities, 1861–1961. *Explorations in Economic History*, 33/3: 384–413.

—— —— 1998. Human capital and city growth in the U.S. Mimeograph.

Vigdor, J. 1998. Was Tiebout wrong? Evidence from Proposition $2\frac{1}{2}$ in Massachusetts. Harvard University mimeograph.

Weitzman, M. 1998. Recombinant growth. *Quarterly Journal of Economics*, 113/2: 331–60.

Chapter 6

Geography or Economics? Conceptions of Space, Time, Interdependence, and Agency

Eric Sheppard

In recent years, the liminal position that economic geography occupies between economics and geography pulled the sub-discipline in different directions. As economics has shed its diverse background and focused on a mainstream paradigm rooted in mathematical models of competitive and quasi-competitive markets, economists' interest in economic geography has been increasingly conditional on insisting that it conform to this mold. As geography has begun to recognize the variety of philosophical approaches that are necessary to a thoughtful interpretation and explanation of the world, geographers have found those aspects of economic geography valued by economists increasingly constraining. Economic geographers have been increasingly attentive to the heterodox traditions of economics that mainstream and geographical economists dismiss (Chapter 2; Sheppard 1995).

As a consequence, two very different groups of scholars are talking of a 'new' economic geography, with apparently incommensurate visions. Economists, led by Paul Krugman, have rediscovered economic geography through the development of new mathematical theories that can model the economics of spatial agglomeration. This has legitimated 'a set of core ideas [in economic geography] that . . . were unacceptable to mainstream economists because they could not at that time be modeled' (Krugman 1995: 37). Among geographers, the 'new' vision is part of a broader cultural turn emphasizing processes of 'identity, meaning and signification . . . [as a cultural practice,] best viewed as it occurs rather than through the lens of some metaphorical end product' (Crang 1997: 5). Despite differences concerning the relative significance of feminist, postmodern, and post-structural approaches, there is consensus rejecting economistic theory and promoting qualitative theoretical languages and research methods.

In this chapter, I seek to interrogate the degree to which geographers and economists share a common vision of how economies work. Given that the language of mainstream economics must be mathematics, such an interrogation should at least initially compare economists and geographers who use this common language as a tool for theory development. A mathematical approach sacrifices complexity for rigor and is out of fashion among geographers. Yet some still insist that numbers matter (Sayer 1997), and others worry about conceding this approach to economists in a world whose outer trappings and academic institutions are pervasively quantitatively oriented (Clark 1998; Martin 1999; Plummer *et al.* 1998). If economists and geographers had similar visions for economic geography, such concerns might be dismissed as little more than disciplinary boundary marking. I will argue, however, that economists and geographers look at economic geography in quite different ways, reflecting distinct disciplinary traditions.

Three recent schools of thought can be identified that focus on the spatiality of economic processes and attempt to represent them within the restrictive language of mathematical theory. Two are dominated by economists and one by geographers, providing a convenient case study of the difference that disciplines make. I will first summarize these different approaches, and then compare them.

Comparing Three Approaches

Attempts to mathematically theorize economic geography in the last decade can be classified into two principal paradigms: the 'increasing returns' approach in economics and the 'regional political economy' approach in geography. The former has been catalyzed by the writings of Paul Krugman, but has a number of other influences. It is important to note, first, that the form of increasing returns emphasized in this approach is different from that emphasized by industrial geographers. Much of the work in economic geography on spatial agglomeration has focused on the idea of Marshallian industrial districts: agglomerations of closely interrelated small firms benefiting from geographic proximity to one another (cf. Amin forthcoming). Other approaches to increasing returns (the idea that increased scale of production in a place results in increased productivity) in economics stem from Cournot and Chamberlin, and Chamberlin's approach has been adopted by Krugman and others (Krugman 1990: ch. 5).[1] Chamberlin's approach is based on monopolistic competition between firms employing production technologies that can take advantage of

[1] Cournot's approach has been applied to geographical economics by Nagurney (1993).

economies of scale. Agglomeration occurs to take advantage of clusters of workers/consumers, not to be close to one another as in Marshall's theory (cf. Krugman 1991; Fujita and Krugman 1995; Fujita and Thisse 1996; Krugman 1996*a*). The use of monopolistic competition as a paradigm for explaining the location of firms dates back to the work of Lösch (Lösch 1954/1940), and was in fact extensively investigated in theories of spatial price equilibrium in the 1980s (cf. Norman 1986; Greenhut *et al.* 1987). This research predates Krugman and addresses different questions, but should be included in any characterization of this paradigm. Taken together, research in this area has examined issues of specialization and trade, the agglomeration of firms, economic growth, and the location and pricing strategies of firms in spatially extensive markets. While often referred to as the increasing returns school, I will rename it the monopolistic competition approach to distinguish it from other conceptualizations of increasing returns.

Another recently developing area of economics deserves attention because it explicitly addresses the space economy: the evolutionary and complexity approach (cf. Anderson *et al.* 1988; Arthur 1994; Arthur *et al.* 1997). As in neo-Austrian and neo-Keynesian economics, it is argued that economic actors have limited information, are heterogeneous in their resources and strategies, and must learn to operate in a changing and uncertain environment. These actors are conceptualized as actively collecting and exchanging information, and trading with their neighbors. The focus is on heterogeneous individuals in competition, on the dynamic processes through which market exchange occurs, and on the locational dynamics that result. A comparison of this paradigm with the monopolistic competition approach will help identify what economists share in their approach to economic geography, whereas a comparison of both with the regional political economy approach will identify commonalties and differences between the disciplines.

The 'regional political economy' paradigm is influenced by the writings of such classical economists as Ricardo and Marx and by Keynes and Kalecki, and builds on the findings of Sraffa and Pasinetti that such classical approaches are not logically inferior to neoclassical economics (Sraffa 1960; Harcourt 1972; Pasinetti 1981).[2] It seeks to examine the locational strategies and unintended consequences of capitalists in an economy made up of different classes of actors with conflicting economic goals (cf. Scott 1980; Clark *et al.* 1986; Webber 1987*a*; Liossatos 1988; Sheppard and Barnes 1990; Webber and Rigby 1996). This approach focuses on the spatial dynamics of capitalism, analyzing urban and regional growth, investment strategies and capital flows, labor markets, specialization and trade, and the role of the state and other social institutions. Recently, the pricing strategies of individual firms have also received attention.

[2] For a distinctive mathematical geographical theory of the space economy see Curry (1998).

Prior to comparing these approaches, I want to emphasize two general points about theory, mathematical theory, and mathematical modeling. First, simplifying the complexity of real economic landscapes is not inherently problematic. All theories do this when they engage in abstract reasoning. In the case of developing a mathematical theory this means making some simplifying assumptions. The assumptions made in mathematical theory and modeling in part ensure that the world can be collapsed into mathematical logic, and in part reflect the standpoint of the theorist—the aspects of reality that she takes for granted.

Secondly, it is crucial to distinguish between assumptions that have minor and those that have major implications for the theories that they underlie. Assumptions whose relaxation does not alter the fundamental tenets of a theory can be seen as minor: making the assumptions more realistic does not qualitatively affect broad theoretical conclusions or policy implications, but presumably improves their pertinence in particular contexts. If relaxing an assumption leads to qualitatively different theoretical conclusions, however, this is a critical assumption with major implications.[3] The critical assumptions of a theory need to be identified, because the theory is not robust in the face of their relaxation. In comparing the different paradigms below, I focus on identifying assumptions that are critical in this sense. Economists and geographers generally will make different kinds of simplifying assumptions reflecting their different disciplinary traditions, but differences in minor assumptions will not lead to qualitatively different understandings of or predictions about the space economy.

The assumptions I focus on here are those that are central to a geographic perspective on economic geography. Of particular importance, of course, is space. Geographers think of space as heterogeneous; places differ, in both their site and situation creating geographical differences between places in the conditions of possibility for economic action. They conceive of distance as a product of societal processes, not as a simple metric. They give importance to geographic scale; to the complex ways in which local, regional, national, and global processes articulate with one another. But space cannot be separated from time. Geographers see landscapes as continually evolving, with the very meaning of space and time varying historically and geographically (cf. Lukermann 1964; Pred 1966; Harvey 1985; Storper and Walker 1989). Finally, geographers take a synthetic perspective, seeking to understand interdependencies between places and individuals, between economic, political, social, and cultural processes, and between societal and biophysical processes. My focus will thus be on the nature and criticality of assumptions about space, time, interdependence, and agency.

[3] An example of this from economics is when the assumption of identical production technologies in different sectors of an economy is relaxed, it no longer can be concluded that wages must equal the marginal productivity of labor in a competitive market (Sraffa 1960).

Monopolistic Competition

Research drawing on models of monopolistic competition is influenced by either Lösch (1954/1940) or Dixit and Stiglitz (1977). There are some common assumptions underlying these frameworks, however: a simplistic treatment of space; a focus on equilibrium; a vertically integrated economy with identical production methods (in non-agricultural sectors); and methodological individualism pursued by perfectly informed representative agents.

Spatiality

In almost all theory within this tradition, *space* is treated as a homogeneous entity. On the one hand, space is assumed to be of the kind familiar in Löschian location theory, where actors are spatially separated from one another in a space with no central or peripheral locations. All locations are equally situated with respect to other locations, eliminating any competitive advantage due to relative location. Space is homogeneous and unbounded. In spatial pricing models, the addition of a spatial separation between producers and consumers, or between producers, does result in market outcomes different from those predicted in a spaceless economy (Greenhut *et al.* 1987).[4] Fundamental theoretical predictions remain consistent with the aspatial economic theory of imperfect competition, however: all firms make zero profits, and sell their goods at identical prices to the same number of customers. A second distinctive insight from introducing space is morphogenesis: even on a homogeneous spatial surface spatial differentiation occurs due to the spatial interactions between economic actors. Core and peripheral locations exist, in the absence of any advantages or disadvantages of relative location. This conclusion, theorized many years ago in geography (Curry 1967), is at the heart of Krugman's (1996*a*) theory of pseudo central place systems on a circle.

Alternatively, space is taken to be a line on which two firms or clusters of firms develop, either at the end-points of the line (Krugman 1991), or at interior but symmetrically placed locations which are equidistant from the end-points of the line (Hotelling 1929; de Palma *et al.* 1986). Space along the line itself is homogeneous, meaning that the two locations of interest are again identical in both site and situation characteristics. The addition of space again results in market equilibria that represent forms of imperfect rather than perfect competition, with different equilibrium scenarios to the spaceless case.

Distance in these models is treated as external to the economy. A variety of devices have been employed, including equating transportation costs with distance, mathematically transforming economic costs of movement into a

[4] Indeed space here need not be geographical at all; it could be differentiation in the quality of products sold by firms (Norman 1986).

homogeneous space, and Samuelson's (1954) 'iceberg' model 'in which only a fraction of the good that is shipped arrives (so that in effect transportation costs are incurred in the good shipped)' (Krugman 1991: 103). In all cases, interaction costs depend on Euclidean distance alone, and are not treated as an endogenous consequence of the geography of economic development. Geographers refer to this as a Newtonian treatment of space, as a metric exogenous to the processes occurring over that space (unlike, for example, Einstein's relativity theory or the relational space of Leibnitz and Whitehead; cf. Harvey 1996). *Scale* only comes up implicitly in these models: aggregate patterns are explained as a consequence of the 'micro-foundations' of individual decision-making, meaning that local actions determine larger scale outcomes.

Time

Most economic research in this tradition focuses on *equilibrium outcomes.* Much is made of how equilibrium thinking has been altered by the monopolistic competition approach: instead of one equilibrium pattern, several different equilibria are possible. As Krugman notes (1990: 88), commenting on the new trade theory:

> What we have learned to do is essentially to live with multiple equilibria, by focusing on models where a good deal can be said without requiring that we know the precise pattern of specialization and trade. . . . To answer a question by changing it is not to everyone's taste. However, the payoff here has been remarkable.

More recently, invoking the language of recent work on complex evolutionary systems, he notes that the possibility of multiple locally stable equilibria means that geographical patterns are not determined in advance, but are 'path dependent'. This means that the particular equilibrium arrived at depends on the previous history of the system.

Little attention has been paid to disequilibrium dynamics. There is increasing awareness that spatial equilibria are only plausible if the system can be shown to converge towards them (i.e. they are at least locally stable). Tests of stability do suggest that this is the case. None the less, far from equilibrium positions and dynamics are not seen as likely positions to find a space economy in, and are not analyzed. This is also true for growth models based on the monopolistic competition approach. In his influential analysis of economic growth with increasing returns, Paul Romer writes: 'One should be able to study convergence to the balanced growth ratio . . . but this analysis is not attempted here' (Romer 1990: S90). The existence of a stable equilibrium in turn enables analysts to ignore the fact that production and marketing take time. Capitalists face uncertainty about whether the money invested at the beginning of a production period will be paid back, at market rates of return, by successful sales at the end of the production period. This uncertainty is a hallmark of Marxian and Keynesian ways of discussing competition, but is irrelevant in equilibrium because everything that is produced is consumed (Walsh and Gram 1980). Production can thus be treated as if it were instantaneous.

Inter-Sectoral Relationships

The monopolistic competition paradigm almost universally employs simplifying assumptions to abstract from the *inter-sectoral nature* of the economy. Unlike the extensive tradition of input–output modeling in regional science, long on empirical analysis but short on theorizing the evolution of input–output flows, firms are not assumed to sell to one another. The economy is seen as multisectoral: each monopolistic firm is conceptualized as representing a different industrial sector, purchasing labor, homogeneous capital and technology, and selling directly to consumers. But firms do not sell to one another. I will dub this simplification of inter-sectoral structure the vertically integrated economy, since it treats production factors as external, non-produced sources of inputs, and consumers as the sinks where products end up. This is conceptually equivalent to aggregate neoclassical economic theory, where a production function converts non-produced production factors into a final product. In addition, and again like neoclassical theory, technology is generally assumed to be identical in all firms/sectors.

The 'capital controversies' in the 1960s established that, taken together, the assumptions of vertical integration and identical technologies are critical to such standard conclusions in neoclassical theory as the Hecksher–Ohlin–Samuelson principles governing specialization and trade, the equation in equilibrium of factor prices with their marginal productivity, and thus the rationality of perfect competition as a foundation for an equitable aggregate distribution of economic output (Harcourt 1972; Steedman 1979; Pasinetti 1981; Sheppard and Barnes 1990).[5] The mathematical rigor of this critique has spawned a heterodox paradigm of post-Keynesian economics.[6]

Because monopolistic competition approaches share with neoclassical theory the assumption of a vertically integrated economy, their application frequently extends rather than challenges the propositions of neoclassical theory.[7]

[5] Karl Marx's transformation problem, the claim that equilibrium prices derive from labor values and thus from exploited workers, is based on the same assumption. Neoclassical economists were quick to recognize the limitation in this case.

[6] Notwithstanding the mathematical rigor of the post-Keynesian critique, its practial implications remain highly contested. Neoclassical theorists assert that the relaxed assumptions favored by post-Keynesians do not usually result in economic conclusions that are so different as to call into question the validity of the neoclassical theory (Burmeister 1980), whereas post-Keynesians claim the opposite (Pasinetti 1981). There is a paucity of data on inter-sectoral flows, a lack of interest in the theoretical issues by those developing such data, and a disinclination of theorists to bother with data.

[7] 'I consider myself a proud neoclassicist. . . . I prefer, when I can, to make sense of the world using models in which individuals maximize and the interaction of these individuals can be summarized by some concept of equilibrium' (Krugman 1996*b*).

For firms in spatial price equilibrium, their prices and relative locations are still such that all firms make zero profits beyond those necessary to pay for fixed capital, although prices generally exceed those in perfect competition. In trade theory, scale economies and product variety are additional sources of comparative advantage to Ricardian comparative cost differences, and intra-sectoral trade (the trade of different industrial goods between countries) also occurs (Helpman 1990; Krugman 1990). Yet continuities with the traditional theory are emphasized, with the focus on cases where the traditional theorems of trade theory continue to hold (Wong 1995). Invoking Lakatos's idea of a research program, in which any paradigm is seen as having a set of 'hard core' ideas whose continued acceptability is essential to the identity of that program and whose validity is taken for granted and vigorously defended by its adherents, McGovern (1994) argues that the new trade theory has been accepted because it embellishes, without challenging, the hard core propositions of orthodox trade theory.

Romer's (1990) model of endogenous economic growth under monopolistic competition ingeniously adds extra steps to the vertically integrated economy: research and design and intermediate goods, as well as final goods. The research sector produces designs under perfect competition, using technology and human capital.[8] Intermediate goods are produced by firms engaged in monopolistic competition, purchasing designs from the research and design sector to convert (forgone) output of the final goods sector into intermediate goods. The final good is again produced under perfect competition, with output depending on human capital and labor and on the variety of intermediate goods. Increases in this variety over time drive increased productivity. All intermediate firms use identical technologies, and factor prices equal their marginal productivity. Wages, for example, appropriately reflect the productivity of workers and should not be manipulated by unions or the state. Post-Keynesian critics argue that endogenous growth theory is still 'new wine in old goatskins', adhering closely to hard core propositions of neoclassical theory (Kurz and Salvadori 1995, 1997).

Applications of this model to economic geography also emphasize continuities with neoclassical regional growth theory (Borts and Stein 1964; Siebert 1969), as economists again have taken up questions of regional economic convergence (Martin and Sunley 1998). Barro and Grilli (1994: 284) argue that if regions have identical technologies, the presence of increasing returns does not undermine the neoclassical conclusion that poorer, labor-intensive regions will grow more rapidly than richer ones. Others, combining Krugman and Romer, focus on identifying equilibria in which both regions have similar economic structures and growth rates, although these frequently are unstable—unlike

[8] This is dubbed an endogenous growth approach because the rate of technical change is endogenously determined from human capital growth, although critics argue that growth in this family of models is in fact determined by technology (Kurz and Salvadori 1995).

equilibria with all industry in one region (Martin and Ottaviano 1996*a*; Walz 1996). As in neoclassical theory, migration is introduced to force balanced regional growth (Bertola 1993; Martin and Ottaviano 1996*b*).

Agency

Methodological individualism is a hallmark of mainstream economic theory. Mainstream economists agree that any macroeconomic theory must have 'micro-foundations': that is, aggregate patterns must be the consequence of instrumental rational choices made by individual economic actors, whose preferences and resources are fixed in advance. This applies *ipso facto* to theories of the space economy. 'Why can't we build models based on more realistic psychological premises . . . a more historically based understanding of institutions, [or] . . . take into account the fact that tastes and motives are . . . socially determined . . . ? I don't have any fundamental answer to these questions' (Krugman 1995: 77). It's just so. It is also assumed that the individual decision-makers can be simplified to identical and fully informed representative agents. The recent evolving complex system approach seeks to move away from this assumption, within a Newtonian spatially heterogeneous landscape.

Evolution and Complexity

Research into the space economy as an evolving complex system employs a computational and simulation approach to theorizing the space economy, rather than pure mathematics. This allows for heterogeneous space, but distance is still assumed to be Newtonian—an exogenous metric. With respect to time, out-of-equilibrium dynamics are emphasized rather than equilibrium solutions. Unstable equilibria are of no substantive interest; and it is felt that the evolutionary path-dependent nature, the sensitivity to initial conditions and exogenous shocks, and the unpredictability of complex non-linear economic processes are neglected in economics (Anderson *et al.* 1988; Silverberg *et al.* 1988; Arthur 1994; Arthur *et al.* 1997).[9] Indeed one of the reasons for a computational approach is to avoid reliance on mathematical simplifications that guarantee tractable solutions while biasing the theory toward equilibrium formulations. Inter-sectoral relationships are ignored in what are usually one or two sector models of the space economy: the economy is vertically integrated, and factors of production are given exogenously. With respect to agency, a modified form of methodological individualism is assumed, with macroeconomic structures determined by rational actions. Yet economists from this

[9] Multiple equilibria and path dependence are also invoked within the monopolistic competition approach, yet it is their implications for equilibrium which matter, not disequilibrium dynamics (Krugman 1996*a*, 1996*b*).

paradigm have been very critical of the idea of representative agents (Kirman 1992; Nelson 1995). Individuals are assumed to have geographically limited information, and have unequal resources and knowledge, and different decisionmaking strategies.

By comparison to the monopolistic competition approach, heterogeneous space, disequilibrium, and heterogeneous agents now are allowed for, but distance remains Newtonian and individual actions drive the economy. Furthermore, since the emphasis often is on comparing this approach to neoclassical theory, equilibria that are an emergent property of out-of-equilibrium dynamics still receive considerable attention.

Research focuses on trade rather than production: examining the out-of-equilibrium dynamics of actors who exchange one or two products with one another. Trade occurs between neighbors when both can gain. For the case of homogeneous space but heterogeneous actors, Albin and Foley (1992) show that an equilibrium does emerge, but prices vary stochastically in spatial waves (whose frequency decreases as the mobility of individuals increases) instead of being uniform, and there is income and welfare inequality. The case of heterogeneous space is exemplified by the 'sugarscapes' of Epstein and Axtell (1996), which employ the genetic algorithms and artificial life models of complexity theory (Holland 1995; Langton 1989). Heterogeneous actors with utility functions for sugar and spice consume, move, reproduce, and trade within a bounded and spatially heterogeneous landscape of renewable resources. In some models utility functions are not exogenous: whenever two actors interact, they may exchange elements of their utility function. In equilibrium, prices vary stochastically across individuals and space and income inequalities persist. In all these models as assumptions conform more with neoclassical approaches so do the results, indicating that mainstream economic approaches to economic geography are modified rather than undermined by these relaxed assumptions.

With respect to regional growth, Arthur (1994) shows that Marshallian local external economies result in the polarization of all industry into a single region (cf. Kaldor 1985), with the actual equilibrium outcome dependent on the stochastic history of firm entry. Models of self-organization describe the dynamics of technological change, trade, and economic growth (Silverberg 1988; Silverberg *et al.* 1988; Dosi *et al.* 1990; Schweitzer 1997). Differentiation between firms in the same sector (in techniques, capital vintage, and prices) is taken seriously, but the economy is vertically integrated. Graphs of economic growth possibilities for two countries (usually a competitive and technologically static 'south' and a monopolistic and technologically dynamic 'north') are constructed, bounded by accounting identities and the assumption of balanced trade.

Introducing heterogeneous space and differences in information, technologies, and resources between individual actors results in theoretical propositions about the space economy that do not deviate dramatically from those of the monopolistic competition paradigm. This is consistent with the neo-Austrian argument that fully informed representative agents and a Walrasian auctioneer are not necessary for markets to clear (cf. von Hayek 1937). Assuming vertically integrated production and exogenous preferences seems critical to this conclusion. When these assumptions are relaxed, the economy begins to behave like an evolving complex system and parallels between the two approaches dissipate.

Regional Political Economy

The term regional political economy describes a research program using mathematical theories applying the classical tradition of Marx, Kalecki, and Sraffa (Morishima 1973; Roemer 1981) to the space economy (Scott 1980; Marelli 1983; Clark *et al.* 1986; Dunford 1988; Liossatos 1988; Sheppard and Barnes 1990; Webber and Rigby 1996).[10] This approach is characterized by further relaxation of assumptions. With respect to spatiality, space is not only treated as heterogeneous, but distance is an endogenous outcome of the evolving space economy: accessibility is produced as a commodity in each region (Sheppard 1990). With respect to time, there is skepticism that any stable equilibria can exist. Conflicts of interest between different groups of economic actors over the distribution of the economic surplus may destabilize any market- or state-induced equilibrium. Considerable attention is paid to disequilibrium adjustments, and to the time taken between the investment of capital in production and its uncertain realization after the commodity is sold (Clark *et al.* 1986; Sheppard and Barnes 1990).

Instead of a vertically integrated economy, inter-sectoral interdependencies are specified, by input–output relationships describing the quantities of inputs bought from and sold between sectors and firms. Capital is thus no longer a homogeneous and exogenously given production factor, but a bundle of interdependently produced capital goods. With respect to agency, different kinds of economic actors are assumed to occupy different class positions within the economic system (defined by the factors of production they own, their position in the hierarchy of economic decision-making, and their relative wealth), differentially conditioning the possibilities available to them as individuals.[11] Common economic interests within classes and conflicts of interest between them create a potential for collective attempts to increase a group's share of the economic surplus. Thus social structures exist which condition action, making methodological individualism an inadequate conceptualization of human

[10] This chapter focuses on just one aspect of this body of research: contributions attempting to develop mathematical theoretical propositions about the space economy. This is just one part of a broader research program that matured in the 1980s (described in Chapter 2).

[11] Individuals are not assumed to belong to a single class. For most individuals, class membership is fuzzy. Wright (1997) has pioneered empirical measures of class.

behavior. In addition, it is assumed that differences exist between individual actors occupying similar class positions, in terms of relative location, resources, preferences, technologies, and so forth, and that actors possess only limited information about the current and future economic landscape. These relaxed assumptions will be treated in two clusters, reflecting their treatment in the literature.

Heterogeneous Space and Incompletely Informed Agents

Theories allowing for these complexities have focused on single sector monopolistic price competition in space. Consider a set of firms using the same technology to produce and sell a homogeneous commodity, to consumers with inelastic demand schedules who are spatially distributed around the firms. Firms occupy fixed locations in a heterogeneous space (i.e. they have different degrees of accessibility to consumers). Consumers are incompletely informed, stochastically choosing to patronize a particular firm based on its price relative to those of other firms in their choice sets (Sheppard *et al.* 1992). This is analogous to monopolistic competition between firms in the monopolistic competition approach, but the two relaxed assumptions result in important differences. First, profits, prices, and output differ between firms in equilibrium. Except for the geographically marginal producer, firms make excess profits reflecting their locational advantage (Sheppard *et al.* 1992). Secondly, and in contradistinction to most mainstream economic theory (Dixit and Stiglitz 1977; Nell 1992), it is rational for firms to maximize the *rate* of profit rather than total profits. Both total profits and the rate of profit may be higher if firms do this (Plummer *et al.* 1998; Sheppard *et al.* 1998). In heterogeneous space this results in distinctive equilibrium pricing, profit, and demand patterns (Haining *et al.* 1996). Thirdly, equilibria are only locally quasi-stable, with numerical simulations suggesting that small price deviations from equilibrium induce price wars (Plummer *et al.* 1998). Instability is enhanced by more complex market structures, such as oligopolists seeking to serve spatially separated and differentiated markets (Plummer 1996*a*, 1996*b*). Thus spatial homogeneity and perfect information may be critical assumptions, the relaxation of which challenges theoretical propositions about competition, prices, and profits in space.

Distance as a Commodity, Inter-Sectoral Interdependence, Social Class

When the assumptions about distance, vertical integration, and agency are also relaxed, further novel theoretical propositions result. Consider the case of a spatially extensive multi-regional economy in which *N* economic sectors engage in the production of commodities, in *R* functional economic regions (such as metropolitan regions). Suppose we know which sectors are found in which regions, employing possibly different production technologies and wage scales for the same industry in different regions. A production technology is defined by the quantity of other commodities, and of labor, used per unit produced, and there are persistent regional differences in technology by sector (Rigby and Essletzbichler 1997). Economic actors may be capitalists, workers, and/or landlords (Sheppard and Barnes 1990), with competing claims on the monetary surplus produced by the economy.[12] Each of these groups is also differentiated; different firms in the same sector employ different production technologies and different mixes of differentially skilled workers, making all theoretical propositions stochastic in nature. Capitalists seek to increase the rate of profit on capital advanced, landlords to increase rents per acre, and workers to increase consumption (real wages).

Transportation is a special commodity: that of accessibility, consumed whenever another commodity or person flows from one place to another. It is produced in every region, not as a direct input to production but as a commodity needed to make the direct inputs geographically accessible. Production methods dictate the other goods required as inputs, but the amount of transportation needed will depend on accessibility to suppliers of those inputs. At the same time, the price of transportation (freight rate), set in the same way as the prices of other commodities, partially determines relative accessibility, and in turn influences decisions of where to purchase inputs from. A major contributor to decreasing the turnover time of capital, reducing production costs, and increasing profits is to introduce communications technologies which lower the price of transportation (Sheppard 1990). David Harvey (1982) refers to this as the historical tendency to annihilate space by time: as a result of which distance is literally produced, and made endogenous to commodity production.

A dynamic equilibrium can be described for any such space economy: a distribution of relative production levels across regions, determined by wage levels, technologies, and transport costs, which reproduces itself and ensures an equal average profit and growth rate in all regions and sectors. Yet the existence of such equilibria is of little interest, since they appear to be unstable, notwithstanding the ad hoc assumptions that can always create equilibrium-seeking dynamics (Sheppard 1983). Furthermore, standard neoclassical conclusions about regional specialization, trade, and growth cannot be assumed to hold (Sheppard and Barnes 1990). The Hecksher–Ohlin rule that regions specialize in and trade commodities which use locally cheaper production methods is not guaranteed, even in an economy with no monopolistic competition. Individual entrepreneurs' rate-of-profit-maximizing choices of production technologies or specialization strategies may eventually reduce average rates of profit (a form of unintended consequences which, as Harvey (1982) notes, is equivalent to Marx's idea of the falling rate of profit). The free movement of capital and labor

[12] For those concerned about microeconomic foundations the parameters chosen to describe an economic equilibrium, including class position, can be assumed to be the result of the constrained optimizing choices of different actors without loss of generality (Roemer 1981, 1988).

in response to wage and profit differentials may enhance, rather than reduce, inter-regional inequalities in the supply of these inputs. Allocation of land through the land market to maximize rents need not maximize efficiency of land use (i.e. the 'highest' use need not be the 'best' one, because land rent cannot be assumed to equal the marginal productivity of land).

There are complex potential conflicts of economic interest between and within actors, conditioned by their class and geographic location. This is reinforced by the spatial nature of the economy, whose high degree of complexity precludes actors from adequately calculating the indirect consequences of their actions. Strategies which maximize landlords' rents per acre, or workers' real wages, need not be the same as those which maximize capitalists' profits, and there is no distribution of income (between wages, profits, and rents) which is Pareto optimal or efficient in a Nash equilibrium sense.[13] Thus there is potential for resistance against any market-induced distribution of income, whether or not it describes an equilibrium situation. Firm strategies include attempts to manipulate labor markets to their advantage (Clark *et al.* 1986), labor organizes to enhance its share of the surplus (Herod 1998), and state intervention is continually necessary to negotiate these conflicts (Aglietta 1979). Workers in competitively advantaged regions can increase their real wages by creating a place alliance with other classes there, which capitalists are willing to join as long as wages are low enough elsewhere to guarantee that local production remains profitable.[14] Strategies by one group of entrepreneurs to enhance their mean profit rate may also reduce the mean profit rates of other fractions of capitalists, locally or non-locally.

Unstable equilibria and unintended consequences, undermining rational expectations, mean that the space economy becomes an arena of constantly shifting competitive advantage, reflecting the economic and political strategies of differently situated actors. Firms' profits, a result of previous production decisions, current demand in different spatial markets, and competitive advantage in those markets, may be invested in higher output, technical change, relocation, or finance markets (from which money may also be borrowed). Finance markets smooth out the redistribution of funds, but interest rates must vary between regions of different sizes in order to maintain dynamic equilibrium (Webber 1987*b*). Regional technological change will depend on firm level processes of innovation, imitation, and the birth and death rates of firms using different technologies (Webber *et al.* 1992; Webber and Rigby 1996). Pricing strategies will depend on supply and demand (competitive advantage), sunk

[13] Pareto optimality is defined with respect to a particular distribution of income; in this case that very distribution is being contested.

[14] While these conclusions may seem to side with Marxian political economy, the same framework calls into question central propositions of Marxian economics, such as the independence of labor values from exchange values, the falling rate of profit theorems, and the unity of economic classes (Sheppard and Barnes 1990).

costs (Clark and Wrigley 1995), and planned technological and growth strategies ('strong competition': Storper and Walker 1989). The resulting fluctuations in wage and unemployment rates affect labor costs and labor migration (cf. Goodwin 1987; Plummer 1999).

A major issue of contention is whether equilibrium conditions are of any relevance at all for understanding out-of-equilibrium dynamics. Michael Webber and David Rigby, for example, argue that equilibrium conditions are smuggled into many of the basic price and output equations used in economic geography. They reject price-based calculations in favor of labor values because the latter do not presume equilibrium, and are beginning to develop the complex envelopes of possible out-of-equilibrium dynamics constrained only by demand and supply constraints (Rigby 1990; Webber 1997; Webber and Rigby 1999). Their approach casts doubt on economic propositions about technological change by relaxing assumptions of equilibrium, although it has not yet been developed into a full multi-regional framework.

Concluding Comments

The three paradigms described above are snapshots of rapidly moving fields. They should not be thought of as complete statements but as continually changing sets of propositions. In each case, however, there is emergent order: stories whose broad outlines can be sketched, and which differ from one another because of the assumptions used by each group. They teach us that the different disciplines of economics and geography do look at the subject matter of economic geography through different disciplinary lenses/norms. Economists tend to be comfortable with equilibrium, insist on methodological individualism and marginal analysis, believe that complex inter-sectoral interdependencies can be abstracted from without difficulty, feel that geography can be approximated by a uniform plain, and treat economic processes as if they can be separated from other societal processes. To a geographer, there are many similarities between the propositions of the monopolistic competition and evolution and complexity schools, notwithstanding strong differences of opinion about economic agents. Geographers tend to see the spaces and places of economic geography as not only differentiated but endogenously created by economic processes, feel that inter-sectoral interdependencies should be treated as seriously as spatial interdependencies, are comfortable with disequilibrium, employ structurationist models of agency (placing individual actions in the context of more durable social structures: Giddens 1979), and insist on embedding economic processes in other societal processes. The resulting, sometimes stark, differences in theoretical propositions about the space economy are differently situated understandings, each of which makes sense within its own community but seems overly narrow from the other community. Neither view can be reduced to the other, making attempts to subsume economic geography into economics, or vice versa, unproductive.

These cases also make clear that the choice of a mathematical language for theory construction, while (like all languages) both limiting and empowering, carries no obligations to employ a particular economic paradigm. Mathematics is not a tool of bourgeois thought, but one whose subject depends on the assumptions made. When the language of mathematics is used, assumptions are easier to pin down, but all theories are based on assumptions, and cannot be critically assessed without analyzing what these are and whether they are critical to the resulting theoretical propositions (Hanson 1994). The greatest challenge lies in developing rigorous but constructive debates across competing sets of assumptions, since our implicit views about what is important and what can be abstracted from tend to reflect our deepest-held personal and disciplinary beliefs.

Acknowledgements

I am grateful for the comments of Trevor Barnes, Paul Plummer, Jun Zhang, and the editors on earlier drafts of this chapter.

Further Reading

An excellent sense of the economists' 'new' economic geography can be found in Paul Krugman's *Geography and Trade* (MIT Press, 1991) and *Development, Geography, and Economic Theory* (MIT Press, 1995). The former summarizes the main approach, and the latter provides a sense of the philosophical foundations behind it. Clive Barnett provides a useful assessment of the cultural turn ('The cultural turn: fashion or progress in human geography?' *Antipode*, 30 (1998): 379–94) and Trevor Barnes (*The Economics of Dislocation*, Guilford, 1996) lays out some philosophical foundations. The most accessible example of the evolution and complexity approach is Brian Arthur's *Increasing Returns and Path Dependence in the Economy* (University of Michigan Press, 1994). Many more ideas are found in the essays by Durlauf, Padgett, and Lindgren in W. B. Arthur, *et al.* (eds.), *The Economy as an Evolving Complex System II* (Addison-Wesley, 1997) and in P. Cohendet, P. Llerena, H. Stahn, and G. Umbauer (eds.), *The Economics of Networks* (Springer, 1998). An older tradition of related research in geography is found in Leslie Curry's *The Random Spatial Economy and its Evolution* (Ashgate, 1998).

The research in regional political economy is inspired by David Harvey's sophisticated dialectical analysis of space in Marxian economic dynamics (*The Limits to Capital*, Blackwell, 1982). Major theoretical contributions taking a mathematical approach are Eric Sheppard and Trevor Barnes's *The Capitalist Space Economy* (Unwin Hyman, 1990) and Michael Webber and David Rigby's *The Golden Age Illusion* (Guilford, 1996). Do not be put off by the mathematics! Everything is also explained in words. Less abstract contributions are Michael Storper and Richard Walker's *The Capitalist Imperative* (Blackwell, 1989), Doreen Massey's *Spatial Divisions of Labour* (Methuen, 1984), Neil Smith's *Uneven Development* (Blackwell, 1984), Anne Markusen's *Profit Cycles,*

Oligopoly and Regional Development (MIT Press, 1985), and Allen Scott's *New Industrial Spaces* (Pion, 1988).

References

AGLIETTA, M. 1979. *A Theory of Capitalist Regulation*. London: New Left Books.

ALBIN, P., and FOLEY, D. K. 1992. Decentralized, dispersed exchange without an auctioneer. *Journal of Economic Behavior and Organization*, 18/1: 27–51.

AMIN, A. forthcoming. Industrial districts. In *A Companion to Economic Geography*, ed. E. Sheppard and T. J. Barnes. Oxford: Blackwell.

ANDERSON, P., ARROW, K. J., and PINES, D., eds. 1988. *The Economy as an Evolving Complex System*. Santa Fe Institute, Studies in the Sciences of Complexity V. New York: Addison-Wesley.

ARTHUR, W. B. 1994. *Increasing Returns and Path Dependence in the Economy*. Ann Arbor: The University of Michigan Press.

—— DURLAUF, S. N., and LANE, D. A. 1997. Introduction. In *The Economy as an Evolving Complex System II*, ed. W. B. Arthur, S. N. Durlauf, and D. A. Lane. New York: Addison-Wesley, 1–14.

BARRO, R., and GRILLI, V. 1994. *European Macroeconomics*. London: Macmillan.

BERTOLA, G. 1993. Models of economic integration and localized growth. In *Adjustment and Growth in European Monetary Union*, ed. F. Torres and E. Giavassi. Cambridge: Cambridge University Press, 159–79.

BORTS, G. H., and STEIN, J. L. 1964. *Economic Growth in a Free Market*. New York: Columbia University Press.

BURMEISTER, E. 1980. *Capital Theory and Dynamics*. Cambridge: Cambridge University Press.

CLARK, G. L. 1998. Stylized facts and close dialogue: methodology in economic geography. *Annals of the Association of American Geographers*, 88/1: 73–87.

—— GERTLER, M., and WHITEMAN, J. 1986. *Regional Dynamics: Studies in Adjustment Theory*. London: Allen & Unwin.

—— and WRIGLEY, N. 1995. Sunk costs: a framework for economic geography. *Transactions of the Institute of British Geographers*, NS 20: 204–23.

CRANG, P. 1997. Cultural turns and the (re)constitution of economic geography: introduction to section one. In *Geographies of Economies*, ed. R. Lee and J. Wills. London: E. Arnold, 3–15.

CURRY, L. 1967. Central places in the random space economy. *Journal of Regional Science*, 7/2 (suppl.), 217–38.

—— 1998. *The Random Spatial Economy and its Evolution*. Aldershot: Ashgate.

DE PALMA, A., LABBÉ, M., and THISSE, J.-F. 1986. On the existence of price equilibria under Mill and uniform delivered pricing policies. In Norman 1986: 30–41.

DIXIT, A. K., and STIGLITZ, J. E. 1977. Monopolistic competition and optimum product diversity. *American Economic Review*, 67/3: 297–308.

DOSI, G., PAVITT, K., and SOETE, L. 1990. *The Economics of Technical Change and International Trade*. London: Wheatsheaf.

DUMÉNIL, G., and LÉVY, D. 1987. The dynamics of competition: a restoration of the classical hypothesis. *Cambridge Journal of Economics*, 11: 133–64.

Duménil, G., and Lévy, D. 1993. *The Economics of the Profit Rate: Competition, Crises and Historical Tendencies in Capitalism.* Aldershot: Edward Elgar.

Dunford, M. F. 1988. *Capital, the State, and Regional Development.* London: Pion.

Epstein, J. M., and Axtell, R. 1996. *Growing Artificial Societies: Social Science from the Bottom Up.* Washington: The Brookings Institution.

Flaschel, P., Franke, R., and Semmler, W. 1997. *Dynamic Macroeconomics: Instability, Fluctuation, and Growth in Monetary Economies.* Cambridge, Mass.: MIT Press.

—— and Semmler, W. 1986. The dynamic equalization of profit rates for input-output models with fixed capital. In *Competition, Instability and Non-linear Cycles,* ed. W. Semmler. Berlin: Springer, 1–34.

Foley, D. K. 1994. A statistical equilibrium theory of markets. *Journal of Economic Theory,* 62: 321–45.

Fujita, M., and Krugman, P. 1995. When is the economy monocentric? Von Thünen and Chamberlain unified. *Regional Science and Urban Economics,* 25: 505–28.

—— and Thisse, J.-F. 1996. Economics of agglomeration. *Journal of the Japanese and International Economies,* 10: 339–78.

Gallup, J. L., Sachs, J. D., and Mellinger, A. D. 1999. Geography and Economic Development, *International Regional Science Review,* 22: 179–232.

Giddens, A. 1979. *Central Problems in Social Theory.* London: Macmillan.

Goodwin, R. M. 1987. Macrodynamics. In Goodwin and Puzo 1987: 3–162.

—— 1990. *Chaotic Economic Dynamics.* Oxford: Oxford University Press.

—— and Puzo, L. 1987. *The Dynamics of a Capitalist Economy.* Boulder, Colo.: Westview Press.

Greenhut, M. L., Norman, G., and Hung, C.-S. 1987. *The Economics of Imperfect Competition: A Spatial Approach.* Cambridge: Cambridge University Press.

Haining, R. P., Plummer, P., and Sheppard, E. 1996. Spatial price equilibrium in interdependent markets: price and sales configurations. *Papers in Regional Science,* 75: 41–64.

Hanson, S. 1994. 'Never question the assumptions' and other scenes from the revolution. *Urban Geography,* 14/6: 552–6.

Harcourt, G. C. 1972. *Some Cambridge Controversies in the Theory of Capital.* Cambridge: Cambridge University Press.

Harvey, D. 1982. *The Limits to Capital.* Oxford: Basil Blackwell.

—— 1985. Money, space, time and the city. In Harvey, *Consciousness and the Urban Experience.* Oxford: Basil Blackwell, 1–35.

—— 1996. *Justice, Nature and the Geography of Difference.* Oxford: Basil Blackwell.

Helpman, E. 1990. *Monopolistic Competition in Trade Theory.* Special papers in international finance, 16. Princeton: Department of Economics, Princeton University.

Herod, A., ed. 1998. *Organizing the Landscape.* Minneapolis: University of Minnesota Press.

Holland, J. H. 1995. *Hidden Order: How Adaptation Builds Complexity.* New York: Addison-Wesley.

Hotelling, H. 1929. Stability in competition. *Economic Journal,* 39: 40–57.

Kaldor, N. 1985. *Economics without Equilibrium.* Armonk, NY: M. E. Sharpe.

Kirman, A. 1992. Whom or what does the representative individual represent? *Journal of Economic Perspectives,* 6/2: 117–36.

KRUGMAN, P. 1990. *Rethinking International Trade*. Cambridge, Mass.: MIT Press.
—— 1991. *Geography and Trade*. Cambridge, Mass.: MIT Press.
—— 1995. *Development, Geography, and Economic Theory*. Cambridge, Mass.: MIT Press.
—— 1996*a*. *The Self-Organizing Economy*. Oxford: Blackwell.
—— 1996*b*. What economists can learn from evolutionary theorists. Paper presented to the European Association for Evolutionary Political Economy, Nov. 1996 (http://web.mit.edu/krugman/www/).
KURZ, H., and SALVADORI, N. 1995. The 'new' growth theory: old wine in new goatskins. Unpublished manuscript.
—— —— 1997. *Theory of Production: A Long-Period Analysis*. Cambridge: Cambridge University Press.
LANGTON, C. G. 1989. *Artificial Life*. Redwood City, Calif.: Addison-Wesley.
LIOSSATOS, P. 1988. Value and competition in a spatial context: a Marxian model. *Papers of the Regional Science Association*, 45: 87–103.
LÖSCH, A. 1954/1940. *The Economics of Location*. New Haven: Yale University Press; 1st pub. 1940.
LUKERMANN, F. 1964. Geography as a formal intellectual discipline and the way in which it contributes to human knowledge. *The Canadian Geographer*, 8: 167–74.
MCGOVERN, S. 1994. A Lakatosian approach to changes in international trade theory. *History of Political Economy*, 26/3: 351–68.
MARELLI, E. 1983. Empirical estimation of intersectoral and interregional transfers of surplus value: the case of Italy. *Journal of Regional Science*, 23: 49–70.
MARTIN, P., and OTTAVIANO, G. I. P. 1996*a*. *Growing locations: industry location in a model of endogenous growth*. Discussion paper No. 1523. London: Centre for Economic Policy Research.
—— —— 1996*b*. *Growth and agglomeration*. Discussion paper 1529. London: Centre for Economic Policy Research.
MARTIN, R. 1999. The new 'geographical turn' in economics: some critical reflections. *Cambridge Journal of Economics*, 23: 65–91.
—— and SUNLEY, P. 1998. Slow convergence? The new endogenous growth theory and regional development. *Economic Geography*, 74: 201–27.
MORISHIMA, M. 1973. *Marx's Economics: A Dual Theory of Value and Growth*. Cambridge: Cambridge University Press.
NAGURNEY, A. 1993. *Network Economics: A Variational Inequality Approach*. Boston: Kluwer Publishers.
NELL, E. 1992. Demand, pricing and investment. In *Transformational Growth and Effective Demand*, ed. E. Nell. New York: New York University Press, 381–451.
NELSON, R. 1995. Recent evolutionary theorizing about economic change. *Journal of Economic Literature*, 33: 48–90.
NORMAN, G., ed. 1986. *Spatial Pricing and Differentiated Markets*. London: Pion.
PASINETTI, L. L. 1981. *Structural Change and Economic Growth*. Cambridge: Cambridge University Press.
PLUMMER, P. S. 1996*a*. Competitive dynamics in hierarchically organized markets: spatial duopoly and demand asymmetries. *Environment and Planning A*, 28/11: 2021–40.
—— 1996*b*. Spatial competition amongst hierarchically organized corporations: prices, profits, and shipment patterns. *Environment and Planning A*, 28/2: 199–222.

Plummer, P. S. 1999. Capital accumulation, economic restructuring and nonequilibrium regional growth dynamics. *Geographical Analysis*, 31: 267–87.

——Sheppard, E., and Haining, R. P. 1998. Modeling spatial price competition: Marxian versus neoclassical approaches. *Annals of the Association of American Geographers*, 88/4: 575–94.

——————1999. Rationality, stability and endogenous price formation in spatially interdependent markets. Manuscript.

Pred, A. 1966. *The Spatial Dynamics of U.S. Urban-Industrial Growth, 1800–1914*. Cambridge, Mass.: MIT Press.

Puu, T. 1991. *Nonlinear Economic Dynamics*. Berlin: Springer Verlag.

Rigby, D. 1990. Technical change and the rate of profit: an obituary for Okishio's theorem. *Environment and Planning A*, 22: 1039–50.

——and Essletzbichler, J. 1997. Evolution, process variety, and regional trajectories of technical change in U.S. manufacturing. *Economic Geography*, 73: 269–85.

Roemer, J. 1981. *Analytical Foundations of Marxian Economic Theory*. Cambridge: Cambridge University Press.

——1988. *Free to Lose*. London: Radius.

Romer, P. 1990. Endogenous technological change. *Journal of Political Economy*, 98: S71–S102.

Samuelson, P. A. 1954. The transfer problem and transport costs, II: analysis of effects of trade impediments. *Economic Journal*, 64: 264–89.

Sayer, A. 1997. The dialectic of culture and economy. In *Geographies of Economies*, ed. R. Lee and J. Wills. London: Arnold, 16–26.

Schweitzer, F., ed. 1997. *Self-Organization of Complex Structures: From Individual to Collective Dynamics*. Amsterdam: Gordon and Breach.

Scott, A. J. 1980. *The Urban Land Nexus and the State*. London: Pion.

Sheppard, E. 1983. Pasinetti, Marx and urban accumulation dynamics. In *Evolving Geographical Structures*, ed. D. Griffith and A. C. Lea. The Hague: Martinus Nijhoff, 293–322.

——1990. Transportation in a capitalist space economy: transportation demand, circulation time and transportation innovations. *Environment and Planning A*, 22: 1007–24.

——1995. Dissenting from spatial analysis. *Urban Geography*, 16: 283–303.

——and Barnes, T. J. 1990. *The Capitalist Space Economy: Geographical Analysis after Ricardo, Marx and Sraffa*. London: Unwin Hyman.

——Haining, R. P., and Plummer, P. 1992. Spatial pricing in interdependent markets. *Journal of Regional Science*, 32: 55–75.

——Plummer, P., and Haining, R. P. 1998. Profit rate maximization in interdependent markets. *Journal of Regional Science*, 38/4: 659–67.

Siebert, H. 1969. *Regional Economic Growth: Theory and Policy*. Scranton, Pa.: International Textbook Company.

Silverberg, G. 1988. Modeling economic dynamics and technical change. In *Technical Change and Economic Theory*, ed. G. Dosi, C. Freeman, R. Nelson, G. Silverberg, and L. Soete. New York: Columbia University Press, 531–59.

——Dosi, G., and Orsegnio, L. 1988. Innovation, diversity and diffusion: a self-organization model. *Economic Journal*, 98: 1032–54.

SRAFFA, P. 1960. *The Production of Commodities by Means of Commodities.* Cambridge: Cambridge University Press.

STEEDMAN, I. 1979. *Trade amongst Growing Economies.* Cambridge: Cambridge University Press.

STORPER, M., and WALKER, R. 1989. *The Capitalist Imperative: Territory, Technology and Industrial Growth.* Oxford: Basil Blackwell.

VON HAYEK, F. A. 1937. Economics and knowledge. *Economica*, NS 4 (Feb.): 33–54.

WALSH, V., and GRAM, H. 1980. *Classical and Neoclassical Theories of General Equilibrium.* Oxford: Oxford University Press.

WALZ, U. 1996. Transport costs, intermediate goods, and localized growth. *Regional Science and Urban Economics*, 26: 671–95.

WEBBER, M. J. 1987*a*. Quantitative measurement of some Marxist categories. *Environment and Planning A*, 19: 1303–22.

—— 1987*b*. Rates of profit and interregional flows of capital. *Annals of the Association of American Geographers*, 77: 63–75.

—— 1997. Profitability and growth in multi-region systems: prologue to a historical geography. *Economic Geography*, 73: 405–26.

—— and RIGBY, D. 1996. *The Golden Age Illusion: Rethinking Postwar Capitalism.* New York: Guilford.

—— —— 1999. Accumulation and the rate of profit: regulating the macroeconomy. *Environment and Planning A*, 31/1: 141–64.

—— SHEPPARD, E., and RIGBY, D. 1992. Forms of technical change. *Environment and Planning A*, 24: 1679–709.

WONG, K.-Y. 1995. *International Trade in Goods and Factor Mobility.* Cambridge, Mass.: MIT Press.

WRIGHT, E. O. 1997. *Class Counts: Comparative Studies in Class Analysis.* Cambridge: Cambridge University Press.

Part II

Global Economic Integration

Section 3

Investment and Trade

Chapter 7

The Geography of International Investment

Howard J. Shatz and Anthony J. Venables

Introduction

THE last fifteen years have seen an enormous growth of activity by multinational corporations, as measured by flows of foreign direct investment (FDI). FDI has grown much faster than either trade or income; whereas worldwide nominal GDP increased at a rate of 7.2 per cent per year between 1985 and 1997 and worldwide imports at 9.2 per cent, worldwide nominal inflows of FDI increased at 17.6 per cent.[1] These figures comprise the financing of new investments, retained earnings of affiliates, and cross-border mergers and acquisitions. Mergers and acquisitions are a large proportion of the whole (especially among the advanced countries), with their value constituting 49 per cent of total FDI flows in 1996 and 58 per cent in 1997 (UNCTAD 1998).

The scale of multinational activity is probably better gauged by looking not at FDI flows, but at sales of multinational firms. In 1996, US multinational parent companies exported $407.4 billion worth of goods out of total US goods exports of $625.1 billion, two-thirds of the total. Much of this trade was intra-firm—of the $407.4 billion, some $182.1 billion, or 44.7 per cent, went to exporters' own foreign affiliates or related companies. Between 1983 and 1995, foreign affiliates of all nationalities accounted for between one-quarter and one-third of worldwide exports, according to figures from UNCTAD (1998).

[1] Much of the data mentioned come from a special extract of the UNCTAD FDI/TNC Database (UNCTAD 1999). The investment flows measured here generally include equity flows and debt between a parent company and an affiliate in which the parent holds at least a 10% ownership interest, as well as retained earnings of the affiliate. However, both the components and threshold differ for some reporting economies.

Some commentators have estimated that multinationals—parents and affiliates combined—are responsible for 75 per cent of the world's commodity trade (Dunning 1993).

The pre-eminence of multinationals is not spread equally across sectors, but instead is concentrated heavily in industries characterized by high levels of research and development, a large share of professional and technical workers, and production of technically complex or differentiated goods. Firms that invest often have some type of intangible asset they want to keep within the firm, rather than exploit through licensing. Furthermore, investing firms are often the larger firms in their industries.[2]

The above figures show that multinational activity now dominates international economic exchange. Our objectives in this chapter are to draw out the main facts about the geographical location of multinational activity and the main theories that seek to explain these facts. Our focus on the location of FDI means that this is not a comprehensive survey of all issues raised by FDI. We do not address the boundaries of the firm (which activities firms transact internally and which they contract out in 'arm's length' trade (see Markusen 1995, for a survey)). Neither do we deal with the implications of FDI for home or for host economies (surveyed by Blomström and Kokko 1994, 1997, and 1998). We start in the next section with an overview of the facts about the location of multinationals then turn, in the following section, to an overview of theory. The penultimate section looks at empirical studies that have sought to explain the pattern of location.

Empirical Overview

Where does FDI come from? The predominant source of supply is, unsurprisingly, the advanced countries.[3] In 1997, they controlled 89.8 per cent of worldwide FDI stock, compared to 10.2 per cent for the developing and transition countries. Recent FDI flows show some decline in the dominance of the advanced countries; whereas during the period 1988–92 they accounted for 92.5 per cent of total FDI outflows, during the five years from 1993 to 1997 this share had fallen to 85.3 per cent. Within advanced countries, the major single investor is the USA which, in 1997, controlled 25.6 per cent of the world's FDI stock, compared to 45.1 per cent for the European Union (EU) 15, and 8.0 per

[2] Caves (1996) gives a comprehensive description of the characteristics of firms that go multinational and in which industries they are most likely to be found.

[3] We classify countries in this section according to UNCTAD (1999) with minor changes. Advanced countries include the EU 15, Gibraltar, Iceland, Norway, Switzerland, Canada, the USA, Australia, New Zealand, Japan, and Israel. Developing countries comprise the rest of the world, including the transition economies of Central and Eastern Europe, as well as South Africa; UNCTAD classifies the transition economies as a separate group and South Africa among the advanced countries.

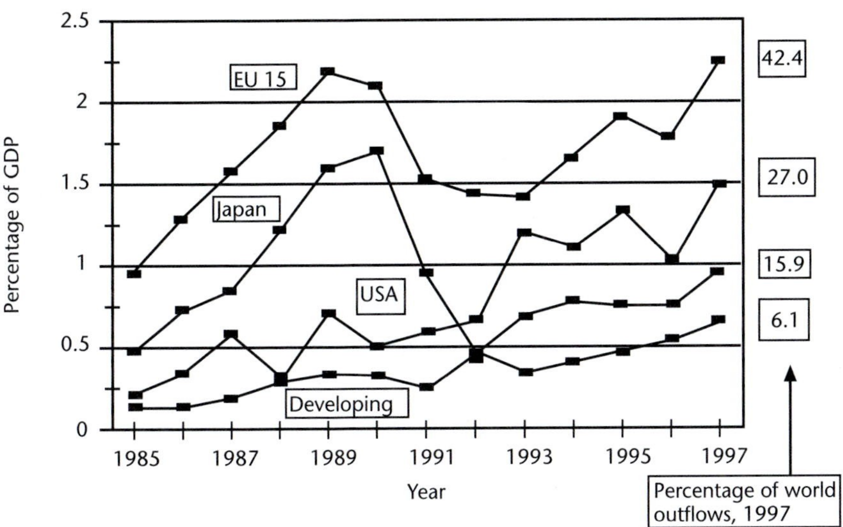

Fig. 7.1. Sources of outward FDI

Sources: UNCTAD FDI/TNC Database and World Bank.

cent for Japan. Japanese and European flows boomed during the late 1980s, although these have now fallen back to a position broadly in line with existing stocks.

Most of the difference between the advanced and developing countries is accounted for by sheer economic size, and the difference in outflows relative to GDP is perhaps less than might be expected. Figure 7.1 maps out the time series of FDI outflows relative to source country GDP. Outward flows from the advanced countries averaged 1.3 per cent of their GDP each year from 1993 to 1997, with the EU having much the highest rate (almost 2 per cent of GDP), largely on the basis of intra-EU investments. For developing countries, outward FDI flows averaged 0.8 per cent of their GDP during 1993 to 1997, compared to 0.3 per cent from 1988 to 1992, a large increase.

Turning to the destination of FDI, most goes to the advanced industrial countries. In the period 1985 to 1997 the developed countries received fully 71.5 per cent of FDI flows. Inevitably, most of this is advanced to advanced country FDI. Of the Group of Seven (G-7) countries, France, Germany, Italy, and the UK sent more than three-quarters of their 1997 FDI flows to the rest of the OECD; Canada, Japan, and the USA sent more than 60 per cent most recently. This pattern of reciprocal FDI shows up strongly at the industry level as well, with a large share of flows appearing as intra-industry investment.

While intra-OECD investment and intra-industry investment within the OECD have been long-established facts, an emerging trend is the rise of FDI to developing countries. The share of worldwide FDI received by the developing

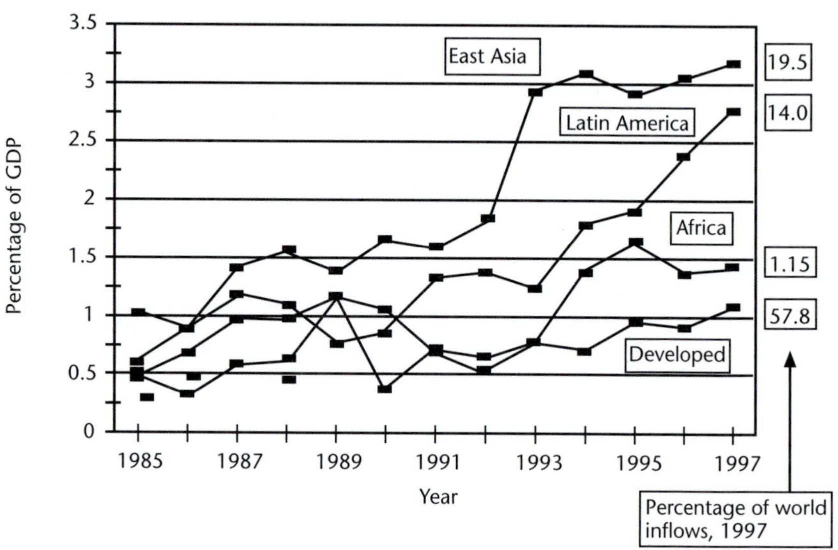

Fig. 7.2. Hosts of inward FDI

Sources: UNCTAD FDI/TNC Database and World Bank.

and transition economies jumped from 21.8 per cent in the 1988 to 1992 period, to 39.8 per cent in the 1993 to 1997 period. The picture is more dramatic if we look at FDI relative to the size of the host country's economy, as shown in Figure 7.2. During the five years from 1988 to 1992, advanced countries received FDI inflows at an average annual rate of 0.90 per cent of their GDP, while developing and transition countries received FDI at an average annual rate of 0.78 per cent of their GDP. By 1993 to 1997, the inflow rate of developing and transition countries had more than doubled to 1.91 per cent of GDP, while that for the advanced countries had decreased slightly to 0.87 per cent of GDP.

Among developing countries, the distribution of FDI is quite uneven. Only ten countries accounted for two-thirds of all inward flows during the most recent five years for which data are available, 1993 to 1997 (Argentina, Brazil, Chile, China, Hungary, Indonesia, Malaysia, Mexico, Poland, and Singapore). China alone received an annual average of 30.6 per cent. Indeed, China accounts for much of the increase in flows to developing countries, with its share of world total FDI flows rising from 2.9 per cent for the period 1988 to 1992, to 12.2 per cent for 1993 to 1997. In nominal dollar terms, inward direct investment to China increased from $3.2 billion in 1988 to $45.3 billion in 1997. The source of all these flows, about 5 per cent of China's GDP in 1997, remains hotly debated. The main sources are considered to be Chinese business groups resident in Asia, Chinese businesses resident in China that send their money out and then bring it back to get certain benefits available to foreign investors (the so-called 'round trippers'), and investors from the advanced industrial economies.

In contrast, all of sub-Saharan Africa, including South Africa, received an annual average of 3.2 per cent of all flows to developing and transition countries between 1993 and 1997, a decrease of almost 2.1 percentage points from the annual average of 5.3 per cent during the 1988 to 1992 period. Relative to world inflows, sub-Saharan Africa's share increased slightly, from around 1.0 per cent between 1988 and 1992, to around 1.3 per cent between 1993 and 1997. This is also reflected in its inflows of FDI relative to host country income, as in Figure 7.2, where we see some increase in FDI to Africa, but at levels dwarfed by inflows to East Asia and Latin America.

Location of Multinationals: Theory

There are two main—and quite distinct—reasons why a firm should go multinational. One is to better serve a local market, and the other is to get lower-cost inputs.

FDI designed to serve local markets is often called 'horizontal' FDI, since it typically involves duplicating parts of the production process as additional plants are established to supply different locations. This form of FDI usually substitutes for trade, since parent firms replace exports with local production. The motive is to reduce the costs involved in supplying the market (such as tariffs or transport costs) or in some other way to improve the firm's competitive position in the market.

In contrast, FDI in search of low-cost inputs is often called 'vertical' FDI, since it involves slicing the vertical chain of production and relocating part of this chain in a low-cost location—for example, assembling electronic goods in Asia even though component manufacture and final sales might take place in the USA. The cheap inputs might be labour—of different skill levels—primary commodities, intermediate goods, or even access to externalities, such as knowledge spillovers. Vertical FDI is usually trade creating, since products at different stages of production are shipped between different locations. The distinction between vertical and horizontal FDI can, of course, become blurred—one plant may serve both functions, and the decision to open a plant to serve a market will depend on local costs—but is nevertheless a fundamental one.

Horizontal FDI and Market Access

A firm can supply a foreign market with its product either by exporting, or by producing locally—becoming multinational. Under what circumstances will it choose to become multinational?

Establishing local production will involve the firm in a variety of additional costs. Some of these are the costs of dealing with foreign administrations, regulations, and tax systems. These may be mitigated by collaboration with local firms through joint ventures, licensing arrangements, or sub-contracting. Some are production costs, both variable and fixed, their size depending on factor prices and technology. The presence of plant-level economies of scale will raise the cost of establishing foreign plants, as compared to producing from a single home plant.

On the other side of the equation, switching from exporting to local production will bring cost savings, the most obvious of which are savings in transport costs or tariffs. To these might be added other benefits of proximity to the market, such as shorter delivery times and ability to respond to local circumstances and preferences.

Theoretical modelling of this sort of FDI has typically posed the issue as one of a trade-off between the additional fixed costs involved in setting up a new plant, and the saving in variable costs (transport costs and tariffs) on exports. Analysis is usually based on a 'new trade theory' model, in which there are distinct firms, and the issues of increasing returns and market structure are addressed explicitly (Smith 1987; Horstmann and Markusen 1987; and Markusen and Venables 1998). What are the main results from this modelling? The first point is that the value of FDI to the firm may exceed the simple calculation of net costs, since establishing local production may have a strategic value. In an oligopolistic environment, each firm's sales depend—in equilibrium—on the marginal costs of all other firms. If one firm reduces its marginal costs then it may induce rival firms to reduce their sales, and this will be of value.[4] Essentially, FDI serves as a commitment to supply the local market, and this commitment may change the behaviour of competitors.

Turning to the location of FDI, the theory predicts that FDI will replace exports in markets where the costs of market access through exports (tariffs and transport costs) are high, or where the costs of setting up a local plant are low. These predictions seem to be at odds with the facts of high (and rising) FDI between economies with low (and falling) trade barriers, for example, within the EU and between North America and Europe, although the apparent contradiction might be resolved by the simple fact that countries with low trade barriers also tend to have low barriers to FDI.

The theory also predicts that FDI is more likely to replace exports the larger is the market. There are two reasons. The first is that the plant-specific fixed cost may be spread over more units of output the larger is the market. The second is that larger markets will tend to have more local firms, and consequently more intense competition than smaller markets. This will lead to a lower price and, if the marginal cost of supply through exports is relatively high, be particularly

[4] This result is model-specific. Cournot oligopolists will reduce their sales. Bertrand oligopolists will increase their sales.

damaging to the profitability of exporting, tipping the firm's decision in favour of local production.

Extending these models to a full multi-country framework, Markusen and Venables (1998) analyse the mix of multinational and national firms operating in each country. They show that multinationals will be prevalent the more similar are countries (in size, and also in other economic dimensions, such as technology and factor endowments). Thus, as Europe has become integrated—essentially increasing market size—it has become more worthwhile for US and Japanese FDI to enter, even though trade barriers and other costs of supplying Europe through trade have been declining.

Vertical FDI and Factor Endowments

A significant part of multinational activity now takes the form of firms shifting a stage of their production process to low-cost locations. The economic analysis of this turns on the idea that different parts of the production process have different input requirements and, since input prices vary across countries, it may be profitable to split production, undertaking unskilled labour-intensive activities in labour-abundant countries, for example.

The classic analysis of this comes from Helpman (1984, 1985) and Helpman and Krugman (1985), and is based on an extended Heckscher–Ohlin trade model with two factors of production and two sectors, one perfectly competitive, producing a homogeneous good under constant returns to scale, and the other producing differentiated products under increasing returns to scale. Firms in the increasing returns sector have distinct 'headquarters' and production activities, which can be separated between countries.

In this model, free trade in goods will bring about the international equalization of factor prices, providing the countries' relative endowments of the two factors are not too different. When this occurs, there is no incentive for firms to separate headquarters and production, so there is no multinational activity. But if the relative endowments are sufficiently different—for example, one economy has a much higher endowment of labour relative to capital than the other—then trade does not equalize factor prices. It is then profitable for firms to divide activities, unsurprisingly putting the more capital-intensive part of the firm (e.g. headquarters) in the capital-abundant country. The capital-abundant economy then becomes an exporter of 'headquarters' services to its production operations located in the labour-abundant economy.

While this analysis provides an elegant way of incorporating multinationals in classical trade theory, its applicability is severely diminished by the maintained assumption that international transactions are frictionless—there are no trade barriers of any sort, and no additional costs are incurred in splitting production. What happens when we allow for such frictions?

FDI, Factor Prices, and Location

Adding trade frictions brings two new forces into play. The first is that transport costs on trade in final goods destroy factor price equalization (unless relative endowments are identical); the consequent factor price differentials increase the incentives to split production. The second is that costs of splitting production—additional costs incurred by having different parts of the firm located in different countries—make multinational production less attractive. Whether firms go multinational—and where they locate different activities—depends on the interaction between these forces.

To analyse this, suppose there are many countries, at varying distances from an economic centre, from which they import goods (including components) and to which they export at least some of their output. Transport costs both on imports (of intermediate goods and final products) and on export sales are higher at more remote locations. If there is some mobile activity—say one stage of a production process—where will it locate?

Locations further away from the centre are unattractive, in so far as firms face heavy transport costs; Radelet and Sachs (1998) show how large these cost penalties can be. On the other hand, since these locations also face transport costs on their other tradable activities, their factor prices will be lower. In particular, the price of factors used intensively in the location's export activity will be low, so investment projects that are intensive users of these factors may be attracted to remote locations. Generally, whether a project will be established in a particular country depends on the factor intensity of the project, relative to the factor intensity of other exports from the country, together with the 'transport intensity' of the project, relative to the transport intensity of other goods traded by the country. These considerations allow us to predict which sort of projects will locate close to established manufacturing regions, and which will go to more remote countries.[5]

Agglomeration

There is some evidence that FDI is spatially more clustered than other forms of production. This could appear in the data for reasons we have already seen. The market size and factor endowment models suggest that although all locations will have some production, only some locations will have FDI. It also appears because of cross-country variations in legal framework, particularly in transition economies, where privatization programmes have been more or less open to foreign investors.

Alternatively, clustering may be due to positive linkages between projects, creating incentives to locate close to other firms. Several mechanisms seem particularly important. One is the spillovers created by research and development;

[5] See Venables and Limao (1999) for analysis of this.

much has been written on this (see Audretsch 1998), although not particularly from the perspective of FDI. Another is confidence, and the possibility that firms 'herd'; firms are uncertain as to whether a particular country is a good location for FDI, and take the success of one firm as a signal of underlying national characteristics. A third mechanism arises from the supply of, and demand for, intermediate goods; once again, this has been extensively analysed, although not particularly from the perspective of FDI.[6]

Location of Multinationals: Empirical Studies

We now review the empirical studies on the determinants of the location of FDI. These have been undertaken for different regions of the world, and each region has presented its own set of patterns. We therefore organize the material by region. The best documented and most heavily researched FDI flows are those from the USA, and we start with these, then turn to outflows from Japan and Europe.

US Outward FDI

Table 7.1 summarizes the US position, showing the direct investment position abroad (the stock of direct investment), sales by US-owned affiliates, and, for comparison, US goods exports, all for 1996. The main determinants of the location of FDI are proximity and host country income level. This 'gravity' relationship has been used extensively in explaining trade flows, and typical findings are that two-thirds of the geographical pattern of trade can be 'explained' by these few variables (see Leamer and Levinsohn 1995). Our own analysis shows that a similar finding holds for multinational affiliate sales.

The interesting question then is to see the ways in which the pattern of FDI differs from that of trade, and the final column of Table 7.1 sheds light on this, giving US affiliate production in each region or country relative to exports from the USA to each region or country. On average, this ratio is equal to 3, so the main outliers are the regions for which this number is markedly different from 3. Three points stand out. First, developing countries do poorly, having less than half the level of affiliate sales relative to trade as do developed countries (1.6 as compared to 4.0). Secondly, neighbouring countries do poorly; this is essentially due to very high trade volumes between the USA and Canada and Mexico. Thirdly, the European Union has a high ratio of affiliate production to exports, and FDI is uneven within the EU, with the UK having the largest share.

To go further we make the distinction between horizontal and vertical FDI.

[6] See Fujita *et al.* (1999) for the analysis of agglomeration patterns created by inter-firm demand and supply linkages.

Table 7.1. USA: direct investment position abroad and sales by affiliates, 1996 (millions of US dollars or percentage)

Area	Direct investment position	Share	Affiliate sales	Share	Share sold in USA	US goods exports	Share	Ratio of affiliate sales to exports
All countries	777,203	100.0	1,861,361	100.0	10.1	625,075	100.0	3.0
Advanced	536,334	69.0	1,434,086	77.0	7.8	356,747	57.1	4.0
of which:								
European Union 15	337,184	43.4	949,648	51.0	4.2	127,711	20.4	7.4
of which:								
United Kingdom	122,692	15.8	286,954	15.4	6.0	30,963	5.0	9.3
Canada	91,301	11.7	231,044	12.4	28.0	134,210	21.5	1.7
Developing	240,869	31.0	427,275	23.0	18.0	268,328	42.9	1.6
of which:								
Latin America	147,535	19.0	178,737	9.6	20.5	109,390	17.5	1.6
of which:								
Mexico	19,900	2.6	46,712	2.5	39.9	56,792	9.1	0.8
Brazil	28,699	3.7	49,814	2.7	4.3	12,718	2.0	3.9
Asia	67,163	8.6	198,298	10.7	15.3	120,105	19.2	1.7
of which:								
Singapore	14,019	1.8	72,593	3.9	21.8	16,720	2.7	4.3
Greater China	18,533	2.4	49,050	2.6	11.8	25,959	4.2	1.9
Africa	6,832	0.9	19,767	1.1	21.6	10,614	1.7	1.9
of which:								
South Africa	1,488	0.2	5,616	0.3	0.5	3,112	0.5	1.8
Middle East	7,793	1.0	10,568	0.6	15.0	19,967	3.2	0.5
East Europe and Former Soviet Union	6,651	0.9	13,699	0.7	0.9	7,623	1.2	1.8

Note: Greater China is China and Hong Kong.

Sources: Multinational direct investment and sales data are from the US Bureau of Economic Analysis, www.bea.doc.gov. Direct investment data are from data file idn0217.exe, 'U.S. Direct Investment Position Abroad, 1982–1997'. Sales data are from data file idn0214.exe, 'U.S. Direct Investment Abroad: Operations of US Parent Companies and their Foreign Affiliates, Preliminary 1996 Estimates'. Figures for direct investment position abroad are for all US affiliates, while sales data are for majority-owned affiliates. Trade data are from the US Census Bureau, www.census.gov, 'Exhibit 13: Exports, Imports, and Balance of Goods by Countries and Selected Areas ... 1996'.

Horizontal FDI was studied by Brainard (1997), who asked the question, how does the USA supply foreign markets? She took as dependent variable the share of exports in total US sales (exports plus affiliate sales) in each market (by country and by industry). Her findings are in line with what we would expect. The share of affiliate sales is higher the higher are trade costs, and lower the lower is per worker income in the host country; this conforms with the poor performance of developing countries we noted above.

Wheeler and Mody (1992) included market size in their analysis of capital expenditures by multinational affiliates, so while their results do not cover the choice of serving a market, they do provide a measure of how market size affects inward multinational activity. They found that market size had a positive influence on capital expenditures by manufacturing affiliates of US multinationals between 1982 and 1988, with an elasticity of 1.57. Elasticity for the highest-income countries was 1.86, while that for the lowest-income countries was 0.74. Other variables that proved important in raising capital expenditures by these affiliates included quality of a country's infrastructure, its degree of industrialization, and the current level of foreign investment. They interpreted these three variables as measures of agglomeration effects.

What about vertical FDI? We can start investigating this by looking at column 5 in Table 7.1, which gives the percentage of US affiliate production that is sold back in the USA. This share is more than twice as high for developing countries (18 per cent) as for advanced countries (7.8 per cent) indicating, as would be expected, that factor price differences play a role in driving such investment. Indeed, Wheeler and Mody alluded to a wage effect in vertical production when they separately tested capital expenditures in the electronics industry, an important offshore assembly industry.[7] They found low labour costs were strongly related to the level of capital expenditures by US electronics affiliates, with larger elasticity in low income countries than high, indicating the importance of labour costs to vertical investment decisions.

Shatz (1999) analyses vertical exports by US-owned manufacturing affiliates in developing countries. He finds that the level of sales back to the USA by these affiliates is higher in countries with low labour costs and tax rates. Low transport costs to the USA and a high degree of trade openness are also important determinants of vertical sales, as the models suggest.[8] These findings

[7] Wheeler and Mody did not note the vertical sales intensity of the electronics industry. However, Shatz (1999) shows using US Bureau of Economic Analysis data that US affiliates in the electric and electronic equipment industry in developing countries sold more than 43% of their output back to the USA between 1986 and 1995. This is the highest proportion of vertical sales of any of the broad industry classes in the data.

[8] The labour cost findings of Shatz and Wheeler and Mody do not appear in every analysis, however. In an early paper investigating vertical investment in the 1960s, Kravis and Lipsey (1982) found a negative association between labour costs and the level of exports in most industries investigated, but this relationship was never statistically significant. Rather, market size regularly emerged as statistically and economically significant, though there was no elasticity computation.

hold true for the ratio of sales back to the USA relative to total sales by these affiliates.

Returning to Table 7.1, Mexico and Singapore stand out as having high sales back to the USA, with Mexico selling almost 40 per cent of its output to the USA and Singapore selling almost 22 per cent.[9] Africa also stands out because of the resource intensity of affiliate production. The one outlier among the advanced countries is Canada, from which US affiliates sell 28 per cent of their output back home. The high level of vertical investment in Canada and Mexico might be explained by three factors—proximity, allowing producers to coordinate their production more easily as they slice it into sections; economic integration, creating a more stable investment climate; and Mexico's maquiladora programme, started in the 1960s, enabling US producers to set up assembly plants to take advantage of Mexico's lower wages. A reform in 1983 simplified the initiation of maquiladora projects, and inward FDI (from all sources) skyrocketed from $478 million in 1983 to $3.6 billion in 1989 (Feenstra and Hanson 1997). Much of this was from the USA (almost $1.7 billion in 1989, for example) and most of it went into maquiladoras. US data show that sales to the USA from US-owned affiliates in Mexico increased 19.6 per cent annually in nominal terms from 1986 to 1995. Worldwide, sales to the USA from US-owned affiliates increased only 8.6 per cent annually.

Japan's Outward FDI

What are the similarities—and differences—between Japanese and US FDI? Table 7.2 gives the basic data, and several points are immediately apparent.

First, the preponderance of investment to advanced countries is as great for Japan as for the USA, with the USA the dominant host. This is almost entirely horizontal FDI. A distinctive feature of Japan's multinationals is the way their export strategy has interacted with their investment strategy. The heaviest Japanese investments in the USA in the 1970s were in distribution rather than production so Japanese companies could market their durable-goods exports, such as automobiles. Subsequent investment in productive facilities occurred in those sectors where widespread distribution networks had been set up.

Another result of this export success was that the threat of quantitative restrictions on exports, starting in the late 1970s, turned into a significant motivator for Japanese FDI in the USA and Europe. Gittelman and Dunning (1992)

Kravis and Lipsey took this finding to imply that there were economies of scale in export production that made output cheaper to produce in larger markets.

[9] When oil, finance, and real estate investments are excluded from the totals (not shown), Singapore's share of output sold back to the USA leaps to almost 36%, while Mexico's increases to nearly 41%.

Table 7.2. Japan: direct investment position abroad (1994) and sales by affiliates (1991) (millions of US dollars or percentage)

Area	Direct investment position	Share	Affiliate sales	Share	Percentage of Japanese affiliate sales sold in Japan
All countries	436,606	100.0	498,000	100.0	14.2
Advanced	316,980	68.4	402,000	80.7	12.8
of which:					
USA	194,429	41.9	229,000	46.0	12.2
European Union 15	84,283	18.2	133,000	26.7	9.5
of which:					
United Kingdom	33,830	7.3	61,000	12.2	7.4
Australia	23,932	5.2	22,000	4.4	37.9
Developing	146,626	31.6	96,000	19.3	20.1
of which:					
Latin America	55,617	12.0	9,000	1.8	28.7
of which:					
Brazil	8,849	1.9	3,000	0.6	41.8
Asia	76,219	16.4	83,000	16.7	18.7
of which:					
Greater China	22,610	4.9	26,000	5.2	19.9
Indonesia	16,981	3.7	1,000	0.2	12.5
Singapore	9,535	2.1	29,000	5.8	20.0
Thailand	7,184	1.5	5,000	1.0	19.5
Malaysia	6,357	1.4	6,000	1.2	19.7
Africa	7,697	1.7	n.a.	n.a.	n.a.
Middle East	4,736	1.0	n.a.	n.a.	n.a.
East Europe and Former Soviet Union	765	0.2	n.a.	n.a.	n.a.
of which:					
Russia	386	0.1	n.a.	n.a.	n.a.
Hungary	338	0.1	n.a.	n.a.	n.a.

Notes: Greater China is China and Hong Kong. EU is the EU 12 for sales data.

Sources: Investment Position is from OECD (1997). Sales data are based on Kimura (1998, table 5.1: 115–16).

found that Japanese investment in both the USA and Europe responded to such threats, though investment activity in the USA seemed to lead investment activity in Europe by several years during the 1980s. While the Japanese were putting most of their efforts into productive facilities in the USA in the early 1980s, they were still expanding their distribution network investments in Europe. In both the USA and Europe, after investment in productive facilities, follow-on investment arrived to establish local production of inputs.[10]

A second characteristic of Japanese FDI is the significant amount of resource-based FDI, particularly in Latin America and Australia (see Caves 1993; and Drake and Caves 1992). We see from Table 7.2 that around one-third of output from Japanese FDI in these regions is exported back to Japan.

The third feature of Japanese FDI is its role in the development of the wider East Asian economy, and the extent to which it has involved relocation of Japanese production to lower wage economies as a base from which to supply the Japanese market and export to third markets. While FDI played only a modest role in the development of some of the first wave of Asian newly industrialized countries (Taiwan and Korea), it has played a much larger role in the second wave, with the share of foreign affiliates in manufacturing sales exceeding 40 per cent in Thailand, the Philippines, Malaysia, and Singapore. In fact, while Japanese manufacturing FDI to developing countries as a group stagnated from the mid-1970s to at least the late 1980s, FDI to Asia increased steadily (Takeuchi 1991). Japanese investments in some of these countries are given in Table 7.2.

Much of this investment is vertical, and column 5 indicates the relatively high levels of sales by these affiliates back to the Japanese market. This figure certainly understates the extent to which this is vertical FDI; less than half the output is sold in the host country, and much goes to other affiliates in the region. Exports to Japan have been particularly important in general machinery, electrical and electronic machinery and equipment, transport equipment, and precision equipment, and most sales back to Japan are to the parent company.

Kimura (1998) contrasted the activities of majority-owned Japanese affiliates in East Asia (specifically, Korea, Taiwan, Hong Kong, Singapore, Malaysia, Thailand, Philippines, Indonesia, and China) with those in the rest of the world. Japan's Asian affiliates are much more likely to be part of vertically integrated production networks, while the non-Asian affiliates are more likely to serve foreign markets horizontally. Not only do the Asian affiliates sell more back to Japan, they also sell a much higher share of their production to Japanese affiliates.

The importance of production costs in choice of locations was confirmed by a firm-level survey, analysed by Mody *et al.* (1998) (MDS). Japanese firms investing in Asia were motivated partly by high Japanese capital costs. Raw

[10] See also Barrell and Pain (1999) for Japanese investments and trade restraints. The experience of Japanese multinational expansion into the USA and Europe points to one other determinant of location, the real exchange rate. A number of authors have found a correlation between a home-country appreciation and increased investment into the market with the depreciated rate, and Japanese investment into the USA is one example of this (Drake and Caves 1992). When assets become cheaper, buyers emerge. For further research, see especially Blonigen (1997) and Froot and Stein (1991).

labour costs did not prove an attractor, but labour quality did, suggesting that unit labour costs rather than raw labour costs mattered, since labour costs throughout Asia are lower than in Japan. Finally, a firm's export propensity from Japan was negatively correlated with the firm's share of investment in Asia. MDS interpret this to mean that Japanese firms have not invested in Asia under threat of trade barriers. Rather, they have gone in search of efficient production and low-cost inputs.

Reviewing changes in the pattern of Japanese FDI since 1972, Kojima (1995) shows both a changing composition of investments, and a geographical broadening of those investments throughout Asia. The concentration in manufacturing has declined, with a rapid increase in service investment; the average labour skill requirements have increased correspondingly. Broadening also took place significantly, with investment spreading in waves from early host countries to neighbours. In 1972, for example, the top three Asian locations for machinery manufacturing (Singapore, Taiwan, and Korea) held 81.5 per cent of total Japanese investment stock in machinery manufacturing in Asia. By 1989, the top three (Thailand, Singapore, and Taiwan) held only 51.3 per cent of the total. And Thailand, which held 5.1 per cent of the total in 1972, moved up to first place by 1989, with 18.6 per cent.

Europe's Outward FDI

Table 7.3 summarizes the European Union 15's outward FDI flows between 1992 and 1994. The first thing to notice is the enormous share of intra-European investment flows. More than two-thirds of FDI flows stayed within Europe during those years, although this share appears to have peaked in 1992, falling to 44 per cent in 1997.

This peak was likely related to the EU's Single Market Programme. Barrell and Pain (1997), based on Pain (1997) and Pain and Lansbury (1997), report that UK and German investment to the rest of the EU from the 1980s up until 1992 rose sharply in those sectors that previously had the highest barriers to cross-border market entry. Among the EU 12, intra-EU investment averaged 29.9 per cent of total outward investment from 1984 to 1988, and 61.7 per cent during the next five years, to 1993 (European Commission 1995, 1997).

EU policy measures have affected more than just the level of intra-EU flows. Baldwin *et al.* (1996) reported above-trend increases in investment into Spain and Portugal after those two countries joined the EU in 1986. Furthermore, during the early years of the creation of the Single Market, foreign investment fell in the European countries not participating, in particular the countries of the European Free Trade Area. After it became clear that many of them would link to the EU through the European Economic Area, investment recovered.

What then can we say about horizontal and vertical investment by the Europeans? Excellent firm-level data exist for Swedish multinationals, and these

Table 7.3. European Union 15: direct investment flows abroad (millions of US dollars or percentage)

Area	1994	1993	1992	Average share 1992–4
All countries	75,952	75,367	87,112	100.0
Advanced	61,364	64,261	81,662	86.6
of which:				
European Union 15	50,342	47,079	63,969	67.4
USA	7,651	16,147	9,010	13.9
Developing	14,588	11,106	5,449	13.4
of which:				
Latin America	5,713	2,968	3,862	5.3
of which:				
Argentina	597	265	395	0.5
Asia	3,464	2,308	1,551	3.1
of which:				
Malaysia	520	665	521	0.7
Greater China	202	364	−243	0.2
Africa	620	126	911	0.7
of which:				
Morocco	259	172	96	0.2
South Africa	83	158	443	0.3
Middle East	335	62	276	0.3
East Europe and FSU	4,006	4,152	3,096	4.8
of which:				
Czech Republic	1,143	951	997	1.3
Hungary	1,002	1,425	1,284	1.6
Poland	736	888	299	0.8
Russia	419	146	n.a.	0.2

Notes: Figures are for equity and other capital outflows to affiliates and do not include reinvested earnings. Greater China is China and Hong Kong.

Source: European Commission (1997).

have become almost as heavily researched as US multinationals.[11] Regarding horizontal investment, Ekholm (1998) found that distance and plant-level scale economies were negatively related to the decision to serve a market through affiliate sales, rather than exports. However, once this decision had been made affirmatively, distance was positively correlated with the level of affiliate sales relative to total Swedish sales (affiliate sales plus exports). Higher transport

[11] The Industrial Institute for Economic and Social Research (IUI) completed six surveys between 1970 and 1994. An early and important study based on these surveys was Swedenborg (1979). The papers in Braunerhjelm and Ekholm (1998) are among the latest making use of these surveys.

costs were also weakly related to higher affiliate sales, even after taking account of distance.

Ireland presents a compelling case study of vertical and horizontal investment by Europeans and by outsiders into Europe. As Barry and Bradley (1997) show, more than 85 per cent of the gross output of foreign-owned manufacturing plants is exported, and more than 65 per cent of intermediates used by these plants are imported, emphasizing that these plants are firmly in a vertical chain of production. However, the destination of exports shows that some are clearly horizontal, while others are probably vertical. For example, UK-owned plants export only 39 per cent of their output, but of this, almost 60 per cent goes to the UK. US-owned plants export 96 per cent of their output, but only 7.9 per cent goes back to the USA—less than the share of total Irish manufacturing exports to the USA. Instead, almost 80 per cent stays within the EU (including Ireland).

One aspect of Ireland's role as an export platform is the importance of agglomeration economies. Barry and Bradley report that surveys of executives in the computer, instrument engineering, pharmaceutical, and chemical sectors show that their decision to locate in Ireland is strongly influenced by the presence of other key firms in their industries.

At the eastern end of the EU, Central and Eastern Europe (CEE) is now integrating into European production networks. European investors are the dominant participants in these newly opened economies, particularly investors from Germany and Austria. The total direct investment position at the end of 1995 in the Czech Republic, Hungary, and Poland was $24 billion, of which 68.7 per cent came from the EU 15, with 34 per cent from Germany and Austria alone.

Hungary offers the best example of the relationship between FDI and trade in Eastern Europe. It has been the primary spot for investment in CEE, attracting the largest absolute and relative (to GDP) flows, on average 5 per cent of GDP annually from 1990 to 1997 (Kaminski and Riboud forthcoming). Kaminski and Riboud show that foreign-invested firms have been the driving forces behind Hungary's increasing exports. In 1989, these firms were responsible for 10.4 per cent of Hungary's exports. By 1997, they were responsible for 74.2 per cent. The authors speculate that many of the exports by foreign-invested firms are actually intra-firm, since many of the firms locating in Hungary are subsidiaries of large multinationals with known international production networks. For example, exports of piston engines leaped from $85 million in 1993 to $1.5 billion in 1997. Not coincidentally, between those two years Volkswagen established Audi Hungaria Motor as a greenfield investment to assemble piston engines. Although not quite as dramatic, other networks have been established, particularly in electronics with subsidiaries of Philips and IBM. One other result of the integration of Hungary with production networks is that exports to the EU have changed from natural resource- and unskilled labour-intensive in 1989, to technology- and skilled labour-intensive in 1997.

One other aspect of European investment deserves special mention. Given the number of Europe's countries with imperial histories, patterns of European FDI show the importance of cultural linkages and colonial heritage. For example, between 1992 and 1994 France's cumulative flows of FDI to Morocco totalled $287 million, while cumulative flows to South Africa totalled $56 million. In contrast, the UK's flows to Morocco totalled only $90 million, while flows to South Africa measured $1.3 billion.

Conclusions

The patterns of FDI and the results of empirical research produce several areas of agreement among scholars regarding the geography of international investment. Distance and market size are extremely important in determining where firms establish their foreign affiliates. Adjusting for market size, a large share of investment stays close to home, and adjusting for distance, a large share of investment heads towards the countries with the biggest markets. In fact, the majority of the world's direct investment is horizontal, designed to serve customers in a host-country market rather than in the worldwide market. As a result, most investment can be found in the advanced industrial countries.

However, the direction of investment has shifted in the 1990s, with a larger share heading towards developing countries. Of these, China dominates. Relative to developed-country investment, much of this is vertical. As seen in the cases of US and Japanese investment, affiliates in developing countries sell a larger share of their output to their home countries than do affiliates in developed countries. Even so, on average, affiliates in developing countries sell a majority of their output in their host economies.

Recently, the competition for FDI inflows has grown fiercer, with the transition countries and other developing countries making efforts to attract multinationals. In addition, technological change and an open world trade environment allow firms to split production processes more easily. Combined with the fact that multinationals are active traders—exports from parents and affiliates together dominate world trade—these patterns raise a number of issues for the future. One is whether the developing countries will continue to attract an increasing share of investment flows. Another is how much higher vertical investment will rise as a share of total investment. The final pattern to watch will be the growth of developing country multinationals. Developing countries control only a small portion of world outward direct investment stock, but their share is rising. Their future activities will confirm what we know about distance, host-country market size, and the dominance of horizontal investment, or suggest new questions about the location of multinational firms.

References

Audretsch, David B. 1998. Agglomeration and the location of innovative activity. *Oxford Review of Economic Policy*, 14/2 (Summer), 18–29.

Baldwin, Richard E., Forslid, Rikard, and Haaland, Jan I. 1996. Investment creation and diversion in Europe. *The World Economy*, 19/6 (Nov.), 635–59.

Barrell, Ray, and Pain, Nigel 1997. Foreign direct investment, technological change, and economic growth within Europe. *Economic Journal*, 107/445 (Nov.), 1770–86.

—— —— 1999. Trade restraints and Japanese direct investment flows. *European Economic Review*, 43/1 (Jan.), 29–45.

Barry, Frank, and Bradley, John 1997. FDI and trade: the Irish host-country experience. *Economic Journal*, 107/445 (Nov.), 1798–1811.

Blomström, Magnus, and Kokko, Ari O. 1994. Home country effects of foreign direct investment: Sweden. In *Canadian-Based Multinationals*, ed. Steven Globerman. Industry Canada Research Series, vol. iv. Calgary: University of Calgary Press, 341–64.

—— —— 1997. How foreign investment affects host countries. Washington: World Bank Policy Research Working Paper No. 1745 (Mar.).

—— —— 1998. Multinational corporations and spillovers. *Journal of Economic Surveys*, 12/3 (July), 247–77.

Blonigen, Bruce A. 1997. Firm-specific assets and the link between exchange rates and foreign direct investment. *American Economic Review*, 87/3 (June), 447–65.

Brainard, S. Lael 1997. An empirical assessment of the proximity-concentration trade-off between multinational sales and trade. *American Economic Review*, 87/4 (Sept.), 520–44.

Braunerhjelm, Pontus, and Ekholm, Karolina, eds. 1998. *The Geography of Multinational Firms*. Economics of Science, Technology and Innovation Series. Boston: Kluwer Academic Publishers.

Caves, Richard E. 1993. Japanese investment in the United States: lessons for the economic analysis of foreign investment. *The World Economy*, 16: 279–300.

—— 1996. *Multinational Enterprise and Economic Analysis*, 2nd edn. Cambridge Surveys of Economic Literature. Cambridge: Cambridge University Press.

Drake, Tracey A., and Caves, Richard E. 1992. Changing determinants of Japanese foreign investment in the United States. *Journal of the Japanese and International Economies*, 6: 228–46.

Dunning, John H. 1993. *Multinational Enterprises and the Global Economy*. Wokingham: Addison-Wesley.

Ekholm, Karolina 1998. Proximity advantages, scale economies, and the location of production. In Braunerhjelm and Ekholm, 1998: 59–76.

European Commission 1995. *European Union Direct Investment, 1984–1993*. Luxembourg: Office for Official Publications of the European Communities.

—— 1997. *European Union Direct Investment—Yearbook 1996*. Luxembourg: Office for Official Publications of the European Communities.

Feenstra, Robert C., and Hanson, Gordon H. 1997. Foreign direct investment and relative wages: evidence from Mexico's maquiladoras. *Journal of International Economics*, 42: 371–93.

Froot, Kenneth A., and Stein, Jeremy C. 1991. Exchange rates and foreign direct investment: an imperfect capital markets approach. *Quarterly Journal of Economics*, 107/4 (Nov.), 1191–1217.

Fujita, Masahisa, Krugman, Paul, and Venables, Anthony J. 1999. *The Spatial Economy: Cities, Regions, and International Trade*. Cambridge, Mass.: MIT Press.

Gittelman, Michelle, and Dunning, John H. 1992. Japanese multinationals in Europe and the United States: some comparisons and contrasts. In *Multinationals in the New Europe and Global Trade*, ed. Michael W. Klein and Paul J. J. Welfens. Berlin and Heidelberg: Springer Verlag, 237–68.

Helpman, Elhanan 1984. A simple theory of international trade with multinational corporations. *Journal of Political Economy*, 92/3: 451–71.

—— 1985. Multinational corporations and trade structure. *Review of Economic Studies*, 52 (July), 443–57.

—— and Krugman, Paul 1985. *Market Structure and Foreign Trade*. Cambridge, Mass.: MIT Press.

Horstmann, Ignatius, and Markusen, James 1987. Strategic investments and the development of multinationals. *International Economic Review*, 28/1 (Feb.), 109–21.

Kaminski, Bartlomiej, and Riboud, Michelle forthcoming. Foreign investment and restructuring: the evidence from Hungary. World Bank Technical Paper in the Europe and Central Asia Poverty Reduction and Economic Management Series.

Kimura, Fukunari 1998. Japanese multinationals and regional integration in Asia. In *Asia & Europe: Beyond Competing Regionalism*, ed. Kiichiro Fukasaku, Fukunari Kimura, and Shujiro Urata. Brighton: Sussex Academic Press, 111–33.

Kojima, Kiyoshi 1995. Dynamics of Japanese direct investment in East Asia. *Hitotsubashi Journal of Economics*, 36/2 (Dec.), 93–124.

Kravis, Irving B., and Lipsey, Robert E. 1982. The Location of overseas production and production for export by US multinational firms. *Journal of International Economics*, 12/3–4 (May), 201–23.

Leamer, Edward E., and Levinsohn, James 1995. International trade theory: the evidence. In *Handbook of International Economics, Volume III*, ed. Gene M. Grossman and Kenneth Rogoff. Amsterdam: Elsevier Science, 1339–94.

Markusen, James R. 1995. The boundaries of multinational enterprise and the theory of international trade. *Journal of Economic Perspectives*, 9/2 (spring), 169–89.

—— and Venables, Anthony J. 1998. Multinational firms and the new trade theory. *Journal of International Economics*, 46/2 (Dec.), 183–203.

Mody, Ashoka, Dasgupta, Susmita, and Sinha, Sarbajit 1998. Japanese multinationals in Asia: drivers and attractors. *Oxford Development Studies*, 27/2 (June), 149–64.

Organization for Economic Co-operation and Development (OECD) 1997. *International Direct Investment Statistics Yearbook 1997*. Paris: OECD.

Pain, Nigel 1997. Continental drift: European integration and the location of UK foreign direct investment. *The Manchester School Supplement*, 65: 94–117.

—— and Lansbury, Melanie 1997. Regional economic integration and foreign direct investment: the case of German investment in Europe. *National Institute Economic Review*, 160 (April, issue 2/97), 87–99.

Radelet, Steven, and Sachs, Jeffrey 1998. Shipping costs, manufactured exports, and economic growth. Mimeo, Harvard University (Centre for International Development/Harvard Institute for International Development Research on Geography and Economic Growth). Presented at the American Economics Association annual meeting, Jan.

Shatz, Howard J. 1999. US multinational exports from developing countries. Mimeo, Centre for International Development at Harvard University and World Bank (Dec.)

SMITH, ALASDAIR 1987. Strategic investment, multinational corporations and trade policy. *European Economic Review*, 31 (Feb.–Mar.), 89–96.

SWEDENBORG, BIRGITTA 1979. *The Multinational Operations of Swedish Firms: An Analysis of Determinants and Effects*. Stockholm: The Industrial Institute of Economic and Social Research.

TAKEUCHI, KENJI 1991. Does Japanese foreign direct investment promote Japanese imports of manufactures from developing economies? *Asian Economic Journal*, 5/1: 19–39.

UNITED NATIONS CONFERENCE ON TRADE AND DEVELOPMENT (UNCTAD) 1998. *World Investment Report 1998: Trends and Determinants*. New York and Geneva: United Nations.

—— 1999. Extract from Foreign Direct Investment/Transnational Corporations Database (electronic communication). New York and Geneva: United Nations.

VENABLES, ANTHONY J., and LIMAO, NUNO 1999. Geographical disadvantage; a von Thunen model of international specialization. Mimeo, World Bank.

WHEELER, DAVID, and MODY, ASHOKA 1992. International investment location decisions: the case of US firms. *Journal of International Economics*, 33/1–2 (Aug.), 57–76.

WORLD BANK 1999. Global Development Finance and World Development Indicators Central Database (electronic database). Washington: The World Bank.

Chapter **8**

Globalization, Localization, and Trade

Michael Storper

Globalization and Specialization

When we think of globalization, it brings to mind the image of rapidly expanding flows of goods, services, and capital across national borders. One day, it seems, our economies will become more global than they are national, just as in the past, regional economies seem to have lost out to national production networks. For many, this means that we will become more dependent on decisions and development processes controlled from outside our nation-states. For most economists, the expansion of trade permits greater specialization, which is the effect of adjustments to a more efficient locational pattern as markets become more integrated. The standard version of trade theory simply upgrades Ricardo, asserting that the factor content of trade is driven by the underlying geographical distribution of factors of production; hence, by working backward from trade, it derives location as the mirror image of trade. More recent versions add in such forces as economies of scale and product differentiation, but they also assume that trade liberalization calls forth determinate locational changes (Helpman and Krugman 1985). This theoretical stance fits well with the state of empirical research, since trade statistics are readily available and it is relatively easy to track the evolution of trade in goods, whereas it is extremely difficult to measure location at an international scale.

Trade theory does correctly predict the rough match between labor-intensive low-wage activities (or low-skill capital-intensive activities) and labor-rich developing areas. This is reflected in the factor composition of a significant

This chapter was initially prepared as a public lecture to the Suntory and Toyota International Centre for Economics and Related Disciplines, at the London School of Economics, 6 November 1998.

amount of trade between poorer and richer areas. It can also provide a starting point for understanding subsequent adjustments of output composition, product prices, and wages in more developed areas in the face of such trade. As an account of the geography of economic development, however, it falls quite short.

When it comes to complexly organized production systems and locational processes among highly developed economies, trade theory cannot be used to explain locational patterns and processes. This is because location is itself driven by complex forces, and it is an independent motor of trade. Among these forces are spatial interdependence and proximity relations, economies of scale, localized technological evolution, and international knowledge flows.[1] Standard notions such as factor content, even when they can be measured at a very fine empirical level, do not help us understand many of the processes underlying location and specialization. Trade certainly affects locational pressures, but there is not a seamless interrelationship between location and trade. Thus, by building a framework based on locational analysis, we can shed clearer light on the causes and consequences of globalization than via trade theory alone.

A Theory Based on 'Moderate Complexity'

Both trade and location studies tend to oscillate between an endlessly complex series of monographic or sectorally specific descriptions and super-complicated modeling exercises. I would like to try something different here, which is based on the principle of moderate complexity in theorizing, hopefully enough to give a reasonable picture of reality, but not so much as to eliminate the possibility of making sensible generalizations.

To do this, I want to make five propositions:

1. to understand location, we have to understand the organization of production, because the latter mediates the relationship between the location of a given kind of activity and geographically differentiated factor and product markets;[2]

[1] More recently, the New Trade Theory has focused its efforts on one of these, economies of scale (Helpman and Kruglan 1985).

[2] For non-economists, this refers to the non-mainstream notion that the mix of economic factors used in an activity comes in a package, and this package is not defined exclusively by economizing on the most expensive factors or even by achieving the cheapest mix of such factors, but by a host of more complex considerations, such as the technology used and the evolution of the product's qualities ('specific factors models'). These create non-separable 'packages' of factor demands, so that the kind of activity found in a given place has a very complex relationship to the costs of factors found there. This finding was empirically validated for world trade in the 1950s by Leontief, who showed that labor-rich poor countries had a higher capital content in their manufacturing exports than rich countries. He called this the 'contrary factor intensities paradox'. Thus, factor content is often a very poor explanation of why a certain activity goes to a certain place, and hence it is very hazardous to try and read location from the factor content of trade.

2. the relationship between the organization of production and location can be roughly captured as two kinds of transactional structures, between an activity and its product markets (downstream) and between the different parts of the production system tied up in intermediate production tasks (upstream). This is an analytical way of describing the relationship between an activity and its two most important environments, its market and its necessary partners and suppliers;
3. traditionally, transactions have been defined as hard exchanges of goods, labor, and money, and expressed through formal instruments such as contracts. As we shall see, however, they also include soft and untraded interdependencies, involving knowledge, ideas, human relations, rules, and conventions;
4. technology is a strong structuring force behind these transactions, and a strong motor of change;
5. the local and international geography of soft transactions or interdependencies has important impacts on technological evolution of sectors, and hence on their locational patterns and trade.

In other words, location has a structuring influence on both trade and on growth rates in different places.

To begin the task of analysis based on these principles, we can start where a lot of economics and location theory has always started, which is with transport costs. The standard and largely correct statement made by trade economists is that transport costs and a host of other costs involved in carrying out market transactions are falling in real terms. All other things equal, this should promote globalization, because many activities can locate at greater distance from their markets than before. Activities concentrate close to their needed inputs, and this generates greater locational concentration and hence, specialization of regional economies. We will call this the TTM part of our model ('transactions and transport to market').

The other part of the locational problem is how economic activities relate to each other. One way to synthesize this complex issue is by drawing on notions of economic organization based in the division of labor. Rather than the firm as a unit of observation, however, we will use physical units of production, for they are the central concerns of an analysis which seeks to understand output and trade. An establishment is a place where transactions between a certain group of tasks or activities are internalized under one roof; so a large-scale business establishment is, in this sense, a large set of transactions internalized under this roof.

Modern economic activity is also carried out through a complex external division of labor between establishments, firms, and industries, which in turn have to relate to each other through transactions: about two-thirds of the buying and selling in advanced economies is at this intermediate level. This intra-

and inter-industry input–output structure has a geography. If an industry has a more fragmented or complex upstream division of labor, there will be more transactions between firms necessary to get to a final product. Under some circumstances, it is efficient for establishments to concentrate together in geographical space and to accept (as a kind of tradeoff) the higher resulting transport costs to market. The standard reasons for firms to depend on spatial proximity to certain kinds of other firms consist of 'hard' transactional efficiencies (ease of inter-firm buying and selling). But recent research has broadened the sources of such proximity relations to include various kinds of 'soft' externalities, such as local knowledge spillovers between firms (Feldman 1993; Audretsch and Vivarelli 1994), and dependence on human relations, rules, and customs which enable firms to coordinate under conditions of uncertainty or complexity (Storper 1997). All of these forces tend to generate locational concentration, intra-industry trade, and territorial economic specialization.[3] In addition to this process of inter-firm agglomeration, the existence of a big plant (i.e. activities clustered 'inside' a plant), would have a similar result: the locational concentration of output.[4] Both stand in opposition to a scattered or random geographical pattern of output.

In order to have a workable shorthand, let us label all of these forces which generate geographical concentration of output as TEKSS (upstream transactions, externalities, knowledge spillovers, and scale). These two groups of forces, TTM and TEKSS, will serve as the horizontal and vertical axes of a conceptual framework to be used for shedding light on some of the major manifestations of globalization and localization today (Fig. 8.1).

The Forces that Generate Proximity

Let us begin by introducing some complexity into the horizontal axis, TTM. The standard story about declining transport cost barriers, though true for many cases, tends to ignore that downstream transactional costs are not just determined by the means of transacting (transport) but by the complexity of what we ask the transport system to do. So, even if transport costs are falling generally, if we have more irregular shipments, smaller lots, or other demands which make the task of transporting more complex or uncertain, it is very possible that transport costs will rise. In an economy where some products

[3] Because we have a more sophisticated idea of the division of labor, outcomes are both dynamic and uncertain. Simple conceptions of the outcomes, such as those of the product cycle, are now replaced by a notion that technological change can bring about locational concentration by creating divisions of labor that create stronger spatial interdependencies, or that it can bring about locational spread by changing the divison of labor so as to create a need for fewer or longer-distance transactions.

[4] Indeed, this problem has been recognized formally via the construction of the Ellison–Glaeser (1997) agglomeration measure, which separates plant size influence from the role of clustering.

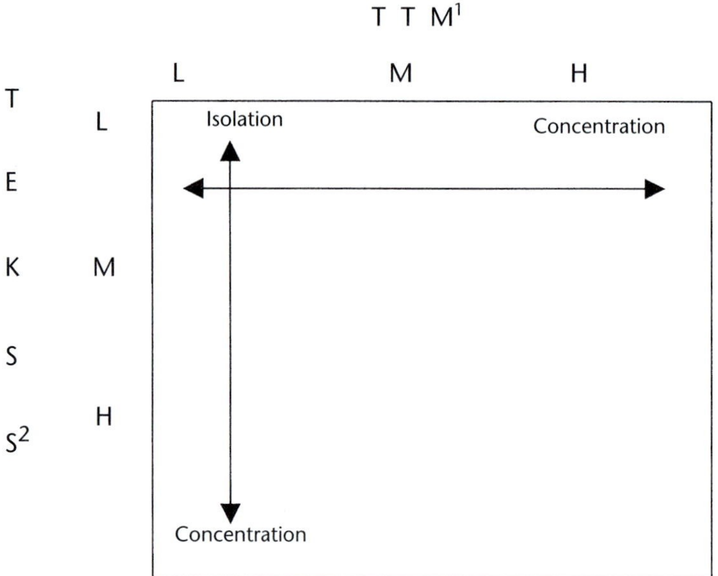

Fig. 8.1. The forces that affect location: proximity and markets

Notes: [1] Transport and transactions to market.
[2] Transaction, externalities, knowledge spillovers, scale.

are becoming more and more tailored to customer demand and increasingly service-intensive, market-oriented locations will thus remain efficient for many goods and services.

It is on the TEKSS, or vertical axis of our model, however, that outcomes are likely to be especially complex and changeable. There are two contemporary forces in the economy which tend to make upstream transactions more complex and more costly. First, in many industries, producers are obliged to organize themselves for great quantitative output flexibility and frequent product changeovers. These sectors include the frontier high technology sectors, design-intensive consumer goods, and some service-intensive or differentiated high quality manufactured goods. They achieve such flexibility in part through recourse to external suppliers. If high fixed costs are avoided through externalization, the latter may also raise transactions costs. One way to ensure immediate availability of a wide range of external resources with low search and transactions costs is via geographical proximity of suppliers (Scott 1988). Thus, there are powerful forces at the center of today's industrial system which may generate locational concentration in spite of declining transport costs.

The importance of scale economies is the centerpiece of the New Trade Theory (Krugman 1991; Helpman and Krugman 1985). In place of constant returns to scale, divisibility and hence perfect competition in geographical space, they introduce scale economies, locational concentration, and imperfect competition over space. The theory predicts greater overall economic specialization, because when market territories for particular goods and services are defined by their scale characteristics, they create territorial 'shadows' or oligopoly effects around them. One particularly important form such specialization will take is that of increased intra-industry trade, as production of intermediate goods is freed to rise to its efficient minimal scale levels, instead of being redundantly present in many places.

There are, however, kinds of linkages between firms other than those which are based on traded input–output relations. For example, firms in many industries cluster together, even though they do not have many of these traded input–output relations at the local level. Most of the surveys on the subject suggest that they stay in the same place as other firms in their business in order to make sure that they are close to the 'action', usually defined as being in a context where they can be sure to get access to the latest ideas on how products or markets are changing (e.g. Saxenian 1994). Often, they cite access to a certain kind of labor, even though much labor may come from outside the local labor market. In still other cases, firms suggest that they use proximity to help with the flow of ideas or negotiations, even though—as we know—information is cheap and easy to transport. What are we to make, analytically speaking, of this kind of evidence?

It suggests that there are what we might call 'soft' and 'indirect', that is, non-traded, interdependencies among firms, essentially having to do with spillovers of knowledge or ideas which those firms consider necessary to stay on top of the competitive process. They seem to be especially important in industries in a particular kind of technological regime—with non-standardized products, complex goods or services involving a lot of customized and negotiated content, or products and services where technology (in the sense of hardware or product designs) changes a lot. These interdependencies are substantively complex, often intangible, only occasionally involving the explicit and formal transaction of ideas or knowledge. This is because some kinds of knowledge or ideas are sufficiently complex or changing that they resist codification, which would in turn make it possible for them to be communicated in an anonymous, depersonalized way and hence to transcend the barriers of distance.

In general, ideas with substantive complexity and low codification will require direct human relations for their successful exchange (Boden and Molotch 1994). Human relations, as vehicles for idea exchange, have quantitative and qualitative dimensions. The quantitative dimension is that it is relatively expensive to transfer people every time we want to transfer an idea, especially in time-opportunity cost. In qualitative terms, the absence of codification implies that a variety of communicative structures and interpersonal processes is needed to get the message through, interpreted correctly, and adjusted and readjusted to concrete circumstances through trial and error and reading between the lines (Cowan and Foray 1997). Communication thus becomes complex and conventional, embedded in webs of relations (Lundvall 1993).[5] This is why most theories of the information age are fundamentally inadequate, because they treat information as disembodied bits of knowledge in relationship to hardware (as in Castells 1996). Because of their conventional and relational content, the cost and time required to make relations cover vast distances and to reach many users can be quite high. The supply structures for these ideas and knowledge are thus characterized by small numbers (due to lack of transparency and easy reproducibility), and hence the 'markets' for exchanging such ideas are strongly imperfect. Knowledge and idea spillovers are not only geographically limited in these cases, but the places where they are produced have the advantages of possessing economically rare, specific, and difficult-to-imitate resources.

Paul Krugman (1995) has argued that while these phenomena may exist, they 'leave no paper trail'. He means that there is no easy way to measure them directly, and he is right. He concludes that therefore we should not bother with them as a possible source of localization externalities, and hence as a driver of specialization and trade. In contrast, the argument is that they may be one of the principal reasons why, in an era of declining transport costs, so many specialized clusters of producers have made or reinforced their appearance on the landscape of contemporary capitalism. It seems impossible to account for such major complexes as Silicon Valley, the pharmaceuticals industry in New Jersey or Switzerland, the City of London, or Hollywood, or a host of other world-important, highly performing regional economies, with any other kind of reasoning.[6] Moreover, the persistence of these clusters in spite of certain forms of internationalization of their knowledge (to which we will return shortly) would seem to be evidence of locational path dependency, in turn rooted in the evolutionary trajectories not so much of their hard input–output structures, but rather of their underlying webs of human relations.

Some Patterns of Development

Now that we have explored some aspects of TTMs and TEKSS, we can put them together to characterize analytically some major geographical patterns of different sectors (or closely interlinked groups of activities) found today. Figure 8.2[7] suggests three levels of intensity for each axis, from low to high transactions

[5] Lundvall (1993) suggests a triad of what kind of knowledge, who has it, and why is it needed?

[6] I argue this point at some lenth in Storper (1997, chs. 1 and 2).

[7] The inspiration for this figure comes from my colleague Allen Scott at the University of California, Los Angeles, especially the top and bottom rows, but I have redefined the axes and added the middle row.

		TTM[1] L	TTM[1] M	TTM[1] H
TEKSS[2]	L	Isolated scattered plants		Market-area locations for isolated plants
	M	Big scattered plants; big interconnected clusters	Big interconnected plants	Big market-oriented plants
	H	Interconnected clusters	Superclusters (Metro economies)	Isolated clusters market-area located

Fig. 8.2. Locational patterns

Notes: [1] Transport and transactions to market.
[2] Transaction, externalities, knowledge spillovers, scale.

and transport to market, and from low to high upstream transactions, externalities, knowledge spillovers, and scale.

In order to use the ideas set forth above, some adjustments are necessary. For the present purposes, there is analytical similarity between a big establishment and a cluster, in that both bring about locational concentration of output and should give rise to economic specialization and interregional or international trade. In practice, however, it is unlikely that the scale of a single establishment will compare to that of a cluster. Hence, in Figure 8.2, we are going to consider big establishments[8] as a medium level of TEKSS, and only the biggest establishments will be classified as high TEKSS cases, that is, quantitatively equivalent to clusters. Having done this, we can now examine a realistic typology of cases.

Take the upper left case, where both TTMs and TEKSS are low: firms have little reason to localize with other producers, nor strong reasons to locate near markets. One would expect a random, scattered pattern of isolated producers, a sort of entropy, unless there are natural resources or other scarce factors

[8] I will define big, for this purpose, as plants with more than 5,000 employees.

involved. Given competitive markets, entry should produce relatively low levels of international trade, but we cannot be sure about this, because low TTMs might also favor such trade. Moving to the upper right case, we find high costs of getting to market, but low upstream interdependencies, and this logically will yield the locational pattern known to geographers as that of Christaller and Losch: market-serving locations, where the only driving factor is the matching of output scale to market scale, resulting in a nested hierarchy of market areas. Only for the most specialized products would we expect high levels of international trade.

On the bottom row, all the cases have high levels of upstream interdependencies. What varies is the relationship to the market. In the lower left-hand case, high upstream interconnections but low costs and difficulty of getting to market generate one of the most typical and complex geographical phenomena today, that of interconnected clusters. In any complex and long production chain, there will be many upstream stages, each with its own intricate division of labor. It is likely, moreover, that each clustered group of intermediate goods producers will serve more than one downstream client, whether in terms of firms or even whole sectors. Thus, the semiconductor industry might cluster in an area and be linked downstream to clusters elsewhere in computers, military hardware, aerospace, and so on. Even within semiconductors, several clusters might form due to differentially intense relationships in parts of the production chain. In so far as TTMs remain low, these clusters can form their own geographical centers of gravity, and ship their intermediate products—which are the 'final' outputs of the clusters—to other clusters. Equally, a large plant might cluster with its suppliers, but in turn—if its products are intermediates—ship them to other clusters. This is a geography of two levels of the division of labor: locally between firms, and interregionally or internationally between clusters. In addition to these hard input–output reasons for a hierarchical system of clusters, there are the soft forms of TEKSS that we explained earlier. Clusters based on communities of knowledge exchange and spillovers are likely to appear and to form specialized nodes in much longer production chains. This is why globalization has become so complex: it involves nested geographies of divisions of labor, knowledge spillovers, and local path-dependent learning communities. Existing industrial statistics are almost entirely incapable of illuminating these dynamics. Yet this sort of locational dynamic is probably behind high and increasing levels of international trade.

This pattern often involves transnational firms as the key agents that bring the clusters together (Blanc and Sierra 1997; Keeble and Wilkinson 1999). There has been quite a lot of polemic about the role of multinational firms in the literature, where frequently it is claimed that localized clustering and the big enterprise are somehow in opposition to each other. The multinational enterprise is said to 'eat' local economies by internalizing everything as intra-firm trade, disconnecting it from the external, market-based local environment. But this is analytically not entirely useful: the most common practice nowadays is for a big transnational to assemble the products of different clusters, often through buying–selling or alliance with other transnationals, who themselves are the key nodes in clusters.

From the standpoint of regions, the key issue is how strong and 'sticky' the local hard or soft TEKSS interdependencies are: how much do they really serve to deter new competitive entrants coming from other regions? In order to answer this question, we need both more sophisticated analyses of upstream intermediate divisions of labor, and a new geography of ideas and learning processes, or what is being defined here as 'the geography of TEKSS externalities'.

The lower right-hand case consists of high interdependencies upstream and high costs to market. In this case we are likely to get a clustered version of Loschian market geography, where what is at the center of the market area is not the firm, but a group of interrelated firms, and the cluster's scale corresponds to that of the demand in a local market area. This is different from the case we just examined, because these market-serving clusters are oriented to final demand rather than intermediate demand. As in the upper right-hand cell of Figure 8.2, international trade will result only when the minimal market area for a cluster exceeds the size of national markets.

In between these two bottom row cases is a particularly interesting set of cases. When the TEKSS forces are very strong, but costs and difficulty of getting to market are moderately strong, we enter into a complex area of elasticities between TTM advantages and TEKSS advantages. We would expect clusters of firms to reduce TTMs by having some locational relationship to their markets. But in so far as their markets are frequently other clusters of firms, the locational logic of these clusters is that of co-location with other clusters. The way that TTMs are managed in many cases is through the appearance of clusters of clusters in proximate geographical space.

There are two aspects to this co-location. On the one hand, in an economy where technological change and innovation are the motors of both hard and soft TEKSS, there is always the risk that clusters of firms will find their previous patterns of interrelationships disrupted (Lundvall and Johnson 1994). To minimize the possible effects of this, they must locate in an area where they can reconstruct such relationships and find new clients, as quickly and easily as possible. This system of co-location as a way of minimizing risk, in the presence of moderate TTMs, is one reason for the metropolitanization of specialized economic activity, as firms try to locate close to the greatest number of potential clients in the face of relationships that are highly unstable (Veltz 1996). But co-location of clusters is not due exclusively to managing change in this negative sense. We observed, in the lower left-hand cell, that separate upstream clusters relate well to each other across long distances where their TTMs are low. But if these are high, then the knowledge spillovers and positive externalities that might flow from inter-cluster relations will also require some degree of spatial proximity. Such positive benefits of soft inter-relationships such as innovation and learning, would depend on co-location of clusters caught up in longer commodity chains. For both these reasons, co-location of clusters results in the appearance of geographical superclusters, which generally take the form of complex metropolitan economies today.[9] These superclusters are increasingly caught up in interregional and international trade, because superclustering implies a distinctively uneven international location pattern.

The Other Face of Globalization: International Knowledge Flows

We arrive, finally, at the analytically most complex set of cases, those of moderate TEKSS forces and moderate TTM forces: big establishments neither entirely indifferent to their final market locations nor inexorably located near them. These cases are complex because there is a big margin of maneuver, both with respect to upstream co-location and with respect to geographical orientation to market. Elaborate supply structures are very likely involved, but they can be extended in geographical space; market relationships have moderate cost and difficulty. Outcomes are particularly difficult to derive analytically here, because the tradeoffs are so many and hence multiple elasticities are at work. There may also be considerable and multiple uncertainties and path dependencies in supply and market structures. Dunning (1995) has argued a similar point at length, claiming that trade theory in general lacks an analytical language for the most important kinds of international, intra-industry relationships today, those characterized by complex substance, and that this includes both inter-cluster and inter-establishment relations.

Predictions of locational concentration and specialization due to reinforcement of TEKSS are likely to be only part of the story. There are new forces and capabilities tugging in the other direction, that of viability for a multiplicity of locations, because of the rise of a new set of more complex international, intra-industry relations. As noted, the existence of strong TEKSS corresponds to a particular kind of technological regime, with significant process or product innovation. In the activities with moderate TEKSS, however, a different kind of technological regime is at hand: innovation occurs, but it is primarily concerned with modifying and perfecting underlying product designs. Knowledge is more codified and stable, but significant evolution is none the less occurring (Utterback 1996).

[9] These two reasons apparently outweigh the obvious disadvantages of metropolitan regions as compared to non-metropolitan areas, but they are also maintained in a state of viability by the internal expansion of metropolitan regions.

The geography of such knowledge is also likely to be quite different from the high TEKSS sectors. On the one hand, there is the well-known tendency for ICTs to become more efficient and cheaper, which permits—within limits—certain forms of even relatively complex knowledge to be transmitted over long distance and relationships to be carried out in real time. But more important are institutional developments. For example, when managers go to the same business schools or to schools that use similar ideas, even when they come from different countries, they learn to 'talk the same language'. Physicists and mathematicians have done this since Newton and Descartes, of course, and the Church did it early on through the generalization of Latin. We are not talking of a literal language here, but of a system of signifiers, which are common ways of constructing understandings so that messages flow more easily: the language of international investment, technology, and management.

This complex web of new structures and practices, of which I have just scratched the surface, is what sociologists call a new 'institutional field' which has been emerging over the last couple of decades (Zucker 1994). It has made the international sharing of economically useful knowledge and ideas more feasible, precisely by specializing in the relationships that make the global–local transfer possible. It constitutes a powerful, though not invincible force, for the long-distance exchange of partially codifiable and partially tacit, and relationally dependent knowledge.

There has been some concern with this process in international economics recently, under the guise of research into international R&D spillovers (Eaton and Kortum 1995; Coe and Helpman 1993; Mansfield and Romeo 1980). There are major productivity-boosting spillovers of US research outside US borders, and this has accelerated sharply in recent years. Less is known about the flows into the USA because of the way patent statistics are structured, but it is a good guess that the flow has been in that direction, too. That research in economics, however, does not dig into the how and where of such flows. We are suggesting that a rapidly expanding institutional field has now made it possible, under certain circumstances, for rather complex ideas and types of knowledge to flow internationally.

The effects of such knowledge exchange on location and trade may be very important, but appear to be underestimated in both the trade and location literatures. Very detailed statistical measurements produced by the CEPII in Paris (Fontagné *et al.* 1997) suggest that in the European Union, for example, intra-industry competition in the routine durable-goods manufacturing industries is accentuating in two ways. For a given, rather narrowly defined kind of output, there are greater quality variations, and within a given general kind of good, there is a greater number of European producers, in part due to their different quality strategies, and in part due to intensified head-to-head competition. Something similar is at work with respect to intermediate outputs as well. Many firms have transformed themselves into more specialized intermediate producers, but they diversify within this field (Greenaway *et al.* 1995).[10] All of this suggests that European companies are successfully restructuring to serve global markets through accentuated quality and variety differentiation, rather than necessarily shutting down some operations and concentrating them elsewhere. This is refleced in some statistical evidence that in many routine, durable-goods sectors in Europe, international trade and the presence of increasingly contestable markets are not leading to US-style patterns of regional specialization (Storper and Chen 1999).[11]

The question of how trade affects location in the presence of international knowledge flows in routine production sectors may now be reformulated. Initially, trade appears to generate some specialization effects, depending on the pattern of winners and losers. But subsequently, local producers may respond positively to this new contestability of markets. And they react using the knowledge which comes in part from trade itself: the products and efficiency levels of their new competitors signal to them what they must do, and the new institutional field described above makes this possible. Trade then becomes a vehicle of knowledge diffusion. This diffusion in turn becomes a force which helps local firms to stabilize their market shares by competing effectively with invaders. At the same time, these local companies may then invade their competitors' territories, resulting in a new international structure of market shares, but with relatively moderate change in aggregate locational patterns. Underlying this aggregate stability, however, there is now a lot more cross-border market serving than there was previously. In other words, a soft form of globalization—knowledge and idea exchange—sustains a much higher level of trade but a relatively stable international output and locational map. Two flows increase dramatically—trade in goods and exchange of ideas—without being propelled by a dramatic increase in locational and output specialization. We could say that the evolutionary technological and product dynamics of these industrial complexes depend in part on their uptake of international knowledge and its use in a specific way within the local production context.

This reasoning leads to a quite different outcome from models based solely on transport costs and imperfect competition. Venables (1996), for example,

[10] One of the most interesting potential implications of this reasoning is how it modifies the standard New Trade Theory notion. Their explanation, as noted, has to do with the way declining trade barriers allow plant-level scale economies to generate new patterns of intermediate production, with increased geographical concentration and specialization. But here we are suggesting that in a routine technological regime, international flows of knowledge might actually bring about the opposite effect, by diffusing knowledge and allowing more producers to get into the intermediates market. Especially where output levels are below the minimal optimal level (frequently the case), there is much 'room' for such intermediate producers to enter. So there could well be a situation of increasing intermediate trade and no geographical concentration for the sector.

[11] We should not forget, relative to the Krugman–Helpman analysis, that minimal-optimal scale economies are reached many times over for many goods, so that the idea of a strong locational concentration effect to reach this scale is not likely in the Triad regions.

suggests that agglomeration occurs at intermediate levels of transport costs, while dispersion comes at high and low levels. In the analysis developed here, at the intermediate level of transport costs, a great deal of spread is likely. Our view is that a broader definition of the nature of intra-industry interdependencies, and then placing them in relation to transport costs, and considering both of them in processual and evolutionary terms, is required to achieve a more plausible view of locational outcomes.

Globalization, in this way, may involve a less radical reshuffling of specializations than we have been led to believe by many theories. If this analysis is correct, the implications for European regional development—especially in contrast to the historical experience of the USA—are considerable. In so far as the location pattern of these industries was established before lowering of trade patterns and hence is relatively widely dispersed—this is the European case—then the fact of moderate TEKSS and TTMs *affects the evolution of their technological regime in a different way from what has occurred in the USA*, leading to the internationally competitive restructuring *in situ* described above. The outcome is high levels of resulting trade, high levels of international knowledge and idea flow, and maintenance of a relatively dispersed locational structure. There may be lessons from this for other regions in the world.

Reconsidering some Common Forms of Globalization

This analytical schema can be used to shed light on some common understandings of globalization (Fig. 8.3). There appear to be four essential 'tiers' in the major developed economies today: these categories consist of activities, or parts of sectors, each of which has a distinctive economic dynamic and different overall degree and type of globalization. The first is *world-serving industrial specializations, and specific-skill-based activities.* This tier consists of the most advanced activities in our economies. The tier has two distinctive parts. On the one hand, are the *winner-take-all products and services.* In industries such as financial services, media, sports, high-level corporate management, business consulting, and science and medicine, there are functions which are assured by individuals who either take part in an international labor market or where the products and services they render are identifiable, scarce, and consumed over an increasingly wide market area. The high-powered corporate attorney, the film or sports star, doctors with a global reputation, are examples. Internationalization enables them to increase their skill-specific rents because international market access now has very low marginal costs (Frank and Cook 1996). They are found in the lower left and middle boxes: they are products of very specific, highly embedded economic contexts, but now they serve world markets. Similar, but taking a very different appearance, is the second part of

TEKS[2] \ TTM[1]	L	M	H
L	Isolated scattered plants (possible international intra-industry supply chains) III		Market-area locations for isolated plants (possible international intra-industry supply chains; imports) II
M	Big scattered plants; big interconnected clusters (exports high; complex supply chains) III, IV	Big interconnected plants (exports high?) (complex supply chains) III IV	Big market-oriented plants (import supply chains)
H	Interconnected clusters (export-oriented) I	Superclusters (export-oriented) I	Isolated clusters Market-area located (import supply chain?) II

Fig. 8.3. Locational patterns and trade

Notes: [1] Transport and transactions to market.
[2] Transaction, externalities, knowledge spillovers, scale.

I: Winner-take-all, skills/expert specialize.
II: Partially or non-tradable goods and services.
III: Import-sensitive manufacturing, with division of labor.
IV: Globally contestable markets with global knowledge flows.

this tier, what we can call *export-oriented specialized industrial clusters*. In most countries, there are certain sectors or parts of sectors which that economy is particularly good at. They show up in each country's export specializations, and we know that the coefficient of difference of exports of the advanced economies has been increasing in the last twenty years, along with the growth in trade. Often these products emerge from distinctive geographical clusters within each country, which have variously been termed 'industrial districts' or 'technology districts' (Storper 1992). They correspond to the two bottom left and middle cases and can analytically now be understood in the terms we have used here.

The second tier is *locally serving partially or non-tradable goods and services*. There are many goods and services which require strong proximity to their points of delivery: their TTMs are high. This may be just the final delivery, as with some services that involve long and complex upstream commodity chains, or it may be that the chain itself is largely localized. In any case, they amount to rather large portions of total output and employment: the part that follows the geographical distribution of population and income. We often forget this in discussions of globalization, and while there is obviously a relationship between mobile and immobile activity, in the sense that population and income redistributions can occur due to the redistribution of mobile activity, in the end much of the economy is less tradable than we are led to believe. It can easily be seen that this tier corresponds to our two market-serving cases, one where there are strong local TEKSS forces, the other where this is not the case. But local delivery of many products and services is the end of a far-away production system. Non-tradables are often the end product of combining many tradables. Hence they may involve more globalization than meets the eye.

The third major tier consists of *globalization through deterritorialization* or, as it is frequently known, *global commodity chains*. This is largely routine manufacturing and services which are susceptible to offshoring to low-wage countries, because of low levels of place-specific assets in the production process. In general, these activities rely on rather low TEKSS upstream, and low TTMs. What is their overall importance? They are very visible in the countries which use them as the basis of their developmental experience, but studies which have attempted to measure their importance indirectly in terms of the degree of competition presented to low-skill workers in the developed countries by low-wage imports almost invariably conclude that it affects about 5 per cent of the total workforce in developed countries and has caused 10 to 15 per cent of the increase in wage inequality there (Mishel *et al.* 1998; Levy 1999).

Finally, there are the manufacturing and service activities which are caught up in increasingly contestable markets (in the sense of Baumol *et al.* 1982). Only some of these fall into the upper left or upper right-hand cases of Figure 8.3. Many of these cases are typified by New Trade Theory, with scale economies permitting them to serve big markets from afar; lowering of trade barriers, which lower TTMs, should lead to a less even geographical distribution of them. A good number of them fall squarely in the middle of the model, involving knowledge and idea exchange with entry, as the basis for a new geography of internationally contestable markets. These involve a more even distribution of activity than we have been led to believe, precisely because of the increasingly wide distribution of competences, initially as a consequence of trade (spurred by it), then as a substitute for further geographical rearrangement.

Two concluding observations can be made here. First, in only a few of the boxes do we find location patterns which presuppose a high degree of locational independence (isolated, footloose plants). Their exports should be perfectly consistent with the factor contents hypothesis, but they are a limited number of cases. Secondly, in virtually all the cases, we can expect rising intra-industry trade (intermediate inputs). This rise in intra-industry trade is, of course, just another way of expressing the complex input–output relationships *between* our different cases and the forms of trade they take. Unfortunately, we do not yet have good theories for such complex relationships, especially at the international level (Dunning 1995).

Growth, Convergence, Divergence: Evolutionary Trajectories of Local Economies

It is an assumption of most international economics that trade is an effective mechanism of growth rate and income convergence: trade in products brings about price and quantity adjustments in local economies and thereby causes their growth rates and income levels to converge in the long run, especially when seen in a general equilibrium framework (Grossman and Helpman 1991). The empirical evidence on growth and income convergence tells a different story, however. At a world level, growth and income convergence is not in evidence. Theory has therefore turned to the notion that convergence can only happen among economies within a certain range of 'structural' similarity, which is known as 'club convergence'. There is considerable evidence in favor of club convergence; but there are major theoretical and empirical problems with the notion (Bouba-Olga 1999; de la Fuente 1995; Barro and Sala-i-Martin 1991). On the one hand, it works only retrospectively: that is, it is not good at predicting convergence among a group of economies, but rather tends to find the structural similarities retrospectively for economies that have experienced convergence. On the other hand, it cannot account for the fact, well documented, that even among the most convergent economies, convergence seems to encounter serious limits. Western Europe experienced considerable catch-up with the USA in the postwar period. Since then, the pattern has been irregular, with countries shooting past each other in one period, and then falling behind in the next (Bouba-Olga 1999). This is true also at the level of sectors: international productivity leadership passes from one nation to the next, with countries falling behind and then catching up or shooting past their competitors. Club convergence seems to be limited and temporally irregular, in other words.

Our framework is consistent with the overall notion that the rate and direction of technical progress will differ between economies, in that the strong localization forces we have described theoretically, and the concomitant observable category of winner-take-all and world-serving specializations, describe activities with localized, strongly endogenous forms of technical change. These differences drive trade and trade does not even them out spatially. At the same time, we have suggested, in agreement with the literature, that there are likely to be processes of international knowledge exchange, and we have argued that they could permit locational patterns to persist, precisely by permitting local producers to attain world levels of productivity and product quality, and this should constitute a force for convergence. So, rather than opting for simple choices of convergence versus divergence, or exogenous versus endogenous growth theories, it is suggested here that a locational approach—rooted in organizational dynamics of production systems and technological dynamics of sectors and places—will shed light on the observable reality of spatial and temporal diversity in growth patterns. It does so specifically by providing an analytical way into the forces that affect the specialization of places. Trade certainly contributes to these dynamics, but in and of itself tells us rather little about them.

Conclusion: Trade is Not a Palimpsest of Globalization

Trade and trade theory, then, are not mirrors of location. They are, variously, complements, outcomes, and partial causes of location. Only by developing the two fields, each in its depth, and through a semi-disaggregated but analytically coherent set of categories—what I have called a moderately complex style of theorizing—can we come to an understanding of their interrelationships, so that when we speak of one we know more accurately what it implies for the other. The analysis advanced here suggests that much of the existing empirical research on globalization which relies uniquely on trade data will have limited utility for understanding the causes, evolutionary tendencies, and consequences of globalization. It will have limited policy relevance. There is a strong need to develop empirical research on globalization which measures international location in its own right rather than reading it off from trade patterns. It follows that by developing both trade and locational analyses in this way, we would have more powerful and realistic things to say about them, and hence about how globalization will influence people's lives.

References

Audretsch, D., and Vivarelli, M. 1994. Small firms and R&D spillovers: evidence from Italy. *Revue d'Économie Industrielle*, 67: 225–38.

Barro, R., and Sala-i-Martin, X. 1991. Convergence across states and regions. *Brookings Papers in Economic Activity*, 2: 107–58.

Baumol, W., Panzar, J., and Willig, J. 1982. *Contestable Markets and the Theory of Industry Structure*. Cambridge, Mass.: Harvard Business School Press.

Bellandi, M. 1993. *Economie di scala e organizzazione industriale*. Milan: FrancoAngeli.

Beyers, W. 1992. Producer services and metropolitan growth and development. In *Sources of Metropolitan Growth*, ed. E. S. Mills and J. F. McDonald. New Brunswick, NJ: Rutgers University Center for Urban Policy Research.

Blanc, H., and Sierra, C. 1997. The geographical dimension of transnational corporations' R&D activities: the organizational trade-off between internal and external proximity. Presented at the conference 'Proximité et coordination économique', 5–7 May, Lyon.

Boden, D., and Molotch, H. L. 1994. The compulsion of proximity. In *Nowhere: Space, Time and Modernity*, ed. R. Friedland and D. Boden. Berkeley and Los Angeles: University of California Press.

Bouba-Olga, O. 1999. Changement technique et espaces. Poitiers: University of Poitiers, Faculty of Economic Sciences, unpublished doctoral dissertation.

Castells, M. 1996. *The Rise of the Network Society*. Oxford: Basil Blackwell.

Coe, D., and Helpman, E. 1993. International R&D spillovers. Cambridge, Mass.: *NBER Working Paper*, No. 4444.

Cowan, R., and Foray, D. 1997. The economics of codification and the diffusion of knowledge. *Industrial and Corporate Change*, 7/2.

de la Fuente, A. 1995. The empirics of growth and convergence: an overview. London: Centre for Economic Policy Research, discussion paper, No. 1275.

Dunning, J. 1995. What's wrong—and right—with trade theory. *The International Trade Journal*, 9/2 (summer), 163–202.

—— 1997. The geographical sources of the competitiveness of firms: some results of a new survey. In *Alliance Capitalism and Global Business*, ed. J. Dunning. London: Routledge, 280–301.

Eaton, J., and Kortum, S. 1995. Trade in ideas: patenting and productivity in the OECD. Boston: Boston University working paper.

Ellison, G., and Glaeser, E. 1997. Geographic concentration of US manufacturing industries: a dart-board approach. *Journal of Political Economy*, 105: 885–97.

Feldman, M. 1993. An examination of the geography of innovation. *Industrial and Corporate Change*, 2/3: 451–70.

Fontagné, L., Freudenberg, M., and Peridy, N. 1997. Intra-EC trade and the impact of the single market. Paris: CEPII (Centre d'Études Prospectives et d'Informations Internationales), working paper 97-07.

Frank, R., and Cook, P. 1996. *The Winner-Take-All Society: Why a Few at the Top get so Much More than the Rest of Us*. New York: Penguin.

Greenaway, D., Hine, R., and Milner, C. 1995. Vertical and horizontal intra-industry trade: a cross-industry analysis for the United Kingdom. *Economic Journal*, 105: 1505–18 (Nov.).

Grossman, G., and Helpman, E. 1991. *Innovation and Growth in the Global Economy*. Cambridge, Mass.: MIT Press.

Hansen, J. D. 1997. Dynamic comparative advantage in a Ricardian model. In *Technology and International Trade*, ed. J. Fagerberg, L. Lundberg, P. Hansson, and A. Melchior. Cheltenham: Edward Elgar.

Helpman, E., and Krugman, P. 1985. *Market Structure and Foreign Trade*, Cambridge, Mass.: MIT Press.

Keeble, D., and Wilkinson, F. 1999. *Networking and Collective Learning in Regionally-Clustered High-Technology SMEs in Europe*. Brussels: Final report to Directorate General 12, European Commission.

Krugman, P. 1987. The narrow moving band, the Dutch disease, and the competitive consequences of Mrs. Thatcher: notes on trade in the presence of dynamic scale economies. *Journal of Development Economics*, 27: 41–55.

—— 1991. *Geography and Trade*. Cambridge, Mass.: MIT Press.

—— 1995. *Development, Geography, and Economic Theory*. Cambridge, Mass.: MIT Press.

Levy, F. 1999. *The New Dollars and Dreams: American Incomes and Economic Change*. New York: Russell Sage Foundation.

Lundvall, B. A. 1993. 'Explaining interfirm cooperation and innovation: limits of the transactions costs approach.' In *The Embedded Firm*, ed. G. Grabher. London: Routledge.

—— and Johnson, B. 1994. The learning economy. *Journal of Industry Studies*, 1/2 (Dec.), 23–42.

Mansfield, E., and Romeo, A. 1980. Technology transfer to overseas subsidiaries by US-based firms. *Quarterly Journal of Economics* (Dec.). 737–50.

Mishel, L., Bernstein, J., and Schmitt, J., eds. 1998. *The State of Working America, 1998–99*. Ithaca, NY: Cornell University Press.

Saxenian, A. 1994. *Regional Advantage: Culture and Competition in Silicon Valley*. Cambridge, Mass.: Harvard University Press.

Scott, A. J. 1988. *Metropolis: From the Division of Labor to Urban Form*. Berkeley and Los Angeles: University of California Press.

Storper, M. 1992. The limits to globalization: technology districts and international trade. *Economic Geography*, 68/1: 60–93.

—— 1997. *The Regional World: Territorial Development in a Global Economy*. New York: Guilford Press.

—— and Chen, Y.-C. 1999. Globalization and localization in the EU and OECD: an empirical analysis and need for alternative explanations. Presented to the DRUID Summer Conference, 9 June, Rebild, Denmark.

Utterback, J. 1996. *Mastering the Dynamics of Innovation*. Boston: Harvard Business School Press.

Veltz, P. 1996. *Mondialisation, villes et territoires: l'économie de l'Archipel*. Paris: Economica.

Venables, A. J. 1996. Equilibrium locations of vertically-linked industries. *International Economic Review*, 37/2 (May): 341–59.

Zucker, L. 1994. The role of insitutionalization in cultural persistence. In *The New Institutionalism in Organizational Analysis*, ed. P. DiMaggio and W. W. Powell. Chicago: University of Chicago Press, 83–107.

Section 4

Development and Underdevelopment

Chapter **9**

Climate, Coastal Proximity, and Development

Andrew D. Mellinger, Jeffrey D. Sachs, and John L. Gallup

Abstract

MOST studies of economic growth have tended to ignore or underplay the role of physical geography. Our recent analyses have shown, however, that physical geography (including climate, access to the sea, soil quality, and so forth) plays an important role in economic development, and can help to account for cross-country differences in the level and growth of per capita GDP. Coastal and temperate-zone economies significantly and consistently outperform landlocked and tropical regions. In this chapter, geographic information systems (GIS) data on global and regional scales are used to examine the relationship between climate (ecozones), water navigability, and economic development in terms of GDP per capita. GDP per capita and the spatial density of economic activity measured as GDP per sq km are high in temperate ecozones and in regions proximate to the sea (within 100 km of the ocean or a sea-navigable waterway). Temperate ecozones proximate to the sea account for 8 per cent of the world's inhabited land area, 23 per cent of the world's population, and 53 per cent of the world's GDP. The GDP densities in temperate ecozones proximate to the sea are on average eighteen times higher than in non-proximate non-temperate areas. We speculate as to why these strong patterns exist and persist, and we propose some future research directions to better integrate physical geography into the study of long-term economic development.

This research is part of an ongoing project at Harvard's Center for International Development investigating the linkages between geography and economic development. The authors wish to thank Karin Johnson, Andrew Warner, and Steve Radelet for their work on this chapter and related efforts.

Introduction

One of the central issues of economics is the enormous disparity in economic performance between rich and poor regions of the world. Modern economics got its start, in fact, with Adam Smith's *Inquiry into the Wealth of Nations* in 1776, in which Smith identified social and geographical factors that could account for differential economic performance across regions of the world. Smith is remembered today mainly for his theory that market institutions would enable societies to develop a richer division of labor, and therefore higher living standards, than societies subject to extensive government controls. He is less remembered for his equally astute geographical observations. Smith asserted that the division of labor is limited by the extent of the market, and that coastal regions, by virtue of their ability to engage in sea-based trade, enjoy a wider scope of the market than interior regions. In Smith's words:

> As by means of water carriage a more extensive market is opened to every sort of industry than what land carriage alone can afford it, so it is upon the sea-coast, and along the banks of navigable rivers that industry of every kind begins to subdivide and improve itself, and it is frequently not till a long time after that those improvements extend themselves to the inland part of the country

Based on the importance of sea-based trade, Smith drew pessimistic conclusions regarding inland Africa and large parts of Russia, Siberia, and Central Asia:

> All the inland parts of Africa, and all that part of Asia which lies any considerable way north of the Black and Caspian Seas, the ancient Scythia, the modern Tartary and Siberia, seem in all ages of the world to have been in the same barbarous and uncivilized state in which we find them at present . . . There are in Africa none of those great inlets . . . to carry maritime trade into the interior parts of that great continent . . .

Smith was less aware of the effects of climate on economic performance. Climatic conditions have pervasive effects on disease, agriculture, human physiology, and other factors that may affect economic performance. Recent studies (Gallup *et al.* 1998; Bloom and Sachs 1999) have noted that tropical areas are consistently poorer than temperate-zone areas, because of the intrinsic effects of tropical ecology on human health and agricultural productivity. Tropical infectious diseases, for example, impose very high burdens on human health, that in turn may lead to shortfalls in economic performance much larger than their direct, short-run effects on health. Another recent study (Gallup and Sachs 1999*a*), found that after controlling for material inputs such as capital, labor, and fertilizers, the productivity of tropical food production still falls far short of the productivity of temperate-zone food production. This poor performance in food productivity probably has serious adverse effects on nutrition levels, with adverse consequences for human capital accumulation, labor productivity, and susceptibility to infectious disease.

In an overview of economic development and geography (Gallup *et al.* 1998), the latitudinal belt between the Tropics of Cancer (23.45 N) and Capricorn (23.45 S) was used to separate the geographical tropics and the rest of the world. They showed that economies in the geographic tropics have lower income levels and lower growth rates than the rest of the world, and that the shortfall is evident after controlling for other standard economic variables that affect economic performance. Indeed, in a ranking of all countries with populations greater than 1 million in 1995, only two economies out of the top thirty countries were predominantly in the geographical tropics: Hong Kong and Singapore. Less than 1 per cent of the population of the richest thirty countries resides in the geographical tropics. Their analysis is extended here by using ecological measures of the tropics rather than the simple latitudinal definitions.

One of the surprising aspects of the modern study of economic growth and development is the almost total neglect of geographical factors. In the hundreds of cross-country studies of comparative economic growth, following the framework established by Barro (1991), almost none has included geographical variables as conditioning variables. Typical cross-country regression studies seek to explain economic growth over an interval of time as a function of the initial income level, the initial level of human capital, and the economic policies and institutions during the period of observation (such as trade policy, fiscal policy, and measures of the rule of law). None the less, when geography variables are added to such equations, they turn out to be highly significant, both economically and statistically. Variables such as climate zone, disease ecology (e.g. the prevalence of malaria), and access to sea-based trade, are important factors in addition to the standard conditioning variables.

The 'new economic geography' which emphasizes the interaction of transport costs, imperfect competition, and increasing returns to scale, treats geography in a wholly different manner. Rather than emphasizing the role of geographical differences across economies, the new geography argues that spatial differences in economic performance—some regions becoming rich while others remain poor—may arise even when the economies are initially similar in structure. The interaction of transport costs and increasing returns to scale impart positive and negative feedback processes to economic development. Some rich regions become even richer as they attract capital and labor from abroad, while other regions become poor (or remain at subsistence), because they fail to reach the scale of population and production needed for economic 'take off'.

While we argue that many important differences between economies have fundamental geographical sources—climate, coastal access, soil quality—the new geography suggests that many differences are accidents of history. The two approaches are potentially complementary, even though their points of view are distinct. It could be, for example, that physical geography helps to explain initial differences in outcomes across regions, and that the new economic geography helps to account for ways in which those initial differences are magnified through positive and negative feedbacks.

In the following sections, we use new GIS data to present evidence on the geographic distribution of per capita GDP, GDP density (defined as GDP per sq km), and population density. These variables are highly influenced by climate and proximity to the sea. We find strong evidence that the ecological tropics, the dry regions, and the sub-tropical regions are systematically poorer than temperate ecozones. Moreover, the temperate ecozones proximate to the sea, though a small part of the world's inhabited landmass, account for a remarkably high proportion of the world's annual economic output. The next section reviews the theoretical debate linking geography and economic development, and clarifies our own hypotheses within this broad debate. The third section describes the data set we developed for this research. The fourth section describes the global distributions of GDP and population across the ecozones. The fifth section examines the distributions within continents. The sixth section offers some further discussion of the results, and explores the ways in which physical geography and the new economic geography might be combined to give a more complete picture of modern economic development.

Linkages of Geography and Development: Perspectives on the Debate

The linkages between geography and economic development have been much debated, and in our view, much misunderstood. Therefore, it is worthwhile stating some basic propositions regarding our hypotheses and empirical approach, to dispel some misunderstandings that might arise. Philosophers, historians, and social scientists have long noted various correlations of geography and development, even though most economists (and indeed geographers) have downplayed or simply ignored those relationships in recent years. At least seven types of hypotheses have been offered.

- Early philosophers, such as Montesquieu, surmised that climate might have direct effects on temperament, work effort, or social harmony.
- Many writers, activists, and politicians have argued that the link from geography to development is the result of a link from race to development.
- Some philosophers and social scientists (such as Karl Wittfogel 1957) have linked geography and climate to the form of government, for example Wittfogel's famous and much contested claim that riparian civilizations are prone to despotism because of centralized control of water systems and the large public works to support irrigation.
- Some social scientists have argued that climate helps to determine the means of production—yeoman farming in the temperate regions, plantation agri-

culture in the tropics—and therefore the organization of society and the propensity to economic development.

- Many commentators have argued that geographical correlations are accidental reflections of historical events: the temperate-zone societies succeeded, in some sense accidentally, in dominating tropical societies through military conquest and colonial rule.
- Another approach argues that geography is important because geographical endowments (climate, access to navigable waterways) directly affect productivity, through transport costs, health and disease, nutrition, population density, and so forth.
- Geography may also affect the pace and diffusion of technological changes. Certain innovations—in health, energy production and use, agriculture—are likely to be ecologically specific, not easily applicable across ecological zones.
- A final approach argues that ecological and geographical conditions were once very important, but are no longer so important because of technological progress. Geographical correlations with economic development would therefore reflect past relationships plus the continuing path dependence of history (early forces, no longer operating, continue to affect present conditions).

Many of these approaches have been discredited. Indeed, as a general matter, the role of geography in economic development has been downplayed in recent decades, partly because of exaggerated claims made in the past (that geography could explain everything about development) and partly because of the deep discrediting of racist theories of development that had been associated with geographical claims. Because of this inherited skepticism, it behoves us to state our own hypotheses more clearly.

First, we are not suggesting any kind of geographical determinism. Geography is but one of several conditioning variables in the case of economic development. We believe that tropical ecozones and landlocked countries face obstacles to development not faced by temperate-zone and coastal economies. None the less, the role of tropical ecology and coastal access are but two of many factors that contribute to the success or failure of economic development. Secondly, we are not claiming any linkages whatsoever between climate and race, work effort, or culture. Such claims have been predominant in past ages, especially during periods of colonial rule and scientific racism associated with social Darwinism. They have been systematically rejected, and deserve to remain so. Thirdly, we hypothesize that geography has direct links to the economy (through effects on health, agriculture, transport, population density) as well as indirect links through effects on the pace and diffusion of new technologies. We suspect that some of the observed correlations of climate and economic development do indeed reflect past patterns that are of declining relevance, but we also find evidence that at least some of the linkages have remained powerful in the past thirty years.

Data and Methods

A new geographic information system (GIS) database was constructed with four key variables: climate zone, population, navigable rivers, and gross domestic product on a per capita basis for 152 countries with a population of 1 million or more in 1995. In 1995 these countries had a combined population of 5.65 billion, 99.7 per cent of the world's population (Tobler *et al.* 1995). GIS is a computer-based relational database used for the storage, analysis, and display of geographically referenced data. The inherent advantage to using a GIS is that data can be analyzed spatially.

A digital map of climate was constructed using the classification devised by Wladmir Köppen (1918) and later revised by his students Geiger and Pohl (1953) to determine climate boundaries that coincided with major vegetation types. The version we use was digitized from Strahler and Strahler (1992). The usefulness of this approach to classification lies in its empirical delineation of climatic boundaries based on either monthly or annual actual temperature and precipitation values. The Köppen–Geiger–Pohl classification designates major climate groups, subgroups within the major groups, and further divides the subgroups to capture seasonal differences in temperature and precipitation. There are, of course, many alternative climate classification systems. We do not believe that our major findings of strong inter-relations among climate, GDP, and population depend on the particular system that we are using, in this case the Köppen–Gieger–Pohl classification, but we are in the process of exploring other classification systems in our ongoing research.

The six major categories of climate zones are designated by a capital letter: A = tropical, rainy; B = dry; C = mild, humid; D = snow, forest; E = polar; and H = highland. The subgroups are classified by the addition of another letter. Adding the lower case *f* used with Af, Cf, and Df indicates climates that are moist with adequate precipitation in all months with no dry season. The *w* used with Aw and Cw denotes a dry winter season in the respective hemisphere. The *m*, which is only used with the A climate, indicates a rainforest climate despite a short, dry season in monsoon-like precipitation cycles. The *s* used with Cs indicates a dry season in the summer of the respective hemisphere. The upper case *W* represents arid, desert climates and the *S* indicates semi-arid, steppe climates. The *W* and *S* are used only with the dry B climates. The H and E zones do not have further subdivision. Figure 9.1 depicts the global extent of the subgroups. We mainly are concerned with the eleven classifications of the second tier, Af, Am, Aw, BS, BW, Cf, Cs, Cw, Df, DW, and H. The E climate is generally excluded because the 4 per cent of the world's land area in this polar zone (e.g. the tundra of Northern Russia) has almost no human population.

Figure 9.2 shows the global distribution of population density as of 1994 (Tobler *et al.* 1995) measured as population per sq km. Tobler *et al.* (1995)

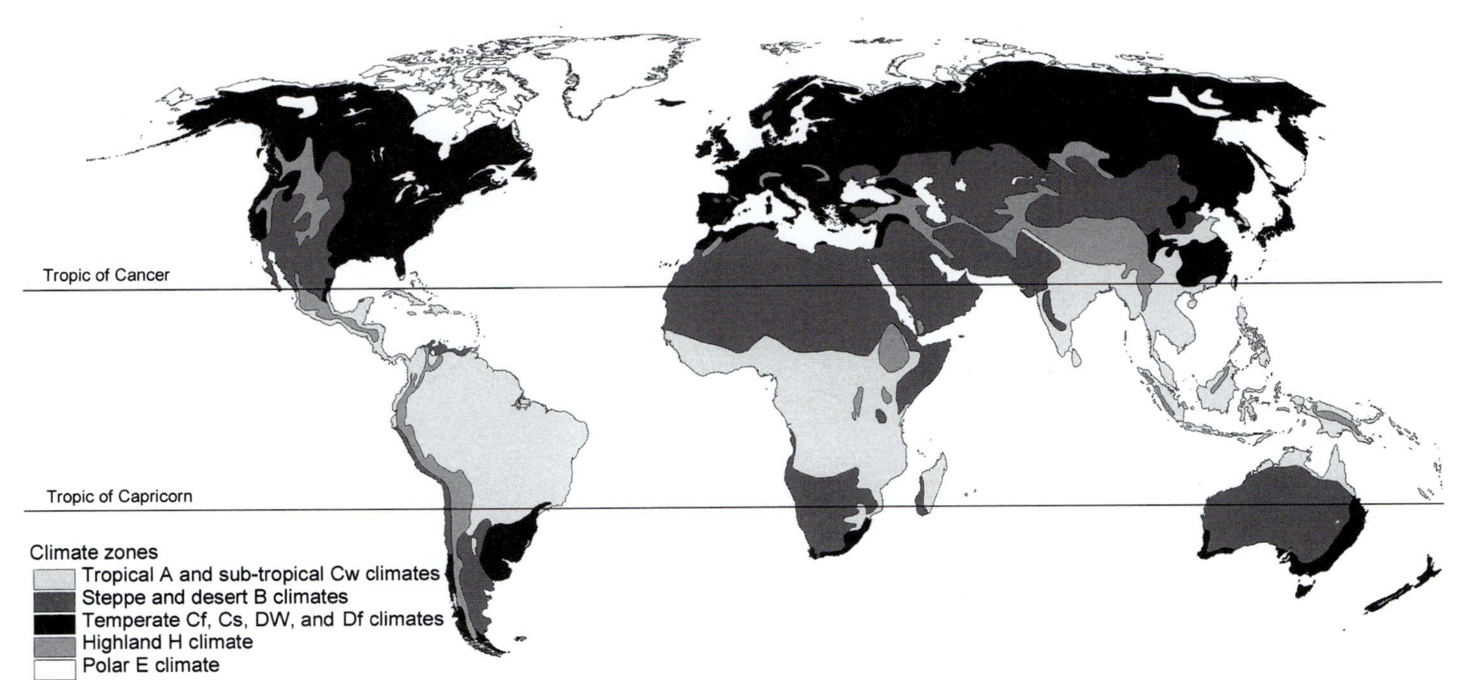

Fig. 9.1. Köppen–Geiger climate zones

Source: Strahler and Strahler (1992).

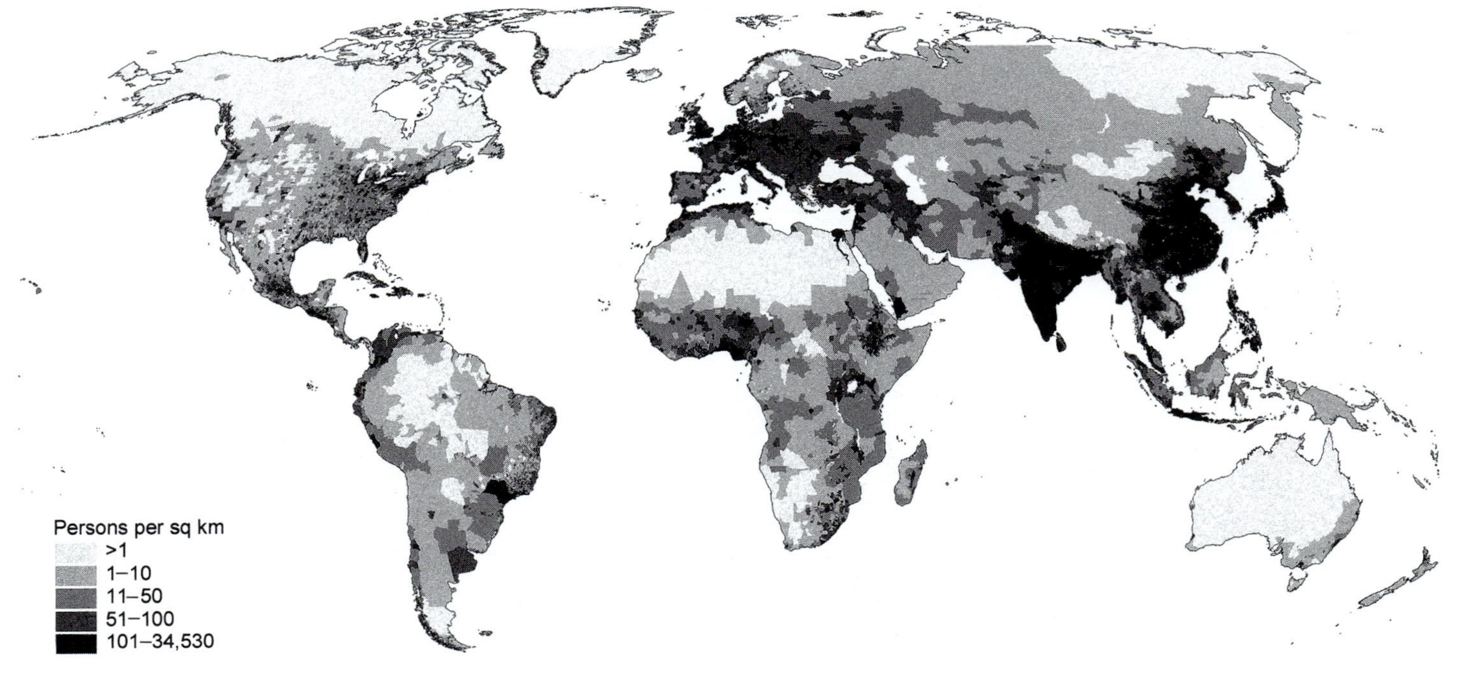

Fig. 9.2. Population density, 1994

Source: See Tobler *et al.* (1995).

obtained a resolution of 5 minutes by 5 minutes, approximately 7.5 sq km at the equator. Some of the underlying data, however, is less refined, with population interpolated to the 5 minute by 5 minute grid. A detailed description of the gridded population data set is in Tobler *et al.* (1995).

Since we are concerned with modern economic development as driven by international trade, rivers were mapped based on navigability for ocean-going vessels. Rivers categorized as navigable in the ArcAtlas (ESRI 1996*a*) database are pared down according to three rules using information taken from Rand McNally (1980), Britannica Online (1998), and *Encyclopaedia Encarta* (1998): whether a river accommodates vessels with a minimum draft of approximately 3 meters (anything smaller is not considered ocean-going); the point at which a navigable river becomes obstructed by falls, rapids, locks, or dams; and whether the river is frozen during winter. The coastline used is free from pack ice throughout the year (ESRI 1996*b*; Rand McNally 1980). Using this classification Figure 9.3 shows the land area in the world that is within 100 km of the ocean coast or a sea-navigable river. As Adam Smith noted, Africa has no sea-navigable rivers that extend from the oceans to the interior of the continent. High continental tableland precludes navigability, even with investment. By contrast, North America has two navigable waterways that link the continent's vast interior with the ocean: the St Lawrence Seaway and Great Lakes system, and the Mississippi River system (and its major tributaries such as the Missouri and Ohio Rivers).[1]

Per capita gross domestic product (GDP) was measured at standardized purchasing power parity (PPP) at both the national and sub-national level. Figure 9.4 depicts global distribution of GDP per capita in 1995. To capture intra-country variance in income distribution, sub-national per capita GDP data was gathered for 19 of the 152 countries in our GIS, including most of the large economies. These are Australia, Belgium, Brazil, Canada, Chile, China, Colombia, France, Germany, Greece, India, Italy, Japan, Mexico, Netherlands, Spain, the UK, the USA, and Uruguay. Since the sub-national data of these countries was collected in local currency rather than on a comparable US dollar purchasing power parity basis, the local-currency measures were adjusted to create internationally comparable sub-national measures.[2] The two major

[1] The St Lawrence Seaway is partly man-made, but the improvements upon its already largely navigable course made this river system fully passable to the Atlantic.

[2] The country-level \$US PPP-adjusted GDP is used for each country for 1995 (GDP per capita below), available from the World Bank (1998), supplemented by CIA (1996, 1997) estimates. For each sub-national region i, the \$US PPP GDP_i is calculated accordingly:

$$\$\text{US PPP GDP}_i = \text{GDP}_c \times (\text{GDP}_i/\text{GDP}_a)$$

GDP_i is the GDP per capita of region i in local currency, and GDP_a is the country-average per capita GDP in local currency. GDP_a is calculated as $\Sigma(GDP_i \times Pop_i)/\Sigma(Pop_i)$. Sub-national regional GDP was collected from national sources, mainly government statistical yearbooks. Thus, provincial populations and provincial income data are used to calculate a country's average GDP per capita,

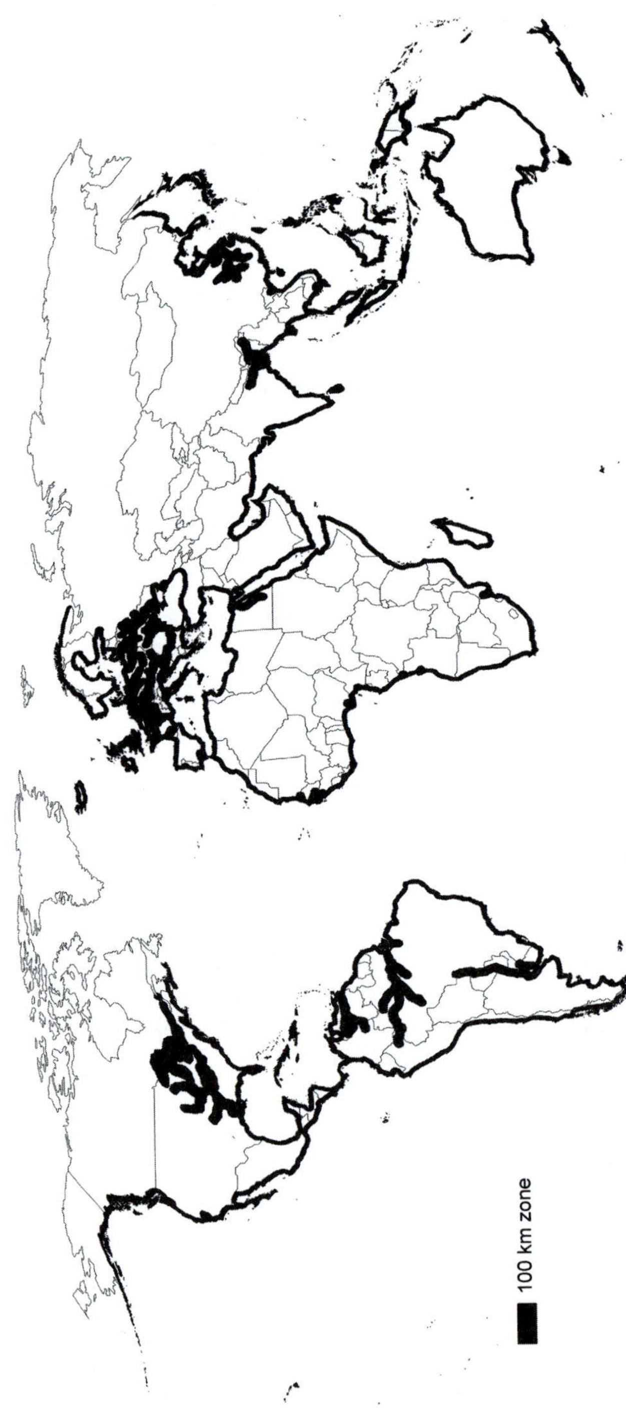

Fig. 9.3. Land within 100 km of an ice-free coast or sea-navigable river

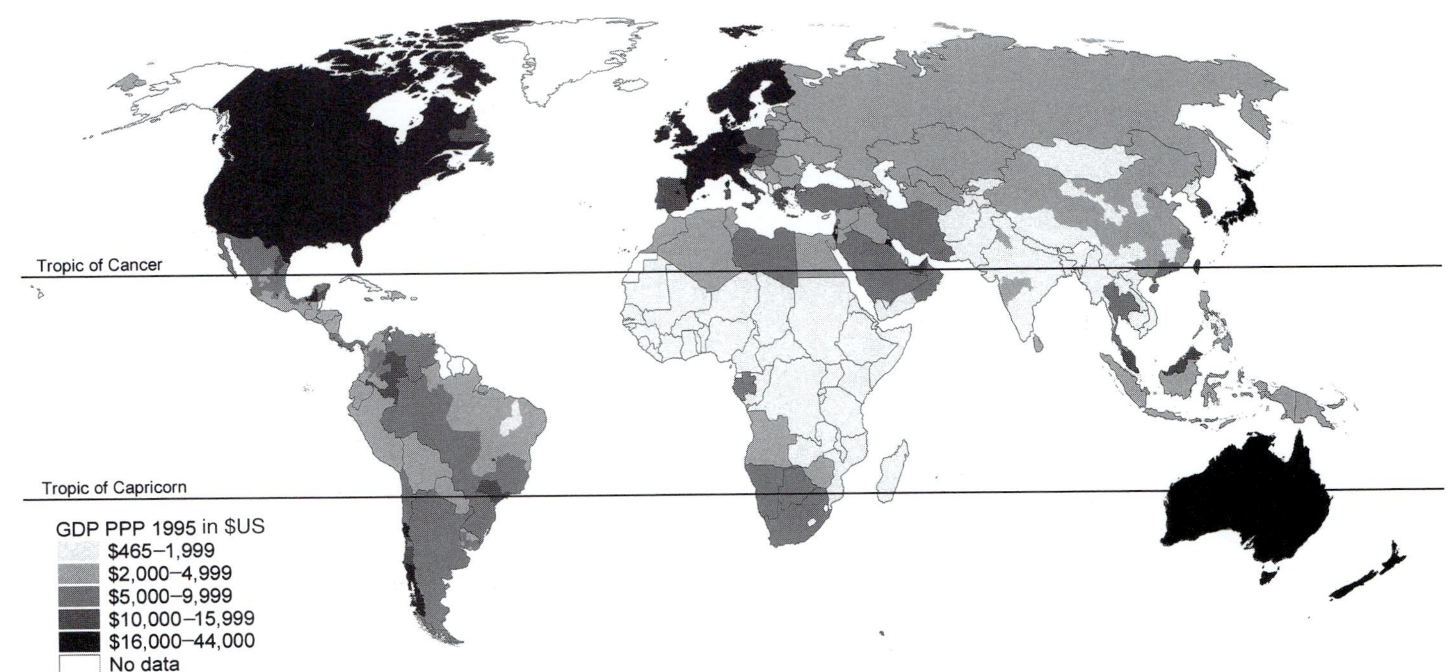

Fig. 9.4. Income per person, 1995 (with sub-national data for 19 countries)

Note: GDP PPP = 1995 Gross Domestic Product per person in purchasing power parity international dollars.
Sources: World Bank (1998) and CIA (1996, 1997).

Table 9.1. Land area by climate zone

Climate zone	Land area (%)		
	Near	Far	Total
Af	1.7	2.3	4.0
Am	0.7	0.1	0.8
Aw	2.5	8.3	10.8
Cw	0.6	3.7	4.3
BS	1.1	11.2	12.3
BW	1.9	15.4	17.3
H	0.4	6.9	7.3
E	0.1	3.9	4.0
Cf	4.8	2.9	7.7
Cs	1.3	0.8	2.2
Df	2.0	21.0	23.0
DW	0.2	6.2	6.4
Tropical[1]	5.5	14.4	19.9
Non-temperate[2]	9.0	51.8	60.8
Temperate[3]	8.4	30.9	39.2
Total	**17.4**	**82.6**	

Notes: 1. Tropical = Af, Am, Aw, and Cw.
2. Non-temperate = Tropical plus BS, BW, H, and E.
3. Temperate = Cf, Cs, Df, and DW.

gradients of per capita GDP that result are climate and distance from the coast. The tropical regions are almost all poor and coastal regions tend to have higher incomes than interior regions. These effects are quantified in the next section.

Spatial Distribution of Population and Economic Density

Using the GIS population data, GDP per capita, and climate zone, the distribution of economic activity and global population according to ecozones and proximity to the sea is calculated. Tables 9.1 to 9.3 show the proportions of global land area, population, and total GDP within each of the eleven climate zones. Each climate zone is separated into two sub-regions: 'near', signifying within 100 km of the sea (i.e. ocean coast or ocean-navigable river); and 'far', signifying beyond 100 km from the sea. Four sub-zones (Cf, Cs, Dw, and Df) are classified as 'temperate'. The Cw zone is mainly sub-tropical but is included here as part of the tropical zone rather than the temperate zone (it encompasses

and then used to calculate the ratio of each province's per capita GDP to the national average. We then multiply that ratio by the $US PPP GDP, to calculate a GDP on a PPP basis for each region. This calculation assumes that the ratio of the regional GDP per capita to national GDP per capita in local currency equals the ratio of the regional GDP to national GDP on a PPP basis.

Table 9.2. Population by climate zone

Climate zone	Population (%)		
	Near	Far	Total
Af	3.8	0.6	4.4
Am	2.3	0.1	2.4
Aw	9.3	8.2	17.5
Cw	6.4	9.6	16.0
BS	2.3	9.4	11.8
BW	2.1	4.1	6.2
H	0.9	5.9	6.8
E	0.0	0.0	0.0
Cf	15.0	4.5	19.5
Cs	3.6	0.7	4.3
Df	2.7	3.1	5.8
DW	1.5	3.8	5.3
Tropical[1]	21.8	18.5	40.3
Non-temperate[2]	27.1	38.0	65.1
Temperate[3]	22.8	12.1	34.9
Total	**49.9**	**50.1**	

Notes: 1. Tropical = Af, Am, Aw, and Cw.
2. Non-temperate = Tropical plus BS, BW, H, and E.
3. Temperate = Cf, Cs, Df, and DW.

Table 9.3. GDP by climate zone

Climate zone	GDP (%)		
	Near	Far	Total
Af	2.5	0.3	2.8
Am	1.0	0.0	1.0
Aw	3.6	3.0	6.6
Cw	3.4	3.6	7.0
BS	1.9	4.6	6.5
BW	1.4	2.2	3.6
H	0.9	4.4	5.3
Cf	36.3	7.4	43.7
Cs	7.9	1.1	9.1
Df	7.3	3.7	11.0
DW	1.4	2.0	3.4
Tropical[1]	10.5	6.9	17.4
Non-temperate[2]	14.7	18.1	32.8
Temperate[3]	52.9	14.3	67.2
Total	**67.6**	**32.4**	

Notes: 1. Tropical = Af, Am, Aw, and Cw.
2. Non-temperate = Tropical plus BS, BW, and H.
3. Temperate = Cf, Cs, Df, and DW.

the Gangetic valley of India, parts of South America south of the Amazon, in Southern Africa, and a small belt in northeastern Australia).

The near temperate zone which is within 100 km of the sea and in a temperate climate plays a dominant role in the world economy (see Fig. 9.5). Note that much of the USA's coasts, Great Lakes, and Mississippi River are included, almost all of Western Europe, much of East Asia, including coastal China, South Korea, and Japan, coastal Australia, New Zealand, South America's Chile, coastal Argentina, and a small part of coastal Brazil, part of North Africa's coast, and the southern tip of South Africa. These regions contain almost all of the world's economic powerhouse economies, and as is demonstrated a significant proportion of global production.

Table 9.1 shows the proportion of global land area in each ecozone. Note that 17.4 per cent of the world's land area is within 100 km of the sea. Moreover 39.2 per cent of the world's land area lies within the four sub-zones designated 'temperate'. By calculating the intersection of the two areas, the near temperate zone constitutes 8.3 per cent of the world's land. Nearly one-third of the world's land area (29.6%) lies in the dry climate zones (desert and steppes), along with a smaller proportion of the world's population (18.0%). The dry zones tend to be among the least densely populated places on the planet; 19.9 per cent of the world's land area lies within the tropics (Af, Am, Aw, and Cw), and 7.3 per cent within the populated highlands.

Table 9.2 repeats this exercise for world population: 34.9 per cent live in the temperate zone, and 49.9 per cent live within 100 km of the sea. The near temperate region includes 22.8 per cent of the world's population, located on 8.4 per cent of the world's landmass, making it a densely populated part of the world. Meanwhile 24.3 per cent live in the tropical A zones, while another 16.0 per cent of the world, mainly in India and China, live in the sub-tropical Cw zone. Only 6.2 per cent of the world's population lives in desert (BW) regions, which comprises 17.3 per cent of the land.

Table 9.3 shows the spatial distribution of the world's GDP by climate zone. For each sub-region, per capita GDP (measured at PPP) is multiplied by the population, giving the total GDP for the sub-region. The world's GDP is the sum of these sub-regional GDPs. A striking 67.6 per cent of the world's GDP is produced within 100 km of the sea, though that area comprises only 17.4 per cent of the world's landmass. Meanwhile 67.2 per cent of the world's GDP is produced in the temperate climates, though these account for only 39.2 per cent of the world's landmass. The near-temperate region, with 8.3 per cent of the world's landmass and 22.8 per cent of the world's population, produces a remarkable 52.9 per cent of the world's GDP.

By dividing the cells of Table 9.2 by those of Table 9.1, as shown in Table 9.4, the population density of the climate zones is shown relative to the global average population density, which is 42.5 inhabitants per sq km (Tobler *et al.* 1995). Thus, the Cf near zone has a relative population density of 3.15, or a population

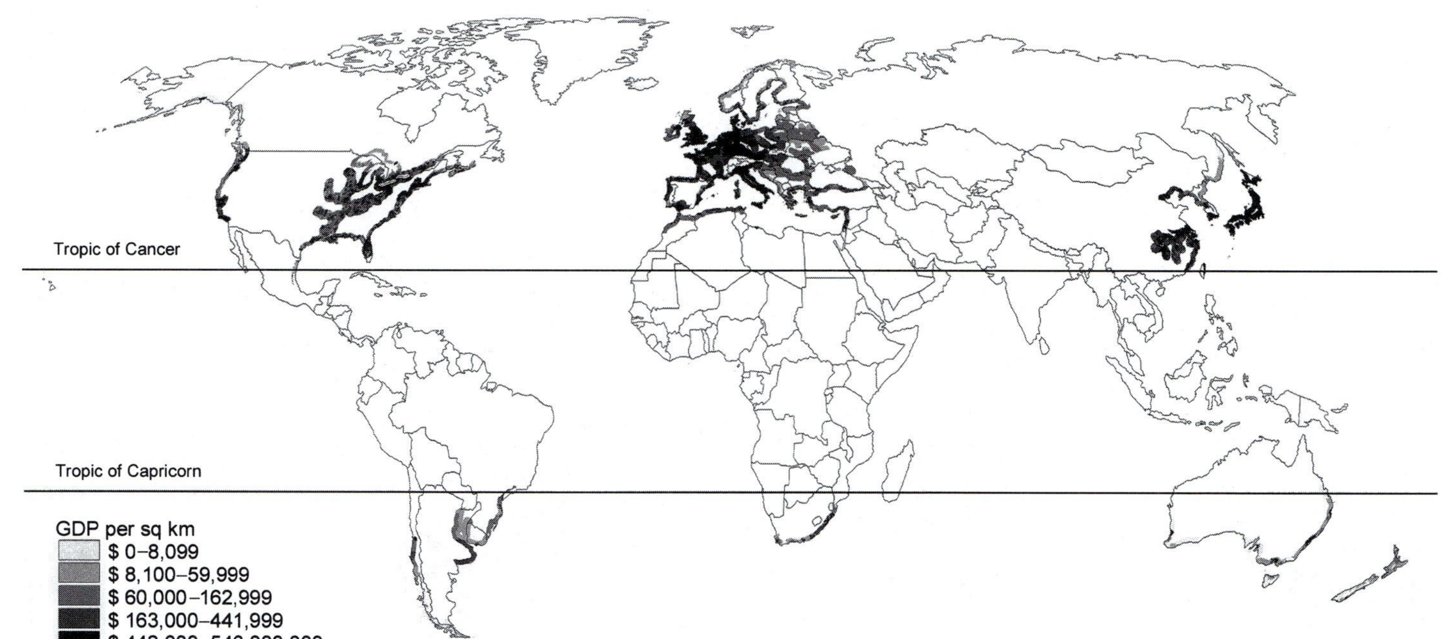

Fig: 9.5. Income density in temperate climate zones 0–100 km from the coast and sea-navigable rivers

Sources: Figs. 9.1, 9.3, and 4.

Table 9.4. Population density by climate zone

Climate zone	Population Near	Far	Total
Af	2.17	0.28	1.10
Am	3.56	0.62	3.16
Aw	3.67	0.99	1.62
Cw	11.03	2.57	3.70
BS	2.19	0.84	0.96
BW	1.12	0.27	0.36
H	2.23	0.85	0.93
Cf	3.15	1.57	2.55
Cs	2.66	0.90	1.99
Df	1.36	0.15	0.25
DW	6.05	0.61	0.82
Tropical[1]	3.95	1.29	2.02
Non-temperate[2]	3.01	0.73	1.07
Temperate[3]	2.72	0.39	0.89
Total	**2.87**	**0.61**	

Notes: 1. Tropical = Af, Am, Aw, and Cw.
2. Non-temperate = Tropical plus BS, BW, and H.
3. Temperate = Cf, Cs, Df, and DW.

density 3.15 times the world average, which is 133.9 people per sq km (= 3.15 × 42.5). The overall near-temperate region is densely populated, with a relative density of 2.72. The near zones are more densely populated than the far zones in every climate zone.

Dividing the cells of Table 9.3 by those of Table 9.2, as shown in Table 9.5, the GDP per capita relative to the world average (or $5,500 at PPP) is presented. The GDP per capita shows two systematic gradients: the near regions are higher than the far regions for every ecozone averaging 1.4 times the world average in the near regions and 0.7 times the world average in the far regions. And the temperate ecozones' GDP per capita is higher than the non-temperate (except in the DW zone which mostly encompasses Siberia), averaging 1.9 times the world average in the temperate zones and 0.5 times the world average in the non-temperate zones. The highest total income ecozone is the Cf (mild, temperate) climate, followed by the Cs (Mediterranean) climate and the Df (snow) climate (the order of these three changes when you compare near and far GDP per capita). Per capita GDP is especially high in the regions that are both temperate and proximate to the sea, with 2.32 times the world average or $12,760 in PPP currency units (2.32 × $5,500). The near-temperate zone has 6 times the per capita GDP of the far tropical zone.

GDP density, measured as total GDP per sq km, is a useful measure for understanding where overall production of goods and services takes place. Since GDP

Table 9.5. GDP per capita (GDP/pop.)

Climate zone	GDP per capita Near	Far	Total
Af	0.66	0.54	0.64
Am	0.41	0.30	0.41
Aw	0.39	0.36	0.38
Cw	0.54	0.37	0.44
BS	0.80	0.49	0.55
BW	0.65	0.54	0.58
H	1.01	0.75	0.78
Cf	2.42	1.63	2.24
Cs	2.22	1.51	2.10
Df	2.67	1.22	1.90
DW	0.92	0.53	0.64
Tropical[1]	0.48	0.37	0.43
Non-temperate[2]	0.54	0.48	0.50
Temperate[3]	2.32	1.18	1.94
Total	**1.35**	**0.65**	

Notes: 1. Tropical = Af, Am, Aw, and Cw.
2. Non-temperate = Tropical plus BS, BW, and H.
3. Temperate = Cf, Cs, Df, and DW.

density is equal to per capita GDP multiplied by population density, and since both GDP per capita and population density are especially high in the near temperate zones, the GDP density is extremely high in those regions. Table 9.6 shows GDP density calculated by dividing the cells of Table 9.3 by those of Table 9.1. The GDP density in the Cf near zone is a remarkable 7.63 times the world average GDP density, equaling $230,000 per sq km. The highest income densities are found in the near zones, the temperate climates, and also the subtropical Cw climate. The latter ecozone is characterized by a relatively low GDP per capita, but an extremely high population density. The near ecozones have on average 10 times the GDP densities of the far zones. The near temperate ecozones produce income densities that average 18 times that of the far non-temperate ecozones.

Thus far averages have been examined for population density, GDP per capita, and GDP per sq km by region. Sharp differences were found according to coastal proximity and ecozone. But how significant are these differences? While *formal* statistical tests of differences of means are not readily usable (there being little justification in assuming that the variables are drawn from any particular underlying distribution), the overall distributions of the variables were examined to assess how different these distributions are across regions. Table 9.7 shows the distribution of GDP per capita by ecozone in both the near and far

Table 9.6. GDP density (GDP/sq km)

Climate zone	GDP Density		
	Near	Far	Total
Af	1.42	0.15	0.70
Am	1.46	0.19	1.28
Aw	1.43	0.36	0.61
Cw	5.91	0.95	1.61
BS	1.75	0.41	0.53
BW	0.73	0.15	0.21
H	2.26	0.64	0.73
Cf	7.63	2.56	5.71
Cs	5.91	1.37	4.18
Df	3.63	0.18	0.48
DW	5.57	0.33	0.53
Tropical[1]	1.90	0.48	0.87
Non-temperate[2]	1.63	0.35	0.53
Temperate[3]	6.32	0.46	1.72
Total	**3.89**	**0.39**	

Notes: 1. Tropical = Af, Am, Aw, and Cw.
2. Non-temperate = Tropical plus BS, BW, and H.
3. Temperate = Cf, Cs, Df, and DW.

regions. The top half of the table refers to regions proximate to the sea, and the bottom half refers to regions far from the sea. For each ecozone, the percentage of the population living at each level of GDP per capita[3] is calculated.

Differences in per capita income across ecozones are reflected in sharp differences in the overall distribution, not just in the means. Among the near regions, for example, no more than 1 per cent of the populations in tropical regions (Af, Am, Aw, or Cw) are in the high-income category ($16,000 or more), while 47 per cent of the populations of the temperate regions are in the high-income category. The tropical regions are nearly uniformly poor, while temperate regions have a wide income range with a small proportion (7%) of the temperate-zone populations at income levels below $2,000, compared with 42 per cent of the tropical zone population.

The same calculations are made for distribution of population density by ecozone, shown in Table 9.8, again dividing the near and far regions for separate analysis. One systematic gradient is that the near ecozones are uniformly more

[3] Note that we have GDP per capita on a national basis for most countries (133 with population of 1 million or more), and a sub-national (provincial or state) basis for 19 countries, giving us 455 administrative units in total for which we have an estimate of average GDP per capita. To make the calculations for Tables 9.3, 9.5, and 9.7, we assume that the entire population within each administrative unit has the average GDP per capita of that unit. Thus, we ignore income inequality *within* administrative units.

Table 9.7. GDP per capita distribution

Zone	Percentage of population within each zone					
	$0–1,000	$1,000–2,000	$2,000–4,000	$4,000–8,000	$8,000–16,000	$16,000+
Near						
Af	16	6	59	8	10	1
Am	4	40	52	3	0	0
Aw	29	37	21	12	1	1
Cw	25	15	34	20	6	0
BS	2	21	55	8	9	5
BW	11	11	50	15	11	2
H	5	3	52	22	8	10
Cf	0	5	15	21	6	53
Cs	1	2	11	30	24	33
Df	0	1	13	30	0	56
DW	22	0	15	39	24	0
Tropical[1]	23	26	35	13	4	1
Non-temperate[2]	19	23	38	13	5	1
Temperate[3]	2	3	14	24	9	47

Table 9.7. Continued

Percentage of population within each zone Zone	$0–1,000	$1,000–2,000	$2,000–4,000	$4,000–8,000	$8,000–16,000	$16,000+
Far						
Af	39	9	18	20	7	7
Am	3	67	30	0	0	0
Aw	35	37	9	12	3	3
Cw	27	29	29	9	3	3
BS	21	26	37	12	2	2
BW	11	47	19	8	7	7
H	24	26	12	29	5	5
Cf	1	10	48	21	10	10
Cs	2	3	32	30	16	16
Df	0	0	8	91	0	0
DW	1	15	59	14	5	5
Tropical[1]	31	32	20	11	3	3
Non-temperate[2]	25	31	23	13	4	4
Temperate[3]	1	9	41	36	6	6
Total						
Tropical[1]	26	29	28	12	4	2
Non-temperate[2]	23	28	29	13	4	3
Temperate[3]	2	5	23	28	8	34

Notes: 1. Tropical = Af, Am, Aw, and Cw.
2. Non-temperate = Tropical plus BS, BW, and H.
3. Temperate = Cf, Cs, Df, and DW.

Table 9.8. Population density distribution (pop. per sq km)

Percentage of regional population Zone	0–20	20–40	40–80	80–160	160–320	320+
Near						
Af	4	7	11	17	13	48
Am	3	1	5	14	26	51
Aw	2	3	7	7	15	67
Cw	0	0	1	3	8	88
BS	3	2	14	15	18	49
BW	9	8	8	7	13	56
H	4	7	13	26	16	34
Cf	2	2	7	16	18	54
Cs	1	3	12	25	24	35
Df	4	5	25	25	13	27
DW	2	0	1	11	20	66
Tropical[1]	2	3	7	13	17	57
Non-temperate[2]	3	3	7	9	14	65
Temperate[3]	2	3	10	18	18	49
Far						
Af	42	16	20	13	7	2
Am	28	11	7	2	11	42
Aw	14	9	14	22	27	14
Cw	4	3	6	16	25	46
BS	11	7	12	11	19	39
BW	24	12	7	16	16	25
H	10	12	19	22	13	24
Cf	5	8	14	20	21	32
Cs	6	20	33	28	11	3
Df	27	20	29	11	3	10
DW	6	3	8	18	25	39
Tropical[1]	12	9	14	21	24	20
Non-temperate[2]	12	8	12	17	21	31
Temperate[3]	12	11	18	17	16	26
Total						
Tropical[1]	5	5	9	15	19	46
Non-temperate[2]	8	6	10	14	18	45
Temperate[3]	6	6	13	18	18	41

Notes: 1. Tropical = Af, Am, Aw, and Cw.
2. Non-temperate = Tropical plus BS, BW, and H.
3. Temperate = Cf, Cs, Df, and DW.

densely populated than the far ecozones. There is much less homogeneity of population density within the tropical and temperate ecozones. The ecozones are less defining of population density than they are of GDP per capita. The tropical zones display regions of both high population densities, 320+

per sq km, and low population densities, 0–20 per sq km. The same is true of temperate ecozones.

Continental Patterns

As a final exercise in this section, the allocation of populations of major continental regions into ecozones and coastal proximity is shown in Table 9.9. The near temperate regions were noted earlier for having much higher levels of income per capita than all other categories. The continental regions differ markedly in the shares of their populations and land areas that fall within these advantaged or disadvantaged zones. We divide the world into nine broad regions: North America, Latin America, Western Europe, Middle East and North Africa, Sub-Saharan Africa, East Asia, South Asia, Oceania, and Eastern Europe and Former Soviet Union.

Four continental regions have large populations living in non-temperate climates; South Asia has no temperate climate, 96 per cent of Sub-Saharan Africans, 88 per cent of Latin Americans, and 70 per cent of Middle Eastern and North Africans live in non-temperate climates. The global average shows 65 per cent of the population residing in non-temperate climates. The global average for population living in non-temperate far regions is 38 per cent. The same four continental regions again have higher shares: 78 per cent of Sub-Saharan Africans, 59 per cent of South Asians, 48 per cent of Latin Americans, and 45 per cent of the Middle Eastern and North Africans live in non-temperate far regions. In Latin America, one-fifth of the population lives in a highland (H) climate far from the coast.

The people living in the other five continental regions are distributed mostly among the temperate climates. East Asia is included in this grouping because its non-temperate far population of 25 per cent is lower than the global average of 38 per cent. East Asia also has an advantage with the majority of its population living in a region near to the sea. Eastern Europe and the Former Soviet Union have 74 per cent of the population in temperate climates, but only 33 per cent in a near temperate zone. For Russia alone, the population share in the near temperate region is only 6 per cent.

Western Europe, North America, and Oceania are all especially favored. Western Europe has a striking 96 per cent of the population in a temperate ecozone, with 87 per cent in near temperate ecozones. North America has 88 per cent of the population in temperate ecozones and 63 per cent of the population in near temperate ecozones. In Oceania, 74 per cent of the population lives in temperate ecozones, with 63 per cent of the population in near temperate ecozones. Figures 9.1 and 9.5 show that the continents with the highest concentrations of near temperate populations, Western Europe, North America, and Oceania, are also the richest. Conversely, the two continents with the highest

Table 9.9. Population by continent (%)

Continent	Tropical[1]		Non-temperate[2]		Temperate[3]		Total	
	Near	Far	Near	Far	Near	Far	Near	Far
Sub-Saharan Africa	15	47	18	78	3	1	21	79
Eastern Europe and Former Soviet Union	0	0	6	20	33	41	39	61
South Asia	38	32	41	59	0	0	41	59
Latin America	31	25	40	48	5	7	45	55
Middle East and North Africa	0	0	25	45	23	7	48	52
Global average	*22*	*18*	*27*	*38*	*23*	*12*	50	50
East Asia	28	14	32	25	26	17	58	42
North America	1	0	3	8	63	26	67	33
Oceania	15	2	17	8	66	8	83	17
Western Europe	0	0	2	2	87	9	89	11

Notes: 1. Tropical = Af, Am, Aw, and Cw.
2. Non-temperate = Tropical plus BS, BW, and H.
3. Temperate = Cf, Cs, Df, and DW.

population in far tropical ecozones, Sub-Saharan Africa and South Asia, are also the poorest.

Discussion and Future Research

Climate and coastal proximity are two key geographical gradients of economic development. Temperate ecozones and regions within 100 km of sea-navigable waterways are home to more than 50 per cent of the world's economic output, but encompass only 8 per cent of the world's inhabited landmass. The near ecozones contain on average ten times the GDP densities of the far ecozones. Comparing the economic density of the near temperate ecozones with the far non-temperate ecozones, the GDP densities are on average 18 times greater. It is the task of the science of economic development to give an interpretation of these patterns.

Following our discussion above, at least three hypotheses seem appropriate for further exploration. The simplest hypothesis is that the intrinsic characteristics of the tropics and interior regions are indeed highly detrimental to long-term economic development. Tropical climates are burdened by much higher levels of infectious disease than temperate climates (Gallup and Sachs 1999*a*, in the case of malaria), and are generally less productive in food production (Gallup and Sachs 1999*b*). Interior regions suffer from much higher transport costs than coastal regions. The combination of being both interior and non-temperate is therefore doubly detrimental. Sub-Saharan Africa has no less than 78 per cent of its population living in far and non-temperate regions.

A second hypothesis is that tropical climates are detrimental, but only modestly so. If the world is subject to increasing-returns-to-scale production technologies, however, then small initial disadvantages can cumulate into larger and larger differences over time. An example might be the following. Suppose that tropical climates were only, say, 25 per cent disadvantaged 200 years ago, but that innovative activity is ecozone-specific (for example in health and agricultural technology) and is determined by the size of the market. A small initial advantage in the temperate zone could then multiply as a result of much larger induced innovative activity in the temperate zones as a result of the initial modest advantage. Modern endogenous growth models would have this property, in which the rate of innovation depends on the scale of the market. In this case, the main policy implication would be the importance of re-directing scientific and technological efforts towards tropical ecozone problems. The importance of the lack of diffusion of innovations across ecological zones is advocated in Sachs (1999).

A third kind of hypothesis would hold that the technological disadvantages of the tropics, or of interior regions, is a thing of the past; that the disadvantages were once important, but no longer are. In this case, the major differences in income levels across regions would tend to diminish over time, except to the extent that increasing-returns-to-scale processes (such as innovative activity, or the agglomeration economies emphasized in the new economic geography) continue to magnify the former disadvantages into permanent differences.

We have been beginning some of this work, by examining the role of climate in the process of technological innovation and technological diffusion. It seems, for example, to be the case that innovative efforts in public health are still overwhelmingly directed at 'temperate-zone diseases', and that the resulting technological innovations do not always cross the ecological divide. There is remarkably little research on malaria vaccines, for example, even though the technological barriers could likely be overcome in just a few years (Hamoudi *et al.* 1999). We have also found that the growth in total factor productivity in agriculture was considerably higher in the temperate zones than the tropical zones during the period 1961–94 (See Gallup and Sachs forthcoming *a*). With regard to coastal proximity, it might be supposed that the vast cost reductions in air and land travel, and in telecommunications and data transmission, during the twentieth century would have greatly reduced the advantages of a coastal location. Such does not seem to be the case, however. In the USA, for example, the proportion of the population living near the sea coast has been rising steadily (Rappaport and Sachs 1999). Also, coastal proximity has given developing countries a clear advantage in the past thirty years in establishing competitive manufacturing export sectors, which in turn have been important contributors to overall economic growth (Radelet and Sachs 1998).

In a recent study of economic growth in Africa, Bloom and Sachs (1999) examined whether geography factors continued to operate directly on economic growth during the time period 1965–90, after controlling for initial income in 1965, human capital in 1965, and economic policies and institutions during the period 1965–90. Using the Barro cross-country growth framework, this study found that Africa's growth shortfall was materially affected by its high prevalence of landlocked populations (only 21% of the Sub-Saharan African population, we have noted, lives within 100 km of the coast), its high concentration of population in the ecological tropics, and the high prevalence of malaria. These factors, together with Africa's low life expectancy (itself a result in large part of the tropical disease environment), accounted for around 1 percentage point per year of Africa's growth shortfall relative to the rest of the developing countries. In general, the analysis underscores the continuing role of coastal access, climate, and disease ecology in the period since 1965, calling into doubt the view that geographical factors are a 'thing of the past'. They have continued to operate with powerful effect in the past thirty years.

A major research priority for economic development is to understand the continuing linkages between ecological zone, disease, agricultural productivity, nutrition, and economic development. In each of these areas, it is surprising how little is known. For example, in the case of malaria, studied recently by Gallup and Sachs (forthcoming, *b*), the basic data on disease incidence and prevalence by region are remarkably incomplete, making difficult a precise measure of the economic burden of the disease. Moreover, the interactions of malaria with nutrition, and with other diseases, is even less well understood. In short, for a major infectious disease that causes more than 1 million deaths per year, and perhaps 200 million clinical cases if not more, very little is understood about the linkages of the disease and broader patterns of economic development—except for the powerful correlation of malarial prevalence and poor economic growth across countries and over time within countries. In general, whether the issue is to analyze the interactions of tropical diseases and growth, or tropical agricultural productivity, nutrition, human capital accumulation, and development, research in this area will require a sophisticated mobilization of cross-disciplinary research approaches.

References

Barro, Robert J. 1991. Economic growth in a cross-section of countries. *Quarterly Journal of Economics*, 106/2: 407–43.

Bloom, David, and Sachs, Jeffrey 1999. Geography, demography, and economic growth in Africa. *Brookings Papers on Economic Activity*, 1999: 1.

Britannica Online. 1998. http://www.eb.com.

CIA (Central Intelligence Agency) 1996. *The World Factbook*. Washington: Central Intelligence Agency.

CIA 1997. *The World Factbook.* http://www.odci.gov/cia/publications/fact book/index.html.

Encyclopaedia Encarta. http://encarta.msn.com.

ESRI (Environmental Systems Research Institute). 1992. *ArcWorld's User Guide and Data Reference.* Redlands, Calif.: ESRI.

—— 1996*a*. *ArcAtlas: Our Earth.* Redlands, Calif.: ESRI.

—— 1996*b*. *ArcWorld Supplement Data Reference and User's Guide.* Redlands, Calif.: ESRI.

GALLUP, JOHN L., and SACHS, JEFFREY D. 1999*a*. Agricultural productivity and geography. Center for International Development, Cambridge, Mass., and forthcoming in the *American Journal of Agricultural Economics.* http://cid.harvard.edu/

—— —— 1999*b*. The economic burden of malaria. Center for International Development, Cambridge, Mass., and forthcoming in the *American Journal of Tropical Medicine and Hygiene.*

—— —— and Mellinger, Andrew D. 1998. Geography and economic development. In *Annual World Bank Conference on Development Economics: 1998*, ed. Boris Pleskovic and Joseph E. Stiglitz. The World Bank. Washington.

GEIGER, R. 1954. Eine neue Wandkarte der Klimagebiete der Erde, *Erdkunde*, 8: 58–61.

—— and Pohl, W. 1953. Revision of the Köppen-Geiger *Klimakarte der Erde.* Darmstadt: Justus Perthes, 4 sheets, 1 : 16 million.

HAMOUDI, AMAR, KREMER, MICHAEL, and SACHS, JEFFREY D. 1999. The case for a vaccine purchase fund. Mimeo. http://cid.harvard.edu/cidmalaria/

KÖPPEN, WLADMIR. 1918. Klassifikation der Klimate nach Temperatur, Niederschlag and Jahreslauf. *Petermanns Geographische Mitteilungen*, 64: 193–203, 243–8.

RADELET, STEVEN, and SACHS, JEFFREY 1998. Shipping costs, manufactured exports, and economic growth. Presented at the American Economics Association annual meeting, Jan. http://www.cid.harvard.edu/economic.htm

RAND MCNALLY and Co. 1980. *Encyclopaedia of World Rivers.* New York: Rand McNally and Co.

RAPPAPORT, JORDAN, and SACHS, JEFFREY 1999. 'The United States as a coastal nation.' Mimeo.

SACHS, JEFFREY D. 1999. Helping the world's poorest. *The Economist*, 352: 8132: 17–20.

SMITH, ADAM. 1976. *An Inquiry into the Nature and Causes of the Wealth of Nations.* 2 vols. ed. Edwin Canaan. Chicago: University of Chicago Press; lst pub. 1776.

STRAHLER, ALAN H., and STRAHLER, ARTHUR N. 1992. *Modern Physical Geography.* 4th edn. New York: John Wiley and Sons, Inc.

TOBLER, WALDO, DEICHMANN, UWE, GOTTSEGEN, JOHN, and MALOY, KELLEY 1995. The global demography project. Technical Report 95–6, National Center for Geographic Information and Analysis, University of California, Santa Barbara, Calif. The data are also freely available on the World Wide Web at CIESIN, Gridded Population of the World, http://www.ciesin.org.html

WITTFOGEL, KARL AUGUST 1957. *Oriental Despotism: A Comparative Study of Total Power.* New Haven: Yale University Press.

World Bank 1998. *World Development Indicators 1998 CD-ROM.* Washington: International Bank for Reconstruction and Development.

Chapter **10**

The Great Tablecloth: Bread and Butter Politics, and the Political Economy of Food and Poverty

Michael J. Watts

Let us sit down to eat
With all those who haven't eaten,
Let us spread great tablecloths,
Put salt in the lakes of the world
Set up planetary bakeries,
Tables with strawberries in snow,
And a plate like the moon itself
From which we will all eat.

For now I ask no more
Than the justice of eating.

(Jorge Luis Borges,
'The Great Tablecloth')

THE whole of human development, Jean-Paul Sartre famously asserted in *The Critique of Dialectical Reason* (1976), 'has been a bitter struggle against scarcity' (p. 23). Indeed for Lionel Robbins it was precisely the universality of scarcity—'We have been turned out of Paradise. We have neither eternal life nor unlimited means of gratification' (1932: 15)—which provided the *unity* of Economic Science in his famous definition of the field as the forms assumed by human behavior in disposing of scarce means. Ironically the economic study of the Third World poor—that is to say those for whom scarcity is *the* defining condition—has never garnered the sort of cachet and legitimacy within academic economics that it properly deserves, perhaps in part because, as the Director of the Harvard Institute of International Development Jeffrey Sachs notes, 'the poorest of the poor are nearly invisible' (1999: 17).

Poverty and hunger are none the less very much part of the landscape of the late twentieth century. As I write, The International Monetary Fund/World Bank, meeting in Washington DC, has acknowledged that the stain of poverty is unacceptably high, and that the absolute numbers living below the poverty line have increased since 1960 (*New York Times*, 2 Oct. 1999: 1).[1] By the conventional measure of hunger, namely the Food and Agricultural Organization's (FAO's) definition of household food security (HFS) ('physical and economic access to adequate food for all household members, without undue risk of losing such access' (FAO 1996: 50)), millions of people are not household food secure. The first FAO report on 'the state of food security in the world' determines that 824 million people (34 million in the developed world) consume so little food relative to requirements that they suffered caloric undernourishment (which often leads to anthropometric deficiency and risk of damaged human development) (FAO 1999). Yet in 1990–2, global food consumption provided 2,720 dietary calories per person which would have been sufficient if distributed in proportion to requirements. In global terms, then, food consumption is so unequal that caloric undernourishment is serious. It is true that the proportion of malnourished people has fallen greatly (more in the past fifty years than in the previous 3,000 according to Michael Lipton *et al.* 1998) but hunger and undernourishment remain endemic in some regions (notably sub-Saharan Africa and South Asia). Paradoxically, there is much evidence to suggest growing hunger in some of the North Atlantic economies and within a number of post-socialist societies. According to the International Food Policy Research Institute (IFPRI) (Von Braun *et al.* 1996), agricultural production fell by 30 per cent in Russia between 1989 and 1994 and hunger is increasingly common. In California (a place seemingly obsessed by eating less and by losing weight), the reform of 'welfare as we know it', has produced 8.4 million who are 'food insecure'. According to a new United Nations Department of Agriculture report, nearly 10 per cent of all US households are 'going hungry or do not have consistent access to adequate food' (*San Francisco Chronicle*, 15 Oct. 1999, p. A7). In 1994, 1.5 million families in the UK could not afford to feed their children an 1876 workhouse diet.

The 742 million poor and hungry souls who reside in the Highly Indebted Poor Countries (HIPCs) have a particular saliency at present—debt relief is on the international agenda once more—and they have drawn the attention of Jeffrey Sachs who sees them as casualties of 'the ecology of underdevelopment' (1999: 17), which, it turns out, is very much about the geography of scarcity. On

[1] In the period since 1980, economic growth in 15 countries has brought rapidly rising incomes to 1.5 billion people, yet one person in three still lives in poverty and basic social services are unavailable to more than 1 billion people. Nowhere is this privation more vivid and pronounced than along gender lines. Of the 1.3 billion people in poverty, 70% are women. Between 1965 and 1988 the number of rural women living below the poverty line increased by 47%; the corresponding figure for men was less than 30% (UNDP 1996).

the one hand, the HIPCs are 'tropical or desert' states, the significance of which resides in the high morbidity and mortality associated with warm climes. Low life expectancy, asserts Sachs, 'is not just the result of poverty but is also a powerful cause of impoverishment' (p. 18). And on the other, the underproduction of food is framed by a sort of double movement: population growth in one corner and the fact that 'the tropics are inherently less productive in annual food crops' (p. 19) in the other. For the geographer, Sachs's account of scarcity is strikingly reminiscent of early twentieth-century, and indeed imperial, geographic theory and before that to a long lineage of neo-Malthusian discourse whose origins lay in the debates around the moral economy of the English poor in the late eighteenth century. Geography and fertility have been, in fact, *the* standard bearers for much modern thinking about scarcity, poverty, and of course hunger in the post-colonial world.

In a rather different vein, Nicholas Xenos (1989) has shown how the experience of scarcity is an invention of modernity, with its own peculiar social practice and self-justification. It was after all the figure of the pauper who, as Karl Polanyi put it in *The Great Transformation* (1957), marked the 'discovery of society', the process by which need provision and security could become part of the public sphere and accordingly enter debates over rights, citizenship, and entitlement. To say that scarcity was invented or constructed in some way is not to deny the existence of material poverty or people too undernourished to work. It is to recognize that lack of well-being has become embedded, at least since the nineteenth century, in a veritable phalanx of institutions, practices, and statistics in which the poor are, to quote Foucault (1972), converted into 'populations', and as such measured, counted, regulated, and institutionalized as particular sorts of subjects. This aspect of what we call 'welfare' represents a sort of third leg of modernity—Marx and Weber represent the other two—in which modern subjects, as dependents, paupers, or welfare mothers, are constituted (Dean 1991). Scarcity in this sense is part of the genealogy of liberal governance.

Scarcity has a more ambiguous relation to modern economics, however, and this is nowhere more the case than in the study of food, hunger, and famine. If the entire edifice of normative and neo-classical economics rests on consumer sovereignty, which is 'the foundation for the market model with consumption as the driving force of the economic system' (Stewart 1998: 269), then there is something paradoxical, if not preposterous, about the idea of acts of individual maximization that confer, as an outcome, extreme hunger or death. As Ben Fine (1997: 620) properly notes:

> it would appear to be impossible to explain how famines occur since no one maximizing utility would choose death . . . even with a low risk. More generally, the new developments within neoclassical economics remain profoundly uncomfortable with questions of power and conflict let alone in instances where rational economic agents die or are killed.

Against this silence, Nobel laureate Amartya Sen's corpus of work—including his new book *Development as Freedom* (1999)—stands as a sharp counterpoint. His approach to the analytical relations between poverty and food insecurity turns on an explicit rejection of both Malthusian doctrine—what he calls 'FAD' or food availability decline—and of utilitarian presumptions about human behavior. Sen's analysis seems out of tune with the timbre of hardcore methodological individualism typified in conventional (that is to say hegemonic) neo-classical economic theory, but it also stands at an angle to the institutionalism of the so-called CDAWN [Coase–Demsetz–Alchian–Williamson–North] school (Bardhan 1989). The Sen lexicon is saturated with the likes of public action, social welfare, inequality, capabilities, and moral philosophy—words somewhat foreign to *cognoscenti* of the profession. Indeed, the very deployment of the language of entitlements, whatever its vagueness and multiple associations (Gasper 1993), marks off Sen as an economist who writes against the grain.

My purpose is not to review the now substantial and almost two decade long debates over entitlements, development, and hunger (see Dreze and Sen 1990; Devereux 1993; Fine 1997; Osmani 1995; de Waal 1997; Watts 1993). Rather I want to explore two areas to which Sen (and some of his critics) have gestured and which geographic research on food systems and provisioning have much to offer. The first concerns the relations that exist between entitlements and what Sen notes in passing as 'the economic class structure as well as the modes of production in the country' (1981: 4). I think one can demonstrate that Sen remains rooted in a somewhat narrow and individualistic model of human behavior, and as Fine (1997) suggests, that his identification of some proximate causes of hunger leaves untheorized the 'economic mechanisms by which social determinants give rise to individual or class-based entitlement outcomes' (p. 633). The second area is the need to understand entitlements in a full and expanded sense and in so doing to identify differing sources of entitlements and the ways in which these sources are politically constituted and struggled over. This permits us, in my view, to go beyond the important but abstract claim that 'No famine has ever taken place in the history of the world in a functioning democracy' (Sen 1999: 23). Curiously, in spite of the regularity with which it appears in his work, politics is the weak reed in Sen's analysis, and I want to suggest how a sensitivity to two differing sorts of politics—of redistribution and recognition (Fraser 1995)—offers a way beyond the oft-cited impasse that Sen's analysis of entitlements has little to say about why the demanding standards of food-enhancing entitlements are rarely met in the real world.[2]

[2] Much of this critical ground has been covered by Fine (1997) in an excellent synthesis of the debate around Sen's work. I have tried to avoid repeating his arguments which in some cases I differ with. I have chosen to emphasize working with entitlements by addressing their social character—something raised by Fine but not developed—and by linking the patterning of social entitlements to both the creation of an anti-famine contract (see de Waal 1997), and the dynamics

Entitlements and Capabilities: Hunger and E-mapping

It is to be expected that something as morally unacceptable as mass hunger in the late twentieth century has a number of contending theoretical points of reference. In a splintered and diverse field, it is demography (so-called neo-Malthusian analyses), technology, production and distribution constraints, weather, and policy failures which loom largest (see Fine *et al.* 1996).[3] The International Food Policy Research Institute (von Braun *et al.* 1999) has, for example, recently offered a synoptic model in its review of the causes of famine in Africa, by identifying on one axis three variables ((1) policy, institutional, and organizational failure, (2) resource poverty and climate, and (3) population pressure), and on the other four 'layers' (namely, 'economic strategy interacting with social discrimination' (p. 7), governance, market failures, and income failure). This produces an unimaginable mix and conflation of all manner of forces and factors which curiously, by the authors' own admission, cannot 'capture political economy issues; nor . . . the relative importance of specific factors . . . nor the important dynamics of famine events' (p. 14)!

Against this body of work, by far the most influential diagnostic account of hunger has been associated with the synoptic work of the brilliant Indian economist Amartya Sen. Sen (1981) approaches hunger, and most especially how hunger and food insecurity on certain parts of the map can degenerate into famine (in his view 'simultaneous' mass mortality due to starvation),[4] from an indisputably micro-economic vantage point. According to Osmani, Sen's 'entitlement approach' calls for the use of 'the general equilibrium method' (1995: 267). Sen indeed begins with the individual endowment which is mapped into a bundle of entitlements, the latter understood as 'the set of alternative commodity bundles that a person can command' (1981: 46) through the use of various *legal* channels of acquirement open to someone of his or her position. Such entitlement bundles confer particular capabilities which ultimately underline well-being. The basic unit of analysis is the individual person, his or her endowment, and his or her entitlement arrangements, though there is considerable ambiguity and slippage in Sen's analysis over the aggregation of such

of political economy as they shape the food system (see also Watts 1991, 1994, and Watts and Goodman 1996).

[3] David Arnold (1988), in his synoptic account of famine, identifies four approaches: climate, population, neo-Malthusianism, and entitlements. For a review of this field see Fine *et al.* (1996), Watts and Bohle (1993), and Dreze and Sen (1990).

[4] There is a legitimate debate over this definition of famine since (1) in famine situations mass mortalities are often caused by disease rather than by starvation *per se*, and (2) the high mortalities due to the existence of serious and prolonged undernutrition and hunger have a 'mass' quality (see de Waal 1997). There is a sense in which Sen's definition and meaning of famine is related to his emphasis on individual entitlements.

individuals into social assemblages such as households or communities or classes. Sen's theory turns on what Fine (1997: 624) properly calls the 'micro (-economic) capability for survival', and on the means by which such individual capabilities fail, producing as a consequence 'excess' individual deaths through generalized individual entitlement failure. In Sen's language, famine as a short-term event characterized by acute deprivation of staple foodstuffs occurs because 'the entitlement set does not include any commodity bundle with enough food' (1981: 46).

Central to Sen's account of why famine occurs is the process of transforming endowments into entitlements, so-called E-mapping. The sorts of entitlements which Sen details are rewards to labor, production, inheritance or asset transfer, and state provisioning (transfers) typically through social security and food relief policies (i.e. anti-famine policies of which the Indian Famine Codes are customarily seen as a model (Dreze and Sen 1990)). In so far as an individual's entitlement set is the consequence of E-mapping on the endowment set, entitlements can only change through transformations in the endowment or E-mapping (see Osmani 1995: 256). Famine occurs through a collapse or adverse change in endowment or E-mapping or both (Sen 1981). Entitlement, in contrast to other theories, 'draws our attention to such variables as ownership patterns, unemployment, relative prices, wage-price ratios, and so on' (1993*a*: 30).

Deploying entitlement in this way, Sen is able to show how famines may occur without a decline in food availability and how entitlements attached to individuals through a generalization of the exchange economy—through markets—may shift in complex ways among differing classes, occupational groups, and sections of the population. In Bengal in 1943, the events of the war years displaced entitlements of certain occupational classes with devastating consequences (over 2.5 million died in 1943–4). Food did not move into famine-stricken Wollo in Ethiopia in 1973 because food prices were not in general higher in Wollo despite starvation, since purchasing power of the local population of peasants and workers had fallen with food output decline. Conversely, a famine '*need not* necessarily occur even when there is a decline of food availability' (Sen 1993*a*: 36–7). Famines can then be seen to have differing dynamics: what he calls 'boom' and 'slump' famines expressing the conditions under which entitlements may fail. Sen is concerned to demonstrate that food supply is not unimportant. The entitlements themselves are influenced *inter alia* by the food system through changes in direct ownership or through contributing to food prices rises (Sen 1993*a*: 37). The real danger resides in concentrating exclusively on food production and availability which can often lull governments into soporific complacency: what Sen calls 'Malthusian optimism': 'Focusing attention on the Malthusian variable of food output per head, the food situation has often appeared to be comfortable even when there have been good economic grounds for expecting terrible troubles for particular occupational groups' (1984: 524).

Sen was of course addressing Third World conditions, but the insight that E-mapping can change in a way in which hunger and even famine may occur amidst plenty, has a particular resonance in a number of post-socialist and advanced capitalist states. A concern with entitlement failure in market circumstances leads Sen (see Dreze and Sen 1990) to emphasize public action through entitlement *protection* (state-funded famine protection through food for work or public food distribution) *and promotion* (a public social security net).

The power of Sen's analysis derives in my view from the fact that it sees the poor and the economically marginal in terms of a set of endowments and the mapping—a complex and largely unexplored term in Sen's corpus—by which they gain command over food. It situates hunger, then, on a landscape, irreducibly social, of the capabilities that individuals, and potentially classes, may mobilize. By examining mapping as an active and transformative process—how the capacity to labor, or access to land can generate an entitlement—it dislodges a concern with output *per se* and focuses on access to and control over food. It offers a *proximate* sort of causal analysis predicated on what immediate or conjunctural forces might shift such forms of access and control and permits a social mapping of such shifts to understand *who* dies or starves (say artisanal craftsmen versus peasants) and *why*. Entitlements—the central mechanism in his intellectual architecture—are individually assigned by virtue of a largely unexamined endowment, and are legally derived from state law (ownership, property rights, contract). Entitlements necessitate making legitimate claims, that is to say, rights resting on the foundations of power (opportunity or actual command) and law (legitimacy and protection).

Running across Sen's scholarship on entitlements are a number of unresolved tensions, a number of which it needs to be said, *contra* his critics, he is acutely sensitive to. One way to reflect upon these tensions is to acknowledge what famines are in practice—a reality that has been immeasurably deepened by the work of geographers (and anthropologists) working on food systems (see Watts 1983; Bohle *et al.* 1991; Swift 1993). Famines have in fact a complex internal architecture, which is to say that the E-mapping is much more complex and dynamic (involving all manner of social, cultural, institutional, and collective actions beyond the entitlements discussed by Sen). E-mapping is a rather passive term for the multiplicity—and the creativity[5]—of coping and adaptive strategies pursued by peasants or petty commodity producers prior to and during a food crisis. In addition, famines must be located historically in terms of the structural tendencies within the political economy, and the crisis proneness of systems of provisioning: proximate causes (Sen's strength) must be

[5] It can legitimately be argued that E-mapping is largely formulaic and almost passive in its characterization of the social dynamics of hunger. What the famine work of geographers, and others, has done, is to demonstrate the agency and graduated forms of flexibility and choice (constrained but choice none the less, even among the poor) with respect to their endowment and the responses to growing food scarcity (see Watts 1983; Richards 1986).

distinguished from longer-term secular dynamics. A famine is inseparable from the historical processes and tendencies which may, quite literally, manufacture it. And not least, as one recent report of famine puts it, 'the study of famine must integrate institutional, political, market, production spheres at both macro and micro levels' (von Braun *et al.* 1993: 73).

It is the relations between the entitlements of the individual and the social group—how are individual (micro) entitlements aggregated for example to account for (macro) class dynamics?—and between the existence of endowments and their social determination which are undeveloped in Sen's corpus. It is not simply that Sen, for example, ignores the role of war in famine genesis—clearly the fundamental cause of famine in much of post-colonial Africa—but that he simply assumes that war displaces production-based entitlements which cause food shortage and famine. But as de Waal (1997) and Keene (1994) have shown, war is often about the political construction of markets. In a similar vein, Sen does not, as Nolan (1993) imputes, ignore socialist famine in China; it is that he attributes it to 'policy failures during the famine years' (1983: 759) without providing an account of how a theory of the state and socialist political economy (a Kornai-like theory of shortage) might provide the reference point for individual entitlements. The social, historical, and structural character of famine is not reducible to individual entitlements any more than the proximate causes of individual entitlement changes have anything to say about the fact that 'the exchange entitlements faced by a person depend, *naturally*, on his position in the economic class structure as well as the modes of production in the country' (1981: 4, emphasis added). Naturally, indeed! In Sen's practice, however, the socio-economic are, as Fine (1997: 638) says, 'necessarily filtered through the analytical framework provided by the microeconomics of entitlements'.

From Entitlements to Entitlement Networks to Modes of Production

I want to offer two ways in which Sen's micro-economics of poverty and food might be pushed forward. One accepts the intellectual originality of entitlements as proximate causes of hunger and famine, but deepens and extends their definition and deployment. The second avenue focuses on class structure and modes of production—political economy—which helps us understand the mechanisms by which social forces give rise, through the food system, to particular entitlement outcomes and forms of E-mapping.[6] While Sen says that

[6] Osmani (1995: 289) notes this lack within Sen's work when he observes that 'the search for causes is then directed backwards to identify the forces that have led to this [entitlement] failure . . . to search . . . for forces that might have impinged upon either endowments or entitlement mappings'.

entitlements are in reality a 'network of entitlement relations' (1981: 159) that depend on economic class structure and a mode of production, he pays scant attention to both the forces which cause entitlements to change or come into being, or to how entitlements are protected and/or promoted.

To begin with entitlements themselves, geographer Charles Gore has noted that 'command over food depends upon something more than *legal rights*' (1993: 433, emphasis added). Indeed, what the geographic work on famine and food systems has shown is precisely the panoply of forms of social interaction—the complex patterns of obligation and duty within communities and households, and collectivities—by which command over food is effected (for example redistributive institutions, forms of charity, gift-giving, and so on, and the multiple forms of livelihood strategy through which command of food is achieved (Richards 1986; Swift 1993; Webb and von Braun 1994)). In part, such rules and norms may be part of a moral economy (Watts 1983), in part they may be forms of sociability which reside within civil and associational life but lie, more pertinently, outside of the law narrowly construed. Sen is sensitive to these 'social entitlements' but his own empirical approach to famine tends to neglect the ethnographic insights into, for example, household, social structural or community institutions, and forms of cultural practice in which command over food may inhere. More importantly, such extended entitlements give reason to question the profoundly individual and legalistic definition of entitlement itself. The legal bias in *Poverty and Famines* (1981) fails to accommodate the obvious fact that illegal acts (food theft by a peasant from a landlord's granary) may be a form of food security.

More precisely, Sen's definition fails to give equal weight to:

- *socially determined entitlements* (a moral economy, indigenous security institutions);
- *non-legal entitlements* (food riots, demonstrations, theft);
- *non-entitlement transfers* (charity).

To include the above under the rubric of entitlements—'extended entitlements' is the term Gore (1993) deploys—highlights a rather different way of thinking about E-mapping. First, entitlements are socially constructed (not just individually conferred); they are forms of social process and a type of representation. Secondly, like all forms of representation, entitlements are complex congeries of cultural, institutional, and political practice which are unstable: that is to say, they are both constituted and reproduced through conflict, negotiation, and struggle. Entitlements are, then, political and social achievements which are customarily fought over in the course of modernization (in this sense one can think about the means by which entitlements enter the political arena in the course of the differing routes to modernity outlined by Barrington Moore in his classic treatise *Social Origins of Dictatorship and Democracy* (1967)). And thirdly, social entitlements confirms Sen's unelaborated observation that the relations between people and food must be grasped as a '*network* of entitlement *relations*' (1981: 159, emphasis added). Food security or famine proneness are the products of historically specific *networks of social entitlements.*

To map such networks, however, requires a theory of entitlements themselves. What are the sources of the entitlements, beyond the fact that they grow in the soil of endowments? Using the work of de Gaay Fortmann (1990), one can conceive of a simple mapping along four dimensions.[7]

- *Institutions*: affiliation to semi-autonomous, rule-making entities in which social networks and positionality determine whether, and what sorts of, entitlements are available.
- *Direct Access*: direct access to forms of legally derived access which turn on property and contract (in Sen's work, ownership and property rights, exchange of labor).
- *State*: forms of instrumental state law (in Sen, social welfare) which identify need and categories of the poor (cf. Fraser's (1989) discussion of discourses of need or dependency in US welfare) and which in turn are rooted in citizenship rights as a bedrock of the modern nation-state.
- *Global Legal Order*: forms of humanitarian assistance grounded in human rights discourse and general principles of freedom, equality, and solidarity for all people as embodied in the Universal Declaration of Human Rights (see Alston (1994) and FAO (1998) on the international 'right to food').

In any setting, the network of entitlements which Sen invokes can be graphically depicted (Fig. 10.1). The strength, depth, and density of the entitlements in each of the four realms will of course vary (one could depict this graphically in terms of the size or shape of the triangular space of each broad category of entitlement), and this differing patterning of entitlements shapes what one might call the architecture of the 'food security system'. Put simply, the geometry of the network for a rural worker in Kerala in South India will look very different from a northern Nigerian peasant. In the former, a regulated agrarian labor market and forms of institutionalized bargaining between state and landlords provides a wage sensitive to price increases; there is in addition a credible and relatively accountable public distribution system which operates effectively in rural areas; and not least there are a number of regional and local civic institutions which provide credit, food for work, and other assistance (see Mooij 1998*b*; Heller 1999). For the Nigerian peasant, state-derived entitlements are almost non-existent, direct access to land is compromised by small holdings incapable of providing self-sufficiency in staple foods, and local food security turns, in some degree, on his or her positionality with respect to local forms of support through lineages, extended families, village redistributive offices, Islamic alms, and the village moral economy (Watts 1983).

[7] I have taken these from de Gaay Fortmann's (1990) excellent working paper but have changed the language.

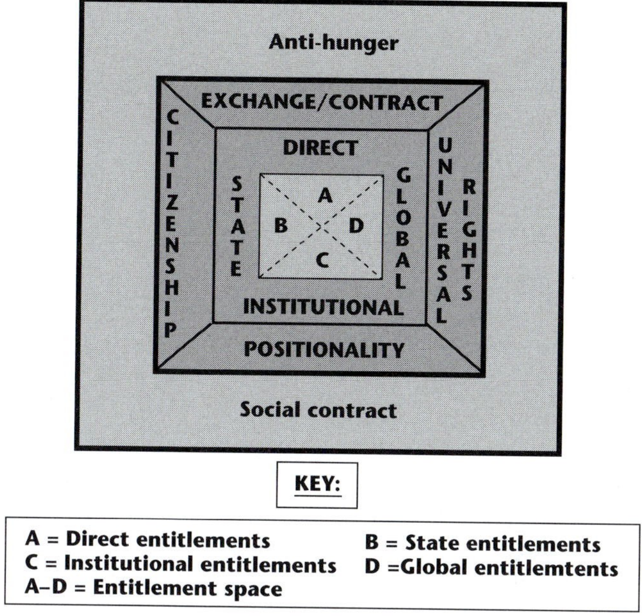

Fig. 10.1. A social contract for food security: a political economy of entitlements

Figure 10.1, in classifying the sources of entitlement, permits a better understanding of both the endowment process and of E-mapping. Endowment embraces not simply assets (land, labor) but *citizenship* (the right to state support), *local group membership* (civic identity in village or community association), and *universal human rights.* The E-mapping then refers to the actual transformative process by which assets, citizenship, and other claims are rendered into effective (i.e. meaningful) entitlement bundles. Put differently, actual state support depends on accountability and transparency (what Sen (1999) simply refers to as democracy). A functioning moral economy rests upon the forms of governance—what others have called social capital—within self-organizing heterarchies (Jessop 1998); humanitarian assistance depends upon the commitment of states and, as de Waal (1997) shows, on the politics and accountability of relief agencies.

In practice, the four sources of entitlement are connected in complex ways. For example, de Waal (1997) has shown how the international humanitarian community is unaccountable in part because local states are decrepit and unaccountable. Much famine relief is channeled through state institutions, the transparency and credibility of which may be open to question. Whether direct access to resources is safe and reliable may turn in large measure on the role of the state, the powers of the judiciary, or the robustness of civil institutions.

Some entitlements in any case are the product of state and civic associations—public–private synergies as Peter Evans (1996) calls them. All of which is to say the network of actually existing entitlements is much more complex that Figure 10.1 depicts. But posing entitlements in this way gives content to the idea of networks and the sources of the network configuration via the differing sources of power, authority, legitimacy, by which the practice of e-mapping actually works out in practice.

The four broad categories of entitlement (and their differing social endowments) raise a number of observations. First, the congeries of social entitlements will be configured in complex bundles in differing settings but they normatively represent what de Waal (1997) calls 'an anti famine political contract' (what I prefer to call a 'food contract'). This contract is both a functional configuration of entitlements to provide food security but also a *political achievement*. Secondly, *the shape* of the contract will change over time, and as a function of the dynamics of the political economy, forms of political regulation, class struggles, and so on. Structural adjustment in Africa and the growing privatization of the humanitarian industry, for example, has reduced an already minimal set of state-based entitlements, and radically reconfigured the space of humanitarian aid (de Waal 1997). And thirdly, the network of social entitlements and the food contract it represents delimits a field or social space of food security, or put differently it defines a 'space of vulnerability' (Watts and Bohle 1993; see also Swift 1993). Vulnerability is here understood as the risks of exposure and the limited capacities to respond to shocks or crises which precipitate entitlement or E-mapping changes. The network of entitlements is more or less inclusive, more or less robust, more or less reliable, and so on. In light of particular perturbations—a drought, an economic recession, price fluctuations, unemployment, and so on—one can begin to think about those who are structurally vulnerable in relation to the extant networks of entitlements.

In pushing entitlements in this way, one inevitably confronts the larger questions of how particular entitlements are distributed and reproduced in specific settings. How is the larger canvas of rights by which social entitlements are defined, fought over and contested, won? How do the structural properties of the political economy precipitate shifts in endowments and E-mapping? These are of course 'classical' questions of political economy (see Kautsky 1899), to which I briefly return in the conclusion.

Bread and Butter Politics and the Great Tablecloth

Sen (1999, 1984) has, of course, linked his account of entitlements to politics both in his work on households—where he links intra-household allocation questions to differing 'perceptions' by household members—and to a general claim about the relations between famine and democracy. But the spheres of both democracy—discussed in large measure as the freedom of the press or more blandly as 'public pressure' (see Dreze and Sen 1990)—and of politics are typically quite abstract and disembodied. There is, for example, little in the way of discussion of food riots, or struggles over the social security net, or an examination of the political discourses over the right to food. For this reason, I want to spend a little time invoking two empirical cases of food politics, struggles over the Great Tablecloth as Borges would say.[8]

The first is drawn from the Indian food system, the Public Distribution System (PDS), and its differential effectiveness in two Indian states: Bihar and Kerala (Mooij 1998*a*). The PDS was set up in part in response to the Bengal famine and institutionalized in 1964, as part of the Nehruvian socialist vision, in tandem with the state-run Food Corporation and the Prices Commission. It is a large-scale rationing program which accounts for 2.5 per cent of government expenditures and 10 to 15 per cent of total production of grains. Staples are purchased in surplus regions, transported and stored and sold in fair price shops. By the 1980s 75 per cent of shops were located in rural areas but the quantity of food allocated through the system varied across states—for example, Kerala distributes 63 kg. per capita while Punjab accounts for a paltry 1 kg. per head—and the 'leakage' is also uneven among states (e.g. for rice from 70–80% loss in Bihar and Orissa to 18% in Kerala).

What Mooij's work (1998*a*, 1998*b*) reveals is how the actual performance of the food security system is largely a function of how and whether food and PDS is 'politicized'. In Kerala a long history of grass-roots activism and political mobilization from below has meant that leakage is low (state accountability and popular mobilization are mutually reinforcing) and distribution reaches the proper constituencies with little loss. In Bihar conversely, leakage is exceptionally high, beneficiaries small, and food security is accordingly low. Mooij's argument turns on how populist politics in the state is of a different sort in which (1) politicians do not require food to increase their popularity, (2) politicians cannot make PDS function in such a way as to make political capital out of it, (3) the diversion of PDS to the black market is a greater source of profit than targeting food insecure constituencies, and (4) some of the households are too poor for PDS. In both cases the actual forms of democracy—one a redistributive politics associated with Marxist parties, and the other a decrepit and corrupt sort of authoritarian populism—have to be grasped in all of their local complexity to identify the ways in which food enters, so to speak, the social contract.

The second example is of some work I conducted in The Gambia, specifically a smallholder irrigation project to increase food security and food productivity. At its heart lay a technological innovation (high yielding seeds and water control) at the point of production involving a crop (rice) for which there was a

[8] See Mooij (1998: 77–101); Watts (1993).

long-standing sexual division of labor by crop (rice was almost wholly a women's crop). Women customarily possessed some direct access to rice land through forest clearance and by inheritance through the female line. Increased output and income had the effect, however, of stimulating struggles *within* the household over entitlements. In so far as a second rice crop was historically unprecedented among Mandinka families, the pressing question at the level of the growers was who would work (longer and harder and in new ways) and for what return? In so far as women lost their traditional rice land and the standing of the improved irrigation was redefined (by men and by local Muslim legal institutions) as male property, the question of entitlements—to land, to the labor of others—carried a powerful valency. The struggles over entitlement in this case were intra-household and took the form of women bargaining with men (their husbands typically) over a share of the crop, over property rights (what claims women had over the improved land), and over the exchange of resources within marriage—that is to say, the content of the conjugal contract. The household as a political arena—of mutual obligations, responsibilities, and entitlements—was converted into a terrain of conflict, negotiation, and struggle. How and whether increased food output at the household level actually enhanced food security of individuals in Mandinka households was in large measure a consequence of the ways women, and wives in particular, could win and establish their claims from their husbands in a patriarchal and patrilocal social structure.

What both of these examples have in common is that they vividly display how differing social entitlements are contested and fought over on the one hand, and how they enter differing sorts of political discourses and practices on the other. One turned on gender and domestic politics, the other on various forms of state populism. Each case suggests that while Sen is right that democracy and famine are related, politics can assume a panoply of forms in numerous arenas (the state, the workplace, the family). They show how entitlements have to be won, enforced, and fought over, and that these struggles rest on the existence and enforcement of civil and political liberties. These political arenas and the struggles over entitlements which ensue are rooted in forms of social power (for example, Hindu populism or Mandinka patriarchy) and in modes of production (for instance, peasant forms of livelihood in The Gambia or social democratic forms of regulated capitalism in Kerala).

But I think that these prosaic illustrations of struggles over food—over food and democracy—also reveal something else: namely, that two different sorts of politics are involved in the creation of an anti-famine contract, and that both are constitutive of what Sen calls democracy. To invoke Nancy Fraser (1995), there is a *politics of redistribution* (in which state redistribution and political parties often play a central role), and there is a *politics of recognition* (often, but not exclusively, a domain of civic and associational life). Linking democracy and food security must necessarily, in my view, build upon such a recoupling of recognition and redistribution, as I think the two case studies show in rather different ways.

New Directions and Future Prospects

One of the great strengths of Sen's approach to hunger is that entitlements are part of a larger architecture of thinking about development as a state of well-being and choice or freedom. In his language, the capability of a person reflects the 'alternative combinations of functioning the person achieves and from which he or she can choose one collection' (1993*b*). Functionings represent parts of the state of a person and especially those things that a person can do or be in leading a life. In seeing poverty or hunger as a failure of capabilities—rather than insufficient income, or inadequate primary goods as in the Rawlsian sense of justice—Sen shows how the freedom to lead different types of life is reflected in the person's capabilities (see Sen 1999).

Without entering here into philosophical debates over capability and its philpsophical basis (see Doyal and Gough 1991; Sen 1993*b*), the point is to recognize that hunger becomes grounded in politics as much as production, in democracy as much as geography, in social capacity and governance as much as technology and distribution. This in turn points to some new directions, and unexplored paths, for the study of development and hunger. I shall briefly mention three here. The first speaks to the need to link governance with food. Sen (1993*b*) properly emphasizes the continued need for public action in the construction of a food contract but one should also think about forms of voluntary association—what Paul Hirst (1997) calls 'associational democracy'—as a complementary frame of reference. Indeed much of the geographical work on governance (see Storper and Salais 1997, and also Jessop 1998) is especially relevant in thinking about how forms of co-ordinations and conventions enter into the food contract. This is especially relevant to understand the genesis of hunger in the North Atlantic economies and provides an avenue to link hunger with debates over the refiguring of the Fordist or social democratic welfare state (van Parijs 1995; Esping-Andersen 1990). Secondly, there is a need to deepen the understanding of the relations between political transitions and the right to food question. How exactly food enters into the discourses of democracy, and through what political forms and institutions, are key questions which can only be explored through a sensitivity to the politics of scale (household, state, global) and to comparative experience. How is the refiguration of the Chinese Iron Rice Bowl since 1978 comparable to food security strategies in the southern cone of Latin America under neo-liberal austerity programs? And thirdly, there is a desperate need to link the increasingly sophisticated work on the political economy of food systems (see Fine 1994; Goodman and Watts 1996)—which is acutely aware of the industrialization and globalization of the agro-food system along its length, and to the specific organic qualities of food provisioning—to the food entitlement and security debate. What does the arrival of Euro-American fast food and recombinant DNA agro-biotechnology imply for the dynamics of food entitlement and the architecture of the contemporary Indian food contract?

In conclusion, perhaps one can productively return to Sen, not to break ranks with his claim that democracy is a prerequisite to resolve hunger, but rather to point to the fact that democracy and democratic forms of social governance are, as Bobbio (1980) says, fundamentally incomplete. In this regard one might say that Sen's entitlements approach has shed some light on proximate causes of famine (entitlement shifts) and the absolute cause of food security (democracy). In between, and awaiting illumination, is on the one hand the great arch of capitalist political economy and its relation to endowments and E-mapping, and on the other the rough and tumble of actual democratic governance—that is to say, democracy which draws from but extends beyond government. In this sense, Sen has, as he is doubtless fully aware, posed sharply the question of the relation between development and freedom in a world in which, to return to Bobbio, the two 'great blocks of descending and hierarchical power'—big business and public administration—continue to hold out against the pressures from below.

References

Alston, P. 1994. International Law and the right to food. In *Food*, ed. B. Harriss-White and R. Hoffenberg. Oxford: Blackwell, 205–16.

Arnold, D. 1988. *Famine.* Oxford: Blackwell.

Bardhan, P., ed. 1989. *The Economic Theory of Agrarian Institutions.* Oxford: Clarendon Press.

Bobbio, N. 1980. *The Future of Democracy.* Cambridge: Polity.

Bohle, H. G., Cannon, T., Hugo, G., and Ibrahim, F. 1991. *Famine and Food Security in Africa.* Bayreuth: Naturwissenschaftliche Gesellschaft.

de Gaay Fortmann, B. 1990. Entitlement and development. *Working Paper Series*, No. 87. The Hague: Institute of Social Studies.

Dean, M. 1991. *The Constitution of Poverty.* London: Routledge.

Devereux, S. 1983. *Theories of Famine.* Hemel Hempstead: Harvester Press.

de Waal, A. 1997. *Famine Crimes.* London: International African Institute.

Doyal, L., and Gough, I. 1991. *A Theory of Need.* New York: Guilford.

Dreze, J., and Sen, A. 1990. *Hunger and Public Action.* Oxford: Clarendon Press.

Esping-Andersen, G. 1990. *The Three Worlds of Welfare Capitalism.* Princeton: Princeton University Press.

Evans, P. 1996. Development stategies across the public-private divide. *World Development*, 24: 1033–7.

Fine, B. 1994. Toward a political economy of food. *Review of International Political Economy*, 1: 579–45.

——1997. Entitlement failure? *Development and Change*, 28: 617–47.
——Heasman, M., and Wright, J. 1996. *Consumption in the Age of Affluence*. London: Routledge.
——and Leopold, E. 1996. *The World of Consumption*. London: Routledge.
Food and Agricultural Organization (FAO) 1996. *Sixth World Food Survey*. Rome: Food and Agriculture Organization.
——1998. *The Right to Food*. Rome: United Nations.
——1999. *The State of Food Security in the World*. Rome: United Nations.
Foucault, M. 1972. *Discipline and Punish*. New York, Harper.
Fraser, N. 1989. *Unruly Practices*. Minneapolis: University of Minnesota Press.
——1995. *Justice Interruptus*. London: Routledge.
Gasper, D. 1993. Entitlements analysis. *Development and Change*, 24: 679–718.
Goodman, D., and Watts, M., eds. 1996. *Globalizing Food*. London: Routledge.
Gore, C. 1993. Entitlement relations and 'unruly' social practices. *Journal of Development Studies*, 29: 429–60.
Heller, P. 1999. *The Labor of Development*. Ithaca, NY: Cornell University Press.
Hirst, P. 1997. *Associational Democracy*. London: Polity.
Jessop, R. 1998. Governance and economic development. *International Social Science Journal*, 168: 56–88.
Kautsky, K. 1899. *La Question agraire*. Paris: Maspero.
Keene, D. 1994. *The Benefits of Famine*. Princeton: Princeton University Press.
Lipton, M., de Haan, A., and Darbellay, E. 1998. 'Food security, food consumption patterns and production patterns'. In *Consumption for Human Development: Background Papers*. New York: United Nations Development Program, 45–120.
Mooij, J. 1998*a*. Real targetting: the case of food distribution in India. *Working Paper Series*, No. 276. The Hague: Institute of Social Studies.
——1998*b*. Food policy and politics. *Journal of Peasant Studies*, 25: 77–101.
Moore, B. 1967. *The Social Origins of Dictatorship and Democracy*. Boston: Beacon.
Nolan, P. 1993. The causation and prevention of famines. *Journal of Peasant Studies*, 21: 1–28.
Osmani, S. 1995. The entitlement approach to famine. In *Choice, Welfare and Development*, ed. K. Basu, P. Pattanaik, and K. Suzumura. Oxford: Clarendon Press, 253–94.
Polanyi, K. 1957. *The Great Transformation*. Boston: Beacon Press.
Richards, P. 1986. *Coping with Hunger*. London: Allen and Unwin.
Robbins, L. 1932. *The Nature and Significance of Economic Science*. London: Macmillan.
Rogers, C., and Gore, C., eds. 1995. *Social Exclusion*. Geneva: International Labor Organization.
Sachs, J. 1999. Helping the world's poorest. *The Economist*, 14 Aug.: 17–20.
Sartre, J.-P. 1976. *The Critique of Dialectical Reason*. London: New Left Books.
Sen, A. 1981. *Poverty and Famines*. Oxford: Clarendon Press.
——1983. Development: which way now? *Economic Journal*, 83.
——1984. *Resources, Values and Development*. Oxford: Blackwell.
——1987. Property and hunger. *Economics and Philosophy*, 4: 57–68.
——1993*a*. The causation and prevention of famines: a reply. *Journal of Peasant Studies*, 21: 29–40.

Sen, A. 1993*b*. Capability and well being. In *The Quality of Life*, ed. M. Nussbaum and A. Sen. Oxford: Clarendon Press, 30–53.

—— 1999. *Development as Freedom*. New York: Knopf.

Stewart, F. 1998. Consumption, globalization and theory. In *Consumption For Human Development Background Papers*. New York: United Nations Development Program, 269–84.

Storper, M., and Salais, R. 1997. *Worlds of Production*. Cambridge, Mass.: Harvard University Press.

Swift, J., ed. 1993. New approaches to famine. *IDS Bulletin*, 24.

United Nations Development Program (UNDP) 1996. *The Human Development Report*. New York: Oxford University Press.

—— 1998. *The Human Development Report*. New York: Oxford University Press.

Van Parijs, P. 1995. *Real Freedom For All*. Oxford: Clarendon.

Von Braun, J. 1991. *A Policy Agenda for Famine Prevention in Africa*. Washington: The International Food Policy Research Institute (IFPRI).

—— Serova, E., Seeth, H., and Melyukhina, O. 1996. *Russia's Food Economy in Transition*. Washington: IFPRI Discussion Paper, No. 18.

—— Teklu, T., and Webb, P. 1993. Famine as the outcome of political, production and market failures. *IDS Bulletin*, 24/3: 73–9.

—— —— —— 1999. *Famine in Africa*. Baltimore: The Johns Hopkins University Press.

Watts, M. 1983. *Silent Violence*. Berkeley: University of California Press.

—— 1991. Entitlement or empowerment? *Review of African Political Economy*, 51: 9–26.

—— 1993. Life under contract. In *Reworking Modernity*, ed. A. Pred and M. Watts. New Brunswick: Rutgers University Press, 65–105.

—— 1994. What difference does difference make. *Review of International Political Economy*, 1/3: 563–71.

—— and Bohle, H. 1993. The space of vulnerability. *Progress in Human Geography*, 17: 43–67.

Webb, P., and Von Braun, J. 1994. *Famine and Food Security in Ethiopia*. New York: Wiley.

Xenos, N. 1989. *Scarcity and Modernity*. London: Routledge.

Section 5

Finance Capital

Chapter **11**

The Regulation of International Finance

Risto I. Laulajainen

Perspective

INTERNATIONAL finance has radically changed shape during the last two decades. The large-scale dismantling of regulatory structures such as exchange and capital controls and cross-border investment rules and increased foreign ownership has widened the geographical scope of international finance. The revolution of information technology has allowed the implementation of financial operations at lightning speed. One perception is that international finance has few limits and that geography has lost much of its meaning in that part of human activity (O'Brien 1992: 1). This interpretation overlooks the original barriers to financial flows that still play a role (Budd 1999: 121; O'Brien 1992: 17–18). Some barriers appear protectionist but intend to safeguard the financial system from abuse, and promote stability and efficiency. These structures reflect the cultural background of their creators and are thereby instrumental in preserving geographical diversity, much to the chagrin of many financial actors.

Hence there is a need to explain this diversity, and to coordinate it. But no matter how apparent the need, creating a plausible international framework and implementing it will take time if it is ever to succeed completely. The regulation of money is very much part of the national legal culture, which is resistant to change, and the national experience of financial abuse, which is long remembered. Countries with a federal structure like the USA and Canada can also have state-level laws further adding to geographical diversity. It does not help either that fiscal law and securities regulations are at the volatile end of the legal spectrum, virtual bus-timetable law (Wood 1995: 251). Coordination by the Bank for International Settlements (BIS), the European Union (EU), the International Organization of Securities Commissions (IOSCO), and similar organizations is of comparatively recent origin, geographically patchy, and often voluntary in implementation. It follows that international finance must largely make do with national regulatory systems.

The oldest and most widespread monetary regulation is the prohibition of usury, or interest in general. The purpose was to protect people in distress at a time when loans were for consumption and large investment projects were realized by forced labour, that is, paid out of cash flow. The moral cause was very strong and had religious connotations, some of which have survived to the present day. Another common ban concerned gambling. Since gambling was also the pastime of the upper social crust, legislation came relatively late. The ruling that gambling debts cannot be collected through courts gained unexpected weight when the idea of hedging was imported from commodity exchanges to the financial world. These financial derivatives were met with great suspicion. They did not involve any tangibles but were 'mere' promises about abstract matters. The verdict was not late in coming: gambling or almost. Countries where such opinions prevailed, or at least surfaced, included some of the world's financial superpowers. In 1991 the House of Lords in the UK freed a number of imprudent local authorities from loss-making swap obligations by referring to their gambling-like nature (Moore 1991). And it was in 1989 when Germany unconditionally abandoned the gambling paradigm. By then the trading of its derivative instruments had already been established in London, whence their repatriation has been an arduous task.

Usury and gambling laws are early examples of legislation intended to protect the small man, the consumer of retail financial services. The regulatory legislation has subsequently been expanded into a vast rule set with appropriate enforcement apparatus. The approach is twofold, to prevent improper behaviour and, when the prevention fails, to compensate victims.

The compensation principle is simple: the government guarantees funds deposited with a financial intermediary either in full or a certain percentage of them, up to a predefined maximum amount. The guarantee is financed by a levy among peers or from tax revenue. Whichever the alternative, it means subsidizing the dishonest by the honest. Yet compensatory schemes are necessary to maintain the confidence of the general public. This is not pure populism because large creditors are likely to be informed and therefore more responsible. But compensation cannot be too generous either because of the imbedded moral hazard. Intermediaries assume larger risks for higher profit and thereby incur losses when things go wrong. An example is US savings banks (thrifts) whose depositors were given a $100,000 guarantee by the federal government. The result was predictable. Investor money flowed in and bankers ventured into increasingly risky lending. This made the ensuing insolvencies more devastating than otherwise. A total of $230 billion, 3.5 per cent of the Gross Domestic Product (GDP), was needed for the rescue of the industry (Warf and Cox 1995, 1996).

The preventive rule set focuses on historically known soft spots such as fraud, misappropriation of funds, and malpractice, and purports to keep a tight rein on professionals. Whether the set is really needed is a matter of some controversy. All developed jurisdictions have a general law about fraud, misrepresentation, and fiduciary duty that makes their codification into a special law more an issue of predictability and accessibility than of principle. The widely publicized enforcement role of US regulators is assumed in Europe by law enforcement authorities in general. There are also customs and codes which, although not legally binding, are nevertheless of substantial potence (Kumar 1997: 64–5; Wood 1995: 255).

Regulators

The basic philosophy is to admit the difference between the small investor and the professional. As long as the financial markets were the realm of professionals and the privilege of the few, the difference did not matter too much. But the coming of the small man who also had the political vote tipped the scales. It became important to protect his interests without jeopardizing the smooth working of wholesale finance. The approach is that of *uberrimae fidei* (full disclosure), while the professional is supposed to take care of himself, the *caveat emptor* principle. Their simultaneous accommodation creates difficulties, which are solved with parallel rule sets and exemptions.

The traditional way was to leave matters to market practitioners. The result was a clubby but professional system that was flexible and kept regulatory cost low but irritated outsiders. Germany is habitually quoted as an example of a club culture. Banks have played a prominent role there, and proper securities legislation came as late as in 1995 when the Federal Supervisory Office for Securities Trading was set up (Covill 1998: 76). The system was rather like in English-speaking post-colonial countries, which continue to rely on stock exchanges for listed securities under the surveillance of the central bank. Codes of conduct for dealers exist but are not legally binding, and ordinary fiduciary law is considered sufficient (Wood 1995: 277). That was also the British way until 1986, when a formal structure was put in place in a sequence of events known as the Big Bang. Still, the practice is liberal when compared with the Continent, drifting forward to increased detail under the guise of the EU (Franks and Schaefer 1993: 21). And the Continent lags behind the USA where a rigid regulation was introduced in the aftermath of the 1929 stock market crash. Equity ownership was spread among large segments of the population and created the necessary political push. Although rigid, the system leaves implementation largely to market practitioners (self-regulation). The US model was then exported to Japan after World War II, although in a diluted form. Administrative judgement is important there, and much of the legal groundwork for massive securitization is lacking (Tett 1998*a*, 1998*b*).

Developing countries tend to follow the same line: compliance with instructions by authorities is an important regulatory goal (merit regulation).

Even where the system follows self-regulatory lines, there must be a supervisory authority. It issues licences, sets rules, and exercises practical supervision. Supervision includes the scrutiny of periodical reports, conduction of on-site inspections, taking corrective and emergency action. To perform its tasks properly the regulator must have autonomy, authority, and capacity, that is, be free of political interference and have competent staff in sufficient numbers. The overall field covers banking, securities, and insurance. How the field is divided administratively varies.

Historically, insurance has had its own regulator, the Department of Labour when the welfare connection has been paramount, or the Department of Industry when economic linkages have taken the front seat. Recalling the different character of life and other types of insurance, both solutions have merit. The unifying force is the accumulation of premium income into funds that need management, more crucial in the life segment than the non-life one.

The next split is into banking and securities regulation. The former is direct and confidential; the latter is largely based on market discipline. Banking regulation is about the soundness of the system at large and the prevention of bank failures that would contaminate it. Securities regulation, in contrast, focuses on market fairness because the business is market-based.

Separate banking and securities regulation prevail in countries with the Anglo-American tradition, because there the underlying businesses are also separate, either by law or custom. There it is natural that banks are supervised by the national central bank. It has the authority and expertise, and also the overall responsibility for the banking system. That responsibility involves the bailing out of troubled banks. In countries where securities markets are weakly developed and financial markets revolve around the banking system, it is also natural that regulatory functions are concentrated in the central bank. Developing countries and those with a strong universal banking tradition follow this model. Germany and Switzerland are quoted as prime examples, and not without reason because their stock exchanges are virtually owned by their largest banks.

Today this stereotype view needs amendments and refinements. The UK recently decided to abandon the decentralized model and consolidate all financial supervision into a single body, the Financial Services Authority (FSA), with banking, exchanges, building societies, insurance, fund management, and pensions under its umbrella (House 1997: 57). The argument was the rapid integration of financial markets, which makes separate supervisors an increasingly untenable concept. How the new system will perform remains to be seen. Denmark and Sweden have implemented the idea successfully but with much smaller and less sophisticated markets (Kumar 1997: 72). Important amendments have also taken place in Germany and Japan. In the former, there has been a shift of power from the central bank to the Federal Banking Supervisory Office, and in the latter the Ministry of Finance has relinquished the regulation of large banks to a new agency.

The decentralized US system may have resisted the winds of change best. The Congress legislates and exercises supreme control at hearings, while the President makes the top nominations. Departments do much routine work in certain fields, in cooperation with state-level regulators. Insurance and pensions fall neatly into the box of the Department of Labor and/or Commerce. The Treasury takes care of all nationally licensed commercial banks and thrifts. This does not yet differ too much from the previous systems. The US speciality is the numerous agencies that are outside the departmental structure. The key agency for bank holding companies with all their parts is the Federal Reserve System (central bank). Investment banks, which are confined to the riskier securities business, are regulated by the powerful Securities and Exchange Commission (SEC). Stock exchanges also belong to its fief, while derivatives exchanges fall under the aegis of the Commodity Futures Trading Commission (CFTC), a historical anomaly. Swaps remain unregulated through a quirk of political horse-trading. SEC's activity rests on disclosure, so that investors are fully informed when making their own decisions. It can investigate, make rules, and pursue civil action in the courts, but its decisions can also be challenged in the same courts.

Costs and Benefits

The total regulatory cost is very much of an enigma. The easiest part is the cost of the regulatory authority itself, more difficult is the hidden cost caused by its action in the field, and most difficult is the change of behaviour that its mere existence will catalyse. There is also the opportunity cost, because compliance resources could be used for other purposes as well. The hidden cost includes the compliance cost of firms and individuals, estimated in the UK at four times the direct cost (Franks and Schaefer 1993: 13). It also arises when immaterial technicalities profoundly affect the normal course of affairs. The privatization of the Polish Telecom is a ready example (Caplen 1998). Changed behaviour is observed when investors and executives assume that the state will bail out insolvent institutions and therefore fail to exercise normal prudence. Imposition of liability on a regulator or an issuing syndicate simply by force of their ability to pay (big-pocket liability), rather than negligence or guilt, will also lead to distorted behaviour.

The direct cost is related best to the number of employees in the financial sector. It varied in 1991–2 between \$90 and \$160 per head in the USA, UK, and France, all countries with substantial self-regulation (Franks and Schaefer 1993, table 2). The staff directly involved is not large: 2,400 at the SEC in 1990 and an estimated 2,100 at the FSA (House 1997: 60; Wood 1995: 253). The FSA figure is a useful yardstick, since it comprises the whole spectrum of financial services. The Swedish market is 5 to 10 per cent of the British one and the regulatory personnel correspondingly less, some 150 persons (Finansinspektionen 1998). The Japanese figures at the new Financial Supervision Agency appear quite modest—only 400, of whom 150 are inspectors, but its sector is also narrow (Smith 1998).

Regulatory cost should be juxtaposed with the savings due to fewer insolvencies, frauds, insider crimes, and so on. Estimating them is a tall order, because only a fraction of such cases comes to light. For example, frauds have a tendency to emerge at insolvencies. The recent track record of UK regulators has been one major disclosed incident every other year, on average. The loss in the Barlow Clowes affair in 1988 was over £100 million, depositors lost hundreds of millions in the bankruptcy of BCCI in 1991, Maxwell pensioners over £400 million in 1992, Barings' shareholders over £800 million in 1995, to take some high-profile examples. The direct annual cost of £93 million in 1991 can be compared with them. That is still easy, but drawing the conclusion is fraught with difficulty. Is it the case that doubling the regulatory resources could have prevented the said incidents? Or did the available resources help by halving the potential losses, to their documented historical level? Nobody knows, and therefore the principle stated by law, that the new FSA should be cost effective, is very bold indeed (Graham 1997).

Banking Rules

The regulation of banking and securities has superseded the traditional regulation of usury and gaming. The basics of bank regulation are rather similar all over the world, be it because of the antiquity of the business or the level-headedness of central bankers, the traditional regulators. Compared with it, securities regulation is as yet unsettled and filled with moralism (Wood 1995: 11–12).

The main characteristic of a bank is that it will accept deposits. A licensed bank should have enough capital for its intended business, shareholders of good moral standing free of conflicts of interest, professional and honest management, a transparent organizational structure amenable to internal control, a sound business plan, and adequate home-country supervision. There will be limits for lending concentration, lending to insiders, a liquidity mismatch, net foreign positions, and stakes in non-financial activity (Folkerts-Landau *et al.* 1998: 32). Details vary by country. For example, a 'large' exposure in the EU is 10 per cent of regulatory capital and the maximum is 25 per cent. Sophisticated foreign exchange banks in the UK can exceed this, however, by permission and without prior notice, but only against a limited list of counterparties. The USA requires 15 per cent for unsecured loans and 25 per cent for loans backed by liquid securities. The EU has an aggregate limit of 800 per cent, while the USA has none (Folkerts-Landau *et al.* 1998: 38; Wood 1995: 387).

The principal source of bank vulnerability is an unstable macroeconomic environment, and little can be done about it except creating reserves to mitigate the shocks. Management shortcomings are more frequent and easier to correct. The normal pattern is that too much risk is taken in order to raise revenue, and too few loan provisions are made to cushion the inevitable defaults. The losses made by imprudent lending to Long Term Capital Management, an unregulated hedge fund, are a current example (Anon. 1998; Shirreff 1998). The microenvironment either inflates or suppresses the effects. The potentially corrupting influence of an official safety net was mentioned above. Banks belonging to conglomerates run the risk of loan concentration. State-owned banks are soft on political lending. Countries practising merit regulation are a variant of the same theme. The purpose need not be sinister. The concentration of national wealth and the lack of capital markets may make it impossible to keep banking interests apart from economic interests in general.

Everyday regulation and surveillance revolve around two concepts, liquidity and solvency. Liquidity means that bills are paid in time. Solvency implies that assets exceed liabilities. A basically sound bank can become temporarily illiquid. It normally has a maturity mismatch, largely beyond its own control. The deposits are redeemable within a year, but the demand for loans is for five years or more, for example. Matching the maturity profiles may be impossible for competitive and other reasons. There can also be systemic failures such as the breakdown of the national payment system. But faulty or not, from a banking perspective, such a bank becomes a bad risk and gets effectively frozen out of the interbank market. The standby facility, the standard remedy, becomes practically worthless for liquidity purposes. Then it is time for the lender of last resort to intervene. This is a sensitive task, because banks typically become insolvent before they become illiquid.

Deciding about insolvency is difficult because most bank assets, and typically loans, have no ready market. A loan market is gradually emerging, but it is unlikely ever to match securities markets, and it is available only in the financially most sophisticated countries. But without a liquid market it is impossible to give loans a fair value. In this respect, securities portfolios are much easier to handle. Another question then is that the incentive to conceal bad loans grows with weakening solvency. They can be renewed in a new shape (novated), reported off the balance sheet, and transferred offshore. When closure becomes inevitable, regulatory speed is vital. This is to prevent asset stripping and systemic panic. To minimize business disruption, the closure is preferably affected after banking hours. The globalization of banking has made this principle increasingly untenable, however, because financial markets are open 24 hours a day, somewhere in the world. It may also be necessary to secure a court order for the closure at the bank's domicile, and that may be available only during the normal business day. That was the case when Luxembourg's regulator wanted to close down the BCCI. Whether a banking regulator should have the authority to sidestep normal bankruptcy proceedings is a delicate question.

When international bankruptcies occur, contradictory legal principles give headaches. For example, should the insolvent be given a chance to sort out problems or be wound up without further ceremony? The USA and France follow the first philosophy, while Germany adheres to the second. Once the winding-up is a fact, the netting of mutual debts irrespective of other creditors becomes an issue. This set-off has been explicitly forbidden in France, Luxembourg, Belgium, Spain, and Greece, although that is bound to change in the context of payment systems. In the UK and associated jurisdictions, the set-off is, in contrast, compulsory. In many other countries, it is permitted by private contract (Wood 1995: 59). Discrimination of foreign debtors and creditors *vis-à-vis* domestic ones is, fortunately, on the way out with the coming of consolidated proceedings (Kelly 1998; Scott 1992).

Securities Rules

Securities include common and preferred shares, bonds, notes, commercial paper, options, and financial futures. It is the realm of non-bank financial institutions (NBFI). They can be independents, bank subsidiaries, or parts of financial conglomerates and universal banks. The regulator's task is more difficult with greater integration. It is not only the larger size and heterogeneity of the organization but also the shuffling of assets and losses between its parts and the conflicts of interest that come into the picture.

Consider an investment-banking arm of a financial conglomerate advising a customer to take over a competitor. The acquisition is to be paid for by the acquirer's equity. The higher the share price, the better the chance of success. The bank also has other customers who deal in these shares, and the temptation to recommend the shares to them is obvious. Then the conglomerate has a fund-management arm. The simplest solution would be if it started buying the shares, whether or not it is in the best interest of the funds. Should the monies be insufficient, the retail-banking arm could lend more from trust funds or deposits made with it by the general public. The conflicts of interest are many, and a crisis in one part of the conglomerate could easily contaminate the rest. To prevent that happening the regulator has set up various hindrances.

The most credible hindrance is to separate banking, securities business, and fund management from each other (fire walling). This is the traditional US policy, also common in Asia. Separate companies, or at least subsidiaries, are pushed to deal with each other at arm's length and simultaneously minimize the contamination risk. The EU policy of having separate capital bases for banking and securities business (banking and trading books), although within the same universal bank, is a diluted form of the same philosophy. Whatever policy is adopted, it is important to bar the use of inside information between the parts, a pursuit for which the metaphor of Chinese walls is used. But in practice it is difficult to prevent people of the same organization, in close physical proximity, to communicate with each other. If it does not happen in the office, it takes place over lunch. One can also close one's eyes and trust in people's honesty, the traditional Continental approach for professionals in the know. Breaking the unwritten rules of the invisible club led to ostracism and loss of business, and was efficient in that sense (Kumar 1997: 3, 67–8). The preferred model depends ultimately on the structure of the financial markets; widespread securities ownership needs the most stringent checks and balances.

NBFIs are either brokers and dealers or funds. Brokers are pure intermediaries, while dealers also take proprietary positions. Dealing is risky because inventories are large and prices are volatile, particularly in private securities. Underwriting tops the scale because the volumes become still larger. Logically, the US policy reserves the most risky segments for investment banks, while commercial banks and even thrifts are allowed to operate in low-risk segments.

US rules are also of interest from a wider angle. Nowhere else is securities legislation as all-embracing and strict as there, which, combined with the country's financial muscle, has induced others to adopt much of its thinking. The registration of issues, the details of the prospectus, the registration and capital adequacy of dealers, the segregation of customer assets from those of the intermediary are standard fare. Registration is followed by annual, semi-annual, and quarterly reports describing important company events, recent financial history, and current financial status. The financials are based on the Generally Accepted Accounting Principles (GAAP). The detail is considerable, becomes expensive, and reveals more than many foreigners are willing to accept. The accounting standard also differs in many important aspects from that prevailing in Continental Europe. All this creates a dilemma because the US market is unsurpassed in its capacity to supply capital.

Cognizant of the demand but also of competition by foreign markets, US authorities have eased the basic rules. Shelf registration was created to enhance competitiveness within euromarkets, which have very little red tape and short lead times. A shelf issue is registered speculatively, its prospectus updated continuously, and the issue can be placed at very short notice when there is a market opening. A popular rule is 144*a* that exempts private placements with Qualified Institutional Buyers (QIB) from registration. A QIB manages at least $100 million of funds, the scale of activity indicating professionalism. An alternative is private investment companies of at most 100 persons, assumed to know each other well enough and be sufficiently sophisticated to take care of themselves. Similar principles about disclosure and professional investors can be found in other jurisdictions. The provision of a sophisticated investor by the EU makes the eurobond market possible, for example.

Eurobonds create special regulatory problems. Securities issued in country *A*, nominated in country *B*'s currency, and intended for international buyers are a widely accepted definition of 'euro' (cf. however, BIS 1997: 21). The market is for professionals and largely self-regulating. When listings are made at exchanges, and the practice is commonplace, the reason is that many funds and trusts are prohibited from buying unlisted securities. Although abroad, eurobonds create headaches for the domestic regulator because of possible tax avoidance and the flouting of securities regulation in general. The bonds are usually in bearer form and, stashed in a vault, pretty much invisible. That problem is fading away, however, with the growing role of pension and insurance funds, which are tax exempt to various degrees.

A more persistent problem is the US prohibition to disclose new information relevant to an issue after the prospectus has been released. The rule applies when there is a direct selling effort in the country, a situation which few large issues can avoid. This creates problems, since company presentations to prospective buyers (road shows) are part of the selling effort. Attendance should be by invitation only, and those invited should be eligible investors. It is prudent to abstain from advertising anywhere because newspapers have international circulation. Once the issue has been placed, a short announcement (tombstone) is routinely published.

Funds assume a key position in securities regulation because of their importance as investment and retirement vehicles. The fundamental rule is that the purpose of a fund must be clearly stated. Particularly stringent is regulation about pools that are marketed to the general public, that is, unit trusts, mutual funds, and open-ended investment companies. The reasons are obvious enough. Fund managers have large discretionary powers, and investors have neither direct control nor voting rights. But investors can easily destabilize a fund by redeeming its capital in an uncontrolled way. When this possibility exists, assets must be in liquid securities, say, at least 85 per cent realizable within seven business days (Kumar 1997: 34–5). Assets must also be repriced daily at the prevailing market rates (marked to market). Since market rates are available only for some securities, investment possibilities are constrained accordingly. That only assets of high rating qualify for money market and pension funds has the same effect. Risky assets like precious metals and commodities are routinely ruled out, and hedge funds dealing in them must locate offshore.

Pensions in the USA and UK are largely based on fund monies, while the EU mostly relies on pay-as-you-go pensions. Nor have investment funds gained the same popularity as in the English-speaking world. Taxation has favoured other types of saving and the great diversity in national pension systems has thwarted the setting up of a uniform regulatory framework. The only EU-wide regulation is for UCITS, mutual funds that can invest only in transferable securities with listing and good liquidity. There are also rules about diversification and risk control, and bans against precious metals, controlling stakes (expensive), short-selling, and guarantees. The legislation does not apply to closed-end funds, which are more common in tax havens such as Luxembourg, Dublin, and the Channel Islands than onshore.

International Cooperation

Internationalization has brought with it new conflicts, due to the human tendency to extend one's legal thinking to other countries. Unlawful marketing in a regulated country, non-compliance with host country disclosure, licensing requirements for foreigners, fraud and market manipulation from abroad, varying margin requirements at exchanges, and the appointment of trustees are among the most frequent sources of abrasion (Wood 1995: 361). The primitive way to deal with them is boycotts, trade sanctions, and confiscations (Irvine 1998). More sophisticated is lobbying at home for action taken abroad. The lobbyist can be a company or other private interest group although often it is a government agency following a legal principle or pursuing an investigation. The pressure can be put on a domestic organization for its foreign activity or the domestic part of a foreign organization. The pressure can be informal and quiet, or it will take the shape of legal action and become high profile. No country is completely free of such behaviour, although the large and mighty are in a better position to practice it than the small and weak. Much acrimony would be spared if countries could agree on some basic rules among which minimum standards and the sharing of information are the most elementary ones.

BIS and EU have made important strides in the former area but suffer from restricted geographical coverage. Both are active in banking and securities regulation, and both are heavily influenced by UK and US practice, which is hardly astonishing. BIS traditionally covers the Western industrialized countries and offers, among other things, a discussion forum for their central bank governors. Recently, membership has been extended to comprise several important Asian and Latin countries. The principal regulatory arm is the Basle Committee on Banking Supervision, which makes decisions by consensus. The implementation is voluntary and depends on the authority of central bank governors. As is usual in decisions by consensus, the guidelines reflect minimum standards.

The key agreement is the Basle Accord, promulgated in 1988 and amended several times thereafter. It regulates the amount of own capital needed to cover credit and, subsequently, also trading risks. The Accord refers only to internationally active banks with good management and diversified portfolios. The original idea was to provide a level playing field, and the sharp end was pointed towards French and Japanese banks, which were thought to enjoy undue advantage internationally because of their state-ownership or implied state guarantees. The formal requirement is at least 8 per cent own capital out of total assets, weighted according to their seniority and perceived credit risk. For example, lending to an OECD sovereign is assumed risk-free, while an OECD bank is risk-weighted at 20 per cent of the credit's nominal value and a non-OECD bank at its full value, as are all business companies.

The Accord leaves many loose ends and is about to be overhauled. The blanket weighting by a borrower's legal status, location, and business is a tremendous oversimplification. The focus is on bank solvency, and there is not a word about liquidity. Maturity mismatch and asset diversification are overlooked. Holding company capital is left unregulated. Trading activities were overlooked in earlier versions, but their growth has led to some regulation. That nut has proved very hard to crack. A previously unheard of solution was to allow banks to choose between their internal value-at-risk (VaR) models and the BIS standard model (Jackson *et al.* 1998: 9). If the choice falls on an internal model, the derived value is multiplied by three to arrive at the regulatory capital. So far there are perhaps forty banks worldwide that have an acceptable internal VaR model (Ito *et al.* 1996: 142 n. 14). The degree of acceptablity is a moot point. VaR assumes that events are normally distributed and markets always liquid, both untenable assumptions during massive market adjustments.

For many BIS members the EU imposes a parallel and partially conflicting regulatory system with its Directives. In contrast to the BIS rules, the Directives are binding and the member states must bring their national legislations into line. The implementation may take time, up to years, because the national systems can differ drastically from the new order. Germany, in particular, with its universal and public law banks, has had difficulty in complying.

The main principles are that banking (and securities business) is subjected to EU-wide minimum controls; banks can branch out into member countries without local authorization; supervision must be effected on a consolidated basis; bank loans and proprietary positions in securities trading ('books') must be separated for the measurement of capital adequacy. If the minimum standards are perceived as too lax, more stringent ones can be applied towards domestic banks but not foreigners. There is one escape, however: the invocation of the General Good. If the national supervisor of a foreign bank is considered inadequate, the foreigner can be denied entry. So far there are no known cases. The handling of the trading book will cause some trouble in the short term because the appropriate Directive did not anticipate VaR and must now be rephrased.

IOSCO is a direct antipode to BIS and EU in having almost all countries with a stock exchange as its members. It is paralleled by several consultative, regional organizations. Its main achievement is a wide network of information-sharing agreements (IOSCO 1998). Memoranda of Understanding (MoU) exist for curbing and punishing securities fraud, protecting customer funds and assets, clarifying default positions, and enhancing cooperation in emergencies. They have been concluded between governments, national supervisors, and exchanges, and are of widely differing importance and content. This can be gauged indirectly from the number of country-by-country treaties. Important financial players like Japan and Switzerland have only minimal MoUs, while some regional groupings, Latin countries in particular, are represented out of proportion to their financial importance. Genuine offshore centres, understandably, prefer a low profile. A typical MoU is about giving information on deeds that violate the laws of the contracting party. It may permit on-site inspection by home country authorities, probably escorted by a host country inspector. IOSCO has the same weaknesses as BIS: decision by consensus and no enforcement power. Logically, the implementation varies widely (Ito *et al.* 1996: 147).

The increasingly 'hot' topics of drug trafficking, and tax fraud and evasion, fall outside IOSCO's domain. There the request by OECD for a tax identification number is likely to have more impact. A customer making a deposit would need to present this identification. And for better effect, the lightly regulated NBFIs would also need to be brought to court. If decreed, the legislation would plug a major loophole, because money outside the home jurisdiction cannot normally be retrieved by authorities (Stoakes 1998: 33). That, indeed, is a major attraction of offshore finance centres.

Evaluation

Offshore investment is the soft underbelly of financial regulation. BCCI was simultaneously incorporated in Luxembourg and the Cayman Islands, and Maxwell foundations were domiciled in Liechtenstein, for example. Both Luxembourg and Liechtenstein lacked the resources for proper surveillance. The Cayman Islands may not have cared either: *caveat emptor*! Nevertheless, it was an orderly place as offshore centres go and in the process of upgrading (Laulajainen 1998: 281–3). That offshore regulation does not compare with onshore regulation is obvious; otherwise offshore would not exist. Still, offshore has almost free access to onshore: a preposterous situation.

Onshore investment has its own weaknesses, of course. The numbers and the professionalism of its regulators is a topic often commented upon. It is partly a question of resources. Two thousand regulators cannot effectively supervise thousands of banks and NBFIs and tens of thousands of investment advisers, for example. Nor are top people available at the salaries of the civil service. When the Blue Arrow fraud case ended in 1992 with a resounding defeat for the Serious Fraud Office (SFO), an anonymous partner in a City law firm was quoted as saying: 'They [the prosecutors] aren't of the calibre of the people they are trying to prosecute. They [SFO] don't pay enough. They aren't a top-flight team' (Waters 1992). What the correct pay would be is more difficult to say. Can any regulator really keep a tight rein on people making $1 million a year in bonuses?

The stakes are against regulators in other ways, too. The financial scene is evolving rapidly and the $1-million people are those behind the change. Regulators should participate in the party to understand it properly. But regulation does not anticipate; by nature it is reactive rather than proactive. The regulatory mandate is also constrained by existing administrative structures and laws. Changing them takes time. Why does the USA need two securities watchdogs, SEC and CFTC, for example? There is no rational explanation, just a historical one.

Should we then have no regulation? Certainly we should. Although many unscrupulous high flyers will escape the net, they cannot develop their skills as freely as without it. The cautious, down-to-earth, and honest have a common guideline to follow. May these people inherit the earth.

References

Anonymous 1998. Luck, leverage and delta$. *Euromoney*, Oct.: 5.

Bank for International Settlements (BIS) 1997. *International Banking and Financial Market Developments*, Feb. Basle: BIS.

Budd, L. 1999. Globalisation and the crisis of territorial embeddedness of international financial markets. In *Money and the Space Economy*, ed. R. Martin. New York, Wiley: 115–37.

Caplen, B. 1998. A strange way to win a mandate. *Euromoney* (Apr.), 28–31.

Covill, L. 1998. 'Made in Germany' doesn't yet appeal. *Euromoney* (Mar.), 75–8.

Finansinspektionen 1998. *A Presentation*. Stockholm: Finansinspektionen.

Folkerts-Landau, D., Lindgren, C.-J., *et al.* 1998. *Toward a Framework for Financial Stability*, Jan. Washington: International Monetary Fund.

Franks, J., and Schaefer, S. 1993. *The Costs and Effectiveness of the UK Financial Regulatory System*. The City Research Project, Report II, Mar. London: London Business School.

Graham, G. 1997. Regulator pledges vigilance over City. *Financial Times* (29 Oct.), 10.

House, R. 1997. Make way for the megaregulator. *Institutional Investor* (Sept.), 55–61.

International Organization of Securities Commissions (IOSCO) 1998. Memoranda of Understanding and Similar Agreements (unpublished). 6 July.

Irvine, S. 1998. Who needs gunboats? *Euromoney* (Mar.), 38–9.

Ito, T., Folkerts-Landau, D., *et al.* 1996. *International Capital Markets, Developments, Prospects and Key Policy Issues*, Sept. Washington: International Monetary Fund, 129–55.

Jackson, P., Maude, D. J., and Perraudin, W. 1998. *Bank Capital and Value at Risk*. Bank of England Working Paper No. 79, May.

Kelly, Jim 1998. Bank's liquidators find way out of $17bn black hole. *Financial Times* (8 July), 4.

KUMAR, A., ed. 1997. *The Regulation of Non-Bank Financial Institutions.* World Bank Discussion Paper No. 362, Washington.

LAULAJAINEN, R. 1998. *Financial Geography.* Department of Human Geography B 93, Göteborg University. Forthcoming in Chinese by Beijing: Commercial Press.

MOORE, P. 1991. Cleaning up the town hall mess. *Euromoney*, Apr.: 31–3.

O'BRIEN, R. 1992. *Global Financial Integration: The End of Geography.* New York: Council of Foreign Relations Press.

SCOTT, H. S. 1992. Supervision of international banking post-BCCI. *Georgia State University Law Review*, 8/3: 487–510.

SHIRREFF, D. 1998. The eve of destruction. *Euromoney* (Nov.), 34–6.

SMITH, C. 1998. Auditing a calamity. *Institutional Investor* (Oct.), 85–6.

STOAKES, C. 1998. Capital on the run. *Euromoney* (Feb.), 33.

TETT, G. 1998*a*. Crucial issue will determine the success of Big Bang. *Financial Times* (26 Mar.), p. vi.

—— 1998*b*. No longer a Cinderella. *Financial Times* (1 May), p. viii.

WARF, B., and COX, J. C. 1995. US bank failures and regional economic structure. *Professional Geographer*, 47/1: 3–16.

—— 1996. Spatial dimensions of the savings and loan crisis, *Growth and Change*, 27 (spring), 135–55.

WATERS, R. 1992. Blue Arrow leaves SFO reputation in tatters. *Financial Times* (17 July), 6.

WOOD, P. R. 1995. *International Loans, Bonds and Securities Regulation.* London: Sweet & Maxwell.

Chapter **12**

Finance and Localities

Adam Tickell

Introduction

THERE are good theoretical reasons for expecting finance —of all the sectors of the economy—to be the least geographical in both its organization and its impacts. Money is, after all, an increasingly intangible commodity which is not only freely exchanged within national borders, but the thrust of political, social, economic, and technological change during the past century have meant that national currencies have increasingly found themselves in internationally competitive markets. For every element of the financial sector these forces have created pressures which ostensibly undermine the economic geography of finance. In wholesale finance, for example, Anglo-American pension funds invest across the capitalist world (Clark forthcoming), while foreign exchange and derivatives markets have flattened space and time (Leyshon 1996) and created novel challenges for financial regulators (see Ch. 11; Tickell 1999). In retail finance, the development of telephonic- and internet-delivered financial services are undermining branch-based services. Such developments led Richard O'Brien to conclude that

> Geographical location no longer matters in finance, or much less than hitherto . . . For financial firms, this means that the choice of geographical location can be greatly widened, provided that an appropriate investment in information and computer systems can be made . . . There will be forces seeking to maintain geographical control . . . Yet, as markets and rules become integrated, the relevance of geography and the need to base decisions on geography will alter and often diminish. (O'Brien 1991: 1–2)

Although economic geographers have only recently begun to explore finance, this chapter argues that the evidence suggests that, while O'Brien's thesis is bold, it is hyperbolic. This chapter explores these issues by examining the slow emergence of work on the economic geography of finance, exploring the ways in which particular localities remain critical in the production and reproduction of even global finance, and discussing the impacts of an uneven geography of finance on localities.

Locating Finance: The Emergence of an Economic Geography of Money

Research on finance and localities within economic geography is a relatively new phenomenon. Although August Lösch, one of the principal influences on the quantitative revolution in geography during the 1960s, planned to write a volume exploring the relationships between finance and location, his early death and the fact that a lengthy paper on the same subject was never translated into English meant that, as Ron Martin has recently pointed out, 'his commentaries on interest rates and price inflation waves across space failed to ignite the passions of economic geographers and regional economists, who focused instead on industrial development and agglomeration' (1999: 3). Even as late as the mid-1970s, geographers largely ignored Charles Kindleberger's (1974) spatially sensitive account of the formation of financial centres, and although the emergence of Marxist and neo-Marxist approaches to the discipline highlighted the fact that money and finance were at the heart of much of the capitalist economy,[1] economic geographers of all interpretative traditions tended either to acknowledge the importance of finance before passing on to other 'more important' matters or to ignore it altogether. Corbridge and Thrift (1994) have argued that there are three explanations for this state of affairs:

> Money, in short, has been neglected in the social sciences in part because of a continuing focus in some quarters on the static and tangible (the fixed points of production). It has also been neglected because of the failure of many economically minded social scientists to engage with the related agendas of political scientists . . . Finally, it has been neglected [because] many on the Left have still remained in thrall to a prevailing 'productionism'. (Corbridge and Thrift 1994: 3)

During the 1980s, economic geographers began to develop an increasingly self-confident approach to the service sector in general (Walker 1985; Allen 1988). Initially, work on finance was largely empirical and, with the notable exception of the political economic analyses of David Harvey which explored the role of finance in shaping urban crisis, it was largely concerned with mapping financial geographies and understanding their evolution. In the UK, for example, research explored the extent to which financial service activities were unevenly distributed over space, demonstrating that there was a heavy

[1] See e.g. David Harvey's insight that 'monetary relations have penetrated into every nook and cranny of the world and into almost every aspect of social, even private life' (1982: 373); see also Harvey and Chaterjee 1973; Leyshon 1995.

concentration of activity in southern England (Marshall 1985; Daniels and Thrift 1987). Not only was London the location for the largest concentration of foreign banks in the world, but also the headquarters location for the entire panoply of an internationally orientated financial sector which included world class stock and derivatives exchanges, the Lloyds insurance market, commodities markets, and a supporting infrastructure of management services. Perhaps unsurprisingly, London's dominance stretched to the UK financial sector, and until the 1990s only the building societies, with their localized histories and mutual ownership arrangements, managed to evade the metropolitan magnet (Gentle *et al.* 1991).

This financial centralization has been an ongoing feature in the UK since the early years of the nineteenth century. For example, in Manchester—the city at the cradle of the industrial revolution—a rapidly growing financial sector developed during the 1820s and 1830s, as new banks were formed and as a local stock exchange was opened (Axon 1886; Killick and Thomas 1970). Yet even at a very early stage the financial sector became subject to surveillance from London. In 1826, the Bank of England established a branch in the city and by the mid-nineteenth century it controlled the local money supply. One hundred years later, there were few English banks not headquartered in London and, as Kindleberger explains, the UK had a highly centralized financial system:

> it is hardly necessary to explain how London became the metropolitan apex of the financial network . . . The system had no choice but to centre in London. London had an ancient banking tradition and it was a major port, the capital seat, and the hub of the railroad network; all forces were brought to bear on this locality . . . The different banking systems in Ireland and Scotland reached across their boundaries and linked up with London. (Kindleberger 1974: 16)

Elsewhere in Europe and in the USA it remained accurate to talk about relatively locally autonomous financial systems until very recently. Italy, for example, still has approaching 1,000 banks and the majority of these remain local (Lane 1994; Allassandrini and Zazzaro 1999), while the Federal German state promoted regional banking structures in order to diffuse economic development and political power. In the USA, the geographically isolated pattern of economic development during the nineteenth and early twentieth centuries initially inhibited the development of a national market (Odell 1992; Martin 1999*a*). During the 1920s, the essentially local nature of US finance was bolstered as fiscal conservatism, small business politics, and a series of legislative responses to the financial panics following the Wall Street Crash in 1929 placed severe controls on inter-state banking. These survived intact until the 1970s, leading to a high degree of spatial dispersion[2] and although liberalization during the 1990s stimulated inter-state banking, the legacy of regulatory controls remains both

[2] See e.g. Lord 1987; Bagchi-Sen 1991; Goldberg *et al.* 1989; Holly 1987; Wheeler 1986; Noyelle 1983; Amos 1992; Cromwell 1990; see also Warf 1989; Cox and Warf 1991; Cox *et al.* 1991.

in restrictions on the creation of new offices by out-of-state holding companies (Martin 1999) and in the patchwork of regulation faced by national bank holding companies which have to report to up to seven separate federal and state supervisory bodies (Bothwell 1996).

Although diversity in the organization of financial systems is common, Sheila Dow (1999) has recently suggested that there are stages in their spatial development, as financial structures and institutions become progressively integrated and move away from locally based financial institutions towards a national and international orientation, characterized by heavy centralization of activity and institutions in key financial centres. As an observation of the long-run history of capitalism, such a trend is certainly discernible, although given the durability of local and regional systems it is important to be clear in explaining it. The spatial organization of the financial system is shaped as much by political decisions as by economic rationality and the recent movement towards 'consolidation' reflects an ideological transformation in the understandings about how economies work (on related matters, see Pauly 1997). Furthermore, while it is important to be sceptical about the theoretical significance of recent empirical phenomena, during the 1990s, industrial reorganization in finance led to employment growth away from the core regions, both to suburbs (Illeris 1996, 1997) and to peripheral cities and regions (Murphy 1998). One substantial change has been the growth of telephone-based delivery mechanisms, undermining the long-standing advantages of service companies with extensive branch networks. Telephone call centres, for example, exhibit a strong tendency to locate in areas with a large stock of—predominantly female—labour which, though better paid better than the regional norm, remains cheap on a national scale (Richardson and Marshall 1996).

Local Finance and Regional Development

One of the stimuli for the rediscovery of the importance of finance in localities came from the exploration of the reasons for the success of what Scott (1988) referred to as 'New industrial spaces', those areas which appeared to be succeeding following the adoption of novel production processes in novel areas out of the ruins of the Fordist economic model (Tickell and Peck 1992). Most notably, analyses of the success of the 'Third Italy' noted the coincidence of a regionally based banking system and a production system based on relationships between small firms (Best 1990). Such observations contributed to an understanding of the importance of financial services on localities. Although the most obvious impact of finance on localities is in terms of direct employment (the economies of cities as distinct as London and Charlotte, North Carolina, depend upon financial jobs), advocates of the central role of local finance claim to have identified a direct causal relationship with local and regional economic prosperity because a large and competitive local financial community may mean that local industry is able to have better access to credit or receive it at a lower price than in centralized systems (Gertler 1984; Hutchinson and McKillop 1990). There is some evidence that localized banking systems, such as in Italy, Germany, and Jutland, have traditionally supported small and medium-sized enterprises and provided them with shock absorbers during cyclical down-turns (e.g. Carnevali 1996; more generally, see Dow 1994; MacKay and Molyneux 1998). Basing their claims on research in Italy, where strong regional banking systems continue to thrive to the extent that there are discernible geographical variations in both interest rates and loan defaults, Alessandrini and Zazzaro argue that regional banking systems act to overcome information asymmetries which develop in national financial systems, allowing smaller firms to access credit:

> Regional banking systems represent the link between local economies and financial centres. On account of the spatial segmentation of credit markets, banks operating in a region (that is, both local and external banks) are indispensable for overcoming the isolation of those local agents who are either so small or so 'new' that the transaction and information costs are usually too high to permit them to access financial centres. Thus, banks operating locally are the main channel . . . through which the financial needs of small and medium-sized enterprises are met. (1999: 75)

As locally orientated financial institutions depend upon the health of the local economy, there is some evidence that they are more likely to support local firms and foster the introduction of innovation than centralized institutions, which have a poorer knowledge of the local area and the businesses within it (Bowles 1998).

Such arguments have parallels even in those countries with heavily centralized financial systems. The management and control of pension funds in the UK, for example, is overwhelmingly concentrated in London and the South East and over two-thirds of domestic investment is made in companies which are themselves based in the same region, with little money trickling back to the regions to stimulate investment or business expansion. As Martin and Minns argue,

> the private occupational pensions system . . . undermines regions by extracting savings from all over the UK and centralising their administration, management and investment in one region, where fees accrue, control over investment policy is concentrated and where tax subsidies are skewed to benefit relatively high income contributors helping to support an investment regime which has little to do with the promotion of capital investment throughout the UK. (1995: 139)

Yet the causal connections between the strength of the local financial system and regional development are more ambiguous than would be expected.[3]

[3] e.g. Warf and Cox (1995) could find no relationship between US commercial bank failure and local economic structures although they (1996) found a strong correlation between failures of Savings and Loans and the local economy.

Although regional financial systems retain and recycle a higher proportion of 'local' money, not only are local banks more vulnerable to localized economic decline, they tend to have assets that are less liquid than in the case of larger, centralized institutions (Martin 1999*a*). Furthermore, the empirical evidence suggests that while some centralized financial systems (such as the UK and France) harm peripheral economies, as important as the geographic structure of the financial system are spatial variations in per capita GDP (MacKay and Molyneux 1998). Therefore, the relationships between local economic performance and the financial infrastructure are, at best, not yet proven.

Situating Finance I: The Global in the Local

While the empirical research reported above undermined analyses which treated space as irrelevant to the current configuration of the financial sector, more theoretical work has explored the mutual constitution of the global and the local (Martin 1994; Clark and O'Connor 1997). The most influential contributor here has been Nigel Thrift (1990: 81) who captures the relationship in an important way: there is not a 'global financial structure "out there", as a *deus ex machina*, but rather a spatially distributed network of money/social power which encompasses the globe . . . [The] local and the global intermesh, running into one another in all manner of ways'.

As the world's financial system has progressively integrated, local pertubations can now rapidly spread instability throughout the international financial system. The twin crises at Barings Bank in 1890 and 1995 illustrate the extent to which superficially similar events have different outcomes. In 1890, Barings Bank was technically insolvent following the growth of bad debts in Argentina but the slow nature of communication and a relatively leisurely pace of change in finance allowed the Bank of England to organize an orderly rescue of the bank over a period of months. By 1995, bad debts in Singapore, precipitated by the Kobe earthquake, not only bankrupted Barings, but threatened to destabilize an integrated international financial system (Tickell 1996).

Yet it is not only crises which illustrate the intimate importance of localities on the international financial system. In an important body of work, Nigel Thrift draws upon the increasing emphasis on the role of cultural and social forms in creating economic geographies (Lee and Wills 1997; Thrift and Olds 1996) to understand the ways in which financial spaces are produced. Thrift shows that although the international importance of the City of London in the international financial system was vigorously promoted by a series of liberal regulatory decisions made by the British authorities (e.g. Pryke 1991; Strange 1999), arguments based primarily on political decisions or economic analysis miss the fact that financial centres develop and are sustained by information, expertise, and contacts (Porteous 1999). In this account, the fact that from a very early stage the City of London was a strongly cohesive centre socially (Cassis 1991; Kynaston 1994, 1995, 1999), whose light-touch supervision relied upon the close economic and social links between regulator and regulated (Moran 1991), had a critical role in the development of the City. As Amin and Thrift (1992: 20) argue, common backgrounds and value systems developed which, 'both maximised face-to-face communication in a small area and also afforded quick assessments of character and, effectively, economic viability. Thus the old City was a trust maximising system and *the knowledge structure was, in effect, the social structure*' (emphasis added).

Critically, however, although the transformation of the financial sector since the 1960s undermined the City's social cohesion, the historical legacy bequeathed by such social practices remain central in understanding its place in the international financial system. As Nigel Thrift has emphasized, this is because international financial centres are not simply locations which have large and liquid financial markets, but they are the centres of representation and, as such, 'the chief points of surveillance and scripting for the global financial services industry' (1994: 335); they are centres of expertise where product innovation and marketing are intimately linked; and they have 'become centres of social interaction on an expanded scale. As a result of the expansion of transportation . . . they have become the meeting places for the global corporate networks of the financial services industry' (335–6). It is important to recognize, however, that such places are constantly produced and reproduced—that the global is created in everyday social and spatial practices in the local. Drawing upon Henri Lefebvre's (1991) understanding of spatial practice, Allen and Pryke (1994: 459) show that

> in the case of finance, the abstract space of the City of London has secured its dominance over time through its ability continually to mould the space around it in its own image. The City *is* finance, and the traces of other uses and routine practices which give meaning to particular spaces within the Square Mile have historically been sidelined.

International financial centres, then, are not just where international financial institutions happen to be located, but are critical in the reproduction of the system itself. Despite the phenomenal transformations in the nature of finance during the latter third of the twentieth century (Leyshon and Tickell 1995), the business of finance still thrives upon close inter-firm and inter-personal relationships. Complex financial transactions are usually shared between financial institutions in order to offset and spread the risk to any particular firm, necessitating a high degree of inter-firm co-operation. However, as financial institutions are simultaneously highly competitive, it is critical that they are able to trust that their collaborators are safe, secure, and as good as their word. Although formal institutions and mechanisms exist which underwrite trust in finance, such as the credit rating agencies Standard and Poor's and Moody's

(Sinclair 1994), informal and personal relationships are an important lubricant in the wheels of international finance (Thrift 1994). As the financial system has become increasingly complex, such trust relationships have become central strategies among traders seeking to reduce risk who, even in an era of frenetic electronic trading and information overload, rely upon both telephone and face-to-face contact to make sense of the world (Boden 1994; Zuker 1986). However, while there is consensus that trust relationships are not novel, neither should they be seen as a panacea. Trust relationships are vulnerable to abuse, as in the case of fraudulent trading at Barings Bank; they rely upon legal frameworks which may themselves change, as in the case of the legality of local government trading (Tickell 1998); and they require an overarching ethical system which may not always exist (Stanley 1996).

An unresolved question in the geography of finance is whether cultural and social processes can survive two pressures. Ron Martin (1999*a*) has recently highlighted that regulatory changes, technological change, and the globalization of markets is 'remapping the financial landscape' and, while sceptical about O'Brien's 'end of geography' thesis, he suggests that the major geographical impacts will be to loosen the bonds between localities and finance. First, since minimum capital adequacy agreements were agreed under the auspices of the Bank for International Settlements in 1987 (Helleiner 1996), central bankers and supervisors have placed increasing emphasis on core standards and regulatory co-operation across the range of the financial services (Tickell 1999). Although such norms and co-operative structures may be relatively timid, Budd has recently argued that they have the capacity to undermine the advantages of particular nodes in the international financial system in his claim that 'Reregulation is leading to a crisis of embeddedness' (Budd 1999: 133). Secondly, technological change is not only undermining much of the face-to-face trading on exchanges such as the London International Financial Futures Exchange, but it is leading to global and continental alliances between financial exchanges: 'the ownership, and thus the territory, of organised exchanges, through their member firms, may become more divorced from their role as information exchanges . . . In this scenario, will the organised exchanges become the residual locations through which contacts are booked in order to conform to prudential regulation?' (Budd 1999: 129).

The lasting theoretical and economic importance of such developments, however, remains uncertain. States remain important arbiters in determining the shape of finance and governments have worked hard to write the international rules in favour of either firms from their territories, most notably in the case of US lobbying of the Bank for International Settlements and the World Trade Organization, or their territorial interests, evident particularly in the way that the Bank of England promotes the interests of the City of London (Cohen 1998).

Situating Finance II: The Local in the Global

> It is clear that one of the contributory factors to the violence in South Central Los Angeles is that financial institutions appear to have turned their backs on the area.
>
> (Senate Banking Committee, cited in Swidler 1994: 387)

As the regulatory frameworks and social concordats which underwrote the geography of national financial systems began to change with the growing hegemony of liberal political economy during the 1980s and 1990s (Tickell 1999), a growing concern with the effects of these became discernible in research on finance and localities. Until the 1980s, the barriers to entry in finance were very high, whether as a result of extensive branch networks of the banks or intermediary structure in insurance in the UK or Canada or as a result of regulatory structures in the USA or Italy. These barriers not only prevented new competitors from entering the market place, but gave financial institutions access to a broad range of information about their clients which was then used to assess creditworthiness.

During the past twenty years, however, such certainties have been undermined—and in cases turned on their heads—by technological change and regulatory reform. Technological change has allowed banks to reduce costs by substituting labour with capital and to take advantage of their potential to reduce the constraints of time and space (Hannan and McDowell 1984; Holly 1987; Warf 1989; Harvey 1989; Marchak 1991). One important result has been that there have been new entrants into an already over-crowded market. On the one hand, brand names with little history in finance, such as Virgin or British Gas in the UK or General Motors in the USA, are targeting particular segments of the financial market, while on the other hand, established companies are establishing direct sales subsidiaries which rely primarily on telephone and internet communication. These organizations have far lower operating costs, greater levels of accessibility, and, on the whole, a much more affluent set of customers. Although the details vary across the developed world, competitive pressures are undermining the revenue streams of long-established firms, while their 'bricks and mortar' branch networks gives them a higher cost base than new entrants who can operate independent of place. Furthermore, the development of generic financial products and sophisticated databases has undermined the intelligence gathering role of the branch and banks have stopped cross-subsidizing customers with profits made from more lucrative clients (Pollard 1999).

For established firms, these factors encouraged them to reconfigure their market approach and their organizational structure:

> The branch networks . . . have figured prominently in these appraisals for, while branches are the distribution points from which the bulk or retail financial services are

sold, they are also responsible for generating most of the costs incurred by such firms . . . Branch restructuring programmes have . . . been informed by a sensitivity to spatial variations in costs and profitability and in levels of debt and perceived risk. (Leyshon and Thrift 1997: 233)

Between 1989 and 1995 the big four banks in Britain, for example, closed over 2,000 branches, contracting their branch networks by more than 20 per cent (Pratt *et al.* 1996). Although this body of work acknowledges that the regulatory changes which stimulated competition unleashed the restructuring movement, it is arguable that it under-specifies the extent to which a wider realignment of the relationship between finance and the state underpinned change. The very different regulatory frameworks in place in different capitalist countries until the early 1980s had, at their core, a common philosophy which held that as the stability of the financial system was central to the smooth operation of the economy as a whole, governments should regulate to ensure that stability. In effect, a social contract was struck to the effect that if financial firms acted as quasi-public utilities by, for example, maintaining branch networks and financing domestic industry, the state would guarantee oligopolistic market conditions (whether nationally or locally). However, economic globalization and the emergence of liberal economic critiques began to undermine this contract during the 1970s and 1980s in the USA and the UK, later spreading to most capitalist countries. In this context, the emergence of newly competitive markets needs to be understood for what it is: a discursively mediated attempt on the part of national states to reform the nature of the economic and social structures (Jessop 1997; Leyshon and Thrift 1997).

Such antecedents notwithstanding, an increasing concern among researchers has been to understand the consequences of these restructuring processes. While early assessments of the ways that technology is used suggest that it is an addition to, rather than a substitute for branch visits Rhoades (1998), Dymski and Veitch (1996) have demonstrated that the costs of this transformation of retail finance is being disproportionately borne by the poor. First, the substitution of a physical infrastructure with an electronic one disproportionately impacts on technologically poor households. Secondly, poor neighbourhoods are increasingly becoming stripped of banks at the same time as more affluent areas are seeing growth (Caskey 1994). Sitting in the shadow of the most powerful financial centre in the world, a 2 square mile area of the Bronx has only one bank branch and no cash machines (Marcus 1996; see also Pollard 1996, 1999). Thirdly, financial institutions in the USA have returned to a crude spatial targeting of poor neighbourhoods by charging very high premiums on insurance products, where they are available at all. In effect, these processes add up to a withdrawal of the 'financial infrastructure' from poor areas and may have very deleterious effects:

The process of financial exclusion has the potential to inflict serious economic and social damage upon communities abandoned by the process of financial infrastructure

> withdrawal . . . In the long term, communities abandoned by the financial system are in danger of entering a slow and painful period of decline due to an inability to gain access to funds necessary for the continuous intensive phase of urban development which supports the maintenance of the built environment and provides the possibility for further economic growth. (Leyshon and Thrift 1997: 237)

Furthermore, as Dymski and Veitch have demonstrated, the withdrawal of the formal financial sector has resulted in the growth of a 'second tier' financial sector consisting of pawnbrokers, money-lenders, cheque-cashing firms, and hire-purchase shops which amplifies

> decay in urban neighbourhoods. Second-tier financial firms which service lower income communities provide no way to pool community savings to finance community investment in new human or physical assets that enhance future economic growth. These new non-banking financial firms meet the financial needs of a community in strictly limited ways. They charge higher fees for services and facilitate households' decumulation of their stock of assets to meet current income crises. In consequence, lower income, higher minority population communities are increasingly isolated from more prosperous communities. Social polarisation is the result. (Dymski and Veitch 1996: 1257)

Financial infrastructure withdrawal and disinvestment was not supposed to happen. Although it passed almost unnoticed by geographers, in 1977 the Community Reinvestment Act (CRA) was passed by the US Congress in an attempt to ensure that banks invested in all of the communities they served. Underlying the CRA was the recognition that banks were, in effect, geographically discriminating in their willingness to accept deposits from, but unwillingness to lend to, poor neighbourhoods (Marcus 1996; Baxter 1996; Immergluck 1999). Therefore, the Act required banks to report on the geographic pattern of their deposits and loans and encouraged them to lend to lower income neighbourhoods. In its initial draft, the Act was to provide for sanctions to be taken if banks were unable to demonstrate that they were meeting their obligations. However, it was eviscerated by fierce rearguard action on the part of the American Bankers Association and other lobby groups and beyond the power of poor publicity, the only effective disciplinary measure was that the CRA evaluation could be used as evidence during merger approval processes (Taibi 1994). Although the CRA became, in effect, a toothless tiger, it did succeed in channelling significant investment into some low income neighbourhoods (Marcus 1996) and lending under the terms of the Act has proved to be at least as profitable as non-CRA lending (Overby 1995), demonstrating that the Act had correctly identified spatial discrimination.

Yet when evaluated from a wider perspective, the CRA failed: financial infrastructure withdrawal during the intervening period has accentuated, redlining and spatial discrimination is worse, and, by the mid-1990s, non-compliance with CRA lending guidelines had been used to block only fifteen expansion or merger applications (Taibi 1994). This has important lessons for geographically based interventions which attempt to ameliorate the effects of global and national financial movements. While the legislation's weakness and the emerging hegemony of a political ideology which eschewed intervention at precisely the moment that the CRA should have begun to impact were perhaps the most significant reasons for its failure, there were other problems. First, as the legislation required banks to report on their loan activity within specified distances from a branch, the closure of a branch with a low or middle income constituency may actually have improved the quality of a bank's overall report. Secondly, the legislation attempted a local solution to what was in effect a wider systemic problem:

> If neighbourhood distress were a by-product of mortgage market imperfections in addition to income and wealth, regulatory actions to eradicate mortgage market discrimination and redlining would be appropriate . . . [Whereas] in reality, neighbourhood distress is likely a by-product of some combination of income and wealth, mortgage market imperfections and housing market imperfections. (Shear *et al.* 1995: 293)

In other words, the failure of the CRA reflects the fact that the problems it attempts to address are wider than it can address (Taibi 1994).

If the Community Reinvestment Act represented a statist response to financial infrastructure withdrawal, the emergence of alternative local currency schemes is an organic, community orientated response. These initially developed in British Columbia in the early 1980s but have since become popular across the USA, Canada, the UK, and Australia and essentially have a similar philosophy to the CRA: to ensure that the unit of exchange is both generated and spent within a local community in an attempt to ground circuits of economic and social reproduction in a locality (Pacione 1999; Lee 1999). In the relatively small number of successful examples, such as in Tomkins County, Ithaca, the schemes have supported the generation of local employment and appear to be a mechanism with which to ground money, to make finance local once again. In some accounts, local currency schemes are seen as a potential force to undermine the effects of global financial flows and economic integration. Pacione, for example (1999: 70; see also Williams 1996; Williams and Windebank 1998; Thorne 1996), has argued that although 'a local currency cannot insulate the local economy from the negative effects of globalisation . . . it can afford a degree of protection against the spatially-insensitive currents of the international financial system'. It is important, however, to take such claims with a healthy pinch of salt. Not only do local currencies remain isolated but the most successful examples have been in small, relatively affluent communities. As such, they can provide little respite for devastated inner city neighbourhoods and the relative failure of legislative interventions should be remembered in assessing the likely impact of voluntarist ones in a period when national economies have been rocked by global financial turbulence. As Roger Lee has recently argued, their power is more symbolic than real:

> Local currencies are a means of political resistance, a vehicle for (re)constructing local communities in opposition to the dictates of global capitalism. They offer an opportunity to move away from valuing people's time and labour not only in conventional (global) monetary terms, and to build community relationships within a system based on mutual respect and reciprocity . . . This is the key issue—the significance of local money lies primarily in the fact that it is *local* in space and time, rather than in the particular economic and social functions that it performs. (Lee 1999: 220, 223–4)

Conclusion

In a relatively short period of time, research on finance and localities has begun to flourish. In its early development, the main emphasis was largely exploratory in its determination to examine the ways in which finance may actually have a geography and the ways in which that geography may affect economic development. While the economic and technological transformations wrought in Western countries during the closing decades of the twentieth century change undoubtedly *altered* the geography of finance they did not undo it. Real economies are not the frictionless planes of neo-classical theory, they are produced and reproduced in complex ways in particular spaces. In other words, despite the intangibility of money, finance has an economic geography. As a growing recognition of the force of this geography emerged, the ways in which this played out politically over space became more explicit. Politically, researchers have been concerned not only with the ways in which corporate restructuring in finance has adversely impacted upon vulnerable groups in society, but there has also been a, somewhat tentative, exploration of alternatives to those trends which undermine the link between local spaces and money. Perhaps most notable, however, has been the emergence of a more theoretical approach to finance and localities, best embodied in the work of Nigel Thrift and Andrew Leyshon who have progressively eschewed a Marxist political economy in favour of an account which privileges the discursive. This, they argue, is because

> we have come to be suspicious of accounts that try to make a clear distinction between the economic sphere (to which money is too often confined) and other spheres (onto which the economic sphere is too often unproblematically mapped), on the grounds that such a distinction itself presumes cultural norms which may indeed be constitutive but by no means need be regarded as inevitable. (Leyshon and Thrift 1997, p. xv)

Such arguments have been powerfully influential on research into the geography of finance because they allow for a nuanced understanding of the mutually constitutive relationship between the two. However, it is important that analyses remain sensitive to the fact that however much financial flows and geographies are socially embedded, culturally inflected, discursively mediated, and symbolically inscribed, financial geographies are also geographies of power and are critical in moulding the quality of people's lives.

References

Allassandrini, P., and Zazzaro, A. 1999. A possibilist approach to local financial systems and regional development: the Italian experience. In Martin 1999*b*: 71–91.

Allen, J. 1988. Service industries: uneven development and uneven knowledge. *Area*, 20: 15–22.

—— and Pryke, M. 1994. The production of service space. *Environment and Planning D: Society and Space*, 12: 453–75.

Amin, A., and Thrift, N. J. 1992. Marshallian nodes in global networks. *International Journal of Urban and Regional Research*, 16: 571–87.

Amos, O. M. 1992. The regional distribution of bank closings in the United States from 1982 to 1988. *Southern Economic Journal*, 58: 805–15.

Axon, A. E. 1886. *Annals of Manchester: A Chronological Record from the Earliest Times to end of 1885*. Manchester: John Heywood.

Bagchi-Sen, S. 1991. The location of foreign direct investment in finance, insurance and real estate in the United States. *Geografiska Annaler*, 73B: 187–97.

Baxter, C. I. 1996. Canals where rivers used to flow: the role of mediating structures and partnerships in community lending. *Economic Development Quarterly*, 10: 44–56.

Best, M. 1990. *The New Competition: Institutions of Industrial Restructuring*. Cambridge: Polity.

Boden, D. 1994. *The Business of Talk*. Cambridge: Polity.

Bothwell, J. L. 1996. Bank oversight: fundamental principles for modernising the US structure. Testimony before the Committee on Banking and Financial Services, House of Representatives, 26 May (available from the General Accounting Office, Washington, 20548-0001).

Bowles, P. 1998. Accessibility and bank mergers in British Columbia. Report prepared for the British Columbia Task Force on Bank Mergers (available at http://www'bankmergersbc'gov'bc'ca/accessibility'html).

Brunskill, I., and Minns, R. 1989. Local financial markets. *Local Economy*, 3: 295–302.

Budd, L. 1999. Globalisation and the crisis of territorial embeddedness of international financial markets. In Martin 1999*b*: 115–37.

Carnevali, F. 1996. Between markets and networks: regional banks in Italy. *Business History*, 38: 84–102.

Caskey, J. P. 1994. Bank representation in low income and minority communities. *Urban Affairs Quarterly*, 29: 617–38.

Cassis, Y. 1991. Financial elites in three European centres: London, Paris, Berlin, 1880s–1930s. *Business History*, 33: 53–71.

Clark, G. forthcoming. *Pension Fund Capitalism*. Oxford: Oxford University Press.

—— and O'Connor, K. 1997. The informational content of financial products and the spatial structure of the global finance industry. In *Spaces of Globalisation*, ed. K. Cox. New York: Guilford.

COHEN, B. J. 1998. *The Geography of Money*. Ithaca, NY: Cornell University Press.

CORBRIDGE, S., and THRIFT, N. J. 1994. Introduction. In Corbridge *et al.* 1994.

—— —— and MARTIN, R., eds. 1994. *Money, Power and Space*. Oxford: Blackwell.

COX, J. C., PRESTON, V., and WARF, B. 1991. The 1987 crash and the spatial incidence of employment changes in the New York metropolitan region. *Urban Studies*, 28: 327–39.

—— and WARF, B. 1991. Wall Street layoffs and service sector incomes in New York. *Urban Geography*, 12: 226–39.

CROMWELL, B. A. 1990. Financial restructuring and regional economic activity. *Economic Review—Federal Reserve Bank, Cleveland*, 26: 13–25.

DANIELS, P. W., and THRIFT, N. J. 1985. *The Geographies of the UK Service Sector: A Survey*. University of Liverpool and University of Bristol, Working Papers on Producer Services, No. 6.

DOW, S. C. 1994. European monetary integration and the distribution of credit availability. In Corbridge *et al.* 1994: 149–64.

—— 1999. The stages of banking development and the spatial evolution of financial systems. In Martin 1999*b*: 31–48.

DYMSKI, G. A., and VEITCH, J. M. 1996. Financial transformation and the metropolis: booms, busts and banking in Los Angeles. *Environment and Planning A*, 28: 1233–60.

GENTLE, C. J. S., MARSHALL, J. N., and COOMBES, M. G. 1991. Business reorganisation and regional development: the case of the British building societies. *Environment and Planning A*, 23: 1759–77.

GERTLER, M. 1984. Regional capital theory. *Progress in Human Geography*, 8: 50–81.

GOLDBERG, M. A., HELSLEY, R. W., and LEVI, M. D. 1989. The location of international financial activity: an interregional analysis. *Regional Studies*, 23: 1–8.

HANNAN, T. H., and MCDOWELL, J. M. 1984. The determinants of technology adoption: the case of the banking firm. *Rand Journal of Economics*, 15: 328–35.

HARRINGTON, R. 1992. The financial system in transition. In *Financial Innovation*, ed. H. Cavanna. London: Routledge, 1–13.

HARVEY, D. 1973. *Social Justice and the City*. Oxford: Blackwell.

—— 1982. *The Limits to Capital*. Oxford: Blackwell.

—— 1989. *The Condition of Post-modernity: An Enquiry into the Origins of Cultural Change*. Oxford: Blackwell.

—— and CHATERJEE, L. 1973. Absolute rent and the restructuring of space by governmental and financial institutions. *Antipode*, 6: 2–36.

HELLEINER, E. 1996. Post-globalisation: is the financial liberalisation trend likely to be reversed? In *States against Markets*, ed. R. Boyer and D. Drache. London: Routledge, 193–210.

HOLLY, B. P. 1987. Regulation, competition and technology: the restructuring of the US commercial bank system. *Environment and Planning A*, 19: 633–52.

HUTCHINSON, R. W., and MCKILLOP, D. G. 1990. Regional financial sector models: an application to the Northern Ireland financial sector. *Regional Studies*, 24: 421–31.

ILLERIS, S. 1996. *The Service Economy: A Geographical Approach*. Chichester: Wiley.

—— 1997. The changing location of service activities in the Copenhagen region. *Geografisk Tidsskrift*, 97: 120–31.

IMMERGLUCK, D. 1999. Intrametropolitan patterns of small business lending: what do the new Community Reinvestment Act data reveal? *Urban Affairs Review*, 34: 787–804.

JESSOP, B. 1997. Capitalism and its future: remarks on regulation, government and governance. *Review of International Political Economy*, 4: 561–81.

KILLICK, J. R., and THOMAS, W. A. 1970. The northern stock exchanges. *Northern History*, 5: 114–30.

KINDLEBERGER, C. P. 1974. *The Formation of Financial Centers: A Study in Comparative Economic History*. University of Princeton, Princeton Studies in International Finance, 36.

KYNASTON, D. 1994. *The City of London, i: A World of its Own 1815–1890*. London: Pimlico.

—— 1995. *The City of London, ii: Golden Years 1890–1914*. London: Pimlico.

—— 1999. *The City of London, iii: Illusions of Gold 1914–1945*. London: Chatto and Windus.

LANE, D. 1994. Italy: from bad to worse. *The Banker*, 19–23 Aug.

LEE, R. 1999. Local money: geographies of autonomy and resistance. In Martin 1999*b*: 208–24.

—— and WILLS, J., eds. 1997. *Geographies of Economies*. London: Arnold.

LEFEBVRE, H. 1991. *The Production of Space*. Oxford: Blackwell. 1st pub. in French as *La Production de l'espace*, 1974.

LEYSHON, A. 1995. Geographies of money and finance. *Progress in Human Geography*, 19: 531–43.

—— 1996. Dissolving distance? Money, disembedding and the creation of global financial space. In *The Global Economy in Transition*, ed. P. Daniels and B. Lever. Harlow: Longman, 62–80.

—— and THRIFT, N. J. 1997. *Money/Space: Geographies of Monetary Transformation*. London: Routledge.

—— and TICKELL, A. 1995. Money order? The discursive constitution of Bretton Woods and the making and breaking of regulatory space. *Environment and Planning A*, 26/12: 1861–90.

LORD, D. 1987. Interstate banking and the relocation of economic control points. *Urban Geography*, 8: 501–19.

MACKAY, R. R., and MOLYNEUX, P. 1998. Bank finance and the regions: a European perspective. In *Inward Investment, Business Finance and Regional Development*, ed. S. Hill and B. Morgan. Basingstoke: Macmillan.

MARCHAK, M. P. 1991. *The Integrated Circus: The New Right and the Restructuring of Global Markets*. Montreal: McGill-Queens University Press.

MARCUS, C. E. 1996. Beyond the boundaries of the Community Reinvestment Act and the fair lending laws: developing a market-based framework for generating low and moderate income lending. *Columbia Law Review*, 3: 710–58.

MARSHALL, J. N. 1985. Services in a post-industrial economy. *Environment and Planning A*, 17: 1155–67.

MARTIN, R. 1994. Stateless monies, global financial integration and national economic autonomy: the end of geography? In Corbridge *et al.* 1994: 253–78.

—— 1999*a*. The new economic geography of money. In Martin 1999*b*, ch. 1.

Martin, R., ed. 1999*b*. *Money and the Space Economy*. Chichester: Wiley.

——and Minns, R. 1995. Undermining the financial basis of regions: the spatial structure and implications of the UK pension fund industry. *Regional Studies*, 29: 125–44.

Moran, M. 1991. *The Politics of the Financial Services Revolution: The USA, UK and Japan*. Basingstoke: Macmillan.

Murphy, L. 1998. Financial engine or glorified back office? Dublin's International Financial Services Centre going global. *Area*, 157–65.

Noyelle, T. 1983. The rise of advanced services: some implications for economic development in US cities. *Journal, American Planning Association*, 49: 280–90.

O'Brien, R. 1991. *Global Financial Integration: The End of Geography*. London: Pinter/Royal Institute of International Affairs.

Odell, K. A. 1992. *Capital Mobilization and Regional Financial Markets: The Pacific Coast States, 1850–1920*. New York: Garland.

Overby, A. B. 1995. The Community Reinvestment Act reconsidered. *University of Pennsylvania Law Review*, 143: 1431–531.

Pacione, M. 1999. The other side of the coin: local currency as a response to the globalisation of capital. *Regional Studies*, 33: 63–72.

Pauly, L. 1997. *Who Elected the Bankers? Surveillance and Control in the World Economy*. Ithaca, NY: Cornell.

Pollard, J. S. 1996. Banking at the margins: a geography of financial exclusion in Los Angeles. *Environment and Planning A*, 28: 1209–32.

——1999. Globalisation, regulation and the changing organisation of retail banking. In Martin 1999*b*: 49–70.

Porteous, D. 1999. The development of financial centres: location, information externalities and path dependence. In Martin 1999*b*: 95–114.

Pratt, J., Leyshon, A., and Thrift, N. J. 1996. Financial exclusion in the 1990s, ii: geographies of financial inclusion and exclusion. *Working Papers on Producer Services*, 38.

Pryke, M. 1991. An international city going global: spatial change in the City of London. *Environment and Planning D: Society and Space*, 9: 197–222.

Rhoades, S. 1996. Competition and bank mergers: directions for analysis from available evidence. *The Antitrust Bulletin*, 41: 339–64.

——1997. Research on IO topics in banking: an introduction and overview. *Review of Industrial Organization*, 12: 1–8.

——1998. The efficiency effects of bank mergers: an overview of case studies of nine mergers. *Journal of Banking and Finance*, 22: 273–91.

Richardson, R., and Marshall, J. N. 1996. The growth of telephone call centres in peripheral areas of Britain: evidence from Tyne and Wear. *Area*, 28: 308–17.

Scott, A. J. 1988. *New Industrial Spaces*. London: Pion.

Shear, W. B., Berkovec, J., Dougherty, A., and Nothaft, F. E. 1995. Unmet housing needs: the role of mortgage markets. *Journal of Housing Economics*, 4: 291–306.

Sinclair, T. 1994. Passing judgement: credit rating processes as regulatory mechanisms of governance in the emerging world order. *Review of International Political Economy*, 1: 133–59.

Stanley, C. 1996. *Urban Excess and Law*. London: Cavendish.

Strange, S. 1999. *Mad Money*. Manchester: Manchester University Press.

SWIDLER, G. M. 1994. Making the Community Reinvestment Act work. *New York University Law Review*, 69: 387–420.
TAIBI, A. D. 1994. Banking, finance and community economic empowerment: structural economic theory, procedural civil rights and substantive racial justice. *Harvard Law Review*, 107: 1463–545.
THORNE, L. 1996. Local exchange trading systems in the United Kingdom: a case of re-embedding? *Environment and Planning A*, 28: 1361–76.
THRIFT, N. 1990. Doing regional geography in a global system: the new international financial system, the City of London and the South East of England, 1984–87. In *Regional Geography: Current Developments and Future Prospects*, ed. R. J. Johnston, J. Hauer, and G. A. Hoekveld. London: Routledge, 180–207.
—— 1994. On the social and cultural determinants of international financial centres. In Corbridge *et al.* 1994: 327–55.
—— and OLDS, K. 1996. Refiguring the economic in economic geography. *Progress in Human Geography*, 20: 311–37.
TICKELL, A. 1996. Making a melodrama out of a crisis: reinterpreting the collapse of Barings Bank. *Environment and Planning D: Society and Space*, 14: 5–33.
—— 1998. Creative finance and the local state: the Hammersmith and Fulham swaps affair. *Political Geography*, 17: 865–81.
—— 1999. Unstable futures: controlling and creating risks in international money. In *Global Capitalism versus Democracy: Socialist Register (1999)*, ed. L. Panitch and C. Leys. Rendleshem: The Merlin Press, 248–77.
—— and PECK, J. A. 1992. Accumulation, regulation and the geographies of post-Fordism. *Progress in Human Geography*, 16: 190–218.
WALKER, R. L. 1985. Is there a service economy? *Science and Society*, 49: 42–83.
WARF, B. 1989. Deindustrialisation, service sector growth, and the underclass in the New York metropolitan region. *Tijdschrift voor Economische en Sociale Geografie*, 81: 332–47.
—— and COX, J. C. 1995. US bank failures and regional economic structure. *Professional Geographer*, 47: 3–16.
—— —— 1996. Spatial dimensions of the Savings and Loan crisis. *Growth and Change*, 27: 135–55.
WHEELER, J. O. 1986. Corporate spatial links with financial institutions: the role of the metropolitan hierarchy. *Annals, Association of American Geographers*, 76: 262–74.
WILLIAMS, C. C. 1996. Local exchange trading systems: a new source of work and credit for the poor and unemployed. *Environment and Planning A*, 1395–415.
—— and WINDEBANK, J. 1998. *Informal Employment in the Advanced Economies: Implications for Work and Welfare*. London: Routledge.
ZUKER, L. 1986. Production of trust: institutional sources of economic structure. *Research in Organisational Behaviour*, 8: 53–111.

Part III

Corporate Structure, Strategy, and Location

Section **6**

Competition, Location, and Strategy

Chapter **13**

Locations, Clusters, and Company Strategy

Michael E. Porter

THINKING about competition and strategy has been dominated by what goes on inside companies. The role of location is all but absent. If anything, the tendency has been to see location as diminishing in importance as globalization allows companies to source capital, goods, and technology from anywhere and to locate operations wherever it is most cost effective.[1] Governments, for their part, are widely seen as losing their influence over competition to global forces.

This perspective, although widespread, does not accord with competitive reality. Competitive success is anything but widely and evenly dispersed. Some nations, regions within nations, and cities contain far more competitive firms than others, even at locations nearby. If we focus on particular industries, and segments of industries, the concentration of competitive companies is even more striking.

In *The Competitive Advantage of Nations* (1990), I put forward a microeconomically based theory of national, state, and local competitiveness within the context of a global economy. This theory gives clusters a prominent role. Clusters are geographic concentrations of interconnected companies, specialized suppliers and service providers, firms in related industries, and associated institutions (e.g. universities, standards agencies, and trade associations) in particular fields that compete but also cooperate. Such clusters are a striking feature of virtually every economy, especially those of more economically advanced areas. While agglomeration has long been part of the economic landscape, the configuration and the role of clusters seem to be taking on a new

This chapter has benefited greatly from assistance by Veronica H. Ingham, and helpful comments from Meric Gertler.

[1] For an example, see Cairncross (1997).

character as competition globalizes and economies become increasingly complex, knowledge-based, and dynamic.

The influence of location and the phenomenon of clusters in one form or another has been recognized and explored in a range of literatures.[2] What has been missing, both in theory and in practice, however, is an understanding of the tight relationship that exists between clusters and competitive strategy at the firm level. Forging this relationship can shed new light on the influence of location as well as the role of government in economic development, as I have developed in other papers.[3] My focus here, however, is on the central but largely unexplored role that location plays in the agenda for companies.

The presence of clusters suggests that *much of competitive advantage lies outside a given company or even outside its industry*, residing instead in the locations of its business units. Competitive success cannot solely depend on managerial and company attributes when many successful firms in a given field are concentrated in just a few locations. Therefore, there is a compelling need to reorient our thinking about corporate strategy in a way that sees location and cluster participation as integral to a firm's success.

Clusters and Competition

What is a Cluster?

A cluster is a geographically proximate group of interconnected companies and associated institutions in a particular field, linked by commonalities and complementarities. The geographic scope of a cluster can range from a single city or state to a country or even a group of neighboring countries.[4] Clusters take varying forms depending on their depth and sophistication, but most include end-product or service companies; suppliers of specialized inputs, components, machinery, and services; financial institutions; and firms in related industries. Clusters also often include firms in downstream industries (i.e. channels or customers); producers of complementary products; and specialized infrastructure providers. Clusters also often involve a number of institutions, governmental and otherwise, that provide specialized training, education, information, research, and technical support (such as universities, think tanks, vocational training providers); and standards-setting agencies. Government departments and regulatory agencies that significantly influence a cluster can be considered part of it. Finally, many clusters include trade associations and other collective private sector bodies that support cluster members.

[2] A discussion of the historical and intellectual antecedents of cluster theory appears in Porter (1998*a*).

[3] See Porter (1995, 1998*a*, 1998*b*)

[4] See Enright (1993*b*) for examples illustrating clusters' varying geographic scope.

Drawing cluster boundaries is often a matter of degree, and involves a creative process informed by understanding the most important linkages and complementarities across industries and institutions (see below). The strength of these 'spillovers' and their importance to productivity and innovation determine the ultimate boundaries.[5]

The boundaries of clusters continually evolve as new firms and industries emerge, established industries shrink or decline, and local institutions develop and change. Technological and market developments spawn new industries, create new linkages, or alter served markets. Regulatory changes also contribute to shifting boundaries, as they have, for example, in telecommunications and transport.

Most cluster participants do not compete directly, but serve different industry segments. Yet they do share many common needs and opportunities and encounter many common constraints and obstacles to productivity. Seeing a group of companies and institutions as a cluster highlights opportunities for coordination and mutual improvement in areas of common concern without threatening or distorting competition or limiting the intensity of rivalry. The cluster can offer a constructive and efficient forum for dialogue among related companies and their suppliers, government, and other salient institutions. Public and private investments to improve conditions for clusters benefit many firms.

Because parts of a cluster often fall within different traditional industrial or service categories, clusters may be obscured or even go unrecognized. In Massachusetts, for example, more than 400 companies, representing at least 39,000 high-paying jobs, were involved in some way in medical devices. The cluster long remained all but invisible, however, buried within several larger and overlapping industry categories, such as electronic equipment and plastic products. Executives in the cluster had never come together before despite the fact that firms shared many common constraints, problems, and opportunities.

Once the cluster was discovered, it started having a productive dialogue with government through MassMedic, an association formed in 1996 which has worked successfully with the US Food and Drug Administration to streamline the approval process for medical devices. This case reveals an important generalization that is important to note here. Managers still rarely see the world in

[5] Clusters occur in many types of industries, in both larger and smaller fields, and even in some local activities, such as hospitality-related businesses. They are present in large and small economies, in rural and urban areas, and at several geographic levels (e.g. nations, states, metropolitan regions, and cities). Clusters occur in both advanced and developing economies, although clusters in advanced economies tend to be more developed. Indeed, the building of clusters is an important condition for middle and advanced economic development. Cluster boundaries rarely conform to standard industrial classification systems, which fail to capture many important actors in competition as well as linkages across industries; see Porter (1998*a*).

terms of clusters, especially in any conscious way. This is a reflection of the near absence of connections between location and firm behavior in the management literature.

Location and Competition

The role of clusters grows out of a broader set of influences of location on competition and competitive advantage.[6] Until the last decade, thinking about the influence of location on competition took a relatively simple view of how companies competed. Competition was seen as largely static and as resting on cost minimization in relatively closed economies. Here comparative advantage in factors of production (labor and capital) is decisive. Subsequent analyses centered on the benefits derived from the presence of economies of scale.

Yet this picture failed to represent real competition. Competition is dynamic and rests on innovation and the search for strategic differences. Three conditions contribute to rendering factor inputs *per se* less valuable: the expanded input supply as more countries open to the global economy; the greater efficiency of national and international factor markets; and the diminishing factor intensity of competition. Instead, close linkages with buyers, suppliers, and other institutions contribute importantly not only to efficiency but to the rate of improvement and innovation. While extensive vertical integration (e.g. in house production of parts, services, or training) may once have been the norm, a more dynamic environment can render vertical integration inefficient, ineffective, and inflexible.

In this broader and more dynamic view of competition, location affects competitive advantage through its influence on firm *productivity* and especially on *productivity growth*.[7] While sound political/legal structures and stable macroeconomic policies create the potential for investment and hence productivity growth, productivity will only increase if a nation (or location) improves its capabilities at the microeconomic level. The microeconomic foundations of development can only be understood by examining the way in which productivity increases at the firm, industry, and cluster levels.

The microeconomic foundations of productivity rest on two interrelated areas: the sophistication of company operations and strategy and the quality of the microeconomic business environment. The sophistication (e.g. technology, skill) with which companies compete ultimately sets national productivity.

[6] In Porter and Sölvell (1998) I suggest that a clearer understanding of firm strategy, organization, and the process of innovation will result from the integration of research on economic geography to issues related to how firms build and sustain competitive advantage.

[7] Scott (1998) has highlighted some of the ways in which location and industrial performance are interconnected.

Unless companies become more productive, an economy cannot become more productive. The sophistication of companies' approaches to competing determines the prices that their products and services can command, and the efficiency with which they produce.

Company sophistication in competing can be divided into two parts. The first and most basic is what I term *operational effectiveness*, or the extent to which companies in a location approach international best practice in their modes of operating, in areas such as production processes, technologies employed, and management techniques.[8] The second dimension of company sophistication relates to the *types of strategies* companies employ in competing. Primitive forms of strategy rely on factor (input) costs, while more advanced forms involve competing based on differentiated products and services and, ultimately, on unique competitive positioning versus rivals.

Yet the sophistication and productivity with which companies compete in a location is strongly conditioned by the *quality of the microeconomic business environment*. Firms cannot employ advanced logistical techniques, for example, unless a high-quality transportation infrastructure is available. Firms cannot operate efficiently under onerous amounts of regulatory red tape that requires endless dialogue with government, or under a court system that fails to resolve disputes quickly and fairly. These circumstances, among others, consume company resources and management time without contributing to customer value.

The effects of some aspects of the business environment, such as the road system, corporate tax rates, and the legal system, cut across all industries. These economy-wide (or horizontal) areas often represent the binding constraints to competitiveness in developing economies. In more advanced economies and increasingly in all economies, however, the more decisive aspects of the business environment are often *cluster specific* (for example, the presence of particular types of suppliers, specialized labor pools, or university departments). Firms located within a cluster are more likely to attain competitive advantage, both in terms of operational effectiveness and types of strategies.

Capturing the nature of the business environment in a location is challenging given the myriad of locational influences on productivity and productivity growth. In *The Competitive Advantage of Nations*, I modeled the effect of location on competition using four interrelated influences, graphically depicted in a diamond, a metaphor that has become a shorthand reference to the theory (see Fig. 13.1).[9]

[8] See Porter (1996).

[9] See Porter (1998*b*) for a discussion of how company operations and strategies, and the business environment must upgrade to support successful development, along with supporting statistical tests.

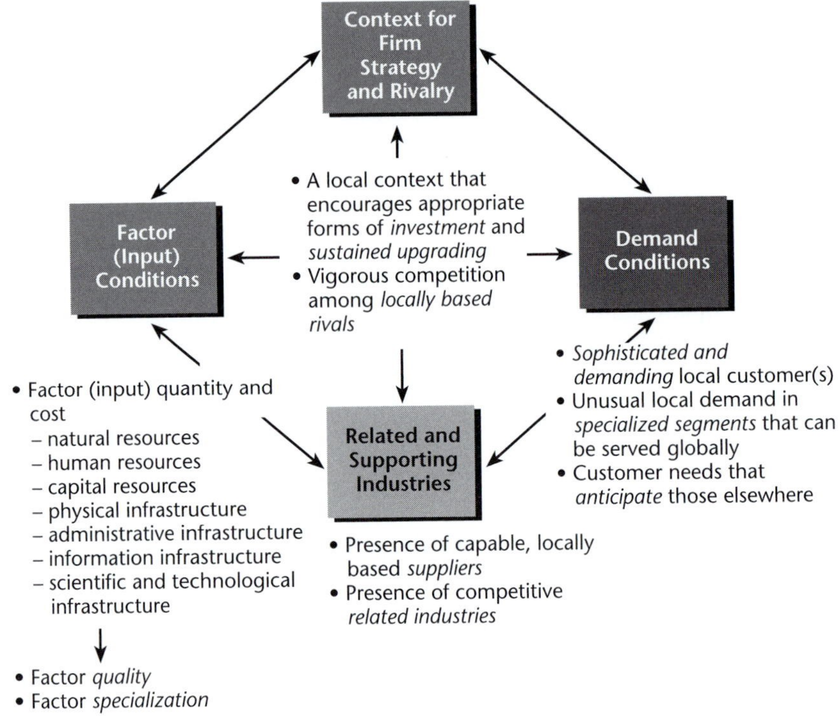

Fig. 13.1. Sources of locational competitive advantage

Clusters contain one facet of the diamond (related and supporting industries), but are best seen as a manifestation of the interactions among all four facets. As noted above, scholars have long sought to explain concentrations of firms in terms of economies of agglomeration.[10] These have normally been seen as arising either at the industry level, or, conversely, in a diversified urban economy.[11] Many treatments of agglomeration economies stress cost minimization due to proximity to inputs or proximity to markets. However, these explanations have been undercut by the globalization of markets, technology, and supply sources, increased mobility, and lower transportation and communication

[10] See Harrison *et al.* (1996) for a good summary. Static agglomeration economies consist of a local concentration of customers (or downstream firms) sufficient to permit suppliers to achieve economies of scale in production or distribution, great enough for local firms to amass sufficient demand to warrant the provision (usually by or via local governments) of specialized infrastructure, and large enough to realize a specialized local division of labor. So-called dynamic agglomeration economies consist of advantages in terms of technological learning and improvement. For a classic early statement on agglomeration and division of labor, see Stigler (1951) and, for an important recent work, see Krugman (1991).

[11] An extensive literature has explored these advantages, including Pascal and McCall (1980), Angel (1990), Rauch (1993), and Glaeser and Maré (1994).

costs. Firms can efficiently source inputs from any location, and efficiently supply international markets in most types of goods and services. Similarly, generalized urbanization advantages offer less weight in explaining competitive success, as there are many urban areas with a substantial concentration of economic activity (see Ch. 5). Simple benefits of concentration can be attained via efficient exchange with other locations. Today, then, economies of agglomeration seem to have shifted in nature.

The locus of agglomeration is increasingly the cluster and not urban areas or narrowly defined industries. Many cluster advantages rest on external economies or spillovers across firms and industries of various sorts. (Many cluster advantages also apply to sub-units *within* firms, such as R&D and production.) A cluster may thus be seen as a system of interconnected firms and institutions whose value as a whole is greater than the sum of its parts.

Clusters and Competitiveness

To understand the link between clusters, competition, and company strategy, it is useful to recognize that clusters influence competition and competitive advantage in three broad ways: first, by increasing the (static) productivity of constituent firms or industries; secondly, by increasing their capacity for innovation and thus productivity growth; and thirdly, by stimulating new business formation that supports innovation and expands the cluster. Some elements of these influences have been recognized in previous literatures, but primarily at the broad theoretical level. Each of the three influences will be discussed in turn, focusing on the connection between clusters and the operations and strategies of individual companies.[12]

Static Productivity

Access to Specialized Inputs and Employees. Locating within a cluster can provide companies with superior or lower-cost access to specialized inputs such as components, machinery, business services, and personnel, as compared to the alternatives—vertical integration, formal alliances with outside entities, or 'importing' inputs from distant locations. The cluster represents a spatial organizational form that can be an inherently more efficient or effective means of assembling inputs—if competitive local suppliers are available.[13] Sourcing outside the cluster may be necessary where competent local suppliers are unavailable, but that is not the ideal arrangement. Sourcing inputs from cluster participants ('local' outsourcing) can result in lower

[12] For a more detailed discussion, see Porter (1998*a*).

[13] Gertler (1995), for example, finds that physical proximity between machinery producers and users facilitates the formation and maintenance of a high-quality, interaction-intensive relationship that in turn bolsters productivity.

transaction costs than those incurred when using distant sources ('distant' outsourcing).

Working against a cluster's advantages in assembling inputs and labor is the possibility that such concentration will render these resources scarce and bid up their cost. Yet a firm's ability to outsource inputs limits any cost penalty relative to other locations. More importantly, the presence of a cluster not only increases the demand for specialized inputs but also *increases their supply*. Where a cluster exists, the availability of specialized personnel, services, and components and the number of entities creating them usually far exceeds the levels at other locations: a distinct benefit, despite the greater competition.

Access to Information and Knowledge. Extensive market, technical, and other specialized knowledge, both explicit and implicit, accumulates within a cluster in firms and local institutions.[14] This can be accessed better or at lower cost from within the cluster, thus allowing firms to enhance productivity and get closer to the productivity frontier. This effect also applies to the flow of information and knowledge between units of the same company.[15] Proximity, supply, and technological linkages, and the existence of repeated, personal relationships and community ties fostering trust, facilitate the information and knowledge flow within clusters.[16] An important special case of the knowledge benefits of clusters is the availability of information about current buyer needs. Sophisticated buyers are often part of clusters, and other cluster participants often gain and share knowledge about their needs.[17]

Complementarities. A cluster enhances productivity not only via the acquisition and assembly of inputs but by facilitating complementarities between the activities of cluster participants. The most obvious form of complementarities is among products. In tourism, for example, the quality of the visitor's experience depends not only on the appeal of the primary attraction (e.g. beaches or historical sites) but also on the comfort and serviceability of area hotels, restaurants, souvenir outlets, airport, and other transportation facilities. As this example illustrates, the parts of the cluster are often truly mutually dependent. Bad performance by one part of the cluster can undermine the success of the others, one reason why clusters relate directly to competitive strategy.

Marketing provides another form of complementarity within clusters. The

[14] The distinction between tacit knowledge and explicit knowledge draws on Polanyi (1966).

[15] Adams and Jaffe (1996), for example, found that the influence of parent firm R&D on plant-level productivity diminishes with geographic distance.

[16] Spender (1998) attempts to develop a geography of organizational knowledge and learning activities. He argues that different kinds of knowledge can, in principle, be associated with different kinds of rent and competitive advantage.

[17] Saxenian (1994) describes the workings of the remarkable information flow within Silicon Valley.

presence of a group of related firms and industries in a location offers efficiencies in joint marketing (e.g. firm referrals, trade fairs, trade magazines, and marketing delegations). It can also enhance the reputation of a location in a particular field, making it more likely that buyers will consider a vendor or manufacturer based there.

Access to Institutions and Public Goods. Clusters make many inputs that would otherwise be costly into public or quasi-public goods. The ability to recruit employees trained in local programs, for example, eliminates or lowers the cost of internal training. Firms can often access benefits, such as specialized infrastructure or advice from experts in local institutions at very low cost. Indeed, the knowledge built up in a cluster can in itself be seen as a quasi-public good. Moreover, public or quasi-public goods at cluster locations often result from *private* investments in training programs, infrastructure, quality centers, and so on. Such investments frequently take place via trade associations or other collective mechanisms.

Incentives and Performance Measurement. Clusters help to solve or mitigate some agency problems that arise in more isolated locations and in more vertically integrated firms. Clusters improve the incentives for several reasons. Foremost is competitive pressure. Rivalry with locally based competitors has particularly strong incentive effects because of the ease of constant comparison and because local rivals have similar general circumstances (e.g. labor costs and local market access) so that competition must take place on other things.

Clusters also facilitate measurement of the performance of in-house activities because, often, other local firms perform similar functions. Managers gain wider opportunities to compare internal costs with arm's-length transactions, and lower employee monitoring costs by comparing employee performance with others locally. The accumulation of cluster knowledge in financial institutions, for example, should make loan decisions and other financing choices better informed and improve customer monitoring.

Many of the advantages of clustering also apply to sub-units *within a single company.* Co-locating R&D, component fabrication, assembly, marketing, customer support, and other activities can facilitate internal efficiencies in sourcing and information flow, as well as complementarities and other benefits. Companies sometimes disperse units in order to lower costs of labor, utilities, or taxes, thus unwittingly sacrificing the powerful system-wide cost benefits of clusters and their advantages in fostering dynamism and innovation.

Clusters and Innovation

Firms within a cluster are often able to perceive more clearly and rapidly new buyer needs and benefit from the concentration of firms with buyer knowledge and relationships.[18] Cluster participation also offers advantages in perceiving new technological, operating, or delivery possibilities. Participants learn early and consistently about evolving technology, component and machinery availability, service and marketing concepts, and so on, facilitated by ongoing relationships with other cluster entities, the ease of site visits, and frequent face-to-face contacts.[19] The isolated firm, in contrast, faces higher costs and steeper impediments to acquiring information and a corresponding increase in the time and resources devoted to generating such knowledge internally.[20]

The potential advantages of clusters in perceiving both the need and the opportunity for innovation are significant, but equally important can be the flexibility and capacity clusters provide to act rapidly to turn these opportunities into advantages in operations or strategy. A firm within a cluster often can more rapidly source the new components, services, machinery, and other elements needed to implement innovations, whether a new product line, a new process, or a new logistical model. Local suppliers and partners can and do get closely involved in the innovation process, thus ensuring that the inputs they supply better meet the firm's requirements. New, specialized personnel can often be recruited locally to fill gaps required to pursue new approaches. The complementarities involved in innovating are more easily achieved among nearby participants.

Reinforcing these advantages for innovation is the sheer pressure—competitive pressure, peer pressure, and constant comparison—occurring in geographically concentrated clusters. The similarity of basic circumstances (e.g. labor and utility costs), combined with the presence of multiple rivals, forces firms to distinguish themselves creatively. The pressure to innovate is elevated. Individual firms in the cluster have difficulty staying ahead for long, but many firms progress faster than do those based at other locations.

Under certain circumstances, however, cluster participation can retard innovation. When a cluster shares a uniform approach to competing, a sort of groupthink often reinforces old behaviors, suppresses new ideas, and creates rigidities that prevent the adoption of improvements.[21] I explore these issues

[18] Audretsch (1998) makes the point that since knowledge is generated and transmitted more efficiently via local proximity, economic activity based on new knowledge has a high prospensity to cluster within a geographic region.

[19] Feldman (1994) examines the spatial dimension of innovation. Her findings confirm that both R&D and innovation tend to cluster in certain regions or areas of production.

[20] Strong empirical support exists for the spillover effects among firms and between universities and firms in R&D and innovation. Jaffe *et al.* (1993) show geographic localization of knowledge spillovers. Audretsch and Feldman (1996) find a strong association between the importance of new knowledge and spatial clustering. Harrison *et al.* (1996) also highlight the geographic dimension of innovation.

[21] Pouder and St John (1996) suggest that in some clusters, competitors' managers may develop similar mental models, leading to homogeneity and inertia, or what the authors call a macroculture that suppresses innovation. Glasmeier (1991) provides an example drawn from the Swiss watch industry.

further elsewhere, in the context of the processes by which clusters emerge and decline.[22]

Clusters and New Business Formation

Many new businesses (i.e. headquarters, not branch offices or ancillary facilities) form within existing clusters rather than at isolated locations. This occurs for a variety of reasons. First, clusters provide inducement to entry through better information about opportunities. The existence of a cluster in itself signals an opportunity. Individuals working somewhere in or near the cluster more easily perceive gaps in products, services, or suppliers to fill. Having had this insight, these individuals more readily leave established firms in order to start new ones aimed at filling the perceived gaps.

Opportunities perceived at cluster locations are pursued there because *barriers to entry are lower than elsewhere.* Needed assets, skills, inputs, and staff, often readily available at the cluster location, can be assembled more easily for a new enterprise. Local financial institutions and investors, already possessing familiarity with the cluster, may require a lower risk premium on capital. The barriers to exit at a cluster can also be lower due to reduced need for specialized investment, deeper markets for specialized assets, and other factors.[23]

While local entrepreneurs are likely entrants to a cluster, entrepreneurs based outside a cluster frequently relocate, sooner or later, to a cluster location. The same lower entry barriers attract them, as does the potential to create more economic value from their ideas and skills at the cluster location or the ability to operate more productively. For all these reasons, cluster thinking is an important missing element in the literature on entrepreneurial management.

The intense competition within a healthy cluster, together with lower entry and exit barriers, sometimes leads to high rates of both entry and exit at these locations. The net result is that many of the surviving firms in the cluster can gain position *vis-à-vis* rivals at other locations. Location and the state of clusters not only affect barriers to entry and exit but most other aspects of industry structure.[24]

Clusters and New Inter-organizational Forms

A number of the mechanisms through which clusters affect productivity and innovation echo findings in other literatures.[25] Management literature shows growing awareness of the importance of close linkages with suppliers and buyers and of the value of outsourcing or partnering. The literature on innovation highlights the role of customers, suppliers, and universities in the

[22] See Porter (1990, 1998*a*).

[23] See Caves and Porter (1977).

[24] See Porter (1998*a*: 14–16).

[25] Enright (1990), building on Porter (1990), provides the foundational treatment of the role of geographic concentration. See also Enright (1993*a*, 1998), and Gabor (1991).

innovation process, while the literature on the diffusion of innovation stresses such notions as demonstration effects, contagion, experimentation, and ease of observability—all clearly influenced by the presence of clusters.[26] Many studies in economics highlight the importance of transaction costs, and others explore the organizational incentive problems that stand in the way of efficiency.[27]

Little of this thinking, however, has been connected to location. It is as if linkages, transactions, and information flow took place outside of time and space. Yet proximity clearly affects linkages and transactions costs. Incentive misalignments difficult to resolve with feasible contracts may right themselves under the influence of repeated interaction and other aspects of location and clusters. The resort to formal partnerships and alliances, undertaken despite complex incentive and governance problems, overlooks the relative ease of achieving many of the same benefits more simply and informally within clusters. Bringing these various theoretical approaches together with an understanding of location and clusters can extend their usefulness and deepen our understanding of the effect of clusters on competition.

More broadly, the geographically proximate cluster of independent and informally linked firms and institutions represents a robust organizational form in the continuum between markets and hierarchies.[28] Location can powerfully shape the tradeoffs between markets and hierarchies. Clusters offer obvious advantages in transaction costs over other forms and seem to ameliorate many incentive problems. Repeated interactions and informal contracts within a cluster structure result from living and working in a circumscribed geographic area and foster trust, open communication, and lower the costs of severing and recombining market relationships.

The mere presence of firms, suppliers, and institutions in a location creates the *potential* for economic value, but it does not necessarily ensure the realization of this potential. Social glue binds clusters together, contributing to the value creation process. Many of the competitive advantages of clusters depend on the free flow of information, the discovery of value-adding exchanges or transactions, the willingness to align agendas and to work across organizations, and strong motivations for improvement. Relationships, networks, and a sense of common interest undergird these circumstances. The social structure of clusters thus takes on central importance. These issues, and the growing literature about networks, are explored elsewhere.[29] Cluster

[26] See e.g. von Hippel (1988), Case (1992), and Rogers (1995).

[27] See e.g. Coase (1937), Williamson (1975, 1985), Klein *et al.* (1978), and Hart (1996).

[28] A variety of literatures, including Lundvall (1988), Cooke and Morgan (1993), Scott (1996), and Storper (1997), explicitly or implicitly view clusters as an intermediate form of governance between markets and hierarchies. The topic, however, has yet to be explored from a managerial perspective.

[29] See Porter (1998*a*).

theory helps illuminate the causes of network structure, the appropriate nature of network activity, and the link between network characteristics and outcomes.

Clusters and the Corporate Agenda

The existence of clusters suggests that much of a company's potential to achieve competitive advantage lies outside the company and even outside the industry. The presence of a well-developed cluster provides strong benefits to productivity and to the capacity for innovation that are difficult for firms based elsewhere to match. We know this because of the strong tendency for competitive firms to be co-located. Often, for a given field, only a few locations in the world provide such an environment.

Despite this, the management literature is only just beginning to incorporate locational considerations. Let me sketch a few of the areas in which location needs to be integrated.

Location and Competitive Strategy

Clusters affect both the ability of firms to attain operational effectiveness and their ability to choose distinctive, rather than imitative, strategic positions (see Fig. 13.2).[30] Both operational effectiveness and strategy can best be understood by disaggregating what firms do into activities, or the discrete economic processes firms perform in competing in any business. Activities are defined more narrowly than are traditional functions.[31]

All companies must continually improve operational effectiveness in their activities. However, sustainable performance differences will most often depend on having a distinctive strategic position. Strategy differences rest on differences in activities, such as the way companies go about order processing, assembly, product design, training, and so on. A strategy is sustainable if it involves tradeoffs, or choices that firms make to offer certain types of value but sacrifice others. A company's unique position is reflected not only in the individual activities tailored to the company's way of competing but also in the fit among them (activity system).

The benefits of clusters for rapid best practice improvement have been discussed earlier. It also appears, however, that operating within a cluster can proliferate opportunities for distinctive competitive positions.[32] A concentration of visible rivals encourages the search for ways of competing that are not head on.

[30] See Porter (1996).

[31] In Porter (1985) I introduced a framework for systematically examining activities, called the value chain.

[32] Some geographic areas have developed competitive strategies for a cluster as a whole. Conejos *et al.* (1997) provide numerous examples drawn from the Catalan experience in Spain.

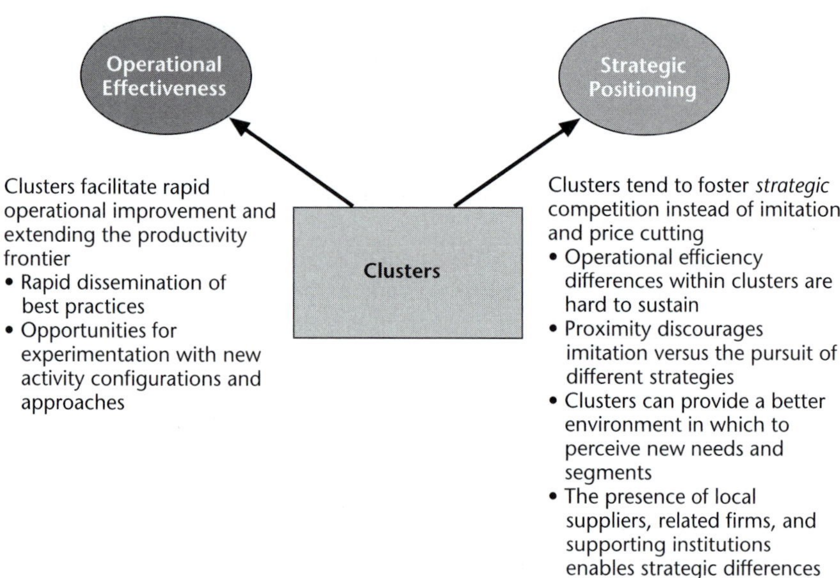

Fig. 13.2. The influence of clusters on the nature of local competition

Niche opportunities overlooked by others can reveal themselves. Ready access to suppliers and partners provides flexibility to configure the value chain in a variety of ways. A more positive-sum form of competition can result when customer choice is widened and different customers are served most efficiently.

Recent managerial literature has emphasized the development of corporate 'capabilities' or 'resources'. Locational considerations are central in defining these resources and capabilities, and clearly play a crucial role in the ability of firms to *access* them.[33] Given the benefits of proximity, location theory provides a rationale for why such advantages might be difficult for firms based elsewhere to access and, hence, are more sustainable.[34]

Location and Global Strategy

Globalization and the ease of transportation and communication have led to a surge of outsourcing, with companies relocating many facilities to locations with low wages, low taxes, and low utility costs. Many companies have lost sight of the importance of location in competitive advantage. While outsourcing some activities to tap lower cost inputs can indeed reduce disadvantages of the home base, cluster theory suggests a more complex view of corporate locational

[33] See Enright (1998). [34] See also Porter (1991).

choices. Cluster thinking makes it clear that corporate location involves far more than simply deciding where to build factories or offices.

First, cluster theory suggests that locational choices should weigh overall productivity potential, not just input costs or taxes. In locating activities, the aim is low total cost or highest value. Locations with low wages and low taxes, however, often lack efficient infrastructure, available suppliers, timely maintenance, and other conditions that clusters offer. Logistical costs and costs of introducing new models may be substantial. Many companies have discovered that such productivity disadvantages can be more than offsetting. Yet the effects of low wages, low taxes, and low utility costs are easy to measure up front, while productivity costs remain hidden and unanticipated.

Locating in an existing or developing cluster, then, often involves lower total systems cost and greatly improves the capacity for innovation. A shift back toward clusters is beginning among companies who once believed in the cost savings of highly dispersed activities. This trend is evident in choices of international locations (with activities being moved back to places such as the USA) and locations within nations (with clusters gaining in appeal over remote sunbelt or other sites). An interesting recent example is Gateway, one of the leading manufacturers of personal computers with a historical location in North Dakota. Gateway relocated many of its headquarters activities to San Diego, citing an inability to attract and retain specialized employees.

Secondly, firms must capture the cost advantages of spreading activities across locations while *also* harnessing the advantages of clusters. The determinants of location differ markedly for various activities. For activities such as assembly plants, manufacture of stable, labor-intensive components, and software translation, locational choices should often be driven by factor cost and market access. For what I term 'home base' activities, however, the basis for choice should be very different. Home base activities are those involved in the creation and renewal of the firm's product, processes, and services. This includes activities, such as fabrication of frequently redesigned components, that involve substantial, ongoing changes.

The location of home base activities should be heavily driven by total systems cost and by innovation potential. Clusters usually provide conditions favorable for innovation. Home base activities should sometimes move to locations outside the company's nation of principal ownership or the nation containing its corporate headquarters—if a more vibrant cluster exists elsewhere. This rule applies especially to product lines, but also to entire business units. The siting of regional headquarters should also involve consideration of clusters, not just tax considerations or the convenience of executives.

Cluster thinking also underscores the desirability of moving groups of linked activities to the same place rather than spreading them across numerous states and nations. Grouping in this way lowers total system costs, eases sharing of internal information, facilitates and spreads innovation, creates critical mass for supporting company infrastructure and facilities, and extends deeper roots into local clusters that increase the ability to capture externalities and spillovers. More companies are beginning to create 'campuses', where they can co-locate a number of related units. Suppliers are being invited to site their facilities nearby. Dell, for example, encourages its suppliers to locate around its plants to minimize logistical costs and the speed of changeovers.

Activities located in places isolated from other firms benefit from efforts to begin building a cluster. The process calls for wooing suppliers to set up shop nearby, encouraging local institutions to make supporting investments, and finding ways to build local capabilities in specialized inputs. Intel is in the process of doing this in Costa Rica where it has recently established its Latin American production base.

All these considerations suggest that corporate location is not something to be delegated to operations departments. It is part of overall strategy. There is an opportunity for major extensions of the corporate location literature, which tends to focus on input cost minimization and static efficiencies, to incorporate the principles and the broader considerations just outlined.

Finally, as global competition nullifies traditional comparative advantages and exposes companies to the best rivals from around the world, a growing number of multinationals are shifting their home bases to more vibrant clusters—often using acquisitions as a means of establishing themselves as insiders in a new location. Nestlé, for example, after acquiring Rowntree Mackintosh, relocated its confectionery business to York, England, where Rowntree was originally based, because a vibrant food cluster thrives there. England, with its sweet-toothed consumers, sophisticated retailers, advanced advertising agencies, and highly competitive media companies, constitutes a more dynamic environment for competing in mass-market candy than Switzerland did. Similarly, Nestlé has moved its headquarters for bottled water to France, the most competitive location in that industry. Northern Telecom has relocated its home base for central office, switching from Canada to the USA—drawn by the vibrancy of the US telecommunications-equipment cluster. A fuller treatment of the role of location in global strategy can be found elsewhere.[35]

Location and Business Growth

A location's competitive advantages provide a means for identifying the industries in which a firm can gain a unique competitive advantage *vis-à-vis* rivals based elsewhere, as well as those industry segments where the home base envi-

[35] See ch. 9 in Porter (1998*a*).

ronment provides the greatest benefits. New business development should concentrate in these areas.

Diversification along cluster lines will better leverage not only companies' own internal assets but also the unique assets of locations to which they have special access, such as suppliers, research centers, and skill pools. Innovations often originate at the interstices between industries and clusters, when related technologies and skills are combined. To get its start in automobiles, for example, Honda drew on its small-engine technology expertise, nurtured in motorcycles. It combined this with assets readily available in the Japanese automobile cluster, including a strong supplier base and demand conditions encouraging compact designs and energy efficiency.

Location and Entrepreneurial Management

Entrepreneurial management, or the study of the creation and growth of new companies, has become a prominent field in the literature on management. This field has developed largely independently of location considerations. Implicitly, the literature assumes that entrepreneurial ideas arise primarily from individuals' personal circumstances, and that any location where capital can be accessed is a good place to establish and develop a new company. Clearly, however, the geographic patterns of new business startups suggest that location plays a much more important role in the entrepreneurial process.[36] The relationship between clusters and new business formation, discussed earlier, reveals some of the connections. New business ideas will tend to bubble up within clusters because of the concentration of firms, ideas, skills, technology, and needs there. Once an idea is perceived, the barriers to entry and growth are lower at cluster locations. Location needs to be integrated into thinking about entrepreneurship, then, and there are many opportunities for further research into the locational patterns of new business formation and their implications.

The Corporate Role in Cluster Development

Cluster theory suggests new tasks and roles for companies. Cluster analysis must become part of competitive assessments, along with company and industry analysis. Private sector roles in cluster upgrading can be found in all parts of the diamond, as shown in Figure 13.3. Improving factor conditions provides the most obvious example, with efforts possible in enhancing the supply of appropriately trained personnel, the quality and appropriateness of local university research activities, the creation of specialized physical infrastructure, and the

[36] Birch *et al.* (1997) begin to sketch, generically, some of the location-specific determinants of entrepreneurship, breaking them into hard and soft variables. The former include the presence of universities, a skilled labor pool, airports, and a high quality of life. The latter relate to a location's culture, in particular its appetite for change and challenge to the existing order.

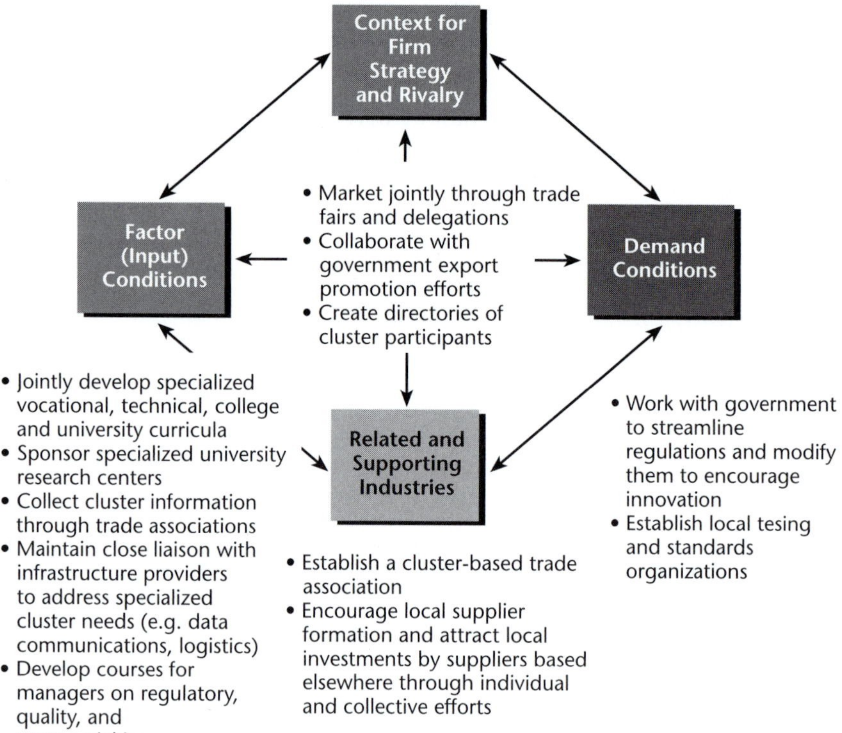

Fig. 13.3. Private sector influences on cluster upgrading

supply of cluster-specific information. Ongoing relationships with government bodies and local institutions, such as utilities, schools, and research groups, are necessary to attain these benefits. There is also a role for private investment by cluster participants to establish common specialized infrastructure, such as port or handling facilities, satellite communication links, and testing laboratories. Often such investments can be made and administered through third parties, for example, universities or trade associations.

In the area of related and supporting industries, firms have a role in attracting suppliers, services, and complementary-product producers to the cluster, as well as in forming supplier businesses to fill gaps. Joint ventures are sometimes used to establish local capability in essential supporting industries.

The need for cluster participants to inform and prod government to address the constraints or weaknesses under its control cuts across all parts of the diamond. Individual departments or units of government that impact on the cluster must be engaged and educated on the effect of regulations and policies and on the quality of government services. An open, constructive dialogue must replace self-serving lobbying or paternalism in these relationships.

Even though clusters offer tangible competitive benefits, the first reaction of managers is often to be wary of them. There are concerns that the expansion of a cluster will invite unwanted competition and drive up the costs of employees and inputs. Managers have nightmare visions of losing valued employees to rivals or spin-offs. As their understanding of the cluster concept grows, however, managers realize that many cluster participants do not directly compete. As I mentioned earlier, although a company may face competition for employees and other inputs, the presence of the cluster expands their supply. The net access to specialized skills, services, technology, and information in a cluster often increases. Any increases in competition come with clusters' benefits in productivity, flexibility, and innovation.

Private Collective Action

Individual companies can independently influence cluster development, and cluster pioneers or leading firms often play this role because they gain major benefits. An example is Genzyme, the biotechnology firm located in Boston. When the company needed a manufacturing facility, its CEO decided to influence the process of creating this capability in Boston. Among other things, Genzyme deliberately chose to work with contractors committed to the Boston area, bypassing many specialized engineering firms located near Philadelphia, a site originally considered for Genzyme's facility.

Given the important externalities and public goods involved in clusters, informal networks and formal trade associations, consortia, and other collective bodies often become necessary and appropriate. Trade associations representing all or most cluster participants can command greater attention and achieve greater influence than can individual members, and an association or collective body (e.g. a joint research center or testing laboratory) creates a vehicle for cost sharing. There is a major opportunity to conduct research in these areas.

Many trade associations do little more than lobby government, compile some statistics, and host social functions. The opportunity for associations to enhance cluster competitiveness, however, is much greater. Associations fulfill especially important functions for clusters consisting of many small- and medium-sized firms (e.g. tourism, apparel, or agriculture). Such clusters have a particularly great need for a collective body to take on scale-sensitive functions. In the Netherlands, for example, grower cooperatives built the specialized auction and handling facilities that constitute one of the Dutch flower cluster's greatest competitive advantages. The Dutch Flower Council and the Association of Dutch Flower Growers Research Groups, in which most growers participate, have taken on other functions as well, such as marketing and applied research.

Most existing trade associations are too narrow; they represent industries, not clusters. In addition, because their role is defined as lobbying the federal government, their scope is national rather than local. National associations, however, are rarely sufficient to address the local issues that are most important to cluster productivity. By revealing how business and government together create the conditions that promote growth, clusters offer a constructive way to change the nature of the dialogue between the public and private sectors. With a better understanding of what fosters true competitiveness, executives can start asking government for the right things.

Summary

Clusters are systems of interconnected firms and institutions that play an important role in competition. While cluster theory is beginning to be prominent in thinking about economic development, the influence of location and the role of clusters is all but absent in the literature on management.

Many of a firm's competitive advantages lie outside the firm and even outside its narrowly defined industry. Locational factors and cluster theory have important implications for strategic positioning, the configuration of global strategies, supply chain management, the analysis of partnering and alliances, and the management of R&D among other areas. Cluster theory reveals 'public' roles for companies that are still rarely understood. Over time, geography and location must become one of the core disciplines in management. There is a compelling need to reorient our thinking about corporate strategy in a way that sees location and cluster participation as integral to a firm's success.

References

Adams, J., and Jaffe, A. 1996. Bounding the effects of R&D: an investigation using matched establishment-firm data. *Rand Journal of Economics*, 27: 700–21.

Angel, D. 1990. New firm formation in the semiconductor industry: elements of a flexible manufacturing system. *Regional Studies*, 24: 211–21.

Audretsch, D. 1998. Agglomeration and the location of innovative activity. *Oxford Review of Economic Policy*, 14: 18–29.

—— and Feldman, M. 1996. R&D spillovers and the geography of innovation and production. *American Economic Review*, 86: 630–40.

Birch, D., Haggerty, A., and Parsons, W. 1997. Corporate demographics: entrepreneurial hot spots, the best places in America to start and grow a company. Cambridge, Mass.: Cognetics.

Cairncross, F. 1997. *The Death of Distance: How the Communications Revolution Will Change Our Lives*. Boston, Mass.: Harvard Business School Press.

Case, A. 1992. Neighborhood influence and technological change. *Regional Science and Urban Economics*, 22: 491–508.

Caves, R., and Porter, M. 1977. From entry barriers to mobility barriers: conjectural decisions and contrived deterrence to new competition. *Quarterly Journal of Economics*, 91: 241–61.

Chandler, A., Hagström, P., and Sölvell, Ö., eds. 1998. *The Dynamic Firm: The Role of Technology, Strategy, Organizations and Regions*. New York: Oxford University Press.

Coase, R. 1937. The nature of the firm. *Economica*, 4: 386–405.

Conejos, J., Duch, E., Fontrodona, J., Hernández, J. M., Luzárraga, A., and Terré, E. 1997. *Cambio Estratégico y Clusters en Cataluña*. Barcelona: Gestíón 2000.

Cooke, P., and Morgan, K. 1993. The network paradigm: new departures in corporate and regional development. *Environment and Planning D: Society and Space*, 3: 543–64.

Enright, M. 1990. Geographical concentration and industrial organization. Ph.D. thesis, Harvard.

—— 1993*a*. The determinants of geographic concentration in industry. Working Paper 93-052, Division of Research, Harvard Business School. Boston, Mass.

—— 1993*b*. The geographic scope of competitive advantage. In *Stuck in the Region? Changing Scales of Regional Identity*, ed. E. Dirven, J. Groenewegen, and S. van Hoof. Utrecht: Netherlands Geographical Studies, 87–102.

—— 1998. Regional clusters and firm strategy. In Chandler, *et al.* 1998: 314–42.

Feldman, M. 1994. *The Geography of Innovation*. Dordrecht: Kluwer Academic Publishers.

Gabor, A. 1991. Rochester focuses: a community's core competence. *Harvard Business Review*, 69: 116–26.

Gertler, M. S. 1995. 'Being there': proximity, organization, and culture in the development and adoption of advanced manufacturing technologies. *Economic Geography*, 71: 1–26.

Glaeser, E., and Maré, D. 1994. Cities and Skills. Working Paper 4728, National Bureau of Economic Research. Cambridge, Mass.

Glasmeier, A. 1991. Technological discontinuities and flexible production networks: the case of Switzerland and the world watch industry. *Research Policy*, 20: 469–85.

Harrison, B., Kelley, M., and Gant, J. 1996. Innovative firm behavior and local milieu: exploring the intersection of agglomeration, firm effects, industrial organization, and technological change. *Economic Geography*, 72: 233–58.

Hart, O. 1996. *Firms, Contracts and Financial Structure*. New York: Clarendon Press.

Jaffe, A., Trajtenberg, M., and Henderson, R. 1993. Geographic localization of knowledge spillovers as evidenced by patent citations. *Quarterly Journal of Economics*, 108: 577–98.

Klein, B., Crawford, R., and Alchian, A. 1978. Vertical integration, appropriable rents, and the competitive contracting process. *Journal of Law and Economics*, 21: 297–326.

Krugman, P. 1991. *Trade and Geography*. Cambridge, Mass.: MIT Press.

Lundvall, Bengt-Åke. 1988. Innovation as an interactive process: from user-producer interaction to the national system of innovation. In *Technical Change and Economic Theory*, ed. G. Dosi *et al.* London: Pinter Publishers, 349–69.

Pascal, A., and McCall, J. 1980. Agglomeration economies, search costs, and industrial location. *Journal of Urban Economics*, 8: 383–8.

Polanyi, M. 1966. *The Tacit Dimension*. London: Routledge & Kegan Paul.

Porter, M. 1985. *Competitive Advantage: Creating and Sustaining Superior Performance*. New York: Free Press.

—— 1990. *The Competitive Advantage of Nations*. New York: Free Press.

—— 1991. Towards a dynamic theory of strategy. *Strategic Management Journal*, 12: 95–117.

—— 1995. The competitive advantage of the inner city. *Harvard Business Review*, 73: 55–71.

—— 1996. What is strategy? *Harvard Business Review*, 74: 61–78.

—— 1998*a*. Clusters and competition: new agendas for companies, governments and institutions. In M. Porter, *On Competition*. Boston: Harvard Business School Press.

—— 1998*b*. The microeconomic foundations of economic development. In *The Global Competitiveness Report 1998*. Geneva: World Economic Forum.

—— and Sölvell, Ö. 1998. The role of geography in the process of innovation and the sustainable competitive advantage of firms. In Chandler *et al.* 1998: 440–57.

Pouder R., and St John, C. 1996. Hot spots and blind spots: geographical clusters of firms and innovation. *Academy of Management Review*, 21: 1192–225.

Rauch, J. 1993. Productivity gains from geographic concentration of human capital: evidence from the cities. *Journal of Urban Economics*, 34: 380–400.

Rogers, E. 1995. *Diffusion of Innovations*. 4th edn. New York: Free Press.

Saxenian, A. 1994. *Regional Advantage: Culture and Competition in Silicon Valley and Route 128*. Cambridge, Mass.: Harvard University Press.

Scott, A. 1996. Regional motors of the global economy. *Futures*, 28: 391–411.

—— 1998. The geographic foundations of industrial performance. In Chandler *et al.* 1998: 384–401.

Spender, J. 1998. The geographies of strategic competence: borrowing from social and educational psychology to sketch an activity and knowledge-based theory of the firm. In Chandler *et al.* 1998: 417–39.

Stigler, G. 1951. The division of labor is limited by the extent of the market. *Journal of Political Economy*, 59: 185–93.

Storper, M. 1997. *The Regional World: Territorial Development in a Global Economy*. New York: Guilford Press.

von Hippel, E. 1988. *The Sources of Innovation*. New York: Oxford University Press.

Williamson, O. 1975. *Markets and Hierarchies: Analysis and Antitrust Implications*. New York: Free Press.

—— 1985. *The Economic Institutions of Capitalism*. New York: Free Press.

Chapter **14**

Places and Flows: Situating International Investment

Peter Dicken

Introduction

WITHOUT doubt, one of the most significant economic-geographic developments of the twentieth century was the growth and spread of international direct investment, and of other forms of international economic involvement (such as collaborative ventures between firms), through the medium of the transnational corporation (TNC). Quantitative evidence of this phenomenon is overwhelming and indisputable (see Dicken 1998; Dunning 1993; UNCTAD annual). What is contested, however, is the *interpretation* of such developments. Whilst it can be accepted that, overall, international direct investment may now be a more powerful force than international trade in integrating the component parts of the world economy (though the two are, of course, intimately linked through the mechanism of intra-firm trade), there is deep disagreement over its transformative influence on the *geography* of the world economy and, conversely, on the role of geography itself in that transformative process.

Globalization zealots argue fervently, using such emblematic aphorisms as 'the death of distance' or 'the end of geography', that we are moving inexorably towards a homogenized world in which geographical differentiation is being obliterated. According to this view, technological developments, in particular, have made capital—and the firms controlling it—'hypermobile', freed from the 'tyranny of distance', and no longer tied to 'place'. In other words, it is implied, economic activity is becoming essentially placeless and de-territorialized. In the words of Manuel Castells (1989, 1996), the traditional 'space of places' has been superseded by a new 'space of flows'. In effect, anything can be located anywhere and, if that does not work out, can be moved somewhere else with ease. In effect, according to this view, economic activity has become de-territorialized. Despite being part of a rather different intellectual discourse, such views resonate strongly with those of much of the contemporary management literature of which Ohmae (1990, 1995) is the extreme exemplar.

Contemporary economic geographers emphatically contest this view of the world. However, a distinction needs to be made between two varieties of the so-called 'new' economic geography. In general, economic *geographers* tend to take a less narrowly economistic stance than in the past, with a stronger emphasis on the fundamentally *social, political, cultural, and institutional* bases of the economy while still emphasizing its inherently *spatial* structure; its intrinsic *territoriality*. Such a perspective is well represented in the work of economic geographers like Amin and Thrift (1994, 1995), Barnes (1996), Dicken (1994, 1998), Gertler (1997*a*, 1997*b*), Grabher (1993), McDowell (1997), Massey (1994, 1995), Peck (1996), Schoenberger (1997), Storper (1997), Yeung (1998*a*, 1998*b*), as well as in the chapters in Lee and Wills (1997). In contrast, the recent (re)discovery of economic geography by *economists* remains firmly within the bounds of economics and focuses particularly on reintegrating it into the disciplinary mainstream through modelling techniques (see, in particular, Krugman 1998; Venables 1998).

The aim of this particular chapter, written from an economic-*geographical* perspective, is to engage critically with one aspect of the 'geography no longer matters' argument: the relationship between geography and international investment as reflected in the structure and competitive behaviour of transnational corporations. My focus is not on the simplistic surface expression of the geography of the stocks and flows of international investment (important though that is) but on a deeper exploration of the relationships between TNCs and geography, notably the significance of place and space. In other words, my focus is upon the essentially dialectical relationship between firms and places: the notion that *places produce firms* while *firms produce places* (see also Dicken and Thrift 1992). Implicit throughout the following discussion is the notion that both 'place' and 'space' are scale-specific, highly contingent, relative concepts and that both are socially produced (Swyngedouw 1997). It recognizes, in other words, what Amin (1998: 153) calls a 'relational logics' approach to globalization which 'replaces a territorial sense of the local, national and the global as separate spheres of social organization and action, by a relational understanding of each as a nexus of multiple and asymmetric *interdependencies* among and between local and wider fields of action, organization and influence'. My approach is consistent with that of Sally (1994: 162) who argues that the TNC may be considered 'as the nodal point of and the interface between two realms: that of *internationalization* in global structures, and that of *embeddedness* in the domestic structures of national/regional political economies'.

Two key questions provide the framework for my discussion. The first might be termed the *placing firms* question. In what ways is the nature of TNCs related to the specific places within which they are embedded? That is, do different places 'produce' different types of firms or are we, indeed, witnessing the convergence of organizational forms towards a universal 'global' form? The second question is, in a sense, the obverse of the first. It might be termed the *firming places* question. How are place (and space) 'used' by TNCs as part of their competitive strategies? That is, is 'placeness' more than simply the fundamental need for all economic activities for spatial fixity (see Harvey 1995)? What are the implications for places (at different geographical scales) of such geographically discriminatory behaviour?

'Placing' Firms: Where Firms Come from is Important

> Country of origin does not matter. Location of headquarters does not matter. The products for which you are responsible and the company you serve have become denationalized.
>
> (Ohmae 1990: 94)

Ohmae's exhortation to corporate managers reflects a pervasive view among many writers: that international firms are inexorably and inevitably abandoning their ties to their country of origin and, by implication, converging towards a universal *global* organizational form. It is not a new idea. The US Under-Secretary of State in the 1960s, George Ball, coined the label 'Cosmocorp' to denote what he saw as the then emerging global corporation (Ball 1967). Barnet and Muller's 1974 book *Global Reach: The Power of the Multinational Corporations* was replete with anecdotal examples of the intentions of US corporate executives to transform their firms into 'placeless' global corporations. They quote the musings of a Chairman of the Dow Chemical Company:

> 'I have long dreamed of buying an island owned by no nation and of establishing the World Headquarters of the Dow company on the truly neutral ground of such an island, beholden to no nation or society. If we were located on such truly neutral ground we could then really operate in the United States as US citizens, in Japan as Japanese citizens and in Brazil as Brazilians rather than being governed in prime by the laws of the United States . . . We could even pay any natives handsomely to move elsewhere.' (cited in Barnet and Muller 1974: 16)

In reality, none of this has actually happened. Although, without doubt, the intensity and geographical extent of competition in many economic sectors has increased markedly in the past few decades, facilitated by both technological developments in transportation, communication, and in production itself and by falling national barriers to trade and investment, the truly global corporation remains, essentially, a myth.

Two kinds of empirical evidence may be used to counter the myth. The first is quantitative and uses statistical data on the operations of the world's leading TNCs.[1] An obvious indicator of the 'globalness' of a TNC's activities is the extent to which its assets and employment are geographically dispersed beyond its home country boundaries. On the basis of their analysis of the *Fortune* 100 largest non-financial companies in the world, Ruigrok and van Tulder (1995: 159) conclude that 'of the largest one hundred core firms in the world, not one is truly "global", "footloose" or "borderless"'. Using an 'index of transnationality'[2] based on the UNCTAD list of the world's largest TNCs, I reach broadly similar conclusions (see Dicken 1998: 193–6). There is no clear evidence to support the view that even the 100 largest TNCs are 'global' in terms of these indicators. Only 42 of the 100 companies have an index of transnationality greater than 50; a mere 13 have an index greater than 75. Significantly, the 13 most transnational firms originate from small countries (Switzerland, the UK, the Netherlands, Belgium, Canada). Conversely, the biggest TNCs in terms of total foreign assets all have relatively low transnationality index scores. On this measure, therefore, there is little evidence of TNCs having the share of their activities outside their home countries which might be expected if they are global firms.

A rather broader approach to this question is provided by Hu (1992). He suggests the following criteria for evaluating the extent to which TNCs are 'global':

1. In which nation or nations is the bulk of the corporation's assets and people located?
2. By whom are the local subsidiaries owned and controlled, and in which nation is the parent company owned and controlled?
3. What is the nationality of the senior positions (executive and board posts) at the parent company, and what is the nationality of the most important decision-makers at the subsidiaries in host nations?
4. What is the legal nationality of the parent company? To whom would the group as a whole turn for diplomatic protection and political support in case of need?
5. Which is the nation where the tax authorities can, if they choose to do so, tax the group on its worldwide earnings rather than merely its local earnings?

On the basis of his empirical analysis of a sample of TNCs, Hu concludes that 'these criteria usually produce an unambiguous answer: that it . . . [the TNC] . . . is a national corporation with international operations (i.e. foreign

[1] The most comprehensive statistical data on the operations of TNCs are provided in the annual *World Investment Report* compiled by UNCTAD.

[2] Calculated as a weighted average of three measures: foreign assets to total assets; foreign sales to total sales; foreign employment to total employment.

subsidiaries)' (1992: 121). Thus, despite many decades of international operations, TNCs—at least in quantitative terms—remain distinctively connected with their home base.

However, such quantitative analysis provides only a partial answer to the questions posed in this section. It tells us something about the relative *geographical extent* of TNC activities outside their home country and, to that degree, demonstrates the continuing emphasis on the home base. But it tells us nothing about the *qualitative* nature of TNC activities and their relationship to place. Neither does it help us to establish whether or not TNCs of different national origins are becoming similar in their modes of operation. It is at least possible that TNCs may retain more of their assets and employment in their home country but still be converging organizationally and behaviourally towards a universal, global form. To address this issue we need a different type of empirical evidence from that which merely measures the geographical dispersion of a firm's activities. We need evidence which explicitly compares TNCs from different countries of origin in a systematic manner.

The theoretical basis for hypothesizing that TNCs 'produced' in different places will continue to display a significant degree of organizational differentiation lies in the much used (and sometimes abused) concept of *social embeddedness*. The most widely quoted proximate authority on this topic is undoubtedly the economic sociologist Mark Granovetter (see Granovetter 1985; Granovetter and Swedberg 1992; Smelser and Swedberg 1994), but its intellectual origins lie with Karl Polanyi's (1957) seminal work, *The Great Transformation*. The intricacies of the embeddedness concept lie beyond the bounds of this chapter. Suffice it to argue that all business firms are rooted within specific social, cultural, political, and institutional contexts which help to influence the ways in which they develop.

> At least in origin, TNCs are 'locally grown'; they develop their roots in the soil in which they were planted. The deeper the roots the stronger will be the degree of local embeddedness, such that they should be expected to bear at least some traces of the economic, social and cultural characteristics of their home country. In other words, they continue to contain elements of the local within their modes of operation . . . the local social-cultural milieu is a major influence on how firms evolve and behave even when their operations are geographically very extensive. This is not to argue a case for cultural determinism or even to argue that all firms of a given nationality are identical. Clearly they are not. But they do tend to share some common features. (Dicken *et al.* 1994: 34)

Although such embeddedness may occur at a variety of inter-related geographical scales, the most significant scale would appear to be that of the national state, the major 'container' within which distinctive practices develop (Porter 1990; Whitley 1992*a*, 1992*b*, 1999). Whitley describes these as 'national business systems' which he defines as:

> distinctive configurations of hierarchy-market relations which become institutionalized as relatively successful ways of organizing economic activities in different institutional environments. Certain kinds of activities are coordinated through particular sorts of authority structures and interconnected in different ways through various quasi-contractual arrangements in each business system . . . They develop and change in relation to *dominant social institutions*, especially those important during processes of industrialization. *The coherence and stability of these institutions, together with their dissimilarity between nation-states, determine the extent to which business systems are distinctive, integrated and nationally differentiated* . . .
>
> The distinctiveness of business systems . . . depends on the integrated and separate nature of the contexts in which they developed. The more that major social institutions such as the political and financial systems, the organization of labour markets and educational institutions, form distinctive and cohesive configurations, the more business systems in those societies will be different and separate . . . (Whitley 1992*a*: 13, 14; emphasis added)

Porter (1990), writing from the more instrumentalist viewpoint of the 'competitiveness of nations', expresses a broadly similar view:

> Competitive advantage is created and sustained through a highly localized process. Differences in national economic structures, values, cultures, institutions, and histories contribute profoundly to competitive success. The role of the home nation seems to be as strong as or stronger than ever. While globalization of competition might appear to make the nation less important, instead it seems to make it more so. (Porter 1990: 19)

Such 'national containers' of distinctive assemblages of institutions and practices help to 'produce' particular kinds of firms. In the TNC literature, Dunning (1979) was one of the first to make the explicit connection between what he terms the 'ownership-specific' advantages of firms and the 'location-specific' characteristics of national states. His view, however, was that 'as an enterprise increases its degree of multinationality, the country specific characteristics of the home country become less, and that of other countries more, important in influencing its ownership advantages' (Dunning 1979: 284). I will return to this latter point in a moment.

Despite these general observations on the hypothesized relationships between firms and the national contexts in which they are embedded, however, there have been very few systematic comparative empirical studies. However, Sally (1994) finds significant differences between French and German TNCs. Biggart and Hamilton (1992) and Yeung (1998*c*) critically analyse the differences between Asian and Western businesses. Whitley (1999) explores the 'divergent capitalisms' of East Asian economies. Gerlach and Lincoln (1992) compare Japanese and US business networks. Each of these studies gives substantial support for the idea that firms from different countries differ, at least in part, because of variations in their national institutional structures. However, the most substantial study of relevance is the recent research by Doremus *et al.*

(1998) (see also Pauly and Reich 1997). These writers explicitly confront the 'convergence' thesis through a detailed empirical comparison of US, German, and Japanese TNCs along a series of structural and behavioural dimensions, including their modes of corporate governance, corporate financing systems, and their strategic behaviour (notably in relation to R&D, direct investment, and intra-firm trade). Their conclusions are unequivocal:

> Despite intensifying international competition, MNCs are not promoting the ineluctable convergence and integration of national systems of innovation, trade and investment, nor are they forcing deep convergence in the national economies in which they are embedded.They cannot do so because they themselves are not converging towards global behavioral norms.
>
> Surface similarities in the behavior of MNCs abound . . . At root, however, the most strategically significant operations of MNCs continue to vary systematically along national lines. The global corporation, adrift from its national political moorings and roaming an increasingly borderless world market is a myth . . .
>
> The empirical evidence . . . suggests that distinctive national histories have left legacies that continue to affect the behavior of leading MNCs. The scope for corporate interdependencies across national markets has unquestionably expanded in recent decades. But history and culture continue to shape both the internal structures of MNCs and the core strategies articulated through them. (Doremus *et al.* 1998: 3, 9)

This notion of the continuing influence of place-specific 'history and culture' is clearly evident in East Asia where, despite the populist perception of 'the Asian firm', there are highly significant, nationally based differences (see e.g. Hamilton 1991; Orru *et al.* 1997; Whitley 1999). There is, in addition, the phenomenon of the Overseas Chinese Business networks which are very different from Japanese and Korean business networks in a variety of ways. In particular, they are not bounded by a specific state framework but are, in effect, a diaspora located in a geographical ring around the edges of the South China Sea. These family-based networks derive their cohesion and influence from very different sources from those characteristic of Western TNCs (East Asia Analytical Unit 1995; Hamilton 1991; Orru *et al.* 1997; Redding 1995; Weidenbaum and Hughes 1996).

However, we should not assume that, because the conditions in which firms develop in their home country environments exert an extremely powerful influence on their behaviour, the impact of the host environments in which they operate is no longer important. On the contrary, although the influence of the home base remains highly significant, this does not mean that it is totally deterministic of how firms operate abroad. For a whole variety of reasons—political, cultural, social—non-local firms invariably have to adapt some of their domestic practices to local conditions. It is virtually impossible, for example, to transfer the whole package of firm advantages and practices to a different national environment (see Abo 1994, 1996; Gertler 1997*a*; Hu 1995). Abo (1994, 1996), for example, points to the 'hybrid' nature of Japanese overseas manufacturing plants. The same argument applies to US firms operating abroad. Even in the UK, where the apparent 'cultural distance' between the USA and the UK is less than in many other cases, there is a very long history of American firms having to adapt some of their business practices to local conditions. What results, therefore, is a varying mix of home-country and host-country influences. But although local adaptation almost invariably occurs, Pauly and Reich (1997: 25) are probably correct in observing that, although TNCs originate from different home bases, they 'appear to adapt themselves at the margins but not much at the core'.

The Russian painter Marc Chagall once observed that 'every painter is born somewhere, and even if later he responds to other surroundings, a certain essence, a certain aroma of his native land will always remain in his work'.[3] It seems to me that Chagall's observation is a better metaphor of the relationship between TNCs and place than Ohmae's quotation at the beginning of this section. It more sensitively captures the complexity of the embeddedness process in which both place of origin and the other places in which TNCs operate influence the ways in which such firms behave and how they, in turn, impact upon such places. Within this essentially dialectical relationship, however, the TNC's *place of origin* remains the dominant influence. But at what geographical scale is that influence manifested? The above discussion focuses on the national scale but there is ample reason to believe that it may well operate at the sub-national scales of region and community. Certainly that has been the case historically with distinctive modes of business operation developing in highly specific geographical clusters. Although technological developments in communications technologies may have blurred some of the distinctiveness between different parts of the same national space, it is unlikely that total uniformity has displaced geographical diversity. Recently, for example, some of the problems facing General Motors have been attributed to 'the ingrained Midwestern focus of GM's top executives' (Simonian and Tait 1999). More systematic evidence of place-specific differences in business behaviour is provided in Saxenian's (1994) comparative study of the Silicon Valley, California and the Route 128, Massachusetts electronics clusters.

'Firming Places': How TNCs use Space and Place

One fruitful way of conceptualizing the transnational corporation is as a complex *relational network*, that is, as a network of internalized, intra-firm relationships embedded within networks of externalized, extra-firm relationships.

[3] Notes to an Exhibition at the Royal Academy of Arts, London, on 'Chagall: Love and the Stage', 1998.

These webs of intra- and inter-organizational relationships are woven across geographical space in ways which not only connect organizations, and parts of organizations, together, but which also connect highly dispersed *places* together through the networked flows coordinated by the TNC. In one sense, therefore, the economies of *places* reflect the ways in which they are 'inserted' into the organizational *spaces* of TNCs either directly, as the geographical locus of particular functions, or indirectly through customer–supplier relationships with other (local) firms. Because the TNC, by definition, is a multi-locational firm operating across national boundaries, it has the potential to manipulate geographical space and to use places as an intrinsic part of its competitive strategies. Thus, the ability to 'control' space and the ability to utilize the resources (in the broadest sense) of specific places are diagnostic characteristics of TNCs, although, of course, the nature and effectiveness of such control varies enormously from firm to firm. Although there is a widespread tendency to regard the relationships between firms and places as being 'top-down', in reality such relationships are essentially dialectical.

The ways in which the organizational structures of firms map on to geographical space (and, in so doing, channel flows differentially) are difficult to disentangle. The pioneer in this respect (as in the early development of the theory of international production) was Stephen Hymer. In a classic 1972 paper concerned with uneven development, Hymer posed the question: does the internal division of labour within the TNC correspond to an international division of labour? Drawing upon theories of organizational hierarchy developed by Alfred Chandler and upon Alfred Weber's theory of location, Hymer argued that such an organizational-geographical correspondence did, indeed, exist:

> the [trans]national corporation tends to create a world in its own image by creating a division of labour between countries that corresponds to the division of labour between various levels of the corporate hierarchy. It will tend to centralise high-level decision-making occupations in a few key cities (surrounded by regional sub-capitals) in the advanced countries, thereby confining the rest of the world to lower levels of activity and income. (Hymer 1972: 59)

Hymer's work was exceptionally influential on later researchers interested in the connections between organizational and geographical processes at the subnational (i.e. regional) level, such as Dicken (1976) and Massey (1984), as well as on the global city theorists like Friedmann (1986) and Sassen (1991). Of course, Hymer's conceptualization was extremely broad-brush and it is also true that the world has changed a great deal in the three decades since he made his observations. Yet there was much truth in the general picture he painted. For example, current empirical observation still shows an extremely strong tendency for both the corporate headquarters of TNCs and their high-level R&D operations to remain highly concentrated in their country of origin, as well as strongly clustered within countries (see Dicken 1998; Office of Technology Assessment 1994; Patel 1995; Patel and Pavitt 1991). Nevertheless, the picture is substantially more complex and dynamic than Hymer's conceptualization implies.

In particular, modes of organization are far more varied than Hymer's simplistic organizational hierarchy suggests. Not only are the internal structures of TNCs far more complex, and the boundaries between which functions are internalized and which are externalized more volatile, but also TNCs are embedded in exceptionally elaborate inter-firm networks involving varying degrees of strategic collaboration and equity/non-equity relationships (see e.g. Bartlett and Ghoshal 1998; Dicken 1998; Dicken *et al.* 1998; Dunning 1993; Nohria and Ghoshal 1997). Hence, the ways in which the TNC's production chain/network is configured and re-configured geographically is far more intricate than suggested either in Hymer's model or in the more recent formulation by Michael Porter (1986), although both models are suggestive and valuable. But we need to go beyond them.

Thus, in addressing the relationships between places and flows—in 'situating' international investment—we must recognize that the global economy is made up of a variety of complex overlapping and interlocking *intra- and inter-organizational networks*. Such organizational networks intersect with *geographical networks* structured around linked agglomerations or clusters of activities. These localized clusters of economic activity consist of a differentiated mixture of independent firms of various sizes as well as of the branch plants and affiliates of multiplant firms, many of which are TNCs (whether domestic or foreign). These different kinds of business establishment are connected into much larger organizational and geographical structures (Amin and Thrift 1992; Dicken 1998; Harrison 1997). In the case of the branches and affiliates, they are obviously part of a specific corporate structure and they will, therefore, be constrained in their autonomy by parent company policy. The extent to which they are functionally connected (or embedded) into the local economy will be enormously variable. Further, the 'independent' firms in the local economy may, in fact, be rather less autonomous than they appear at first sight. Some, at least, will be integrated into the customer–supplier networks of larger firms, again including TNCs whose decision-making functions may be very distant geographically. Others may be linked together through strategic alliances or may be part of so-called flexible business networks coordinated by a lead firm or 'broker'.

In other words, it is extraordinarily difficult to generalize across the board about the precise ways in which firms and places are mutually interconnected. What we can say is that the global economy is made up of intricately interconnected localized clusters of economic activity which are embedded in various ways into different forms of corporate network. Such corporate networks vary greatly in their geographical extent and organizational complexity. Some TNCs are globally extensive; most have a more restricted geographical span. Either way, however, firms in specific places—and, therefore, the firms themselves—are increasingly connected into international and even global networks. The precise roles played by firms, and parts of firms, in these networks will inevitably have very significant implications for the communities in which they are based. In that sense, we can think of places as being 'firmed'. At the same time, as we saw in the previous section of this chapter, firms are 'placed'; they, and their component parts, are themselves embedded in places whose attributes actively impinge upon them.

These highly complex connections—between the component parts of firms and between firms and the places in which they operate—are fundamentally embedded within asymmetrical, multi-scalar *power structures*. From the perspective of the present discussion, four highly interconnected sets of relationships are especially relevant:

- *intra-firm relationships*: between different parts of a transnational business network, as each part strives to maintain or to enhance its position *vis-à-vis* other parts of the organization;
- *inter-firm relationships*: between firms belonging to separate, but overlapping, business networks as part of customer–supplier transactions and other inter-firm interactions;
- *firm-place relationships*: as firms attempt to extract the maximum benefits from the communities in which they are embedded and as communities attempt to derive the maximum benefits from the firms' local operations;
- *place–place relationships*: between places, as each community attempts to capture and retain the investments (and especially the jobs) of the component parts of transnational corporations

Each of these sets of relationships is embedded within and across *national/state* political and regulatory systems which help to determine the parameters within which firms and places interact. Notwithstanding changes in the international political economy which are re-configuring the role and functions of nation-states, the state remains fundamentally important as both a regulator of economic transactions and as a container of distinctive institutional practices. In addition, each of the three sets of relationships is closely connected with the others. Let me outline very briefly how these relationships work in general terms.

Even in the archetypal hierarchical business organization, in which decisions are essentially top-down, it is by no means the case that each component part simply operates as a passive recipient of decisions handed down from on high (for an analysis of the differential roles of subsidiaries within TNCs, see Bartlett and Ghoshal 1998; Birkinshaw and Morrison 1995). On the contrary, intra-firm relationships within all firms are highly contested processes—the manifestation of internal power structures and bargaining relationships (see

Schoenberger 1997)—and these have profound implications for national, regional, and local economies. As Cawson and his colleagues observe: 'firms are themselves systems of power with constituent groups (e.g. of engineers, managers, workers, R & D staff) challenging each other's power . . . [and] . . . in which different kinds of interests within the firm try to pursue their own . . . strategies' (Cawson *et al.* 1990: 8, 27). In a similar way, the individual affiliates of a firm (its subsidiaries, branches, and so on) are continuously engaged in competition to improve their relative position within the organization by, for example, winning additional investment or autonomy from the corporate centre. At the same time, the performance of each affiliate is continuously monitored against the relevant others (internal benchmarking) and this is used as an integral part of the internal bargaining processes within the firm. In a transnational firm, operating in a diversity of national/cultural environments, the very nature of these environments—the *places* in which parts of the firm are embedded—will exert an influence on these internal bargaining processes.

Indeed, because each affiliate is itself grounded in a specific geographical community, there is a strong stimulus for that community to try to influence the outcome of these intra-firm bargaining processes by, for example, making concessions or improving local conditions which may enhance the likelihood of the local affiliate winning out in its struggle for additional investment. Such a stimulus is even greater, of course, when a parent company uses threat of closure or downsizing of a specific plant. It is in these circumstances that concessions (usually by the workforce) are most often sought. The dilemma for the local community is that it is often extremely difficult to ascertain whether the threat is real or merely a bargaining ploy. In this respect, the bargaining process between the firm and a local community is highly asymmetrical because multi-locational firms have a substantial degree of potential flexibility to switch and to re-switch their operations between locations, both within and between countries.

Thus, one aspect of the firm–place relationship is that between firms and those places in which they already have operations. The other aspect concerns the search by firms for new investment locations and by communities attempting to attract such investments. It is here, above all, that the firm–place and place–place bargaining processes meet through what are sometimes termed 'investment tournaments'. Indeed, one of the most striking developments of the last two or three decades has been the enormous intensification in *competitive bidding* between states (and between communities within the same state) for the relatively limited amount of internationally mobile investment. Such 'cut-throat' bidding undoubtedly allows TNCs to play off one state against another to gain the highest return for their investment. In fact, much of the actual financial investment may be provided by the host government itself in the form of various kinds of financial and fiscal (tax) deals as well as in the form of physical and social infrastructure. A recent study by UNCTAD (1995) found that only 4 countries out of 103 did not offer some kind of fiscal incentive to inward investors during the early 1990s while financial incentives were offered in 59 out of 83 countries surveyed.

States, like firms, therefore, engage in *price competition* in their attempts to capture a share of the market for mobile investment. Like firms, states also engage in *product differentiation* by creating particular 'images' of themselves such as the strategic nature of their location, the attractiveness of the business environment, the quality of the labour force, and so on. States (and local communities) undoubtedly face a major dilemma. If they do not join the bidding battle, they face the probability of being left out of TNCs' investment plans. On the other hand, UNCTAD's view is that

> incentives are not among the main determinants of FDI locational decisions. Nevertheless, competition among countries to attract and keep investment through incentives is strong and pervasive. This is partly so because, other things being equal, incentives can induce foreign investors towards making a particular locational decision by sweetening the overall package of benefits and hence tilting the balance in investors' locational choices. Incentives can be justified if they are intended to cover the wedge between the social and private rates of return for FDI undertakings that create positive spillovers. However, incentives also have the potential to introduce economic distortions (especially when they are more than marginal) . . . It is not in the public interest that the cost of incentives granted exceeds the value of the benefits to the public. But, as governments compete to attract FDI, they may be tempted to offer more and larger incentives than would be justified, sometimes under pressure from firms that demand incentives to remain in a country. (UNCTAD 1995: 299)

This quotation serves to remind us that, in attempting to unravel the complexities of the economic geography of international investment we have to move way beyond the bounds of the 'economic'. The processes are those of intricate power and bargaining relationships involving both firms and the multiscalar geographical contexts in which they are embedded.

Conclusion

The central argument of this chapter has been that, contrary to much received wisdom, place and geography still matter fundamentally in the ways in which firms are produced and in how they behave. Despite the unquestioned geographical transformations of the world economy, driven at least in part by the expansionary activities of transnational corporations, we are not witnessing the convergence of business-organizational forms towards a single 'placeless' type. Organizational diversity, related at least in part to the place-specific contexts in which firms evolve, continues to be the norm. That, at least, seems to me to be a reasonable interpretation of existing empirical evidence. But that should not be seen as the end of the story. Much of the evidence we have is suggestive rather than conclusive. There is a real need to unravel the complexities of firm–place relationships in a more theoretically sophisticated and empirically rigorous manner. Such a research agenda needs to involve more than an intellectual exercise *per se*. If, as I have argued in this chapter, firms from different geographical contexts are different in significant respects, then this has enormous implications for economic development policy at national, regional, and local levels. To understand these implications requires meticulous comparative international analyses of firm–place relationships. In this regard, such research forms part of the broader intellectual effort devoted to understanding the nature and characteristics of the persistently varied and divergent forms of capitalism (Berger and Dore 1996; Hollingsworth and Boyer 1997; Whitley 1999).

References

Abo, T., ed. 1994. *Hybrid Factory: The Japanese Production System in the United States.* New York: Oxford University Press.

——1996. The Japanese production system: the process of adaptation to national settings. In *States Against Markets: The Limits of Globalization* ed. R. Boyer and D. Drache. London: Routledge.

Amin, A. 1998. Globalization and regional development: a relational perspective. *Competition and Change*, 3: 145–65.

——and Thrift, N. J. 1992. Neo-Marshallian nodes in global networks. *International Journal of Urban and Regional Research*, 16: 571–87.

————eds. 1994. *Globalization, Institutions and Regional Development in Europe.* Oxford: Oxford University Press.

————1995. Institutional issues for the European regions: from markets and plans to socioeconomics and powers of association. *Economy and Society*, 24: 41–66.

Ball, G. 1967. Cosmocorp: the importance of being stateless. *The Columbia Journal of World Business*, 2/6 (Nov.–Dec.): 25–30.

Barnes, T. 1996. *Logics of Dislocation: Models, Metaphors and Meanings of Economic Space.* New York: Guilford.

Barnet, R. J., and Muller, R. E. 1974. *Global Reach: The Power of the Multinational Corporations.* London: Jonathan Cape.

Bartlett, C. A., and Ghoshal, S. 1998. *Managing across Borders: The Transnational Solution.* 2nd edn. New York: Random House.

Berger, S., and Dore, R. 1996. *National Diversity and Global Capitalism.* Ithaca, NY: Cornell University Press.

Biggart, N. W., and Hamilton, G. G. 1992. On the limits of a firm-based theory to explain business networks: the western bias of neoclassical economics. In Nohria and Eccles 1992.

Birkinshaw, J. M., and Morrison, A. J. 1995. Configurations of strategy and structure in subsidiaries of multinational corporations. *Journal of International Business Studies*, 26: 729–55.

Castells, M. 1989. *The Informational City.* Oxford: Blackwell.

—— 1996. *The Rise of the Network Society*. Oxford: Blackwell.

Cawson, A., Morgan, K., Webber, D., Holmes, P., and Stevens, A. 1990. *Hostile Brothers: Competition and Closure in the European Electronics Industry*. Oxford: Clarendon Press.

Cox, K. R., ed. 1997. *Spaces of Globalization: Reasserting the Power of the Local*. New York: Guilford.

Dicken, P. 1976. The multiplant business enterprise and geographical space: some issues in the study of external control and regional development. *Regional Studies*, 10: 401–12.

—— 1994. Global-local tensions: firms and states in the global space-economy. *Economic Geography*, 70: 101–28.

—— 1998. *Global Shift: Transforming the World Economy*. 3rd edn. London: Paul Chapman Publishing; New York: Guilford.

—— Forsgren, M., and Malmberg, A. 1994. The local embeddedness of transnational corporations. In Amin and Thrift 1994.

—— Kelly, P. F., Olds, K., and Yeung, H. W.-C. 1998. Chains and networks, territories and scales: towards a relational framework for analyzing the global economy. Paper presented at the Annual Meeting of the Association of American Geographers, Boston.

—— and Thrift, N. J. 1992. The organization of production and the production of organization: why business enterprises matter in the study of geographical industrialization. *Transactions of the Institute of British Geographers*, 17: 279–91.

Doremus, P. N., Keller, W. W., Pauly, L. W., and Reich, S. 1998. *The Myth of the Global Corporation*. Princeton: Princeton University Press.

Dunning, J. H. 1979. Explaining changing patterns of international production: in defence of the eclectic theory. *Oxford Bulletin of Economics and Statistics*, 41: 269–96.

—— 1993. *Multinational Enterprises and the Global Economy*. Reading, Mass.: Addison-Wesley.

East Asia Analytical Unit 1995. *Overseas Chinese Business Networks in Asia*. Parkes, Australia: Department of Foreign Affairs and Trade.

Friedmann, J. 1986. The world city hypothesis. *Development and Change*, 17: 69–83.

Gerlach, M. L., and Lincoln, J. R. 1992. The organization of business networks in the United States and Japan. In Nohria and Eccles 1992.

Gertler, M. S. 1997*a*. Between the global and the local: the spatial limits to productive capital. In Cox 1997.

—— 1997*b*. Globality and locality: The future of 'geography' and the nation-state. In *Pacific Rim Development: Integration and Globalization in the Asia-Pacific Economy*, ed. P. J. Rimmer. St Leonards, NSW: Allen & Unwin.

Grabher, G. 1993. *The Embedded Firm: On the Socioeconomics of Industrial Networks*. London: Routledge.

Granovetter, M. 1985. Economic action and social structure: the problem of embeddedness. *American Journal of Sociology*, 91: 481–510.

—— and Swedberg, R., eds. 1992. *The Sociology of Economic Life*. Boulder, Colo.: Westview Press.

Hamilton, G. G., ed. 1991. *Business Networks and Economic Development in East and South East Asia*. Hong Kong: University of Hong Kong Centre of Asian Studies.

Harrison, B. 1997. *Lean and Mean: The Changing Landscape of Corporate Power in the Age of Flexibility*. New York: Guilford.

Harvey, D. 1995. Globalization in question. *Rethinking MARXISM*, 8: 1–17.

Hollingsworth, J. R., and Boyer, R., eds. 1997. *Comparing Capitalisms: The Embeddedness of Institutions*. Cambridge: Cambridge University Press.

Hu, Y.-S. 1992. Global firms are national firms with international operations. *California Management Review*, 34: 107–26.

—— 1995. The international transferability of the firm's advantages. *California Management Review*, 37: 73–88.

Hymer, S. H. 1972. The multinational corporation and the law of uneven development. In *Economics and World Order*, ed. J. N. Bhagwati. London: Macmillan.

Krugman, P. 1998. What's new about the new economic geography? *Oxford Review of Economic Policy*, 14/2: 7–17.

Lee, R., and Wills, J., eds. 1997. *Geographies of Economies*. London: Arnold.

McDowell, L. 1997. *Capital Culture: Gender at Work in the City*. Oxford: Blackwell.

Massey, D. 1984. *Spatial Divisions of Labour: Social Structures and the Geography of Production*. London: Macmillan.

—— 1994. *Space, Place and Gender*. Cambridge: Polity Press.

—— 1995. *Spatial Divisions of Labour: Social Structures and the Geography of Production*. 2nd edn. London: Macmillan.

Nohria, N., and Eccles, R. G., eds. 1992. *Networks and Organizations: Structure, Form, and Action*. Boston: Harvard Business School Press.

—— and Ghoshal, S. 1997. *The Differentiated Network: Organizing Multinational Corporations for Value Creation*. San Francisco: Jossey-Bass.

Office of Technology Assessment 1994. *Multinationals and the US Technology Base*. Washington: Office of Technology Assessment.

Ohmae, K. 1990. *The Borderless World: Power and Strategy in the Interlinked Economy*. New York: The Free Press.

—— 1995. *The End of the Nation State: The Rise of Regional Economies*. New York: The Free Press.

Orru, M., Biggart, N. W., and Hamilton, G. G. 1997. *The Economic Organization of East Asian Capitalism*. Thousand Oaks, Calif.: Sage Publications.

Patel, P. 1995. Localized production of technology for global markets. *Cambridge Journal of Economics*, 19: 141–53.

—— and Pavitt, K. 1991. Large firms in the production of the world's technology: an important case of 'non-globalization'. *Journal of International Business Studies*, 22: 1–21.

Pauly, L. W., and Reich, S. 1997. National structures and multinational corporate behaviour: enduring differences in the age of globalization. *International Organization*, 51: 1–30.

Peck, J. A. 1996. *Work-Place: The Social Regulation of Labor Markets*. New York: Guilford.

Polanyi, K. 1957. *The Great Transformation: The Political and Economic Origins of Our Time*. Boston: Beacon Press.

Porter, M. E. 1986. Competition in global industries: a conceptual framework. In *Competition in Global Industries*, ed. M. E. Porter. Boston: Harvard Business School Press.

—— 1990. *The Competitive Advantage of Nations*. London: Macmillan.

Redding, S. G. 1995. Overseas Chinese networks: understanding the enigma. *Long Range Planning*, 28: 61–9.

Ruigrok, W., and van Tulder, R. 1995. *The Logic of International Restructuring*. London: Routledge.

Sally, R. 1994. Multinational enterprises, political economy and institutional theory: domestic embeddedness in the context of internationalization. *Review of International Political Economy*, 1: 161–92.

Sassen, S. 1991. *The Global City: New York, London, Tokyo*. Princeton: Princeton University Press.

Saxenian, A. 1994. *Regional Advantage: Culture and Competition in Silicon Valley and Route 128*. Cambridge, Mass.: Harvard University Press.

Schoenberger, E. 1997. *The Cultural Crisis of the Firm*. Oxford: Blackwell.

Simonian, H., and Tait, N. 1999. Midwest giant struggles to find forward gear. *Financial Times*, 4 Jan.: 24.

Smelser, N., and Swedberg, R., eds. 1994. *The Handbook of Economic Sociology*. Princeton: Princeton University Press.

Storper, M. 1997. *The Regional World: Territorial Development in a Global Economy*. New York: Guilford.

Swyngedouw, E. 1997. Neither global nor local: 'glocalization' and the politics of scale. In Cox 1997.

United Nations Conference on Trade and Development (UNCTAD annual). 1995. *World Investment Report, Annual*. New York: United Nations.

—— *World Investment Report, 1995*. New York: United Nations.

Venables, A. J. 1998. The assessment: trade and location. *Oxford Review of Economic Policy*, 14/2: 1–6.

Weidenbaum, M., and Hughes, S. 1996. *The Bamboo Network: How Expatriate Chinese Entrepreneurs are Creating a New Economic Superpower in Asia*. New York: The Free Press.

Whitley, R. D. 1992*a*. *Business Systems in East Asia: Firms, Markets and Societies*. London: Sage.

—— ed. 1992*b*. *European Business Systems*. London: Sage.

—— 1999. *Divergent Capitalisms: The Social Structuring and Change of Business Systems*. Oxford: Oxford University Press.

Yeung, H. W.-C. 1998*a*. Capital, state and space: contesting the borderless world. *Transactions of the Institute of British Geographers*, 23: 291–309.

—— 1998*b*. The social-spatial constitution of business organizations: a geographical perspective. *Organization*, 5: 101–28.

—— 1998*c*. *Transnational Corporations and Business Networks: Hong Kong Firms in the ASEAN Region*. London: Routledge.

Chapter **15**

The Globalization of Retail Capital: Themes for Economic Geography

Neil Wrigley

Introduction—Whatever Happened to Distribution in the Globalization Debates?

THE many excellent volumes which now exist documenting and debating globalization and the transformation of the world economy typically state an intention to explore the globalization of production *and* distribution networks or, alternatively, the role of multinational/transnational corporations 'in globalizing the production and distribution of goods and services' (Held *et al.* 1999: 237). However, it rapidly becomes clear that *distribution* systems and industries are, at best, a very minor, and more frequently, a totally neglected topic. Almost inevitably, the focus of those volumes locks on to the globalization of production and to the emergence of a 'global manufacturing system in which production capacity is dispersed to an unprecedented number of developing as well as industrialised countries' (Gereffi 1994: 25), although that focus is usually complemented by consideration of the shifting patterns of global finance and the structure of evolving global financial markets (Held *et al.* 1999: 189–235). Whilst the latter usually promotes wider consideration of the growing importance of services, not only financial services, in the global economy (e.g. Dicken 1998: 387–421), distribution is likely to be mentioned only fleetingly, in the context of a post-production service input necessary to final sales.

The choice of case studies of industrial sectors and transnational corporations (TNCs) in these volumes is also instructive. Distribution industries and firms rarely merit consideration and, in particular, studies of retail-industry TNCs, despite providing some of the most potent motifs of global consumption, are notably absent. So, whilst case studies of Toyota, Volkswagen, Hyundai,

Sony, Siemens, and IBM abound in these volumes—supplemented increasingly by studies of the leading commercial and investment banks, and even by the fund management organizations of what Clark (1999) refers to as 'pension fund capitalism'—retail-industry TNCs ranging from Gap Inc. to Royal Ahold or Carrefour are never mentioned, and the world's largest retailer, and rapidly emerging TNC, Wal-Mart, fails to make an appearance. Yet, established retail-industry TNCs such as Royal Ahold and Carrefour (the Dutch and French food retailers) were by the late 1990s very significant global firms—operating in 17 and 21 countries respectively (26 countries with annual sales exceeding $55 billion following the completion of Carrefour's merger with Promodès), and obtaining a large proportion of their sales and profits from their international activities (75% in the case of Ahold and 40% in the case of Carrefour/Promodès). Moreover, many of these established, and also emerging retail-industry TNCs, such as Wal-Mart and Gap Inc., had market capitalizations which dwarfed their manufacturing-TNC rivals—$205 billion and $41 billion respectively for Wal-Mart and Gap Inc. in early 1999. And, of course, beyond such store-based retail-industry TNCs lie the emerging non-store electronic retailers—the Amazon.com's of the world of e-commerce. Not only are such firms proto-twenty-first century versions of the 'virtual firm'/'hollow corporation' TNCs that Donaghu and Barff (1990) and Korzeniewicz (1994) had recognized in the early 1990s in the form of businesses such as Nike, but their emergence also raises fundamental questions about the nature of global commerce if the distribution of goods and services goes 'virtual'. Again, surprisingly, questions which find no place within the standard accounts of global transformation.

Indeed, almost the only occasion that global retail distribution finds any mention in these volumes relates to the rather atypical case of Benetton—incessantly invoked in the globalization literature to illustrate a TNC which employs 'innovative methods to link together its production and distribution networks' (Dicken 1998: 308), which 'utilizes advanced communications systems to monitor its global network' (Castells 1996: 162), and whose devolved systems are claimed to reduce risk and confer a high level of flexibility. However, whilst in some respects a global clothing retailer, Benetton is certainly not a retailer in the true sense. Rather, it is a firm best viewed as an apparel manufacturer and multi-brand owner and manager. Moreover, its 'quasi-franchising' method of operating a global network of retail outlets, whilst reducing significantly the level of fixed asset investment the company has to make, has proved increasingly problematic in a late 1990s environment in which the true clothing retailers such as Gap Inc. have exploited the competitive advantages of tight control over store image and product merchandising during their international expansion. So whilst the intrinsic interest of this highly complex TNC faced with constant pressure to renew itself is undeniable, it is in no sense representative of retail-industry TNCs or, indeed, emblematic of future trends in global distribution.

Not least, its small scale as a global operator with a market capitalization in early 1999 of barely 9 per cent of a clothing-retailer competitor such as Gap Inc. or 2 per cent of that of Wal-Mart, and with annual sales less than 4 per cent of a European food-retail TNC such as Carrefour/Promodès should be borne in mind.

It is the contention of this chapter, therefore, that despite numerous statements to the contrary, the literature which documents and debates globalization and the transformation of the world economy has, in practice, shown a myopic neglect of distribution systems and industries. In particular, the lack of consideration and insight into the increasingly global nature of retail distribution is profound, and even the most respected of the globalization volumes convey little sense of the rapid rise of retail-industry TNCs up the rankings of the world's largest global corporations during the 1990s. Take, for example, Royal Ahold which curiously does not feature in Dicken's (1998: 194) table of the 100 largest TNCs in the world in 1994 in terms of total foreign assets. Based on Dicken's three indicators of 'transnationality'—foreign sales, foreign assets, and foreign employment—just five years later, by 1999, Ahold with over 75 per cent of its sales, employment, and assets focused in its international operations would emerge unambiguously as one of the top fifteen 'global' TNCs.

Within the context of a *Handbook of Economic Geography* the question which must be posed, however, is not simply whether a neglect of the increasingly global nature of retail distribution has occurred and is of importance. Rather, it must be what themes for conceptual debate in economic geography are highlighted by the emergence of large globally operating retailers, and what perspectives does that emergence offer? In this chapter, I identify several important themes, ranging from the cost-of-capital issues and merger and acquisition benefits driving global economic transformation, through the scale of first-mover advantages accruing to initial entrants into emerging markets, and the mechanisms of within-firm 'best practice' knowledge transfer, to the myths and realities of global sourcing and the short-circuiting of existing product and service chains by e-commerce.

Aspects of Global Retailing in the Late 1990s

But first, and briefly, it is necessary to provide some of the essential background on retail-industry TNCs in the late 1990s missing from the globalization volumes. Figure 15.1 begins that task by outlining the world's top 35 retailers in mid-1999 ranked by pro forma annual retail sales—that is to say, taking into account acquisitions and mergers announced but perhaps not formally completed at that point (e.g. Carrefour/Promodès). The figures, relate to 1998 sales, are standardized to a euro billions basis, and have been adjusted to reflect true

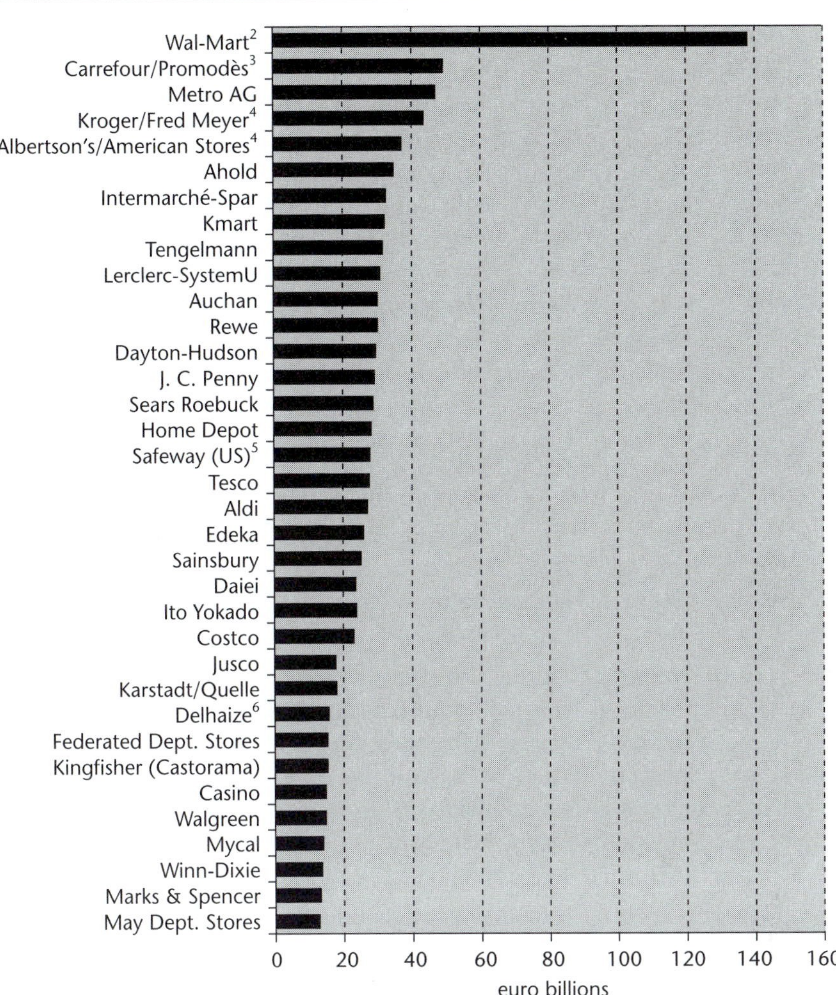

Fig. 15.1. World's top 35 retailers, mid-1999, ranked by pro forma 1998 retail sales[1]

Notes: [1] Any significant non-retailing revenue of firms stripped out of figures to provide true retail turnover.
[2] Includes sales of Asda plc following takeover announcement June 1999.
[3] Following merger announcement Aug. 1999.
[4] Mergers completed May 1999 (Kroger), July (Albertson's).
[5] Includes sales of aquisitions: Dominick's, Carr Gottstein, and Randall's.
[6] Includes sales of Delhaize America companies: Food Lion, Kash n'Karry, and Hannaford (aquisition announced Aug. 1999).

Source: Significantly adapted by author from Merrill Lynch (1999*a*).

retail turnover. That is to say, they strip out the significant non-retailing activity of certain firms—for example, the element within the overall $41 billion turnover reported by Sears Roebuck in 1998 which related to its substantial credit card operations and its appliance servicing business. Sometimes, as in the case of Pinault Printemps-Redoute (the French distribution conglomerate), non-retail sales were a considerable proportion of the whole (48% of a total euro 16.5 billion turnover), serving to remove that firm from the table. A ranking of the world's top retailers in mid-1999 by market capitalization rather than retail sales would include virtually identical firms. However, because of the buoyancy of the US equity market during the late 1990s, several of the major US retailers (e.g. Home Depot, Walgreen) would occupy significantly higher rankings, and other US retailers (e.g. Gap Inc.), on the margins of inclusion in Figure 15.1 on a retail sales basis, would enter the table—indeed, in the case of Gap Inc. with its high equity rating, into a top five position.

Four trends which underlie the information reported in Figure 15.1 are worthy of note:

1. the massive growth in scale of many of these retail firms during the 1990s, particularly since the mid-point of the decade, powered by a wave of acquisition- and merger-driven consolidation of retail markets throughout the world;
2. the increasingly international nature of much of that merger and acquisition activity;
3. the rapid emergence within this listing of the world's largest retailers of an elite group of firms with proven international capability and ambition—Ahold, Carrefour/Promodès, Kingfisher, Casino, Delhaize, Metro, Auchan, and so on—with international sales in the 25 to 75 per cent range, active across a range of developed (mature) and emerging (growth) markets, and potentially including within their number firms such as Wal-Mart and Tesco who prior to the mid-1990s had very little international exposure;
4. the importance of food retailing, both within the real-terms growth in scale of the world's largest retailers during the 1990s, and as a core component of the activities of that elite group of retail-industry TNCs.

Illustrative of the rapid conversion to global expansion of many of the leading retailers during the period since the mid-1990s are Wal-Mart and Tesco. Following the announcement of Wal-Mart's acquisition of the UK food retailer Asda, and taking into account Asda's £7.9 billion turnover in 1998, Wal-Mart's total sales had increased by over 60 per cent in just three years. However, during that period its international sales (on a pro forma basis) had increased no less than sixfold, taking Wal-Mart from a firm which in 1995 drew less than 4 per cent of its sales from outside its domestic market to one with almost 17 per cent of sales from its international operations. By 1999, Wal-Mart had entered Mexico, Canada, Argentina, Brazil, Puerto Rico, China, Indonesia, South Korea, Germany, and the UK and, although still dwarfed by its domestic sales, Wal-Mart's international operations (with pro forma 1998 sales of almost $25 billion) would, if considered as a stand-alone company, have been large enough to have placed it within the world's top 25 retailers. Critical to that expansion, both domestically and internationally, was Wal-Mart's emergence, via the growth of its supercenter format, as a major food retailer. Similarly, Tesco, the leading UK food retailer, which in 1994–5 had only 2 per cent foreign assets and was in the early stages of entering merely its second international market (Hungary) had, by 1999, developed important international operations in Poland, the Czech Republic, Slovakia, the Republic of Ireland, Thailand, and South Korea and was considering further diversification into Malaysia and Taiwan. In the process its international sales had increased to more than 10 per cent. But more significantly, over 25 per cent of Tesco's trading space was by that point outside the UK and the firm was positioned to see that reflected in a differentially rapid rate of expansion of its international sales and profits. The level of its foreign investment was continuing to rise and, for the first time, the company was growing its international space organically (via new store development/store expansion) at a faster rate than that of its UK core holdings.

A second way to provide insight into the characteristics of global retailing in the late 1990s is to consider the emerging markets of regions such as South East Asia, Central Europe, and Latin America which in the early 1990s were relatively untouched by transnational retail activity. Figure 15.2, for example, shows the penetration of international retailers into Central Europe by 1998–9 and highlights Tesco's presence in the region via a network of 97 stores. In a remarkably short period during the mid to late 1990s almost 80 per cent of the turnover of major retailers in Poland and 60 per cent in the Czech Republic had become dominated by foreign market entrants, many of which feature in the listing of the world's top retailers in Figure 15.1. In a similar fashion, Table 15.1 outlines the extent of the expansion of the larger Western retail TNCs into South East Asia and China by 1998–9. Despite the economic difficulties of that region during the late 1990s, these companies continued to invest heavily in what they perceived to be an important growth market within their overall global strategies.

Finally, a third perspective on the scale and characteristics of global retailing in the late 1990s can be obtained from a consideration of the activities of an established retail TNC such as Royal Ahold. Ahold's frequently quoted view during the late 1990s was that the global food retail industry would become dominated during the early part of the twenty-first century by just four to six major groups, and its stated ambition was to position itself as the corporate parent of such a group (ABN-AMRO 1999*a*). To that end, as the US food retail industry consolidated in a dramatic fashion which will be considered below, Ahold actively participated in the process whilst, at the same time, maintaining a rapid pace of expansion in emerging markets. By the end of the 1990s with sales in the USA of $20 billion, Ahold had firmly established itself as part of the elite group of US food retailers. Between 1996 and 1999 as Figure 15.3 illustrates, it had added, or attempted to add, to its operations three major chains

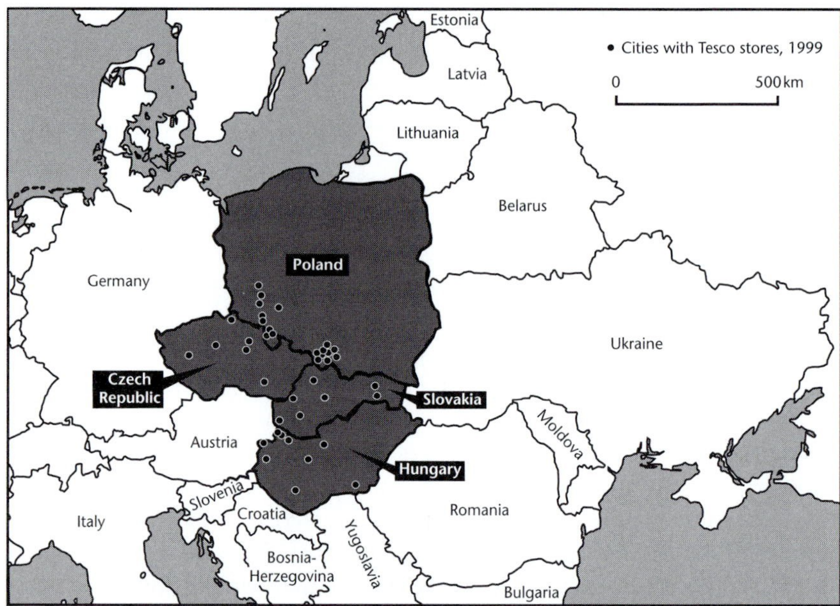

	Poland	Czech Republic	Hungary	Slovakia
Number of foreign entrants among top 10 retailers	8	7	6	2
% of turnover of major retailers controlled by foreign firms	80	61	49	19
Total large international retail entrants	16	13	8	2
Top 35 world retailers in country	Metro, Ahold, Carrefour, Intermarché, Tengelmann, Lerclerc, Auchan, Rewe, Tesco, Kingfisher, Casino	Metro, Ahold, Carrefour, Intermarché, Tengelmann, Rewe, Tesco, Marks & Spencer	Metro, Intermarché, Tengelmann, Rewe, Auchan, Tesco, Marks & Spencer	Rewe, Tesco

Fig. 15.2. Penetration of retail TNCs into Central Europe by 1998–99, highlighting Tesco operations (97 stores) in region[1]

Notes: [1] Stores: Hungary (47), Poland (33), Czech Republic (10), Slovakia (7).

Sources: Author, from information in Tesco plc Annual Report (1999) and Merrill Lynch (1998).

in the densely populated Boston–Washington DC corridor—Stop & Shop (the market leader in southern New England), Giant Food (the leader in Washington DC/Baltimore), and Pathmark (the leader in the metro markets of New York/New Jersey). Although the final acquisition (Pathmark) was blocked by opposition from the Federal Trade Commission (Cotterill 1999), the acquisition of Stop & Shop and Giant Food increased Ahold's existing presence in the

Table 15.1. Large Western retail transnational corporations in South East Asia and China 1999

	China	Hong Kong	Indonesia	Malaysia	Philippines	Singapore	South Korea	Taiwan	Thailand	Total
Ahold	40	—	70[3]	45	—	14	—	—	39	208
Carrefour	14	4	1	5	—	1	8	22	8	63
Makro[1]	4	—	8	7	3	—	—	7	16	45
Delhaize	—	—	12	—	—	22	—	—	5	39
Casino	—	—	—	—	—	—	—	1	20	21
Tesco	—	—	—	—	—	—	2	—	13	15
Kingfisher[2]	1	—	—	—	—	7	—	4	—	12
Marks & Spencer	—	10	—	—	—	—	—	—	—	10
Wal-Mart	5	—	—	—	—	—	4	—	—	9
Costco	—	—	—	—	—	—	3	1	—	4
Promodès	1	—	3	—	—	—	opening 1999	—	—	4
Metro AG	2	—	—	—	—	—	—	—	—	2
Store Totals	67	14	94	57	3	44	17	35	101	432

Notes: 1. These stores remained owned and operated by SHV-Makro and *not*, as was the case with the Makro stores in Europe, by Metro AG.
2. Kingfisher figures relate to mid-1999, others to early 1999.
3. Indonesian stores franchised owing to foreign ownership restrictions.

Sources: Author, adapted from Merrill Lynch (1999*b*, 1999*c*), JP Morgan (1998, 1999*a*).

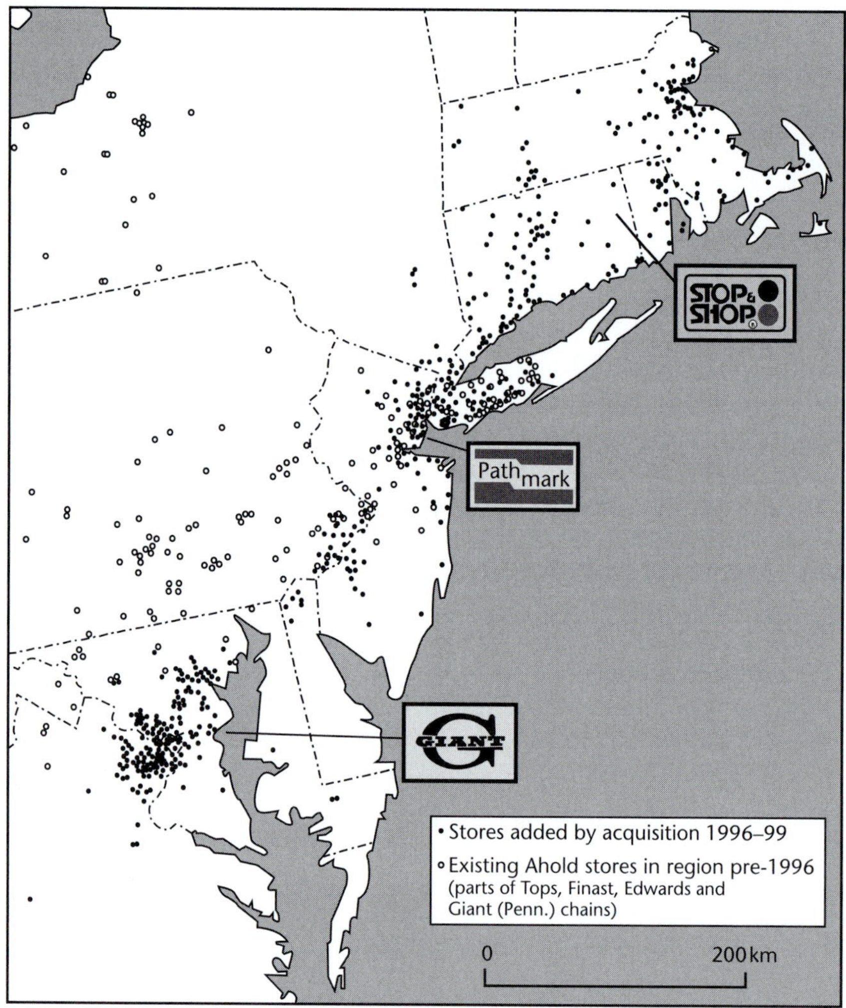

Fig. 15.3. Royal Ahold operations in North East USA 1999 showing chains acquired (and proposed for acquisition) 1996–99[1]

Note: [1] Ahold withdrew from acquisition of Pathmark, Dec. 1999, following opposition to acquisition from Federal Trade Commission.

Source: Author, from data supplied by Royal Ahold, Giant Food, and Pathmark.

US market by $10 billion of annual sales and gave it the opportunity and critical scale to extract considerable operating synergies from its previously somewhat dispersed US activities. In the process, as the proportion of Ahold's global sales and profits derived from the USA increased to almost 60 per cent, its credibility as the potential corporate parent of a global retail mega-group was significantly enhanced.

Securing Global Scale by Merger and Acquisition

The wave of acquisition- and merger-driven consolidation of retail markets throughout the world which has characterized the period since the mid-1990s and provided the path to global scale for many of the leading retailers in Figure 15.1, has occurred during a period of low and declining inflation in which leading retailers have faced significant pressures on traditional components of their growth. But why, and what perspectives does this offer for areas of conceptual debate in economic geography?

In simple terms, the overall sales growth recorded by retailers can be divided into three components—that due to price inflation, that deriving from newly opened additional retail space, and that deriving from 'volume' (identical-store or 'like-for-like') growth within the retailer's pre-existing store portfolio. Since the mid-1990s, leading retailers have been faced in their core markets with a rapidly declining inflationary component—potentially an increasing problem because of the differential cost inflation which the retail industry suffers as a result of its high gearing in relation to labour costs. In addition, in many markets—particularly those in Western Europe—the contribution to growth which the leading retailers have been able to obtain from newly opened retail space has become increasingly problematic due to a significant tightening of the regulatory environment—for example, the *Loi Rafferin* in France, revised *Planning Policy Guidance (PPG) Note 6* in the UK, and the *Ley de Ordenancio del Commercio* in Spain (see Wrigley and Lowe (2000, ch. 4) for details)—which has made the opening of new retail space increasingly difficult. Finally, the volume growth experienced by these retailers in their core markets, albeit increasing in relative importance as a component of recorded overall sales growth, has—particularly in sectors such as food and clothing—been low, frequently minimal.

Although there are clearly exceptions—for example, certain firms such as Gap Inc. achieved robust volume growth in their core markets during the late 1990s—many of the leading retailers in Figure 15.1 have, since the mid-1990s, faced a world of low inflation in which each of the traditional constituents of their sales growth—inflation, new retail space, and 'like-for-like' volume—has been under pressure. In response, those firms have sought new avenues of growth. Three of these stand out:

1. innovations in retail format—Wal-Mart's move into the combination food and general merchandise 'supercenter' format during the 1990s, and the conversion of over 500 of its existing US discount stores to the format by 1999, provides a classic example;
2. international diversification into less mature markets;

3. attempts to extract synergistic cost savings and scale benefits from mergers and acquisitions.

The latter, in particular, has significance for conceptual debate in economic geography as it provides some particularly useful insights into the cost reductions and buying power benefits which can be extracted in attempts to acquire global scale by merger and acquisition.

Table 15.2 which outlines some of the major mergers and acquisitions (M&A) in the food retail sector during 1998–9 suggests the scale of retail M&A activity taking place in the late 1990s. One of the most dramatic examples of market consolidation produced by such activity was provided by US food retailing—a huge industry with annual sales of $432 billion in 1997 in which consolidation had been held back for several decades, first as a result of regulation (Mueller and Paterson 1986; Wrigley 1992) and then as a result of the intense period of financial re-engineering during the LBO wave of the late 1980s (Cotterill 1993; Denis 1994; Wrigley 1999*a*, 1999*b*). In just three years, 1996–9, powered by mergers such as those of Kroger/Fred Meyer and Albertson's/American Stores and the multiple acquisitions of Safeway and Ahold, the market share of the top four firms increased by 80 per cent. In the process, embryonic national US food chains emerged, and the annual turnovers of the top four firms shifted significantly from the $12–20 billion to the $20–50 billion range (Wrigley 1999*b*). However, even in markets which had traditionally been much more highly concentrated, for example, those of Scandinavia and Canada, consolidation and the drive for significantly increased scale by the major firms characterized the late 1990s—as illustrated by the mergers and acquisitions involving Dagab/D-Gruppen, ICA/Hakon, Sobeys/Oshawa, and Loblaw/Provigo.

A consideration of the economics of the major US food retail mergers and acquisitions in this period helps to suggest why. The merger of Kroger and Fred Meyer, for example, produced a firm with combined 1998 sales of $43 billion from over 2,200 supermarkets in 31 US states. By year three of the merger (i.e. in 2002) Kroger suggests that the synergistic cost savings it will achieve in areas such as distribution/logistics, administration, systems and advertising, plus the extraction of scale benefits from coordinated purchasing and the sharing of best practices between the two companies, will produce fiscal year savings of $225 million, that is, cost reductions of around 1.4 per cent of the added firm's (Fred Meyer's) historic sales. Similar figures, ranging to around 3 per cent, were also identified in most of the other US food mergers and acquisitions of the late 1990s. Not surprisingly, with each of the traditional constituents of their sales growth under pressure, the extraction of scale benefits from merger and acquisition offered the leading firms a more secure route to value-creating earnings growth. In seizing this opportunity, the valuations placed on acquisition targets—the so-called 'acquisition multiples' rose significantly (from a 5.5–6.5

Table 15.2. Food retail sector: merger and acquisition activity, Europe and North/South America: December 1997 to December 1999

Country	Deal	Country	Deal
USA	Fred Meyer/Ralphs merger	**Germany**	Wal-Mart (US) acquires Wertkauf
	Fred Meyer/Quality Food Centers merger		Wal-Mart (US) acquires Interspar
	Albertson's acquires Buttrey, Seessel's		Metro acquires Allkauf
	Albertson's/American Stores merger		Metro acquires Kriegbaum
	Kroger/Fred Meyer merger		Tengelmann acquires Tip
	Safeway acquires Carr Gottstein	**Argentina**	Ahold (Neth) acquires stake in Disco
	Safeway acquires Dominick's		Casino (Fr) acquires stake in Libertad
	Ahold (Neth) acquires Giant Food		Promodès (Fr) acquires stake in Norte
	Ahold (Neth) acquires Pathmark[1]		Promodès (Fr) acquires Tia
	Sainsbury (UK) acquires Star Markets		Casino (Fr) acquires San Cayetano
	Safeway acquires Randall's		Ahold (Neth)/Disco acquires Gonzalez, Supamer
	Delhaize (Bel) acquires Hannaford	**Brazil**	Ahold (Neth) acquires stake in Bompreço
Canada	Loblaw acquires Provigo		Carrefour (Fr) acquires Planaltão, Mineirão, Roncetti, Raihna
	Sobeys (Empire) acquires Oshawa		Sonae (Port) acquires Real, Candia, Big, Mercadorama, Nacional, Coletão, Marmungar
France	Carrefour acquires Comptoirs Modernes		Ahold (Neth)/Brompreço acquires PetiPreço
	Casino and Cora create buying group		Casino (Fr) acquires stake in Pão de Açucar (CBD)
	Carrefour/Promodès merger	**Colombia**	Casino (Fr) acquires stake in Exito
Netherlands	De Boer Unigro/Vendex Food merger (renamed Laurus)	**Chile**	Ahold (Neth) acquires stake in Santa Isabel
UK	Somerfield/Kwik Save merger		Ahold (Neth)/Santa Isabel acquires Tops
	Wal-Mart (US) acquires Asda		
Sweden/Norway	Dagab/D-Gruppen merger		
	ICA/Hakon merger		
	Ahold (Neth) acquires stake in ICA		

Note: 1. Ahold withdrew from acquisition of Pathmark, December 1999, following opposition to acquisition from Federal Trade Commission.

times range in the early 1990s to a typical 8–12 times range by the end of the decade—see Wrigley 1999*b*).

Outside the USA, similar synergistic cost reductions and scale benefits from consolidated purchasing and the sharing of best practices in areas such as logistics, marketing, working capital management, store construction, and IT systems operation were also identified. For example, in the European mergers and acquisitions outlined in Table 15.2, Carrefour's transactions involving Comptoir Modernes in 1998 and Promodès in 1999 were both expected to yield cost reductions of around 3 per cent of the smaller company's sales after three years. Although it has been argued (ABN-AMRO 1999*a*) that cross-border mergers and acquisitions are likely to offer retailers lower synergistic cost savings—largely as a result of the limited range of products which are likely to overlap between countries and which can benefit from the retailer's increased purchasing scale—those savings have nevertheless been estimated to lie in the order of 1 per cent of the acquired sales. Moreover, having once established a presence in another market via M&A activity, the acquisition of additional sales in that market (e.g. Ahold's successive purchases in the USA) produce synergy benefits at the within-market level.

The rapid growth in scale of the major retail firms which has characterized the global economy since the mid-1990s is of importance to conceptual debate in economic geography not least, therefore, for the insight which it offers into the nature of contemporary M&A activity in the global economy. Frequently, the financial logic of that activity is left undiscussed, and certainly unquantified, in the literature.

Leveraging Scale, Know-How, and the Cost of Capital in Emerging Markets

Consolidation of retail markets and the significant growth in scale of many of the leading firms during the 1990s was driven to a major extent by the relatively secure earnings growth which those retailers were able to derive from the synergistic cost savings associated with mergers and acquisitions. However, those firms also realized that in order to sustain their earnings growth in the longer term, together with their advantageous growth-company equity valuations, they must use free cash flow (Jensen 1986) generated in their core markets to seek expansion in emerging markets offering the prospects of much faster sales/revenue growth. It is for this reason, rather than simply a defensive objective of reducing dependence on a domestic market, that the mid to late 1990s were characterized by the rapid market entry and expansion in Latin America, South East Asia, Central/Eastern Europe, and Southern Europe of an elite group of international retailers—perhaps 15 to 20 in total with Carrefour/Promodès, Ahold, Casino, Delhaize, Wal-Mart, and Tesco increasingly at its core.

Emerging markets offered the attractions of potentially rapid economic development and rising levels of affluence, consumer spending, and retail sales, combined with extremely low levels of penetration of Western forms of large-store corporate retailing and associated distribution systems. Indeed, up to 90 per cent of retail sales in such markets were often in the hands of very small independent retailers or informal retail channels. The opportunity existed for the leading retailers to enter these markets, leveraging their scale, their lower costs of capital, and their superior distribution/logistics and IT systems operation know-how to obtain rapid revenue growth and high returns on investment.

Those firms (particularly Carrefour) which led the push into the emerging markets by the elite group of retail TNCs were initially able to achieve super-normal returns on their investment. Rapid organic growth was possible in markets in which competition to Western-style large-store corporate retailing was minimal. Licences to open new stores were easy to obtain (in marked contrast to the position in Western Europe), capital requirements for site acquisition and store construction were low, and the existing retailers in those markets typically had little purchasing scale and operated in an inefficient manner. Very rapid rates of revenue growth and market share gains were achieved (Carrefour, for example, had captured 19% of the Brazilian food market by 1998) and exceptionally high returns on invested capital, in the 25 to 30 per cent range, were often recorded from operations which had very low levels of capital intensity. Indeed, Carrefour was required to make minimal recourse to shareholders' equity or debt financing to expand in emerging markets in the 1980s and early 1990s. Not only was this the result of the intrinsically low capital requirements but because, in practice, much of the funding required was provided by *negative working capital* on the back of supplier's credit—that is, when a retailer is able to turn over its stock faster than the supplier's credit period working capital becomes a source of cash flow.

The super-normal returns which firms like Carrefour were able to achieve in emerging markets in the early 1990s attracted, in turn, an influx of capital from other members of the elite group of international retailers—the case of Poland (see Fig. 15.2) provides a classic example of the scale and rapidity of that influx. By the late 1990s, therefore, retail industries in the emerging markets had become far more capital intensive. In essence this was because of rising land costs and real estate asset prices in those countries, and increasing competition from other well-capitalized retail TNC market entrants, which required matching investment from the initial entrants in terms of store renewal and more sophisticated logistics and IT systems operations. As a result, the asset turnover levels (a measure of how many dollars of annual sales are generated by a dollar of total assets—see Wrigley 1998: 21) of those initial entrants fell steadily during the mid to late 1990s. For example, Carrefour's asset turnover which had been 13× in 1994 at a time when Wal-Mart in its pre-internationalization period was achieving merely 3.8×, had halved to just 6× by 1999 with Wal-Mart achieving a very similar level (JP Morgan 1999*c*: 23).

Nevertheless, in comparison to the position which the elite group of retail TNCs often faced in their core/mature markets during the late 1990s, the attractions of the emerging markets remained essentially unchanged. Although more capital intensive than in the early 1990s, those markets continued to offer lower labour costs and lower capital investment per store requirements, whilst offering the potential of the rapid revenue/earnings growth and return on capital (when discounted for currency and political risk) increasingly difficult to achieve in the retailers' core markets. The Asian and Latin American economic crises of the late 1990s had relatively limited impact on the perception of those advantages by the retail TNCs. Indeed they were as likely to be viewed, particularly in the context of South East Asia, as an opportunity to acquire retail and real-estate assets at discounted prices. However, partnerships and joint ventures with local operators were often used by the retail TNCs in both South East Asia and Latin America during the late 1990s to attenuate some of the risks of market entry. (Ahold, for example, entered Latin America by acquiring 50% of the voting shares of Brazilian retailer Bompreço and forming a 50/50 joint venture with Velox Holdings to acquire stakes in (subsequently full control of) Disco the leading Argentinian food retailer, and Santa Isabel a retailer operating in Chile, Peru, Paraguay, and Ecuador.) In many cases, the retail TNCs subsequently increased their stakes in such partnerships—Promodès, for example, after taking an initial 49 per cent stake in the leading Argentinian retailer Norte in 1998, subsequently raised that stake to 67 per cent after the acquisition and integration of a second Argentinian chain, Tia, in 1999.

Global retailing was characterized during the mid to late 1990s then by the efforts of an elite group of firms to leverage their increasing core-market scale and the free cash flow for expansionary investment which those markets provided, in order to secure the longer-term higher growth opportunities offered by the emerging markets. Ahold's operations in Latin America with 292 stores in six countries and 11.5 per cent of its global selling space in the region by the end of 1998 is representative. In summary, those firms both perceived their competitive advantages to lie, and exploited those advantages, in five main areas:

1. In the area of logistics and distribution systems where, during the 1980s and early 1990s in their core markets, those firms had learned how to restructure their operations and increase their return on capital by adopting a range of innovations in logistics to reduce inventory levels (Fernie 1992, 1995; Smith and Sparks 1993; Sparks 1994; Walker 1994). In this way, they had been able to raise the yield on inventory—one of the largest pieces of capital that a retailer deploys. By transferring their distribution-system know-how to their emerging market acquisitions or joint-ventures, the retail TNCs were,

as a result, able to reduce their distribution costs as a percentage of sales, to decrease shrinkage levels, and to cut the working capital tied up in inventory.

2. In the area of IT systems operation and supply-chain management, where aspects of the sophisticated 'demand-pull' electronic data interchange (EDI)-based systems of Western Europe and North America could be used to marked effect.
3. In relation to their access to low-cost capital. Debt financing for expansionary growth could be raised very cheaply in Europe and the USA in the low-inflation environment of the late 1990s and some of the European TNCs could also exploit favourable taxation arrangements.
4. In relation to the transfer of 'best practice' knowledge. Ahold, for example, employs an international 'mentor' system to formalize this process in which its emerging market subsidiaries are paired with its mature market chains—for example, the management of Bompreço from Brazil meets regularly with that of Stop & Shop from the USA. That system is then supplemented by four international support centres—one in the Netherlands, the others in Atlanta, Buenos Aires, and Singapore.
5. In relation to the depth of their human/management capital resources—with senior management in firms such as Carrefour and Ahold providing and being offered a wide range of international management experience.

But what of global sourcing competitive advantages in this list? In practice, these seem to have been less important in the movement of the retail TNCs into emerging markets in the mid to late 1990s than has often been suggested. Although some of the major manufacturers supplying the food and general merchandise retailers (Procter & Gamble, Unilever, and so on) did begin to change their organizational structures from a geographical region to global product group basis, most analysts of these industries do not believe that the huge wave of retail M&A activity in both mature and emerging markets came *in response* to a globally reorganizing supply base—'we certainly do *not* believe food retail consolidation is a reaction to a consolidating supply base' (ABN-AMRO 1999*a*: 16).

Yet global sourcing by retailers clearly increased significantly during the 1990s, with most retailers sourcing clothing and electronic products on a global scale by the late 1990s and with the retail TNCs increasingly attempting to capture the important synergies to be derived from coordinated international purchasing. The fact remains, however, that most of the elite group of retail TNCs active in the emerging markets in the late 1990s were food and general merchandise retailers, with combination food/non-food hypermarkets being the primary vehicle for the entry of 'modern' Western-style corporate retailing into these markets. It was the non-food consumer product categories in those hypermarkets which offered retail TNCs the greatest scope to leverage global purchasing scale—the potential in food products was more limited due to differences in national tastes and preferences, perishability issues, and the more restricted overlap between countries in the food products stocked by retailers than might first appear. Nevertheless, buying centres serving the major global markets of the retail TNCs did begin to emerge—Ahold's Latin America purchasing centre, for example, located in Argentina, helped the firm to lower the procurement costs of key products for all its chains in the region relative to their competitors. And, even in the perishable fresh produce area, there were increasing examples of combined purchasing and international sourcing across several chains within a TNC.

As in the case of retail M&A activity and consolidation of mature markets during the late 1990s, the rapid push into emerging markets by an elite group of retail TNCs during that period serves, therefore, to highlight a number of themes of considerable importance for conceptual debate in economic geography. Of these five stand out—costs-of-capital issues driving global economic transformation in the late 1990s; the scale and nature of first-mover advantages accruing to initial entrants into emerging markets; the potential for corporate restructuring via inventory yield management; the mechanisms of within-firm 'best practice' knowledge transfer and between-firm differences in the culture of that 'best practice' transfer (see Gertler 1995); and the myths and realities of global sourcing.

Global Retailing in a World of E-Commerce

Finally, to what extent are the economic geographies of globalizing retail capital which developed in the late 1990s likely to be destabilized by the emergence of 'virtual' global commerce and the rapid rise of the non-store electronic retailers of the world of e-commerce? Here, as in the case of global sourcing by the retail TNCs, myth and reality are often widely separated. However, the conceptual issues raised are of fundamental importance—'the wider implications of e-commerce stem from its ability to lower barriers to entry and to short-circuit existing product and service chains (disintermediation)' (ABN-AMRO 1999*b*: 3).

The potential of e-commerce to reshape the global retail landscape is a well-rehearsed topic. E-commerce, particularly via the internet, offers a market place in which barriers to entry are very low—firms can sell products without the need to establish a significant 'physical' presence and with a substantially lower element of fixed and sunk costs. In particular, the internet is borderless, offering the opportunity to sell globally without many of the traditional costs associated with entering foreign markets. In the view of many, the internet provides 'the ultimate technology for shortening channels of distribution between the supplier and the consumer' and will create new lead firms 'committed to the new technology in a way that firms pre-dating the technology can never be' (Jones and Biasiotto 1999: 77–8). However, in the context of this chapter, there are four interrelated questions which must be posed about the potential of e-commerce. First, what is the total size of the market likely to be in the early twenty-first century? Secondly, to what extent, in practice, is the world of e-commerce significantly less bound by geography? Thirdly, what sectors of retailing are likely to see the greatest impact from the opening up of e-commerce as an alternative distribution channel? Fourthly, to what extent are the store-based ('bricks and mortar') retail TNCs potentially threatened by the emergence of non-store electronic retailers?

Estimates of the total volume of e-commerce place it at between $7 and $8 billion in 1998, that is to say, an insignificant share of total retail sales, which in the USA alone were $2.7 trillion in 1998, and dwarfed even by the retail sales of single sectors—for example, US foodstore sales approaching $450 billion per annum in the late 1990s. Projections suggest internet retail sales of anywhere between $35 and $75 billion in 2002, with the consensus placing the figure in the $40–50 billion range (Merrill Lynch 1999*d*)—a sixfold increase in just four years. The bulk of those sales are likely to be generated in the US market where household personal computer ownership levels in the late 1990s were substantially higher than in other countries (40% of households compared to 22% in the UK and 12% in France) and where the number of internet users is predicted to grow from 29 to 50 million between 1998 and 2002. Indeed, best estimates (Forester Research in Merrill Lynch 1999*d*) suggest that US internet retail sales accounted for a 79 per cent market share of the world's e-commerce in 1998, followed by Western Europe with 9 per cent, and Japan and Canada at 4 per cent each.

Why then, given the potential competitive advantages of e-commerce, is its projected growth not more explosive? After all, a single retail TNC such as Ahold, with estimated global retail sales of more than $50 billion in 2002, may be of equivalent size to the entire e-commerce market. And that market is certain to be dwarfed by the retail sales of Wal-Mart which are likely to exceed $240 billion in 2002. The answer relates to the fact that e-commerce remains bound by geography to a far greater extent than is often suggested. At the heart of e-commerce is the logistical problem of what is termed *fulfilment*. An infrastructure to distribute products ordered via the internet is essential—one which is of necessity place-bound and expensive to operate, involving specialized logistics, and the creation of a network of fulfilment centres, the numbers and locations of which depend on the size and density of the market and the nature/perishability of the products being distributed. As analysts at Merrill Lynch (1999*d*: 125) have noted:

> Fulfillment is very expensive. So expensive in fact that it is one of the major reasons why the catalogue industry, whose genesis goes back to the late 1800s . . . only generates

about $55 billion today or 9% of total US general merchandise retail sales. Fulfillment costs keep catalogue prices from being significantly different than prices at bricks and mortar retailers. Catalogue companies also do not give you instant gratification of being able to take the item home when you purchase it. Nor do they enable you to touch, feel or wear the item before you buy it. These limitations of the catalogue industry also seem to apply to most e-commerce operations.

Extensive store networks offer major advantages in terms of the fulfilment problems of e-commerce, with the capacity to be used in a distribution role and, more importantly, being available to consumers as sites for 'pick up' and/or return and exchange of products.

The Merrill Lynch observations also provide insight into the sectors of the retail industry likely to see the greatest impact from e-commerce. These are likely to be those handling commodity products, particularly where distribution costs are low as a percentage of total costs, which are of standard specification and possibly also branded (i.e. where potential quality variation does not have to be assessed by the consumer by inspection and touch), where price comparisons are relatively easy, and where the 'sociality' of the purchasing process is unimportant. Early evidence from the UK market (Verdict Research in ABN-AMRO 1999*b*) confirms this view, with internet retail sales estimated to have captured between 3 and 10 per cent of the music/video, book, and computer-software/game markets in 1998 but only a tiny 0.01 per cent of the food and clothing markets. It is a view supported by detailed studies of relative cost structures in food retailing in the late 1990s by accountants Coopers & Lybrand—studies which demonstrate the unambiguous operating cost, profit margin, and 'total economic margin' competitive advantages retained by store-based retailing relative to various configurations of e-commerce.

The elite group of retail TNCs which emerged in the late 1990s was, as we have seen, primarily composed of food and general merchandise retailers. Not only were these retail TNCs largely in sectors where the competitive advantages of e-commerce were potentially at their lowest, but they were also firms which during the 1980s and 1990s had increasingly focused on distribution and inventory management issues. Relative to the purely non-store electronic retailers who, during their rapid emergence in the late 1990s, had struggled to achieve profitability because of the costs of fulfilment and the challenges and scale-requirements of the buying process and inventory control, the store-based TNCs retained considerable competitive advantages. They had the warehouse infrastructures, supply-chain and inventory systems, distribution systems, customer-support centres, and product-return networks already in place, and could seek to leverage those strengths by adding e-commerce operations to their existing businesses. In many cases, that process was confined within the firm, with the retail TNC seeking to learn from and avoid the heavy start-up losses that the first movers into e-commerce incurred. Other retail TNCs, however, chose to outsource parts or all of the e-commerce order processing and fulfilment process, in the same way that the European and US food retailers had contracted out distribution/logistic functions in the 1980s and early 1990s (Fernie 1992). Wal-Mart, for example, in 1999 contracted out its internet order fulfilment to Fingerhut Inc.

The potential threat of the growth of e-commerce and the emerging non-store electronic retailers to the elite group of retail TNCs is likely, therefore, to be rather muted. The retail TNCs are learning to adapt their businesses to the new distribution channels, and will inevitably become multiple-channel ('bricks and clicks') retailers to a greater or lesser extent. They will use e-commerce as part of a dual strategy in which the new electronic channels are employed both to extend and protect their customer franchise and markets, and also to drive additional customers into their existing store networks. Whilst there are clearly longer-term threats—not least the challenge to flexibility which derives from the need to adapt organizational structures historically rooted in the physical world—and whilst the competitive landscape of global retailing will clearly be altered by emergence of e-commerce, it seems unlikely that the economic geographies of globalizing retail capital that developed in the late 1990s will be destabilized by the rise of the non-store retailers—'ultimately, we still believe that Wal-Mart and not another pure play e-tailer, will become the "Wal-Mart of the Web"' (Merrill Lynch 2000: 3).

Conclusion

The globalization of retail distribution and the rapid emergence of retail-industry TNCs during the 1990s is a profoundly neglected topic in economic geography. Virtually no academic literature currently exists on either the wave of retail mergers and acquisitions that has provided the path to global scale for the leading firms in the industry, or the market entry and expansion of an elite group of international retailers in the emerging markets of Latin America, South East Asia, Central/Eastern Europe, and Southern Europe. Debates about the processes of global economic change in the discipline retain much of their traditional focus on production and global manufacturing systems—albeit softened to a certain extent by the global commodity chain perspectives (Gereffi 1994) that centre on the dynamics of production/consumption/distribution linkages and have attracted increasing attention from geographers (Leslie and Reimer 1999). Yet, simultaneously, the late 1990s has seen both rapidly developing new economic geographies of globalizing retail capital, and the rise of e-commerce as a potentially destabilizing force within those geographies. It is the contention of this chapter that an 'economic geography' worthy of its name can no longer afford to neglect these developments. They are neither peripheral in substantive terms, nor in terms of the wider themes for conceptual debate which their consideration serves to highlight.

Acknowledgements

This chapter developed out of research on 'The Post-LBO Reconfiguration of US Food Retailing' supported by The Leverhulme Trust under a 1997 Individual Research Award. The author is grateful for ongoing discussions with leading analysts of the retail industry at Merrill Lynch, Donaldson, Lufkin & Jenrette, JP Morgan, Deutsche Bank, ABN-AMRO, and Credit Suisse First Boston, and for the opportunity to participate in meetings with the management of the leading firms in the industry organized by those investment banks.

References

ABN-AMRO 1999*a*. *European Food Retail: Short Cut to Consolidation*. London: ABN-AMRO Equities Ltd., 12 Mar.

—— 1999*b*. *E-Commerce*. London: ABN-AMRO Equities Ltd., 17 Feb.

Castells, M. 1996. *The Rise of the Network Society*. Oxford: Blackwell.

Clark, G. L. 1999. The retreat of the state and the rise of pension fund capitalism. In Martin 1999: 241–60.

Cotterill, R. W. 1993. Food retailing: mergers, leveraged buyouts and performance. In *Industry Studies*, ed. L. Duetsch. Englewood Cliffs, NJ: Prentice Hall, 157–81.

—— 1999. *An Antitrust Economic Analysis of the Proposed Acquisition of Supermarkets General Holdings Corporation by Ahold Inc*, Research Report No. 46, Food Marketing Policy Center, University of Connecticut.

Denis, D. J. 1994. Organizational form and the consequences of highly leveraged transactions: Kroger's recapitalization and Safeway's LBO. *Journal of Financial Economics*, 36: 193–224.

Dicken, P. 1998. *Global Shift: Transforming the World Economy*. 3rd edn. London: Paul Chapman.

Donaghu, M. T., and Barff, R. 1990. Nike just did it: international subcontracting and flexibility in athletic footware production. *Regional Studies*, 24: 537–52.

Fernie, J. 1992. Distribution strategies of European retailers. *European Journal of Marketing*, 26/8–9: 35–47.

—— 1995. International comparisons of supply chain management in grocery retailing. *Service Industries Journal*, 15: 134–47.

Gereffi, G. 1994. The organization of buyer driven global commodity chains. In Gereffi and Korzeniewicz 1994.

—— and Korzeniewicz, M., eds. 1994. *Commodity Chains and Global Capitalism*. Westport, Conn.: Praeger.

Gertler, M. S. 1995. Being there: proximity, organization and culture in the development and adoption of advanced manufacturing technologies. *Economic Geography*, 71: 1–26.

Held, D., McGrew, A., Goldblatt, D., and Perraton, J. 1999. *Global Transformations*. Cambridge: Polity Press.

Jensen, M. C. 1986. Agency costs of free cash flow, corporate finance and takeovers. *American Economic Review*, 76: 323–9.

JONES, K., and BIASIOTTO, M. 1999. Internet retailing: current hype or future reality? *International Review of Retail, Distribution and Consumer Research*, 9: 69–79.

JP MORGAN 1998. *Metro AG: Restructuring, Refocusing, Rerating*. London: JP Morgan Securities Ltd., 24 Nov.

—— 1999*a*. *Kingfisher: Angling for the 'A' List*. London: JP Morgan Securities Ltd., 26 May.

—— 1999*b*. *Latin American Retailing*. New York: JP Morgan Securities Inc., 28 June.

—— 1999*c*. *Carrefour: Moving the Goal Posts*. London: JP Morgan Securities Ltd., 30 June.

KORZENIEWICZ, M. 1994. Commodity chains and marketing strategies: Nike and the global athletic footwear industry. In Gereffi and Korzeniewicz 1994.

LESLIE, D., and REIMER, S. 1999. Spatialising commodity chains. *Progress in Human Geography*, 22: 401–20.

MARTIN, R. L., ed. 1999. *Money and the Space Economy*. Chichester: John Wiley.

MERRILL LYNCH 1998. *Tesco: Fit Enough to Survive?* London: Merrill Lynch & Co., 4 Dec.

—— 1999*a*. *Leaders Emerging: Trends in Retail Consolidation*. London: Merrill Lynch & Co., 29 Apr.

—— 1999*b*. *The European Food Retail Guide, Issue 4*. London: Merrill Lynch & Co., 16 Apr.

—— 1999*c*. *Ahold: Portfolio Approach to Global Growth*. New York and London: Merrill Lynch & Co., 16 July.

—— 1999*d*. *E-Commerce: Virtually Here*. New York: Merrill Lynch & Co., Apr.

—— 2000. *Wal-Mart Stores*. New York: Merrill Lynch & Co., 22 Feb.

MUELLER, W. F., and PATERSON, T. W. 1986. Policies to promote competition. In *The Organization and Performance of the US Food Industry*, ed. B. W. Marion. Lexington, Mass.: Lexington Books, 371–412.

SMITH, D. L. G., and SPARKS, L. 1993. The transformation of physical distribution in retailing: the example of Tesco plc. *International Review of Retail, Distribution and Consumer Research*, 3: 35–64.

SPARKS, L. 1994. Delivering quality: the role of logistics in the post-war transformation of British food retailing. In *Adding Value: Brands and Marketing in Food and Drink*. ed. G. JONES and N. J. MORGAN. London: Routledge, 310–35.

TESCO PLC 1999. *Annual Review and Summary Financial Statement 1999*. Cheshunt, UK: Tesco plc.

WALKER, M. 1994. Quick response: the road to lean logistics. In *Logistics and Distribution Planning*, ed. J. Cooper. London: Kogan Page.

WRIGLEY, N. 1992. Antitrust regulation and the restructuring of grocery retailing in Britain and the USA. *Environment and Planning A*, 24: 727–49.

—— 1998. Understanding store development programmes in post-property-crisis UK food retailing. *Environment and Planning A*, 30: 15–35.

—— 1999*a*. Corporate finance, leveraged restructuring, and the economic landscape: the LBO wave in US food retailing. In Martin 1999: 185–205.

—— 1999*b*. Market rules and spatial outcomes: insights from the corporate restructuring of US food retailing. *Geographical Analysis*, 31: 288–309.

—— and LOWE, M. S. 2000. *Reading Retail: A Geographical Perspective on Retailing and Consumption Spaces*. London: Edward Arnold.

Section 7

Remaking the Corporation

Chapter **16**

The Management of Time and Space

Erica Schoenberger

Introduction

THIS chapter takes a critical look at how geographers have conceived the relationship between corporations and spatial form. The big questions are what kind of world do corporations make as they go about their business, why does this happen, and what does it mean for all of us. I focus here mainly on the history of economic geography in the post-World War II period. This history is not altogether a glorious one, as we will see, and this has been most true when the big questions have been lost sight of and when the analytical trajectory has most closely adhered to mainstream economic analysis.

Following on this review, there are three objectives. The first is to find a way to talk about corporations as truly *strategic* actors who are seen to be creating the world they live in and not merely responding to disembodied price signals. The second is to demonstrate that the management of temporal and spatial processes is an essential part of the strategic work the corporation needs to do in order to remain competitive. This means countering the idea that corporate behaviors fill up space as a by-product of strategies related solely to products, markets, and production processes. The third aim, more generally, is to show why the big questions are the right ones to ask, although they are impossible to answer definitively.

The Discussion So Far

In postwar economic geography, the discussion about corporate behavior and spatial form was early on marked by the enthusiastic embrace of mainstream

My thanks to Anno Saxenian, Gerald Autler, Larry Barone, Gary Fields, Larissa Muller, Abby Siegal, and Matt Zook for comments on an earlier draft. I hold them absolutely responsible for the outcome.

equilibrium economic theory. This constrained both the conception of what managers do, how they think, and what is strategic about their work. Ironically, it also limited the conception of location and spatial form.

Location Theory and its Discontents

Industrial location theory became the organizing principle for much economic geographic research. In a landscape where factors of production were unevenly distributed and immobile, factor costs varied across places, and transportation costs were a function of distance and weight, location choice was a reasonably straightforward tradeoff between transportation costs to market and factor costs (see Isard 1956; Alonso 1975; Webber 1984; Ch. 2). In this way, location became simply an add-on to a standard production function.

Note that in this model, specific industry characteristics and the choice of technique are set a priori and location simply follows from these parameters. No history and no problems of spatial fixity enter into the story: capital is perfectly mobile across space. Moreover, location itself has no strategic content and no influence on any other variable such as choice of technique.

The resulting economic landscape is simply the aggregate outcome of many small, unconnected location decisions by individual firms. Interdependencies might be realized in practice in terms of access to factor and output markets in the form of so-called agglomeration or localization economies, but again these exist a priori through the blind workings of a competitive market and there is nothing particularly *strategic* about the resulting location decision. There is certainly no sense in which firms might, for example, actively construct these conditions through, say, the recruitment of immigrants or suppliers.

One might predict a tendency for regional specialization given the cost topography, but the theory maintained a discreet silence about interregional trade and general growth and development issues.[1] This includes the factor cost implications of particular regional development trajectories.

An important variation on the location theory theme, which introduced the problem of imperfect competition, was offered by Hotelling (1929). This approach was unconcerned with issues of production and focused on jockeying for superior access to markets. Since products were assumed homogeneous, location became *the* strategic issue and locational clustering a likely outcome. Locational rivalry, in a sense, substituted for the product rivalry more familiar from writings on oligopolistic competition (see e.g. Caves 1974). Although broaching the subject of imperfect competition was an important move

[1] One exception to this would be the tie-in between location and regional development made by export base theory (see North 1955). While the latter theory was important in geographical and planning circles, it wasn't so much because of the tie to location theory but rather because of its connections to interest in natural resource endowments as the basis for economic development and its apparent susceptibility to fairly simple policy interventions.

theoretically, Hotelling's work did not really underwrite a broad research program.[2]

Disequilibrium economics entered in most strongly through growth pole theory as Scott notes in Chapter 2 of this volume.[3] It proposed a spatial analog to the hypothesized *industrie motrice*: a geographical cluster driving growth and development in a region. Indeed, innovative growth industries do often cluster geographically, but the understanding of how and why this occurs historically was weak. Though the idea underwrote a policy of intervening in the locational behavior of firms to construct growth poles in peripheral regions, the results were generally disappointing.

The Multi-locational Corporation: Product Cycles and the New International Division of Labor

The foregoing largely took place in a world of small, single-plant firms. In the 1960s and afterwards, geographers followed at least some economists and business historians into the domain of the large, multidivisional firm with a national and international reach (Chandler 1962; Hymer 1972; Kindleberger 1973). If, in location theory, the person of the manager was merely implied and indeed was hardly necessary since market signals took care of all decisions, here management practice as it works through organizational and spatial form begins to emerge as an issue in its own right.

The management problem is now to optimize the location of a variety of corporate activities. A key parameter is variations in labor process depending on corporate function and industrial sector. A spatial division of labor—intricately connected to divisions of labor across industries and within firms—emerges as something corporations must construct and reconstruct as a normal part of doing business (Hymer 1972; Massey 1984; Storper and Walker 1974). Two models became especially important in this context. The first, product cycle theory, was centrally concerned with products and production technique. The second, the New International Division of Labor (NIDL) model, shared many features of the product cycle, but was more attentive to labor process and labor relations.

Both describe a trajectory in which manufacturing processes located in advanced industrial areas are eventually decentralized to peripheral regions. For both, costs become a growing problem over time and the solution to this problem is to employ low-cost workers who are, of course, found in low-cost

[2] His hypotheses, though, were indirectly borne out many years later in Knickerbocker's (1973) work on oligopolistic reaction in the location of multinational firms—again, a line of work that remained somewhat isolated from the mainstream.

[3] Disequilibrium analysis was, of course, more generally important in regional development theory (again, see the citations in Ch. 2) but I want to focus here on that segment of it which specifically bears on the behavior of firms in space.

regions. The product cycle optimistically sees this process in terms of a continually self-replenishing supply of innovative products at the core quite naturally drifting outwards. The NIDL, its dark twin, sees the process more in terms of corporate functions than products, and envisions a more deliberate class strategy underlying corporate decisions. Thus, corporate control and R&D functions might stay in the core while manufacturing is aggressively de-skilled and moved offshore.[4]

The two theories taken together were extraordinarily influential in geography and other disciplines. Nevertheless, they suffered from being too closely tied to particular kinds of industry at a particular historical juncture and from a rather mechanistic reading of the evolutionary and adjustment possibilities of firms, industries, and technologies.[5] Thus, although both had at least implicitly a conception of a manager/decision maker pursuing a project of market and/or class domination and, in so doing, creating a global social and economic landscape, the theoretical understanding of this social actor remained sketchy.

The New Institutionalism, Industrial Organization, Industrial Space

The new institutionalism challenged the behavioral assumptions underlying neoclassical economics, allowing for a more historicized and acculturated economic actor whose strategies are appropriate to a particular institutional setting and set of incentives (see North 1990). In short, context matters, although there is still an uneasy vacillation between what Granovetter (1985) describes as the under-socialized *homo economicus* of mainstream economic theory and the over-socialized 'history made me do it' drone who populates the most one-dimensionally functional accounts.

At the same time, it became apparent that firms couldn't be treated merely as atomized production functions divorced from the welter of complicated transactional activity that enables the transformative operations of the firm. This move revived a line of inquiry that focused on why the economy is organized at all, and why it is organized differently depending, for example, on time, place, and sector (Coase 1937; Demsetz 1988; Williamson 1985; North 1990).

Both lines of analysis are converging on a view of the economy as being more socially embedded and possessed of a more historically bounded character. Significantly, this is a world that allows for the coexistence of differing organi-

[4] Essential texts include Vernon (1966), Storper and Walker (1974), Hymer (1972), Frobel *et al.* (1980); Massey and Meegan (1982), Bluestone and Harrison (1982), and Massey (1984). An important variation on the product cycle theme was offered by Markusen (1985) who proposed that a 'profit cycle' better reflected the historical trajectory of many industries, and drew special attention to those which managed to stave off the advent of increasingly open price competition. Though the profit cycle offered much greater theoretical flexibility to cope with complicated processes of industrial change, it was not as broadly influential as the original product cycle in subsequent empirical research.

[5] See especially Markusen (1985), Storper (1985), Clark *et al.* (1986), Schoenberger (1989), and Storper and Walker (1989).

zational and social forms and in which the relationship between social and institutional structures and the behavior of individuals becomes central (Granovetter 1985; Piore and Sabel 1984; Ostrom 1990; Sabel 1982; Storper and Salais 1997; Scott 1988). Accordingly, the scope for meaningfully strategic behavior, whether of a cooperative or competitive sort, is broadened. It is, finally, a world in which actual people have actual relationships that, through deepening local knowledge and building mutual trust, reduce uncertainty and enable a range of economic activities that might not otherwise be possible.

This is an analytical trajectory that actually hearkens back to a strong geographic tradition of close analysis of regional and historical differentiation and cultural adaptation (Ch. 2). The emphasis on institutions and transactional complexity seemed to validate an old geographic preoccupation with the particularities of place and an expectation of continuing geographical and historical diversity rather than the general convergence anticipated by mainstream economists.

This may help to explain why the efflorescence of discussion about 'flexible specialization' had perhaps a larger impact among geographers than among economists. For geographers, the flexible specialization thesis was attractive on several fronts. First, it rather decisively broke with the sense of inevitability surrounding the model of the huge firm coasting along on economies of scale, relatively footloose and indifferent to the characteristics of the places it happened to inhabit. Secondly, it valorized precisely the *local* social, cultural, and institutional setting, hence unavoidably the historical and the geographic. The whole idea of an industrial district depended on the historical accretion of tacit understandings and specialist knowledge that develop and circulate within a bounded area in which people metaphorically and literally speak the same language and in which the people who run firms have complex social identities and behaviors. By articulating a strongly historicized and spatialized account of a social economy, the model reopened an analytically respectable way of dealing with economic and geographical diversity.

The most well-elaborated follow-ons within geography emphasized variously the formal problem of transaction costs or the more diffuse analysis of cultural and institutional ensembles in particular places. The 'new industrial spaces' approach, for example, stressed the efficiency gains of clustering among vertically disintegrated production units as well as the contributions to quality, innovation, and market responsiveness thought to result from smaller-scale, destandardized production trajectories (Scott 1988). The idea of 'worlds of production' organized around geographically and sectorally differentiated social conventions insists more on the existence of relational assets that can be mobilized to add value and underwrite success in the market (Storper and Salais 1997).

In either case, the practice of management is inherently spatialized in the sense of being dependent on a particular social and geographical location for its character and validation. This is really the first strong argument we get that the behavior of the firm does more than fill up space—it is directly subject to spatial conditions and the fact that the spatiality of the firm is productive. This is still shy, however, of an assertion that space is a strategic problem for the firm.

The Production of Space

Finally, there is a strong Marxist tradition that, as in economics, reasserted itself in the 1970s but had a bigger impact in geography.[6] This tradition is reasonably diverse but there are several unifying threads.

The first is an underlying commitment to the notion that spatial forms and relationships are socially constructed and emerge out of complex and contentious social processes. By the same token, social processes are not merely inherently spatial in the sense that they must, after all, take place *somewhere*, but in the stronger sense that in constructing our social and economic world we necessarily create the spaces and places in which we live and, in so doing, create ourselves. From this flows an interrelated set of theoretical claims:

- space is both socially produced and producing;
- the production of the built environment is a necessary underpinning for all social and economic activity and it stands in a very particular relationship to normal processes of capitalist industrialization and capital accumulation;
- spatial processes and relations are always socially contested; eventual spatial outcomes are produced in and through this social struggle.

The earth is not merely a natural surface on which we play out our social and economic lives—a necessary background which does not, however, affect who we are and what we do in the world. We must, of course, build *on* the earth the dwellings and factories and cities in which we live and work and the transportation and communications networks that allow movement of people, goods, and information among these places. One might say that this process of building makes our social and economic life possible. More strongly, one might say that this process of building *is* a deeply important part of our social and economic life because in constructing these places and connections, we create the possibility for certain kinds of social and economic relationships and constrain others.

The gathering together in very particular kinds of spaces of different social groups and activities registers in both material and symbolic ways. For example, the massing of huge numbers of workers in one factory and housing them in nearby working-class suburbs was a characteristic feature of large-scale industry that shaped the nature of labor–management relations inside the factory and the character of local politics outside it. Creating places is a way of creating an industrial history and a socio-technical trajectory that bear strongly on

[6] Key texts include Harvey (1982); Smith (1984); and LeFebvre (1991).

long-run issues of industrial change and competitiveness as well as the general character of social relations.

Secondly, the process of building is simultaneously a process of investing in a built environment. In the best circumstances, this built environment will substantially facilitate the production of wealth: the buildings, roadways, communications networks, and so forth allow production to happen. The most appropriate buildings and the latest and best transportation networks allow production to happen most efficiently. But the longevity of these investments means that, over time, they may also constrain productivity growth in the system as new methods require different building configurations or transportation networks become congested or do not serve emerging markets or sources of raw materials. In other words, the very investments that enable productive activities, because they are so long-lived and spatially fixed, may eventually constitute barriers to further productivity gains and the continued generation of wealth.

Thirdly, this process of creating a built environment also channels the distribution of the social product, by whom it will be consumed or reinvested, and how. This includes the impact of rent on profit and wage incomes. It also involves exposure to the various kinds of negative and positive externalities common to industrial and urban life (e.g. proximity to museums, polite police, and good schools versus waste incinerators, drug markets, and dilapidated public infrastructure).

This hints at why spatial relationships and processes are so deeply conflictual within and across social classes. A remarkable amount of normal social life is spent fighting over the control and valorization of turf in one way or another—from who gets to say how life will be lived on the shop floor to whether or not downtown business interests can defend themselves against competition from other places by building yet another stadium and convention center.

In sum, a continuing historical process of investment/disinvestment, wealth generation or stagnation, distributions of income, particular kinds of consumption and reinvestment, marks places and people simultaneously. This is one important sense in which space is both socially produced and producing and it is also why the production of the built environment is such an important, contentious, and contradictory part of normal economic and social life. Once we can envision the production of space as inescapably entwined with capitalist development processes in general, it becomes more apparent how it may also be necessarily part of the management function of the firm.

The Management of Time and Space

Here we can posit a further set of theoretical claims that bear more specifically on management practice and strategy:

- spatial and temporal processes are intimately connected;
- the management of space and time is a strategic problem for the firm;
- corporate spatial form is an indeterminate result of a number of processes that may be in considerable tension.

We readily recognize the strategic value of time management in corporate life. This was, of course, the great message of the scientific management approach, enshrined in the time-motion study and brought stunningly to life in Henry Ford's moving assembly line. Time compression in production and product development has remained central to the managerial project to this day.[7] Current management mantras such as 'lean production' and 'flexibility' are about nothing if they are not about time compression.

The geographers' claim is that the management of temporal processes is always caught up in the management of spatial processes. Both are invested with strategic value, and both are the subject of social conflict and shifting distributions of social power.

Consider, for example, the shift from American-style mass production techniques to the currently favored just-in-time approach. Just in time (JIT) is about time compression in processing and transfer activities in manufacturing accompanied by an obsessive concern with reducing the time in which goods are tied up unproductively either in inventory or waiting around for further processing. It is also more generally about time management, and in particular ensuring that the time of workers is always occupied, either by charging them with the operation of multiple machines or moving them around the shop floor at will.

From the local to the global level, this form of time management in production alters the set of feasible or desirable spatial arrangements. Machines need to be grouped in a U around a single worker rather than strung out on a line, one machine to one worker. Practices bearing on plant specialization and plant loading change so that inter-plant dependencies may be vastly enlarged.[8] Suppliers preferentially cluster near the final assembly facility or even set up shop within it so as to ensure timely delivery of exactly the material needed. Where JIT is linked to a strategy of compressing product life cycles, even R&D may be drawn more closely into contact with manufacturing.

However, as many firms are discovering, it's not easy to reconfigure an established system to conform to the new rules of just in time. One problem is over-

[7] For a formal Marxist analysis of why this is, which is more interesting than you might think, see Marx, Vols. 1 and 2; Harvey (1982); Smith (1984). For a more detailed account of how this may be related to corporate competitive strategy, see Schoenberger (1997) and citations therein. Management texts that bear on this issue include Stalk and Hout (1990) and Smith and Reinertsen (1991).

[8] This was quite evident as recently as the summer of 1998 when strikes at one General Motors parts plant in the USA caused a cascade of plant closures elsewhere in the corporate empire (*Financial Times* 1999).

coming the legacy of fixed investment whose spatial character reflected the needs of the earlier production regime and whose overhaul may expose the firm to a considerable burden of sunk costs (Mair 1994; Clark 1994).

At the same time, the new temporal and spatial practices are caught up in changing social relations in production. Management practices and ways of thinking may require considerable renovation as a consequence. For example, just in time works better with multi-tasking and cross-training of workers so they can competently operate a wide variety of machines and intervene in case of normal malfunctions. This implies more worker mobility on the shop floor, both to oversee the larger number of machines per worker and to allow a greater degree of task flexibility. Both the temporal and spatial requirements, in turn, benefit from a higher degree of self-supervision and self-motivation than was characteristic of just-in-case methods.

In sum, the pursuit of greater efficiencies in production and a more commanding position in the market operates through interlinked transformations in temporal, spatial, and social practices, relations, and ways of thinking. An entire production culture and way of life is at stake.

The Indeterminate and the Strategic

We have come a long way from the determinate, static, and derivative world of traditional location theory. The indeterminacy results in part from insisting on the socialness of the categories of time and space—on the *construction* of temporal and spatial practices, rhythms, and meanings in everyday life and how they are caught up in real social struggles. This implies that social, spatial, and temporal outcomes depend very much on who is engaged in these struggles, the resources they bring to them, and how they are played out over time.

These struggles take place between social classes; for example, struggles between management and labor over the pace of work or outsourcing to suppliers overseas. But, importantly for our purposes, they also take place within classes as the people who run firms vie for advantage in the market by altering socio-spatio-temporal practices and ways of thinking. Thus, as Toyota emerges as a powerful competitor to Ford and GM, a whole set of industrial practices involving time and space is thrown into question.

The indeterminacy, finally, is what allows management to be conceived of as a strategic activity. The task of the high-level manager is not merely to run the algorithm that will reveal optimal production techniques, locations, and all the rest. The really important task is to be able to imagine and bring into being an ensemble of social practices, relations, and ways of thinking that will allow a given firm to compete successfully against its rivals. The manager, in this context, is in competition with others of his type[9] and his central task is to confront existing conditions and alter them to the benefit of his firm.

[9] Or hers, but let's recall that it's mostly his.

I want to focus here on top management, the people responsible for setting the strategy of the firm and for mobilizing the resources to put that strategy into play. Part of their work involves creating a distinctive world in which the corporate 'community' is defined or redefined, different types of person and activity are valued in very particular ways, and in which time and space acquire specific meanings. The assets they bring to bear in this work, and which underwrite their power to define this distinctive world, include both material resources (control over capital, people, knowledge) and the social weight of their position or what elsewhere has been described as social and cultural capital (Bourdieu 1984). Their social power, needless to say, can be challenged in many ways, but that doesn't nullify its existence.

Change and Stability

What, then, do they need to do—or try to do—with these resources and this power? In a nutshell, they need to do at least as well as but preferably better than the competition in obtaining a return on the resources invested, and in reinvesting them to continue the cycle. Because the penalty for failure is death, there are tremendous incentives to innovate (in products and processes) and change the rules of the game. Yet because major innovations devalue so much existing investment and throw into doubt a whole range of social assets—including, potentially, the manager's own social assets—there are also tremendous incentives to stabilize the system around a known set of rules.

This means that the system is always characterized by conflict and tension, even when it's operating well. There is a permanent tension between stability and change and, since people's social positions and ways of life are directly affected by which changes occur when, this implies permanent conflict over the trajectory of the system. Note that this doesn't imply a blanket resistance to change *tout court*. It does mean that which kinds of changes are embraced, and which rejected, depends on who wins. This tension also means that no operational problems are ever definitively solved—they just move around or change shape. An apparently stable configuration of practices and meanings can be abruptly destabilized even though a lot of people have a stake in defending the status quo.

For example, we can trace the consequences of Ford's innovation of the assembly line inside and outside the firm according to the categories deployed here. Certain kinds of skilled work that had been valued in the previous production regime were devalued; the accumulated social assets of most craft autoworkers became unimportant. They represented a kind of social sunk cost: skills that had value in one setting have none in a transformed environment (Clark 1994). Other kinds of work (e.g. line supervision) gained value. Certain kinds of people—unskilled, inexperienced, non-English speakers, blacks—became now eligible to work at Ford who wouldn't have been candidates before.

The community was altered and the principles of valuation of different kinds of work and different categories of person changed.

Spatio-temporal practices changed in tandem. Workers no longer moved from station to station to do their jobs; they became fixed in place on the shop floor. The pace of work increased and was controlled by the machinery, not the worker; the labor content of goods produced drastically diminished (Hounshell 1984). The whole experience of work was transformed and the social relations surrounding it put under new kinds of stress. The conflict that ensued as workers challenged the new practices and principles and management insisted on their enforcement was often bloody and most certainly protracted.

Meanwhile, competitors whose way of life was organized around the pre-Fordist processes and understandings had to either change drastically to stay in the game or disappear. Mostly they disappeared and the industry in the USA was stabilized at a handful of final assemblers.

In the auto and other sectors, this stability anchored an industrial regime and an industrial culture that was defined by particular conceptions of how markets worked, how competition would take place within them, how production would be organized, how workers and suppliers would be valued, and how all of this would be organized and managed temporally and spatially. This amounts to the institutionalization of historically specific rules of the game and a distinctive and enduring ensemble of social practices and ways of thinking. Change could occur within the boundaries of this ensemble—faster line speeds, more or less chrome, and so on—but the viability of massive social resources depended on the basic set of rules and understandings remaining intact.

The advent of new competitors from abroad who brought markedly different practices and understandings to bear on these issues threw the system into crisis. They changed the world that the existing firms lived in and undermined the value of the social and material assets that had guaranteed their dominance in the market for some decades.

What we might think of as the period of high mass production stabilized a spatio-temporal regime that *appeared* to be determined by the technology and scale of production. These included a continual, planned throughput of product without regard to the short-run fluctuations of the market; steady, fairly rapid (e.g. annual) turnover of external design features of products; slow and intermittent (e.g. five to fifteen years) turnover of major product features; huge production facilities dominating a particular geographic space; and inter-plant and production-to-market coordination over huge distances nationally and internationally. Distance, in this system, was a solved problem so long as product configurations remained relatively stable and homogeneous.

The dominance of this system gave it an air of inevitability and evolutionary supremacy. It seemed, in a word, natural. Accordingly, it became easy to overlook the quite significant tradeoffs that were being made and institutionalized all along the line and that could be made in other ways. Here is one example.

In a capitalist world, all firms face extraordinary pressure to keep their capital continuously on the move, earning profits that are reinvested and so on. This means that machines ought to be in use as much as possible, workers working all the time, and product rolling out of the door and thence into the hands of consumers. This all seems very straightforward and conceptually uncomplicated, but the minute one commits to a particular way of doing things, all sorts of compromises and tradeoffs are forced into existence *even when the system is functioning well.*

In the American mass production system, one of the cardinal virtues was getting product out of the door steadily, rapidly, and continuously. Within this general compulsion, priority was given to keeping machines in use as much of the time as possible, also to capturing scale economies. But to keep the machine in use without interruption implied two things. One is that changing what the machine did was anathema because that detracted from the amount of time it could be producing *stuff*. This was a given. Accordingly, it was not worthwhile developing faster ways of changing what the machine did.

Secondly, it seemed axiomatic that workers should wait for machines rather than that machines should wait for workers. In the American system, individual workers were appendages of individual machines. They were there to continually feed, monitor, and tend their machine. While the machine performed its task, the worker/servant would wait until it was done. Then he or she would start the cycle over again. Plainly, for many tasks there was no waiting at all and the real problem was that the intensity of work would wear people out. But machine pacing of work created pockets of idle time in some places while it ran people off their legs elsewhere. This represented a cost to the system, but one that seemed both unavoidable and normal.

Notice, in this context, that whole categories of question are removed from the arena of strategy. To the extent that particular practices appeared natural and inevitable, they simply could not be the subject of strategy or the avenue for altering the competitive environment. If it is natural that assembly lines are specialized to produce one product, then the strategists will not take up the question of how to gain competitive advantage by fielding a constantly changing mix of products.

In the Japanese mass production system by contrast, priority was given to eliminating waste rather than producing as much as possible. Machine idle time automatically becomes more tolerable, while idle time for workers becomes anathema. It's an exact reversal of the US system of temporal values. Hence, the problem becomes how to arrange workers *vis-à-vis* multiple machines so that the workers are always moving even while any individual machine is performing its task or not working at all. As noted, the whole spatial layout of the plant changes, and workers become mobile in the plant, able to move to different stations as needed rather than fixed in place. Meanwhile, the idea of stopping a machine in order to change what it does is no longer inconceivable. This promotes the development of new ways of shortening changeover times and hence allows an entirely different and vastly more flexible array of product types to be produced at acceptable cost.

We don't need to romanticize or over-culturalize Japanese industrial practices to appreciate how thoroughly different the operating principles and strategic possibilities of the system are. First of all, even Japanese firms have their problems; flexibility does not immunize against such normal features of capitalist history as hideous overcapacity. Secondly, these very different practices do not emerge 'naturally' from a culture that values harmony or flowers or respect for the elderly. They came out of real historical-geographical processes and circumstances and have, in turn, helped to create a specific Japanese industrial culture and set of strategic possibilities and constraints (see Cusumano 1985; Fruin 1992).

In short, real histories in real places create the world in which corporate strategies must be produced and valorized. These strategies in turn are bound to affect how history happens on the ground.

Conclusion

While we are used to thinking of competitive strategy as bearing principally on products, prices, and market entry considerations, arguably a much deeper competitive challenge is embodied in major shifts in spatio-temporal practices. These are harder to appreciate because we tend to think about time and, especially, space as natural categories rather than strategizable processes.

Spatial form, however, is not merely a by-product of decisions taken according to the more compelling specifics of products, markets, and production processes. Firms produce and use and are shaped by spatial relations as a normal part of doing business and must continually create and seek to validate spatio-temporal processes and understandings as a condition of staying alive. Another way of saying this might be that spatial and temporal processes are very deeply part of the production function and the growth trajectory, not artifacts of them.

The strategic and productive value of spatio-temporal practices and ways of thinking exists, moreover, whether or not managers are specifically aware of them and act upon them with strategic intent. It may even be the case that misrecognition of altered spatio-temporal processes is an important way that corporations get blind-sided in the market and are unable to respond effectively to certain kinds of competitive challenge (Schoenberger 1997).

If space and time are strategic, then there can be no expectation of an optimal spatial form or any prospect of spatial equilibrium. Spatio-temporal practices *must* change, sometimes spectacularly, as part of the normal workings of the system and as part of the competitive struggle of the firm.

By the same token, if spatial and temporal processes are necessarily *social*, then they will always be caught up in social relations of all sorts, whether these be conflictual or competitive or cooperative. The way in which these relations are worked out historically, whether between classes (as between managers and workers on the shop floor) or within them (as when people who run corporations seek competitive advantages against others who are doing the same thing), will be saturated with competing visions of the rightness and productiveness of different spatio-temporal models. This again guarantees change in general, but what *kind* of change and who will fight for it and who will resist it depends on particular historical-geographical conditions.

This is exactly why it is interesting and worthwhile to study how these struggles take place, on what grounds, with what resources, and to what effect in the real world. We know that the rivalries and the strategizing and the commitment of resources to gain particular ends will always go on. We have a good idea of which social actors will be involved, the resources they can draw upon, what they have at risk, and what they stand to gain. But we don't know in advance who will prevail and how this will structure the conditions for the next round of struggle.

A particular ensemble of practices and ways of thinking—what we might call an industrial culture—may be stabilized for some period of time during which the struggle is muted and diverted into less momentous channels (e.g. pricing, product configuration, and differentiation, and so on). But sooner or later, the big issues related to how the world works or *ought to* work will resurface and in that moment, the industrial and social landscape stands to be radically transformed. New understandings and practices related to the meaning and value of work, institutional identities (e.g. who is included in the corporate 'community'—temporary workers? workers with seniority? suppliers?), time and space, competition, and so on will emerge to be fought over in their turn. The stakes involved in who wins and who loses are very high and no one escapes their impact.

In analyzing how the struggle takes place and what it means, we need to pay close attention to the rich particularities of firms and industries on the ground. But in order to make sense out of all this, we have to examine it through the optic of larger questions and analytical categories. This means that figuring out what the struggle is really about is utterly crucial.

It's not immediately evident that the big struggles may be about seemingly arcane issues such as spatial and temporal processes and meanings. These seem to us natural—that's just the way the world works—and beyond our individual control. What I've tried to suggest here is that the veneer of the 'natural' obscures a highly strategic and contentious site for working out how the world will be. This is why the 'big' questions, including questions about the meaning of space and time and how it changes, are the ones we must ask.

References

Alonso, W. 1975. Location theory. In *Regional Policy: Readings in Theory and Applications*, ed. J. Friedmann and W. Alonso. Cambridge, Mass.: MIT Press.

Bluestone, B., and Harrison, B. 1982. *The Deindustrialization of America.* New York: Basic Books.

Bourdieu, P. 1984. *Distinctions: A Social Critique of the Judgment of Taste.* Cambridge, Mass.: Harvard University Press.

Caves, R. 1974. Industrial organization. In *Economic Analysis and the Multinational Enterprise*, ed. J. Dunning. New York: Praeger.

Chandler, A. 1962. *Strategy and Structure.* Cambridge, Mass.: MIT Press.

Clark, G. 1994. Strategy and structure: corporate restructuring and the scope and characteristics of sunk costs. *Environment and Planning A*, 26: 9–32.

—— Gertler, M., and Whiteman, J. 1986. *Regional Dynamics: Studies in Adjustment Theory.* Boston: George Allen and Unwin.

Coase, R. H. 1937. The nature of the firm. *Economica*, 4: 16: 33–55.

Cusumano, M. 1985. *The Japanese Automobile Industry.* Cambridge, Mass.: Harvard University Press.

Demsetz, H. 1988. *Ownership, Control and the Firm.* Oxford: Blackwell.

Financial Times 1999. A strong year for US car industry. 7 Jan.: 4.

Frobel, F., Heinrich, J., and Kreye, O. 1980. *The New International Division of Labour.* Cambridge: Cambridge University Press.

Fruin, W. M. 1992. *The Japanese Enterprise System.* Oxford: Clarendon Press.

Granovetter, M. 1985. Economic action and social structure: the problem of embeddedness. *American Journal of Sociology*, 93: 481–510.

Harvey, D. 1982. *The Limits to Capital.* Oxford: Blackwell.

Hotelling, H. 1929. Stability in competition. *Economic Journal*, 39 (Mar.), 41–57.

Hounshell, D. 1984. *From the American System to Mass Production, 1800–1932.* Baltimore: Johns Hopkins University Press.

Hymer, S. 1972. The multinational corporation and the law of uneven development. In *Economics and World Order*, ed. J. Bhagwati. New York: Free Press.

Isard, W. 1956. *Location and Space-Economy.* New York: Wiley.

Kindleberger, C. 1973. *International Economics.* Homewood, Ill.: R. D. Irwin.

Knickerbocker, F. 1973. *Oligopolistic Reaction and Multinational Enterprise.* Boston: Harvard Business School Press.

LeFebvre, H. 1991. *The Production of Space.* Oxford: Blackwell.

Mair, A. 1994. *Honda's Global Local Corporation.* New York: St Martin's Press.

Markusen, A. 1985. *Profit Cycles, Oligopoly and Regional Development.* Cambridge, Mass.: MIT Press.

Marx, K. 1967*a*. *Capital*, i. New York: International Publishers.

—— 1967*b*. *Capital*, ii. New York: International Publishers.

MASSEY, D. 1984. *Spatial Divisions of Labour: Social Structures and the Geography of Production.* London: Macmillan.

MASSEY, D., and MEEGAN, R. 1982. *The Anatomy of Job Loss.* London: Methuen.

NORTH, D. 1955. Location theory and regional economic growth. *Journal of Political Economy*, 63/3: 243–58.

—— 1990. *Institutions, Institutional Change and Economic Performance.* Cambridge: Cambridge University Press.

OSTROM, E. 1990. *Governing the Commons: The Evolution of Institutions for Collective Action.* Cambridge: Cambridge University Press.

PIORE, M., and SABEL, C. 1984. *The Second Industrial Divide.* New York: Basic Books.

SABEL, C. 1982. *Work and Politics.* Cambridge: Cambridge University Press.

SCHOENBERGER, E. 1989. Multinational corporations and the new international division of labor: a critical appraisal. In *Work Transformed?* ed. S. Wood. London: Unwin Hyman.

—— 1997. *The Cultural Crisis of the Firm.* Oxford: Blackwell.

SCOTT, A. 1988. *New Industrial Spaces.* London: Pion.

SMITH, N. 1984. *Uneven Development.* Oxford: Blackwell.

SMITH, P., and REINERTSEN, D. 1991. *Developing Products in Half the Time.* New York: Van Nostrand.

STALK, G., and HOUT, T. 1990. *Competing Against Time.* New York: Free Press.

STORPER, M. 1985. Oligopoly and the product cycle: essentialism in economic geography. *Economic Geography*, 61/3: 260–82.

—— and SALAIS, R. 1997. *Worlds of Production.* Cambridge, Mass.: Harvard University Press.

—— and WALKER, R. 1974. The spatial division of labor. In *Frostbelt/Sunbelt*, ed. W. Tabb and L. Sawers. New York: Oxford University Press.

—— —— 1989. *The Capitalist Imperative: Territory, Technology and Industrial Growth.* Oxford: Blackwell.

VERNON, R. 1966. International investment and international trade in the product cycle. *Quarterly Journal of Economics*, 80/2: 190–207.

WEBBER, M. 1984. *Industrial Location.* Beverly Hills, Calif.: Sage Publications.

WILLIAMSON, O. 1985. *The Economic Institutions of Capitalism.* New York: Free Press.

Chapter 17

Corporate Form and Spatial Form

David B. Audretsch

Introduction

As with all other types of economic activity, the corporate form of organization has been shaped by the forces of geography. A disparate set of literatures spanning a broad group of academic disciplines such as economics, management, international business, geography, and sociology provide rich insights into the manner in which corporate form has been influenced by geography. The purpose of this chapter is to weave together these disparate literatures to identify the most salient and compelling forces shaping the geography of the firm.

The starting point for this chapter draws on Chandler's (1990) seminal work documenting the emergence of the corporation in the USA. In the second section, the implications of the corporation for spatial relationships are identified. In particular, the era of mass-production, dominated by the corporate structure and accompanied by a strategy of cost-minimization of standardized products, resulted in a geographic concentration of ownership along with a high degree of concentration among owners. The actual geographic pattern of production tended to be concentrated, but as a result of multi-plant production proved to be less concentrated than that of ownership.

The third section of this chapter focuses on the extension of multi-plant ownership beyond national borders—the phenomenon of the multinational corporation, or foreign direct investment. Whereas the earliest theories of the multinational corporation focused on the firm leveraging its firm-specific advantages across geographic space, more recent theories focus on accessibility to assets that are non-transferable across geographic space.

The fourth section links a shift in the fundamental source of comparative advantage to firms based in high-cost countries—knowledge—to three important shifts in corporate structure and strategy—an increased importance in the role for geographic proximity as a strategy to access knowledge, a pronounced shift towards decentralization in decision making and an increased role for small firms, and an emerging emphasis on deploying geography to foster learning and dynamic capabilities. Policy implications and suggestions for future research are provided in the last section of the chapter.

The Emergence of the Corporation within and across Geographic Space

Prior to the middle of the nineteenth century, production was typically at a small scale (Chandler 1977). The minimum efficient scale (MES), or smallest level of output where the minimum average cost was attained, was minimal and involved just a handful of employees. Production was typically undertaken in small-scale craft establishments and was centered on family-owned businesses. Piore and Sabel (1984) conclude that prior to the middle of the nineteenth century, a flat average cost curve was not a bad approximation for most firms in most industries. Thus, both production and ownership of economic activity tended to be linked in a single enterprise at a single geographic location. At the same time, much of production tended to be diffused across geographic space in a decentralized series of independently owned enterprises.

The fundamental cost structure changed dramatically with the advent of the corporation and the accompanying managerial revolution. The corporation had emerged as the most efficient instrument of resource management during the American industrial revolution. If the application of British inventions had served as the catalyst underlying US industrialization, the revolution in management techniques—the modern corporate structure—enabled its implementation. Through the organizational structure of the modern corporation, the new managerialism emerging after the US Civil War excelled at amassing large quantities of raw materials, labor and capital inputs, and at applying particular manufacturing processes, thereby achieving a very specific use of these resources. The emergence of mass-production made feasible by the organization of the corporation combined with the managerial revolution triggered a dramatic shift in the underlying cost structure of firms and industry. The MES increased dramatically in many manufacturing industries, resulting in a shift in the long-run average cost curve from essentially flat to downward sloping.

The response to a decreasing cost curve had three aspects. The first was, for the first time in American history, small-scale production was threatened. The second aspect involved massive increases in output as a result of the unprecedented productivity increases generated by large-scale production. The third aspect involved the emerging large corporations, which generally did not prove capable of mastering the business environment sufficiently to ensure the viability of mass-production.

Just as the organization of the corporation combined with modern management to achieve the coordination of production within the firm, it analogously sought to extend that control to the external environment. An important aspect of this centralization involved both a concentration of ownership and an increased concentration across geographic space. While the emerging dominant corporations in an industry engaged in a strategy of geographic diversification through multi-establishment ownership across geographic space, the overall impact of mergers and consolidation typically led to a drastic increase in geographic concentration. This was clearly the case in the automobile industry, which ended up being centered in Detroit; steel, which ended up being concentrated in Pittsburgh; and tires, which ended up being geographically concentrated in Akron, Ohio.

This increase in ownership concentration was accomplished partially through plant closures resulting from mergers and consolidation, which led to an increase in geographic concentration, and partially through the advent of multi-plant ownership, which resulted in less geographic concentration even in the face of an increase in ownership concentration. The ownership of multiple establishments across geographic space by a single enterprise led to an increased concentration of ownership while preserving a more decentralized geographic production. Scherer (1970) identified a number of dimensions of scale economies yielded by multi-plant ownership across geographic space. First, 'multi-plant operations may be able to economize on management services by sharing a common overhead pool of accountants, finance planners, market researchers, production planning specialists, labor relations specialists, purchasing agents, and lawyers' (Scherer 1970: 90). Secondly, there may be economies of scale in conducting centralized R&D. The third source of potential multi-plant economies involves economies of massed reserves, particularly raw materials and other inputs.

Extending the Geographic Market: The Multinational Corporation

The simultaneous geographic centralization of ownership but decentralization of production transcending national boundaries, or foreign direct investment, has exploded at the end of the twentieth century. During the 1970s, annual flows of foreign direct investment averaged $27.5 billion. Kozul-Wright and Rowthorn (1998) report that annual foreign direct investment flows subsequently rose to $50 billion in the first half of the 1980s and $155 billion in the second half. With the publication of Stephen Hymer's (1976) Ph.D. thesis, *The International Operations of National Firms: A Study of Direct Foreign Investment*, scholars began to notice that the phenomenon of ownership concentration across geographic space using a strategy of multi-plant operations also applied across national borders. The fundamental challenge of this growing literature was to address the question, 'Why do firms engage in ownership control of assets located beyond national borders rather than resorting to trade relationships or licensing agreements?' Most of the explanations have built on Hymer's seminal study by focusing on firm-specific advantages. Such firm-specific advantages enable rents to be created which compensate for the various costs arising in foreign direct investment (Hymer and Rowthorn 1970; and Rowthorn 1992).

Dunning (1993) points out that the literature on the multinational corporation has identified four major strategies motivating outward foreign direct investment: (1) market seeking, (2) resource seeking, (3) efficiency seeking, and (4) strategic asset seeking.

According to the theories focusing on the geographic extension of firm-specific attributes, production by a corporation begins locally. After production has become established, the firm then expands geographically via shipping the product across geographic space. Thus, the product gains geographic exposure, while production and ownership remain local. In order to reduce costs and exploit the types of (multi-plant) economies of scale described above, firms then substitute multi-plant production for single establishment production and shipping the product across geographic space. Pursuing a strategy of foreign direct investment simply involves further scale economies to be gained across geographic space. As Kozul-Wright and Rowthorn (1998: 76) observe,

> The two decisive elements in this process are firm size and market penetration. When sufficient sales have been achieved in the new market, it becomes feasible to set up local production facilities on a scale large enough to exploit economies of scale. Since large firms tend to have large exports and more capital at their disposal, they will normally do most investing and this investment will generally be attracted to large and expanding markets.

John Dunning (1993) has argued that no single theory of foreign direct investment can adequately and comprehensively explain transnational economic activity, and in particular, multinational corporations. Instead, Dunning proposes combining several of the most widely accepted theories into an *eclectic paradigm*. In particular, this eclectic paradigm embraces both the neo-technology theories of trade and the theories of imperfect competition. The neo-technology theories are a direct offshoot of the fundamental theorem for international trade, the Heckscher–Ohlin theory, later extended to the Heckscher–Ohlin–Samuelson model (Leamer 1984). According to the Heckscher–Ohlin theory, the proportion of productive factors determines the trade structure. If there exists an abundance of physical capital relative to labor, a country will tend towards the export of capital-intensive goods; an abundance of labor relative to physical capital leads to the export of labor-intensive goods. While the focus of the model was originally on the factor inputs of capital and labor, it was later expanded to include human capital and skilled labor, and technology. The neo-technology theories focus on the role of R&D and the creation of new economic knowledge in shaping the comparative advantage and flows of foreign direct investment. Gruber *et al.* (1967) suggest that R&D expenditures reflect a temporary comparative advantage resulting from products and production techniques that have not yet been adapted by foreign competitors. Thus, industries with a relatively high R&D component are considered to be conducive to the comparative advantage of firms from the most developed nations.

By synthesizing the neo-technology theories of trade and models of imperfect competition, Dunning (1981) proposes an eclectic theory of foreign direct investment. This synthesis suggests that enterprises that benefit the most from internalizing activities will tend to gain the competitive advantage in global markets. Such advantages vary across industries, countries, and enterprises. In particular, the propensity for an enterprise to engage in foreign direct investment is shaped by three fundamental sets of factors. The first is that the enterprise must have an endowment of capabilities oriented towards specific foreign markets that are superior to firms located in other countries. Such firm-specific characteristics, which Dunning terms as *ownership advantages*, are principally in the form of intangible assets. While such asset specificity may not last indefinitely into the long run, the enterprise has an exclusive access to such assets in the short and medium terms.

The second set of factors influencing the propensity for firms to engage in foreign direct investment is that the benefits accruing to the enterprise from exploiting such firm-specific ownership advantages must exceed those gained from selling or licensing them to foreign firms. That is, the benefits from internalization of the asset and extending the enterprise's activities to include production in a foreign country must exceed externalizing the property rights through mechanisms such as licensing, management contracts, franchises, technical services agreements, turnkey projects, and subcontracts.

Finally, the third set of factors influencing the propensity for firms to engage in foreign direct investment are those bestowing advantages upon the enterprise to extend production from its home country into some foreign country. That is, there must exist at least some factor inputs (including natural resources) outside the home country that provide an advantage to production in the foreign country. Otherwise, the enterprise would choose to produce solely in its home country and export the product to foreign markets. In general, the greater the advantages of internalization within the enterprise, the greater is the incentive to enterprises to engage in foreign direct investment.

Knowledge and Globalization

The Heckscher–Ohlin–Samuelson model of international trade is and remains one of the most powerful theories in economics. It has been, and remains, the foundation for understanding the basis for comparative advantage among countries. While the comparative advantage for the USA subsequent to World War II was generally assumed to be in economic activity requiring capital-intensive production, the famous Leontief Paradox empirically challenged this. The resolution to the paradox during the 1960s and 1970s suggested that the comparative advantage of the USA lies not in capital-intensive industries, but rather in industries requiring a high degree of skilled labor (Magee 1989).

More recently, however, many studies have documented a shift in the comparative advantage of the high-wage countries toward an increased importance for knowledge-based economic activity. For example, Kortum and Lerner (1997: 1) point to 'the unprecedented recent jump in patenting in the United States', as evidenced by the rise in applications for US patents by American inventors since 1985, which exceeds the increase in any other decade in this century. Throughout this century, patent applications fluctuated within a band of between 40,000 to 80,000 per year. By contrast, in 1995 there were over 120,000 patent applications. Similarly, Berman *et al.* (1997) have shown that the demand for less skilled workers has decreased dramatically throughout the OECD, while at the same time the demand for skilled workers has exploded.

Geographic Networks and Clusters

Why has it proven so difficult for incumbent corporations to shift economic activity out of the traditional industries where the products are now fairly standardized and where production can be easily transferred out of high-cost locations? Established corporations have what is called their core competence in traditional products. They have limited capacity for shifting their activity out of these traditional industries and into new industries.

Part of this inability to shift into new knowledge-based industries is that large corporations excelled in an economy where it was more or less known what was to be produced and how to produce it. The large corporations excelled at bringing together the essential inputs of machinery, workers, and natural resources to generate manufactured products. Knowledge is a qualitatively different input in the production process to machinery or workers who serve as cogs in an assembly line. While a consensus can arise about the contribution of a worker in an assembly line process, no such consensus exists for new ideas that workers have. New ideas are inherently uncertain. What one worker thinks is a good idea may be disputed by colleagues and bosses. Sometimes opportunities to try out new ideas can be found within existing firms. But often people with new ideas find that, because of the fundamental uncertainty, starting a new firm is the only way in which the idea can be pursued and commercialized.

Starting in the mid-1970s, the trend toward increased concentration reversed itself. A wave of studies confirmed that in virtually every developed country, small firms were accounting for a greater share of economic activity (Loveman and Sengenberger 1991). For example, the share of manufacturing employment accounted for by small firms increased in the UK from 30.1 per cent in 1979 to 39.9 per cent in 1986; in Germany it increased from 54 per cent in 1970 to 58 per cent in 1987; and in Italy it increased from 44.3 per cent in 1981 to 55.2 per cent in 1987.

While the organization of production was centered upon *mass-production* during the first three decades of this century, an alternative system of industrial organization, *flexible specialization*, has seen something of a re-emergence during the last several decades of this century.[1] Flexible production consists of producing smaller series of specially designed goods of a specific quality for a niche market. Such goods typically command a higher price (van Dijk 1995).

There is considerable evidence supporting the hypothesis that not only does flexible production provide a viable alternative to mass-production as a system of industrial organization, but also that such systems centered around flexible production actually outperform those based on mass-production. And this evidence spans both developed and less developed countries.

The evidence also suggests that firms employ different organizational and production methods that more than offset what might otherwise be scale economies' disadvantages. For example, certain new technologies have a *decentralizing* impact on economic organization. Numerically controlled machine tools have apparently contributed to a reduction in the minimum efficient scale (MES), or the level of output required to exhaust scale economies.

Dynamic Organizational Capabilities

The theories of Michael Porter (1990) suggest that enterprises need not passively accept their fate as determined by the factor endowments of the country in which they are operating, but rather may actively engage in strategies and investments to generate their own dynamic capabilities that ultimately bestow international competitiveness. David Teece and Gary Pisano (1994) point out that well-known corporations, such as IBM, Texas Instruments, and Phillips, have generally followed a resource-based strategy that targets the accumulation of valuable technological assets. These assets are typically closely guarded through an aggressive intellectual property stance. While the resource-based strategy seemingly guaranteed success for decades, Teece and Pisano (1994: 538) observe that more recently,

> This strategy is often not enough to support a significant competitive advantage. Winners in the global market place have been firms that can demonstrate timely responsiveness and rapid and flexible production innovation, coupled with the management capability to effectively coordinate and redeploy internal and external competencies. Not surprisingly, industry observers have remarked that companies can

[1] Piore and Sabel (1984) argue that the first industrial divide, which occurred over a century ago, represented a distinct choice away from craft production to mass production.

accumulate a large stock of valuable technological assets and still not have many useful capabilities.

The concept of dynamic capabilities refers to a source of competitive advantage that emphasizes two key aspects that have generally been overlooked from traditional strategy perspectives. The first of these is that the external market environment is rapidly changing. This means that certain strategic responses are required when time-to-market and timing is critical, the pace of innovation is accelerating, and the nature of future competition and markets is shrouded in uncertainty. The second of these is that the term capabilities emphasizes the key role played by strategic management in successfully adapting, integrating, and re-configuring internal and external organizational skills, resources, and functional competencies in rising to the challenge posed by a constantly shifting external environment. In particular, dynamic capabilities are the subset of the competencies or capabilities of an enterprise enabling it to generate new products and processes, and ultimately maintain or even improve its competitiveness. According to Iansiti and Clark (1994: 560), 'Dynamic capability is the capacity of an organization to consistently nurture, adapt, and regenerate its knowledge base, to develop and retain the organizational capabilities that translate that knowledge base into useful actions'.

Kogut and Zander (1992) point out that the distinctive feature of enterprise competencies is that they cannot be duplicated through market exchange. That is, by creating a core competence, the firm as a whole is able to produce value in excess of what could otherwise be created simply through a nexus of contracts. Most of the literature has, to date, treated the core competencies of a firm within a static context. It is not well understood where these core competencies come from, and it is generally assumed that they will continue well into the future.

By contrast, focusing on the dynamic capabilities of firms shifts the emphasis both to the origins of core competencies as well as to their continued evolution. Managerial and organizational processes shape such dynamic capabilities of enterprises, the endowment of technology and intellectual property, and set of technological trajectories available to the enterprise.

Managerial and organizational processes within an enterprise have been termed by Nelson and Winter (1982) as constituting a *routine*. A routine refers to the 'regular and predictable' aspects regulating the behavior of the firm. Thus, Nelson and Winter (1982: 99) argue that,

> It is easy enough to suggest that a plausible answer to the question, 'Where does the knowledge reside' is 'In the organization's memory.' But where and what is the memory of an organization? We propose that the routinization of activity in an organization constitutes the most important form of storage of the organization's specific organizational knowledge.

The notion of a routine emerges as an organizational mechanism for dealing with Simon's (1957) concept of bounded rationality. Confronted with incomplete information, and ill equipped for digesting an abundance of information—much of it uncertain—organizations resort to their routines for guiding not only actions but also the decision-making process. As the agents employed by an enterprise accumulate experience and knowledge, they incorporate them into the routines characterizing the enterprise and define its core competencies. Nelson and Winter (1982) assume that, although these routines may change in the long run, they are stable over the short and medium run. Most importantly, the routines are stable enough to yield predictions as to how a given enterprise will cope with a change in its external environment.

According to Nelson and Winter (1982), the enterprise can actively engage in searching for new economic knowledge. This function is distinct from that embedded in routines. The two key distinguishing features of what they term as *search* are irreversibility and uncertainty.

The organizational and managerial processes of enterprises provide at least some of the sources of dynamic competence in an organization. This source of competence can come from the way that production is organized by management inside the enterprise (Garvin 1994).

A second source of dynamic capabilities is learning. Cohen and Levinthal (1989) argue that enterprises can influence their ability to adopt new technologies by expanding the boundaries of what they term as absorptive capacity. While R&D and high levels of human capital are generally considered to generate new knowledge, a dual purpose may be served—to assimilate and exploit existing knowledge, or to facilitate the adoption of existing technology. Cohen and Levinthal (1989: 569) argue that, 'While R&D obviously generates innovations, it also develops the firm's ability to identify, assimilate, and exploit knowledge from that environment', what they term as a firm's learning or *absorptive capacity*.

An emerging literature suggests that in order to generate the dynamic capabilities of the type described in the above studies, corporations deploy geographic strategies. For example, Cantwell and Piscitello (1997) find evidence suggesting that multinational corporations are increasingly engaging in foreign direct investment to obtain access to particular knowledge sources at specific locations. According to Cantwell (1998, p. iv), 'Multinational firms have increasingly been able to utilize this locational differentiation between alternative but complementary streams of technological innovation, by constructing a cross-border network as a means of furthering their own recent corporate diversification'.

An earlier line of literature (Buckley and Casson 1976; and Teece 1981) focused on the non-codifiability of knowledge as a motivation for outward foreign direct investment, rather than licensing. As a result of the transfer of technological and other types of know-how from the host country via outward foreign direct investment, Cantwell (1995) has identified the existence of spillovers from the home country to firms in the host country, suggesting that there are externalities associated with inward foreign direct investment.

Cantwell and Noonan (1999) examine the interaction between local firms and large foreign firms engaged in inward direct investment in Germany. They examine the relative technological advantage of indigenous firms and foreign firms within the six most innovative regions of Germany. They find that there is little evidence that the initial technological advantages of indigenous firms in an earlier period influence that of foreign firms in subsequent periods. Similarly, there is no evidence that the initial technological advantages of foreign firms influence the subsequent technological advantages of indigenous firms. Rather, the empirical evidence clearly suggests that the primary determinants of the performance of foreign firms in one period are the success in the previous period. Similarly, the primary determinant of the performance of indigenous firms in one period is the success in the previous period. These results are consistent with the theory of path dependency.

However, knowledge spillovers from the host country to the home country via outward foreign direct investment are less substantiated. According to Blomström and Kokko (1998: 251),

> Although the existing literature on FDI has not discussed the home country effects of foreign investments in terms of productivity spillovers, it is still clear that some of the potential benefits from FDI to the home economy can be interpreted along these lines. In particular, outward FDI focusing on foreign industry clusters with leading technologies may be a way to get access to valuable foreign technology. However, in the home country context, it is often more difficult to identify productivity spillovers.

Analyzing foreign direct investment as a strategy to access localized knowledge spillovers for transfer back to the home country is clearly an important topic that will see considerable attention in the coming years.

Conclusions

There are two important types of conclusions to be reached from the state of knowledge linking management and corporate form to geography. The first involves implications for policy. The second involves the areas and topics where future research is needed.

The first type of conclusion, involving implications for public policy, stems from the fact that globalization combined with the telecommunications revolution has drastically reduced the cost of transporting not just material goods but also information across geographic space. High wages are increasingly incompatible with information-based economic activity, which can be easily transferred to a lower-cost location. By contrast, the creation of new ideas based on tacit knowledge cannot easily be transferred across distance. Thus, the comparative advantage of the high-cost countries of North America and Western

Europe is increasingly based on knowledge-driven innovative activity. The spillover of knowledge from the firm or university creating that knowledge to a third-party firm is essential to innovative activity. Such knowledge spillovers tend to be spatially restricted. Thus, an irony of globalization is that even as the relevant geographic market for most goods and services becomes increasingly global, the increased importance of innovative activity in the leading developed countries has triggered a resurgence in the importance of local regions as a key source of comparative advantage.

As the comparative advantage in Western Europe and North America has become increasingly based on new knowledge, public policy toward business has responded in two fundamental ways. The first has been to shift the policy focus away from the traditional triad of policy instruments essentially constraining the freedom of firms to contract—regulation, competition policy or antitrust in the USA, and public ownership of business. The policy approach of constraint was sensible as long as the major issue was how to restrain footloose multinational corporations in possession of considerable market power. This is reflected by the waves of deregulation and privatization along with the decreased emphasis of competition policy throughout the OECD. Instead, a new policy approach is emerging which focuses on enabling the creation and commercialization of knowledge. Examples of such policies include encouraging R&D, venture capital, and new-firm startups.

The second fundamental shift involves the locus of such enabling policies, which are increasingly at the state, regional, or even local level (Gray and Dunning 1998). Many scholars have interpreted the downsizing of federal agencies charged with the regulation of business in the USA and Great Britain as the eclipse of government intervention. But to interpret deregulation, privatization, and the increased irrelevance of competition policies as the end of government intervention in business ignores an important shift in the locus and target of public policy. The last decade has seen the emergence of a broad spectrum of enabling policy initiatives that fall outside the jurisdiction of the traditional regulatory agencies. Sternberg (1996) documents how the success of a number of different high-technology clusters spanning a number of developed countries is the direct result of enabling policies, such as the provision of venture capital or research support. For example, the Advanced Research Program in Texas has provided support for basic research and the strengthening of the infrastructure of the University of Texas, which has played a central role in developing a high-technology cluster around Austin (Feller 1997). The Thomas Edison Centers in Ohio, the Advanced Technology Centers in New Jersey, and the Centers for Advanced Technology at Case Western Reserve University, Rutgers University, and the University of Rochester have supported generic, pre-competitive research. This support has generally provided diversified technology development, involving a mix of activities encompassing a broad spectrum of industrial collaborators.

Such enabling policies which are typically implemented at the local or regional level are part of a silent policy revolution currently under way. The increased importance of innovative regional clusters as an engine of economic growth has led policy makers to abandon the policy cry frequently heard two decades ago, 'Should we break up, regulate, or simply take over General Motors, IBM and US Steel' for a very different contemporary version, 'How can we grow the next Silicon Valley?'

The second type of conclusion stemming from this chapter involves future research. There are a number of important holes in our knowledge about the management of geographic space as a strategic instrument of corporate and economic policy. The first one involves a more precise understanding of the types of communication and exchange that constitute information and can be transmitted at zero marginal cost across geographic space versus those constituting tacit knowledge, where the cost of transmission across geographic space is prohibitively high. A related issue is the manner in which specific new technologies impact on the classification of particular types of communication between tacit knowledge and information. It may be that firms and agents are learning how to shift tacit knowledge to information in some situations, thus reducing the importance of geographic proximity.

Another topic of importance to future research is how the management of geographic location and proximity varies systematically across industries. Since the role of tacit knowledge and information is not identical in every industry, the role of geographic location and proximity would also be expected to vary systematically across industries. Factors such as the stage of the product life cycle and types of technologies underlying the industry may be important in determining the way that geographic location and proximity are managed for strategic advantage. But these are only speculations. Future research must determine the exact links between organizational structure and the strategic management of geographic location and proximity.

References

Almeida, P., and Kogut, B. 1997. The exploration of technological diversity and the geographic localization of innovation. *Small Business Economics*, 9/1: 21–31.

Arrow, Kenneth, J. 1962. Economic welfare and the allocation of resources for invention. In *The Rate and Direction of Inventive Activity*, ed. R. R. Nelson. Princeton: Princeton University Press, 609–26.

Audretsch, D. B. 1995. *Innovation and Industry Evolution*. Cambridge, Mass.: MIT Press.

——and Feldman, M. P. 1996. R&D spillovers and the geography of innovation and production. *American Economic Review*, 86/3 (June): 630–40.

——and Stephan, P. E. 1996. Company-scientist locational links: the case of biotechnology. *American Economic Review*, 86/3 (June): 641–52.

Berman, E., Bound J., and Machin, S. 1997. Implications of skill-biased technological change: international evidence. Working Paper 6166, National Bureau of Economic Research (NBER), Cambridge, Mass.

Blomström, M., and Kokko, A. 1998. Multinational corporations and spillovers. *Journal of Economic Surveys*, 12/3: 247–77.

Buckley, Peter J. 1997. International technology transfer by small and medium-sized enterprises. *Small Business Economics*, 9/1: 67–78.

——and Casson, M. 1976. *The Future of the Multinational Enterprise*. London: Macmillan.

Cantwell, J. 1995. The globalization of technology: what remains of the product cycle model?' *Cambridge Journal of Economics*, 19: 155–74.

——1998. Technology and the firm: introduction. *Research Policy*, 27, pp. iii–v.

——and Iammarino, S. 1998. MNCs, technological innovation and regional systems in the EU: some evidence in the Italian case. *International Journal of the Economics of Business*, 5/3: 383–408.

——and Noonan, C. 1999. The regional distribution of technological development by foreign-owned firms in Germany. Paper presented at the International Conference on 'Knowledge Spillovers and the Geography of Innovation: A Comparison of National Systems of Innovation.' St Etienne, July.

——and Piscitello, L. 1997. Accumulating technological competence—its changing impact on corporate diversification and internationalisation. Discussion Papers in International Investment and Management, University of Reading, No. 232.

Chandler, A. D., Jr. 1977. *The Visible Hand: The Managerial Revolution in American Business*. Cambridge, Mass.: Harvard University Press.

——1990. *Scale and Scope*. Cambridge, Mass.: Harvard University Press.

Cohen, W., and Levinthal, D. 1989. Innovation and learning: the two faces of R&D. *Economic Journal*, 99/3: 569–96.

Dunning, J. 1981. *International Production and the Multinational Enterprise*. London: George Allen & Unwin.

——1993. *Multinational Enterprises and the Global Economy*, Boston: Addison-Wesley.

Eden, L., Levitas, E., and Martinez, R. J. 1997. The production, transfer and spillover of technology: comparing large and small multinationals as technology producers. *Small Business Economics*, 9/1: 53–66.

Feldman, M. 1994*a*. Knowledge complementarity and innovation. *Small Business Economics*, 6/3: 363–72.

Feldman, M. 1994*b*. *The Geography of Innovation*. Boston: Kluwer.

——and Audretsch, D. 1999. Science-based diversity, specialization, localized competition and innovation. *European Economic Review*, 43: 409–29.

Feller, Irwin 1997. Federal and state government roles in science and technology. *Economic Development Quarterly*, 11/4: 283–96.

Garvin, D. 1994. The process of organization and management. Harvard Business School Working Paper No. 94-084.

Glaeser, E., Kallal, H., Scheinkman, J., and Shleifer, A. 1992. Growth of cities. *Journal of Political Economy*, 100: 1126–52.

Gomes-Casseres, B. 1997. Alliance strategies of small firms. *Small Business Economics*, 33–44.

Gray, H. Peter, and Dunning, J. H. 1998. Towards a theory of regional policy. Unpublished manuscript, Rutgers University.

Griliches, Z. 1992. The search for R&D spill-overs. *Scandanavian Journal of Economics*, 94(S): 29–47.

Gruber, W. H., Mehta, D., and Vernon, R. 1967. The R&D factor in international trade and international investment of the United States. *Journal of Political Economy*, 75 (Feb.): 20–37.

Hymer, S. 1976. *The International Operations of National Firms: A Study of Direct Foreign Investment*, Cambridge, Mass.: MIT Press.

—— and Rowthorn, R. 1970. Multinational corporations and international oligopoly: the non-American challenge. In *The International Corporation*, ed. C. P. Kindelberger. Cambridge, Mass.: MIT Press.

Iansiti, M., and Clark, K. 1994. Integration and dynamic capability: evidence from product development in automobiles and mainframe computers. *Industrial and Corporate Change*, 3/3: 557–605.

Jacobs, J. 1969. *The Economy of Cities*. New York: Random House.

Jaffe, A. 1989. Real effects of academic research. *American Economic Review*, 79: 957–70.

—— Trajtenberg, M., and Henderson, R. 1993. Geographic localization of knowledge spillovers as evidenced by patent citations. *Quarterly Journal of Economics*, 63: 577–98.

Kindleberger, C. P., and Audretsch, D. B. 1984. *The Multinational Corporation in the 1980s*. Cambridge, Mass.: MIT Press.

Kogut, Bruce, and Zander, Udo 1992. Knowledge of the firm, combinative capabilities, and the replication of technology. *Organization Science*, 46/1: 143–62.

Kortum, S., and Lerner, J. 1997. Stronger protection or technological revolution: what is behind the recent surge in patenting? Working Paper 6204, National Bureau of Economic Research (NBER), Cambridge, Mass.

Kozul-Wright, R., and Rowthorn, R. 1998. Spoilt for choice? Multinational corporations and the geography of international production. *Oxford Review of Economic Policy*, 14/2: 74–92.

Krugman, P. 1991. *Geography and Trade*. Cambridge, Mass.: MIT Press.

Leamer, E. E. 1984. *Sources of International Comparative Advantage: Theory and Evidence*. Cambridge, Mass.: MIT Press.

Loveman, G., and Sengenberger, W. 1991. The re-emergence of small-scale production: an international perspective. *Small Business Economics*, 3/1: 1–38.

Magee, S. P. 1989. The competence theory of comparative advantage. In *The Internationalization of U.S. Markets*, ed. D. B. Audretsch and M. P. Claudon. New York: New York University Press, 11–24.

Nelson, R. R., and Winter, S. G. 1982. *An Evolutionary Theory of Economic Change*. Cambridge, Mass.: Harvard University Press.

Penrose, E. T. 1959. *The Theory of the Growth of the Firm*. Oxford: Basil Blackwell.

Piore, M. J., and Sabel, C. F. 1984. *The Second Industrial Divide*. New York: Basic Books.

Porter, M. 1990. *The Comparative Advantage of Nations*. New York: Free Press.

Reich, R. B. 1983. *The Next American Frontier*. New York: Times Books.

Romer, P. M. 1994. The origins of endogenous growth. *Journal of Economic Perspectives*, 8/1 (winter): 3–22.

ROWTHORN, R. 1992. Intra-industry trade and investment under oligopoly: the role of market size. *The Economic Journal*, 102/411: 402–14.

SAXENIAN, A. 1990. Regional networks and the resurgence of Silicon Valley. *California Management Review*, 33: 89–111.

SCHERER, F. M. 1970. *Industrial Market Structure and Economic Performance*. Chicago: Rand McNally.

SIMON, HERBERT A. 1957. *Models of Man*. New York: John Wiley.

STERNBERG, R. 1996. Technology policies and the growth of regions. *Small Business Economics*, 8/2: 75–86.

TEECE, D. J. 1981. The market for know-how and the efficient international transfer of technology. *The Annals of the American Academy of Political and Social Science*, 458: 81–96.

—— and PISANO, G. 1994. The dynamic capabilities of firms. *Industrial and Corporate Change*, 3: 537–56.

VAN DIJK, M. P. 1995. Flexible specialisation, the new competition and industrial districts. *Small Business Economics*, 7/1: 15–28.

VENABLES, A. J. 1996. Localization of industry and trade performance. *Oxford Review of Economic Policy*, 12/3: 52–60.

VON HIPPLE, E. 1994. Sticky information and the locus of problem solving: implications for innovation. *Management Science*, 40: 429–39.

Part IV

The Geography of Innovation

Section 8

National and Localized Learning

Chapter **18**

Nation States and Economic Development: From National Systems of Production to National Systems of Knowledge Creation and Learning

Bengt-Åke Lundvall and Peter Maskell

> . . . social invention, is an indispensable prerequisite for modern economic growth.
>
> (Kuznets 1960: 32)

Introduction

More than forty years ago most mainstream neo-classical theorizing could rightly be accused of residing in a 'wonderland of no spatial dimensions' (Isard 1956: 25). Things have changed since then, but not much. Though implicitly present in any neo-classical macro analysis of the open economy, spatially defined entities still appear explicitly only in trade theory. Even in the emerging literature on 'increasing returns endogenous growth' it is usually assumed that national differences in institutions, structure, and culture can safely be disregarded as their impact on innovations, investments, and economic growth is considered trivial or negligible.

It is our assertion that not all combinations of institutions, structures, and culture are equally prone to enhance a nation's economic growth and that old and new growth theories alike still grossly underestimate the importance of specific institutions, structures, and cultures for a nation's long-term economic performance.

The experience of small, open economies may be especially relevant in this context (Menzel 1980; Senghaas 1982). What exactly might be meant by 'small' or 'large' countries is, however, the object of long-standing differences of opinion. In his influential analysis, Katzenstein (1985) links the size of the national economy with an inclination towards a policy of free trade and openness, and a strong affinity towards corporatism, resulting from a general perception in small countries of common fate and the spread of common fears. Additionally, he detects in the small countries a penchant for neutrality; a weakness of the political right; a dependence on foreign capital to supplement internal savings, and a tenor of domestic political stability induced by the need to secure access to export markets. As a response to their position in the international economy, small countries have developed specific institutions to maintain competitiveness in key industries and mechanisms compensating domestic losers when readjustment becomes necessary because of imported disruptions.

In contrast to their larger counterparts, small nations are generally characterized by the absence of scale economies and, with few exceptions, by being specialized in low-technology products (see Table 18.1), normally characterized by slow growth in terms of technological opportunities and market volume (Freeman and Lundvall 1988). In spite of these apparent handicaps many smaller nations have successfully matched the bigger countries in terms of income per capita, and sometimes even outstripped them (Maskell *et al.* 1998).

In the following sections we will focus on some recent theoretical approaches all trying to come to grips with this 'unexplained' portion of growth differences between nations, by giving prominence to factors that distinguish each nation from all others.

First, we consider an approach that gives emphasis to the production structure (National System of Production). Secondly, we will discuss one that emphasizes the institutional set-up (National Business Systems). Thirdly, we introduce National Innovation Systems as an attempt to integrate the analysis of structural and institutional characteristics. Finally, we argue that the next step must include analysing and comparing 'national systems of knowledge creation and learning', focusing on the fundamental role of intellectual, social, and natural capital.

National Systems of Production

The first major attempt to put the nation state at the centre of economic development and analysis goes back more than 150 years to Friedrich List (1841) who contrasted his own national system approach with what he characterized as Adam Smith's 'cosmopolitan' approach. Behind his criticism of Adam Smith there was a mixture of political and analytical differences.

List identified himself with the need for the rising German state and for the

Table 18.1. Some key data for groups of nations, 1992

	Large nations	Medium-sized nations	Small nations Non-Nordic	Small nations Nordic
GDP per capita (US$)	22,887	18,910	16,725	25,843
Openness ((exports/imports)/ manufacturing production)	11	28	50	42
Exports				
High-tech products	26%	13%	9%	11%
Medium high-tech products	50%	48%	38%	33%
Medium low-tech products	10%	15%	15%	16%
Low-tech products	14%	24%	38%	40%
Production				
High-tech products	13%	7%	6%	6%
Medium high-tech products	32%	31%	19%	22%
Medium low-tech products	18%	22%	25%	21%
Low-tech products	37%	40%		50%
GERD (Gross domestic expenditure on R&D) as percentage of GDP	2.79	2.11	1.60	2.43

Note: 'Large nations' include the USA and Japan (both with an annual output exceeding US$2,750 billion and more than 100 million inhabitants); 'Medium-sized nations' include Germany, the UK, Italy, France, and Spain (all with an annual output exceeding US$275 billion and with 30–100 million inhabitants); 'Small nations' include Canada, Australia, New Zealand, Austria, Belgium, the Netherlands, Greece, Portugal, and the five Nordic nations: Sweden, Denmark, Finland, Norway, and Iceland (all small nations with an annual output of less than US$275 billion and with less than 30 million inhabitants). Together, these twenty OECD countries account for roughly 70% of the world economy, whether measured by production volume, value added, or exports.

Sources: The OECD structural analyses database (STAN) and OECD (1997).

USA to catch up with England, but he also had original theoretical ideas. He juxtaposed the mechanisms that secured an efficient allocation of resources in the short run ('theory of value') with those that contributed to the long-term economic development ('theory of productive forces'). He argued that Smith only contributed to the analysis of the first type of mechanisms. In order to understand the creation of new productive forces, he argued, it is necessary to bring in the nation state and national institutions explicitly.[1]

[1] List has become known mainly as an economist in favour of protectionism and for his 'infant industry' argument for protectionism. However, as pointed out by Freeman (1995*a*), his work may be regarded as the first major contribution to the literature on National Innovation Systems. He emphasizes the need for lagging countries to invest in training, to extend their knowledge base, and to build infrastructures at the level of the nation state in order to catch up. Like the contemporary inventors and users of endogenous growth models, List did, however, not believe in the viability of small nation states (Hobsbawm 1990). We submit that on this point they are wrong (see below).

In the 1960s and 1970s, French structuralist economists developed an analysis of national systems of production that was rooted in the Marxian reproduction schemes. They assumed that different sectors affect growth differently and that the most dynamic elements in the system were located upstream. This led them into ordering national systems in a hierarchy. It was assumed that countries such as the USA and Germany had a stronger economy than France because their production systems were specialized in the production of machinery to produce machinery (machine tools), while France was specialized in the production of machinery for the production of semi-manufactured goods (GRESI 1976). It also led them to recommend developing countries to establish, at an early stage, activities belonging to the sector producing machinery (Bernis 1966).

The basic mechanisms involved were not always made clear but the general idea was that the strong presence of a sector that produces machinery to produce machinery makes it easier to develop new process technology for the whole production system. Some economists tried to develop this approach further using input–output analysis (Brookfield 1975). Others applied a more dynamic approach to vertical linkages in the production system and got closer to development issues (Dahmén 1950; Hirschman 1958; Stewart 1977). Dahmén and Hirschman, in particular, introduced the conscious creation of disequilibria as an important element in the promotion of the development process.

These different perspectives were brought together and combined with a life-cycle perspective on national systems by Esben Sloth Andersen in a number of publications in Danish in the late 1970s (Andersen 1978, 1979). Some of the ideas were later presented for an international audience in Andersen and Lundvall (1988) and Andersen (1992). Andersen significantly revised the French approach. First, he introduced the importance of backward linkages in the form of flows of information from user sectors. Secondly, he introduced both learning by doing and searching in the model. Thirdly, he made a distinction between different stages in the development of industrial complexes as seen from a life-cycle perspective. Fourthly, he introduced, explicitly, the open economy as an analytical framework.

With these revisions, the focus was now, explicitly, on the development of new technology in an interaction between user sectors and producer sectors. The *quality* of demand became an important element in the process. And, while the approach of the French structuralists left small countries very limited prospects in terms of growth and wealth, as does the new growth theory today, Andersen's revision pointed to a less gloomy future for these countries by emphasizing the *qualitative characteristics* of the home market.

However, because of its focus on production and intellectual capital, the National Production System approach has little to say about the role of institutions for economic growth. One way of introducing the institutional dimension is to focus on how firms and markets are organized in different countries. This is the approach of the National Business System literature, to which we shall turn next.

National Business Systems

The central concern of the business system approach (Whitley 1994*a*, 1994*b*, 1996) is to explain international differences in the diversity of firm activities and the extent to which radical discontinuities occur over time in firms' activities and capabilities. The focus is on the co-ordination of economic activities and on governance issues. National differences in the organization of firms and markets are explained by differences in culture and in formal institutions.

One important implication of the analysis is that there is no single, best practice, mode of organization of the firm. Another important point is that it is not true that 'anything goes' when different organizational traits are combined. Some combinations are easier to establish than others. 'Remote property rights owners' and 'market-based financial systems' will, for instance, typically be combined with 'isolation of economic actors', while 'credit-based systems' and 'a culture making it easy to establish trust between non-kin' will favour 'industrial networking'.

The approach of National Business Systems is interdisciplinary, combining elements of economic reasoning with sociological perspectives. The starting point is a sociological perspective on business activities (Whitley 1987) and one important historical reference is to Maurice *et al.* (1986). The specification of the analytical elements has been inspired by analyses of the newly industrialized Asian countries such as that of Hamilton and Biggart (1988). However, there are also references to theoretical work by some of the most important heterodox industrial economists such as Penrose (1959/1995) and Richardson (1972).

In its initial formulation (Whitley 1994*a*), the model of National Business Systems was extremely complex, making it difficult to identify the most important, among the model's many possible causal relationships. Most variables were, furthermore, multidimensional: they could not be reduced to one indicator or to one scale, but frequently implied two or more analytical dimensions.

The problems of introducing so many and such relatively diffuse variables in an explanatory scheme were addressed by Whitley (1996), simplifying the model in important respects and strongly reducing the number of causal relationships. The two initial sets of exogenous variables were brought together into one set and the number of dependent variables cut from thirteen to five. Of the background institutions representing a nation's cultural endowment, only one remains: 'Strength of institutions governing trust relations

Institutional features (x)
Strength of institutions governing trust relationships and extra-family collective loyalties
Extent to which state dominates economic systems
Level of state risk-sharing with private economic actors
State support for intermediate associations and inter-firm co-operation
Formal regulation of market boundaries, entry, and exit
Credit-based financial system
Significance of labour movement in strategic decision-making
Centralization of bargaining and negotiation
Collaboration in skill training and certification

Characteristics of economic actors (y)
Diversity of activities and capabilities co-ordinated through authoritative communication
Extent of radical discontinuities in activities and capabilities over time
Isolation of economic actors from other organizations and agencies
Delegation of control to salaried manager
Dominance of growth goals with weak profit constraints

Fig. 18.1. The basic causal relationships in the new National Business Systems approach

Source: Whitley (1996).

and extra-family collective loyalties'. In addition, the line of reasoning was simplified.

A strategic intermediate variable is 'the degree of isolation of the firm' and this variable is assumed to reflect national institutions governing trust as well as the type of credit system. The basic line of reasoning is the following: in nations where the institutional set-up supports the establishment of trust between non-kin agents, and especially where this is combined with a credit-based financial system, firms will tend to be involved in co-operative networks. *Therefore, they will be able to share their risks with network partners.*

In such an economy, firms will not fear the potentially damaging consequences of a high degree of specialization and division of labour, and their expansion will be based on incremental growth in terms of capabilities and assets. Government support for inter-firm co-operation will reinforce these characteristics. It is also assumed that a strong position of labour in the National Business System reduces the risk of radical discontinuities by establishing a barrier to mergers.

It might be assumed that the specific design of National Business Systems will have a substantial impact on economic growth but it is probably fair to say that the relationship has not yet been sufficiently spelled out.[2]

[2] Other analyses of national governance systems go further in this respect (Freeman 1987). The Japanese success in specific production fields has, for instance by Tylecote (1994), been explained by its governance form, emphasizing the Japanese business system's predilection for long-term commitments as opposed to Anglo-Saxon short-termism. Others emphasize how the internal organization of the Japanese firm promotes rapid product innovation and high quality output in specific sectors (Clark and Fujimoto 1991; Fransman 1995).

National Innovation Systems

From Innovation as an Interactive Process to Innovation Systems

While the National Production System approach neglected the institutional dimension, the major limitation of the National Business System approach is that it neglects the national production structure. No consideration is given to the fact that the organization of firms and markets differs between sectors, reflecting the prevailing technologies and their specificities. The causal relationships going from the production structure to the organizational and the institutional level are neglected.

It may be argued that the National Innovation System approach represents a kind of synthesis of National Production Systems and National Business Systems in the sense that it tries to capture the co-evolution of structural and institutional characteristics in a systemic perspective. However, the literature on National Innovation Systems is diverse. Different scholars have approached the phenomenon by different tracks (McKelvey 1991). There is not, as in the National Business Systems literature, one standard reference and there are significant nuances in the interpretation of the concept among leading scholars. The set of publications captured by a recent bibliographic search[3] illustrates how the concept of National Innovation Systems has stimulated efforts to locate *regional*, *technological*, as well as *sectoral* systems of innovation.

The concept 'innovation system' was first introduced in a booklet on user–producer interaction in the middle of the 1980s (Lundvall 1985: 55) to capture the relationships and interactions between R&D laboratories and technological institutes, on the one hand, and the production system, on the other.[4] In this context, it was also referred to as 'the innovative capacity of national systems of production' (Lundvall 1985: 66). The first widely disseminated publication applying the concept of National Innovation Systems was the analysis of Japan by Christopher Freeman (1987). The concept was definitely established as a result of the collaboration between Freeman, Nelson, and Lundvall in the collective work on technology and economic theory (Dosi *et al.* 1988).[5]

The National Innovation Systems approach gained ground as previous prevailing theories were discredited by empirical findings through the 1970s

[3] The search, though preliminary, came up with 255 titles that explicitly make use of the concept 'innovation system'. Of these, 30 were published before 1992 and about the same number has been forthcoming in each of the following years, until 1997, when the number of annual publications reached 40.

[4] The concept was, however, implicit in the National Production Systems approach developed by Andersen at the end of the 1970s.

[5] More recent contributions are Lundvall (1992), Nelson (1993), Edquist (1997), and Boyer *et al.* (1997). Porter (1990) did not explicitly use the concept but his approach is akin in important respects.

and 1980s. Attempts to reduce the driving force behind innovation to either demand or supply factors were unsuccessful. The Sappho study pursued by Freeman and his colleagues at Science Policy Research Unit (SPRU) at the beginning of the 1970s (Rothwell 1977) had already given strong support for the idea that success in innovation has to do with long-term relationships and close interaction with external agents. The presentation of 'the chain-linked model', by Kline and Rosenberg (1986), was important because it gave a specific form to an alternative to the cherished linear model, where new technology is assumed to develop directly on the basis of scientific efforts, and, thereafter, to be materialized in new marketed products. On the contrary, empirical studies revealed how innovations reflect a process where feedbacks from the market and knowledge inputs from users interact with knowledge creation and entrepreneurial initiatives on the supply side. All this constituted the first step towards the development of the idea of National Innovation Systems.

The second step was to realize that the relationships and interactions between agents had to involve non-market relationships. These relationships were presented as *organized markets* with elements of power, trust, and loyalty (Lundvall 1985). These relationships of co-ordination and co-operation were identified as the only possible solution to the conundrum of product innovations: on the one hand, pure market interactions were found incapable of transmitting the qualitative information between users and producers. On the other hand, the transformation of markets into hierarchies proposed by transaction cost theory did not materialize.

The third step was to realize that different national contexts offered disparate possibilities for establishing organized markets. A series of studies pointed, for instance, to the long-term development of selective inter-firm relationships in Japan and contrasted them with the arm's length relationships predominating in the Anglo-Saxon countries (Dore 1986; Sako 1990). Other important differences between nations were found in the organization of the financial markets, the interaction between universities and industry, the education and training system, and the kind of interaction it fostered among specialists, and so on, which was gradually incorporated into the National Innovation Systems approach.

Within the National Innovation Systems approach, Johnson (1992) and Edquist and Johnson (1997) represent the most developed understanding yet of organizations and institutions, understood as norms, habits, and rules. There is a fundamental difference in the perspective chosen in these contributions and the ones of the National Business Systems approach. While Whitley and his colleagues employ institutions and culture to explain business organization, Edquist and Johnson are primarily interested in how institutions and organizations affect innovation performance. Four kinds of institutions are especially important in the context of learning and innovation: the *time horizon* of agents, the role of *trust*, the *actual mix of rationality*, and the way *authority* is expressed.

The now almost generally accepted distinction between a more short-term perspective as characterizing corporate governance in Anglo-Saxon countries and a more long-term one in, for instance, Japanese investment decisions is one important example of how institutional differences have had a decisive influence on the conduct and performance at national level.

Trust is a multidimensional and complex concept. It refers to mutual expectations regarding consistency in behaviour and full, truthful revelation of relevant information and to loyalty in difficult times. Trust can be very local or it can be extended to a wider set of actors. The strength, the extension, and the kind of trust embedded in markets will affect transaction costs and this will determine to what degree interactive learning can take place in connection with the market relationship.

Economic transactions in the form of single and isolated exchange acts in a capitalist environment tend to support patterns of behaviour corresponding to instrumental rationality. When we take into account the importance of learning, including learning new skills through interaction with other agents, it is no longer the only generalized kind of behaviour that will establish itself. Learning, and especially learning tacit skills in an interaction with others, will not thrive in a context where the individuals involved are driven by instrumental rationality.

Finally, it is necessary to consider different forms of 'authority' in connection with industrial relations and also in relation to organizations. As pointed out by Polanyi (1966), the learning of new skills will typically take place in the context of a master–apprenticeship relationship where a mixture of trust and authority is necessary. In traditional societies, age and seniority play a key role in establishing authority, in others, the control of financial resources might substitute for these, and in yet others the key to authority may be merits in terms of knowledge and skills.

It is important to note that all these four 'institutions' are more easily undermined than produced anew and that they form different dimensions of what has been coined 'social capital'. They are especially important when it comes to understanding international differences in learning regimes and learning styles.

Structure and Specialization

Some authors, especially coming from, or inspired by, the US Science and Technology tradition, tend to regard the concept of National Innovation Systems simply as a follow-up and an incremental broadening of earlier analyses of national science systems and national technology policies (Mowery and Oxley 1995). To them, the key issue is to map indicators of national specialization and performance regarding innovation, R&D efforts, and the science and technological set-up. They are reluctant to emphasize too strongly the national dimension since they see it as evoking a threat in terms of increased techno-nationalism.

In contrast, the 'European' approach to National Innovation Systems developed by Christopher Freeman (1987) and the 'Aalborg group' (see Lundvall 1985 and Lundvall 1992) goes further. In particular, it takes as its starting point the fact that important parts of the knowledge base are tacit and emanate from routine-based learning-by-doing, learning-by-using, and learning-by-interacting, and not only from search activities related to science and technology. The differences between the US and the European approach might reflect some characteristic features of the scholars' home base. Both agree that economic performance is based on the national knowledge base. In small and even in medium-sized countries, it is, however, obvious that formalized scientific knowledge does not constitute the most important source of economic growth (Maskell 1998*a*; Maskell *et al.* 1998). In a big country, such as the USA, with dominating firms operating at the technological and scientific frontier, this is far less evident.

The pivotal constituent in the 'European version' of the National Innovation Systems approach, pursued in this chapter, is the specific national *interaction* between the prevailing economic structure and the institutional set-up. The fundamental assumption is that interactive learning is rooted in routine activities, and most search activities will be oriented towards problems emanating from the existing set of economic activities. It should not be too controversial to claim that *the economic structure* differs between countries. If institutions define *how things are done* and how learning takes place, it is the economic structure that affects *what is done* and therefore what is learnt.

By using a combination of trade specialization data and patenting data, recent research has proved the existence of such a correlation between a nation's pattern of specialization in production and trade, on the one hand, and the national knowledge base on the other (Archibugi and Pianta 1992). A nation's economic structure and its specific economic activities thus reflect accumulated national learning while at the same time pointing to the route of future learning and innovation.

Among those scholars who recognize that national differences are important, some have argued that the differences emanate mainly from structural characteristics (Breschi and Malerba 1997), while others are assuming the reverse causality thus analysing how national institutional specificities affect the location of certain industries (Guerreri and Tylecote 1997). Both these perspectives capture important characteristics of industrial dynamics at the national level. It is reasonable to assume that the historical pattern of specialization has affected the institutional set-up through a composition effect. Once a dominating specific institutional pattern has been established, it will attract those industries most compatible with it. The two perspectives converge in demonstrating the *interdependence* of the two dimensions in the innovation system: the economic structure and the institutions.

Some care should, nevertheless, be exercised to avoid simplistic functionalist reasoning. In fact, the main reason for differences in performance between national systems may be that the degree of *matching* between structure and institutions differs among countries (Freeman 1995*b*). Institutions may be rooted far back in social history and they may be slow to adapt to the change in economic structure. Therefore no one-to-one correlation should be expected, and empirical studies continuously add to our understanding of why a complete match is seldom found and how different degrees of mismatch affect the performance of systems of innovation. Mismatches and tensions between structure and institutions may hamper economic growth but they may also be regarded as the fundamental motor behind social and economic change in innovation systems. A classical example of how a lack of social invention hampered economic growth was the British problems with establishing new institutions and organizations that could support the new growth industries related to steel and chemistry (Freeman 1995*a*). An example of how a crisis and a mismatch triggered a successful social invention was the establishment of a democratic and popular training system in Denmark inspired by Grundtvig in the last part of the nineteenth century.

Globalization and National Innovation Systems

The rediscovery of the magnitude of globalization before World War I[6] reveals that transnational markets are delicate arrangements that might break down at some point in the future. Not only military action but also less dramatic incidents such as congestion, infrastructure under-investments, and trade wars may raise the relative cost of transporting tangible or intangible goods and thereby reverse the process of globalization. Even if no such event occurs, any reduction in the cost of producing a good will, of course, make its movement over space *relatively* more expensive. Continued globalization thus hinges on the prospect of matching any future cost-saving improvement in production with an equally cost-saving improvement in transportation and communication.

Though the present process of globalization shares important features with

[6] See e.g. Feis (1934), Bairoch (1996), and Maddison (1991).

the pre-World War 1 'empire' model of internationalization, it also contains genuinely novel elements such as the new 'ethos of globalization' that makes many former national loyalties dwindle. Consumers increasingly choose commodities primarily based on price, quality, and reputation (brand), making considerations of producer nationality of secondary importance. International business standards, insurance systems, and banking facilities for swift and secure transfer of payments have also contributed to a considerable transformation and growth in transnational interaction on most business-to-business markets. Moreover, investments and innovations in transport and communication systems, and the success of governmental efforts to remove most former barriers to trade (General Agreement on Tariffs and Trade (GATT), World Trade Organization (WTO)), have jointly made national frontiers more porous.

It may be considered a paradox that analytical concepts, such as National Innovation Systems and National Business Systems, are increasingly adopted both by analysts and policy-makers in a period where globalization and integration seem to be accelerating. However, no such paradox or conflict exists. The reason is that competitiveness[7] can only be built on heterogeneity: on firms having control over something wanted by others or by firms being able to do something that the competitors cannot do as well, as fast, or as cheap. Little progress would be made in a world of clones. Or in the words of Alfred Marshall: 'Every locality has incidents of its own which affect in various ways the methods of arrangement of every class of business that is carried on in it . . . The tendency to variation is the chief cause of progress' (Marshall 1890: 355).

The process of globalization simply compels firms and governments alike to focus on the remaining *localized* (immobile) capabilities: the ones that have not yet become *ubiquitous*, equally available to firms regardless of their location (Maskell *et al.* 1998).

National Innovation Systems are, by definition, localized and immobile and thus able to provide firms with valuable capabilities and framework conditions *not available* to competitors located abroad, even under the most open market conditions imaginable. In an age of accelerating globalization, National Innovation Systems thereby play an increasingly crucial role by *preserving heterogeneity* across space. Careful governmental intervention might, furthermore, rectify identified weaknesses in the nationally specific interaction between structure and institutions (i.e. the core of National Innovation Systems), adding to the variation in the business environment between nations.

[7] Competitiveness may be defined as 'the ability of companies, industries, regions, nations or super-national areas to generate, while being and remaining exposed to international competition, relatively high factor income and factor employment levels on a sustainable basis' (Hatzichronoglou 1996).

Summing Up and the Challenges Ahead

In the preceding sections, we have tried to demonstrate the usefulness of an approach that puts the interaction between structure and institutions at the centre of the analysis. Systemic features that differ between countries are important in explaining differences in dynamic conduct and performance.

The National Innovation Systems approach is, however, not completed once and for all, and at least three aspects of contemporary economic development deserve closer attention in the future: the role of knowledge, learning, and innovation; the role of social capital; and the role of the natural environment. In the remaining part of this chapter, each of these challenges will be considered in turn.

When the elimination of former international barriers to trade confront firms in high-cost nations with new competitors with lower labour costs, some firms react by raising their capital–labour ratio and others by outsourcing or relocating activities to low-cost areas. An increasing number of firms in high-cost environments have, however, met the challenge differently, by pursuing dynamic improvements through enhanced knowledge creation (Nonaka 1991; Spender 1994; Gibbons *et al.* 1994). The resulting very rapid rate of change gives a premium to those who are swift learners (Johnson and Lundvall 1994; Maskell and Malmberg 1999). This is reflected in the forms of organization inside firms, new mixes of co-operation and competition, as well as in new forms of governance. So far, the studies of National Innovation Systems have given too little emphasis to the subsystem related to human resource development. This includes formal education and training, the labour market dynamics, and the organization of knowledge creation and learning within firms and in networks. This subsystem will be confronted with very strong needs for social invention in the near future in all national systems and quite a lot of the peculiarities of national systems are rooted in this subsystem.

At a more aggregate level, globalization has dramatically enhanced the importance of what modern authors (Bourdieu 1977; Coleman 1988, 1990; Burt 1992; Putnam 1993; Fukuyama 1995; Woolcock 1998) have called *social capital*, which enables firms to exchange knowledge and conduct other business transactions without much fuss. Historically this kind of localized resource has constituted the major comparative advantage of certain small nations (Kuznets 1960), and possibly also of some subnational regions like the Italian industrial districts (Malmberg and Maskell 1997). Seen from the perspective of National Innovation Systems, a major role of the nation state may, actually, be to accumulate, reproduce, and protect valuable social capital—some of which might originate from local pre-industrial traditions (Maskell 1998*b*). The dissimilar form and unequal distribution of social capital across nations might thus account for at least some national differences in economic growth rates that remain unexplained by old and new growth theories.[8]

Such nationally specific social capital accumulated through the years might easily be eroded with the formation of broader territorial entities such as, for instance, the European Union:

> . . . the institutions of the highly organized welfare state give an indication of how many national ties need to be complemented by corresponding international ties in order to approach international integration. The welfare idea is so deeply rooted that its manifestations within the national framework can be superseded only by corresponding institutions of an international welfare community. How this can be made is an important subject for investigation. (Svennilson 1960: 9–10)

Forty years later it remains an important theoretical and practical task to find out how social capital can be reproduced at the transnational European level. The lack of consensus regarding the strengthening of the social dimension of the European project might be seen as an indicator of these difficulties. Furthermore, the popular resistance to the European project in many quarters might also be less irrational and nostalgic than it appears: it reflects, at least in part, the insight that the direct access of vested interests to the European bureaucracy and the lack of democratic transparency are factors hampering the accumulation of social capital, thereby weakening the economic foundation of some of the small nations.

Finally, National Innovation Systems can be regarded as a tool for analysing economic development and economic growth. It has in common with growth accounting that it tries to bring together the major factors that affect technical progress as registered in standard neo-classical growth models. Such a perspective may be too narrow, however, and as pointed out by Freeman (1997), the ecological challenge ought to be integrated in any strategy for economic development.

Table 18.2 illustrates that economic growth is faced with a double challenge in terms of sustainability and that there is an immanent risk of undermining not only the material basis of material production.[9] The creation of tangible

[8] Scholars have interpreted 'social capital' in different ways, sometimes regarding the 'civic networks' as its core, and thus in conflict with the extension of the welfare state. Our understanding is closer to the definition of Woolcock (1998), who distinguishes between micro- and state-level relationships. Somewhat parallel to Woolcock's (1998: 180) 'beneficent autonomy' we conceive social capital as fundamentally supportive of, rather than undermining, the design of welfare state policies in small and economically successful nations. We also regard the production of 'intellectual capital' as highly dependent on the stock and reproduction of 'social capital', regardless of how far globalization might progress.

[9] The 'model' indicated in the table is closely related to the growth model by Irma Adelman (1963: 9) referred to by Freeman (1997: 9). The major difference is that labour is not introduced in our table. This reflects the fact that we do not regard labour as a resource on the same lines as the four kinds of 'capital'. The human factor is the one that puts in motion, integrates, and coordinates the different kinds of capital.

Table 18.2. Resources fundamental for economic growth: combining the tangible and reproducible dimensions

	Reproducible resources	Non-reproducible resources
Tangible resources	1. Production capital	2. Natural capital
Intangible resources	3. Intellectual capital	4. Social capital

capital may also be threatened by a neglect of environmental sustainability. We would argue that the production and efficient use of intellectual capital is fundamentally dependent upon social capital in terms of trust, a long-run perspective, authority, and discursive rationality. Technical innovation, for instance in terms of developing substitutes to natural raw products, may help to overcome the fact that natural capital cannot be reproduced. Social innovation and institutional design may help to overcome a crisis where the social capital is foundering.

In both cases, it is important to note that the workings of unhampered market forces will erode the basis of economic growth. This perspective indicates a broader and more interdisciplinary approach to economic growth than prevails within mainstream economics. It also differs in being more explicit in terms of the institutional assumptions made and especially in avoiding any assumption about factors being independent. This reflects the perspective of National Innovation Systems with its emphasis on virtuous and vicious circles or match and mismatch between elements and subsystems.

References

Adelman, I. 1963. *Theories of Economic Growth and Development.* Stanford, Calif.: Stanford University Press.

Andersen, E. S. 1978. *Industriel udvikling og industrikrise.* Serie om industriel udvikling no. 4. Aalborg: Aalborg Universitetsforlag.

—— 1979. *Industriel udvikling og international konkurrenceevne.* Serie om industriel udvikling no. 6. Aalborg: Aalborg Universitetsforlag.

—— 1992. Approaching national innovation systems. In Lundvall 1992.

—— and Lundvall, B.-Å. 1988. Small national innovation systems facing technological revolutions: an analytical framework. In Freeman and Lundval 1988.

—— —— 1997. National innovation systems and the dynamics of the division of labor. In Edquist 1997.

Archibugi, D., and Michie, J. 1995. The globalization of technology: a new taxonomy. In *Cambridge Journal of Economics*, 19/1: 121–40.

—— and Pianta, M. 1992. *The Technological Specialization of Advanced Countries.* Dordrecht: Kluwer Academic Publishers.

Bairoch, P. 1996. Globalization myths and realities: one century of external trade and foreign investment. In *States against Markets. The Limits of Globalization*, ed. R. Boyer and D. Drache. Routledge: London, 173–92.

Bernis, G. D. de 1966. Industries industrialisantes et contenu d'une politique d'intégration régionale. *Économie Appliquée*, 19/3–4 (July–Dec.), 415–73.

Bourdieu, P. 1977. Cultural and social reproduction. In *Power and Ideology in Education*, ed. J. Karabel and H. A. Halsey. New York: Oxford University Press.

Boyer, R., Amable, B., and Barré, R. 1997. *Les Systémes d'innovation a l'ère de la globalization.* Paris: Economica.

Breschi, S., and Malerba, F. 1997. Sectoral innovation systems. In Edquist 1997.

Brookfield, H. 1975. *Interdependent Development: Perspectives on Development.* London: Methuen.

Burt, R. S. 1992. *Structural Holes: The Social Structure of Competition.* Cambridge, Mass.: Harvard University Press.

Cantwell, J. A. 1995. The globalization of technology: what remains of the product cycle model? *Cambridge Journal of Economics*, 19/1: 155–74.

Carlsson, B., and Jacobsson, S. 1997. Diversity creation and technological systems: a technology policy perspective. In Edquist 1997.

Clark, K. B., and Fujimoto, T. 1991. *Product Development Performance: Strategy, Organization and Management in the World Auto Industry.* Boston: Harvard Business School Press.

Cohendet, P., and Llerena, P. 1997. Learning, technical change and public policy: how to create and exploit diversity. In Edquist 1997.

Coleman, J. 1988. Social capital in the creation of human capital. *American Journal of Sociology*, 94 (suppl.), 95–120.

—— 1990. *Foundations of Social Theory.* London: Harvard University Press.

Dahmén, E. 1950. *Svensk industriell företagarverksamhet. Kausalanalys av den industriella utvecklingen 1919–1939.* Lund: Industriens Utredningsinstitut.

Dore, R. 1986. *Flexible Rigidities: Industrial Policy and Structural Adjustment in the Japanese Economy 1970–1980.* London: Athlone Press.

Dosi, G., Freeman, C., Nelson, R. R., Silverberg, G., and Soete, L., eds. 1988. *Technology and Economic Theory.* London: Pinter Publishers.

Edquist, C., ed. 1997. *Systems of Innovation: Technologies, Institutions and Organizations.* London: Pinter Publishers.

—— and Johnson, B. 1997. Institutions and organizations in systems of innovation. In Edquist 1997, 41–63.

—— and Lundvall, B.-Å. 1993. Comparing the Danish and Swedish Systems of Innovation. In Nelson 1993.

Eliasson, G. 1996. *Firm Objectives, Controls and Organization.* Amsterdam: Kluwer Academic Publishers.

Ernst, D., and Lundvall, B.-Å. 1997. Information technology in the learning economy—challenges for developing countries. *DRUID Working Paper* No. 97-11. Aalborg: Department of Business Studies.

Feis, H. 1934. *Europe—The World's Banker 1870–1914.* Reprinted 1974 with a new introd. by the author and by C. P. Howland. Clifton: Augustus M. Kelley.

Fransman, M. 1995. *Japan's Computer and Communications Industry.* New York: Oxford University Press.

Freeman, C. 1987. *Technology Policy and Economic Performance: Lessons from Japan.* London: Pinter Publishers.

—— 1995*a*. The National Innovation Systems in historical perspective. *Cambridge Journal of Economics*, 19/1: 5–24.

—— 1995*b*. History, co-evolution and economic growth. In *IASA Working Paper 95-76.* Laxenburg: IASA.

—— 1997. Innovation systems: city-state, national, continental and sub-national. Mimeo. Paper presented at the Montevideo conference, University of Sussex, SPRU.

—— and Lundvall, B.-Å., eds. 1988. *Small Countries Facing the Technological Revolution.* London: Pinter Publishers.

Fukuyama, F. 1995. *Trust: The Social Virtues and the Creation of Prosperity.* London: Hamish Hamilton.

Gibbons, M., Limoges, C., Nowotny, H., Schwartzman, S., Scott, P., and Troiw, M. 1994. *The New Production of Knowledge.* Sage: London.

Groupe de reflexion pour les strategies industrielles (GRESI) 1976. *La Division internationale du travail*, i–ii. Paris.

Guerreri, P., and Tylecote, A. 1997. Interindustry differences in technical change and national patterns of technological accumulation. In Edquist 1997.

Habermas, J. 1984. *The Theory of Communicative Action*, i. Boston: Beacon Press.

Hamilton, G., and Biggart, N. W. 1988. Market culture and authority: a comparative analysis of management and organization in the Far East. *American Journal of Sociology*, 94: 552–94.

Hatzichronoglou, T. 1996. *Globalisation and Competitiveness: Relevant Indicators.* Organization for Economic Co-operation and Development (OECD), Directorate for Science, Technology and Industry, Working Papers, IV, 16, Paris.

Hirschman, A. O. 1958. *The Strategy of Economic Development.* Clinton, Mass.: Yale University Press.

Hobsbawm, E. J. 1990. *Nations and Nationalism since 1780: Programme, Myth, Reality.* Cambridge: Cambridge University Press.

Isard, W. 1956. *Location and Space-Economy.* Cambridge, Mass.: MIT Press.

Johnson, B. 1992. Institutional learning. In Lundvall 1992.

Katzenstein, P. J. 1985. *Small States in World Markets: Industrial Policy in Europe.* New York: Cornell University Press.

Kline, S. J., and Rosenberg, N. 1986. An overview of innovation. In *The Positive Sum Game*, ed. R. Landau and N. Rosenberg. Washington: National Academy Press.

Kuznets, S. 1960. Economic growth of small nations. In Robinson 1960.

List, F. 1841. *Das Nationale System der Politischen Ökonomie.* Basel: Kyklos. (Trans. and pub. under the title *The National System of Political Economy* by Longmans, Green and Co., London 1841.)

Lundvall, B.-Å. 1985. *Product Innovation and User-Producer Interaction.* Aalborg: Aalborg University Press.

—— ed. 1992. *National Innovation Systems: Towards a Theory of Innovation and Interactive Learning.* London: Pinter Publishers.

—— and Borras, S. 1999. *The Globalising Learning Economy: Implications for Innovation Policy.* Brussels: DGXII-TSER, The European Commission.

Lundvall, B.-Å., and Johnson, B. 1994. The learning economy. *Journal of Industry Studies*, 2/1: 23–42.

McKelvey, M. 1991. How do National Innovation Systems differ?: A critical analysis of Porter, Freeman, Lundvall and Nelson. In *Rethinking Economics: Markets, Technology and Economic Evolution*, ed. G. M. Hodgson and E. Screpanti. Aldershot: Elgar Publishing House.

Maddison, A. 1991. *Dynamic Forces in Capitalist Development*. Oxford: Oxford University Press.

Malmberg, A., and Maskell, P. 1997. Towards an explanation of regional specialization and industry agglomeration. *European Planning Studies*, 5/1: 25–41.

Marshall, A. 1890. *Principles of Economics*. 8th edn. 1920. London: Macmillan.

Maskell, P. 1998*a*. Low-tech competitive advantages and the role of proximity—the case of the European furniture industry in general and the Danish wooden furniture production in particular. *European Urban and Regional Studies*, 5/2: 99–118.

—— 1998*b*. Learning in the village economy of Denmark: the role of institutions and policy in sustaining competitiveness. In *Regional Innovation Systems: The Role of Governance in a Globalized World*, ed. H. J. Braczyk, P. Cooke, and M. Heidenreich. London: UCL-Press, 190–213.

—— Eskelinen, H., Hannibalsson, I., Malmberg, A., and Vatne, E. 1998. *Competitiveness, Localised Learning and Regional Development: Specialisation and Prosperity in Small Open Economies*. London: Routledge.

—— and Malmberg, A. 1999. Localised learning and industrial competitiveness. *Cambridge Journal of Economics*, 23/2: 167–86.

Maurice, M., Sellier, F., and Silvestre, J. J. 1986. *The Social Foundation of Industrial Power*. Cambridge, Mass.: MIT Press.

Menzel, U. 1980. Der entwicklungsweg Dänemarks (1880–1940): Ein Beitrag zum konzept autozentrierter entwicklung. Projekt Untersuchung zur grundlegung einer praxisorientierten theorie autozentrierter entwicklung. Forschungsbericht no. 8. Bremen: Bremen Universität.

Mowery, D. C., and Oxley, J. E. 1995. Inward technology transfer and competitiveness: the role of National Innovation Systems. *Cambridge Journal of Economics*, 19/1: 67–93.

Nelson, R. R., ed. 1993. *National Innovation Systems: A Comparative Analysis*. Oxford: Oxford University Press.

—— 1996. *The Sources of Economic Growth*. Cambridge, Mass.: Harvard University Press.

Nonaka, K. 1991. The knowledge-creating company. *Harvard Business Review*, 69/6: 96–104.

—— and Takeuchi, H. 1995. *The Knowledge Creating Company*. Oxford: Oxford University Press.

OECD 1997. *Industrial Competitiveness: Benchmarking Business Environments in the Global Economy*. Paris: OECD.

Ostry, S., and Nelson, R. R. 1995. *Techno-nationalism and techno-globalism: Conflict and Co-operation*. Washington: Brookings Institution.

Patel, P. 1995. Localized production of technology for global markets. *Cambridge Journal of Economics*, 19/1: 141–53.

Pavitt, K. 1984. Sectoral patterns of technical change: towards a taxonomy. *Research Policy*, 13: 343–73.

Penrose, E. 1959/1995. *The Theory of the Growth of the Firm*. Oxford: Oxford University Press. 1st pub. 1959.

Polanyi, M. 1958/1978. *Personal Knowledge*. London: Routledge & Kegan. 1st pub. 1958.

—— 1966. *The Tacit Dimension*. London: Routledge & Kegan.

Porter, M. 1990. *The Competitive Advantage of Nations*. London: Macmillan.

Putnam, R. D. 1993. *Making Democracy Work—Civic Traditions in Modern Italy*. Princeton: Princeton University Press.

Richardson, G. B. 1972. The organization of industry. *Economic Journal*, 82: 883–96.

—— 1996. Competition, innovation and increasing return. *DRUID Working Paper* No. 10. Copenhagen Business School, Department of Industrial Economics and Strategy.

—— 1997. Economic analysis, public policy and the software industry. *DRUID Working Paper* No. 4. Copenhagen Business School, Department of Industrial Economics and Strategy.

Robinson, E. A. G., ed. 1960. *Economic Consequences of the Size of Nations*, Proceedings of a conference held by the International Economic Association. London: Macmillan.

Romer, P. M. 1990. Endogenous technological change. *Journal of Political Economy*, 98.

Rothwell, R. 1977. The characteristics of successful innovators and technically progressive firms. *R&D Management*, 7/3: 191–206.

Sako, M. 1990. Buyer-supplier relationships and economic performance: evidence from Britain and Japan. Ph.D. thesis. University of London.

Saviotti, P. 1997. Innovation systems and evolutionary theory. In Edquist 1997.

Senghaas, D. 1982. *Von Europa lernen*. Frankfurt am Main: Suhrkamp. (Trans. to English and pub. under the title: *The European Experience: A Historical Critique of Development Theory*. Leamington Spa: Berg Publishers, 1985.)

Sørensen, O. J., and Kuada, J. forthcoming. Institutional context of Ghanaian firms and cross national inter-firm relations. In *Understanding Business Systems in Developing Countries*, ed. G. Jacobsen and J. E. Tork. New Delhi: Sage.

Spender, J.-C. 1994. The geographies of strategic competence: borrowing from social and educational psychology to sketch an activity and knowledge-based theory of the firm. In *The Dynamic Firm: The Role of Technology, Strategy, Organizations, and Regions*, ed. A. D. Chandler, P. Hagström, and Ö. Sölvell. Oxford: Oxford University Press, 417–39.

Svennilson, I. 1960. The concept of the nation and its relevance to economics. In Robinson 1960.

Stewart, F. 1977. *Technology and Underdevelopment*. London: Macmillan.

Tylecote, A. 1994. Financial systems and innovation. In *Handbook of Industrial Innovation*, ed. R. Dogson and D. Soskice. Cheltenham: Edward Elgar.

Whitley, R. 1987. Taking firms seriously as economic actors: towards a sociology of economic actors. *Organization Studies*, No. 8: 125–47.

—— 1994*a*. Societies, firms and markets: the social structuring of business systems. In *European Business Systems*, ed. R. Whitley. London: Sage Publications.

Whitley, R. 1994*b*. Dominant forms of economic organization in market economies. *Organization Studies*, 15/2: 153–82.

—— 1996. The social construction of economic actors: institutions and types of firm in Europe and other market economies. In *The Changing European Firm*, ed. R. Whitley. London: Routledge.

Woolcock, M. 1998. Social capital and economic development: toward a theoretical synthesis and policy framework. *Theory and Society*, 27/2: 151–207.

Chapter 19

Location and Innovation: The New Economic Geography of Innovation, Spillovers, and Agglomeration

Maryann P. Feldman

Introduction

HISTORIANS Leslie and Kargon (1996) conclude that there are too many unique factors that created Silicon Valley to ever duplicate its success. This view is not very satisfying to an economist: our objective is to find systematic patterns between location and innovation. Towards that end, a substantial literature is beginning to emerge. Innovation, either product, process, or organizational, is the novel application of economically valuable knowledge. The ability to harness knowledge and to reap the resulting economic benefits is critical to economic development, technological change, and industrial evolution.[1] New methods of modeling innovation have placed agglomeration economies and knowledge spillovers, especially within a limited spatial context, at the heart of the analysis. Within the new empirical literature there is an appreciation for locational context and the diversity of landscape that condition economic activity. The concept of location is now being defined as a geographic unit over which interaction and communication is facilitated, search intensity is increased, and task coordination is enhanced.[2]

There are two major intellectual traditions in the empirical study of innovation and location. The first tradition is predicated on the concept of

[1] See Romer (1986 and 1990), Lucas (1993), and Krugman (1991*a* and 1991*b*) as well as chapters in this volume. Stephan (1996) provides a useful complementary review.

[2] In studying the networks in California's Silicon Valley, Saxenian (1994) emphasized that it is the communication between individuals that facilitates the transmission of knowledge across agents, firms, and even industries.

geographically mediated spillovers and includes a geographic dimension to the determinants of innovation. Studies in this tradition are conducted over a common geographic unity and are based upon the logic of the production function which employs some measure of innovation as the dependent variable against a set of explanatory variables. These studies try to quantify the geographic impact of knowledge spillovers on innovation.

The second tradition is motivated to understand differences in economic outcomes such as economic growth or productivity across locations. This focuses on growth or productivity as the dependent variable and considers how location relates to these outcomes. In this tradition, innovation may enter as a potential intermediate link; for example, agglomeration economies drive innovation, which then drives growth. Most importantly, when we account for differences in geographic characteristics, location becomes exogenous, which makes it possible to distinguish economic effects.

This chapter is organized around the two traditions: first, considering studies that attempt to measure geographically mediated spillovers; and secondly, related studies with a geographic dimension. The first part of this review identifies four separate strains: (1) empirical studies employing innovation production functions; (2) empirical studies on the linkages between patent citations, defined as paper trails; (3) studies that measure the impact of the mobility of skilled labor on innovation based on the notion that knowledge spillovers are transmitted through people; (4) empirical studies based on the assumption that knowledge spillovers are embodied in traded goods. The second part of this review considers the composition of agglomeration economies, the attributes of knowledge, and the characteristics of firms as they relate to location. This review begins with a discussion about the choice of measure of innovation and the geographic unit of observation and concludes with some insight into further questions to address.

Defining Innovation

It is useful first to define innovation and how it may be measured in empirical studies. The simplest distinction is between process and product innovation. Process innovation focuses on incorporating new technology into the methods of production.[3] It is usually associated with firm-level productivity effects that lower productive costs or increase product quality. In contrast, product innovation focuses on the creation of new products that range from radical breakthroughs that create new product categories to simple, incremental improvements. While ideally, we would like data on the economic impact of innovation, typically counts of either patents or new product announcements are the only data available.

[3] Helper (1995), for example, provides an example of an empirical study of the diffusion of a new process technology that allows machine tools to be programmed in the automobile industry.

Another useful distinction is based on what we may term the impact of the innovation. Innovations may be either radical or incremental. For example, most innovation creates small incremental improvements to existing products. Other innovations are radical in that they create entirely new product categories, require new competencies, and render existing ideas, techniques, and perhaps companies obsolete. Finally, in considering innovation, another difference lies in the distinction between the commercialization of innovation (the non-linear and interactive process of translating knowledge into economical value (Kline and Rosenberg 1987)), and the process of diffusion in which that new innovation is adopted by users (Brown 1981; Trajtenberg 1990). Both concepts are social and economic processes and each may have a geographic dimension.

There are many ways in which innovation and innovative activity have been measured as outcomes or dependent variables in the literature. The earliest empirical studies relied on R&D activities, measured by the number and location of industrial laboratories, the number of R&D employees, or the amount of R&D expenditures (see Malecki 1987 for a review). These concepts are more likely to be inputs to the innovation production rather than measures of innovative output.[4]

Empirical work requires the definition of a measurable output. Thompson (1962) provides the first locational study of patents and notes the difficulty of obtaining data. The computerization of the US patent office enabled Jaffe (1989) to assemble large volumes of patent data with geographic precision. These data provide a rich geographic time series which has been further characterized into patent families—patents that reference or cite each other and are used to indicate the flows of knowledge from one invention to another (Jaffe *et al.* 1993; Jaffe and Trajtenberg 1996).[5] A limitation to patent data is that not all patented inventions are economically valuable nor are all innovations patented. Other work uses innovation citations which represent the market introduction of new commercial products (Feldman 1994*b*; Audretsch and Feldman 1996).[6] These data consist of new product announcements compiled from technology, engineering, and trade journals.[7]

[4] R&D is frequently used as an independent variable in innovation studies. A further problem is that while there is reliable industry data and geographic data exist, there are no data currently available in the USA that are both at the industry and sub-state geographic level.

[5] Griliches (1990) provides a survey of the uses and limitations of patent data.

[6] The United States Small Business Administration's Innovation Database consists of new product introductions compiled from the new product announcement sections of over 100 technology, engineering, and trade journals spanning every industry in manufacturing. An innovation is defined in the database as a process that begins with an invention, proceeds with the development of the invention, and results in introduction of a new product, process, or service to the market place. A detailed description of the US Small Business Administration innovation data is contained in Feldman (1994*b*).

[7] There are many patented inventions that are never realized commercially, indicating the importance of new product introductions.

These data are limited in that they only exist for the USA as a cross-section for the year 1982.[8]

Other measures associated with innovative activity are used as dependent variables. For example, the creation of new firms is generally perceived to be associated with innovative activity since firm formation is associated with new ideas that cannot be absorbed by existing firms. Audretsch and Vivarelli (1994) look at new firm start-up and survival as an indicator of innovative activity. Zucker *et al.* (1998*b*) specifically focus on the formation of New Biotech Entities (NBE) as a measure of innovative output.

New investment is another factor associated with innovative activity. Head *et al.* (1995 and 1999), and Smith and Florida (1994) use new Japanese manufacturing plant investment to test if agglomeration economies influence location choices. Feldman and Lichtenberg (1998) rely on investment in funded research projects as a measure of innovative activity in the European Community.

Other studies use economic variables such as wage or employment growth for which innovation is seen as a driving force. For example, Beeson and Montgomery (1992), and Glaeser *et al.* (1992) use wages and employment growth as a dependent variable under the assumption that these will be the measurable effects of innovation and new economic knowledge. Similarly, J. V. Henderson (1986, 1997) compares total factor productivity for industries and regions. Adams and Jaffe (1996) measure total factor productivity at the firm level to capture the effect of process innovation. In conclusion, the choice of dependent variable is dictated by the research question under investigation.

Reflections on the Choice of Geographic Unit

In contrast to most economic analysis, where we can clearly identify the unit of analysis, studies of location face difficulty in defining the appropriate unit of analysis. There is a prior tradition that reduced the definition of location to a simple distance metric. These studies, based on urban rent gradients, assume a distance decay function that may be more appropriate when we consider a fixed central point.

The new empirical work in economic geography builds on the idea of knowledge spillovers using distance and geographic space differently. The concept of location that empirical studies attempt to measure is the geographic unit over which interaction and communication is facilitated. Consider that popular accounts of innovative activity focus on geographic units defined as Silicon Valley and Route 128. This type of descriptor is so effective that names for these types of geographic concentrations have proliferated, but the boundaries are not clearly defined and many times overlap or ignore political jurisdictions.

The earliest US studies used state-level data, while acknowledging that states are not the most appropriate level of analysis. This choice was dictated more by

[8] See National Science Foundation (1998) for a description of new data collection efforts.

data availability than conceptual preference.[9] Still, states are important political jurisdictions that are easy to identify and understand. Head *et al.* (1995) argue that groups of contiguous states that contain related activity may create regional industrial units.

More recent studies have used the concept of cities as either Metropolitan Statistical Areas (MSA) or Consolidated Metropolitan Statistical Areas (CMSA), where applicable (Jaffe *et al.* 1993; Feldman and Audretsch 1996). Other studies, in order to refine the unit across which location might affect innovation, have used smaller units such as counties, Bureau of Economic Analysis (BEA) areas (Zucker and Darby 1996) or even US postal zones (Lerner 1999). In contrast, some studies are content to test whether spillovers are greater within countries than they are between countries or internationally (Irwin and Klenow 1994). Consequently, there is no general consensus for the correct unit of analysis in empirical studies and variation in findings may be due to differences in the unit of analysis.

Empirical Studies of Geographically Mediated Knowledge Spillovers

Griliches (1992) defines knowledge spillovers as 'working on similar things and hence benefitting much from each other's research'. As an example, Jaffe (1986) found that a significant fraction of the total flow of spillovers that affects a firm's research productivity originates from other firms. This work reveals that firms benefit from the R&D efforts of other firms that are in close technological proximity. Once we believe that knowledge spillovers can easily cross firms, then the possibility that spillovers may be geographically mediated becomes credible. An empirical testing of the effect of geographic proximity is a logical extension of this line of inquiry. This review now considers four approaches to the study of knowledge spillovers.

Geographic Innovation Production Functions

In the first study to examine geographically mediated knowledge spillovers, Jaffe (1989) modified the knowledge production function approach introduced by Griliches (1979) to account for spatial and product dimensions:

$$I_{si} = IRD^{\beta_1} * UR_{si}^{\beta_2} * \varepsilon_{si}$$

where I is the measure of innovative output, *IRD* is private corporate expenditures on R&D, and *UR* is the research expenditures undertaken at universities.[10]

[9] Adams and Jaffe, looking at the relationship between plants, test alternative specifications within states and within a 100-mile radius.

[10] Jaffe's formulation also included a measure of the geographic coincidence of university and corporate research to compensate for the use of the state as the unit of analysis.

This conceptualization changed the observation from the traditional unit of the firm to the geographic level.

Jaffe found that patents occur in those states, *s*, where public and private knowledge-generating inputs are the greatest. Even after controlling for industrial R&D, the results indicated that the knowledge generated at universities spilled over for higher realized innovative output. Feldman (1994*b*) adapted the knowledge production function framework to data on new market introduction in order to test the model against a more direct measure of innovative output than patent data. Since commercial innovations were closer to the market than patents, Feldman added related industry presence and the receipts for business services as two additional knowledge-generating inputs suggested by the case-study literature. The basic result held: geographic regions with greater amounts of knowledge-generating inputs produce more innovation. These findings confirm that knowledge spillovers tend to be geographically bounded within the region where new economic knowledge was created. That is, there are geographic limits to the spillovers of new economic knowledge.

While the earliest studies to estimate the knowledge production function used state-level data, the robustness of the basic results using sub-state data hold (Anselin *et al.* 1997). The geographic estimation of the knowledge production function is conceptually limited because there is no understanding of the way in which spillovers occur and are realized at the geographic level. The pre-existing pattern of technology-related activities makes it difficult to separate spillovers from the correlation of variables at the geographic level. Economic activity may be co-located, but the pattern of causality is difficult to decipher.

Jaffe (1989) found an important indirect or induced effect as university research increases industry R&D which thereby increases patents. This effect is quantitatively larger than the direct effect of a given increase in university research.

The knowledge production function implies that innovative activity should cluster in regions where knowledge-generating inputs are the greatest and thus where knowledge spillovers are the most prevalent. Audretsch and Feldman (1996) follow Krugman's (1991*b*) example and calculate Gini coefficients for the geographic concentration of innovative activity to test this relationship.[11]

[11] The Gini coefficients are weighted by the relative share of economic activity located in each state. Computation of weighted Gini coefficients enables us to control for size differences across states. The Gini coefficients are based on the share of activity in a state and industry relative to the state share of the national activity. The locational Gini coefficients for production are based on industry value-added and are calculated as the amount of value-added in an industry and a state divided by state share of national value-added for the industry. This ratio is normalized by the state share of total manufacturing value-added in order to account for the overall distribution of manufacturing activity. An industry which is not geographically concentrated more than is reflected by the overall distribution of manufacturing value-added would have a coefficient of 0. The closer the industry coefficient is to 1, the more geographically concentrated the industry.

The results indicate that a key determinant of the extent to which the location of production is geographically concentrated is the relative importance of new economic knowledge in the industry. Even after taking into account the geographic concentration of production, the results suggest a greater propensity for innovative activity to cluster spatially in industries in which industry R&D, university research, and skilled labor are important inputs. In this work, skilled labor is included as a mechanism by which knowledge spillovers may occur as workers move between jobs in an industry, taking their accumulated skills and know-how with them.

These studies provide evidence of the existence of geographically mediated spillovers. These findings do not address the path that spillovers take or the mechanisms by which spillovers are realized. These have been provided by work reviewed in the next section.

Paper Trails

Persuasive evidence about the existence of knowledge spillovers is found by examining what may be termed the *paper trails* left by patent citations. Krugman (1991*a*: 53) argues that economists should abandon any attempts at measuring knowledge spillovers, because 'knowledge flows are invisible, they leave no paper trail by which they may be measured and tracked'. However, Jaffe *et al.* (1993: 578) point out that, 'knowledge flows do sometimes leave a paper trail'—in particular, in the form of patented inventions and new product introductions.

Building on Trajtenberg's (1990) approach of linking an originating or major patent application to the other patents that reference or cite it, this work explores both the temporal and geographic span of knowledge spillovers. For example, starting with 1,450 patents that originated in 1980, Jaffe *et al.* trace the characteristics of approximately 5,200 citations that occurred to these originating patents from 1980 to 1989. The relationships between the originating patents and the citing patent are used to identify knowledge spillovers.

To adjust for bias due to the existing geographic distribution of technical activity, a control sample that closely resembles the citing patent in terms of technology and timing was selected. The frequency of the match between the originating patent and the control patent provide a baseline against which the frequency of originating patent-citing patents matches are normalized (Jaffe *et al.* 1993: 581–3). This allows a test for the extent to which spillovers are localized relative to what would be expected given the existing distribution of technological activity.[12]

Jaffe *et al.* (1993) find evidence that patents cite other patents originating in the same city more frequently. Citations are five to ten times as likely to come

[12] In a further attempt to capture true spillovers, this work also excludes self-citations, that is, patents that are owned by the same organization as the originating patent.

from the same city as the control patents.[13] For every geographic level, and adjusting for different organizational types, such as universities, top corporation, and other corporations, citations are statistically significantly more localized than the controls; these results hold for two cross-sections. It is important to point out that the effects, though statistically significant, are fairly small.

This research further uncovers factors that condition localization. For example, citations are more likely to be localized in the first year following the patent. This effect fades with time: citations show fewer geographic effects as knowledge diffuses. This work also highlights factors that condition spillovers by concluding that the frequency and duration of citations depends on the scientific field. For example, Jaffe and Trajtenberg (1996) find that electronics, optics, and nuclear technology enjoy high immediate citation but, due to quick obsolescence, experience a rapid fading of citations over time. The effect of the patent on subsequent citations also depends on the institutions from which they originated. For example, government patents tend to be less 'fertile', having fewer citations than university and corporate patents. University patents are more fertile than corporate patents. Additionally, these results are variant to time, suggesting that technological opportunity may be changing. For example, citation intensity, defined as the average number of citations that a patent receives, declined in the late 1980s across all institutions and categories.

The same methodology has been applied by Almeida and Kogut (1997) to study patenting in the semiconductor industry. The basic results agree: patent citations are highly localized, indicating that there are geographic limits to knowledge spillovers. There has not, to date, been an empirical study that considers how geographic spillovers may be affected by new telecommunications technology. We might expect an 'internet effect' in which new technology may diminish the advantages of co-location by increasing access to knowledge and speeding its diffusion.[14]

Ideas in People

None of the above studies addresses the mechanism by which knowledge spillovers are realized. One avenue that has been explored by Zucker and Darby (1996) is that ideas are embodied in individuals who have the skill, knowledge, and know-how to engage in technological advance. Zucker and Darby (1996) summarize a series of papers that examine the role of 'star scientists' as a source of intellectual capital that drives the transformation of bioscientific knowledge into commercial applications. This work demonstrates that localized intellectual capital is key in the development of the biotech industry and that know-

[13] For example, 12.6% of the university patents and 21.9% of the top corporate patents were localized from the 1980 cohort.

[14] Glaeser (1998) suggests that there is no evidence that the internet will destroy the locational advantage of cities.

ledge generates externalities that tend to be geographically bounded within the region where these scientists reside.

A 'star scientist' is defined as a highly productive individual who discovered a major breakthrough. Using this criterion, there are 337 stars that authored 4,315 articles related to biotechnology. In addition, there is a group of collaborators who co-authored with the stars, yielding a total of 4,196 observations in the USA.[15] These individuals embody the intellectual capital necessary to commercialize breakthrough discoveries in biotech. These scientists are geographically concentrated in 141 universities, 74 research institutes, and 48 firms in a relatively small number of locations in the USA.

The start-up of New Biotech Entities (NBEs) is localized in regions in which this intellectual capital resides. These scientists embody knowledge of breakthrough techniques that is initially only available at the lab bench of these scientists, making it costly for others to obtain or use. Zucker *et al.* (1998*b*) find localized linkages between the stars and the NBEs. The number of publications in these bench-level working relationships predicted higher subsequent firm productivity in terms of products in development, products on the market, and employment growth in the firm. Firms with access to leading edge scientists performed better than enterprises lacking such access.

Zucker *et al.* (1998*b*) find that intellectual capital (in terms of the number of stars and their collaborators in a given area) is predictive of NBEs, controlling for presence of universities and federal funds. The Zucker paper empirically demonstrates boundary spanning between universities and NBEs via star scientists at universities who have made scientific breakthroughs. Using panel data on the number of NBEs within a local labor market,[16] knowledge spillovers from the star scientists are demonstrated.

Almeida and Kogut (1997) extend this approach of following intellectual capital by considering the inter-firm mobility of star patent holders in order to trace the transfer of ideas in semiconductors. Their results suggest that inter-firm mobility results in the transfer of ideas as demonstrated by the subsequent assignment of patents and that these knowledge spillovers are geographically confined.

In conclusion, this work demonstrates that localized intellectual capital is key in the development of the new industry and that knowledge-generated externalities tend to be geographically bounded within the region where these scientists reside. In related work, Audretsch and Stephan (1996) examined the scientific advisory boards of NBEs and find that these relationships were not necessarily geographically mediated. This indicates that further work is needed to reconcile the conditions and stages of the industry life cycle when location

[15] Zucker *et al.* (1998*b*) find that firm scientists had a higher total number of citations than scientists in universities or in research institutes and hospitals.

[16] The local labor market is defined using Bureau of Economic Analysis (BEA) units. There are 183 functional units.

and proximity matter. Sokoloff (1988), in an investigation of nineteenth-century patenting activity, finds that the regional concentration of patenting was geographically concentrated but then became less concentrated as industrialization occurred.

The work of Zucker and Darby focuses on the human capital of key individuals rather than the average human capital in a local labor market. In contrast, Lucas (1988) suggests that the ability to develop and implement new technology depends on the average level of human capital in the local economy. Glaeser *et al.* (1992) find that higher average levels of human capital are tied to higher rates of growth in cities. It may be that key individuals are important to new company start-ups but are not sufficient to anchor an industry in a location. This hypothesis can be tested, and the results would have implications for places that are trying to develop technology-intensive industries.

Ideas in Goods

Knowledge spillovers may be embodied in goods in which the innovator is unable to appropriate all the surplus from the trade.[17] There are a series of empirical studies which assume that trade is the prime mechanism by which spillovers are mediated. Coe and Helpman (1995) find that international R&D spillovers mediated by trade are strong and significant. Import-weighted foreign R&D spillovers are significantly correlated with domestic productivity levels. Similarly, Park (1995) considers both public and private R&D sources and further disaggregates by sector. Park uses sectoral allocation of R&D to measure technological proximity and finds evidence of international R&D spillovers.

Keller (1998) compares the elasticity of domestic productivity with respect to foreign R&D with an elasticity based on counterfactual, randomly created international trade patterns. Using a Monte-Carlo simulation, Keller creates a series of randomly generated bilateral trade relationships and trade-weighted foreign R&D stocks. He also concludes that the randomly generated trade patterns give rise to large estimated international R&D spillovers. He concludes that R&D spillovers must be estimated in a model which allows simultaneously for trade-related international technology diffusion. Keller's results cast doubt on the previous studies; however, it should be noted that studies of this type are based on estimations of a knowledge production function with aggregate data for which no means of control for heterogeneity between firms, industries, and countries exists. Branstetter (1998) uses firm-level data to assess international and intra-national spillovers and finds that knowledge spillovers are primarily intra-national in scope, indicating that spillovers are confined within a country.

To summarize, these four approaches demonstrate the existence of geographically mediated knowledge spillovers, the persistence and importance of

[17] Branstetter (forthcoming) provides a comprehensive review of international knowledge spillovers.

localized knowledge, and one path, skilled labor, that provides a mechanism for knowledge spillovers. The next section seeks to integrate what we have learned from empirical studies of firms' production and investment decisions that have added a geographic dimension. The objective is to establish what we have learned about the factors that condition the relationship of location and innovation.

Location, Location, Location

This section organizes the empirical literature that adds a geographic dimension to the study of economic phenomena such as growth, productivity, and investment decisions. These studies suggest several key considerations that condition the effects of location on innovation, and subsequently other economic outcomes. First is the composition of agglomeration economies, second are the attributes of knowledge that condition the effect of location on economic activity, and last, there are characteristics of industries that provide general parameters on the interaction of innovation and location.

Agglomeration Economies

In seeking to understand how location affects economic activity, empirical research has classified agglomeration economies into either localization economies or urbanization economies. This distinction was first noted by Loesch (1954). Localization economies are external to a firm but internal to an industry within a geographic region. In contrast, urbanization economies are scale effects associated with city size or density. These definitions imply different concepts of the composition of economic activity and have implications for industrial location and innovation (J. V. Henderson 1983). Each of these is addressed in empirical studies with their subsequent impact on knowledge spillovers and innovation.

Localization economies, or what Glaeser *et al.* (1992) define as *Marshall–Arrow–Romer* externalities, are knowledge spillovers external to firms, yet internal to an industry within a city. A local industry agglomeration may increase innovation directly by providing industry-specific complementary assets and activities that may either lower the cost of supplies to the firm or create greater specialization in both input and output markets. We expect that industries in which complementary assets are important would more likely be concentrated geographically and realize greater innovative productivity.

The empirical evidence on localization economies is inconclusive. Henderson (1986) finds that localization raises factor productivity for the USA and Brazil. In contrast, neither Glaeser *et al.* (1992) nor Feldman and Audretsch (1996) find that industry localization increases either growth or innovative activity. This may be due to the fact that industries which have a high degree of concentration in a local economy may be mature industries that have large-scale production facilitates, therefore dominating certain locations. A high concentration of an industry in a location may measure geographic specialization, but not dynamic localization economies.

One reason why industries may concentrate geographically is locational factor endowments. Head *et al.* (1995: 227), drawing on the international trade literature, provide an alternative hypothesis of endowment-driven localization. Under this formulation, industries may be localized due to differential factor endowments among places. For example, sawmills might congregate in a particular state to take advantage of the supply of high quality timber. This reason would be distinct from localization due to knowledge spillovers. The location of Japanese investment in the USA provides a quasi-experiment that allows Head *et al.* (1995) to trace the degree to which Japanese investment reflects either of these sources of localization. The evidence is that Japanese investments are influenced by the location of prior investment in the same industry, suggesting that firms locate near other firms in order to benefit from information externalities and not for factor endowment reasons.

In contrast, urbanization economies come from the scale effects that are external to industries but internal to geographic units such as cities. Lucas (1993) describes urbanization economies when he asserts that the only compelling reason for the existence of cities would be the presence of increasing returns to scale that make these locations more productive. Urbanization economies have been measured by population size and density in the literature: again, the empirical evidence has been somewhat inconclusive. Henderson (1986) finds evidence of urban diseconomies or congestion effects on productivity growth. Nakamura (1985) and Moomaw (1988) find evidence that urbanization economies are more important in specific industries such as apparel, food products, and printing, but not in heavy, durable product industries.

Jacobs (1969) argues that urbanization economies are realized through the exchange of complementary knowledge across diverse firms and economic agents within geographic regions. In economics this is the concept of cross-product increasing returns—one activity increases the marginal product of another activity and the effect is directly related to proximity. In a theoretical context, Jacobs's agglomerations may reduce search costs and also increase the opportunity for serendipitous events that would provide innovative opportunities.

Empirical studies have supported the idea that location brings together closely related activities to benefit innovation. Jaffe *et al.* (1993) find evidence that knowledge spillovers are not confined to closely related technologies, as approximately 40 per cent of citations do not come from the same primary patent class as the originating patent. Glaeser *et al.* (1992) provide the first empirical test of Jacobs's externalities using the concentration of the top five industries in a city and find that more diversity in the local economy is associated with higher rates of growth.

One question in empirical work is how we might define diverse yet complementary knowledge that would create economically useful spillovers. Feldman and Audretsch (1996) use survey data from Levin *et al.* (1987) to discern the disciplines that form a common science base that contributes to the basis for cross-industry increasing returns. This work finds that industries that rely on the same science base tend to cluster geographically and the presence of diverse industries within the same science base in a city leads to increased innovation.

The concept of agglomeration economies also includes the presence of intermediate suppliers and service providers. The empirical question is what types of industries and activities constitute an agglomeration. For example, industrial R&D and university research are inputs in the formulation of the knowledge production function. This is predicated on an understanding that universities are important suppliers of knowledge (Mansfield 1995). There are many empirical studies that establish the importance of local universities to innovation. For example, Beeson and Montgomery (1992) examine the relationship between universities and labor market conditions. They find that universities raise the average skill level of the surrounding area and positively affect wage and employment rates. The study focuses on employment growth rates for the time periods 1975–80 and 1980–9 and finds that employment growth is related to increases in university R&D funding as well as to the number of nationally rated science and engineering programs at local universities. These results are consistent over the two time periods.[18]

For specific industries, it may be possible to define a set of relevant suppliers. For example, Smith and Florida (1994), in a study of Japanese investment in the automobile industries and auto-related parts suppliers, find that suppliers locate near the automobile assembly plants to form the sort of industrial district agglomeration that Marshall discusses. We expect that an agglomeration of related suppliers would result in increased innovation or productivity. There have been no general tests of this hypothesis using a source such as input–output tables or commodity flows. Justman (1994) uses this type of data to demonstrate that local demand influences industry location decisions. It would be useful to extend his approach.

In conclusion, the external economies associated with location have been defined in a variety of ways, either same industry localization, urban scale economies, Jacobs's concept of diversity, or the idea of specialized supplier

[18] The results on income, employment rate, and net migration are somewhat mixed. Choice of time period does not include the turnaround prompted by innovation in the computer industry known as the Massachusetts Miracle nor does it capture the computer revolution which certainly are two incidents of high innovative activity that anecdotally are associated with increased local earnings, higher employment rates, and net in-migration.

networks. Each of these measures attempts to discern the effects of composition activity within a region. Another way to consider the interaction of location and innovation is based on attributes of knowledge which condition the ways in which different industries might benefit from location. These are considered in the next section.

Attributes of Knowledge

Knowledge has certain characteristics, which may condition the effects of location on innovation. Since knowledge is one of the most decisive inputs for innovation, this section looks at what empirical work suggests about the tacit nature of knowledge, technological opportunity, and the appropriability of knowledge for the location of innovation.

Knowledge varies to the degree that it is tacit or articulable. Knowledge with a low degree of tacitness may be easily standardized, codified, and transmitted via journal articles, project reports, prototypes, and other tangible mediums. In contrast, tacit knowledge has a higher degree of uncertainty and the precise meaning is more interpretative and is less easily conveyed through a standardized medium. As a consequence, when knowledge is more tacit in nature, face-to-face interaction and communication are important and geographic proximity may promote commercial activity (Von Hipple 1994). That is, the less codified and articulated the knowledge, the greater the degree of centralization in geographic organization.

A problem arises in the measurement of the tacitness of knowledge. Using data on the results of publicly supported R&D projects in the European Community, Feldman and Lichtenberg (1998) construct several indicators of tacitness based on the degree to which projects result in prototypes, which might be easily transferred to others, or result in know-how that is knowledge that is less able to be transmitted. The results indicate that the more tacit the knowledge generated by the R&D, the greater the extent of geographic and administrative centralization of R&D activities.

Knowledge, rather than being a continuous flow, is affected by new discoveries and breakthroughs that provide different opportunities to realize technological advance and innovation. Caballero and Jaffe (1993) argue that the extent of knowledge spillovers depends on both the rate at which new ideas outdate old ideas (i.e. the obsolescence of ideas), and on the rate at which knowledge diffuses among users. Their empirical results, based on patent citations, conclude that the stock of existing knowledge that is useful in generating new inventions has been declining. This suggests that current inventors face higher costs on searching for useful knowledge and may imply that location provides a means to lower search costs. Industries with high average annual rates of knowledge obsolescence, we may hypothesize, would face the greatest pressures to locate near the sources of new knowledge.

Tests of the effects of technological opportunity on the interaction between location and innovation have mostly been indirect. Some studies have made cross-industry comparisons and have found a high degree of spatial clustering in particular industries that face high technological opportunity. For example, Jaffe and Trajtenberg (1996) conclude that both the frequency and the duration of the citation of a patent are highly dependent on the field. Some fields, such as electronics, optics, and nuclear technology are marked by high immediate citation, but due to quick obsolescence a rapid fading of citations over time. Furthermore, this work reveals that citations are more localized in the first year following a patent but that geographic effects dissipate quickly over time. Unfortunately, this work does not address the interaction of location and technology. Similarly, Audretsch and Feldman (1996) find a direct relationship between the propensity for industries to concentrate geographically and the knowledge intensity of the industry's activity and Henderson (1983) concludes that both localization and urbanization effects are important for high tech industries. If we assume that knowledge-intensive industries also face high technological opportunity this suggests that location appears to matter most for those activities.

The effects of the appropriability of knowledge on either encouraging or discouraging innovation are rather ambiguous (Cohen 1995). There have been no direct general tests of the effects of differences in appropriability on location and geographic clustering. There are some interesting conjectures that warrant further investigation. For example, Liebeskind *et al.* (1996) argue that the rapid pace of innovation in biotechnology is fueled by strict property rights regimes. The first firm to claim property rights over innovation will reap economic benefits causing firms to enter into patent 'races'. This will be complicated as organizations may not have the required internal knowledge, making it imperative to balance the need to cooperate in order to share new economic knowledge with the need to compete in order to benefit economically. The result may be the existence of social networks defined as a 'collectivity of individuals among whom exchanges take place that are supported only by shared norms of trustworthy behavior' (Liebeskind *et al.* 1996: 7). Location may facilitate the social contacts necessary for the development of these networks and may decrease the costs of monitoring untrustworthy behavior. Certainly, if firms could innovate without sharing knowledge then we might expect them to locate in geographic isolation. In that case, the resulting locational patterns of innovative firms would be very different from what we observe.

An interesting insight into the effect of appropriability on innovation may be seen by contrasting the work of Zucker and Darby (1996) with Audretsch and Stephan (1996). Both studies focus on biotech but at slightly different stages of the commercialization process. Zucker and Darby find that firm formation is more geographically concentrated at the time when appropriability is low. In contrast, at the stage of an initial public offering (IPO), when firms have acquired patent rights and are revealing information in order to raise funds, Audretsch and Stephan (1996) find a greater geographic reach in the organization of scientific advisory boards. The answer may be that close geographic collaboration is useful before the appropriation of commercial rewards. When property rights have been assigned, a company can identify key individuals who may have required knowledge or who may add credibility to the endeavor through their expertise. These issues raise questions of firm characteristics that are addressed in the next section.

Firm Characteristics

Empirical work has considered the effects of location on firm characteristics such as the stage of industry development, firm size, and strategy. A fundamental question concerns what types of firms are able to absorb and benefit economically from knowledge spillovers.

The expected economic value of new knowledge to a firm is shaped by what is termed as the core competency of the firm. As Cohen and Levinthal (1989) point out, the costs associated with innovation, such as learning new techniques and absorbing new research results, are less if the new knowledge is relevant to the firm's ongoing activity and existing expertise. Henderson (1993) compares new industry entrants' and incumbents' ability to exploit significant change in new technology and finds that new entrants are more likely to commercialize radical new innovation. The fact that small firms generate a disproportionate share of innovation supports this view. Indeed, small firms may be a mechanism for the commercialization of knowledge.

Location may allow small firms to achieve the economies of scope and scale associated with larger operations by co-locating with complementary, external resources. Feldman (1994*a*) uses the knowledge production function to establish that third parties, firms, or research institutions may provide geographically localized knowledge inputs to benefit small firms. Knowledge spillovers from a large R&D firm or research institution may benefit smaller firms who are receptive to more radical innovation that may be competency destroying in the larger firm. The new innovation would be attributed to the smaller firms; however, knowledge spillovers from the external environment make the innovation possible. Indeed, the work of Zucker and Darby (1996) concludes that it is the star scientists who transfer knowledge in order to realize economic returns from the human intellectual capital developed at universities.

Beyond the initial stages of a new company, location may facilitate access to resources that allow firms to grow, develop, and innovate. Lerner (1999) finds evidence that small start-up firms benefit from being in a location that is attracting venture capital investment. This work tracks the long-run growth patterns of Small Business Innovation Research (SBIR) grant recipients against matched samples of similar firms and finds that employment and sales growth were significantly higher if the award was made to a firm located in a postal code that received private venture capital activity. These results suggest that firms benefit from rich information exchanges within these locations. Adams and Jaffe (1996) find that geographically distant R&D is almost worthless to the R&D productivity of drug companies.

Reflective Conclusions

In recent years, economists have returned to the study of location and innovation with a sizeable empirical literature, which examines the phenomenon of geographic clustering—specifically the factors or conditions that give rise to them, the existence and span of local externalities, and whether these pertain to certain industries or certain stages of industries' development. The empirical work reviewed here provides insights into the emerging understanding of the effect of location on innovation.

Most of the empirical work reviewed here has been conducted in the USA. There has been significant work done in other countries that this review has not incorporated (cf. Antonelli 1994; Autant-Bernard and Massard 1998; Beise and Stahl 1999; Capron and Cincera 1995; Carrincazeaux *et al.* 1999; Lung *et al.* 1996). These studies could be incorporated in a review so that we may gain a greater appreciation of how the effects of location vary across national borders and the role that the institutions and systems of innovation play.

Most importantly, we still have a limited understanding of the way in which knowledge spillovers occur and benefit innovative activity. Marshall (1949: 152–3) tells us that knowledge 'is in the air' and although we may cite Marshall, this answer is simply not very satisfying. To date, the mechanisms of externalities and knowledge spillovers have not yet been made explicit. Many researchers have tried to estimate the geographic boundaries of knowledge spillovers. The consensus is that knowledge spillovers are geographically bounded within a limited space over which interaction and communication is facilitated, search intensity is increased, and task coordination is enhanced. Due to language, cultural, and other institutional differences, we expect that knowledge spillovers will be more easily captured within national boundaries. In addition, there is also a literature that documents the importance of social interaction, local networks, and personal communication in knowledge transmission, but we do not know how social interaction is initiated, how it evolves into a working relationship, and how economically useful knowledge is created.

References

Adams, J. D., and Jaffe, A. B. 1996. Bounding the effects of R&D: an investigation using matched establishment-firm data. *The RAND Journal of Economics*, 94 (winter), 700–21.

ALLEN, R. 1983. Collective invention. *Journal of Economic Behavior and Organization*, 4: 1–24.

ALMEIDA, P., and KOGUT, B. 1997. The exploration of technological diversity and the geographic localization of innovation. *Small Business Economics*, 9: 21–31.

ANSELIN, L., VARGA, A., and ACS, Z. 1997. Local geographic spillovers between university research and high technology innovation. *Journal of Urban Economics*, 42: 422–48.

ANTONELLI, C. 1994. Technological districts localized spillovers and productivity growth: the Italian evidence of technological externalities in the core regions. *International Review of Applied Economics*, 18–30.

APPOLD, S. J. 1991. The location processes of industrial research laboratories. *Annals of Regional Science*, 25: 131–44.

ARORA, A., and GAMBARDELLA, A. 1990. Complementarity and external linkages: the strategies of large firms in biotechnology. *The Journal of Industrial Economics*, 38: 361–79.

ARROW, K. J. 1962. Economic welfare and the allocation of resources for invention. In Nelson 1962.

AUDRETSCH, D. B., and FELDMAN, M. P. 1996. R&D spillovers and the geography of innovation and production. *American Economic Review*, 86/3: 630–40.

——and STEPHAN, P. E. 1996. Company-scientist locational links: the case of biotechnology. *American Economic Review*, 86/3: 641–52.

——and VIVARELLI, M. 1994. Small firms and R&D spillovers: evidence from Italy. *Small Business Economics*, 8/3: 249–58.

AUTANT-BERNARD, C., and MASSARD, N. 1998. Innovation and externalities: does geographic proximity matter? CREUSET Working Paper.

BANIA, N., EBERTS, R. W., and FOGARTY, M. S. 1993. Universities and the startup of new companies: can we generalize from Route 128 and Silicon Valley? *Review of Economics and Statistics*, 75/4 (Nov.), 761–6.

BARTEL, A., and LICHTENBERG, F. 1987. The comparative advantage of educated workers in implementing new technologies. *Review of Economics and Statistics*, 69: 1–11.

BEESON, P., and MONTGOMERY, E. 1992. The effects of colleges and universities on local labor markets. *Review of Economics and Statistics*, 75: 753–61.

BEISE, M., and STAHL, H. 1999. Public research and industrial innovations in Germany. *Research Policy*, 28/4 (Apr.), 397–422.

BOLLINGER, L., HOPE, K., and UTTERBACK, J. M. 1983. A review of the literature and hypothesis on new technology-based firms. *Research Policy*, 12: 1–14.

BRANSTETTER, L. 1998. Are international spillovers international or intranational in scope? Microeconometric evidence from the U.S. and Japan. *Annales D'Économie et de Statistique*, 49/50.

——forthcoming. Looking for international knowledge spillovers: a review of the literature with suggestions for new approaches. *Journal of International Economics*.

BRAUNDERHJELM, P., and SVENSSON, R. 1996. Host country characteristics and agglomeration in foreign direct investment. *Applied Economics*, 28/7: 833–40.

BROWN, L. A. 1981. *Innovation Diffusion: A New Perspective*. New York: Methuen.

CABALLERO, R. J., and JAFFE, A. B. 1993. How high are the giants' shoulders: an empirical assessment of knowledge spillovers and creative destruction in a model of economic growth. In *NBER Macroeconomics Annual 1993*, ed. O. Blanchard and S. Fischer. Cambridge, Mass. and London: MIT Press, 15–74.

Capron, H., and Cincera, M. 1995. Opportunités et externalités technologiques de la productivité des grandes firmes mondiales. In *Technologie et Performances Économiques*, ed. J. A. Héraud Haudevill and M. Humbert. Paris, Economica 279–309.

Carrincazeaux, C., Lung, Y., and Rallet, A. 1997. De la localisation à l'organisation spatiale des activités de recherche-développement des entreprises: hypothéses théoriques et résultats empiriques dans le cas de la France. Paper presented at the 46th AFSE Congress, Sept. Paris 16.

Coe, D. T., and Helpman, E. 1995. International R&D spillovers. *European Economic Review*, 39: 859–87.

Cohen, W. 1995. Empirical studies of innovative activity. In *Handbook of the Economics of Innovation and Technological Change*, ed. P. Stoneman. Cambridge, Mass.: Blackwell. Publishers 182–264.

—— and Levinthal, D. A. 1989. Innovation and learning: the two faces of R&D. *The Economic Journal*, 99: 569–96.

Darby, M. R., and Zucker, L. G. 1996. Star scientists, institutions and the entry of Japanese biotech enterprises. NBER Working Paper No. 5795.

Davelaar, E., and Nijkamp, P. 1989. The role of the metropolitan milieu as an incubator center for technological innovations: a Dutch case study. *Urban Studies*, 26: 516–29.

David, P., and Rosenbloom, J. 1990. Marshallian factor markets externalities and the dynamics of industrial localization. *Journal of Urban Economics*, 28: 349–70.

Dorfman, N. S. 1983. Route 128: the development of a regional high-technology economy. *Research Policy*, 12: 299–316.

Feldman, M. P. 1994*a*. Knowledge complementarity and innovation. *Small Business Economics*, 6: 363–72.

—— 1994*b*. *The Geography of Innovation*. Boston: Kluwer Academic Publishers.

—— and Audretsch, D. B. 1996. Science-based diversity, specialization, localized competition and innovation. Mimeo.

—— and Lichtenberg, F. R. 1998. The interaction between public and private R&D investment: cross-country evidence from European Community's R&D information service. *Annales D'Économie et de Statistique*, 49–50: 199–222.

Fors, G., and Zejan, M. forthcoming. Location of R&D by Swedish multinationals and technological specialization of host countries. *Scandinavian Journal of Economics*.

Frankel, J., and Romer, D. 1997. Trade and growth: an empirical investigation. NBER Working Paper No. 5476.

—— —— and Cyrus, T. 1997. Trade and growth in East Asian countries: cause and effect. NBER Working Paper No. 5732.

Glaeser, E. 1998. Are cities dying? *Journal of Economic Perspectives*, 12/2 (spring), 139–60.

—— Kallal, H. D., Scheinkman, J. D., and Shleifer, A. 1992. Growth in cities. *Journal of Political Economy*, 100: 1126–52.

Griliches, Z. 1979. Issues in assessing the contribution of R&D to productivity growth. *Bell Journal of Economics*, 10: 92–116.

—— 1990. Patent statistics as economic indicator: a survey. *Journal of Economic Literature*, 28: 1661–707.

Griliches, Z. 1992. The search for R&D spillovers. *Scandinavian Journal of Economics*, 94 (suppl.), 29–47.

Harrison, B., Kelley, M. R., and Gant, J. 1996. Innovative firm behavior and local milieu: exploring the intersection of agglomeration, firm effects, and technological change. *Economic Geography*, 72/3 (July), 233–58.

Head, C. K., Ries, J. C., and Swenson, D. 1995. Agglomeration benefits and location choice: evidence from Japanese manufacturing investment in the United States. *Journal of International Economics*, 38/3–4 (May), 223–47.

——————1999. Attracting foreign manufacturing: investment promotion and agglomeration. *Regional Science and Urban Economics*, 29/2 (Mar.), 197–218.

Helper, S. 1995. Supplier relations and adoption of new technology: results of survey research in the U.S. auto industry. NBER Working Paper No. 5278.

Henderson, J. V. 1974. The size and types of cities. *American Economic Review*, 64: 1640–56.

——1983. Industrial base and city size. *American Economic Review*, 73: 164–8.

——1986. Efficiency of resource usage and city size. *Journal of Urban Economics*, 19: 47–70.

——1997. Externalities and industrial development. *Journal of Urban Economics*, 42/3 (Nov.), 449–70.

Henderson, R. 1993. Underinvestment and incompetence as responses to radical innovation: evidence from the photolithographic alignment equipment industry. *The RAND Journal of Economics*, 24/2 (summer), 248–70.

——1994. Managing innovation in the information age. *Harvard Business Review*, 72 (Jan.–Feb.), 100–5.

——and Cockburn, I. 1996. Scale, scope, and spillovers: the determinants of research productivity in drug discovery. *The RAND Journal of Economics*, 27: 32–59.

Irwin, D. A., and Klenow, P. J. 1994. Learning by doing: spillovers in the semiconductor industry. *Journal of Political Economy*, 102/6: 1200–27.

Jacobs, J. 1969. *The Economy of Cities*. New York: Random House.

Jaffe, A. 1986. Technological opportunity and spillovers of R&D. *American Economic Review*, 76: 984–1001.

——1989. The real effects of academic research. *American Economic Review*, 79: 957–70.

——and Trajtenberg, M. 1996. Flows of knowledge from universities and federal labs: modeling the flows of patent citations over time and across institutional and geographic boundaries. NBER Working Paper No. 5712.

————and Henderson, R. 1993. Geographical localization of knowledge spillovers as evidenced by patent citations. *Quarterly Journal of Economics*, 108: 577–98.

Justman, M. 1994. The effect of local demand on industry location. *The Review of Economics and Statistics*, 76 (Nov.), 742–53.

Keller, W. 1997. Trade and the transmission of technology. NBER Working Paper No. 6113.

——1998. Are international R&D spillovers trade-related? Analyzing spillovers among randomly matched trade partners. *European Economic Review*, 42/8 (Sept.), 1469–81.

Kline, S., and Rosenberg, N. 1987. An overview of innovation. In *The Positive Sum Strategy*, ed. R. Landau and N. Rosenberg. Washington: National Academy Press.

Kogut, B., and Chang, S. J. 1991. Technological capabilities and Japanese foreign direct investment in the United States. *Review of Economics and Statistics*, 73: 401–14.

Krugman, P. 1991*a*. Increasing returns and economic geography. *Journal of Political Economy*, 99: 483–99.

—— 1991*b*. *Geography and Trade*. Cambridge, Mass.: MIT Press.

Lamoreaux, N. R., and Sokoloff, K. L. 1997. Location and technological change in the American glass industry during the late nineteenth and early twentieth centuries. NBER Working Paper No. 5938.

Lazonick, W. 1993. Industrial clusters versus global webs: organizational capabilities in the American economy. *Industrial and Corporate Change*, 2/1: 1–24.

Lerner, J. 1999. The government as venture capitalist: the long run impact of the SBIR program. *Journal of Business*, 72/3 (July), 285–318.

Leslie, S., and Kargon, R. 1996. Selling Silicon Valley. *Business History Review*, 70/4 (winter), 435–72.

Levin, R. C., Klevorick, A. K., Nelson, R. R., and Winter, S. G. 1987. Appropriating the returns from industrial research and development. *Brookings Papers on Economic Activity*, 3: 783–820.

Liebeskind, J. P., Oliver, A. L., Zucker, L. G., and Brewer, M. 1996. Social networks, learning and flexibility: sourcing scientific knowledge in new biotechnology firms. *Organization Science*, 7 Feb.

Loesch, A. 1954. *The Economics of Location*. New Haven: Yale University Press.

Lucas, R. 1988. On the mechanics of economic development. *Journal of Monetary Economics*, 22: 3–39.

—— 1993. Making a miracle. *Econometrica*, 61: 251–72.

Lung Y., Rallet, A., and Torre, A. 1996. Innovative activity and geographical proximity. European Regional Science Association, 36th European Congress. ETH Zurich, Switzerland, 26–30 Aug.

Malecki, E. J. 1987. The R&D location of the firm and creative regions: a survey. *Technovation*, 6: 205–22.

Mansfield, E. 1995. Academic research underlying industrial innovations: sources, characteristics, and financing. *Review of Economics and Statistics*, 1: 55–65.

Marshall, A. 1949. *Elements of Economics of Industry*. London: Macmillan.

Moomaw, R. 1988. Agglomeration economies: localization or urbanization? *Urban Studies*, 25: 150–61.

Nadiri, M. I., and Mamuneas, T. P. 1996. Public R&D policies and cost behavior of the US manufacturing industries. *Journal of Public Economies*, 63/1 (Dec.), 57–81.

Nakamura, R. 1985. Agglomeration economies in urban manufacturing industries: a case of Japanese cities. *Journal of Urban Economics*, 17: 108–24.

National Science Foundation 1998. *Science & Engineering Indicators—1998*. Washington: Government Printing Office.

Nelson, R. R., ed. 1962. *The Rate and Direction of Inventive Activity.* Princeton: Princeton University Press.

Park, W. G. 1995. International R&D spillovers and OECD economic growth. *Economic Inquiry*, 33: 571–91.

Piore, M. J., and Sabel, C. F. 1984. *The Second Industrial Divide: Possibilities for Prosperity*. New York: Basic Books.

Porter, M. 1990. *The Competitive Advantage of Nations*. New York: The Free Press.

Romer, P. M. 1986. Increasing returns and long run growth. *Journal of Political Economy*, 94: 1002–37.

—— 1990. Endogenous technological change. *Journal of Political Economy*, 98/5: 71–102.

Rosenberg, N. 1982. *Inside the Black Box: Technology and Economics*. Cambridge: Cambridge University Press.

—— 1994. *Exploring the Black Box: Technology, Economics, and History*. New York: Cambridge University Press.

Saxenian, A. 1994. *Regional Advantage*. Cambridge, Mass.: Harvard University Press.

Scott, A. J. 1993. *Technopolis: High-Technology Industry and Regional Development in Southern California*. Berkeley: University of California Press.

Smith, D., and Florida, R. 1994. Agglomeration and industry location: an econometric analysis of Japanese-affiliated manufacturing establishments in automotive related industries. *Journal of Urban Economics*, 36: 23–41.

Sokoloff, K. L. 1988. Inventive activity in early industrial America: evidence from patent records, 1790–1846. *Journal of Economic History*, 48/4: 813–50.

Stephan, P. E. 1996. The economics of science. *Journal of Economic Literature*, 34/3: 1199–235.

Stiglitz, J. 1987. Learning to learn, localized learning and technological progress. In *Economic Policy and Technological Performance*, ed. P. Dasgupta and P. Stoneman. Cambridge: Cambridge University Press.

Storper, M. 1995. Regional technology coalitions: an essential dimension of national technology policy. *Research Policy*, 24: 895–911.

Thompson, W. R. 1962. Locational differences in inventive effort and their determinants. In Nelson 1962.

Trajtenberg, M. 1990. *Economic Analysis of Product Innovation: The Case of CT Scanners*. Cambridge, Mass.: Harvard University Press.

Valente, T. 1995. *Network Models of the Diffusion of Innovation*. New Jersey: Hampton Press.

Von Hipple, E. 1994. Sticky information and the locus of problem solving: implications for innovation. *Management Science*, 40: 429–39.

Zeckhauser, R. 1996. The challenge of contracting for technological information. *Proceedings of the National Academy of Sciences of the United States of America*, 93: 12,743–8.

Zucker, L. G., and Darby, M. R. 1996. Star scientists and institutional transformation: patterns of invention and innovation in the formation of the biotechnology industry. *Proceedings of the National Academy of Science*, 93 (Nov.), 12,709–16.

—— —— and Armstrong, J. 1998*a*. Geographically localized knowledge: spillovers or markers? *Economic Inquiry*, 36/1 (Jan.), 65–86.

—— —— and Brewer, M. B. 1998*b*. Intellectual human capital and the birth of U.S. biotechnology enterprises. *American Economic Review*, 88/1: 290–306.

Chapter **20**

Restructuring and Innovation in Long-Term Regional Change

Cristiano Antonelli

Introduction

Regions are simultaneously a source of major hysteretic constraints and a source of innovation opportunity. Hysteretic constraints result from the duration and irreversibility of fixed and intangible capital. Locations may thus be characterized by long-term rigidity and irreversibility or may provide a context for technological communication, external knowledge, and learning opportunities. Location is thus an important factor in assessing the rate and direction of technological change and economic fortune.

All changes in relative prices and desired output levels oblige incumbents to change the existing combination of superfixed and variable factors. Irreversibility, however, makes technical substitution impossible and pushes firms to out-of-equilibrium conditions. Such conditions can become a powerful inducement factor to try and introduce localized technological changes. To avoid technical inefficiency, induced innovations are introduced along the endowment line defined in terms of the original amounts of superfixed production factors.

The access to collective knowledge and the opportunities for technological pooling provided by effective communication systems, within technological districts, favor the efficiency of innovation activities within firms and the eventual introduction of localized technological changes. In turn, enhanced efficiency of innovation activities of firms and faster rates of introduction of innovations increase the amount of collective knowledge available in the

The comments of Maryann Feldman on preliminary versions are gratefully acknowledged as well as the support of the European Union TSER project industrial districts and localised technological knowledge and the support of the Consiglio Nazionale delle Ricerche (research grants Nos. 98.03795.PS10 and 97.05173.CT10).

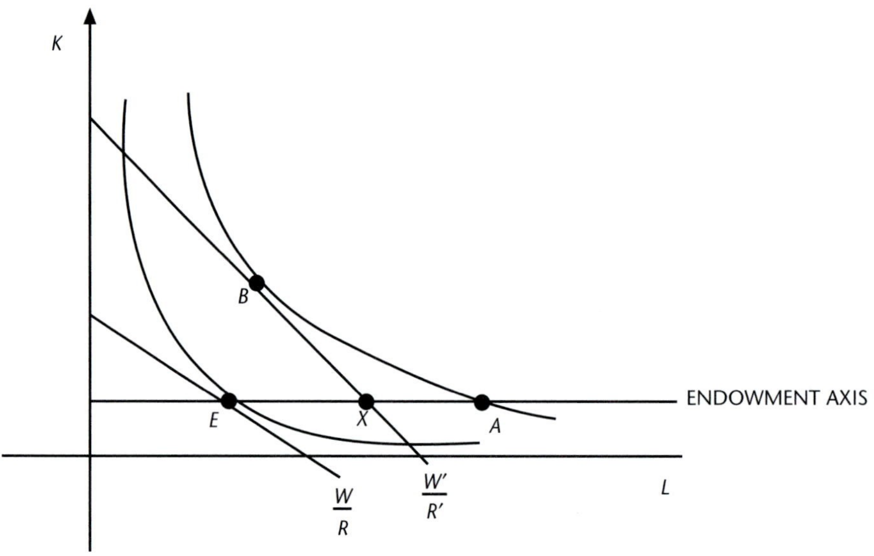

Fig. 20.1. Irreversibility, technical inefficiency, and the inducement to innovate

region. A spiraling interaction fueled by the localized positive feedback between firms and regions can take place with significant effects in terms of dynamic increasing returns both at the regional and the firm levels.

Regions are a major factor in making technological change hysteretic. Because of regional institutions and place-specific opportunities, innovations are introduced along technological paths that are defined in terms of factor intensity and technological continuity and based upon complementarity and interoperability and reflect different technological vintages. The interaction of the dynamics of localized technological changes and communication processes explains the clustering of innovations in well-defined technological districts as well as the rate and direction of introduction of technological changes.

This chapter elaborates an interpretative framework to understand the long-term interactions between location in regional space, irreversibility, and localized technological change. In the second section, a simple model shows how changes in demand and factor prices together with superfixed production factors induce the endogenous introduction of localized technological changes. In turn the interaction of endogenous technological change and communication processes, presented in the third section, explains the clustering of innovations in well-defined regional spaces, as well as the key role of knowledge-intensive business services and technological cooperation in assessing the innovative capability of regional innovation systems. The implications for economic analysis and the relevant policy issues are considered in the conclusions.

The Inducement of Localized Technological Change

An array of detailed empirical analyses, especially in industrial economics, has highlighted the key role of superfixed production factors (Antonelli 1999). Superfixed production factors are long-lasting, tangible, and intangible assets which once installed can be replaced only with huge costs and a long time span. Recent advances in the theory of investment are now dealing with such empirical evidence (Dixit 1992). The analysis of sunk costs has made important contributions to the theory of the firm and markets because it has provided a better understanding of the long-term effects of historic time in assessing the conduct of firms and the results of their strategic interaction in the market place (Sutton 1991).

Technical interrelatedness, which takes the form of major technical constraints among phases of the production process and between capital, intermediary goods and skills, subsystem bottlenecks and complementary assets, dedicated and idiosyncratic competence are all factors that keep the firm in a limited region of existing production frontiers or isoquants. Sunk costs are especially relevant when the discrepancy between purchasing costs of capital goods and resale prices in secondary markets is high: this is the case of most intangible assets. The idiosyncratic characteristics of the production process of each firm—such as reputation in both product and factor markets, type of managerial organization, standard operating procedures, capital structure and shareholder expectations, and last but not least traditions—add on to make evident the superfixed character of a significant portion of their production factors. Finally and most importantly, location in a well-defined regional space is a major factor of rigidity. Location roots firms in a variety of ways: plants and buildings are often difficult to change and expand; user–producer relations in intermediary markets have a strong regional aspect, as well as internal and external labor markets. Regions are a major factor of irreversibility also for the important role of infrastructures such as transportation, telecommunications networks, and research institutions.

When superfixed production factors are relevant, in that they constitute a major part of total production factors, all adjustments of firms to the changing conditions of the business environment are subject to significant constraints. Changes in the production mix and output size expose firms to relevant price and output 'Farrell' inefficiency, with the eventual emergence of 'quasi-losses'. In these circumstances, firms are pushed in out-of-equilibrium conditions that induce them to try and find a solution in the form of a new technology. In this case, they will incur innovation costs, that is, the costs of implementing their tacit knowledge and actually changing their technology.

In these circumstances, the implementation of tacit knowledge, the generation of localized technological knowledge, and the introduction of new technologies that make it possible to re-establish the efficiency conditions become a viable alternative to the quasi-losses.

On this basis, we can now turn to a brief formal exposition of the model.

Let us consider a firm in equilibrium with a given level of superfixed production factors and a ratio of wages W to capital rental costs R at point E. After a change in relative prices creating a new level of wages W' and rental costs R', the firm of the standard microeconomics textbook would choose the new technique B where the new marginal rate of substitution equals the slope of the new relative prices. A similar process takes place when the firm is exposed to increases in the level of demand. When demand increases, textbook firms should increase the levels of inputs, with a given technique, in order to expand output to the new desired level. Now that firm would reach the point B on the new isoquant placed further to the right on the same map. The combination of both changes makes the situation even more evident.

Such solutions however imply change in the levels of superfixed production factors: typically it is a very long-term solution that engenders relevant costs and may actually be impossible. It is now clear that our context of analysis is an extension of the time horizon of the traditional short-term cost and production analysis.

The firm with superfixed production factors cannot do any better than selecting the technique A, defined by the intersection between the isoquant and the endowment axis. This implies higher costs. Alternatively the incumbent can select the technique defined by the intersection between the new isocost and the endowment axis, but for a given map of isoquants and hence for a given technology, the new solution implies clear output inefficiency in terms of lower levels of output. In these conditions, it is clear that a firm exposed to significant changes either in the demand for its product or in the relative price of production factors is bound to experience either a decline in price efficiency or an emerging output efficiency (Farrell 1957). More directly, we can define the effects of such situations as quasi-losses.

We can write the quasi-loss function associated with both the changes in the relative prices of inputs and in the demand for incumbents characterized by relevant superfixed production factors, as follows:

$$QL = f(\mathrm{d}AX), \tag{1}$$

where QL are the quasi-losses measured in terms of the technical distance between A at the intersection between the endowment axis and the new isoquant and any new solution X on the endowment axis.

The introduction of a new localized technology can help the firm to restore equilibrium and even reduce costs. All new technologies that reshape the isoquant map along the endowment axis so as to make the solution X 'viable', enable the productive factors to be used rationally so as to restore the general price efficiency of the firm and can lead to an overall increase in efficiency and eventually in total factor productivity.

We can now turn our attention to the role of technological knowledge and technological change. In order to change their technology, firms must capitalize on the tacit knowledge acquired through the learning that has been going on in the techniques being used, and invest in formal R&D activities. Systematic search for available external knowledge is also necessary and relevant communication costs are associated with this. This research process can stop when the new technology is such that the firm reaches the equilibrium where the marginal rate of substitution again equals the slope of the new isocosts yet remaining on the endowment axis. Further movements along the endowment axis however are welcomed. They are actually likely to generate an increase in total factor productivity in monetary terms.

The costs of innovation activities necessary to move the isoquant along the endowment axis towards (and possibly beyond) the point *X* are a function of the leftward distance from:

$$CTI = g(\mathrm{d}XA), \tag{2}$$

where *CTI* represents the innovation costs borne in implementing learning procedures, acquiring external knowledge, and hence building technological communication channels with other firms and with other research institutions, operating R&D laboratories, and broadly of all the activities directed towards the introduction of the technological changes that are necessary to reshape the isoquant so as to move it along the endowment axis between the technique *E* towards and beyond the new point *X*.[1]

A firm that chooses to stay in technique *A* incurs a decline in general efficiency but avoids all innovation costs. Conversely, a firm that chooses the new technology *X* avoids the decline in efficiency, but incurs substantial innovation costs which are necessary to find the new technology that enables the firm to produce as much as it would have done on the old isoquant but next to and actually beyond the intersection between the new isocost and the endowment line.

We are now in a position to portray the decision process of the firm with the standard tools of profit maximization. The profit equation for the firm reads as follows:

$$P = R(\mathrm{d}AX) - CTI(\mathrm{d}XA) \tag{3}$$

where *R* stands for the gross revenue from adjusting to the new factor prices, measured in terms of the reductions in production costs, with respect to technique *A*, made possible by the introduction of technological changes that reduce price and output inefficiency. In other words, the revenue of changing the technology along the endowment axis consists of the reduction in the total

[1] The 'necessary' assumption that $g > 0$ seems plausible.

costs in A. $CTI(dAX)$ are the innovation costs and can be measured in terms of the distance on the endowment line between A and X.

Standard maximization of the profit equation enables the identification of the 'correct' amount of innovation costs a firm can bear, for a given technology production function 'g', that is, for a given technological capability to create new technological knowledge and eventually introduce new technologies with a given amount of economic resources.

This geometric approach makes it possible to relate the amount of innovation selected directly to the technical inefficiency arising from superfixed production factors so as to establish a trade-off between technical inefficiency and technological innovation. Maximization here identifies the 'best' distance on the endowment axis a firm can travel by means of the introduction of localized technological changes, induced by the twin constraints of a production process characterized by heavy superfixed inputs and changes both in product and factor markets.

The introduction of localized technological changes along the endowment axis will make it possible for firms that cope with the increase in demand levels and changes in the relative prices of production factors to adjust the ratio of marginal productivities, actually changing the usage intensity of the superfixed production factor. The direction of technological change will be shaped by the endowment of superfixed production factors. Technological innovations introduced in this context will be strongly characterized by high levels of sequential cumulability, interoperability, complementarity, and technological continuity with respect to the existing and irreversible production factors. The rate of technological change in turn will be affected by the levels of turbulence of the business environment and the share of superfixed production factors of total costs. The larger are the former and the latter, the larger is the inducement to rely upon technological change in order to cope with the new factor and product market conditions.

The actual rate of technological change, for given levels of superfixed production factors and entropy in the product and factor markets, will be clearly determined by the effective capability of firms to generate new technological knowledge and hence technological innovations. With high innovation costs, incumbents will be unable to meet the quasi-losses with the introduction of innovation and will eventually decline. With medium innovation costs, incumbents are induced to make only incremental innovations so as to reduce the distance on the endowment axis between A and the intersection between the isocost and the endowment axis. In these circumstances, incumbents can only reduce quasi-losses and come closer to the best practice. With low innovation costs and large technological opportunities, incumbents can meet the emerging quasi-losses with the successful introduction of radical innovations that make possible a quantum leap on the endowment axis and actually go beyond the 'equilibrium' point with a substantial increase of total factor productivity.

It is now clear that location within regions plays a twin role. On the one hand, it is a major source of irreversibility: regions reduce the capability of firms to perform standard technical substitution on the existing map of isoquants, but on the other they can provide access to important sources of technological knowledge. Location within a region can increase the access to technological opportunities routed in a specific system of embedded relations and help increase the general efficiency of the technological production function '*g*' and hence can favor the introduction of technological innovation. Location within a region may introduce significant technological changes that enable the substantial increase of total factor productivity.

In this context, the access conditions to external knowledge and the levels of technological opportunities that stem from the interaction and technological communication among firms and between firms and local research institutions within a region play a major role.

The Role of Local Communication in the Dynamics of Localized Technological Change

The notion of localized technological knowledge emerges at the crossroads of the debates in the economics of knowledge about its codified or tacit character and its public or quasi-private nature as an economic good. The notion of localized knowledge stresses the process by means of which new knowledge is generated. In this approach, the production of technological knowledge is heavily dependent on the multiplicative relationship of: (1) internal learning processes which lead to the accumulation of tacit knowledge, (2) internal R&D activities which enable codified knowledge to be gathered, (3) the access to external tacit knowledge by means of the socialization of experience and competence among firms, and (4) the access to and eventual recombination of existing external codified knowledge. In such a complex mix, each element is complementary and indispensable (Antonelli forthcoming).

This approach has many implications. First, the localized character of technological knowledge increases its appropriability but reduces its spontaneous circulation in the economic system. Technological knowledge in fact is viewed as strongly embedded: it is industry-specific, region-specific, and firm-specific; and because of this it is costly to use elsewhere: respectively in other industries, other regions, and other firms. The transfer and adaptation of localized technological knowledge from one industry, region, and firm to another involves specific actions of firms and costs that need to be assessed. Secondly, localized knowledge is now viewed as a basic, indivisible, and single intermediary input into the production process of new knowledge. Hence knowledge has the typical codified characteristics of public goods, and yet it is dispersed and embedded in a variety of specific and localized contexts of application and partly appropriated by a myriad of users: as such its collective character is stressed.

Access to collective knowledge in turn depends on the extent to which effective communication among innovators takes place through the innovation system. In this context, the properties of economic systems, conceived as communication networks into which information flows, matter in explaining the capability of each agent to generate new technological knowledge. The conditions for technological communication become relevant and their assessment contributes significantly to the analysis of local innovation systems (Freeman 1991 and 1997; Nelson 1993; Antonelli 1999).

Localization within regional innovation systems characterized by effective communication channels can play a major role in this context. Agglomeration favors interaction and repeated exchanges; reduces opportunistic and free-riding behaviors. Agglomeration reduces transactions costs associated with the absorption of technological externalities (Lundvall 1985; Von Hippel 1988; Utterback 1994; Lamberton 1996 and 1997; Engelbrecht 1998; Antonelli forthcoming).

Technological communication differs from technological externalities. Too much emphasis has been put in the innovation systems literature on technological externalities as if external technological knowledge could be acquired freely in the 'atmosphere' without dedicated efforts. The notion of technological externalities is consistent with the Arrovian notion of technological information, a public good with low levels of appropriability and excludability. The notion of technological communication seems far more appropriate to the new theorizing about the quasi-private and hence collective nature of localized technological knowledge (Lamberton 1971, 1996, 1997; Cohen and Levinthal 1989; Lundvall 1985; Krugman 1996).

Recent progress in the analysis of communication processes suggests the application to communication processes of the methodology of spatial stochastic interactions. Within communication networks, we see in fact that at each point in time, the magnitude and the impact of the effective flow of information which is both emitted and received by each agent can be thought to be the outcome of the interaction between two classes of stochastic events: (1) the connectivity probability that the flows of effective communication and the exchange of information take place within information networks and (2) the receptivity probability that the results of the research and learning efforts of each firm in the system are effectively assimilated and eventually implemented by the amount of external information available in the technological environment. In turn the distribution of connectivity and receptivity probabilities is influenced by but not deterministically dependent upon the quality of connectivity links, their density, and the distance among firms and other research institutions and the distribution and intentional efforts of receptive agents. This methodology, moreover, makes it possible to reproduce analytically the dynamic laws of a process where the actual transfer of technological information can either take place or decay: stochastically, in fact, communication fails (David and Foray 1994; Krugman 1996; Antonelli 1999).

Location plays a major role in this context, not only as a factor of constraints in terms of rigidity and irreversibility, but also for its connectivity-enhancing effects. The quality of connectivity among agents can be probabilistically influenced by intentional connectivity-enhancing strategies such as active technological outsourcing, technological cooperation, and location in close vicinity to other innovators. Such communication strategies can in fact be better implemented by location in well-defined regional and local systems where the density of 'technological communicators' is high. Proximity and spatial density enhance technological connectivity on many counts: user–producer relations are easier as well as informal exchanges, labor market mobility, university–firms interactions (Allen 1983; Becattini 1987; Feldman 1994 and 1999; Von Hippel 1988; Castells 1989; Freeman 1991; Lundvall 1985; Utterback 1994).

Technological districts, that is regions which provide high levels of technological communication, are likely to be conducive to a virtuous cycle where irreversibilities and hence out-of-equilibrium conditions lead to fast rates of introduction of new technologies and hence fast increases of total factor productivity which in turn engender new turbulence in the product and factor market places. Regions with low levels of technological communication and high levels of irreversibility cannot resist markets' turbulence and are likely to experience a fast decline of efficiency and market shares. The different levels of effective communication among innovators, as measured by the mixed probability of the communication process, are likely to significantly affect the productivity of the total amount of resources devoted by each firm to research and learning activities and hence substantially reduce innovation costs (Nelson 1987).

This approach makes it possible to appreciate the characteristics of regions in terms of sectoral composition and technological strategies of firms. The variety of firms in terms of size and competence and hence sectoral distribution is an important factor of technological communication. Firms are less reluctant to share their knowledge with firms that are not direct competitors. Mobility of skilled and competent labor within local labor markets is an important factor of technological communication and increases the rates of accumulation of collective knowledge. The distribution and quality of knowledge-intensive business service industries also have important effects on the local economic systems in terms of communication and hence innovative capacity. The local supply of the services of consultants and advisers improves connectivity between agents, sharing learning experiences and creating learning opportunities, and thus advances receptivity. An active supply of knowledge-intensive business services, in terms of distribution, capillarity, competence, and access, can stimulate the technological outsourcing demand by small and medium-sized firms in particular, with in-house R&D. Advanced telecommunication networks, including high speed data communication and high-definition images, play an important role in favoring the local division of innovative labor among research units and learning firms. As growing evidence confirms, digital communication can complement rather than substitute for person-to-person communication. Technological districts with high-quality communication infrastructure can benefit from the spiraling interactions between digital and face-to-face communication. Finally, the quality of local academic infrastructure is an important factor in enhancing the capability of firms to absorb collective knowledge and make productive use of it because of increased opportunities to take advantage of technological externalities and benefit from interaction with the academic community. Agglomeration again can favor formal as well as informal university–enterprises interaction and hence successful technological communication (Mansfield 1991; Bania *et al.* 1993; Jaffe *et al.* 1993; Audretsch and Stephan 1996; Feldman and Audretsch 1999).

Agglomeration favors *de facto* technological cooperation among agents as well. Locally, technological cooperation takes place often within the context of outsourcing strategies with the active participation of suppliers and subcontractors in the identification of new processes and new products. Technological cooperation at the local level can play a major role in assessing the communication probability and hence the innovative capability for it enhances: (1) the circulation of tacit knowledge and its socialization; (2) the opportunity for external learning; (3) the opportunity for accelerated recombination of the bits of codified knowledge generated by each cooperating firm; (4) the scope for capitalizing on potential complementarities between the variety of firms and between the different R&D activities performed by each firm.

The characteristics of each technological district in terms of technological communication conditions should not be thought to be given and/or exogenous. On the contrary, communication conditions are themselves the—partly—intentional outcome of long-term routines, codes of conduct, and actual investments implemented by the strategic behavior of agents and governments to increase the innovation capabilities of economic systems. In fact, effective connections are the result of deliberate action and should be considered to be endogenous: an effort has to be made to establish each effective connection.

In sum, high levels of innovation activities, as induced by good technological communication conditions, are likely to increase the amount of collective knowledge available. This in turn affects positively the efficiency of research activities and further pushes firms along the endowment axis. All the characteristics of a self-reinforcing mechanism, based upon positive feedbacks, are now in place. Localization in a technological district increases the productivity of resources invested in innovation activities and the likelihood of the introduction of technological innovations that actually increase total factor productivity. Increased levels of innovation activities funded by each firm and augmented efforts in activating communication mechanisms increase respectively the amount of collective knowledge available in the districts and the communication probabilities. Fast rates of introduction of innovation push further the demand for the firms, which, for given levels of irreversibility, fuel the inducement to innovate. Higher levels of local technological opportunities, based upon the augmented stock of collective knowledge and the increased levels of open communication channels in place, further increase the efficiency of innovation activities.[2] This process is especially evident within technological districts such as Turin in Piedmont, Modena and Bologna in central Italy, Toulouse in western France, and the local innovation systems of Route 128 and Silicon Valley in the USA.

It is now clear that location in well-defined regions is a factor itself of long-term rigidity and irreversibility and hence potential losses in a turbulent environment and at the same time an opportunity for growth because it provides the context in which technological communication can take place and is hence a factor enhancing the rate of introduction of technological innovations along well-defined directions shaped by the intensity of superfixed production factors.

The stochastic nature of communication processes, however, makes such self-reinforcing feedback mechanisms random. Mixed communication probabilities are especially sensitive to all perturbations in both connectivity and receptivity probabilities. In such conditions, local innovation systems may eventually experience a sharp reduction in general communication efficiency, and reverse negative feedback may take place with major discontinuities in long-term growth patterns.

When technological communication fails, the generation of new knowledge and the related introduction of technological changes become more expensive; firms with a large endowment of superfixed production factors can face the increase in demand and the changes in the relative prices of variable production factors only with a substantial decline in technical efficiency and limited rates of introduction of technological innovations. The advantages of agglomerations decline and industrial districts decay. This is also the story of many traditional industrial districts in central England and northern France. The conditions for technological communication become a key issue of central relevance for a dedicated economic and innovation policy.

Conclusions

Standard microeconomics assumes the adaptive behavior of firms. Firms adapt quantities to prices and vice versa without any possibility of generating

[2] Moreover, local communication probabilities at time t are likely to affect the behavior of agents not only with respect to the levels of their R&D expenditures, but also to the levels of deliberate action taken to build up connections and receptivity which can enhance the efficiency of the funds invested in R&D. Hence the local communication probability at time $t+1$ is influenced, but because of its stochastic nature, not determined by the conduct of the firms at time t.

endogenous changes in their technologies. Adaptive responses, however, are often made difficult by the irreversibility of production factors and relevant sunk costs. In these circumstances, firms can react. In so doing firms change their technology and modify their production conditions. Reactivity, as opposed to adaptivity, is the underlying theme of this chapter. Some limitations to adaptations have been explored and the conditions for reactivity have been assessed with reference to regional change. Economic analysis can make important progress when endogenous structural change, consisting in the intentional introduction of new production and utility functions, as induced and focused by economic factors, is fully acknowledged.

As a matter of fact, regions play a major role in both reducing the scope for adaptation and favoring the conditions for reactivity.

Superfixed production factors are a pervasive condition which economic theory is more and more taking into account. Technical interrelatedness, system bottlenecks, long-term obsolescence, limited span of application of intangible assets, location in well-defined regions are all factors that reduce the capability of firms to adjust, even in the long term, significant chunks of their stock of intangible and tangible capital.

In these conditions, all changes in relative prices and desired output levels are likely to induce a significant decline in both output and price efficiency: firms are unable to produce with the 'correct' combination of flexible and fixed production factors. Emergent technical inefficiency becomes all the more cogent in competitive markets with high levels of technical variety: firms with larger shares, in relation to total costs, of superfixed production factors are soon exposed not only to a decrease of technical efficiency but also to an actual decline of market shares and profits. Such an emergency can be accommodated by established firms with the endogenous generation of localized knowledge and the eventual introduction of localized technological changes that are compatible with superfixed production factors.

Regions and local innovation systems, characterized by high levels of superfixed production factors, business turbulence, and conducive conditions for technological communication are likely to experience fast rates of introduction of technological changes. Location within well-defined regions becomes at the same time a factor of irreversibility and inducement to introduce technological changes and a factor favoring the generation of technological knowledge in highly productive conditions. A local recursive hysteretic process is likely to take place in these circumstances. Much evidence, provided by industrial economics and economic history, about the increasing specialization of regions in the use of specific combinations of inputs, finds a consistent interpretative framework in the model so far elaborated. The stochastic nature of local communication processes and their key role in long-term growth can play a major role in explaining discontinuities in such self-reinforcing mechanisms with sudden declines of the local performances.

In this recursive context, the pervasive role of technological communication adds understanding to explain the dynamics of hysteretic and localized technological change. With high levels of mixed communication probabilities and hence innovation opportunities, firms' reactive responses to all changes in their business environment favor the introduction of localized technological change. The better are the access conditions to external technological knowledge, which flow within communication systems, the higher are the chances of introducing localized technological changes (Freeman 1991 and 1997; Nelson 1993).

Analysis of the interaction of the dynamics of localized technological changes and local communication processes provides important tools with which to understand the clustering of innovations in well-defined regional spaces as well as the emergence of technological systems characterized by the introduction of complementary innovations. In this context, the growing effect of new communication technologies, the diffusion of technological cooperation schemes, and the supply of knowledge-intensive business services play a key role in assessing the innovation capabilities of local innovation systems.

The approach so far elaborated seems useful in many ways. First, it provides a theory and an interpretative framework to understand why local economic systems exposed to similar shocks, in terms of changes of factor and product markets, can react with the introduction of compatible technological changes that increase total factor productivity or assist its eventual decline.

Secondly and most importantly, we now have a theory to understand the dynamics of agglomeration within regional clusters of innovative firms. The virtuous interaction between changes in the business environment and rates of introduction of localized technological changes, as shaped by the characteristics of local communication processes, is such that in regions with high levels of technological communication, the conditions for circulation and actual assimilation of technological information and the introduction of technological innovations reinforce each other with a self-propelling mechanism based upon the dynamics of positive feedback. The dynamics of localized technological change and communication processes can explain the emergence of regional clusters of innovative firms especially around centers of academic excellence.

Thirdly, we now have new elements to understand the role of regions in assessing the persistent dynamic variety of firms within industries. The dynamics of local feedback between regions and firms helps us to understand why firms, located in different regions, react with different strategies and achieve different performances. The regional context of embedment and action of firms needs to be fully taken into account, both in terms of irreversibility and technological environment, when assessing industrial dynamics.

In this context, the traditional outcomes of the analyses about the 'tragedy of commons' can be reversed (Stiglitz 1994). The positive effects of the renewable and ever-expanding commons of technological knowledge, embedded in well-defined regions, can be appreciated. The notion of collective knowledge, viewed as the result of a dynamic accumulation process characterized by the synchronic and diachronic complementarity between the research and learning activities of a myriad of co-localized agents, opens the way to new research into the economics of 'technological commons'. The study of technological commons can help us to understand the dynamics of increasing returns in the production of knowledge, the emergence of new technological systems, and the key role of technological opportunities stemming from the interdependent innovation capabilities of firms within local innovation systems.

Finally, receptivity-enhancing strategies can become the target of dedicated strategies at the company level. Receptivity and connectivity can be intentionally implemented by firms better aware of the role of technological communication to acquire and make use of external knowledge generated by other firms, reducing the communication lags and the not-invented-here syndrome.

The implications for industrial and innovation policies are far reaching. The appreciation of the factors governing the technological communication and the internalization of local technological externalities among firms which are involved in complementary innovation activities become a possible strategy for public intervention in that such activities will lead to an increase in the productivity of resources invested in innovation activities. More specifically, public subsidies to enhance technological communication in terms of better trade conditions for disembodied technological knowledge, local supply of knowledge-intensive business services, technological cooperation both among firms and between firms and universities, accelerated licensing of patents and know-how, can offer firms the opportunity to internalize the spillover of localized technological knowledge and take better advantage of available external knowledge with the active participation of both parties in the trade: vendors and customers. Enhanced rates of introduction of technological changes and faster rates of increase of total factor productivity may be obtained with the implementation of local communication processes.

References

Allen, Robert C. 1983. Collective invention. *Journal of Economic Behavior and Organization*, 4: 1–24.

Amendola, Mario, and Bruno, Sergio 1990. The behaviour of the innovative firm: relations to the environment. *Research Policy*, 19: 419–34.

Antonelli, Cristiano 1986*a*. *L'Attività innovativa in un distretto tecnologico.* Turin: Edizioni della Fondazione Agnelli.

—— 1986*b*. Technological districts and regional innovation capacity. *Revue d'Économie Régionale et Urbaine*, 5: 695–705.

—— 1987. The determinants of the distribution of innovative activity in a metropolitan area: the case of Turin. *Regional Studies*, 21: 85–94.

—— 1990. Induced adoption and externalities in the regional diffusion of new information technology. *Regional Studies*, 24: 31–40.

——1994. Technological districts, localized spillovers and productivity growth: the Italian evidence on technological externalities in the core regions. *International Review of Applied Economics*, 8: 31–45.

——1995. *The Economics of Localized Technological Change and Industrial Dynamics*. Boston: Kluwer Academic Press.

——1999. *The Microdynamics of Technological Change*. London: Routledge.

——forthcoming. Collective knowledge communication and innovation: the evidence of technological districts. *Regional Studies*.

Arora, Ashish 1995. Licencing tacit knowledge: intellectual property rights and the market for know-how. *Economics of Innovation and New Technology*, 4: 41–60.

——and Gambardella, Alfonso 1990. Internal knowledge and external linkages: theoretical issues and an application to biotechnology. *Journal of Industrial Economics*, 38: 361–79.

Arrow, Kenneth J. 1962. Economic welfare and the allocation of resources for invention. In *The Rate and Direction of Inventive Activity: Economic and Social Factors*, ed. Richard R. Nelson. Princeton: Princeton University Press.

Audretsch, David B., and Stephan, Paula 1996. Company-scientist locational links: the case of biotechnology. *American Economic Review*, 86: 641–52.

Bania, Neil, Eberts, W. Randall, and Fogarty, Michael S. 1993. Universities and the startup of new companies: can we generalize from Route 128 and Silicon Valley. *Review of Economics and Statistics*, 75: 761–6.

Becattini, Giacomo, ed. 1987. *Mercato e forze locali: il distretto industriale*. Bologna: Il Mulino.

Castells, Manuel 1989. *The Informational City: Information Technology, Economic Restructuring, and the Urban-Regional Process*. Oxford: Blackwell.

Cohen, Wesley M., and Levinthal, Daniel A. 1989. Innovation and learning: the two faces of R&D. *Economic Journal*, 99: 569–96.

David, Paul A. 1975. *Technical Choice Innovation and Economic Growth*. Cambridge: Cambridge University Press.

——1993. Knowledge property and the system dynamics of technological change. *Proceedings of the World Bank Annual Conference on Development Economics*. Washington: The World Bank.

——and Foray, Dominique 1994. The economics of EDI standards diffusion. In *Global Telecommunications Strategies and Technological Changes*, ed. Gerard Pogorel. Amsterdam: North-Holland.

Dixit, Avinash 1992. Investment and hysteresis. *Journal of Economic Perspectives*, 6: 107–32.

Engelbrecht, Hans-Jurgen 1998. A communication perspective on the international information and knowledge system. *Information Economics and Policy*, 10: 359–67.

Farrell, M. J. 1957. The measurement of productive efficiency. *Journal of the Royal Statistical Society*, Series A, 120: 253–81.

Feldman, Maryann P. 1994. *The Geography of Innovation*. Dordrecht: Kluwer Academic Publishers.

——1999. The new economics of innovation spillovers and agglomeration: a review of empirical studies. *Economics of Innovation and New Technology*, 8: 5–26.

——and Audretsch, David B. 1999. Innovation in cities: science-based diversity specialization and localized competition. *European Economic Review*, 43: 409–30.

FREEMAN, CHRISTOPHER 1991. Networks of innovators: a synthesis of research issues. *Research Policy*, 20: 499–514.

—— 1997. The national system of innovation in historical perspective. In *Technology Globalisation and Economic Performance*, ed. Daniele Archibugi and Jonathan Michie. Cambridge: Cambridge University Press.

GRILICHES, ZVI 1992. The search for R&D spillover. *Scandinavian Journal of Economics*, 94 (suppl.), 29–47.

JAFFE, ADAM, TRAJTENBERG, MANUEL, and HENDERSON, REBECCA 1993. Geographic localization and knowledge spillovers as evidenced by patent citations. *Quarterly Journal of Economics*, 108: 577–98.

KRUGMAN, PAUL 1996. *The Self-Organizing Economy*. Oxford: Blackwell.

Lamberton, Don, ed. 1971. *Economics of Information and Knowledge*. Harmondsworth: Penguin.

—— ed. 1996. *The Economics of Information and Communication*. Cheltenham: Edward Elgar.

—— ed. 1997. *The New Research Frontiers of Communications Policy*. Amsterdam: Elseviers.

LUNDVALL, BENGT-ÅKE 1985. *Product Innovation and User-Producer Interaction*. Aalborg: Aalborg University Press.

MANSFIELD, EDWIN 1991. Academic research and industrial innovation. *Research Policy*, 20: 1–12.

METCALFE, STAN 1995. The economic foundation of technology policy: equilibrium and evolutionary perspectives. In *Handbook of the Economics of Innovation and Technological Change*, ed. Paul Stoneman. Oxford: Basil Blackwell.

NELSON, RICHARD R. 1987. The role of knowledge in R&D efficiency. *Quarterly Journal of Economics*, 97: 453–70.

—— ed. 1993. *National Systems of Innovation*. Oxford: Oxford University Press.

SCITOWSKY, TIBOR 1954. Two concepts of external economies. *Journal of Political Economy*, 62: 143–51.

STIGLITZ, JOSEPH E. 1994. *Whither Socialism*. Cambridge, Mass.: MIT Press.

SUTTON, JOHN 1991. *Sunk Costs and Market Structure*. Cambridge, Mass.: MIT Press.

SWANN, PETER, PREVEZER, MARTHA, and STOUT, DAVID 1998. *The Dynamics of Industrial Clustering*. Oxford: Oxford University Press.

UTTERBACK, JAMES M. 1994. *Mastering the Dynamics of Innovation*. Boston: Harvard Business School Press.

VON HIPPEL, ERIC 1988. *The Sources of Innovation*. London: Oxford University Press.

Section 9

Districts and Regional Innovation Systems

Chapter **21**

Industrial Districts: The Contributions of Marshall and Beyond

Bjørn T. Asheim

Territoriality and Economics—On the Contribution of Industrial Districts

THE seemingly paradoxical role played by traditional, pre-capitalistic, socio-cultural structures in competitive, modern economies has motivated new research on industrial districts. There is general agreement that what made districts so successful was their combination of functional and territorial integration: the territorial dimension of the socio-cultural structures represented the basic input promoting flexibility and dynamism. While, on the one hand, the continual influence of socio-cultural structures was said to make the districts vulnerable to changes in the global capitalist economy, on the other hand, much work has evaluated the adaptability and replicability of the district model to other regions in need of development strategies. The European experience of industrial districts had become a major point of reference in the international debate on regional policy promoting endogenous development (Asheim 1994).

The main lesson learned from the rapid growth of industrial districts and other specialized areas of production was to view industrialization as a territorial process. The importance of agglomeration and non-economic factors (i.e. culture, norms, and institutions) for the economic performance of regions gained ascendancy. Another factor contributing to the generalization of the experiences of industrial districts was the new theoretical understanding of innovation as a social process. Compared to the previous dominating linear model of innovation, this implies a more sociological view, in which interactive learning is looked upon as a fundamental aspect of the innovation process, which, thus, cannot be understood independently of its institutional and cultural contexts (Lundvall 1992).

What this broader understanding of innovation as a social, non-linear, and interactive process meant was a change in the evaluation of the importance and of the role played by socio-cultural structures in regional development. Instead of being looked upon as mere reminiscences from pre-capitalist, although still productive, civil societies, social and cultural infrastructure was viewed as a necessary prerequisite for regions in order to be innovative and competitive in a post-Fordist global economy. According to Amin and Thrift (1995: 8), this forces a re-evaluation of 'the significance of territoriality in economic globalisation'.

This re-evaluation is part of the development towards what Storper (1997) and others call the new heterodoxy in economics, which according to Porter (1994: 38) ought to imply that 'economic geography must move from the periphery to the mainstream' (of economics—my addition). In a wider evaluation of the importance of the original as well as later formulations of the concept of industrial districts, one must look at the broad context and not only use a narrow accounting of the actual diffusion of industrial district in the global economy. Seen in this broad perspective, it is not at all paradoxical that Alfred Marshall, typically referred to as the founder of neo-classical economics, is a forerunner for the contemporary new economic heterodoxy. In his writings on industrial districts and related themes, as they appear in *Principles of Economics* and *Industry and Trade*, Marshall is not very typical of a neo-classical economist. Marshall talks about the existence of different categories of firms; the importance of proximity in order to achieve external scale economies; the relevance of broader environmental factors;[1] and finally, he refers to entrepreneurship as 'the best educators of initiative and versatility, which are the chief sources of industrial progress' (Marshall 1921: 249). To further strengthen this line of thought the main new theoretical achievement of Marshall's Italian followers (e.g. Becattini 1989, 1990, 1991 and Brusco 1986, 1989, 1990, 1992) was to change the focus from the cluster of small firms to the broader perspective of the merger of community and inter-related firms, thus strengthening the non-economic, socio-territorial dimension of the concept. This has represented, as we shall examine, a major contribution in the development of the new heterodoxy in contemporary economics.

Towards a Definition of Industrial Districts—On the Theoretical and Empirical Origins of the Concept

Industrial districts are 'essentially a territorial system of small and medium-sized firms' (Goodman 1989: 21). According to Brusco (1986: 187), 'what is rel-

[1] This expands the concept of agglomeration economies to take into account factors that reduce transaction costs and stimulate (informal) networking (e.g. trust) as well as factors pointing to (informal) labour skills such as tacit knowledge, as part of what Marshall called industrial atmosphere.

evant are no longer the characteristics of one single firm, but the characteristics of the industrial district of which the small firm is a part'.

The original rationale for industrial districts rests on the creation of external economies of scale, economies that are external to the firm but internal to the area, for groups of small firms. This provides a competitive alternative to the internal economies of scale of big companies (Asheim 1994). According to Marshall, 'the economies arising from an increase in the scale of production of any kind of goods, . . . fell into two classes—those dependent on the general development of the industry and those dependent on the resources of the individual houses of business engaged in it and the efficiency of their management; that is, into *external* and *internal* economies' (Marshall 1930: 266; emphasis in original). Thus, external economies concern the productivity of the single firm and the efficiency of the production system, obtained through an external, technical division of labour between firms, 'which can often be secured by the concentration of many small businesses of a similar character in particular localities: or, as is commonly said, by the localisation of industry' (Marshall 1930: 266). Marshall introduces the possibilities of dividing 'the process of production into several stages, each of which can be performed with the maximum of economy in a small establishment' (Marshall in Whitaker 1975: 196–7; here quoted from Becattini 1989: 131).

Brusco (1989: 259) refers to 'the progressive specialisation of all the firms working in the same sector in the same area' as characteristic of industrial districts. With reference to products, it is possible to distinguish between three categories of firms in an industrial district: firms having a direct connection with the final market, stage firms, and firms of the vertically integrated sector (Brusco 1990: 14). These firms can be linked in three different ways: vertically, when different stages of a process are involved; laterally, where the same stage in a like process is involved; and diagonally, when service processes are involved (Bellandi 1989: 137).

To Marshall (1930: 266), the normal case is to obtain external economies through localization economies and Bellandi considers external economies as 'one of the most important factors in explaining the efficiency of the industrial system of a district' (Bellandi 1989: 139). Nevertheless, external economies do not fully explain the advantages of agglomeration, or, as Bellandi (1989: 139) puts it: 'we are in the field of external economies, not yet in the field of agglomeration economies'.

In contrast to traditional regional economics, Marshall attaches a more independent role to agglomeration economies as the specific *territorial* aspects of a geographical agglomeration of industrial production. Marshall focuses on traditional socio-cultural factors, which concern the quality of the social milieu of industrial districts, and which only indirectly affect the profits of firms. Among such factors Marshall emphasizes in particular the mutual knowledge and trust that reduces transaction costs in the local production system; the industrial atmosphere which facilitates the generation and transfer of skills and qualifications of the workforce required by local industry; and the effect of both these aspects in promoting (incremental) innovations and innovation diffusion among small firms in industrial districts. By defining agglomeration economies as socially and territorially integrated properties of an area, originating in pre-capitalist civil societies, Marshall abandons 'the pure logic of economic mechanisms and introduces a sociological approach in his analysis' (Dimou 1994: 27).

The industrial atmosphere of industrial districts can enhance the potential of small firms for acquiring (especially) tacit knowledge and other forms of informal skills in order to support the development, adoption, and diffusion of innovations. Such processes are strongly conditioned by the spatial proximity and cultural homogeneity of industrial districts. The transactional problem of the diffusion of innovations among competitive firms requires the setting up of formal or informal arrangements allowing innovative co-operation. This may be facilitated through the relatively high degree of trust and consensus among and between firms, employers, and workers, often present in an established industrial district (Bellandi 1989).

When using the term industrial atmosphere, Marshall refers to factors of a public good character emerging within industrial districts 'in which manufacturers have long been domiciled, a habit of responsibility, of carefulness and promptitude in handling expensive machinery and materials becomes the common property of all' (Marshall 1986: 171). In this way 'the agglomeration of industry in a district generates, in time, an aptitude for industrial work, and this aptitude communicates itself to most of the people who live in the district' (Bellandi 1989: 143).

Lastly, it should be remembered that Marshall, in his writings on the progressive role of industrial districts in generating industrial and economic growth, is strongly influenced by the ideas of Spencer that evolutionary progress meant differentiation and integration (Hodgson 1993; Sunley 1992). While Sunley (1992: 306) argues that Marshall's biological analogies result in a 'consequent exaggeration of the efficiency and potential of industrial localization', Hodgson (1993), from a perspective of the history of ideas of economics, sees the introduction of biological analogies as representing an improvement towards making economic theory more dynamic ('bringing life back into economics') compared with the dominating mechanical, static analogies. According to Hodgson (1993: 99), 'Marshall saw the limitations of mechanical reasoning, and turned to biology in his search for inspiration and metaphor'.[2]

[2] It is from this perspective that the often quoted statement of Marshall (also quoted by Sunley 1992) that 'the Mecca of the economist lies in economic biology rather than in economic dynamics' should be understood. Hodgson (1993) points out that the rest of the paragraph is very seldom referred to. Marshall continues: 'But biological conceptions are more complex than those of mechanics; a volume on Foundations must therefore give a relatively large place to mechanical analogies; and frequent use is made of the term "equilibrium", which suggests something of a statical analogy' (Marshall, *Principles of Economics*, 9th edn., London: Macmillan, 1949, p. xii; here quoted from Hodgson 1993: 99).

The Italian Reinterpretation of the Concept of Industrial District—The Characteristics of Neo-Marshallian Districts of the Third Italy

One of the major contributions by the Italian economists to the formulation of the neo-Marshallian approach was the strong focus on the social and territorial dimensions of the concept. Becattini, perhaps the most well known of these Italian economists, has termed the Marshallian industrial district a socio-economic notion, and has defined the industrial district as 'a socio-territorial entity which is characterised by the active presence of both a community of people and a population of firms in one naturally and historically bounded area. In the district, unlike in other environments, such as manufacturing towns, community and firms tend to merge' (Becattini 1990: 38). This contribution to the theory of economic geography is summarized by Martin (1999: 79) who maintains that these Italian economists 'differ significantly from their spatial agglomeration and regional convergence modelling counterpart in that their approach is firmly rooted in detailed empirical work on specific regions and stress the social, cultural and institutional foundations of local industrial growth'.

Bellandi (1989) emphasizes that the economies of the districts originated from the thick local texture of interdependencies between the small firms and the local community. Becattini (1990: 40) maintains that 'the firm becomes rooted in the territory, and this result cannot be conceptualised independently of its historical development'. Thus, it is necessary to conceive of industrial districts as 'a social and economic whole . . . The success of the districts, then, lies not just in the realm of the economic. Broader social and institutional aspects are just as important' (Pyke and Sengenberger 1990: 2).

What is expressed here is the idea of embeddedness as a key analytical concept in understanding the formation as well as the functioning of industrial districts (Granovetter 1985). Harrison (1992: 478) points out that 'the industrial district model posits a very strong form of the embedding of economic (business) relations into a deeper social fabric, providing a force powerful enough to provide for the reproduction of even so apparently paradoxical a practice as co-operative competition'. Fua (1983: 376) emphasizes that 'the continuity with local history and traditions is doubly valuable. It is something positive in itself, and it is a source of strength in achieving other positive results: hence the system's merits' (Fua 1983: 376). He concludes by stressing

> in this model, industrialization finds fertile soil in the local (if still latent) supply of entrepreneurial energies, labour and saving, and in the existence of a well-run society with its institutions, its culture and material infrastructures. The success of the model relies on its capacity to combine all the strong points and resources of the existing organisation and harness them to modern development. (Fua 1983: 355)

According to Harrison (1992), this mode of theorizing is fundamentally different from the one found in conventional regional economics or in any other neo-classical-based agglomeration theory. It is precisely this embeddedness in broader socio-cultural factors, originating in a pre-capitalist civil society, that is the material basis for Marshall's view of agglomeration economies as the specific *territorial* aspects of geographical agglomeration of economic activity (Asheim 1994).

The existence of agglomeration economies distinguishes industrial districts from regions such as Perrouxian development poles or Japanese just-in-time production systems. Another important factor supporting the emphasis on the *territorial* dimension in the definition of industrial districts is the fact that many independent small firms characterize Marshallian industrial districts ensuring that no single big company acts as a centre for strategic decision-making. In contrast, the key or 'motor' industries of Perroux (1970) are large companies having a decisive, growth-generating effect on the growth pole as a whole due to their greater innovative capacity than that of small firms, resulting in an increase in the production of the pole that is considerably larger than in the rest of the economy.

The structural characteristics of industrial districts could be summarized in the following way (Garofoli 1991*a*: 95):

1. an extensive division of labour between firms in the local production system, which represents the basis for a close network of intra- and inter-sectoral input–output relations;
2. a strong product specialization at the firm and company level, which limits the production spectrum, stimulates the acquisition of specialized knowledge, facilitates the introduction of new technology, thus leading to an increased independence of the production systems of the districts;
3. the existence of an effective information network at the district level, which guarantees a broad and fast circulation of information about markets, alternative production techniques, new raw materials, components, and other input goods being used in the production process, and also new administrative techniques, which all contribute to convert individual knowledge to collective competence for the whole district. These processes are being facilitated by the geographical proximity in industrial districts, providing good opportunities for frequent face-to-face contacts especially between suppliers and users of means of production and various producer services; and
4. the high competence level of the work force, which partly is a result of intergenerational transfer of tacit knowledge about labour processes and production techniques, and partly is a result of formal training from technical schools and so on.

The first two attributes refer to the functional dimension of external economies and the last two to the territorial dimension of agglomeration economies (Asheim 1992).

Potentials and Problems of Industrial Districts—On Locational Efficiency and Innovative Capacity

An important factor in the diffusion of the concept of industrial districts has undoubtedly been the contextualization of the concept by Bagnasco (1977), in his book *Tre Italia.* This sociological analysis identified a specific path of modernization based on clusters of Small and Medium-sized Enterprises (SMEs) in the Third Italy (i.e. the Central and North Eastern regions). These were qualitatively different from the developed North West as well as from the underdeveloped South of Italy. Sforzi (1990) identified the existence of 61 Marshallian industrial districts, mainly in the Third Italy. Last, but not least, the seminal book by Piore and Sabel (1984), *The Second Industrial Divide*, used the Italian industrial districts as the main example in their global, macro-historical analysis of the transformation from Fordist standardized mass production to the flexible specialization of the post-Fordist model of organizing the world of production.

However, some observers started to raise questions about the long-run stability of industrial districts, arguing that they will be fragmented either through the take-over of the most successful SMEs by Trans-National Corporations (TNCs) or the formation of hierarchies of firms inside the districts lead by the most dynamic SMEs (Harrison 1994*a*, 1994*b*). Others suggest that some industrial districts will develop a post-Marshallian organization of production, that is to say, become Marshallian nodes within global networks (Amin and Thrift 1992). As this will imply a reduced level of vertical disintegration locally, one could ask how Marshallian such nodes eventually became (Harrison 1994*b*).

While this position treats the changing role and function of industrial districts as problematic, caused by the globalization process, another position looks at industrial districts as a specific stage of development in a process of industrialization (Dimou 1994). Garofoli (1992) has presented a typology of Italian industrial districts that represents a redynamization of the concept. This implies that industrial districts can pass through a possible development process from areas of productive specialization via local productive systems to system areas as the most advanced form. In this view, industrial districts do not represent a stable (or static) organizational model of industrial production. On the contrary, development and change should be looked upon as a natural part of the history of industrial districts.

Such a process of change could either result in a strengthening and reproduction of the typical Marshallian characteristics of the districts or, in a post-Marshallian organizational model, a circular and cumulative process of fragmentation leading to stagnation and decline in previously prosperous districts. Most observers seem to agree, however, that technological capabilities are an important differentiating factor concerning the development and future prospects of industrial districts (Asheim 1994; Bellandi 1994; Brusco 1990; Crevosier 1994; Garofoli 1991*a*). Crevosier (1994: 259) emphasizes the importance of understanding how industrial districts 'react to or generate radical innovations. Without making this point clear, it is not possible to make any prediction about the reproduction and the duration of such systems'. Thus, the endogenous innovative capacity of the districts becomes of strategic importance for their future development. More specifically this means the capability of SMEs in industrial districts to break path dependency and change technological trajectory through radical innovations. Piore and Sabel (1984) also pointed at permanent innovation as a vital characteristic, and a precondition for continuous growth, of industrial districts. According to Piore and Sabel (1984: 275), 'the fusion of productive activity, in the narrow sense, with the larger life of the community' will secure the reproduction of the balance between co-operation and competition as well as the permanent innovation and adoption of new technologies.

However, how functional are agglomeration economies in promoting innovations? On the one hand, Marshall maintains that the two most important aspects of agglomeration economies, mutual knowledge and trust and the industrial atmosphere, will have a positive effect on the promotion of innovations and innovation diffusion among small firms within industrial districts. On the other hand, Marshall was also aware of the fact that agglomeration economies as such do not give any guarantee for product and process innovations taking place.

Indeed, studies have shown that the industrial atmosphere of industrial districts can support the imitation, adaptation, and diffusion of innovations between SMEs (Asheim 1994). In the same way, the presence of trust can bring about the introduction of new technology into industrial districts, since mutual trust—in addition to reducing transaction costs—seems to be crucial for the establishment of non-contractual inter-firm linkages. Becattini (1990: 47) conceives of this as a social process of collective self-awareness in which the decision to introduce a new technology, partly owing to the common system of values and attitudes prevailing in the districts, is perceived as an opportunity to defend an already acquired position. It is in this sense that Becattini's (1991: 102) statement that 'a MID [i.e. a Marshallian Industrial District] is either creative or it is not a (true) MID' should be understood.

The importance of territorial embedded agglomeration economies in promoting innovations concerns largely incremental innovations. As Marshall noted, 'industrial districts can generate innovations by incremental steps, through a gradual improvement of the final product, of the process and of the overall production organization' (Bianchi and Giordani 1993: 31). Garofoli (1991*b*) also maintains that industrial districts have a larger capacity to deal with gradual innovations than with 'ruptures'. In this way, agglomeration economies can represent important basic conditions and stimulus to incremental innovations through informal 'learning-by-doing' and 'learning-by-using', primarily based on tacit knowledge (Asheim 1994). As Bellandi (1994) suggests, such learning, based on practical knowledge (experience) of which specialized practice is a prerequisite, may have significant creative content. Thus, because of 'decentralized industrial creativity' (DIC), the collective potential innovative capacity of small firms in industrial districts is not always inferior to that of large, research-based companies (Bellandi 1994). However, the fact remains that, in general, the individual results of DIC are incremental, even if 'their accumulation has possible major effects on economic performance' (Bellandi 1994: 76).

However, in an increasingly global world economy it is rather doubtful whether incremental innovations will be sufficient to secure the competitive advantage of SMEs in industrial districts. Crevosier (1994: 259) argues that the reliance on incremental innovations 'would mean that these areas would very quickly exhaust the technical paradigm on which they are founded'. In addition, Bellandi (1994: 80–1) underlines that 'consistency [between DIC and MID] does not mean necessity. A number of difficulties may arise which can constrain and even bring to a halt DIC within an industrial district'.

In his advocacy of a transition from the original industrial district without local government intervention, Mark I, to an industrial district with considerable government intervention, or Mark II, Brusco points out that 'industrial districts eventually face the problem of how to acquire the new technological capabilities which are necessary to revive the process of creative growth. It is here that the need for intervention appears' (Brusco 1990: 17). In another context, Brusco has claimed, 'industrial districts are slow to adopt new technologies, lack expertise in financial management, have little of the know-how required for basic research, and are unable to produce epoch-making innovations' (Brusco 1992: 196). Along the same lines, Varaldo and Ferrucci (1996) maintain 'the district firm presents a barrier to organizational innovation, if changes are linked to the assimilation of new competencies very different from the entrepreneur's technical culture. In this way, these firms have deficits in marketing and R&D activities' (Varaldo and Ferrucci 1996: 30).

Bellandi (1994) precisely emphasizes the private and public institution making as a condition for the reproduction of dynamic industrial districts with growth potentials. When difficulties with institution making or supporting local industrial policy arise, 'the basic conditions which sustain DIC are easily impaired, and the life-expectancy of such a district is relatively short' (Bellandi

1994: 81). Such institution making is part of what Amin and Thrift (1994: p. v) call institutional thickness, which they claim is of critical importance for the performance of local economies in a global economy.

However, perhaps a more fundamental problem of Marshallian industrial districts is that their basic characteristics do not represent the most adequate means to meet the challenge of a post-Fordist global economy. Marshall's perspective was to secure the productivity and competitiveness of small firms through economies of localization achieved by an extensive division of labour and strong product specialization between firms in industrial districts. The standard of comparison was the internal economies of scale of large firms. Even if the specific Marshallian interpretation of agglomeration economies can be said to stimulate the innovation process at the district level, their major impact was to secure the (informal) skills and social and ideological qualifications of the workforce.

These characteristics of a traditional (Marshallian) industrial district represent at least two fundamental problems with respect to generating endogenous technological development in contemporary industrial districts. The first problem is the one-dimensional focus on efficiency and productivity as understood within a Fordist frame of reference, that is, productivity growth because of standardized production. One of the constraining factors in moving beyond the domination of incremental innovations in industrial districts is the fierce competition between subcontractors specializing in the same products or phases of production, and vertically linked to the commissioning firms.

The second problem concerns the functionality of Marshallian agglomeration economies with respect to endogenous innovation capacity. As already pointed out, the territorial embedded agglomeration economies can promote incremental innovations. However, if a lock-in situation occurs, for example as a result of the inability of SMEs in industrial districts to change technological trajectory, the existence of a strong industrial atmosphere could be used to squeeze wages to remain competitive, which consequently, would result in a functional incapacity of the system of SMEs to promote technological development (Glasmeier 1994). On the other hand, the presence of industrial atmosphere can provide additional competitive strength through the willingness of committed workers to engage in the formation and workings of the district firm in more dynamic industrial districts with a less strong path dependency.

The neo-Marshallian industrial district has also been criticized by the GREMI group (Groupement de Recherche Européenne sur les Milieux Innovateurs) for representing a static perspective as it 'considers the local relationships mainly in terms of locational efficiency' (Camagni 1991: 2). As an alternative, the GREMI group has introduced the concept innovative milieu, that is, 'the set, or the complex network of mainly informal social relationships on a limited geographical area, . . . which enhance the local innovative capability through synergetic and collective learning processes' (Camagni 1991: 3).

From this perspective, creativity and continuous innovation is considered to be a result of 'a collective learning process, fed by such phenomena as intergenerational transfers of know-how, imitation of successful managerial practices and technological innovations, interpersonal face-to-face contacts, formal and informal cooperation between firms, tacit circulation of commercial, financial or technological information' (Camagni 1991: 3). According to Maillat (1998: 118), 'the existence of a milieu provides a measure of trust and convergence of viewpoints which . . . prompt firms to transcend the usual barriers of competition to discuss common technological problems, to learn from each other and, possibly, to seek collective solutions'. Defined in this way, however, the innovative milieu approach does not represent any alternative or new perspective compared to, for example, Brusco's industrial district Mark II, where the aim is public intervention to support organizational innovations. Examples such as centres of real services in the industrial districts of Emilia-Romagna have turned out to be successful in modernizing the economic structure of the districts and, thus, have strengthened their competitive advantage.

The Importance and Development of Industrial Districts—On the Role of Competition and Co-operation in Post-Fordist Learning Economies

The International Institute for Labour Studies in Geneva published three books with a strong focus on the industrial districts of the Third Italy (Pyke *et al.* 1990; Pyke and Sengenberger 1992; Cossentino *et al.* 1996). The titles and themes of the three books describe the development of theoretical perspectives as well as empirical trends with respect to the change and growth of industrial districts. The opening chapter of Pyke and Sengenberger (1996) asks the strategic question whether the industrial districts will continue to have the capacity in the future of competing 'on the basis of innovation, productivity, constant improvement and good labour standards', or will they be forced, due to increased global competition, to compete by resorting to 'short-term cost-cutting exercises, engaging in cut-throat low wage, low quality competition?' (Pyke and Sengenberger 1996: 3).

According to the reviews of the three most important regions in the Third Italy, Veneto, Emilia-Romagna, and Tuscany, the basic message is one of continuous positive development trends, thus following the high road path of development in most of the districts. Concerning key factors such as income and employment, earnings are at least equal to, and often above, the national average, and job creation is reported to be at least as good as or better than national average figures. In addition, in the mid-1990s unemployment is generally well below levels in other parts of Italy, e.g. 6 per cent in both Veneto and

Emilia-Romagna compared to 11 per cent for Italy as a whole. These results are achieved in districts still heavily dominated by small firms, which appear to be able to reproduce a sufficient competitive advantage to secure a high overall export rate.

However, not every industrial district is doing equally well, which basically concerns the competitiveness of the small firms in the districts. The problems of reduced competitive advantage in certain districts have to be considered as a challenge to every district, which has resulted in structural changes in many of the districts, such as growing concentration among SMEs in the form of group formations, problems and potentials connected to the entrance of multinational companies, and a decentralization of certain production stages to areas outside the region, for example to East European countries or countries in the Third World. The least impressive reading in the reviews from the three regions concerns their innovative capability, and especially their capacity to carry out radical innovations, which is often required in order to change technological trajectories. The outcome of these changes, and not least their effect on the innovativeness and competitiveness of the firms, will play a decisive role in determining the future economic prospects of the districts. Concerning Emilia-Romagna, which is looked upon as perhaps the most successful of the Third Italy regions, it is maintained that this success has much to do with the region's highly developed adaptive and innovative capacity due to a close and fruitful co-operation between small firms and the local and regional authorities (Cooke and Morgan 1994).

This formation of innovative capacity and successful fostering of competitive advantage at the regional level has turned many traditional industrial districts, especially in Emilia-Romagna, into *technological districts*, which have been capable of taking on international competition through making dynamic use of new technologies (Storper 1992). New demand for a different kind of production and services has created a need for *new technological districts*, 'directed not at a mass public, or catering for the demands of industry, but oriented towards promoting a better quality of life and environment' (Capecchi 1996: 176). The future challenge in the industrial districts is to do this without endangering the endogenous innovation potential from which they grew in the earlier development phases.

Learning from the Emilia-Romagna model of policy-making, it is important to understand that the economic development of the region has not simply been 'the result of a spontaneous development but, rather, it has been assisted by a process of institutional building aimed at the creation of an intermediate governance structure capable of establishing a positive enabling environment for firm development' (Bianchi 1996: 204). This points to the relevance of experiences in the third phase of the development of the Emilia-Romagna model, as this is the stage when enterprise support of a more proactive kind has been introduced by agreement amongst SMEs, the regional government, and the intermediary agencies. Furthermore, the creation of networks of supporting institutions, such as service centres are 'not intended merely to supply technical advice that firms cannot find locally. . . . Rather, the aim should be for a service center to act as a kind of social catalyst, including groups of firms and institutions, both public and private, to interact and establish virtuous circuits of knowledge diffusion' (Bianchi 1996: 205). There are a myriad of cases of business centres throughout Europe, which, operating on this basis, have failed to change the efficiency of local firms.

The perspective on the importance of agglomerations in promoting innovations can find support from modern innovation theory, originating from new institutional economics, which argues that 'regional production systems, industrial districts and technological districts are becoming increasingly important' (Lundvall 1992: 3). Accordingly, the most important theoretical contribution to the development of heterodox economics of bringing territoriality (back) into economics comes precisely from evolutionary and institutional economics. Especially central to the understanding of the workings and future prospects of industrial districts has been the work of Lundvall and his colleagues. They have worked on national innovation systems and the learning economy (Lundvall 1992; Lundvall and Johnson 1994). The reading of their work resulted in mutual benefits for both subjects. For economic geography, the explanatory power of the new definition of innovation as interactive learning could be used to argue why industrial districts, often producing traditional, artisan-based consumer goods such as textiles, shoes, and ceramics, could stay innovative and competitive in a global economy. For evolutionary economics, the identification and documentation by economic geographers of existing and working industrial districts and other post-Fordist industrial spaces provided empirical evidence for the importance of interactive learning in a post-Fordist learning economy.

The emphasis on interactive learning as a fundamental aspect of the process of innovation points to *co-operation* as an important strategy in order to promote innovations. The rapid economic development in the Third Italy, based on territorial agglomerated SMEs, has drawn increased attention towards the importance of co-operation between firms and between firms and local authorities in achieving international competitiveness.

> This willingness to co-operate is indispensable to the realization of innovation in the ID which, due to the division of labour among firms, takes on the characteristics of a collective process. Thus, for the economic dynamism of the district and for the competitiveness of its firms, they must be innovative but, at the same time, these firms cannot be innovative in any other way than by cooperating among themselves. (Dei Ottati 1994: 474)

Thus, if these observations. are correct, this represents new forces in the promotion of technological development in capitalist economies implying a modification of the overall importance of competition between individual capitals. Lazonick argues, referring to Porter's empirical evidence (Porter 1990), that

> domestic cooperation rather than domestic competition is the *key* determinant of global competitive advantage. For a domestic industry to attain and sustain global competitive advantage requires continuous innovation, which in turn requires domestic cooperation. Domestic rivalry is an important determinant of enterprise strategies. But the substance of these competitive strategies—specifically whether they entail continuous improvement or cut-throat price cutting—depends on how and to what extent the enterprises in an industry cooperate with one another. (Lazonick 1993: 4; emphasis in original)[3]

The literature on industrial districts from Piore and Sabel's book (1984) onward has underlined that 'the central feature of the industrial district is the balance between competition and co-operation among firms' (You and Wilkinson 1994: 259). Dei Ottati asserts that 'the cooperative elements contribute in a decisive way to the integration of the system, while forces of competition keep it flexible and innovative. This is because competition in the particular socio-economic district environment encourages better utilization of available resources and above all, development of latent capabilities and diffuse creativity' (Dei Ottati 1994: 476).

This ambivalence regarding the relationship between, and the relative importance of, competition and co-operation is basically caused by a traditional, Marshallian perception of industrial districts and of the achievement of external economies through vertical co-operation with subcontractors along the value chain.[4] This limits the potential for horizontal technological co-operation between principal firms and suppliers, thus hindering the transformation of local production systems into learning systems (Patchell 1993).

Conclusion: Industrial Districts as Learning Regions

In securing the continuing successful development of industrial districts, the possibilities and potentials of the learning economy to meet the challenges of the globalizing economy are not fully recognized. In a learning economy, the competitive advantage of firms and regions is based on innovations, and innovation processes are seen as social and territorial embedded, interactive learning processes. Thus, based on modern innovation theory, it could be argued that

[3] In addition, the emphasis on the importance of domestic rivalry and competition in influencing factor creation (Porter 1990), could reflect the survival of the view of 'the orthodox economics in which co-operation is regarded exclusively as an attempt to distort prices and is therefore inefficient' (You and Wilkinson 1994: 275).

[4] Porter (1990) has an explicit reference to Marshall (in a footnote) when he discusses the relation between domestic rivalry and external economies.

SMEs in industrial districts could develop and strengthen their competitive advantage in the contemporary global economy (Asheim 1997). Furthermore, in addition, this broader view on the central importance of innovation as interactive learning extends the range of branches that could be viewed as innovative from typical high-tech branches of Silicon Valley to traditional, non-R&D-intensive branches of industrial districts.

Taken together, this theoretical development has dramatically changed the basis for launching industrial and technology policies towards SMEs with the intention of promoting endogenous regional development. Such a localization strategy can be seen as an alternative strategy to achieving competitiveness in a global economy, a position often neglected in the globalization debate.

However, one problematic aspect of the learning economy has been its focus on 'catching up' learning based on incremental innovations, and not on radical innovations requiring the creation of new knowledge. Thus, in order to underline the dynamic and rapid change in the contemporary globalizing economy, it is necessary to pay attention to knowledge creation as a process of equal importance to learning and forgetting.

The perspective of the learning economy emphasizes the importance of organizational and institutional innovations to promote co-operation, primarily through the formation of dynamic flexible learning organizations. Such learning organizations must be based on strong involvement of workers in work organizations inside firms, on horizontal collaboration between firms in networks, and on bottom-up, interactive-based innovation systems at the regional level and beyond, representing a systemic and networked approach to the formation of innovation supportive regions. Networked regional innovation systems represent a planned interactive enterprise support relying on close university–industry co-operation, where large and smaller firms establish network relationships with other firms, universities, research institutes, and government agencies based on public–private partnerships. As such, this could be said to represent a development towards a 'learning region' (Asheim 1996) understood as a 'development coalition' (Ennals and Gustavsen 1999). Such regional knowledge infrastructures must take into account the complex interactions and relationships which characterize the innovation process of SMEs in the vertically disintegrated, local production systems of industrial districts in order to promote innovation, change, and improvement.

Finally, the importance of co-operation should remind us of the significance of non-market and non-economic factors, such as social capital (e.g. trust) and institutions, for the economic performance of regions and nations (Putnam 1993). According to Lazonick (1991: 8), 'history shows that the driving force of successful capitalist development is not the perfection of the market mechanism but the building of organizational capabilities'. Thus, a major challenge for future research on industrial districts as well as for policy implementation is to demonstrate the potential of regional clusters and social capital, so typical of industrial districts, for promoting a learning-based strategy of endogenous regional development that can be applied on a broader scale. The growth of existing industrial districts (e.g. in the Third Italy) has shown that the necessary requirements concerning socio-cultural and socio-economic structures are to be found in relatively well-off regions, and sufficient techno-economic and political institutional structures only in relatively developed countries. Thus, it is important to keep in mind that such a strategy cannot be applied across the board without some form of public intervention as well as public–private co-operation, stimulating cluster creation and network formation through the building up of social capital on a regional basis.

References

Amin, A., and Thrift, N. 1992. Neo-Marshallian nodes in global networks. *International Journal of Urban and Regional Research*, 16/4: 571–87.

—— —— eds. 1994. *Globalization, Institutions, and Regional Development in Europe.* Oxford: Oxford University Press.

—— —— 1995. Territoriality in the global political economy. *Nordisk Samhällsgeografisk Tidskrift*, No. 20: 3–16.

Asheim, B. T. 1992. Flexible specialization, industrial districts and small firms: a critical appraisal. In *Regional Development and Contemporary Industrial Response: Extending Flexible Specialization*, ed. H. Ernste and V. Meier. London: Belhaven Press, 45–63.

—— 1994. Industrial districts, inter-firm co-operation and endogenous technological development: the experience of developed countries. In *Technological Dynamism in Industrial Districts: An Alternative Approach to Industrialization in Developing Countries*? New York and Geneva: UNCTAD, 91–142.

—— 1996. Industrial districts as 'learning regions': a condition for prosperity? *European Planning Studies*, 4/4: 379–400.

—— 1997. Learning regions in a globalised world economy: towards a new competitive advantage of industrial districts? In *Interdependent and Uneven Development: Global-Local Perspectives*, ed. M. Taylor and S. Conti. Aldershot: Ashgate, 143–76.

Bagnasco, A. 1977. *Tre Italia: La Problematica Territoriale dello Sviluppo Italiano.* Bologna: Il Mulino.

Becattini, G. 1989. Sectors and/or districts: some remarks on the conceptual foundations of industrial economics. In Goodman and Bamford 1989: 123–35.

—— 1990. The Marshallian industrial district as a socio-economic notion. In Pyke *et al.* 1990: 37–51.

—— 1991. The industrial district as a creative milieu. In Benko and Dunford 1991: 102–14.

Bellandi, M. 1989. The industrial district in Marshall. In Goodman and Bamford 1989: 136–52.

—— 1994. Decentralised industrial creativity in dynamic industrial districts. In *Technological Dynamism in Industrial Districts: An Alternative Approach to Industrialization in Developing Countries*? New York and Geneva: UNCTAD, 73–87.

Benko, G., and Dunford, M., eds. 1991. *Industrial Change and Regional Development.* London: Belhaven Press.

Bianchi, P. 1996. New approaches to industrial policy at the local level. In Cossentino *et al.* 1996: 195–206.

—— and Giordini, M. G. 1993. Innovation policy at the local and national levels: the case of Emilia-Romagna. *European Planning Studies*, 1/1: 25–41.

Brusco, S. 1986. Small firms and industrial districts: the experience of Italy. In *New Firms and Regional Development in Europe*, ed. D. Keeble and E. Wever. London: Croom Helm, 184–202.

—— 1989. A policy for industrial districts. In Goodman and Bamford 1989: 259–69.

—— 1990. The idea of the industrial district: its genesis. in Pyke *et al.* 1990: 10–19.

—— 1992. Small firms and the provision of real services. In Pyke and Sengenberger 1992: 177–96.

Camagni, R. 1991. Introduction: from the local 'milieu' to innovation through co-operation networks. In *Innovation Networks: Spatial Perspectives*, ed. R. Camagni. London: Belhaven Press, 1–9.

Capecchi, V. 1996. New technological districts for promoting quality of life and the environment. In Cossentino *et al.* 1996: 175–94.

Cooke, P., and Morgan, K. 1994. Growth regions under duress: renewal strategies in Baden-Württemberg and Emilia-Romagna. In Amin and Thrift 1994: 91–117.

Cossentino, F., Pyke, F., and Sengenberger, W. eds. 1996. *Local and Regional Response to Global Pressure: The Case of Italy and its Industrial Districts*. Research series 103. Geneva: International Institute for Labour Studies.

Crevoisier, O. 1994. Book review (of G. Benko and A. Lipietz, eds., *Les Régions qui gagnent*, Paris, 1992). *European Planning Studies*, 2: 258–60.

Dei Ottati, G. 1994. Cooperation and competition in the industrial district as an organization model. *European Planning Studies*, 2/4: 463–83.

Dimou, P. 1994. The industrial district: a stage of a diffuse industrialization process—the case of Roanne. *European Planning Studies*, 2/1: 23–38.

Ennals, R., and Gustavsen, B. eds. 1999. *Work Organisation and Europe as Development Coalition*. Amsterdam and Philadelphia: John Benjamin's Publishing Company.

Fua, G. 1983. Rural industrialization in later developed countries: the case of northeast and central Italy. *Banca Nazionale del Lavori Quarterly Review*, 147: 351–77.

Garofoli, G. 1991*a*. The Italian model of spatial development in the 1970s and 1980s. In Benko and Dunford 1991: 85–101.

—— 1991*b*. Local networks, innovation and policy in Italian industrial districts. In *Regions Reconsidered*, ed. E. M. Bergman, G. Maier, and F. Tödtling. London: Mansell, 119–40.

—— 1992. Diffuse industrialization and small firms: the Italian pattern in the 1970s. In *Endogenous Development and Southern Europe*, ed. G. Garofoli. Aldershot: Avebury, 83–102.

Glasmeier, A. 1994. Flexible districts, flexible regions? The institutional and cultural limits to districts in an era of globalisation and technological paradigm shifts. In Amin and Thrift 1994: 118–46.

Goodman, E. 1989. Introduction: the political economy of the small firm in Italy. In Goodman and Bamford 1989: 1–30.

—— and Bamford, J. eds. 1989. *Small Firms and Industrial Districts in Italy*. London: Routledge.

Granovetter, M. 1985. Economic action and social structure: the problem of embeddedness. *American Journal of Sociology*, 91/3: 481–510.

Harrison, B. 1992. Industrial districts: old wine in new bottles? *Regional Studies*, 26/5: 469–83.

—— 1994*a*. The Italian industrial districts and the crisis of the cooperative form: part I. *European Planning Studies*, 2: 3–22.

—— 1994*b*. The Italian industrial districts and the crisis of the cooperative form: part II. *European Planning Studies*, 2: 159–74.

Hodgson, G. 1993. *Economics and Evolution: Bringing Life Back into Economics*. Cambridge: Polity Press.

Lazonick, W. 1991. *Business Organization and the Myth of the Market Economy*. Cambridge: Cambridge University Press.

—— 1993. Industry cluster versus global webs: organizational capabilities in the American economy. *Industrial and Corporate Change*, 2: 1–24.

Lundvall, B.-Å. 1992. Introduction. In *National Systems of Innovation*, ed. B.-Å. Lundvall. London: Pinter Publishers, 1–19.

—— and Johnson, B. 1994. The learning economy. *Journal of Industry Studies*, 1/2: 23–42.

Maillat, D. 1998. From the industrial district to the innovative milieu: contribution to an analysis of territorialised productive organisations. *Recherches Économiques de Louvain*, 64/1: 111–29.

Marshall, A. 1921. *Industry and Trade*. 3rd edn. London: Macmillan.

—— 1930. *Principles of Economics*. 8th edn. London: Macmillan.

—— 1986. *Principles of Economics*. 8th (reset) edn. London: Macmillan.

Martin, R. 1999. The new 'geographical turn' in economics: some critical reflections. *Cambridge Journal of Economics*, 23: 65–91.

Patchell, J. 1993. From production systems to learning systems: lessons from Japan. *Environment and Planning A*, 25: 797–815.

Perroux, F. 1970. Note on the concept of growth poles. In *Regional Economics: Theory and Practice*, ed. D. McKee, R. Dean, and W. Leathy. New York: The Free Press, 93–103.

Piore, M., and Sabel, C. 1984. *The Second Industrial Divide: Possibilities for Prosperity*. New York: Basic Books.

Porter, M. 1990. *The Competitive Advantage of Nations*. London: Macmillan.

—— 1994. The role of location in competition. *Journal of the Economics of Business*, 1: 35–9.

Putnam, R. 1993. *Making Democracy Work: Civic Traditions in Modern Italy*. Princeton: Princeton University Press.

Pyke, F., and Sengenberger, W. 1990. Introduction. In Pyke *et al.* 1990: 1–9.

—— —— eds. 1992. *Industrial Districts and Local Economic Regeneration*. Geneva: International Institute for Labour Studies.

—— —— 1996. Introduction. In Cossentino *et al.* 1996: 1–15.

—— Becattini, G., and Sengenberger, W. eds. 1990. *Industrial Districts and Inter-Firm Co-operation in Italy*. Geneva: International Institute for Labour Studies.

Sforzi, F. 1990. The quantitative importance of Marshallian industrial districts in the Italian economy. In Pyke *et al.* 1990: 75–107.

Storper, M. 1992. The limits to globalization: technology districts and international trade. *Economic Geography*, 68/1: 60–93.

—— 1997. *The Regional World: Territorial Development in a Global Economy*. New York and London: The Guilford Press.

SUNLEY, P. 1992. Marshallian industrial districts: the case of Lancashire cotton industry in the inter-war years. *Transactions Institute of British Geographers*, NS 17: 306–20.

VARALDO, R., and FERRUCCI, L. 1996. The evolutionary nature of the firm within industrial districts. *European Planning Studies*, 4/1: 27–34.

WHITAKER, J. K. ed. 1975. *The Early Economic Writings of Alfred Marshall, 1867–1890*, ii. London: Macmillan.

YOU, J.-I., and WILKINSON, F. 1994. Competition and co-operation: toward understanding industrial districts. *Review of Political Economy*, 6/3: 259–78.

Chapter 22

Innovation Networks, Regions, and Globalization

Beat Hotz-Hart

KNOWLEDGE and its application for market success has become the primary source of competitiveness in the developed economies of the world. Innovations involve creative and interactive processes between various forms of knowledge and market needs. The importance of these issues has been reflected in both politics and academia over the last decade. The OECD has examined them extensively within its Technology/Economy Programme, TEP, launched in 1988, and the resulting report discusses the context: globalization, intangible investment, the role of networks in technological innovation, the new approaches to competitiveness and growth and urgent problems facing developing countries (OECD 1992). The OECD programme on 'National Innovation Systems' (NIS), developed from this framework, focused on innovative firms and innovative firm networks, clusters, mobility of human resources, organizational mapping, and catching-up economies. The report *Managing National Innovation Systems* summarizes the main theoretical and empirical findings (OECD 1999*c*).

This chapter builds on the debate. National innovation systems are well researched; however, what is missing in most approaches are the vertical links and interactions between local/regional, national, and global actors and the resulting differentiated global innovation network. There are fewer and fewer reasons why the nation should be seen as the predominant perspective for a system of innovation. This chapter focuses on the following four questions:

1. How can the process of innovation be understood?
2. To what extent are innovation processes localized, and does innovation have a particular regional base?
3. How are R&D and the innovation process globalized?

4. What impact does globalization have on regional innovation networks? What impact do globally oriented innovation processes have on the 'system of innovation'?

Innovation as a Process within Networks

The 1996 OECD report on technology, productivity, and job creation noted that innovative firms are efficient learning organizations that seize technological and market opportunities creatively in order to expand production frontiers. The report found that firms that innovate more consistently and rapidly, employ more workers, demand higher skill levels, pay higher wages, and offer more stable prospects for their workforce. The innovativeness of firms is the key element and depends on the incentives firms face, and their own competence.

Competitiveness is becoming more dependent upon the ability to apply new knowledge and technology in products and production processes. But, with the rapid advancement of knowledge, firms are forced into an active search process. For complementary knowledge and know-how, firms increasingly rely on interaction with a variety of actors. Inter-firm collaboration is by far the most important channel of knowledge sharing and exchange. Networking has become an effective innovation technique in its own right.

Empirical findings show that relationships between firms within networks with respect to innovation have increased during the last ten or twenty years substantially. Statistically this can be measured by numbers of co-operations, alliances, or joint ventures in R&D (OECD 1999*c*: 57). It can also be seen in the vast range of types of interactions: supplier–user co-operation, outsourcing, and contractual R&D. Empirical studies confirm that companies with a high intensity of co-operation are more innovative than those that co-operate little (Smith 1995).

Innovation is an interactive learning process that requires knowledge exchange, interaction, and co-operation among various actors in a production network or value chain: interaction-based innovation theory. In the interaction several actors are included: other companies, both large and small, contractors and subcontractors, equipment and component suppliers, users or customers (particularly the innovation-stimulating lead users), competitors, internal and external, private and public research labs, universities and other institutions of higher education, providers of consultancy and technical services, state authorities and regulatory bodies. All these actors form a network where new ideas and new solutions to problems are developed with respect to market success. There is empirical evidence that by far the most important channel of knowledge sharing and exchange is inter-firm collaboration (OECD 1999*c*: 53).

The concept of '*systems of innovation*' as used by OECD is a framework of conceptual thinking and analytical research, based on a strong interdisciplinary approach, rather than a full-blown theory. The following sets out the most important success factors for the functioning of innovation processes within a network:

- *better access of firms to information, knowledge, skills and experiences* and more rapid and effective interchange in innovation networks: there are better opportunities for learning, informal exchanges, and reducing time to market for new products and processes; participating firms exchange information and experience and engage in mutual learning in their role as customers, suppliers, and subcontractors;
- *more intense linkages and co-operation* between particular agents and actors, first of all between user and supplier; the contract behaviour and the competence of the firms' leading customers may be a signal for the companies and the network as a whole; networking results in a better use of complementarity and synergy, for example, between engineers, designers, marketing specialists, PR managers, and/or financiers;
- *higher response capacity*, greater ability of the participating firms to change their perception about the future, the technology base, and the organizational routine; increased learning capacity of firms and other organizations;
- *reduction of risks, moral hazard, information and transaction costs:* a multitude of partnerships between firms with complementary assets creates cost-reducing synergies via internalization of transactions within networks. The relationships within a network allow the joint assessment of risks. A well-functioning innovation network is based on strongly positive and reciprocal external economies and spillovers, both pecuniary and non-pecuniary;
- *better trust base and social cohesion:* the communal non-economic institutions and various attributes of 'trust' embedded in local society permit the various actors both to compete and to collaborate (Harrison 1992: 478).

Networks of innovation are not always successful *per se*. The factors and arguments outlined above describe rather a potential or a chance that has to be used and exploited successfully. In the worst case, networks can have a negative impact on innovation activities: they might stabilize existing structures via cartels and cause a sclerosis. Competition policy is confronted with a dilemma: regulators have to assess and decide whether an existing or growing network will increase the innovation performance, or whether it will hinder competition and structural change.

Regional Base of Innovation Networks

Empirical evidence shows that firms and innovations in particular have a localized character; they tend to cluster spatially, in a particular geographic region. Regions frequently specialize in certain technological or industrial areas. Examples of regional clusters are pharmaceutical innovation in the New

Jersey/New York area, the automobile industry in Michigan, the watch industry in the Jura, Switzerland, or packaging firms in Lombardy, Italy. Piore and Sabel (1984) showed how networks of mostly small, linked, but loosely coupled manufacturing firms had produced many specialized industrial districts across Europe.

Regional innovation networks have their particular characteristics and way of functioning. This is shown by Saxenian (1994) in a comparison between Silicon Valley and Route 128, Massachusetts. Substantial differences exist in terms of local institutions and culture as well as in industrial structure and corporate organization. All of these factors have an impact on the outcome. They were differentiated as follows:

- relationships between companies are open and intense in Silicon Valley or closed and distant in Route 128;
- in Silicon Valley inter-company mobility of labour is frequent and expected; in Route 128 seldom;
- exchange of information and experiences within the region is free and open in Silicon Valley or reluctant and guarded in Route 128.
- in Silicon Valley employees are fascinated by technology, in Route 128 by a company.

Furthermore, empirical studies show differences in links between science and technology between regions. According to the findings of the OECD NIS study (1999*c*: 40), some innovation systems show a strong link between the science system and industrial innovation (e.g. Denmark, Ireland, UK, and USA). In other countries, innovation has been geared more towards engineering excellence and the rapid adoption and adaptation of technological innovation (e.g. Japan, Korea, Germany).

Theoretical arguments to explain these phenomena have quite a tradition. Perroux (1964) analysed spatial polarization and developed the concept of development and growth poles. Modern industries may be considered as industries *motrice*: active components in development poles where their role assumes a central tertiary function such as research and development, management or marketing. The traditional sectoral perspective was taken over by the cluster approach that has received a great deal of attention since the mid-1980s. The case study approach, mainly using Porter's diamond network approach, was applied as a framework for analysing the competitiveness of the local production structure (Porter 1997; OECD 1999*a*: 13). For a region, advantages arise from highly specialized clusters of related skills, technologies, and infrastructure, especially when these are hard to duplicate. In Porter's analytical framework, groups of domestic rivals are integrated into the operation of industry clusters. An industry cluster is defined as 'industries related by links of various kinds' (Porter 1990: 131). These links are both vertical (connecting users and suppliers), and horizontal (connecting enterprises that have common customers, employ related technologies, and use the same channels of communication) (Porter 1990: 149).

The aim of the research programme of the OECD Focus Group on Cluster Analysis and Cluster-Based Policy was to get a better understanding of successful innovative behaviour (OECD 1999*a*: 13, 414). It defines clusters as networks of strongly interdependent firms, knowledge-producing institutions (universities, research institutes, technology-providing firms, knowledge-intensive business services), bridging institutions (e.g. brokers, providers of technical or consultancy services) and customers, linked in a production chain that creates added value. In this perspective, clusters are seen as reduced-scale innovation systems.

Many of the country contributions in the OECD Proceedings (1999*a*) describe networks of strongly interdependent firms or industry groups based on trade linkages, innovation linkages, knowledge flow linkages, common knowledge base, or common factor conditions. In any case, in order to innovate successfully, firms need cross-sectoral networks, made up of dissimilar and complementary firms specializing around a specific link or knowledge base in the value chain.

Why or when are clusters successful? For Porter, the major determinants of global competitive advantage are—according to his diamond concept—actor conditions, demand conditions, related and supporting industries, and firm strategy, structure, and rivalry. What determines the competitive advantage of nations is, first of all, 'the pressure on firms to invest and innovate', and, secondly, 'the institutional mechanisms for specialised factor creation' (Porter 1990: 71, 80).

By pressure, Porter means the social forces that motivate companies to develop and employ productive resources. Pressures to invest and innovate are generated by factor scarcities, sophisticated demand, and domestic rivalry. Of these pressures, Porter clearly views domestic rivalry as the most critical. 'In global competition successful firms compete vigorously at home and pressure each other to improve and innovate . . . Only intense domestic rivalry (or the threat of entry) can pressure such behaviour' (Porter 1990: 162).

What is increasingly required for firms to be successful is co-operation in clusters. Co-operation can reduce costs. Firms that acquire external knowledge and thus meet their needs more cheaply than by producing that knowledge in-house, create greater opportunities for learning. From a regional perspective this may make economies of scale and scope possible, enabling the sharing of R&D costs and risks, allowing greater flexibility, and reducing the time to market for new products and processes. But, this argument needs extension: a critical factor for success is a good mix of rivalry and co-operation, advanced supplier firms, flexible organizations and management, continuous upgrading of knowledge, and attractiveness of the industry for talented people.

Finally, innovation systems have national characteristics. Countries differ with regard to the extent, nature, and motives of inter-firm collaboration. Patterns of interaction between firms and the technology infrastructure are country-specific, reflecting differences in institutional frameworks and the organization of public policies. The propensity to collaborate with foreign actors is influenced by country size and industrial specialization, the location and strategies of multinational firms, and country-specific public policies.

Substantial theoretical and empirical research has been undertaken under the particular aspect of National Innovation Systems (NIS). Key elements of NIS vary widely: innovation, system, national, and institutional are interpreted quite differently by various scholars (for an overview, see Edquist 1997; OECD 1999*c*). Metcalfe (1995) sees NIS as a set of institutions which jointly and individually contributes to the development and diffusion of new technologies and which provides the framework within which governments form and implement policies to influence the innovation process. As such, it is a system of interconnected institutions to create, store, and transfer the knowledge, skills, and artefacts that define new technologies.

In several studies, major advantages of localized systems are identified. At the same time, localized factors are sources of diversity between regions (Krugman 1991; Feldman and Audretsch 1999). Dimensions or factors that exhibit some degree of country specificity and advantages for the localized innovation network are internationally immobile factors:

- *Regional labour market:* specific qualifications of human resources are available in some regions only. Middle management and technicians with high professional qualification show low regional mobility. This contributes to unequal innovation performances and income of different regions. A regional difference with respect to human capital endowment is particularly the case in Europe, to a lesser extent in the USA or Japan where labour mobility is generally higher.
- The *educational system* and particularly the achievement of specialized knowledge and skills are based on the traditional economic activities of the region. An example is the interplay between the watch industry, schools for watchmakers, and a regional labour market of highly qualified craftsmen; a concentration of highly skilled and specialized labour allows for a pooled labour market of workers.
- *R&D institutions* in a region with high expertise in a special field that interact with local companies, for example, textile machine companies and their R&D departments, have an interest in co-operation with textile factories in their neighbourhood for the successful development of new machines, for testing and optimizing.
- *Professional traditions and experiences* which go with specific technologies or economic activities have passed by generations and become the tacit knowledge of the workforce of the region; collective knowledge includes social

aspects which are incorporated in social networks such as culture, trust, or tradition of the region. The social network has an impact on collective learning and flexible adjustment, risk taking and entrepreneurship, or loyalty for companies of the region.

- *Economies in information flows and knowledge spillovers* can be achieved. Tacit knowledge can be internal to an area or region but external to the individual firm; better communication may result through 'facilitators of information flow' such as personal relationships due to schooling, ties through the scientific community, or professional associations (Porter 1990: 153).
- The *institutional setting* and related incentive structure are developed historically and are country-specific. Aspects which are particularly relevant for innovative behaviour are the *financial system and corporate governance*, including the legal and regulatory framework.

The localized and immobile factors mentioned are structural by character and impact on the region in the long run. Firms are better able and more inclined to do things that are similar to what they have done in the past. Search processes for new technologies are path dependent and also dependent on the region. The outcomes are self-enforcing patterns of specialization of regional and technological capabilities. The specialization within a region itself increases path dependency.

There are, however, some risks associated with tight networks. A firm or network can lock in to an old technology or specialization because its technological system might not provide the right technology and forecasts for the future. The network may support prejudice, narrow-mindedness, or limit oversight of changes in trajectories that are going on globally. It fosters path-following behaviour at times when path breaking would be more appropriate.

The assumed complementarity of national and sectoral systems of innovation approaches is shown by Guerrieri and Tylecote (1997: 107). The authors argue that the technological performance of countries can be explained by the degree of fit between the behavioural and the external technological requirements of specific industries and the extent to which countries meet these requirements. They demonstrate that both sectoral composition and organizational and institutional characteristics matter for innovation performance and that patterns are country specific and rather stable over time. Several other authors confirm strong stability in national patterns of technological specialization (e.g. Patel and Pavitt 1994).

Internationalization and Globalization of R&D and Innovation Processes

Globalization is a process of change generated through a combination of increasing cross-border activity and information technology. It enables virtually instantaneous communication worldwide and allows everyone everywhere access to the world's best. Kanter (1995: 41) identifies four broad processes which are associated with globalization: mobility of capital, people, and ideas; simultaneity: everywhere at once; bypass: increased alternatives, multiple choice; and pluralism: a relative decline of monopolistic centres and dispersion to multiple centres of expertise and influence.

Globalization of the economy is applicable to companies as well as to the economy as a whole. In both cases national, political, and cultural boundaries are loosened. But globalization is more than internationalization. Globalization takes place if networks arise which go beyond nationalities, if economic actors do not identify themselves anymore with a particular country.

Globalization is shaped by companies and changes their structure. The growth and structure of Foreign Direct Investment (FDI) gives perhaps the best-documented measure of globalization. FDI grew more quickly than OECD GDP from the early 1970s, with very high growth rates in the latter half of the 1980s. It grew faster than imports and exports. Empirical evidence is provided by studies about foreign direct investments: globalization through FDI has had different effects where R&D is performed and where technology is applied. As Vickery (1996: 107 f.) reports from his empirical research:

- the share of R&D carried out in foreign subsidiaries is rising in many countries;
- R&D has tended to remain concentrated in the home country of the foreign investor relative to the spread of production capacity and employment;
- diffusion and application of new technology, particularly process technology, tend to be very rapid in subsidiaries of international firms;
- foreign-owned subsidiaries have higher labour productivity, economies of scale, superior technology, better co-ordination and organization.

In the 1990s joint ventures and strategic alliances boomed. The co-existence of increased competition with an increased number of network relations and strategic alliances was called alliance capitalism (Dunning 1997). As a consequence, the national character of many companies or products is fading away. Production performances and value chains are becoming processes across countries; people and cultures are being brought together and interwoven.

Together with globalization, international competition has become more and more a competition via innovations. For companies from highly industrialized countries, new market shares are only available through new, creative, or original products and services. The competitiveness of such economies is highly dependent on their innovativeness.

Traditional objectives for internationalization of company activities were the improvement of turnover and cash flow and/or a reduction of cost. Up to the 1980s internationalization of company activities has brought mostly a direct improvement of company results in the short term, for example, improved return on investment (ROI). Reasons for internationalization in the 1990s, however, go together with the increasing relevance of R&D, innovation, and the development of advantages in competitiveness in the long term.

The main objectives for globalization of R&D and innovation are:

- *input-oriented:* companies intend to gain access and therefore to benefit from globally distributed but locally bound pools of know-how, qualifications, and creativity; access to the worldwide best human resources such as R&D experts and specialists (local scientific community), access to regional information and communication networks to exploit pockets of innovation;
- *output-oriented:* in some cases companies intend to develop their products in close contact with regional markets and customers. They pursue R&D in the regions for adjustment to regional market needs; adjustment to local production processes; closeness to lead users;
- *political and socio-cultural:* companies adjust to national, or political and legal habits and regulations. They intend to use historically grown structures; to fulfil local content clauses, or to overcome protectionist barriers.

In order to benefit from the perspective of organizational learning, companies look for an intercultural and interdisciplinary learning process by involving several locations. With multi-local activities, they expect more and better ideas as well as better information about new trends.

Obviously, there are also reasons against an internationalization of R&D; for example, high information and co-ordination costs; failing to reach a critical mass by missing economies of scale when compared with centralized R&D; missing the synergy of centralized R&D; and loss of protection of its own basic research. But, empirical evidence shows that the advantages predominate and globalization of R&D expands.

Multinational corporations (MNCs) apply a variety of strategies to capitalize worldwide on technological advantages. The degree and nature of globalization of the companies' strategy are different according to their size, business area, technological field, and/or competence and business culture. By sector, market, and company structure, advantages of *globalization* (e.g. economies of scale, bypassing national protectionism) or advantages of *localization* (e.g. contacts with local markets and increased understanding and know-how about local preferences and tastes) can be identified. Therefore, companies can choose between or combine *four strategic options* (Bartlett and Ghosal 1990):

- *international strategy:* there are no particular advantages through globalization nor through localization; the company has a national identity and exports from the home base (ethno-centric structure);
- *multi-local strategy:* a strong pressure to adjust to particular local characteristics with little advantages from globalization; subsidiaries in local markets to improve local presence (poly-centric structure);

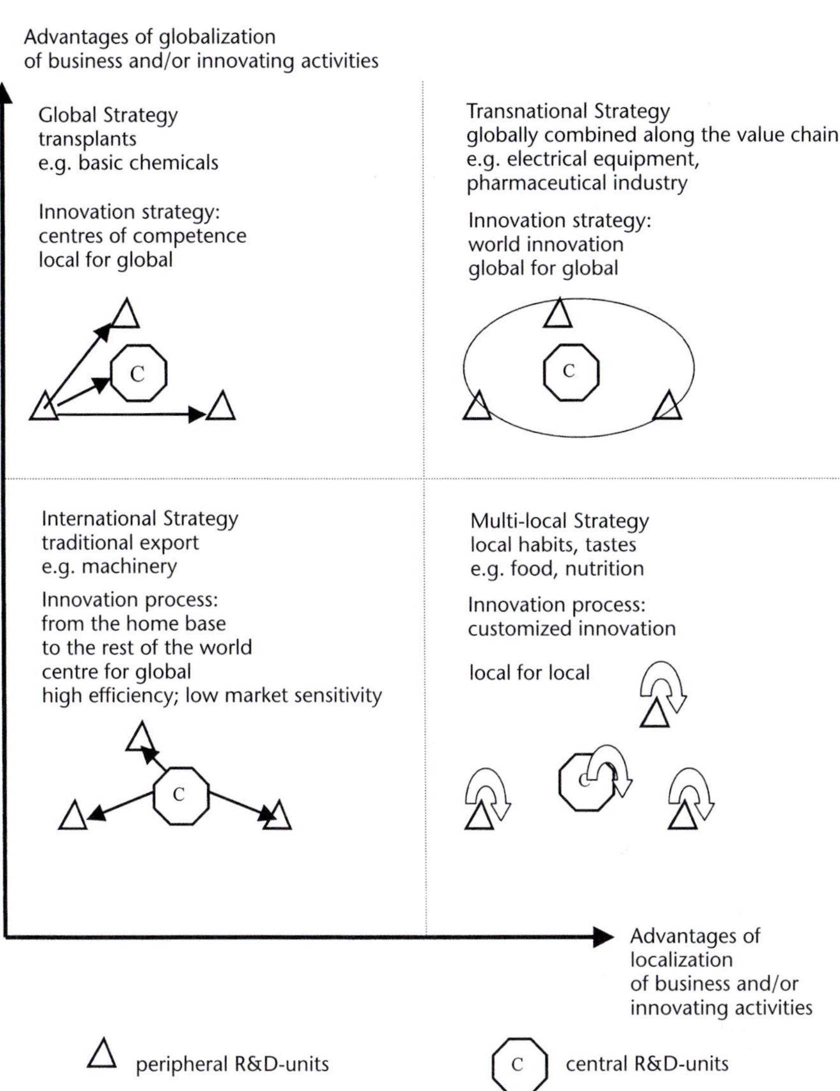

Fig. 22.1. International positioning of business and innovation strategies of firms

Sources: Developed according to Bartlett and Ghosal (1990); Gassmann and von Zedtwitz (1996).

- *global strategy:* the target markets are similar worldwide; major economies of scale; standardized production facilities in many locations (transplants);
- *transnational strategy:* particular local characteristics are relevant; simultaneously economies of scale can be implemented.

Different company innovation strategies in a global context shall be integrated into this framework. We distinguish the location or place of the generation and of the use of knowledge and innovation. In company strategies, four patterns of innovation strategies can be classified: centre for global; local for local; local for global and global for global. Each of them has its strengths and weaknesses. A simple best practice valuable for all companies does not exist. Each company, maybe each business unit within a company, has to choose one of these strategies according to its products or its target markets, although these are not mutually exclusive.

The result is a *differentiated global innovation network*. National borders and their meaning as economic boundaries are loosening. National economies' (national) systems of innovation are progressively becoming more integrated, interwoven, and globally connected. Driving forces are companies, particularly MNCs. They gain access to immobile resources and find ways of gaining indirect leverage in their exploitation within the corporate system. They provide a bridge for a form of arbitrage for the different localized resources.

Many of the sources of competitive advantage are localized and relatively immobile. The internationally immobile factors of innovation must be incorporated wherever they exist; hence there is a need to create international links between agents that are located in different national systems. An increasing number of the phases of the innovating activity are conducted by agencies that collaborate across borders with the aim of producing the best possible technology. Innovating activities themselves are delocalized.

Globalization of business activities takes place in phases: in the beginning are exports; what follows are different stages of manufacturing with the opening of subsidiaries abroad; FDI and intra-firm trade increase. Foreign R&D investment tends to follow production abroad. The more production is located abroad, the more likely research and development will be, too. Research and development by MNCs complements their manufacturing and sales activities in major markets. For most countries, there is a strong correlation between foreign affiliate shares of R&D expenditures and their domestic sales. But most MNCs have kept their core technologies or strategic projects in their home economies, and do design and development abroad to adapt products to local markets (Reger 1998).

Much evidence points to a growing international dispersion of multinational corporations' research activities. Key know-how is increasingly scattered internationally, although predominantly within the Triad of Europe, Japan, and North America. International innovation management is more than the configuration and co-ordination of R&D locations. Companies strive to achieve a market-oriented perspective that goes beyond simple co-operation with a narrow R&D unit abroad. There should be an interaction between all actors in the innovation process marketing and/or customers. Empirical evidence shows that innovation processes are particularly successful if there is a close collaboration between central R&D units and internationally distributed lead users (Von Hippel 1988).

Multinationals are constantly striving to find an appropriate balance among the alternatives of exporting, or investing and thereby avoiding obstacles to trade, or licensing its skills for others to exploit by putting their own capital at risk. In management literature, the two-way pulls on managers are recognized. They have to strike a balance between the forces for integrating operations across borders and those for recognizing and exploiting the differences among national markets (Bartlett and Ghosal 1989). Kanter (1995: 111) sums it up: 'network locally—grow globally'.

Porter (1990) states that it is the home base that determines most of the technological competence of multinational firms as well as receiving most of the benefits. This has been challenged by authors like Dunning (1992) and Cantwell (1991). Cantwell showed that in both host and home areas, various forms of interaction between firms and the environment determined the firm's technological potential and, depending on the specific strategies of the firms and the geographical context, its overall territorial impact. He provides evidence showing that the specific geographical structure of multi-plant firms is an important determinant of their innovative capabilities. Subsidiaries of multi-plant firms may act as vital hubs in regional economic development, depending on the nature of their embeddedness in local as well as wider networks.

The impact on regions or countries and on the home base involved may be different. Kuemmerle (1997) identified two types of foreign-affiliate R&D laboratories

- *home base exploiting laboratories:* import company-specific knowledge from home to better satisfy local demand abroad, and therefore are substituting for local research;
- *home base augmenting laboratories:* the company is assessing specialized knowledge found in foreign markets and transferring it back to the home base to create new products for global markets. MNCs locate home-base-augmenting laboratories in the most dynamic and attractive technology markets; that is, regions that offer specialized poles of expertise are more likely to attract home-base-augmenting types of R&D FDI.

Dunning (1992) refers to two typical scenarios that can be followed by a foreign investor: an 'easy pickings' scenario where host regions may lose intellectual assets, and an upgrading scenario including the creation of partnerships with local firms and institutions, aimed at improving the local skill base and support to the development of small and medium-sized enterprises (SMEs). It is obvious but not always made explicit that globalization of innovation can also be addressed from the perspective of regions or countries in their position in wider added value chains and knowledge transfer. There may be substantial differences in the interests pursued by MNCs and regions or countries.

Although empirical research shows there are wide differences between countries in the level of openness and the rate and types of globalization of their NIS, smaller industrial countries (like the Netherlands, Switzerland, or Sweden) show a higher degree of internationalization of their R&D activities and a higher level of flows of scientific and technological knowledge and embodied technology crossing their borders. But while Niosi and Bellon (1996) conclude that flows have increased, NIS may appear less national today than twenty years ago.[1]

Differences between countries depend on:

- the attraction of the domestic research base, the local supply base, and linkages between local suppliers and foreign investors;
- the ability to attract foreign direct investors in particular technology-intensive investments on a global basis;
- how externally owned capital may fit in a concept of innovation at a regional level.

A core component of innovation systems is *absorptive capacity* rather than the generation of new knowledge. For most regions and nations, the most important asset is to have a market system that is able to capture new forms of knowledge and apply them within the context of the local production system. Multinational firms can act as important vehicles of technology transfer; this depends on whether there are adequate mechanisms for information exchange and trading, whether the right incentives exist for co-operation and dialogue between local and foreign actors, and whether the foreign players fit into the existing institutional system of economic development and technology transfer.

Consequences for Regional Systems: Globalization and the Emergence of New Systems of Innovation

Systems of innovation are increasingly complex and intertwined, with regional, national, and international levels of integration of innovating activities. They interact from the top, and from below in a synergistic way. Schumpeter's (1934) creative destruction goes on, including not only firms and industries, but also regions, national systems of innovation, and international networks.

Local or regional networks still exist, develop, renew themselves, and compete with each other. International networks of innovators develop and modify

[1] Empirical evidence suggests that only one major supranational system of innovation is currently emerging, around Europe. Canada and the USA show similar, but less intense, interpenetration of their R&D activities. There seems to be no supranational system emerging around Japan (OECD 1999*b*).

existing local and national networks. During this process, some previously regional or national activities are transferred to international networks. Globalization and intertwining is an ongoing and growing process that has important implications for the NIS. The established NIS concept has to be adjusted and elaborated.

The local/regional, national, and global systems of innovation can be interpreted as layers of the new world order. The prime dynamics are sometimes rooted in global systems of innovation and sometimes in local or regional ones, sometimes in large organizations and companies and sometimes in small and medium-sized enterprises. It is not clear—as de la Mothe and Paquet (1996: 278) conclude from their studies—how they interact, what determines the origin of dynamics, and why this changes.

On the one side, globalization supports *convergence*, a higher degree of homogeneity of regional economies and technological systems because globalization implies imitation, diffusion of knowledge and practices, where organizational forms, technology, and science move from the innovating countries to followers. There are equalizing interactions and exchange of many different innovating units under flexible and complex forms of co-ordination that include technological alliances, de-localized R&D, international scientific co-operation and technology transfer. Globalization implies huge mobility of all productive factors (labour, capital organization, technology, and natural resources). However, theories of globalization underestimate the fact that most technology is industry- and resource-specific, and therefore still limited in mobility.

But, globalization leads also towards *specialization*. It appears to reinforce national patterns of economic specialization because of regionally unequal distribution of innovation capabilities. The innovative potential of regions depends on internationally immobile factors such as highly skilled labour, niche markets, research institutions, or regulation. Countries, and even similar sectors in different countries, specialize around their national knowledge base and comparative advantages. Flows may cause specialization, when factors of production move towards the countries presenting the best endowment profiles for specific activities.

International trade, technology transfer, and diffusion are in a state of flux and tend to distribute innovations uniformly over the world economic system. But globalization is only an acceleration of the processes of flux present in the system and not the disappearance of innovation. Globalization implies only a faster rate of diffusion of practices. Although globalization can change substantially the nature of the NIS, it is unlikely to eliminate completely national or local specificity. It does not eliminate the local heterogeneity created by innovations. We cannot expect a complete convergence of NIS. A particular specificity remains and will be used by each region to defend and fight for its own competitiveness. Finally, it is the balance between the rate of innovation and the rate of diffusion that determines the degree of convergence of economic systems.

As a consequence: present trends toward *globalization with specialization* seem more likely than sheer adjustment and levelling. The new international political economy is presenting us with a paradox: 'greater globalisation and greater nationalism in the determinants of competitiveness', as Stopford puts it (1996: 118). A cliché reflects the paradox: the multinationals' objectives are to be global and local simultaneously. The new paradoxical logic appears to drive the world production system towards both an increasing degree of globalization and an increasing degree of sub-national regionalization. A key issue can be seen as one of balancing spatial convergence and divergence, concentration and dispersion, homogeneity and heterogeneity, or standardization and diversity. A world with multiple poles of excellence may arise while differences and contrasts between regions and countries may even increase.

Important for the success of systems of innovation is the (regional) diversity and variety, particularly with respect to culture and education, the region's knowledge base. The latter is based on culture. Both belong to the identity of a country or a regional system of innovation and animate the innovative performance. Variety and diversity between regions are essential sources of innovation. They should be strengthened in order to strengthen the competitiveness of regions.

In contrast to this, a standardization of science and technologies takes place through transfer and diffusion. In some cases this is compelling in order to apply a particular technology, for example, in information and communication technologies standards and norms have to be applied worldwide. It is the challenge of companies and governments to optimize diversity and variety on the one hand and standardization on the other.

The evolutionary dynamics of such a global innovation system can be seen as a feedback or a dialectical process:[2]

- some strengths of a region based on immobile factors generate innovation, uniqueness, and therefore some temporary advantages of the region in international competition;
- multinationals find novel combinations of such immobile resources with globally mobile ones—a form of arbitrage, from which can emerge new sources of advantage;
- the process of globalization results in diffusion, imitation, adjustment of the advantages, a process of convergence between regions;

[2] In this context, it might be attractive to reflect on the contribution of the theories of regional imbalance introduced by Myrdal (1957: 17 and 26) and Perroux (1964). A rethinking of the virtuous and vicious circle arguments and growth induction as a combination of scale, productivity, and innovation could help to explain the dynamics of a globalized innovation system.

- but originating in regional peculiarities based on immobile factors, new innovations and advantages arise; this might attract more specific sources;
- the process begins again.

Although there is diffusion and growing globalization of technologies and management styles, in most countries companies, universities, public R&D laboratories, and the legal system have a national character. It is argued that the home base as well as neighbourhood plays a continuing, even enhanced, role for the competitiveness of companies. 'The process of creating skills and the important influences on the rate of improvement and innovation are intensively local. Paradoxically, then, more open global competition makes the home base more, not less, important' (Porter 1990: 158).

Under the influence of the feedback process and the openness of NIS, regions and networks are exposed to increased competition. In this environment, the role of competition on the home base is assessed differently. One side argues that intensive competition in the home base supports and improves international competitiveness. On the other side, Lazonick (1993: 8) argues, to fight foreign rivals requires a suspension of rivalry in order to build value-creating industrial and technological communities. The balance between domestic rivalry and domestic co-operation that yields global competitive advantage will change when domestic industry faces a new competitive challenge from abroad. More domestic rivalry will not result in global competitive advantage when foreign rivals, innovating on the basis of their industry clusters, have already acquired a sustainable competitive advantage.[3] Global competition advantages require the building of supportive business communities within a domestic economy and industry (Harrison 1992). Internationalization goes hand in hand with strengthening domestic or regional networks. In order to be competitive firms build on the regional system of innovation. The OECD analysis shows that inter-firm collaboration is still predominantly inward oriented (OECD 1999*c*: 54).

A region or a country should reach and occupy attractive positions in the global value-added chains. Therefore, policy should develop its own base of knowledge and expertise. It should improve immobile factors such as particular skills, regulatory framework, or financial system. It should foster collective identities and trust to support the formation and elaboration of local networks. In such an approach, the role of the state is more that of a broker than investor or procurer, matching firms that had so far little or no contact with each other, and matching university researchers with firms.

[3] And referring to Porter's argument of rivalry, Lazonick (1993) assesses that the basic problem for US industry in international competition is not insufficient rivalry but insufficient co-operation.

Conclusion

In order to be successful in the process of globalization, regional innovation networks have to become stronger. For high innovative performances, there has to be a strong root in a regional cluster, a strong regional knowledge base with an endowment of particular factors such as specific skills, knowledge infrastructure, an adequate (institutional and regulatory) framework and financial system, and a technologically sophisticated home market. This includes a certain degree of regional specialization and adequate positioning in the global value-added chains.

At the same time, global interdependencies are increasing and getting more important. In combining some regional innovation systems, new, problem-oriented networks are constituted in order to innovate jointly. They go beyond regional or national innovation systems, are both short-term oriented and highly flexible or longer-term oriented and relatively stable. The result is interaction and collaboration between regional innovation systems. Success depends on the complementarity and synergy the networks involved are able to mobilize with respect to market success. Role and relevance as well as the way of interaction of the different regional systems of innovation can differ. Hierarchies are likely, as is the capability to learn and absorb knowledge and technologies of increasing relevance (see Fig. 22.1). Leadership and management of the new and higher systems of innovation are needed. There should be more research in order to understand what the role and impact of multinational companies is in this context, and how R&D behaviour is changing.

One of the impacts is the development towards new forms of organizing business such as network companies, virtual enterprises, or virtual economic complexes. In a similar way, Dunning (1997) points to the rising of alliance capitalism. This will include the creation of new products and services and a complete reorganization or re-engineering of value-added chains. The driving force is the company with strong roots in one or more regional systems of innovation. A new way of competing arises and spreads out. It is not yet clear what will be the optimal way of competing and the corresponding optimal form of business organization. A phase of experiments and turbulent changes in organization in network building is likely, including trial and error in new groupings in the sectors and business areas involved. During this process, some regions may rise, others decline, with chances limited in time like windows of location opportunities.

The system of innovation approach is a framework of conceptual thinking and analytical research. Its power of explaining needs further elaboration and the empirical evidence needs strengthening. This includes the interplay of the following key elements: processes of innovation in networks; regionally based systems of innovation, mainly in the form of clusters; combination and interlocking in the process of globalization; and finally, the impact of new technological developments and its application particularly in the field of information and communication technologies. Companies, politicians, and academics will be highly interested in research contributions, particularly concerning the explanation of the development of business strategies, of regions, and the development of new forms of the economy in this context.

References

Bartlett, C. A., and Ghoshal, S. 1989. *Managing across Borders.* Cambridge, Mass.: Harvard Business School Press.

—— —— 1990. Managing innovation in transnational corporations. In *Managing the Global Firm*, ed. C. A. Bartlett, Y. Doz, and G. Hedlund. London: Routledge.

Berger, S., and Dore, R., eds. 1996. *National Diversity and Global Capitalism.* Ithaca, NY and London: Cornell University.

Camagni, R. 1991. Local 'milieu', uncertainty and innovation networks: towards a new dynamic theory of economic space. In *Innovation Networks: Spatial Perspectives*, ed. R. Camagni. London: Belhaven Press, 121–44.

Cantwell, J. A. 1991. The theory of technological competence and its application to international production. In *Foreign Investment, Technology and Growth*, ed. D. G. McFertridge. The Investment Canada Research Series. Calgary: University of Calgary Press, 33–70.

de la Mothe, J., and Paquet, G. 1996. *Evolutionary Economics and the New International Political Economy*. London: Pinter.

Dunning, J. H. 1992. The competitive advantage of countries and the activities of transnational corporations. *Transnational Corporations*, Feb., 135–68.

—— 1997. *Alliance, Capitalism and Global Business.* London: Routledge.

Edquist, C., ed. 1997. *Systems of Innovation—Technologies, Institutions and Organizations.* London: Pinter.

Feldman, M., and Audretsch, D. 1999. A science-based diversity, specialization, localized competition and innovation. *European Economic Review*, 43: 409–29.

Gassmann, O., and von Zedtwitz, M. 1996. *Internationales Innovationsmanagement.* Munich: Vahlen.

Guerrieri, P., and Tylecote, A. 1997. Interindustry differences in technical change and national patterns of technological accumulation. In Edquist 1997: 107–29.

Harrison, B. 1992. Industrial districts: old wine in new bottles? *Regional Studies*, 26/5.

Kanter, R. M. 1995. *World Class.* New York: Simon & Schuster.

Krugman, P. 1991. Increasing returns and economic geography. *Journal of Political Economy*, 99: 483–500.

Kuemmerle, W. 1997. The globalisation of industrial research—an investigation into its determinants and implications for public policy. Unpublished paper. Paris: OECD.

Lazonick, W. 1993. Industry clusters versus global webs: organizational capabilities in the American economy. *Industrial and Corporate Chance*, 2/1: 1–24.

Lundvall, B. A., ed. 1992. *National Systems of Innovation: Towards a Theory of Innovation and Interactive Learning*. London: Pinter.

Metcalfe, S. 1995. The economic foundations of technology policy: equilibrium and evolutionary perspectives. In *Handbook of the Economics of Innovation and Technical Change*, ed. P. Stoneman. Oxford: Blackwell.

Morgan, K. 1997. *Learning by Interacting: Inter-firm Networks and Enterprise Support, Local Systems of Small Firms and Job Creation*. Paris: OECD.

Mowery, D. C., and Oxley, J. E. 1995. Inward technology, transfer and competitiveness—the role of national innovation systems. *Cambridge Journal of Economics*, 19/1: 67–93.

Myrdal, G. 1957. *Economic Theory and Underdeveloped Regions*. London: Duckworth.

Niosi, J., and Bellon, B. 1996. The globalisation of national innovation systems. In de la Mothe and Paquet 1996: 138–59.

OECD 1992. *Technology, Economy and Productivity* (TEP). Paris: OECD.

—— 1996. *Technology, Productivity, and Job Creation: Best Policy Practices*. Paris: OECD.

—— 1999*a*. *Boosting Innovation: The Cluster Approach*. OECD Proceedings. Paris: OECD.

—— 1999*b*. *Globalisation of Industrial R&D: Policy Issues*. Paris: OECD.

—— 1999*c*. *Managing National Innovation Systems*. Paris: OECD.

Patel, P., and Pavitt, K. 1994. The nature and economic importance of national innovation systems, *STI Review*, 14. Paris: OECD.

Perroux, F. 1964. *La Firme motrice dans la région motrice: L'économie du XXe siècle*, ii. Paris: University Press of France.

Piore, M. J., and Sabel, C. F. 1984. *The Second Industrial Divide: Possibilities for Prosperity*. New York: Basic Books.

Porter, M. E. 1990. *The Competitive Advantage of Nations*. New York: Free Press.

—— 1997. Knowledge-based clusters and national competitive advantage. Paper presented at Technopolis 97, 12 Sept. Ottawa.

Reger, G. 1998. Changes in the R&D strategies of trans-national firms: challenges for national technology and innovation policy. *STI Review*, 22. Paris: OECD.

Saxenian, A. 1994. *Regional Advantage. Culture and Competition in Silicon Valley and Route 128*. Cambridge, Mass.: Harvard University Press.

Schumpeter, J. 1934. *The Theory of Economic Development*. Cambridge, Mass.: Harvard University Press.

Smith, K. 1995. Interactions in knowledge systems: foundations, policy implications and empirical methods. *STI Review*, 16: 69–102.

Stopford, J. 1996. The globalisation of business. In de la Mothe and Paquet 1996: 118–37.

Vickery, G. 1996. The globalisation of investment and trade. In de la Mothe and Paquet 1996: 83–117.

Von Hippel, E. 1988. *The Sources of Innovation*. Oxford: Oxford University Press.

Part V

Localities and Difference

Section **10**

Labour and Locality

Chapter **23**

Local Labour Markets: Their Nature, Performance, and Regulation

Ronald L. Martin

The Changing Question of Labour in Economic Geography

Modern economic geography has long been aware of differences in labour force characteristics across space, but the importance accorded to these differences, and how they have been conceptualized, have changed in recent years. From the 1930s to the mid-1970s, labour was viewed simply as a *location factor*, a 'factor cost' that varied from location to location. In much the same way that mainstream economics regards labour just as a variable input in a firm's, industry's, or economy's production function, so in economic geography labour was looked upon merely as an input to a firm's or industry's 'location function' (see e.g. Smith 1966, 1981; Lloyd and Dicken 1972). With the rise of radical Marxist economic geography in the late 1970s, the focus shifted to the *spatial division of labour* (Massey 1984), the idea that regional development and the distribution of employment are spatial expressions of the technical and social organization of the labour process. Labour was no longer seen as just another commodity or 'factor', but as subject to control and exploitation. Moreover, the complex interactions involved in labour utilization and control were argued to vary from place to place, and to depend on the spatial organization of production on the one hand, and the pre-existing geography of employment, social relations, and class structures on the other. As Storper and Walker (1984, 1989) argued, although capital and technology have become increasingly mobile and malleable, labour remains unique because of its relative immobility and the peculiarities of labour performance, control, and reproduction in particular places. It is this tension that is at the centre of the spatial division of labour.

Since the late 1980s, the treatment of labour in economic geography has shifted once again. The emphasis now is much more on the *geographies of the labour market.* Basic to this new approach is the belief that the labour market has an *intrinsically local level of operation and regulation*, that the creation and destruction of jobs, and the processes of employment, unemployment, and wage setting, and the institutional and social regulation of these processes, to some extent at least, are locally constituted. It is within specific spatial settings and contexts—'local labour markets'—that workers seek employment and employers hire and fire workers, that particular forms of employment structures evolve, that specific employment practices, work cultures, and labour relations become established, and particular institutionalized modes of labour regulation emerge or are imposed. Research into these and related issues by economic geographers has been growing apace (e.g. Martin 1981, 1986; Peck 1989, 1992, 1996; Clark 1989; Hanson and Pratt 1992, 1995; Martin *et al.* 1996; Allen and Henry 1997; McDowell 1997; Lawless *et al.* 1998; Herod 1995). While it would certainly be an exaggeration to claim that this growing literature constitutes a fully articulated spatial theory of labour and labour markets (and most geographers would argue that the search for any single, all-encompassing theoretical framework would in any case be misguided), it does seem that labour is at last firmly established as a key subject of geographical enquiry.

It is not possible here to provide a comprehensive account of the growing corpus of literature in this field. In what follows, I focus instead on what I believe to be some of the basic issues that loom large in the study of contemporary labour market geographies, namely the transition that is occurring in the world of work, and the implications of this transition for how we think about the nature, performance, and regulation of local labour markets. I shall seek to distil the key elements of these themes, but I have to ask the reader's indulgence, for although all are big questions, limitations of space preclude any detailed discussion.

New Landscapes of Labour

One reason for the new-found interest in labour by geographers is that it reflects the more general socio-institutional and regulationist 'turns' that have characterized economic geography as a whole in recent years. The spatialities of socio-economic regulation and the institutional bases of local and regional development have become key topics of research. In this context, since the labour market is a prime site of social, institutional, and regulatory practices (see Solow 1992; Peck 1996; *Regional Studies* 1996), it is not surprising that local labour markets should assume prominence as part of the new socio-institutionalist economic geography. In addition, however, the rise of labour market geography (or what some prefer to call labour geography) has unquestionably been stimulated by the dramatic changes that have been transforming the geographies of work, workers, and welfare across the advanced nations.

At one level, major differences in labour market performance have opened up between nations. For example, the performance of the US labour market over the past two decades has been in stark contrast to that of Europe. In the USA, several million new jobs have been created and unemployment has remained relatively low. However, at the same time, wage inequalities have widened considerably (Freeman and Katz 1993; OECD 1994*a*; Krugman 1994*a*, 1994*b*). In most of the European Union countries, on the other hand, wage inequalities have not widened to the same extent (except in the UK), yet employment growth has been minimal and unemployment has increased. But at the same time, the transformation of the labour market is re-configuring the *local* geographies of work, wages, and welfare within nations. While some areas are attracting concentrations of highly skilled, highly paid employment, entrenched joblessness or inferior forms of low-skill, low-wage work have dominated others. Within most major cities, areas of mass unemployment, poverty, and social exclusion co-exist with other areas of successful, high-income professional workers. Compared to barely two decades ago, the landscape of labour market inequality is now a much more rugged terrain (Lawless *et al.* 1998; Madanipour *et al.* 1998).

This *increased spatiality* of the labour market poses economic geographers with a series of important empirical and theoretical challenges, not only in terms of making sense of the new patterns that are emerging, but also in terms of understanding how local labour markets function and what form local labour market policy interventions should take. Such is the salience of these issues that even economists have begun to take the geography of the labour market much more seriously. Traditionally, economists have not assigned much significance to the geography of the labour market (Corina 1972). Over the past decade or so, new theoretical perspectives and policy models have proliferated in labour economics (for reviews, see Sapsford and Tzannatos 1993; Fine 1998). Although much of this work has continued to be aspatial, a small but influential literature has developed which has an explicit geographical stance, with themes dealing with regional employment and wage dynamics, spatial unemployment disparities, and local skill formation and human capital development (Adams 1985; Marston 1985, Topel 1986; Blanchard and Katz 1992; Eichengreen 1993; Benabou 1994; Blanchflower and Oswald 1994; Evans and McCormick 1994; Decressin and Fatas 1995). This interest by economists in local labour markets is arguably part of a more general 'geographical turn' that is occurring in economics (see Krugman 1998; Martin 1999).

For their part, economic geographers have tended to see the new landscapes of labour in regulation-theoretic terms, as inextricably bound up with the passage from Fordism to post-Fordism. This has led them to counterpoise typical previous 'Fordist' local labour markets with what are viewed as typical emerging 'post-Fordist' local labour markets (see Table 23.1 for a summary). While this depiction certainly throws the marked changes taking place in the world of work into sharp relief, and usefully situates the transformation of labour and labour markets within a wider set of economic, social, and political changes (see Boyer 1988; Harvey 1989; Knudsen 1996), it also has problems (see Fine 1998). The distinction between 'Fordist' and 'post-Fordist' local labour markets is by no means as obvious or clear cut as protagonists might suggest. Indeed, it is debatable whether Western capitalism has in fact entered a new stable form of post-Fordist development: it is probably more accurately portrayed as being caught up in a still-ongoing period of 'after-Fordism'. Further, the structural and spatial 'typicality' of these two respective local labour market forms is easily exaggerated. Each is idealized, and at best captures only a small part of the diversity and complexity of local labour in each era. There is no doubt that a key feature of emerging local labour market forms is the growing emphasis—by firms and governments—on *labour flexibility.* But, as Fine (1998) and others have argued, the drive towards flexible capitalism and flexible labour markets may only be an interim phase in the search for a new economic and regulatory 'fix'. Understanding the upheavals and shifts that are reworking local labour markets is thus clearly a vital, but difficult task, not least because in the midst of change it is far from easy to separate what may eventually prove to be ephemeral and interim developments from the more fundamental and transformative changes. Thus while 'post-Fordist' and 'flexible accumulation' accounts may well provide useful interpretative backcloths, these have their own limitations, and neither provides a theoretical framework for specifically conceptualizing the nature and functioning of *local* labour markets.

Conceptualizing the Nature and Workings of Local Labour Markets

Nearly half a century ago, in what are generally regarded as two of the classic papers on the nature of labour markets, Kerr (1950, 1954) argued that geography acts as a form of 'balkanization', or discontinuity, in the labour market, imparting strong, though not fixed, local boundaries. On the demand side, the local labour market can be defined as the 'labour supply shed' or 'worker recruitment space' of local employers. On the supply side, a local labour market is the geographical area in which workers can change jobs without changing their residence: the 'employment field' or 'job search space' of workers. Clearly, the more that the 'employment field' of workers and the 'labour supply shed' of employers spatially coincide, the more easily defined and more self-contained the local labour market will be. It is this notion which underpins the idea of defining local labour markets as 'travel-to-work' areas.

	Fordist labour markets	Post-Fordist labour markets
Labour process	Taylorist, mass production involving large workforces within firms. Productivity achieved by division of labour into detailed standardized tasks.	Flexible, specialized production. Productivity achieved by division of labour within firms into 'core' and 'peripheral' categories, with functional flexibility of core workers and numerical flexibility of peripheral workers.
Employment	Substantial proportion in manufacturing. Predominantly male. Most jobs full-time. Considerable labour hoarding over economic cycle. High degree of job security ('life-time' jobs). Generally full employment.	Small proportion in manufacturing, most in services. Many jobs part-time and temporary. Low labour hoarding. High flows into and out of employment. Increasing job insecurity. High levels of unemployment and non-employment.
Wages	Most set by collective bargaining (by industry-wide or nation-wide unions). Complex systems of occupational wage differentials. Stable or falling income inequalities.	De-collectivization and localization of wage determination. Breakdown of established systems of differentials. Increased polarization between high-paid, full-time workers and low-paid, part-time, and other contingent workers
Labour relations	Highly formalized and confrontational. Labour organized into strong unions. Steady growth of union membership. Collective strike action by workers common and protected in law.	Much more individualistic and cooperative. Unions in decline, even in historic 'heartland' areas. Solidaristic labour cultures in retreat. Collective labour action generally low and highly circumscribed by anti-union laws.
Labour market regulation	Macroeconomic demand management to maintain full employment. Welfare-orientated. Benefits unconditional and funded by progressive taxation system. Extensive panoply of employment protection and workplace regulations.	Abandonment of full employment policies. Shift from welfare to workfare and training-fare. Benefits increasingly conditional. Deregulation of employment and workplaces (but stringent regulation of labour unions) to promote labour flexibility.
Spatial features	Relatively self-contained local labour markets. Distinct local employment structures and labour cultures. Typified by centres of mass production industry. Local disparities in unemployment minimal.	Continued importance of local labour markets, but greater segmentation within than between them. Typified by new local centres of flexible production and service activity. Substantial local disparities in unemployment and growth of localized concentrations of social exclusion.

However, such 'travel-to-work' areas not only vary substantially in geographical extent, some are much more diffuse than others. On the one hand, the boundaries of the local labour market are shaped by the pecuniary and psychological costs of extensive daily travel to work by labour, and the similar but greater costs of migration between different areas. On the other, the geographical differentiation of local labour markets is also shaped by the spatial networks of labour communications which link workers and employers, both formal (e.g. employment agencies and local news media) and informal (e.g. word of mouth and personal recommendations). Thus in spatial terms, the 'local market' for the supply of labour may be thought of as a series of 'information-mobility' contours extending outwards in declining relative significance from each locality (Loveridge and Mok 1979). Such boundaries obviously differ for different groups of worker. In practice, then, local labour markets are necessarily 'fuzzy at the edges', as well as constantly evolving over time.

Nor are local labour markets internally homogeneous. There are important distinguishing features between different groups of worker in terms of skill, journey-to-work patterns, and attachment to place of residence, both socio-cultural attachment and relative (im)mobility within the housing market. So important is attachment to place of residence for many workers that they will change their job (or even occupation) rather than their residence. There are clear national differences in this attachment to place of residence—for example, the overall geographical mobility of labour is considerably greater in the USA than in European countries (European Commission 1998)—but, in general, lower income groups are most likely to change their job rather than their place of residence. Indeed, many unskilled low-income workers are not so much attached to, as *trapped in*, particular locations by virtue of their being unable to afford to move. These same groups are also less able to bear the costs of extensive daily travel to work in more distant parts of the local labour market (let alone to other nearby local labour markets), so that the range of employment opportunities open to such workers is often very restricted, making them more vulnerable to prolonged unemployment if they lose their local jobs.

This 'attachment to place' gives local labour markets two of their key characteristics. The first is the relative *spatial fixity of local labour* compared to the potential geographical mobility of capital. Of course, firms are not perfectly mobile: commitments in the form of sunk capital and local ties in the form of networks of suppliers or customers, for example, impart a degree of locational inertia. Nevertheless, in general, firms are able to switch capital investments and disinvestments between localities more easily than most workers move between areas. Again, of course, workers do move between local labour markets—especially so in the USA—yet (and even in the USA), their mobility is less than that of capital. Firms and industries that have been major sources of local employment can, and often do, shut down suddenly. The problem is that it takes time for the expelled workers to find alternative jobs, and even longer for them to move out of economically depressed local labour markets into more buoyant ones.

Secondly, the relative immobility of workers residentially, even between different zones of the same broad travel-to-work area, means that local labour markets are also internally 'balkanized', both occupationally and spatially. Different groups of workers are segmented by residential location in ways that depend, on the one hand, on their incomes—and hence their employment—and, on the other, on the intersection of the spatial structure (by type, age, and price) of the local housing stock and the way that local housing market institutions (such as mortgage companies, or local public authorities) allocate that stock. Thus the operation of employment and housing processes tends to be mutually reinforcing, producing distinct spatialities of socio-economic advantage and disadvantage within local labour markets (Lawless and Smith 1998; Madanipour *et al.* 1998). The local labour market is thus itself a complex assemblage of segmented submarkets, each having its own geographies, its own employment and wage processes, and its own specific modes of social regulation, an assemblage of non-competing submarkets which, nevertheless, are linked together to varying extents via direct and indirect webs of local economic dependency and exchange.

How to conceptualize the functioning of these internally structured local labour markets has become a contested issue (see Table 23.2). There are economists who treat local labour markets as if they are inherently no different from *ordinary commodity markets*. Such models—common in neo-classical and 'new classical' analyses—assume that local labour markets function and 'clear' like any other markets, or rather that they *ought* to. In this sense, these models are often used as ideological platforms from which to attack labour market institutions for impeding the 'market-clearing' process. But labour markets are not like ordinary commodity markets, and they do not equilibrate in a textbook 'market-clearing' way. A more realistic approach recognizes that local labour markets by their very nature are a *special market form*, consisting of complex social relations and institutional arrangements, and characterized by 'stickiness' and hysteresis effects in the way that local employers and employees adjust to the impact of demand, supply, technological change, and other shocks.

Moreover, as mentioned above, local labour is balkanized into various submarkets. It is this feature that is emphasized by those approaches which see the local labour market as *an arena of segmentation*, in which employers utilize processes of stigmatization, discrimination, and stratification to partition the local labour force into various non-competing groups (differentiated not just by skill, but also by gender, ethnicity, age, and even location) with different employment conditions, job security, and pay structures. There are both radical and orthodox versions of this segmented labour market approach (see Fine 1998). Still others take this focus further by viewing the local labour market as *a socially embedded institutional space*. Here, processes and patterns of

Table 23.2. Different perspectives on the local labour market and its functioning

Conceptions of local labour market	Underlying theoretical frameworks	Basic tenets of approach	Main focus
As a perfectly competitive and equilibrating submarket	Neo-classical economics and microeconomics of the labour market.	Labour no different from other commodities. Local labour markets no different from other markets.	Focus is on mechanisms of 'market clearing'. Failure of local labour markets to clear (e.g. presence of local unemployment) seen as evidence of 'barriers' and 'impediments' to free, efficient workings of local labour market.
As an imperfect market	Various, including efficiency wage theory, labour contract models, bargaining theory, insider–outsider models, and disequilibrium approaches.	Labour market different from other markets (because of social and institutional features). Local labour markets need not clear.	Focus is on why spatial disparities in unemployment, wages, job conditions, etc., may exist in equilibrium, and on the local adjustments to demand, supply, and technological shocks.
As a localized system of labour segmentation and inequalities	Segmented and dual labour market theories.	Labour market as a nexus of job differentiation and worker discrimination practices within and between workplaces.	Focus is on how segmentation processes operate in specific local settings and how the spatial structure of labour markets both reflects and reinforces segmentation.

As a socially embedded institutional space	Draws upon institutional economics and other heterodox schools of economic theory.	Local labour markets vary in their socialized and institutionalized systems of employment practices, workplace norms, work cultures, and labour traditions.	Focus is on the 'institutional thickness' and composition of local labour markets and how different institutional forms develop in, and infuence the employment, wage, and other outcomes of, different areas.
As a regulatory space	Combines several theoretical approaches, including regulation theory, post-Fordist 'theory', and institutional and social economics.	Local labour market is a site of processes of social regulation and politico-economic governance.	Focus on how local and non-local (national and international) systems of informal and formal (institutionalized) rules, norms, legal structures, and governance mechanisms intersect to shape local employment, wage, and welfare conditions.
As an arena for the social differentiation and reproduction of the workforce	Human capital models. Endogenous growth theory. Social economics.	Labour market as a basic determinant of social inequalities.	Focus is on the social determinants of the local labour force, processes of skill formation, household income inequalities, and problems of labour market exclusion.

employment, wage determination, labour segmentation, discrimination, and inequality are linked to the formal and informal practices of socially constituted institutions, not just firms but also labour unions, business associations, and local regulatory organizations (such as private and public employment and training agencies). Drawing on certain elements of institutional economics (e.g. Hodgson 1993) and the economics of 'social embeddedness' (Granovetter and Swedberg 1992), geographers stress the ways in which institutional configurations, workplace cultures, and labour traditions vary from area to area, and how these spatial variations in 'institutional thickness' influence local labour market performance (see Herod 1992; Martin *et al.* 1996).

Related to this perspective, the local labour market can also be seen as a *regulatory space* (Jonas 1996; Peck 1996; *Regional Studies* 1996), the sphere where local and non-local (national and international) systems of social rules, norms, customs, legal structures, and governance mechanisms intersect to shape and institutionalize the behaviour of both workers and employers. State policies and interventions play a particularly important role in this respect, not only through macroeconomic measures of demand management, but also through the legal regulation of employment relations within local firms (e.g. with respect to employment rights, health and safety, minimum wages, and union recognition), and the social regulation of the local labour force (e.g. via the tax and benefit systems, housing provision, education, and training). Even ostensibly nationally uniform interventions in the labour market may impact differently, and with different consequences, from one local labour market to another. And in some cases, state intervention and regulation have an explicit local dimension (e.g. the variation in union recognition legislation amongst the US states—see Clark 1989, and different legal minimum wages amongst the Japanese prefectures—see Martin and Sunley 2000). Finally, local labour markets can be seen as *spaces of social reproduction* in which various market, institutional, and regulatory mechanisms combine to influence and reproduce the social conditions and differentiation of the nation's workforce, its patterns of income inequality, social inclusion and exclusion, and skills and human capital.

These various conceptions provide distinct, often competing but also in some cases overlapping, views about how local labour markets function. At one extreme, the local labour market is assumed to function as a set of impersonal demand and supply interactions; at the other, as a power-saturated, institutionally constructed social process. Thus, for example, under the competitive-market view, the existence of persistent unemployment disparities between local labour markets is construed as evidence of local barriers and impediments to the 'free working' of labour demand and supply adjustment processes (wage movements, mobility of labour, and so on). Policy should focus on removing those impediments. Under a segmentationalist or institutionalist perspective, however, persistent local unemployment disparities have as much if not more to do with the interaction between firms' internal labour markets, their stratification of workers into core and peripheral groups, the institutionalized discrimination and stigmatization exercised against the unemployed, and the vicious spiral of labour market exclusion in which the unemployed can all too easily become entrapped. The policy emphasis under this perspective is on reforming labour market institutions and practices—both inside the firm and in the external labour market—so as to get the unemployed gainfully and securely reabsorbed into employment.

Flexibility, Globalization, and Local Labour Markets

The question of how local labour markets function takes on special significance in relation to the flexibilization issue referred to earlier. For employers and governments alike, the slogan for the contemporary era is *flexibility*. Labour market flexibility, the OECD (1994*b*, 1996) stresses, will be essential for securing job creation and full employment in the twenty-first century. As various authors have emphasized, however, flexibility takes various forms, with quite different consequences for employers and workers. In the case of employers, it means greater freedom to hire and fire workers, to use non-standard forms of employment (of part-time, contract, casual, and temporary workers), to deploy workers readily across different functions and tasks, to individualize employment contracts, to dilute worker rights, and to exert much greater control and discretion over wages. But while flexibility may be extolled by employers and governments as being essential to labour market and economic success, the implications for many workers are much less celebratory (see Sayer and Walker 1992; Hudson 1989; Pollert 1988, 1991; Standing 1992), typically entailing a deterioration in their employment conditions and their pay, and compelling many to combine more than one job in order to secure a living wage.

One of the factors singled out by academics and governments alike as driving this new imperative of 'flexibility' is economic globalization. The growth of global markets, global companies, and global competition, so the argument goes, is 'delocalizing' local labour markets. The domestic prices of consumer goods, financial assets, and even labour are governed less and less by local and national conditions: they increasingly react to and reflect prices elsewhere in the global system. Multinational companies break up the chain of production of their products or services and locate the links in different localities around the world, depending on what appears to be most profitable at the time. Global capitalism is leading to the intensification of economic relations and the displacement of activities from their local connections and contexts into networks of relationships whose reach is distant or worldwide. Local labour thus becomes vulnerable to economic changes and developments happening in remote locations.

However, at the same time, globalization also 'relocalizes' local labour markets. The specific characteristics and qualities of different individual local labour markets—the skills, productivity, wages, and workplace attitudes of their workers—have assumed heightened importance in the locational strategies and decisions of multinational companies in their search for competitive advantage in global markets. Locationally fixed labour finds itself at the mercy of globally mobile capital. In the new battleground of global trade, local workers are forced into direct conflict with other, often geographically distant, local workers over jobs. Under these conditions, many argue, unless local labour is flexible—in terms of skills, working arrangements, employment conditions, and especially wages—local workers risk losing their jobs to other, more flexible, and cheaper workers elsewhere. Both the OECD and the European Commission subscribe to versions of this argument, and individual governments (as in the UK, for example), respond to public outcries stemming from the local closure of foreign plants by pleading that, while they sympathize, it is 'all part of the global economy', and thus beyond their control.

The importance of flexibility in today's global, high technology economy is typically pointed up by contrasting the experience of local labour markets in Europe and those in the USA. In the former, it is alleged, because of the institutionalized inflexibilities of labour markets, unskilled workers have been particularly hit by the growth of manufacturing trade with the developing world, leading to entrenched localized problems of high unemployment and rising welfare bills (see Wood 1994). In the USA, it is argued, because wages are more flexible within, and workers more mobile between, local labour markets, the same global trade pressures have not led to high unemployment. The message is that Europe should emulate the 'American model' and flexibilize its labour markets. But as Freeman (1993), Krugman (1994*b*), and even Paul Samuelson (1997) point out, the cost of greater flexibility in the USA has been downward pressure on the wages of the low skilled and a marked increase in wage inequality. The 'American model' (i.e. deregulated labour and lower wages) is, therefore, a dubious route by which local labour markets in Europe should meet the challenges of global competition (see Freeman 1995; Mishel and Schmitt 1995; Philpott 1997). The more so since the empirical evidence suggests that local wages in Europe are not in fact less flexible than those in the USA (Blanchflower and Oswald 1994; Baddeley *et al.* 2000). Instead of a 'low-road' flexibilization solution, therefore, attention should focus on a 'high-road' policy of investing in human capital (education and (re)training) so as to upgrade the quality and productivity of labour in the advanced economies (Reich 1991; Wood 1994).

In any case, the 'globalization threat' to local labour markets may possibly have been exaggerated (Krugman 1994*c*; Lawrence 1996; Freeman 1997).

Typically, most advanced economies trade much more with one another than with developing countries. Most local labour markets in Europe are in direct competition with those in the USA or in Japan, and vice versa. Of course, local wage differences may still matter, but productivity differences between local workforces are probably more important. This reinforces the need for investment in skills and training. And even in this context, there is the 'lump of labour fallacy', the erroneous argument that there is a set quantity of jobs in the global economy for which different groups of workers in different local labour markets are in constant struggle one against another. Furthermore, few local labour markets in Europe and the USA are primarily dependent on manufacturing: most now depend on service industry for their employment. Indeed, the tertiarization of the employment structures of local labour markets has been one of the most significant and widespread developments in Western capitalism over the past quarter century. And it is within service industries that some of the most worrying aspects of the contemporary trend towards greater labour 'flexibility' are occurring.

The service sector, of course, covers a wide variety of jobs, skills, and wages. There is a world of difference between the very highly paid careers of (usually male) 'city' professionals such as lawyers and financiers (see McDowell 1997), on the one hand, and the low-paid, often part-time or casual jobs of (typically female) unskilled office cleaners, restaurant waiters, or laundry workers on the other (Reimer 1998). Notions of flexibility also differ dramatically as between different types of worker. For service professionals, increased flexibility is likely to mean self-determined 'flexi-time', split home–office working arrangements, high salaries, and generous social and non-wage benefits. For part-time cleaners, increased flexibility invariably means working unsocial shifts and hours, short-term contracts, loss of employment rights and entitlements, and depressed pay and conditions.

For many service workers—and for unskilled workers in manufacturing—*increased insecurity* of employment and pay has become a growing feature of local labour markets everywhere in the advanced countries (Elliot and Atkinson 1998; Heery 1999). It results both from the growth of demand for the sorts of activities where low-skilled part-time employment, casual work, temporary, and high-turnover jobs tend to be concentrated (such as cleaning, catering, hotels and hospitality, leisure, security, distribution, and some types of retailing), and from the strategies of employers seeking to capitalize on changed labour market conditions (high unemployment, rising female participation, deregulation, and privatization) in order to reduce their commitments to and expenditure on labour. Although many low-skilled manual service activities are being internationalized by large multinationals, the services provided depend on localized demand, whilst typically requiring only unskilled labour and little local sunk capital by the firm in the form of equipment or premises. These companies are thus neither able—nor indeed concerned—to play one local labour market against another as alternative locations in which to invest: to the contrary, their very success depends on being able to win customers across as many localities as possible. Instead, they use their monopoly advantages and aggressive pricing to drive out local service firms, putting downward pressure on the local and employment conditions and wages of workers in this sector, and upward pressure on the flexibilization of labour inputs.

As a consequence, for workers in these and similar activities, the local labour market has become increasingly characterized by *risk* (Allen and Henry 1997; Reimer 1998), a place of precarious employment and low income. Even the most prosperous and buoyant local labour markets have a sizeable *contingent* workforce of this kind, in which levels of job and worker turnover—or 'churning'—are high: a sort of 'throw away' or 'Kleenex' workforce, hired and fired at will by employers. In the USA, high job and labour turnover regimes are seen as a sign of a healthy and adaptive local economy (see Davis *et al.* 1996; but cf. Martin and Sunley 1999). As Allen and Henry (1997) show in the UK context, it is indeed within the most dynamic regions and localities of the economy that the growth of high turnover peripheral employment is most marked, stimulated by the expanding service needs of the prospering primary activities and sections of the local population. But this is not so much a welcome sign of prosperity as a disturbing source of widening employment conditions and incomes. According to Hutton (1995*a*, 1995*b*) what we are seeing is the emergence of a '30-30-40' society, consisting of an advantaged group (40%) of well-paid workers who hold stable, tenured jobs and have relatively certain income prospects, a newly insecure layer of people (30%) who, while in work, are in forms of employment which are structurally insecure and often poorly paid, and a third, disadvantaged layer (30%) consisting of the unemployed and economically inactive, dependent on welfare for their main source of income. If the flexibilization of work and labour is an inherent structural feature of the shift towards a new post-Fordist (or after-Fordist) phase of globalized capitalism, the price would thus far seem to be increased labour market insecurity, inequality, and social polarization.

The key question, then, is whether increased inequality and insecurity constitute a price worth paying for enhanced flexibility? Indeed, does flexibilization necessarily lead to more employment, or to intensified stratification within employment? Because it also widens labour market inequalities and increases poverty and dependence on social welfare, is increasing labour market flexibility ultimately contradictory and dysfunctional for the economic system? Flexibilization, therefore, may well create its own set of social policy challenges. In the European Union, the access of individuals to employment opportunities, regardless of where those individuals happen to live, and a more equitable distribution of income with minimal levels of poverty are the two key defining features of the Union's model of 'social cohesion' (see European Commission

1996). How this goal can be reconciled with the emphasis now also given to the pursuit of labour market flexibilization is far from clear.

The (Re)regulation of Local Labour

Local labour markets in the advanced nations are now caught in a powerful predicament. On the one side, advancing technologies and intensifying global competition are constantly restructuring regional and local economies, with destabilizing consequences for their workforces. On the other side, states are busy deregulating and reregulating local labour markets and decentralizing labour market policies so as to increase the flexibilities of regions and localities, whilst at the same time seeking ways of curbing expenditure on welfare and social security as part of their attempts to control public spending and reduce personal taxation. To these ends, labour market polices have become more supply-side orientated and more targeted to the needs of labour market flexibility. The USA and UK are leading the way in this shift in the mode of labour market regulation, with the UK borrowing policy ideas from the USA, and the UK in turn being seen as the model other European states, such as Germany and Sweden, want to emulate.

The central pillar of this emergent new model of labour market regulation is the 'workfare' system pioneered in the USA and recently copied (in the form of the New Deal) by the Labour government in the UK. There are two key features of this new 'Anglo-American' regulatory model (Philpott 1997; Peck 1998; Peck and Theodore 1999). The first is the move to make social benefits *conditional* on compulsory participation in state-subsidized work and training programmes. This conditionality element is founded on the new (so-called 'third way') precept of 'no entitlements without obligations': the local unemployed have a right to state help and support, but also a responsibility to improve their 'employability'. Local 'workfare' and 'training-fare' measures are intended to provide the means by which unemployed individuals can fulfil that responsibility. The second feature of this new workfare model is precisely that it is quintessentially local: the regulatory powers and institutional capacities for implementing workfare have been decentralized to the local level, to local partnerships of state employment agencies, local government, quasi-state, and even local private sector organizations whose interventions and activities are assumed to be closer to local labour markets and their specific employment problems (OECD 1999).

However, whilst in theory this 'decentralization' and 'localization' of labour market regulation may well increase the local adaptability and impact of workfare-type schemes, by the same token the very success of such schemes is in turn dependent on local labour market conditions. Local labour markets with high unemployment are also those which tend to have the lowest new job creation and new hire rates (Jones and Martin 1986; Davis *et al.* 1996). Thus, unless workfare is accompanied by policies that boost the creation of new jobs locally, it will tend to be least successful in the very local labour markets where help for the unemployed is most needed (Turok and Webster 1998; Martin *et al.* 2000). Indeed, the fear is, and US evidence already suggests, that in such areas workfare may simply serve to (re)produce a peripheral labour force which 'churns' through the contingent segments of the local labour market (Peck and Theodore 1999).

The temptation is to see workfare as an essentially post-Fordist mode of labour market regulation. For example, whilst admitting that workfare may take a number of different national forms (in the same way that Keynesian welfarism did under postwar Fordism), Jessop (1994) argues we are likely to witness its continuing consolidation in successful capitalist economies because 'the hollowed out Schumpeterian workfare state could prove structurally congruent and functionally adequate to post-Fordist accumulation regimes' (p. 27). Such a view can be challenged on various grounds. For one thing, it is still unclear what the 'post-Fordist' or 'after-Fordist' labour market will eventually look like. Secondly, we do not know whether the 'Schumpeterian workfare state' is indeed the new post-Fordist successor to the Keynesian welfare state, or merely the latest stage in an ongoing search for a new mode of social regulation. The argument prosecuted by Jessop (1991, 1994) and others that the flexibility-workfare model is the 'most congruent' post-Fordist solution to the regulation of local labour is thus not only suspect and dangerously functionalist, it would seem to allow local labour itself little or no role in shaping that regulation process.

Which brings us to a central issue: how should labour itself respond to the new and rapidly changing world of global capitalism, flexibility, and workfare experiments? The problem for labour in forging a response is that the main traditional vehicle for worker voice and activism—trade unionism—is itself in decline in almost every OECD nation (Edwards *et al.* 1986; Ferner and Hyman 1992; Hyman and Ferner 1994; Jacoby 1995). Local labour markets are being emptied of their labourist traditions, and workers are losing their collective power in the determination of their work conditions and pay (Martin *et al.* 1996). Some see this de-unionization and de-collectivization of local labour markets as not only integral to the shift to post-Fordist global capitalism (see Jessop 1992), but also as necessary if local labour markets are to be able to respond flexibly to the new global competition. The prospects for local worker activism would thus seem to be highly limited. Yet, it may be that the new post-Fordist regime of localized flexible accumulation, the associated return to pre-welfare localized modes of labour regulation, and the shift to decentralized, enterprise-based industrial relations which post-Fordism is promoting actually create new potential for organized labour to reassert its influence at the local scale. By abandoning their increasingly outmoded nation-wide spaces of mass organization and representation and 'going local' instead, labour unions may be better able to identity with both employers and workers and thereby revive their local memberships and workplace significance accordingly (Locke 1990; Murray 1994; Martin *et al.* 1996).

In opposition to this view, many argue that place-based local labour politics of this sort—especially local 'enterprise unionism'—are doomed to failure (Harvey 1996). Local regulation of work and organization of workers is not enough. Instead of scaling down labour organization to the local level, it should be rescaled upwards to the national, and indeed to the international, level. What is required is a new labour transnationalism to confront global capital (Herod 1995; Wills 1998). There is a powerful logic in this argument, although it too is problematic. If labour unions need to organize transnationally, they no less need to unite and protect the fragmented and segmented groups of workers within individual local labour markets. The challenge for labour, therefore, is one of forging transnational solidarity so as to protect labour standards at a global scale, whilst at the same time responding to the specific employment, wage, and unemployment problems that local workers and local union officials and organizers have to confront. The 'local living wage campaigns' in the USA, in which local unions team up with other local organizations to lobby for city-wide labour standards for the diverse sections of service workers in an area, testify to the need for and possibilities of such locally based activism (Pollin and Luce 1998; Walsh 1999; Herzenberg *et al.* 1999). The issue for a 'new unionism' is one of finding ways of articulating spaces of worker organization and representation at a variety of spatial scales, from the local to the international.

The future of work and welfare in the contemporary climate is undoubtedly going to be a difficult one. But what is clear is that it is within local labour markets that the ongoing transformation of work and workers is being most keenly felt, and that the unfolding policy debate will be increasingly focused. Economic geographers thus have a key role to play in informing our understanding of these processes. The development of a vibrant and committed labour market geography could not be more timely.

References

Adams, J. D. 1985. Permanent difference in unemployment and permanent wage differentials. *Quarterly Journal of Economics*, 100: 29–56.

Adnett, N. 1996. *European Labour Markets.* London: Longman.

Allen, J., and Henry, N. 1997. Ulrich Beck's risk society at work: labour and employment in the contract services industries. *Transactions of the Institute of British Geographers*, 22/2: 180–96.

Baddeley, M., Martin, R. L., and Tyler, P. 1998. European regional unemployment disparities. *European Urban and Regional Studies*, 5/3: 195–215.

——————2000. Regional wage rigidity: Europe and the United States compared. *Journal of Regional Science*, 40/1: 115–42.

BENABOU, R. 1994. Human capital, inequality and growth: a local perspective. *European Economic Review*, 38: 817–26.

BLANCHARD, O. J., and KATZ, L. 1992. Regional evolutions. *Brookings Papers in Economic Activity*, 1: 1–75.

BLANCHFLOWER, D. G., and OSWALD, A. J. 1994. *The Wage Curve*. Cambridge, Mass.: MIT Press.

BOYER, R. 1988. *The Search for Labour Market Flexibility: The European Economies in Transition*. Oxford: Clarendon Press.

CLARK, G. L. 1989. *Unions and Communities under Siege: American Communities and the Crisis of Organized Labour*. Cambridge: Cambridge University Press.

CORINA, J. 1972. *Labour Market Economics: A Short Survey of Recent Theory*. London: Heinemann.

DAVIS, S. J., HALTIWANGER, J. C., and SCHUH, S. 1996. *Job Creation and Destruction*. Cambridge, Mass.: MIT Press.

DECRESSIN, J., and FATAS, A. 1995. Regional labour market dynamics in Europe. *European Economic Review*, 39: 1627–55.

EDWARDS, R., GARONNA, P., and TODTLING, F., eds. 1986. *Unions in Crisis: Perspectives from Six Countries*. London: Auburn House.

EICHENGREEN, B. 1993. European monetary integration and regional unemployment. In Ulman *et al.* 1993: 188–223.

ELLIOT, L., and ATKINSON, D. 1998. *The Age of Insecurity*. London: Verso.

European Commission 1996. *Social Cohesion: First Report*. Luxembourg: European Commission.

—— 1998. *Employment in Europe*. Luxembourg: European Commission.

EVANS, P., and MCCORMICK, B. 1994. New patterns of regional unemployment. *Economic Journal*, 104: 633–47.

FERNER, A., and HYMAN, R., eds. 1992. *Industrial Relations in the New Europe*. Oxford: Basil Blackwell.

FINE, B. 1998. *Labour Market Theory: A Constructive Reassessment*. London: Routledge.

FREEMAN, R. B., ed. 1993. *Working under Different Rules*. New York: Russell Sage Foundation.

—— 1995. The limits of wage flexibility in curing unemployment. *Oxford Review of Economic Policy*, 11/1: 63–72.

—— 1997. Does globalization threaten low-skilled western workers? In *Working for Full Employment*, ed. J. Philpott. London: Routledge, 132–50.

—— and KATZ, L. F. 1993. Rising wage inequality: the United States versus other countries. In Freeman 1993: 29–62.

GRANOVETTER, M., and SWEDBERG, R. 1992. *The Sociology of Economic Life*. Boulder, Colo.: Westview Press.

HANSON, S., and PRATT, G. 1992. Dynamic dependencies: a geographic investigation of local labour markets. *Economic Geography*, 68: 373–405.

—— —— 1995. *Gender, Work and Space*. London: Routledge.

HARVEY, D. 1989. *The Condition of Postmodernity*. Oxford: Blackwell.

—— 1996. *Justice, Nature and the Geography of Difference*. Oxford: Blackwell.

HEERY, E., ed. 1999. *The Insecure Workforce*. London: Routledge.

HEROD, A. 1992. The production of scale in United States labour relations. *Area*, 23: 82–8.

——1995. The practice of international labour solidarity and the geography of the global economy. *Economic Geography*, 71: 341–63.
——1997. From a geography of labour to a labour of geography: labour's spatial fix and the geography of capitalism. *Antipode*, 29/1: 1–31.
HERZENBERG, S. A., ALIC, J. A., and WIAL, H. 1999. *New Rules for a New Economy: Employment and Opportunity in Post-Industrial America*. Ithaca, NY: Cornell University Press.
HODGSON, G. 1993. *The Economics of Institutions*. Aldershot: Edward Elgar.
HOOVER, E. 1948. *The Location of Economic Activity*. New York: McGraw-Hill.
HUDSON, R. 1989. Labour market changes and new forms of work in old industrial regions: maybe flexibility for some, but not flexible accumulation. *Environment and Planning, D: Society and Space*, 7: 5–30.
HUTTON, W. 1995*a*. *The State We're In*. London: Jonathan Cape.
——1995*b*. The 30-30-40 society. *Regional Studies*, 29/8: 719–21.
HYMAN, R., and FERNER, A., eds. 1994. *New Frontiers in European Industrial Relations*. Oxford: Basil Blackwell.
JACOBY, S. M., ed. 1995. *The Workers of Nations: Industrial Relations in a Global Economy*. Oxford: Oxford University Press.
JESSOP, B. 1991. Thatcherism and flexibility: the white heat of a post-Fordist revolution. In *The Politics of Flexibility*, ed. B. Jessop, H. Kastendiek, K. Neilson, and O. Pederson. London: Edward Elgar.
——1992. Fordism and post-Fordism: critique and reformulation. In Storper and Scott 1992.
——1994. The transition to post-Fordism and the Schumpeterian workfare state. In *Towards a Post-Fordist Welfare State*, ed. R. Burrows and B. Loader. London: Routledge, 13–37.
JONAS, A. 1996. Local labour control regimes: uneven development and the social regulation of production. *Regional Studies*, 30/4: 323–38.
JONES, D., and MARTIN, R. L. 1986. Voluntary and involuntary turnover in the labour force. *Scottish Journal of Political Economy*, 33: 124–44.
KERR, C. 1950. Labour markets: their character and consequences. *American Economic Review, Papers and Proceedings*, 40: 278–91.
——1954. The balkanisation of labour markets. In *Labour Mobility and Economic Opportunity*, ed. F. Wright Bakke. New York: Wiley.
KNUDSEN, D. C., ed. 1996. *The Transition to Flexibility*. Dordrecht: Kluwer.
KRUGMAN, P. 1993. *Inequality and the Political Economy of Eurosclerosis*. London: Centre for Economic Policy Research.
——1994*a*. *The Age of Diminished Expectations*. Cambridge, Mass.: MIT Press.
——1994*b*. Europe jobless: America penniless. *Foreign Policy*, fall.
——1994*c*. Does Third World growth hurt First World prosperity? *Harvard Business Review*, July–Aug., 113–21.
——1998. What's new about the new economic geography? *Oxford Review of Economic Policy*, 14/2: 7–17.
LAWLESS, P., MARTIN, R. L., and HARDY, S., eds. 1998. *Unemployment and Social Exclusion: Landscapes of Labour Market Inequality*. London: Jessica Kingsley.
——and SMITH, Y. 1998. Poverty, inequality and exclusion in the contemporary city. In Lawless *et al.* 1998: 201–16.

Lawrence, R. Z. 1996. *Single World: Divided Nations? International Trade and OECD Labour Markets*. Paris: OECD.

Lloyd, P., and Dicken, P. 1972. *Location in Space: A Theoretical Approach to Economic Geography*. London: Harper and Row.

Locke, R. 1990. The resurgence of the local union: industrial restructuring and industrial relations in Italy. *Politics and Society*, 18: 327–79.

Loveridge, R., and Mok, A. L. 1979. *Theories of Labour Market Segmentation*. London: Martinus Nijhoff.

McDowell, L. 1997. *Capital Culture: Gender at Work in the City*. Oxford: Blackwell.

Madanipour, A., Cars, G., and Allen, J., eds. 1998. *Social Exclusion in European Cities*. London: Jessica Kingsley.

Martin, R. L., ed. 1981. *Regional Wage Inflation and Unemployment*. London: Pion.

——1986. Getting the labour market into geographical perspective. *Environment and Planning, A*, 18: 569–72.

——1997. Regional unemployment disparities and their dynamics. *Regional Studies*, 31: 235–50.

——1999. The new 'geographical turn' in economics: some critical reflections. *Cambridge Journal of Economics*, 23/1: 65–91.

——Nativel, C., and Sunley, P. 2000. The local impact of the New Deal: does geography make a difference? Paper presented at the Annual Conference of the RGS-IBG, University of Sussex, UK.

——and Sunley, P. 1999. Unemployment flow regimes and regional unemployment disparities. *Environment and Planning, A*, 31: 523–50.

————2000. The geographies of the national minimum wage, *Environment and Planning, A*.

————and Wills, J. 1994. The decentralisation of industrial relations? New institutional spaces and the role of local context in British engineering. *Transactions of the Institute of British Geographers*, NS 19/4: 457–81.

——————1996. *Union Retreat and the Regions: The Shrinking Landscape of Organised Labour*. London: Jessica Kingsley.

Marston, S. T. 1985. Two views of the geographic distribution of unemployment. *Quarterly Journal of Economics*, 100: 57–79.

Massey, D. 1984. *Spatial Divisions of Labour: Social Structures and the Organisation of Production*. London: Macmillan.

Mishel, L., and Schmitt, J. 1995. *Beware the US Model: Jobs and Wages in a Deregulated Economy*. Washington: Economic Policy Institute.

Murray, G. 1994. Structure and identity: the impact of union structure in comparative perspective. *Employment Relations*, 16/2: 24–40.

OECD 1994*a*. *The Jobs Study: Part I: Labour Market Trends and Underlying Forces of Change*. Paris: OECD.

——1994*b*. *The Jobs Study: Part II: The Adjustment Potential of the Labour Market*. Paris: OECD.

——1996. *Employment Outlook: United Kingdom*. Paris: OECD.

——1999. *The Local Dimension of Welfare-to-Work*. Paris: OECD.

Peck, J. 1989. Reconceptualising the local labour market: space, segmentation and the state. *Progress in Human Geography*, 13: 42–61.

—— 1992. Labour and agglomeration: control and flexibility in local labour markets. *Economic Geography*, 68/4: 325–47.
—— 1996. *Workplace: The Social Regulation of Labour Markets*. New York: Guilford.
—— 1998. New labourers? Making a new deal for the 'workless class'. Paper given at the Annual Conference of the Royal Geographical Society–Institute of British Geographers, Kingston University, Jan.
—— and Theodore, N. 1999. Insecurity in work and welfare: towards a trans-Atlantic model of labour regulation. Paper presented at the Annual Conference of the Royal Geographical Society–Institute of British Geographers. University of Leicester, Jan.
Philpott, J. 1997. *Anglo-Saxon Economics and Jobs*. Economic Report. London: Employment Policy Institute.
Pollert, A. 1988. Dismantling flexibility. *Capital and Class*, 34: 42–75.
—— ed. 1991. *Farewell to Flexibility?* Oxford: Blackwell.
Pollin, R., and Luce, C. 1998. *The Living Wage: Building a Fair Economy*. New York: The Free Press.
Regional Studies 1996. Special issue: geographies of labour market governance. *Regional Studies*, 30/4: 319–441.
Reich, R. B. 1991. *The Work of Nations: Preparing Ourselves for 21st Century Capitalism*. London: Simon and Schuster.
Reimer, S. 1998. Working in a risk society, *Transactions of the Institute of British Geographers*, NS 23/1: 116–27.
Robinson, P., ed. 1991. *Unemployment and Local Labour Markets*. Aldershot: Avebury.
Rutherford, T. 1996. The local solution? The Schumpeterian workfare state, labour market governance and local boards for training in Kitchener, Ontario. *Regional Studies*, 30/4: 413–28.
Samuelson, P. 1997. Wherein do the European and American models differ? Address delivered at the Bank of Italy, 2 Oct.
Sapsford, D., and Tzannatos, Z. 1993. *The Economics of the Labour Market*. London: Macmillan.
Sayer, A., and Walker, R. 1992. *The New Social Economy: Reworking the Division of Labour*. Oxford: Blackwell.
Smith, D. 1966. A theoretical framework for geographical studies of industrial location. *Economic Geography*, 42: 95–113.
—— 1981. *Industrial Location: An Economic Geographical Analysis*. London: Wiley.
Solow, R. 1992. *The Labour Market as a Social Institution*. Oxford: Basil Blackwell.
Standing, G. 1992. Alternative routes to labor flexibility. In Storper and Scott 1992: 255–75.
Storper, M. 1995. Boundaries, compartments and markets: paradoxes, of industrial relations in growth pole regions of France, Italy and the United States. In Jacoby 1995: 155–81.
—— and Scott, A. J., eds. 1992. *Pathways to Industrialization and Regional Development*. London: Routledge.
—— and Walker, R. 1984. The spatial division of labor: labor and the location of industries. In *Sunbelt-Snowbelt: Urban Development and Regional Restructuring*, ed. L. Sawers and W. Tabb. Oxford: Oxford University Press, 19–47.
—— —— 1989. *The Capitalist Imperative: Territory, Technology and Industrial Growth*. Oxford: Basil Blackwell.

TOPEL, R. H. 1986. Local labour markets. *Journal of Political Economy*, 94 (suppl.), 111–43.

TUROK, I., and WEBSTER, D. 1998. The New Deal: jeopardised by the geography of unemployment? *Local Economy*, 1–20.

ULMAN, L., EICHENGREEN, B., and DICKENS, W. T., eds. 1993. *Labor in an Integrated Europe*. Washington: The Brookings Institution.

WEBER, A. 1929. *Theory of the Location of Industries*. Chicago: University of Chicago Press.

WALSH, J. 1999. Organizing the scale of labour regulation: the living wage labor-community alliance model. Paper presented at the Annual Conference of the Institute of British Geographers. University of Leicester, Jan.

WILLS, J. 1998. Taking on the CosmoCorps? Experiments in transnational labour organization. *Economic Geography*, 74: 111–30.

WOOD, A. 1994. *North-South Trade, Employment and Inequality: Changing Fortunes in a Skill-Driven World*. Oxford: Clarendon.

Chapter 24

Firms, Workers, and the Geographic Concentration of Economic Activity

Gordon H. Hanson

Introduction

In the last decade, there has been a renewed interest in urban and regional economics. Part of this interest has originated in other fields, especially international economics and macroeconomics, as economists have used regional economies as laboratories in which to examine a variety of questions. Central to this line of inquiry has been an attempt to understand the factors that explain why economic activity tends to concentrate geographically. As it turns out, if we can explain geographic concentration, then we can also explain important aspects of international and interregional trade and the process of economic growth.

This chapter discusses recent academic research on the location of economic activity. My interest is in the incentive of firms and workers to locate in densely concentrated regions. Consider the economic geography of the USA. In 1950, the location of production in the country told the story of US industrialization. Manufacturing was concentrated in cities within an industrial belt that stretched from Maine in the northeast to Wisconsin in the northern mid-west (Perloff *et al.* 1960). This industrial development created urban areas, which, in turn, amassed the necessary capital and labor to sustain further growth. Half a century later, the location of production in the USA tells the story of the country's transformation into a diversified, service-oriented economy. Traditional manufacturing cities in the north have declined, while new, broadly specialized cities have emerged in the south and west (Blanchard and Katz 1992; Glaeser *et al.* 1995; Black and Henderson 1998). The northern cities that have managed to survive this transition, such as Chicago and New York, have refashioned themselves as centers for the provision of business services.

There are at least two important lessons from the US experience. The first is that despite changing patterns of industrial specialization and location, the agglomeration of production in cities is a constant feature of the economic landscape (Glaeser 1998). In 1990, the 150 largest metropolitan areas in the continental USA accounted for 70.4 per cent of total employment, but only 13.9 per cent of total land area. While there have been important changes in the size ranking and internal organization of cities (Dobkins and Ioannides 1998; Black and Henderson 1998), the overall concentration of economic activity in metropolitan areas has been relatively stable. In 1970, the 150 largest US cities accounted for 68.7 per cent of employment and 13.8 per cent of land area. The geographic concentration of production is not, of course, unique to the USA. Industrialization and urbanization have also been coincident events in Europe, Asia, and Latin America (Bairoch 1988; Williamson 1991).

A second lesson from the US experience is that the location of major production centers can change considerably over time (Blanchard and Katz 1992; Dumais *et al.* 1997). Shifts in regional production patterns require the migration of labor and capital. In the USA, the high-growth cities of the late twentieth century, such as Atlanta, Houston, and Los Angeles, could not have flourished without importing workers and firms from other regions. Spatial agglomeration appears to be a dynamic process, involving a high degree of interregional and intersectoral mobility of labor and capital.

In this chapter, I will focus on the characteristics of regions that attract workers and firms. A central theme of recent theoretical work is that the existence of well-developed markets for consumer goods, industrial goods, and factors of production help make densely concentrated regions attractive places to live and work. Part of why Los Angeles is a logical place to film a movie or make a musical recording, for instance, is the presence of specialized firms and workers that supply key inputs into the production process, such as video and sound editing and script and song writing. Explaining why labor and capital are attracted to particular regions is essential to unlock the mystery of why economic activity spatially agglomerates. The literature on this subject is vast. To contain my enterprise, I choose papers that illustrate important concepts and do not attempt an exhaustive survey of the field.

To complement the other chapters in this volume, I will focus almost entirely on empirical research, though a brief discussion of recent theoretical literature will be helpful for context. Also, to keep the scope of this chapter manageable, I will mainly discuss research by economists. Other disciplines have unquestionably made important contributions to our understanding of the location of economic activity. My motivation for limiting the scope of the chapter is solely to sharpen the analytical focus.

Theory and Empirical Methodology

Theory

Recent theoretical literature explains the geographic concentration of economic activity as the result of increasing returns to scale in production. If average production costs decline as the scale of production, at the firm, industry, or regional level, rises, then there are advantages to concentrating production in a particular location. The link between scale economies and agglomeration has long been recognized by urban and regional economists (Fujita and Thisse 1996). In this section I briefly discuss recent theory in order to identify the channels through which scale economies contribute to spatial agglomeration.

In an early strand of literature, agglomeration economies arise from positive spillovers between firms that share the same locality (Henderson 1974 and 1988). The source of these externalities is not made explicit, but one can imagine that the dense concentration of firms promotes learning and the exchange of knowledge, as in Marshall (1920). Location-specific externalities give firms an incentive to locate near large concentrations of other firms in their own industry or related industries.

The externalities that Henderson (1974) has in mind are static. Lucas (1988) proposes a dynamic version of this story, in which workers learn from one another. When one worker becomes more productive, through education or training, all workers in a locality also become a bit more productive.[1] In the Lucas model, each region is a closed economy, so there is no spatial agglomeration *per se*. Black and Henderson (1999), building on work by Eaton and Eckstein (1997), present a dynamic model of city formation, which combines the agglomeration economies in Henderson (1974) with the localized human capital spillovers of Lucas (1988).

In another recent strand of literature, agglomeration results from demand linkages between firms, which are created by the interaction of fixed production costs and transport costs (Krugman 1991). In this case, scale economies are internal, rather than external, to the firm, and the externalities associated with agglomeration arise endogenously from the location decisions of economic agents. Fixed production costs imply that firms prefer to serve consumers from a single location, while transport costs imply that firms prefer to locate near large consumer markets. These two effects create demand linkages within a region that contribute to spatial agglomeration. Firms are drawn to densely concentrated regions by the possibility of serving a large local market from a

[1] In both Henderson (1974) and Lucas (1988) externalities are assumed rather than derived. Acemoglu (1996) presents a model in which externalities from human capital accumulation arise endogenously, due to costs in matching skilled workers with firms.

single plant at low transport costs; the more firms that locate in the region, the more attractive the region becomes.[2] Similar results obtain if there are increasing returns in the production of non-traded inputs (Fujita 1988; Rivera-Batiz 1988) or if there are input–output linkages between industries (Venables 1996).

Whether increasing returns are internal or external to firms, the logical consequence of location-specific externalities is the geographic concentration of economic activity in a small number of locations. The force working against such an outcome is congestion costs, which arise from the existence of non-traded goods or immobile factors. Housing is one example. The agglomeration of economic activity requires workers to live in a limited geographic area, which drives up housing prices in industry centers relative to outlying locations. To attract workers to the region, firms must compensate workers for congestion costs by paying them relatively high wages. In equilibrium, the degree of spatial agglomeration depends on the strength of scale economies, the magnitude of transport costs, and the importance of congestion costs.

Empirical Methodology

Recent theoretical literature shares an emphasis on increasing returns to scale as a key motivation for spatial agglomeration. Two important tasks for empirical work are to verify whether scale economies in fact contribute to spatial agglomeration and to identify which types of scale economies are at work. To isolate the forces that influence industry location, most theoretical work abstracts away from the natural characteristics of regions, such as climate or natural resource supplies. While this abstraction does not limit the generality of theory, it is quite important for considering how to apply theory to data. The issue arises because spatial agglomeration is not in and of itself evidence that increasing returns to scale are at work. Spatial agglomeration due to scale economies is observationally equivalent to spatial agglomeration due to exogenous regional characteristics (Ellison and Glaeser 1997).

Consider the Los Angeles entertainment industry. One explanation for why the industry is highly concentrated in Los Angeles is that there are location-specific externalities associated with providing entertainment services. Musicians or actors may learn techniques from their colleagues, which improve their performances, or the expansion of the local industry may make it feasible for local firms to provide a wider variety of specialized services, such as recording sessions in specialized studios or more realistic movie special effects, which raise the productivity of local recording artists and movie producers. This hypothesis, drawn from recent theory, is consistent with the industry's concentration in Los Angeles. But without further evidence on the characteristics of the industry and region it is impossible to distinguish this hypothesis empirically from the hypothesis that the entertainment industry is concentrated in Los

[2] For recent related work, see Puga (1999) and Ottaviano and Thisse (1998).

Angeles because it has pleasant weather (which is useful for filming movies) and attractive natural geography (which inspires actors and musicians).

Empirical work on spatial agglomeration thus confronts an identification problem. The externalities that contribute to spatial agglomeration, such as spillovers between workers, learning across firms, or cost and demand linkages between local industries, are difficult to observe. We are left to infer their existence from the covariance of observed variables, such as wages, employment, and output. One way to document the evolution of empirical work on spatial agglomeration is to trace different approaches that researchers have developed to statistically identify the impact of scale economies on industry location. Evaluating the strengths and limitations of these different approaches will be an important task of this chapter.

Workers and Spatial Agglomeration

Why are workers attracted to cities? An obvious explanation is that workers receive a higher economic return for their efforts in cities than elsewhere. It is well known that urban workers tend to receive higher wages than workers in outlying areas. In 1990, the average wage for wage and salary workers in the 150 largest US cities was 23.3 per cent higher than in the rest of the country; in 1970, the figure was 25.0 per cent. The urban wage premium falls only slightly when one controls for the fact that workers with higher observable skill levels tend to concentrate in cities (Glaeser and Mare 1994). These urban–rural wage differences are in *nominal* terms. Since housing prices are also higher in cities, *real* regional wage differences are smaller.

Several recent strands of literature use the variation in wages across regions to uncover the forces that contribute to spatial agglomeration. There are at least two broad explanations for regional wage differences. A first possibility is that variation in wages across space simply reflects differences in the inherent desirability of regions as places to live and work. A second possibility is that workers are attracted to cities because agglomeration, through location-specific externalities, raises the return to their skills.

To dispense with an alternative explanation, in the USA, at least, regional differences in unemployment cannot fully explain regional wage differences. Blanchard and Katz (1992) find that for US states over the period 1950–90 regional differences in unemployment rates tend to die out quickly over time. The lack of persistence is due in part to labor migration between regions. Migration also helps arbitrage away some portions of interregional wage differences (Topel 1986), but regional differences in nominal wages are never fully eliminated, suggesting they are not due to regional variation in business cycles alone. The US experience stands in stark contrast to that of the European continent, where regional differences in unemployment are large, persistent, and not offset by regional adjustment in wages (Abraham 1996). Higher labor mobility within the USA relative to Europe probably accounts for at least part of these differences in regional labor-market dynamics.

Regional Wage and Rent Differentials

One source of regional wage differences is regional variation in resource endowments or exogenous supplies of amenities that consumers value (Rosen 1979; Roback 1982). Florida, for instance, has lots of sunshine and an abundant supply of beaches. If workers value pleasant weather or proximity to the coast, they will congregate in Florida and be willing to accept lower wages in the state than in locations without such amenities. Consumers who value these amenities will be willing to pay relatively high prices for housing in Florida. Even with migration, the presence of such amenities will contribute to regional variation in nominal wages and housing prices. The exogenous characteristics of a region may also affect the productivity of labor. In regions with endowments that raise labor productivity, firms will be willing to pay workers high wages relative to other locations. High wages will attract workers to the region and the resulting agglomeration will drive up land prices relative to other regions.

The standard empirical approach to estimate the impact of exogenous regional characteristics on wages and land prices is hedonic price estimation (Rosen 1974). In this framework, the dependent variable is either the wage of an individual worker or the imputed rent for a particular housing unit. The independent variables include individual characteristics (e.g. education, age, gender of a worker; size, age, heating/cooling system of a housing unit) and exogenous regional characteristics (climate indicators, proximity to the coast, air quality). Roback (1982) finds that in a cross-section of US cities the wages a worker earns are positively correlated with local measures of heating degree-days, total snowfall, and the number of cloudy days and negatively correlated with the number of clear days. This suggests that workers attach a negative (positive) value to poor (good) weather and require a higher (lower) wage as compensation. Subsequent research extends the hedonic approach to address regional productivity and fiscal differences (Beeson and Eberts 1989; Gyourko and Tracy 1991).

While the exogenous characteristics of regions influence wages and housing prices, it seems clear that one needs to account for the endogenous characteristics of regions, such as those created by the agglomeration of economic activity, to fully explain why wages and housing prices vary across space. Consider the cases of Silicon Valley and lower Manhattan. These two locations have some of the most expensive commercial real estate in the world. Yet, microelectronics firms continue to agglomerate in Silicon Valley and investment-banking firms continue to agglomerate near Wall Street. Firms are willing to pay dearly for the privilege of being near other firms in their industry (Lucas 1988). It is difficult to ascribe this behavior to exogenous regional characteristics, since in either location uncrowded sites with virtually identical exogenous features can be found within an hour's drive. We need to appeal to the *acquired* characteristics of regions to understand why these locations are attractive.

Agglomeration, Education, and Labor Productivity

The theories of Lucas (1988), Eaton and Eckstein (1997), and Black and Henderson (1999) suggest that if there are spillovers in the accumulation of human capital, a worker will be more productive the more educated are the workers with whom he or she shares a given location. Several recent papers examine this possibility.

Using hedonic price estimation, Rauch (1993) finds that both wages and housing rents are higher in US cities with higher average education levels. These regressions include controls for individual worker characteristics, in the case of wage regressions, or individual housing unit characteristics, in the case of rent regressions. The interpretation is that workers benefit in terms of higher productivity from being around more educated workers and that, in regions with a highly educated labor force, this shows up in terms of higher wages and higher demand for housing. While the positive correlation between wages, housing rents, and average regional education levels is not direct evidence of agglomeration economies, it is consistent with the existence of location-specific human capital spillovers. In related work, Glaeser *et al.* (1995) find that US cities that begin with a more educated population have higher population growth in the future.

Peri (1998) explores the mechanisms underlying Rauch's results. Most of the effect of average education on wages is due to the fact that the returns to education for individual workers are increasing in the average local education level. The benefit in terms of higher labor earnings from additional years of schooling appears to be higher in cities with a more educated labor force. This gives more-educated workers a stronger incentive to agglomerate in cities than less-educated workers. In related work, Borjas *et al.* (1992) find that migrants with higher education levels are attracted to regions with higher returns to education.

Human-capital spillovers are just one type of externality that could contribute to regional variation in wages. Ciccone and Hall (1996) examine whether labor productivity is higher in US states where economic activity is more densely concentrated. Based on a production function in which the density of employment is presumed to influence productivity, they derive and estimate a specification that expresses labor productivity at the state level as a function of the education level of workers in the state and employment densities for counties within the state. They find that doubling the employment density in a region raises local labor productivity by 6 per cent. This is consistent with the idea that the close proximity of workers to each other makes them more productive and allows them to command higher wages.

Additional sources of variation in wages across space are the cost and demand linkages proposed in Krugman (1991) and related work. A key prediction of this model is that firms are willing to pay workers higher wages in regions that are close to large consumer markets, since firms in these regions are able to deliver goods to market at low transport cost. This idea is related to Harris's (1954) market-potential function, which states that the demand for goods produced in a location is the sum of the purchasing power in all other locations, weighted by transport costs. Hanson (1997, 1998*a*) looks for evidence of demand linkages between regions by examining the correlation between wages and proximity to consumer markets across states in Mexico and counties in the USA. In both cases, he finds that, controlling for other factors (including worker education levels), wages are higher in locations that are closer to large consumer markets, which is consistent with the demand-linkage hypothesis proposed by Krugman. These results suggest that demand linkages between firms create location-specific externalities that contribute to spatial agglomeration.

Spatial variation in wages and housing prices contains important information about the benefits that firms and workers derive from agglomeration. The observed variation in the exogenous characteristics of regions appears to be insufficient to explain regional price differences. Existing empirical work suggests that spatial wage differences are consistent with benefits from proximity to more educated workers, dense concentrations of economic activity, and high areas of consumer or industrial demand. One limitation of existing empirical work is that most studies tend to look at a given explanation for spatial agglomeration, in isolation from other possible effects. Thus, we do not know whether there are multiple types of externalities that contribute to agglomeration or whether each of these apparent effects simply captures a different aspect of a single unified force behind the location of economic activity.

Firms and Spatial Agglomeration

Why are firms attracted to densely concentrated regions? Since we have already established that wages and land prices are higher in these regions, for firms to be willing to locate in industry centers it must be that such locations have higher productivity for some factors or lower costs for other factors. Several recent strands of literature examine whether factor productivity is related to the local agglomeration of economic activity. Early contributions along this line include Sveikauskas (1975) and Moomaw (1981) (see Quigley 1998).

Accompanying the overall agglomeration of economic activity in cities is a tendency for individual industries to cluster geographically. Kim (1995) finds that the geographic concentration of individual manufacturing industries in the USA rose substantially from 1860 until 1914, during the first stage of the US industrial revolution, stabilized in the interwar period, and then declined between 1947 and 1986. Kim claims that declining localization is inconsistent with external economies being a motivation for agglomeration, but this view seems unwarranted in light of the results in Dumais *et al.* (1997). They find that while industry localization declined slightly between 1972 and 1992, the *location* of industry clusters did not. The birth and death of manufacturing plants has led to large shifts in industrial activity across regions. Though the death of manufacturing plants may lead to the decline of an industry cluster in a particular location, the birth of new plants recreates clusters of firms in the same industry in entirely new locations. This is compelling evidence that it is the acquired characteristics of regions that attract firms to particular locations.

Agglomeration, Productivity, and the Firm Location Decision

One strategy to examine whether firms expect to be more productive in regions where other firms in their industry are concentrated is to examine the location decisions of new firms.[3] By examining new firms, one can control for the impact that sunk investments have on business location decisions. Carlton (1983) examines the location decision of US firms in a subset of industries that tend to ship their goods long distances. Controlling for local labor costs, energy costs, and tax rates, new firms are more likely to choose a city the larger is own-industry employment in the city. In related work, Wheeler and Mody (1992) examine the foreign investment decision of US multinational enterprises. Controlling for differences in labor cost, economic openness, and political risk across countries, foreign investment by a firm is higher in countries with larger markets, a larger initial concentration of foreign firms, and higher quality of infrastructure. Both findings are interpreted as supporting agglomeration effects: firms are attracted to locations that have large concentrations in their industry or related industries.

Alternatively, one can examine directly whether productivity is higher in regions with larger concentrations of industry. Nakamura (1985) and Henderson (1986) estimate production functions for Japanese (Nakamura) and US and Brazilian (Henderson) manufacturing industries to see whether total factor productivity is higher in a regional industry when own-industry production or employment in the region is also higher. Both authors find that, controlling for factor costs, productivity is higher in a regional industry the larger is the scale of production in the industry. Again, these results are

[3] A large literature examines the impact of local tax rates, unionization, and other government policies on business activity and the plant location decision. Since this body of work does not explicitly address agglomeration, I do not discuss it. See Bartik (1985) for an early study and Holmes (1998*b*) for a recent contribution. Feldstein *et al.* (1995) and Hines (1996) discuss the impact of taxes on the location of foreign direct investment.

interpreted as evidence of agglomeration economies. A large literature uses this approach to estimate agglomeration effects.

Controlling for observable cost and other differences across regions, firms are attracted to locations with large concentrations of firms in their industry and appear to be more productive in these locations. The difficulty in interpreting these findings as evidence of agglomeration effects is that there are many unobserved factors which may also influence firm location and productivity, but which are not controlled for in standard regressions. The shrimp packing industry, for instance, is concentrated near coastal areas with abundant shrimp populations. Not surprisingly, one tends to find that new shrimp packing factories tend to locate near large concentrations of other shrimp packers. The agglomeration of shrimp packers likely has much more to do with exogenous regional characteristics than with externalities. Yet, much empirical research would attribute the agglomeration of shrimp packers to externalities, since few studies control for exogenous regional characteristics at a sufficiently detailed level.

Several recent studies of industry location make creative use of available data to address this issue. Head *et al.* (1995) examine the location decision of new Japanese manufacturing plants in the USA. They find that, controlling for the local concentration of US plants in the same industry, Japanese plants are more likely to choose a location the higher is the existing local concentration of Japanese manufacturing plants in the same industry. This finding is similar to Carlton's that firms are attracted to large concentrations of firms in their industry. But, by focusing on Japanese plants and controlling for the location of overall US manufacturing activity, this approach goes further than previous studies in controlling for the effects of unobserved, site-specific characteristics. Smith and Florida (1994) and Aitken *et al.* (1997) provide related results on agglomeration and plant behavior.

Agglomeration and Regional Growth and Innovation

An alternative strategy to empirically distinguish the effects of agglomeration economies on industry location from those of unobserved site-specific factors is to examine variation in industry growth or innovation across regions. By examining the growth process one can control for the time-invariant characteristics of regions that influence firm behavior.

Using data on long-run changes in industry employment in US cities, Glaeser *et al.* (1992) find that employment growth in a city industry is positively correlated with the initial diversity of industrial activity in the city, but not with initial own-industry employment in the city. They interpret this result to mean that the benefits firms derive from agglomeration come from interacting with many different types of firms rather than from interacting with firms in their own industry. Henderson *et al.* (1995) examine annual employment growth for a subset of manufacturing industries across US cities. They find that for new industries employment growth in a city is positively correlated with initial industrial diversity in a city, but for mature industries employment growth is positively correlated with initial own-industry employment in the city and uncorrelated with initial industrial diversity. They interpret these results to imply that the benefits to agglomeration depend on the stage of development of the industry. Firms in newer industries benefit from exposure to ideas drawn from many different sources, while firms in industries with more established production techniques benefit more from proximity to firms in similar lines of activity.

Those industries tend to have higher growth rates in regions where industrial diversity is higher or where own-industry employment is higher, consistent with agglomeration economies. These results are silent, however, about the precise source of benefits to agglomeration. Many types of agglomeration economies (or perhaps other industry characteristics) could explain persistence in regional industry employment growth. To identify the acquired regional characteristics that influence industry location, Dumais *et al.* (1997) examine the correlates of industry employment growth for US cities. Industry employment growth is higher in cities where industries (1) use workers in similar occupations to the industry in question, and (2) are relatively specialized in inputs demanded or supplied by the industry in question. It appears that firms are attracted to regions that have a relatively abundant supply of workers they are likely to hire and of firms in upstream and downstream activities.

Another way to identify the source of agglomeration benefits is to focus on a narrow set of possible externalities. Jaffe *et al.* (1993) examine the geographic localization of US patent citations. When the government issues a new patent, the patent holder is required to cite any previous patents that relate to the innovation contained in the new patent. Patent citations thus delimit the property right conferred by the new patent and identify its intellectual antecedents. Jaffe *et al.* (1993) find that new patents and cited patents are much more likely to have originated in the same city than are new patents and a control group of patents, where the control group is selected randomly from patents issued at the same date and in the same industry as the new patent. They interpret this result to mean that there are location-specific spillovers associated with innovation, which contribute to industry localization. In related work, Audretsch and Feldman (1996) find that innovations are concentrated in locations with relatively high spending on R&D, employment of skilled labor, and spending on university research, suggesting that innovations cluster near knowledge-intensive activities.

Industrial Linkages, Trade Policy, and Agglomeration

Following the logic of Krugman (1991) and Venables (1996), agglomeration may raise the productivity of firms if it expands local demand for their goods, either through market size effects or input–output linkages between industries.

For demand linkages to matter, it must be that, due to transport costs or other trade costs, most output is traded locally or regionally. Wolf (1997) finds that for the USA, consumer products, such as footwear, apparel, and electronics, tend to be shipped longer distances, while intermediate inputs, such as cement, glass, lumber, and petroleum products, tend to be shipped shorter distances. This suggests that downstream firms tend to locate near upstream supplier industries (and vice versa). As further evidence of regional input–output linkages, Wolf finds that trade between two states is higher the more similar are production patterns in the states and that states that are closer to one another tend to have more similar production patterns. In related work, Holmes (1998*a*) finds that plants in more localized industries tend to have a higher ratio of purchased inputs to total sales, suggesting that plants in these industries are less vertically integrated (and thus may purchase a higher fraction of their inputs locally) than other plants.

That regional input–output linkages exist is not, in and of itself, evidence that such linkages raise productivity or promote spatial agglomeration. The empirical literature has just begun to address this issue. The previously mentioned papers by Dumais *et al.* (1997) and Hanson (1998*a*) both find evidence consistent with the hypothesis that regional demand linkages contribute to spatial agglomeration. Davis and Weinstein (1999) offer other evidence of such effects. They find that regional production by an individual Japanese manufacturing industry increases more than one for one with the regional consumption of goods from an industry. This suggests that there is an excess concentration of production in regions where demand for a good is relatively high. Such an effect could work through consumer markets—with firms concentrating production near relatively large sources of final demand, as in Krugman (1991)—or through markets for intermediate inputs—with firms concentrating near their buyers or suppliers, as in Venables (1996). In related work, Justman (1994) also finds strong positive co-movements between local supply and local demand for manufacturing industries in US cities.

An alternative way to identify the impact of demand linkages on industry location is to exploit variation in economic policy, either across regions or time. Variation in trade policy is a particularly useful tool in this regard, since trade barriers determine the cost of trade across borders and hence influence the incentive of firms to locate in particular regions. Krugman and Livas (1996) model how trade policy can alter the location of economic activity. In a closed economy, where industry agglomerates may be indeterminate, many domestic locations may be equally viable candidates for industry centers. Following a liberalization of trade, firms that export or that use imported inputs may choose to relocate to regions that have relatively low-cost access to foreign markets, which may cause entire industry centers to relocate.

Several recent empirical papers examine whether industry location is influenced by trade policy. Ades and Glaeser (1995) find that countries with higher trade barriers and lower exposure to international trade have a higher concentration of population in the country's largest city. This suggests that locating near large sources of domestic demand is more important where firms have poor access to foreign markets. Hanson (1996, 1998*b*) examines regional employment growth in Mexico before and after a dramatic liberalization of trade. For Mexico, the USA is the major source of foreign demand. Prior to trade reform, nearly half of the country's manufacturing labor force was agglomerated in a single location, Mexico City. After trade reform, the fastest growing regions were those closest to the USA, and relatively far from Mexico City. Trade reform thus appears to have contributed to a relocation of economic activity away from the closed-economy industry center in Mexico City and towards the border region with the USA. These findings suggest that proximity to market demand has a strong effect on industry location.

Concluding Thoughts

The spatial agglomeration of production is a persistent feature of the economic landscape. One factor that draws workers to agglomerated regions, is higher wages, which suggests that labor productivity is higher near dense concentrations of economic activity. These productivity effects appear to be capitalized into land values, which accounts for why housing rents are also higher in agglomerated regions. Firms are willing to incur higher labor and land costs in agglomerated regions if the productivity of labor and other factors in these regions is also higher. There is abundant evidence that this is the case, which is an indirect confirmation of location-specific externalities associated with geographic concentration.

There is now a large body of empirical evidence that suggests that economic benefits to agglomeration exist and have quantitatively important effects on the migration of labor and the location of industry. However, our knowledge of why agglomerations form and how they evolve over time remains incomplete. There are a number of unresolved issues confronting future empirical work on geographic concentration.

A first issue is that we have relatively little understanding of the precise type of externalities that contribute to agglomeration. Is it learning across firms and workers that drive agglomeration? Or is it the formation of regional industrial complexes that lower transport costs and permit firms to achieve greater economies of scale? Individual studies find evidence consistent with human capital spillovers across workers in the same city, localized knowledge spillovers in the innovation process, and regional cost and demand linkages between firms. There is little work that attempts to estimate the relative impact of these different effects (Dumais *et al.* 1997 and Hanson 1998*a* are exceptions). One reason for this is that few empirical studies attempt to estimate explicit structural economic models, in which it is possible to nest different hypotheses about which factors contribute to spatial agglomeration. Another reason is that theoretical models tend to focus on a single explanation for geographic concentration, in isolation from other factors. Developing richer theoretical models and taking these models to the data are two important tasks for future research.

A second issue is that empirical work is plagued by simultaneity problems. In the presence of agglomeration economies, the location decisions of firms and workers are interdependent, which makes it difficult to ascribe causal influence to any particular factor. For instance, if cost and demand linkages between firms matter, as in Krugman (1991) and Venables (1996), then upstream industries will wish to locate near downstream industries and vice versa. Shocks to one segment of the industry are likely to influence other segments of the industry in the same location, making it difficult to identify the impact that the location of one segment of the industry has on the location of other segments. One solution to this problem is to look for natural experiments in the data, such as those created by large (and hopefully exogenous) changes in economic policy. Examining industry location in Mexico before and after trade liberalization is one example of this approach (Hanson 1998*b*). Exploiting variation in policies across US states (Holmes 1998*b*) or countries (Ades and Glaeser 1995; Hines 1996) are other examples. The transition from central planning to market economies in former communist-bloc countries would seem to offer many possible cases for study.

A third issue is that much empirical work on economic geography actually has a small geographic component. The standard approach in much of the literature is to treat regions as distinct and physically separate small open economies, ignoring any interregional linkages that may exist. In literature on why industry employment growth varies across cities or regions, for instance, there is no consideration of wage adjustment between regions.[4] The implicit assumption is that regions can import unlimited supplies of workers at a given real wage. We should expect, however, that high employment growth in one region would put upward pressure on wages in that region and in regions from which it attracts workers. Additionally, an important message of recent theory (e.g. Krugman 1991) is that the level of economic activity in different regions is interrelated. Cost and demand linkages between firms are one source of this interrelationship, as are knowledge spillovers that spread across neighboring regions. The solution to this problem is to move away from using *partial equilibrium* empirical techniques to test *general equilibrium* theories. A promising development on this front is recent work that takes the spatial distribution of economic activity as the focus of analysis and examines the properties of this distribution and how it evolves over time (Quah 1996; Eaton and Eckstein 1997;

[4] Topel (1986) and Blanchard and Katz (1992) consider wage adjustment between regions explicitly, but do not address the spatial agglomeration of economic activity.

Black and Henderson 1998*a*; Dobkins and Ioannides 1998). This line of research is returning to an emphasis on viewing individual agglomerations as part of an urban hierarchy or a system of cities, which was one of the early theoretical insights (Henderson 1974) that helped launch modern research on regional economies.

References

Abraham, F. 1996. Regional adjustment and wage flexibility in the European Union. *Regional Science and Urban Economics*, 26: 51–75.

Acemoglu, D. 1996. A microfoundation for social increasing returns in human capital. *Quarterly Journal of Economics*, 111: 779–804.

Ades, A., and Glaeser, E. L. 1995. Trade and circuses: explaining urban giants. *Quarterly Journal of Economics*, 110: 195–228.

Aitken, B., Hanson, G. H., and Harrison, A. E. 1997. Spillovers, foreign investment, and export behavior. *Journal of International Economics*, 43: 103–32.

Audretsch, D., and Feldman, M. 1996. R&D spillovers and the geography of innovation and production. *American Economic Review*, 86: 630–40.

Bairoch, P. 1988. *Cities and Economic Development*. Chicago: University of Chicago Press.

Bartik, T. J. 1985. Business location decisions in the United States: estimates of the effects of unionization, taxes, and other characteristics. *Journal of Business and Economic Statistics*, 14–22.

Beeson, P. E., and Eberts, R. 1989. Identifying productivity and amenity effects in interurban wage differentials. *Review of Economics and Statistics*, 71: 443–52.

Black, D., and Henderson, V. 1998. Urban evolution in the U.S.A. Mimeo. Brown University.

—— —— 1999. A theory of urban growth. *Journal of Political Economy*, 107/2 (Apr.), 252–84.

Blanchard, O., and Katz, L. 1992. Regional evolutions. *Brookings Papers on Economic Activity*, 1: 1–75.

Borjas, G. J., Bronars, S. G., and Trejo, S. J. 1992. Self-selection and internal migration in the United States. *Journal of Urban Economics*, 32: 159–85.

Carlton, D. W. 1983. The location and employment choices of new firms: an econometric model with discrete and continuous endogenous variables. *Review of Economics and Statistics*, 65: 440–9.

Ciccone, A., and Hall, R. 1996. Productivity and the density of economic activity. *American Economic Review*, 86: 54–70.

Davis, D. R., and Weinstein, D. E. 1999. Economic geography and regional production structure: an empirical investigation. *European Economic Review*, 43/2 (Feb.), 379–407.

Dobkins, L. H., and Ioannides, Y. 1998. The evolution of city size distributions in the United States. Mimeo. Tufts University.

Dumais, G., Ellison, G., and Glaeser, E. 1997. Geographic concentration as a dynamic process. NBER Working Paper No. 6270.

Eaton, J., and Eckstein, Z. 1997. Cities and growth: theory and evidence from France and Japan. *Regional Science and Urban Economics*, 27: 443–74.

Ellison, G., and Glaeser, E. L. 1997. Geographic concentration in U.S. manufacturing industries: a dartboard approach. *Journal of Political Economy*, 105: 889–927.

Feldstein, M., Hines, J. R., and Hubbard, R. G., eds. 1995. *The Effects of Taxation on Multinational Corporations.* Chicago: University of Chicago Press.

Fujita, M. 1988. Monopolistic competition and urban systems. *European Economic Review*, 37: 308–15.

——and Thisse, J. F. 1996. Economics of agglomeration. *Journal of the Japanese and International Economies*, 10: 339–78.

Glaeser, E. L. 1998. Are cities dying? *Journal of Economic Perspectives*, 12: 139–60.

——Kallal, H., Sheinkman, J., and Shleifer, A. 1992. Growth in cities. *Journal of Political Economy*, 100: 1126–52.

——and Mare, D. C. 1994. Cities and skills. NBER Working Paper No. 4728.

——Scheinkman, J. A., and Shleifer, A. 1995. Economic growth in a cross-section of cities. *Journal of Monetary Economics*, 36: 117–43.

Gyourko, J., and Tracy, J. 1991. The structure of local public finance and the quality of life. *Journal of Political Economy*, 99: 774–806.

Hanson, G. 1996. Localization economies, vertical organization, and trade. *American Economic Review*, 86: 1266–78.

——1997. Increasing returns, trade, and the regional structure of wages. *Economic Journal*, 107: 113–33.

——1998*a*. Market potential, increasing returns, and geographic concentration. NBER Working Paper No. 6429.

——1998*b*. Regional adjustment to trade liberalization. *Regional Science and Urban Economics*, 28: 419–44.

Harris, C. D. 1954. The market as a factor in the localization of industry in the United States. *Annals of the Association of American Geographers*, 44: 315–48.

Head, K., Ries, J., and Swenson, D. 1995. Agglomeration benefits and location choice: evidence from Japanese manufacturing investments. *Journal of International Economics*, 38: 223–48.

Henderson, J. V. 1974. The sizes and types of cities. *American Economic Review*, 64: 640–56.

——1986. Efficiency of resource usage and city size. *Journal of Urban Economics*, 19: 47–70.

——1988. *Urban Development: Theory, Fact, and Illusion*. New York: Oxford University Press.

——Kuncoro, A., and Turner, M. 1995. Industrial development and cities. *Journal of Political Economy*, 103: 1067–81.

Hines, J. R. 1996. Altered states: taxes and the location of foreign direct investment in America. *American Economic Review*, 86: 1076–94.

Holmes, T. J. 1998*a*. Localization of industry and vertical disintegration. Mimeo. University of Minnesota.

——1998*b*. The effects of state policies on the location of manufacturing industry: evidence from state borders. *Journal of Political Economy*, 106: 667–705.

Jaffe, A., Trajtenberg, M., and Henderson, R. 1993. Geographic localization of knowledge spillovers as evidenced by patent citations. *Quarterly Journal of Economics*, 108: 577–98.

Justman, M. 1994. The effect of local demand on industry location. *Review of Economics and Statistics*, 76: 742–53.

Kim, S. 1995. Expansion of markets and the geographic distribution of economic activities: the trends in U.S. regional manufacturing structure. *Quarterly Journal of Economics*, 110: 881–908.

Krugman, P. 1991. Increasing returns and economic geography. *Journal of Political Economy*, 99: 483–99.

—— and Livas, R. 1996. Trade policy and the Third World metropolis. *Journal of Development Economics*, 49: 137–50.

Lucas, R. E. 1988. The mechanics of economic development. *Journal of Monetary Economics*, 22: 3–42.

Marshall, A. 1920. *Principles of Economics*. New York: Macmillan.

Moomaw, R. L. 1981. Productivity and city size: a critique of the evidence. *Quarterly Journal of Economics*, 96: 675–88.

Nakamura, R. 1985. Agglomeration economies in urban manufacturing industries: a case of Japanese cities. *Journal of Urban Economics*, 17: 108–24.

Ottaviano, G., and Thisse, J. 1998. Agglomeration and trade revisited. CEPR Discussion Paper.

Papageorgiou, Y. Y., and Thisse, J.-F. 1985. Agglomeration as spatial interdependence between firms and households. *Journal of Economic Theory*, 37: 19–31.

Peri, G. 1998. Human capital externalities and U.S. cities. Mimeo. University of California.

Perloff, H. S., Dunn, E. W., Jr., Lampard, E. E., and Muth, R. F. 1960. *Regions, Resources, and Economic Growth*. Lincoln, Nebr.: University of Nebraska Press.

Puga, D. 1999. The rise and fall of regional inequalities. *European Economic Review*, 43/2 (Feb.): 303–34.

Quah, D. 1996. Regional convergence clusters across Europe. *European Economic Review*, 40: 951–8.

Quigley, J. M. 1998. Urban diversity and economic growth. *Journal of Economic Perspectives*, 12: 127–38.

Rauch, J. E. 1993. Productivity gains from geographic concentration of human capital: evidence from the cities. *Journal of Urban Economics*, 34: 380–400.

Rivera-Batiz, F. L. 1988. Increasing returns, monopolistic competition, and agglomeration economies in consumption and production. *Regional Science and Urban Economics*, 18: 125–53.

Roback, J. 1982. Wages, rents, and the quality of life. *Journal of Political Economy*, 90: 1257–78.

Rosen, S. 1974. Hedonic prices and implicit markets: product differentiation in pure competition. *Journal of Political Economy*, 82: 34–55.

—— 1979. Wage-based indexes of the urban quality of life. In *Current Issues in Urban Economics*, ed. P. Mieszkowski and M. Straszheim. Baltimore: Johns Hopkins University Press.

Smith, D. F., and Florida, R. 1994. Agglomeration and industrial location: an econometric analysis of Japanese-affiliated manufacturing establishments in automotive-related industries. *Journal of Urban Economics*, 36: 23–41.

Sveikauskas, L. 1975. The productivity of cities. *Quarterly Journal of Economics*, 89: 393–413.

Topel, R. H. 1986. Local labor markets. *Journal of Political Economy*, 94 (suppl.), 111–43.

Venables, A. J. 1996. Equilibrium locations of vertically linked industries. *International Economic Review*, 37: 341–60.

Wheeler, D., and Mody, A. 1992. International investment location decisions. *Journal of International Economics*, 33: 57–76.

Williamson, J. 1991. Migration and urbanization. In *Handbook of Development Economics*, i, ed. H. Chenery and T. N. Srinivasan. Amsterdam: North-Holland, 425–65.

Wolf, H. C. 1997. Patterns of intra- and inter-state trade. NBER Working Paper No. 5939.

Section 11

Gender, Race, and Place

Chapter **25**

Feminists Rethink the Economic: The Economics of Gender/ The Gender of Economics

Linda McDowell

Recognizing the significance of gender divisions—and the associated body of feminist scholarship—has the potential, indeed has begun, to transform economics and economic geography. An engagement with feminist scholarship has already had an impact on theorizations of economic change, uneven development, globalization, migration patterns, work, employment, local labour markets, the structure of the firm, locational strategies, employment practices, the care of dependants, and the relationships between domestic divisions of labour and paid employment. And yet economic geography remains uneven in its analyses of gendered social relations, at least in comparison with class divisions, and the ways in which they are both partly constituted by and affect economic processes. One of the primary aims of this chapter, therefore, is to introduce some of the growing volume of work about gender—not all of it undertaken from a feminist perspective—to explain its relevance and endeavour to persuade economic geographers, at present unaware of or unconvinced by the challenge that these literatures offer to their work, of the salience of feminist perspectives.

My task is, however, ludicrously ambitious such has been the rate of expansion of the relevant literatures, and their growing engagement with new approaches to economic analyses that recognize the necessity of taking 'difference' into account. But this is not the only, nor indeed the major, reason for its ambition. The implications of feminist arguments are challenging because they demand nothing less than a transformation of the very definition of 'the economic' itself, of the subject material designated as economic and of dominant methodological approaches, rather than the addition of a set of research questions which can be subsumed under a separate category 'economics and gender', tucked away in an odd corner and presumed to be of interest only to women, or indeed a minority female subcategory: feminists.

My argument here is not new. For two decades or more, feminist scholars across the social sciences—from anthropology to sociology—have argued that the analysis of the significance of gender divisions transforms their subject. As Henrietta Moore, in the context of anthropology, noted

> [C]orrecting male bias in reporting, and building up new data on women and women's activities, could only be a first step—albeit a very necessary one—because the real problem about incorporating women into anthropology lies not at the level of empirical research but at the theoretical and analytical level. Feminist anthropology is, therefore, faced with the much larger task of reworking and redefining anthropology theory. (Moore 1988: 2)

As Moore noted, anthropology, with its interest in families and kinship, had at least included women in its disciplinary gaze, whereas, as I demonstrate below, economics was defined to exclude activities conventionally associated with women.

Geographers have also developed feminist critiques of their discipline, showing how the central distinction between public and private spaces depends on the masculinist assumptions of liberal theory (Mackenzie and Rose 1983; McDowell 1992, 1999; Massey 1994; Rose 1993; WGSG 1984 and 1997) and powerful surveys of gender and economics (see e.g. Humphries 1995) as well as explorations of the economics of gender (Jacobsen 1994) have been published. While I want to review some of this material through an explicitly geographical lens, I shall begin by reversing the emphasis of earlier surveys, looking first at the gender of economics. By this phrase I intend not a survey of how many women scholars are economists and economic geographers (not enough), nor a survey of how 'women's issues' are neglected (some of that comes later); instead I want to argue that a broader way of conceptualizing the field[1] would increase both its scope and influence.

[1] This rather feeble or evasive term 'the field' has to stand in for what economics (or perhaps 'the economic') is, for the moment at least, although I shall broaden my definition later in the chapter. Broadly I understand economics—as it is conventionally defined—to be about production and exchange in which 'the market' is a key concept. Indeed a number of economists have traced the origin of the discipline to the ascendance of the market system over other economic systems. The market (in neoclassical economic theory) is a clearing mechanism which produces an efficient allocation of goods with equilibrium prices between individual rational agents with stable preferences making choices which are constrained by income. Although the agents are often individuals they may also be households, firms, and even nations: indeed in economic geography these agents are more usual than individuals *per se*. In this definition and the related comments in the text above, I am aware that I am over-simplifying to make a point and that my remarks are more relevant to neoclassical approaches than to Marxist economics. I deal briefly with the relationship between feminism and Marxism later in the chapter.

Gendered Metaphors and Concepts

Long termed the dismal science by its detractors, economics is arguably the most masculinist of the social sciences, distinguished by an insistence on scientific rationality and objectivity in certain guises or its grand claims to truth in others. It has stoutly resisted, at least until the recent past, all challenges to positivist and empiricist claims even though the work of the more abstruse modellers is based on versions of the world that by their abstraction and elegance are ideal illustrations of the discursive construction of 'reality'.[2]

While this notion—that reality is a discursive construction—is still contested by most economists, there is an interesting growth of books and papers exploring the ways in which disciplinary gazes are constituted through the use of metaphors. Trevor Barnes's (1996) work has been key in the growing understanding of the metaphorical construction of the economic. However, his critique of *homo economicus* was on grounds other than his gender. Barnes (p. vi), accepts that feminist scholarship is not reflected in his work but, as he links feminism to what he terms 'the posts-' (postmodernism, post-colonialism, and so on), he misses the significance of feminist critiques of rationality.

To understand the ways in which particular ways of thinking about gender have become implicated in thinking about economics we have to look elsewhere. Julie Nelson (1992) was one of the originators of this task and I draw on her work here. Nelson argued that, 'dualistic, hierarchical metaphors for gender have permeated the way we think about what economics is and how it should be done, . . . an alternative metaphor provides a more adequate basis of understanding' (Humphries 1995: 103). The association between hierarchical dualisms and gendered categories is now well established in feminist scholarship. Although, as social scientists in several disciplines have demonstrated, the cultural attributes, activities, skills, and behaviours that are perceived to be feminine vary over time and space, typically they are defined in relation and as inferior to those attributes, activities, skills, and behaviours that are coded as masculine.[3] This devaluation of the feminine and the valorization of masculine attributes lies behind the social construction of economics: in the way in which it is constructed as a science and in the way in which its boundaries are drawn to distinguish it from other social sciences. The same arguments apply to economic geography and its distinction from other

[2] In parts of economics that feminists have criticized most strongly, the work of Becker (1965, 1976, 1981, 1985) about rationality in household and marriage decisions is an appropriate example.

[3] It surely is not necessary to note that the cultural designation of certain traits as masculine or feminine does not mean that men and women necessarily exhibit these characteristics.

subdisciplines of the subject. The economic end of the social sciences conventionally is characterized as rational, hard, scientific, and factual and, in its adherence to quantitative modelling and mathematical representations, as rigorous, spare, and elegant: all masculinist traits, which are drawn on to distinguish economics from the 'softer' social sciences. But as Nelson notes, compared with mathematics or 'real' science, economics itself might be seen to occupy the softer end of the disciplinary spectrum as, after all, it does relate to human behaviour, even if the application of market principles to all forms of behaviour including familial and sexual relations—as, for example, Becker (1976, 1981, 1985) is wont to do—might seem to be an inadequate portrayal of most people's behaviour. Nelson (1992, 1993) suggests that the position of economics among the human sciences leads to a defensive attitude among some economists, anxious to prove their masculinity and their hard scientific credentials.

While the linguistic construction of the economic as masculine is relatively easy to illustrate, the question of why economics, and by association economic geography, is at the masculinist end of the social sciences is harder to answer. Numerical dominance by men is not the reason. There are after all plenty of (well, some) women economists and economic geographers.[4] Nelson (1992) suggests two interconnected reasons '. . . economics is blessed with a natural unit of measure—money—which makes quantitative analysis easier' (p. 109).[5] Michel Foucault in *The Order of Things* (1973) identifies economics as one of the three essential sciences, as its central focus is value (the other two are biology and philology treating, respectively, natural life and representation). As those activities traditionally associated with women are not valued, at least in monetary terms, so they are worthless and excluded from the definition of what is necessary or essential. Secondly, Nelson suggests that the tendency to use money as the unit of measurement and markets as the central organizing principle is associated with a certain way of theorizing human behaviour. 'The economist's conception of a person [is] as an autonomous agent' (1992: 109) whose choices are made on the basis of competition and utility maximization, rather than as an individual or member of a social group faced with limited choices in a set of complex and multiple social relations. As Nelson (1992) notes

> Homo economicus is the personification of individuality run wild. 'Economic man' . . . springs up fully formed, with preferences fully developed, and is fully active and self-contained. He has no childhood or old age, no dependence on anyone, no responsibility for anyone but himself. The environment has no effect on him, but rather is the passive

[4] although only eight of the forty-one contributors to Roger Lee and Jane Wills's (1997) collection *Geographies of Economies* were women, and this collection reflects the 'new' economic geography which is less quantitative in style and also influenced by recent work in economic sociology and the sociology of organizations.

[5] and an association between money, masculinity, and power is common: see e.g. McDowell (1997).

> material, presented as 'constraints', over which his rationality has play . . . Homo economicus is the central character in a romance of individuality. (ibid. 115–16)

But the romance is crumbling, despite the recent resurgence of rational choice theory, as the messy, complicated, and interdependent relations of nature and society increasingly intrude into economic analyses.

The Construction of Gendered Subjects

As is now well documented (see e.g. Bordo 1986; Chodorow 1980; Gilligan 1982; Harding 1986; Pateman and Grosz 1986), the association between femininity, nature or the natural, and inferiority had the effect of banishing certain subjects and subject matters from the definition of the economic. The Cartesian view of the world, which privileges separation over connection, dividing the public from the private, and assuming women's natural sphere is the latter, results in the gendered construction of the sciences and social sciences. But, to quote from Nelson again:

> The projection of autonomy onto masculinity and connection to nature and society onto femininity is 'embarrassingly empirical' to borrow a phrase from Catherine Keller (1986, p. 201). Abstract philosophy connects with gendered experience in everyday distinctions between who does the thinking and who does the dishes . . . What could be a recognition of physical embodiment and social connectedness, as well as individuality, within each person becomes a negative complementarity. The male's 'transcendence' of nature and society is made possible only through the subjection of the female to full-time maintenance of the social and physical connections that are, after all, indispensable for human existence. (Nelson 1992: 116)

This passage contains within it an indication of the different ways in which feminists have challenged the definition of the economic: that women's work in 'the maintenance of social and physical connections' should be part of the subject; that the assumption of masculine 'transcendence' and feminine 'immanence', of masculine disembodiment and female embodiment, has structured the public world of economic production, exchange, and the labour market in particular ways and finally, that economic activities are connected to and embedded within relations of 'social connectedness' which vary across space and between places rather than existing in an idealized space with no connections, boundaries, barriers, or constraints.

In the next sections, I address each of these feminist criticisms in turn, illustrating the argument with recent work by economists and economic geographers. I then suggest that the 'embarrassingly empirical' gendered associations are being challenged by contemporary economic change and restructuring in ways that necessitate rethinking assumed binary gender divisions and their connection with other key social divisions, especially class position.

Recognizing Women's Work

Counting Domestic Labour as Work

There has been a long struggle, waged in the main by feminist economists, to make women count (Waring 1988). Economic statistics in most nations, for example, are an inadequate basis for the construction of descriptions, let alone explanations, of women's economic position. Accurate time series data comparing men's and women's status and income figures are an exception. Figures for income and wealth are often collected on a household basis, disguising inequalities in the intra-household allocation of resources. Figures for women's labour market participation are notoriously inaccurate—as, of course, are those for many men in societies where formal labour market participation is restricted—as casual, part-time, and multiple job holding is often under-enumerated. Unemployment figures are affected by benefit regulations which have a systematic sex bias.

The net result of these exclusions, compounded by the definition of domestic labour—all that caring work and maintenance done within the household and the local community for 'love'—as 'non-work', at least in the collection of national statistics, is to seriously underestimate the gross domestic product of nations. For many years, feminists have argued that estimates of unpaid labour should be included in national accounting systems.[6] Finally in 1997, after more than thirty years of pressure, the British government acknowledged that the value of domestic labour, if counted, might more than double the size of the economy. A national time budget survey revealed that people spent one and a half times as long doing domestic tasks as they spent at 'work'. The Office of National Statistics calculated that if the time spent on unwaged work was valued at the same average rate as paid employment, its worth would be a huge £739 billion per annum. If the imputed value is calculated by disaggregating tasks and applying the average wage rate for nannies and childminders for looking after children, the rate for cleaners of housework, for painters and decorators for DIY, and so forth, the overall figure declines to £341 billion as these jobs are among the lowest paid in the labour market. But even so, the figure is 56 per cent of current GDP and its value is greater than the whole of the UK manufacturing sector. While there is little prospect of actual monetary reward for these tasks, it is a step forward to see them included in national accounts and for the government to recognize feminist arguments, that unpaid or not, domestic tasks that

[6] The arguments have a long history. In 1878, for example, the Association for the Advancement of Women (AAW) protested against the US Census's exclusion of 'homemakers' from the category of gainful workers. In a letter to Congress they wrote, 'We pray your honorable body to make provision for the more careful and just enumeration of women as laborers and producers' (quoted by Folbre 1991: 463).

are undertaken within the confines of the home, primarily, although not only, by women,[7] are work nevertheless.

Recognizing domestic and community labour undertaken outside the cash nexus has wider implications than the statistical definition of the economy. It demands a refocus of emphasis away from the satisfaction of demands in the market to a more comprehensive analysis of the multiplicity of ways in which both wants and needs—the necessities of life—are met through various ways of making a living or surviving, including self-provisioning and mutual exchange, and extending to the provision of non-material goods and services such as love, care, and respect (Nelson 1993). Glucksmann (1995) has argued the word 'work' should be replaced by a more accurate term, suggesting 'the total social organisation of labour' as an alternative.

There have been a number of ways in which such a broad definition has begun to enter economic analyses. There is a growing body of work about unwaged domestic labour—both small-scale empirical analyses of who does what in different periods and places (Momsen and Kinnaird 1993; Oberhauser 1995) and a longer tradition of theoretical analyses of domestic labour (Barrett 1981; Folbre 1991; Hartmann 1979; Seccombe 1974; and see Gardiner's (1997) useful summary). This work unpacks social relations within the household, challenging assumptions of reciprocity and mutual exchange and foregrounding questions of power and coercion, as well as cooperation. Economic questions about monetary flows, poverty, and financial inequality and power thus enter the analysis at the micro-scale of the household, as well as in the macroeconomy.

Interesting work on domestic relations by geographers brings an explicit spatial emphasis to the analysis, as a growing number of studies show how domestic and waged labour are connected and change over time and between places. Great variety in gendered social relations within and outside the home, in participation in paid and unpaid servicing work are being revealed. Studies are also beginning to unpack connections between class, ethnicity, and gender, for example in studies of women from the Third World and diasporic women in the West who are drawn into networks of servicing more affluent women and children from different ethnic backgrounds to their own. In the USA, there is an interesting set of work about the current racialization of women's waged domestic labour (England and Stiell 1997; Enloe 1989; Pratt 1997; Romero

[7] Figures produced by the Office of National Statistics for men and women's use of time in Great Britain in 1995 showed that women spent an average of 68 minutes a day cooking, 86 minutes looking after children, 25 minutes doing the washing, 70 minutes cleaning, and 46 minutes shopping. Men, by comparison, spent only 28 minutes in the kitchen, 55 minutes with their children, 3 minutes doing laundry, 43 minutes cleaning or doing other household chores, and 26 minutes shopping. Other research has shown that when women are also in paid work, their contribution to domestic work declines although not substantially. The time their male partners put into housework and child care does rise somewhat, interestingly in direct proportion to the woman's earning capacity (Morris 1992).

1992; Salzinger 1997; Stiell and England 1997) and its relation to international migration flows, national immigration policies, and local labour market changes, as well as historical analyses of the position of African-American women in servicing work inside and outside the home (Glenn 1992). In Britain, connections between the marketization of domestic labour, overall changes in women's labour market participation rates, regional variations, and the restructuring of the welfare state have begun to be investigated (Gregson and Lowe 1994).

Gender, Economics, and Care

Rethinking domestic labour has led to a wider debate about the concept and ethics of caring, challenging the conceptualization of individual economic actors. Feminist and environmental critics coincide in the introduction of ethical questions into economic discourses. While environmentalists have found Amartya Sen's (1984) concept of 'capability' a useful tool, feminist economists have focused more directly on care *per se* (DeVault 1991; Folbre 1994, 1995; Gardiner 1997; Tronto 1987, 1993). Jean Gardiner (1997) identifies the emotional and personal nature of care as differentiating it from other forms of work, and she distinguishes different forms of domestic labour. Some tasks are routine and may be replaced by commodified substitutes—cooking and cleaning are good examples here. Others cannot be replaced by market substitutes without a fundamental change in their nature—these are the tasks that Gardiner defines as caring. She suggests that emotional and personal caring work is now the dominant part of domestic labour in industrial societies, while recognizing that a growing number of even these services can be commodified. Indeed, they are a significant element of the 'new service economy' in advanced industrial nations, and feminist analyses of the changing nature of waged labour have also begun to emphasize the significance of 'emotional work'.

In a range of occupations in the service sector—and not only in those that might be classified as caring (nursing, elder care, domiciliary care, and personal therapies of different sorts)—in which face-to-face interactions are an essential aspect of service provision, emotions have to be managed. Building on Arlie Hochschild's (1983) innovative analyses of the emotional labour involved in debt collecting and in airline stewarding, the ways in which strategies of emotional control and manipulation, as well as the presentation of a particular bodily style and repertoire of exchanges, form an essential part of service sector work have been documented in occupations ranging from fast food and insurance selling to nursing and merchant banking (Adkins 1992, 1995; Halford *et al.* 1997; Leidner 1993; McDowell 1997). Carol Wolkowitz (1998) suggests 'body-work' as a useful summary term for the rapid expansion in the numbers of people employed to look after, care for, survey, and decorate other people's bodies or display their own. As she notes: 'analyses based on the study of labour processes in the manufacturing industries are only partly able to explain the production of these workers, their training systems, appraisal schemes and wage structures, and, especially the ways in which they interact with the objects and consumers of their labour'.[8]

I want to look at some new work on the connections between gendered and emotional labour or bodywork, but first, I briefly summarize earlier analyses of gender and waged work.

How 'Immanence' Structures Economic Activities: Gender in the Labour Market and the Firm

There is a huge volume of work about the ways in which hierarchical assumptions about gender and gendered social relations structure the differential participation of women and men in the labour market, their occupational segregation, status, and differential monetary rewards (as well as a distinct but related literature modelling variations in women's labour market participation over space and time which is not explicitly feminist, as it accepts gender as variable rather than as a factor that needs explanation). As summaries of approaches to the question of why there are gender differentials in participation and earnings (see e.g. Bradley 1989; Blau and Ferber 1992; Hanson and Pratt 1995; Humphries 1995; Jacobsen 1994; McDowell 1989, 1999; Walby 1986, 1997) as well as detailed case studies of men and women's labour force participation and case studies of their working lives across time and space (Cavendish 1983; Kobayashi 1994; Pollert 1982; Pringle 1989, 1998) are now widely available, I only briefly outline the nature of recent changes in these patterns, before turning to case studies to illustrate in detail the ways in which gender relations are implicated in service sector occupations and in current patterns of economic restructuring.

Despite the growing feminization of the labour force at a global scale—albeit with marked national and regional variations connected, *inter alia*, to levels of economic development, patterns of international capital investments, the structure of local labour markets, variations in familial structures, levels of welfare provision, and religious and social attitudes about women's position—one of the most enduring features of women's labour market participation is their segregation into a narrow range of occupations and jobs that are regarded as appropriate for women (Bradley 1989; Fuentes and Ehrenreich 1983; Jackson and Pearson 1998; Mies 1986; Mitter 1986; Stichter and Parpart 1988; Walby

[8] although David Harvey (1998) has recently made claims for the utility of a Marxian approach to questions about the labouring body.

1997). Indeed these occupations are themselves coded as feminine, regarded as inferior in status to 'male' jobs and so are differentially remunerated. This segregation—horizontal segregation—is paralleled by vertical segregation: women's over-representation in the bottom end of status and pay hierarchies compared with men in the same occupations. These two features combine to produce a gender pay gap which, despite equal opportunity legislation and women's growing penetration of 'male' jobs in advanced industrial economies, seems to remain stubbornly at 20 per cent—that is, women in full-time work receive 80 per cent of the average wage for men in full-time employment (Hakim 1996, 1998).

There are various explanations of these patterns whose emphasis depends on the theoretical school within which they are developed (Jacobsen 1994; McDowell 1989). They include variants of human capital and rational choice theory in which women's lower pay is variously attributed to lower skill levels, fewer educational and vocational credentials, and hence a rational household decision for women and men to specialize in domestic and waged labour respectively (Becker 1976, 1985). Alternative models emphasize institutional and structural features of labour markets, including notions of dual and segmented labour markets (Humphries and Rubery 1995), whereas an explicitly Marxist approach argues that women form part of the reserve army of labour that capitalism pulls into and expels from the social relations of waged labour depending on levels of profitability (Beechey 1987). All of these models, but especially the first and last, are challenged by empirical evidence of the changing nature of both the demand for and supply of female labour (Hanson and Pratt 1995; McDowell 1989, 1992, 1999; Walby 1989; Walby and Bagguley 1989). In many nations women's educational capital is rising, their domestic responsibilities are falling with new technologies, more widely available contraception, and better health care, and in general the growing feminization of the labour force seems unrelated to economic cycles. Yet, segregation remains. Indeed, as a growing body of work is beginning to demonstrate, gender is an integral part rather than a consequence of economic restructuring across time and space (Bagguley *et al.* 1990; Kerfoot and Knights 1993; Knights and Morgan 1991).

In the next section, therefore, I turn to three case studies in different sectors of the British economy which document the different and often subtle ways in which assumptions about masculine and feminine attributes, skills, and talents are the very basis of the organizational structure of the firms and their employment strategies. I have chosen case studies not of manufacturing—of which there are many excellent feminist analyses—but from different parts of the service sector: high-tech R&D, merchant banking, and retail banking. While the first two are 'leading edge' sectors which are spatially concentrated, the last is a classic example of a spatially ubiquitous consumer service.

High-Tech Monasteries

In their book *High Tech Fantasies*, Massey *et al.* (1992) began to unpack the geographies of high-tech science-park-based firms, drawing out the links between their structure and locational strategies and dominant cultural values about science. However, they did not explicitly investigate the gendering of organizational cultures and of recruitment and employment practices. Massey began to address this absence in work on gendered social relations in the workplaces and homes of workers in Cambridge's science park (Massey 1995). Here I draw not on her empirical findings but on the provocative theoretical parallels she suggested between science and religion. Both activities, she argues, construct their high status by a link to masculinity, and to compartmentalism into specialized time-spaces. Monasteries and high-tech workplaces are ' "masculine" spaces not in the sense that it is mainly men[9] who work here, but in the sense that their construction *as spaces* embodies the elite, separated, masculine concept of reason dominant in the West' (ibid. 27; emphasis in original). Massey is interested in the histories that lie behind the constitution of these spaces as elite, exclusive, masculine spaces, leading to a different story about locational strategies from more usual economic geographies, where the rise of high-tech science parks is linked to the origins of Western science in an older European clerical culture. Massey recognizes that the general story of 'the relation of "big dualisms" to sex and gender has of course been widely analysed' (ibid. 28); her aim is 'to provide a more grounded history of its practical social establishment in the Western world' (ibid. 28). Particular ideas about space and spatial relations were a crucial part in the establishment of ideas about gender and identities in this history. 'The masculinization of scientific culture, and the contemporaneous definition of (a specific form of) masculinity, went hand in hand with the development of the notion of science/rationality as necessitating separation from nature/the body/sexuality. Moreover, the material spatialization of these separations both depended upon and reinforced the discursive counterpositions' (ibid. 33–4). This separation and masculinization effectively excludes women as workers, and produces a culture in which values traditionally associated with femininity are absent. The ideal scientific worker is, once again, that elusive rational individual without dependants and, preferably, a body.

Embodied Bankers

The previous study clearly demonstrated the associations between disembodied rationality and masculinity. This next uncovers more complex relationships

[9] In fact as Massey shows elsewhere, the workforce is numerically dominated by men. Interesting questions remain about whether women scientists feel 'out of place' in these spaces and how their presence changes the everyday cultures and practices. Anecdotal evidence from university departments illustrates the impact of a critical mass—which seems to be at least three women in a department.

between gender and embodiment than a simple binary division in a contemporary workplace that is also constructed as an elite, spatially separated institution—merchant banks in the City of London (McDowell 1997). Financial workforces include somewhat more women than high-tech research laboratories and, more significantly, the construction of masculinity is more variable and is contested. In City merchant banks, there are two versions of hegemonic masculinity. In the dealing rooms and on the (fast being replaced) trading floors, masculinity is constructed around a vital, noisy celebration of masculine bodily attributes such as exuberance, high spirits, horse play, and aggressive oral performances. The disembodied and cerebral rational masculinity that Massey found in research laboratories is reserved for the corporate end of the business. Thus, gender differences are linked both to the type of work and to the places where it is carried out.

However, bankers—be they traders or corporate advisers—do have something in common. Unlike the scientists studied by Massey, leading cloistered, isolated lives, merchant banking crucially consists of selling: be it advice about mergers and acquisitions or derivatives, futures and options, and in both cases bodies matter. As I argued above, embodiment—the personal bodily attributes of a service provider—is an integral part of selling any service. Here the 'natural' attributes of femininity are perceived as advantageous and in banks I found contested domains as men and women struggled to assert versions of gendered performances that ran counter to their embodiment. Some women became honorary men; some men co-opted 'feminine' attributes such as empathy and caring in personal interactions, as well as a demonstrable concern with their looks and weight; others acted in ways more congruent with their sexed bodies. Although my work was limited to three banks in which there were singularly few women in the very highest positions, it was significant that, for both men and women, a feminized gender performance seemed most successful, although it is important not to exaggerate the extent of changes in the particular class-based and patriarchal cultures of merchant banks.

Patriarchal Attitudes

The final example is also drawn from banking, but retail rather than merchant banking. The focus here is more explicitly on the ways in which gender is used to divide a workforce to achieve restructuring and regrading in order to cut staff costs. As Halford *et al.* (1997) argue in their work on gender and organizations, 'the very process of restructuring is bound up with redefining the workforce' (ibid. 69) and the ways in which gender relations are embedded in an organization is a key aspect of such redefinition. Halford *et al.* documented the ways in which changes in the organizational culture of a high street bank, in combination with the growing employment of women with appropriate credentials, challenged both the patriarchal career structure and internal culture of the bank. As retail banking expanded in the 1970s, it 'had to project a respectable and trustworthy image. This traditional image and culture was strongly linked to masculine images and to men as responsible and trustworthy. Bank staff had to cultivate a sober and reliable image, which drew upon masculine and paternalistic imagery' (Halford *et al.* 1997: 73). But by the late 1980s when personal accounts were commonplace, customers had to be persuaded to take out other services. 'Sellbank (a pseudonym) tried to introduce a "sales culture" to the bank [and rethought] the types of staff quality valued by the bank' (ibid. 74). Men—especially branch managers who literally embodied all the austere, remote attributes of masculinity—found their positions usurped by women who took over the front-of-bank specialist functions, showing the 'human' face of banking. Here traditional attributes of femininity, including accessibility and good looks, became important. There was also a shift in the culture of masculinity with reorganization, where new regional structures and management styles encouraged forms of competitive masculinity. Although women were achieving 'back-stage' positions in this reorganization, the new competitive ethos tended to maintain the earlier patterns of exclusion, albeit through different mechanisms.

As these organizational studies show, economic geographers and sociologists are producing innovative analyses of the forms of employment increasingly dominating industrial Western economies. These studies are part of a wider reconsideration of theoretical and methodological approaches within economics and economic geography, as the significance of the social and cultural attributes not only of organizations but also of localities, regions, nation states, and international forms of economic organization become a new focus of research. Elsewhere in this handbook, the social and institutional character of markets, their connectivity, and embeddedness have been emphasized. Feminist work has, in the main, tended to be undertaken at the smallest spatial scale—within the organization, as I illustrated in the examples above (there are many other excellent studies of the gendered cultures of organizations and professions: Casey 1995; Cockburn 1991; Cornwall and Lindisfarne 1994; Davies 1995; Fine 1987; Grossberg 1990; Kanter 1977; Kondo 1990; Kunda 1992; Pringle 1998), or at the level of the local labour market where specific and comparative analyses have been undertaken of issues such as gender-specific migration flows, journeys to work, job search strategies and patterns, and participation rates in numerous localities, as well as of the ways in which women in different localities combine different forms of work (Deseran and Wojtkiewicz 1993; England 1995; Garcia-Ramon and Monk 1996; Gordon *et al.* 1989; Molho 1983; Momsen and Kinnaird 1993; Oberhauser 1995; Odland and Ellis 1998; Preston *et al.* 1993; Ward and Dale 1992). Through careful empirical work, the multiple ways in which gender relations are constituted in place and the spatial particularities of women's domestic and workplace lives are beginning to be unpacked. Kobayashi (1994), for example, in a wonderful study of the lives of Japanese

Canadian women, shows how traditional patriarchal notions about women's place in Japanese culture are paradoxically restrictive and supportive for Japanese Canadian women in Canadian cities. Hanson and Pratt (1995) in their in-depth analysis of the gendered structure of local labour markets in Worcester, Massachusetts, have demonstrated how occupational segregation is constructed, illustrating the importance of differences that occur at a very fine spatial scale, both in a locality and within workplaces. There is a need for many more studies like these that span the spatial scales in their analysis of the distinctive ways in which gender is constituted in place.

Thinking about 'Difference' and Challenging Capitalism

Feminist critiques of the definitions of the economic and of economics/economic geography have had a dual focus. On the one hand, a key task has been to reveal the masculinist basis of the assumptions that prop up liberal theory and neoclassical approaches. On the other hand, there has been a somewhat vexed relationship with Marxist theories in debates about the nature of domestic labour, the characterization of women as part of a reserve army, and the attempts to weld patriarchal structures to capitalism as either a dual or single system, showing how gender as well as class divisions are a key part of capitalist social relations (Hartmann 1979; Mies 1986; Walby 1990). In this task, household work practices inevitably were explored through the lens of an economistic or productionist model. The assumptions behind the social construction of the explanation (as in neoclassical models) and the representation of the world to be explained were thus those of capitalism, notwithstanding the important work on theorizing caring that I outlined above. In her/their[10] provocative text *The End of Capitalism (As We Knew It)*, J.-K. Gibson-Graham (1996) challenged this productionist emphasis and recast political economy through a wide-ranging feminist critique. Instead of interpreting economic restructuring and changes in workplace practices and household relations as part of a story about the changing nature of global capitalism and adjustments to it, Gibson-Graham suggested that different stories—or representations—are possible which might both be more interesting and open up spaces for resistance. Instead of interpreting change through the lens of capitalist adaptations perhaps

> unstable gender identities, inabilities to adapt to the new shiftwork schedule, and non-capitalist economic activities should be emphasized instead of swept under the rug. The

[10] In their desire to challenge the authority of the author, as well as the 'citation culture' of the contemporary academy, Kathie Gibson and Julie Graham write together and publish as a composite person.

visions of households, subjects and capitalist industry operating in harmony (and in fact coming together in a new phase of capitalist hegemony) might be replaced by alternative social representations in which noncapitalist practices proliferated, gender identities were renegotiated and political subjects actively resisted industrial restructuring, thereby influencing its course. (ibid., pp. viii–ix)

If we depict 'social existence at loose ends with itself, rather than producing social representations in which everything is part of the same complex and therefore ultimately "means the same thing" (e.g. capitalist hegemony)' (ibid., p. ix), then new opportunities for social existence can be glimpsed. 'Rich and prolific disarray' may be a more progressive way to represent and theorize economies and economic change rather than a representation as a seamless hegemonic capitalist system. Gibson-Graham link postmodernist ideas about discursive representation to a progressive political project, in a thought-provoking way that has similarities with Nancy Fraser's (1996) stimulating analyses of economic participation, household work, and welfare regulations.

Rethinking Gender Divisions

Gibson-Graham's claim for complexity and diversity parallels the growing emphasis in contemporary feminist analyses that gender relations should be theorized as unruly and complicated. Despite the continuing theoretical dominance of the social construction of gender identity as binary (at least outside feminist theorizing), with a corresponding normative discourse of heterosexuality, the diversity of gender relations, in action as it were, is increasingly evident. In the economic arena, as I have illustrated above, interactive service sector occupations have recut and reconnected gendered performances to sexed bodies in diverse ways. New forms of work, related to changing family relationships and household structures, growing economic uncertainty, casualization, and the perniciously named 'flexibility', demand that men and women rethink long-established gender divisions and responsibilities and take on new ways of being men and women, workers and parents (Bianchi 1995). Further, the ways in which gender, ethnicity, and class divide and unite individuals and groups on different issues need attention. Class and income differentials among women in the UK and the USA are currently wider than in any other period since World War II, exacerbated, especially in the USA, by ethnic divisions (Walby 1997) and regional variations in labour market structures, job opportunities, and unemployment rates lead to growing diversity in working patterns and standards of living between households. The differential number of multiple earners, households with no earners, and those dependent on women's wages is redrawing maps of poverty and affluence, as well as affecting opportunities for marriage and family formation. Interesting work in the USA, for example, has shown not only how women's labour market participation rates vary by localities, but by choices about marriage, child rearing, and child-care strategies too (Deseran *et al.* 1993; Lichter *et al.* 1991; Odland and Ellis 1998; Seeborg and Jaeger 1993). These complex patterns, in combination with recent theoretical approaches, have led to an insistence on diversity in the definition and analysis of gender relations, challenging the over-simple distinction between man and woman, as social constructs and categories for analysis.

Conclusions: Gender, Gender Everywhere?

What to include and what to exclude from this chapter was a difficult decision. It is hard enough to delimit the scope of what is 'economic', especially as recent changes in the definition and nature of economics and economic geography have expanded their boundaries and blurred distinctions between them and other disciplines, let alone to link these changes to analyses of gender relations. But as I have argued, taking feminist scholarship seriously means rethinking not only boundaries and methods of economics and economic geography but also their philosophical and theoretical bases, with implications that stretch beyond the boundaries of this chapter.

Two inter-related questions remain—is there anything that still distinguishes the economic or is it now so flexible and complex that economics is everything and everywhere? And is there anything distinctive about feminist approaches? I want to answer a provisional 'yes' to both questions. Despite expanding the definition of the economic to include making a living/provisioning/getting by in the widest sense, and how these activities are affected by and affect the uneven division of space, the economic sphere is not undifferentiated from the concerns of other disciplines, despite closer links in subject matter and approach in recent work. If the core definition of the economic is broadened to 'how humans try to meet their need for material goods and services', it returns it to 'the etymological roots of the term in the Greek words meaning "household management"' (Nelson 1992: 119). It is here that feminism has been so successful, challenging masculinist biases, introducing new issues, and asking different questions about old ones.[11] Care and caring have become part of 'the economic', notions about the household as a consensual or cooperative unit have been unpicked, and concepts of power and conflict have been introduced at this scale as well as to economic analyses at other spatial scales.

I also believe that it has been from the basis of feminist critiques of knowledge and of the social construction of categories, including gender and economics,

[11] There is also some interesting work by feminist economists demonstrating the costs and benefits of equal opportunities policies (see e.g. Humphries and Rubery 1995) but space precludes its consideration here. The other major absence is a discussion of the relationship between gender relations and economic change in Third World economies: again space constraints do not permit its consideration.

that exciting work about diversity in ways of knowing has been developed. This work has revitalized those parts of economics and economic geography that have moved away from quantitative modelling and idealized views of the world as a marketplace to become a complex and challenging subject.

References

Adkins, L. 1992. Sexual work and the employment of women in the service industries. In *Gender and Bureaucracy*, ed. M. Savage and A. Witz. Oxford: Blackwell, 207–28.

—— 1995. *Gendered Work: Sexualility, Family and the Labour Market*. Buckingham: Open University Press.

Bagguley, P., Mark-Lawson, J., Shapiro, D., Urry, J., Walby, S., and Warde, A. 1990. *Restructuring: Place, Class and Gender*. London: Sage.

Barnes, T. 1996. *Logics of Dislocation: Models, Metaphors and Meanings in Economic Space*. New York: Guilford.

Barrett, M. 1981. *Women's Oppression Today: Problems in Marxist Feminist Analysis*. London: Verso.

Becker, G. 1965. A theory of the allocation of time. *Economic Journal*, 75: 493–517.

—— 1976. *The Economic Approach to Economic Behaviour*. Chicago: University of Chicago Press.

—— 1981. *A Treatise on the Family*. Cambridge, Mass.: Harvard University Press.

—— 1985. Human capital effort and the sexual division of labor. *Journal of Labor Economics*, 3 (suppl.), 33–58.

Beechey, V. 1987. *Unequal Work*. London: Verso.

Bianchi, S. 1995. Changing economic roles of women and men. In *State of the Union: America in the 1990s*, i: *Economic Trends*, ed. R. Farley. New York: Russell Sage Foundation, 107–54.

Blau, F., and Ferber, M. 1992. *The Economics of Women, Men and Work*. Englewood Cliffs, NJ: Prentice-Hall.

Bordo, S. 1986. The Cartesian masculinization of thought. *Signs: Journal of Women in Culture and Society*, 11: 439–56.

Bradley, H. 1989. *Men and Women at Work*. Cambridge: Polity.

Casey, C. 1995. *Work, Self and Society: After Industrialism*. London: Routledge.

Cavendish, R. 1983. *Women on the Line*. Basingstoke: Macmillan.

Chodorow, N. 1980. Gender, relation and difference in psychoanalytic perspective. In *The Future of Difference*, ed. H. Eisenstein and A. Jardine. Brunswick, NJ: Rutgers University Press, 3–19.

Cockburn, C. 1991. *In the Way of Women: Men's Resistance to Sex Equality in Organisations*. London: Macmillan.

Cornwall, A., and Lindisfarne, N. 1994. *Dislocating Masculinity*. London: Routledge.

Davies, C. 1995. *Gender and the Professional Predicament in Nursing*. Buckingham: Open University Press.

Deseran, E., Li, J., and Wojtkiewicz, R. 1993. Household structure, labor market characteristics and female labor force participation. In *Inequalities in Labor Market Areas*, ed. J. Singelmann and F. Deseran. Boulder, Colo.: Westview Press, 165–90.

DeVault, M. L. 1991. *Feeding the Family: The Social Organisation of Caring as Gendered Work*. Chicago: University of Chicago Press.

England, K. 1995. Girls in the office: recruiting and job search in a local clerical labour market. *Environment and Planning A*, 27: 1995–2018.

——and Stiell, B. 1997. 'They think you are as stupid as your English is': constructing foreign domestic workers in Toronto. *Environment and Planning A*, 29: 195–215.

Enloe, C. 1989. *Bananas, Beaches and Bases*. London: Pandora.

Fine, G. 1987. One of the boys: women in male dominated settings. In *Changing Men: New Directions in Research on Men and Masculinity*, ed. M. Kimmel. Newbury, Calif.: Sage.

Folbre, N. 1991. The unproductive housewife: her evolution in nineteenth century economic thought. *Signs: Journal of Women in Culture and Society*, 16: 463–84.

——1994. *Who Pays for the Kids? Gender and the Structures of Constraint*. New York: Routledge.

——1995. 'Holding hands at midnight': the paradox of caring labour. *Feminist Economics*, 1: 73–92.

Foucault, M. 1973. *The Order of Things*. New York: Vintage. (1st publ. in French in 1966 as *Les Mots et Les Choses*. Paris: Gallimard.)

Fraser, N. 1996. *Justice Interruptus*. London: Routledge.

Fuentes, A., and Ehrenreich, A. 1983. *Women in the Global Factory*. Boston: South End Press.

Garcia-Ramon, D., and Monk, J., eds. 1996. *Women of the European Union: The Politics of Work and Daily Life*. London: Routledge.

Gardiner, J. 1997. *Gender, Care and Economics*. Oxford: Clarendon Press.

Gibson-Graham, J.-K. 1996. *The End of Capitalism (As We Knew It): A Feminist Critique of Political Economy*. Oxford: Blackwell.

Gilligan, C. 1982. *In Different Voice*. Cambridge, Mass.: Harvard University Press.

Glenn, E. 1992. From servitude to service work: historical continuities in the racial division of paid labour. *Signs: Journal of Women in Culture and Society*, 18: 1–43.

Glucksmann, M. 1995. Why work? Gender and 'the total social organisation of labour'. *Gender, Work and Organisation*, 2: 275–94.

Gordon, P., Kuman, A., and Richardson, H. 1989. Gender differences in metropolitan travel behaviour. *Regional Studies*, 23: 499–510.

Gregson, N., and Lowe, M. 1994. *Servicing the Middle Classes*. London: Routledge.

Grossberg, M. 1990. Instituting masculinity: the law as a masculine profession. In *Meanings for Manhood: Constructions of Masculinity in Victorian America*, ed. M. Cranes and C. Griffen. Chicago: University of Chicago Press.

Hakim, C. 1996. *Key Issues in Women's Work: Female Heterogeneity and the Polarisation of Women's Employment*. London: Athlone.

——1998. *Social Change and Innovation in the Labour Market: Evidence from the Census SARs on Occupational Segregation and Labour Mobility, Part-Time Work and Student Jobs, Homework and Self-Employment*. Oxford: Oxford University Press.

Halford, S., Savage, M., and Witz, A. 1997. *Gender, Careers and Organisations: Current Developments in Banking, Nursing and Local Government*. Basingstoke: Macmillan.

Hanson, S., and Pratt, G. 1995. *Gender, Work and Space*. London: Routledge.

Harding, S. 1986. *The Science Question in Feminism*. Ithaca, NY: Cornell University Press.

Hartmann, H. 1979. *Capitalist Patriarchy and the Case for Socialist Feminism*. New York: Monthly Review Press.

Harvey, D. 1998. The body as an accumulation strategy. *Society and Space D: Society and Space*, 16: 401–22.

Hochschild, A. 1983. *The Managed Heart: The Commercialisation of Human Feeling*. Berkeley: University of California Press.

Humphries, J., ed. 1995. *Gender and Economics*. Aldershot: Edward Elgar.

——and Rubery, J., eds. 1995. *The Economics of Equal Opportunities*. Manchester: Equal Opportunities Commission.

Jackson, C., and Pearson, R., eds. 1998. *Feminist Visions of Development: Gender Analysis and Policy*. London: Routledge.

Jacobsen, J. P. 1994. *The Economics of Gender*. Oxford: Blackwell.

Kanter, R. 1977. *Men and Women of the Organization*. New York: Basic Books.

Keller, C. 1986. *From a Broken Web: Separation, Sexism and Self*. Boston: Beacon Press.

Kerfoot, D., and Knights, D. 1993. Management, masculinity and manipulation: from paternalism to corporate strategy in financial services in Britain. *Journal of Management Studies*, 30: 659–78.

Knights, D., and Morgan, G. 1991. Management control in sales: a case study from the labour process of life insurance. *Work, Employment and Society*, 4: 369–89.

Kobayashi, A. 1994. *Women, Work and Place*. London: McGill-Queens University Press.

Kondo, D. 1990. *Crafting Selves: Power, Gender and Discourse of Identity in a Japanese Workplace*. Chicago: University of Chicago Press.

Kunda, G. 1992. *Engineering Culture: Control and Commitment in a High-Tech Organisation*. Philadelphia: Temple University Press.

Lamphere, L., Ragone, H., and Zavella, P., eds. 1997. *Situated Lives: Gender and Culture in Everyday Life*. London: Routledge.

Leidner, R. 1993. *Fast Food, Fast Talk: Service Work and the Routinisation of Everyday Life*. Berkeley and Los Angeles: University of California Press.

Lee, R., and Wills, J., eds. 1997. *Geographies of Economies*. London: Arnold.

Lichter, D., Leclere, F., and McLaughlin, D. 1991. Local marriage markets and the marital behaviour of black and white women. *American Journal of Sociology*, 96: 843–67.

McDowell, L. 1989. Gender divisions. In *The Changing Social Structure*, ed. C. Hamnett, L. McDowell, and P. Sarre. London: Sage, 158–98.

——1991. Life without Father and Ford: the new gender order of post-Fordism. *Transactions, Institute of British Geographers*, 16: 400–19.

——1992. Space, place and gender relations, part 1: feminist empiricism and the geography of social relations. *Progress in Human Geography*, 17: 305–18.

——1997. *Capital Culture: Gender at Work in the City*. Oxford: Blackwell.

——1999. *Gender, Identity and Place: Understanding Feminist Geographies*. Cambridge: Polity.

Mackenzie, S., and Rose, D. 1983. Industrial change, the domestic economy and home life. In *Redundant Spaces? Industrial Decline in Cities and Regions*, ed. J. Anderson, S. Duncan, and R. Hudson. London: Academic Press.

Massey, D. 1994. *Space, Place and Gender*. Cambridge: Polity.

Massey, D. 1995. Masculinity, dualisms and high technology. *Transactions, Institute of British Geographers*, 20: 487–99.

——1997. Economic/non-economic. In *Geographies of Economies*, ed. D. Lee and J. Wills. London: Arnold, 27–36.

——Quintas, P., and Wield, D. 1992. *High Tech Fantasies: Science Parks in Society, Science and Space*. London: Routledge.

Mies, M. 1986. *Patriarchy and Accumulation on a World Scale: Women in the International Division of Labour*. London: Zed Books.

Mitter, S. 1986. *Common Fate, Common Bond: Women in the Global Economy*. London: Pluto Press.

Molho, I. I. 1983. A regional analysis of the distribution of married women's labour force participation rates in the UK. *Regional Studies*, 17: 125–34.

Momsen, J., and Kinnaird, V., eds. 1993. *Different Voices, Different Places*. London: Routledge.

Moore, H. 1988. *Anthropology and Feminism*. Cambridge: Polity Press.

Morris, L. 1992. *The Workings of the Household*. Cambridge: Polity.

Nelson, J. 1992. Gender, metaphor and the definition of economics. *Economics and Philosophy*, 8: 103–25 (reprinted in Humphries 1995).

——1993. The study of choice or the study of provisioning? Gender and the definition of economics. In *Beyond Economic Man: Feminist Theory and Economics*, ed. M. A. Ferber and J. A. Nelson. Chicago: University of Chicago Press, 23–36.

Oberhauser, A. 1995. Gender and household economic strategies in rural Appalachia. *Gender, Place and Culture*, 2: 51–70.

Odland, J., and Ellis, M. 1998. Variations in the labour force experience of women across large metropolitan areas in the United States. *Regional Studies*, 32: 333–47.

Pateman, C., and Grosz, E. 1986. *Feminist Challenges: Social and Political Theory*. Sydney: Allen and Unwin.

Pollert, A. 1982. *Girls, Wives, Factory Lives*. London: Macmillan.

Pratt, G. 1997. Stereotypes and ambivalence: the construction of domestic workers in Vancouver. *Gender, Place and Culture*, 4: 159–78.

Preston, V., McLafferty, S., and Hamilton, E. 1993. The impact of family status on black, white and Hispanic women's commuting. *Urban Geography*, 14: 228–50.

Pringle, R. 1989. *Secretaries Talk*. London: Verso.

——1998. *Sex and Medicine: Gender, Power and Authority in the Medical Profession*. Cambridge: Cambridge University Press.

Romero, M. 1992. *Maid in the USA*. London: Routledge.

Rose, G. 1993. *Feminism and Geography*. Cambridge: Polity.

Salzinger, L. 1997. A maid by any other name: the transformation of dirty work by Central American immigrants. In Lamphere *et al.* 1997: 271–91.

Seccombe, W. 1974. The housewife and her labour under capitalism. *New Left Review*, 83.

Seeborg, M., and Jaeger, K. 1993. The impact of local labor markets on black and white family structure. *Journal of Socio-Economics*, 22: 115–30.

Sen, A. 1984. *Resources, Values and Development*. Cambridge, Mass.: Harvard University Press.

Stichter, S., and Parpart, J., eds. 1988. *Women, Employment and the Family in the International Division of Labour*. London: Macmillan.

Stiell, B., and England, K. 1997. Domestic distinctions: constructing difference among paid domestic workers in Toronto. *Gender, Place and Culture*, 4: 339–60.

Tronto, J. 1987. Beyond gender difference to a theory of care. *Signs: Journal of Women in Culture and Society*, 12: 644–63.

—— 1993. *Moral Boundaries: A Political Argument for an Ethic of Care*. New York: Routledge.

Walby, S. 1986. *Gender at Work*. Cambridge: Polity.

—— 1989. Flexibility and the sexual division of labour. In *The Transformation of Work?* ed. S. Wood. London: Unwin Hyman, 127–49.

—— 1990. *Theorising Patriarchy*. Oxford: Blackwell.

—— 1997. *Gender Transformations*. London: Routledge.

—— and Bagguley, P. 1989. Gender restructuring: five labour-markets compared. *Environment and Planning D: Society and Space*, 7: 277–92.

Ward, C., and Dale, A. 1992. Geographical variation in female labour force participation: an application of multi-level modelling. *Regional Studies*, 26: 243–55.

Waring, M. 1988. *If Women Counted: A New Feminist Economics*. New York: Harper and Row.

Wolkowitz, C. 1998. Not 'just a job': the conceptualisation of bodywork in the 1990s. Paper given at the Work, Employment and Society conference, University of Cambridge, 14–16 Sept. (copy available from the author at the University of Warwick, UK).

Women and Geography Study Group (WGSG) 1984. *Geography and Gender*. London: Hutchinson.

—— 1997. *Feminist Geographies: Exploration in Diversity and Difference*. London: Longman.

Chapter **26**

Racial and Economic Segregation in US Metropolitan Areas

John F. Kain

Introduction

This chapter examines social science research concerned with racial/ethnic and economic segregation in US metropolitan areas. Of the two topics, racial/ethnic segregation, which is examined in the first two-thirds of the chapter, is by far the most important.

Several decades of racial discrimination, particularly discrimination in housing markets, created massive central city ghettos in American cities. Constrained by serious limitations on their residential choices, most black households limited their search for housing to the ghetto. As their numbers increased, they bid up housing prices and crowded out white households who would have preferred for reasons of job access or other preferences to remain in the city. These dynamics in turn profoundly affected the residential location decisions of middle and upper income white families. During the past two to three decades, racial prejudice has declined and the former nearly absolute barriers to black movement to all or predominantly white neighborhoods have clearly been reduced. Consequently, the levels of black–white segregation have declined, although they remain very high.

The last third of this chapter reviews research on economic segregation, including the somewhat more extensive body of research on concentrated poverty. Because black Americans have significantly lower incomes on average than white Americans, their concentration in central city ghettos is the dominant factor in determining economic segregation within metropolitan areas. Therefore, virtually all studies of economic segregation examine economic segregation within race/ethnic groups. Because of its obviously great policy implications, moreover, researchers have paid somewhat more attention to the geographic concentration of the poor, what is termed concentrated poverty.

Both racial segregation and concentrated poverty have large and pervasive impacts on the welfare of minorities and on the larger society. As important as these issues are, space limitations preclude their consideration in this review.[1]

The Extent of Racial Residential Segregation

Massey and Denton (1993) and Cutler *et al.* (1999) perform a service that is similar to that provided by Taeuber and Taeuber (1965) three decades earlier. Taeuber and Taeuber (1965) summarized earlier studies of racial segregation in American cities, and prepared quantitative estimates of the extent of racial segregation in 1940, 1950, and 1960 for 109 large US cities and 1960 indexes for the 207 cities with more than 1,000 non-white households. Using the index of dissimilarity, the Taeubers clearly demonstrated that the levels of residential segregation were very high in cities throughout the country. A value of 100 is obtained for this index when there is total segregation, that is, all of the geographic areas (usually blocks or census tracts) used in the analysis are either 100 or zero per cent black. Using block data for 207 cities in 1960, they found the index of dissimilarity ranged from 60.4 to 98.1. Only 8 cities had scores below 70, and only 31 had values below 79. The dissimilarity index is not without weaknesses and most of the authors identified in this survey calculate other indexes. Space precludes either a discussion of the differences among these several indexes or the results obtained using them.[2]

In an analysis of a panel of 109 cities in 1940, 1950, and 1960, Taeuber and Taeuber (1965: 38) found that 83 of them were more segregated in 1950 than in 1940 and that the average change was 2.1 points. These increases occurred during a period of tight housing and labor markets and of unprecedented levels of migration by southern blacks to northern and western cities. Tight labor and housing markets resulted from rapid industrial expansion during World War II and strict wartime controls on residential construction. During the 1950s, segregation decreased in slightly more than half (64 out of 109) of the same cities and the mean dissimilarity index declined by 1.2 points as a postwar housing boom increased the supply of urban housing.

[1] Housing market discrimination and the racial segregation which is a consequence have been shown to increase the price of comparable housing for black households, to reduce black ownership rates and thus hamper capital accumulation, concentrate black children in low-quality schools, and reduce the employment and earnings of black workers. The following sources are but a small sample of the extensive literature that documents these adverse consequences: Cutler and Glaeser (1997); Holzer (1991); Ihlanfeldt (1991); Ihlanfeldt and Sjoquist (1990); Jencks and Mayer (1990); Kain (1968, 1992); Kain and Quigley (1975); Yinger (1995); Zax and Kain (1996).

[2] Discussions of these several indexes are provided by Taeuber and Taeuber (1965); Massey and Denton (1993); Cutler *et al.* (1999).

Several authors used 1970 and 1980 census data to update Taeuber and Taeuber's findings, and, possibly for this reason, there was less agreement about the direction and extent of changes in segregation between 1970 and 1980 (Sørenson *et al.* 1975; Van Valley *et al.* 1977). Cutler *et al.*'s (1999) study of racial segregation for census years from 1890 through 1990 clarify these trends. Their analysis has the great advantage of having used a consistent methodology to quantify the extent of black–white segregation for over a century. For reasons of data availability, they use central cities as the unit of analysis for years before 1940 and metropolitan areas for the post-World War II period. Since they include only cities or metropolitan areas with at least 1,000 blacks in their analyses, their sample sizes varied from a low of 54 cities in 1900 to a high of 313 metropolitan areas in 1990. Using these data, Cutler *et al.* found that from 1890 to 1940 segregation rose dramatically to levels that we think of as the modern ghetto; from 1940 to 1970, segregation expanded or leveled off; and after 1970, segregation declined.

Changes in Racial Segregation, 1970–1990

Anticipating an argument that is more fully developed in *American Apartheid* (1993), Massey and Gross (1991: 32) found that declines in segregation between 1970 and 1980 'were limited to a select set of SMSA's [metropolitan areas] that are uncharacteristic of the urban areas where most blacks live'. Massey and Denton (1993: 63) similarly conclude that there was virtually no sign of progress in residential integration between 1970 and 1980 'among the oldest and largest northern ghettos—places where the riots of the 1960s were most severe'. In contrast to most other authors, they subtract Hispanics from both the white and black population groups before computing their black–white segregation indexes.

Farley and Frey's (1993) analyses of changes in segregation for 232 metropolitan areas during the subsequent decade (1980–90) caused them to be much more optimistic than Massey and Denton about the prospects for racial integration.[3] They employed the more usual convention of comparing all whites to all blacks and used block group data instead of tracts.[4] Block groups are smaller than tracts and generally provide a more sensitive measure of the extent of segregation and higher scores than tract indexes. Farley and Frey (1993) found that the black–white index of dissimilarity fell in 194 areas between 1980 and 1990.

[3] These areas had 20,000 or more blacks or blacks were at least 3% of the population in 1990.

[4] About 6% of white and 3% of black residents of the 232 areas identified themselves as Hispanic. Citing the results of an earlier joint paper, Farley and Frey (1993: 21) note that black–white dissimilarity indexes are smaller 'when the Hispanic and Asian population were large relative to blacks'.

Farley and Frey also used multivariate statistical methods to analyze both variations in 1990 segregation levels and changes in segregation between 1980 and 1990. They found that residential segregation in 1990 was greater in the northeast and midwest, in larger metropolitan areas, and in metropolitan areas with large fractions of retired persons, and was lower in metropolitan areas with unusually large shares of university, government, or military employment, in areas with high rates of new construction, and in areas with higher black to white income ratios. Their 1980–90 percentage change regressions similarly indicated that segregation in the average metropolitan area declined by 12.1 per cent during the decade and that southern metropolitan areas generally experienced larger decreases in segregation than areas in other parts of the country. Finally, they determined that metropolitan areas with large fractions of retired persons and in communities with high levels of white exposure to blacks in 1980 experienced larger increases or smaller decreases in racial segregation and that segregation declined by more in areas with high rates of new construction.[5]

In assessing the impacts of urban structure and fair housing efforts on levels of segregation, Farley and Frey endorse Massey and Denton's (1987: 18) observation that 'Cities built before the end of the Second World War have ecological structures that are more conducive to segregation'. They add that independent suburbs are much less important in southern metropolitan areas and point out that southern whites less often have the option of moving to a white suburban community with an exclusively white school system than the residents of northern metropolitan areas. Finally, they note that places with large fractions of their housing stock built after 1969 when discrimination in housing became illegal are 'less segregated'.

Because Farley and Frey do not present separate estimates for the 30 metropolitan areas with the largest black population, they do not directly consider the argument made by Massey and Denton in *American Apartheid*. This and other questions are addressed in Table 26.1. The top panel presents the author's calculations of mean dissimilarity indexes using the individual estimates for 1980 and 1990 prepared by Harrison and Weinberg (1992*b*). They demonstrate that the mean absolute decline in the level of segregation for all metropolitan areas with more than one million population in 1980 and for the areas used by Massey and Denton was larger than those for smaller metropolitan areas. Since these large metropolitan areas had higher levels of segregation in 1990, the percentage decline was somewhat smaller than for the smaller areas. Thus, the changes in segregation for the 30 metropolitan areas with the largest black populations in 1980 do not appear to be appreciably different from those for all metropolitan areas. Jargowsky (1996*a*: 139), similarly, found that

[5] Farley and Frey's findings about the effects of higher rates of new construction were anticipated by Massey and Gross (1991: 27) in their analysis of changes in segregation in 60 large metropolitan areas between 1970 and 1980.

Table 26.1. Dissimilarity indexes for 1980 and 1990

	1980	1990	1980–90 change	Percentage change
Black vs. White (H&W)				
Metropolitan areas >1 million	78.3	73.9	4.4	5.6
Metropolitan areas 500,000–1 million	68.5	64.3	4.2	6.1
Metropolitan areas <500,000	61.3	57.5	3.8	6.2
30 metropolitan areas with most blacks	78.2	73.8	4.4	5.6
All metropolitan areas (H&W)				
Black vs. white	73.6	69.4	4.2	5.7
Hispanic vs. white	50.0	50.4	–0.4	–0.8
Asian vs. white	39.7	40.9	–1.2	–3.0
232 metropolitan areas (F&F)				
Black vs. non-black	68.8	64.3	4.5	6.5
Hispanic vs. non-Hispanic	42.2	42.7	–0.5	–1.2
Asian vs. non-Asian	40.7	43.0	–2.3	–5.7

Notes: H&W refers to Harrison and Weinberg (1992*b*); F&F refers to Farley and Frey (1993).

the black–white dissimilarity index for the quartile of metropolitan areas with the largest percentage of blacks (80 of 318) declined by 0.03 points between 1980 and 1990 while the indexes for the remaining three declined by 0.06 points.

The second and third panels in Table 26.1 present estimates of black/non-black, Hispanic/non-Hispanic, and Asian/non-Asian segregation in 1990 prepared by Harrison and Weinberg and by Farley and Frey. While the authors define these groups somewhat differently and use different geography (tracts vs. block groups), the results are generally consistent. In particular, they support the findings of earlier studies which indicated that black–white segregation is substantially greater than Hispanic/non-Hispanic segregation and Asian/non-Asian segregation. In addition, these estimates indicate that mean levels of Hispanic/non-Hispanic and Asian/non-Asian segregation increased over the decade, although in both cases the levels of segregation remain much lower than those for blacks and non-blacks.

The Causes of Racial Residential Segregation

It is much easier to quantify the extent of racial residential segregation than to explain its causes. Three, not necessarily mutually exclusive, primary hypotheses have been set forth as explanations for both the intensity and persistence of black–white segregation in American cities. They are: (1) black–white differences in income and other socio-economic-demographic characteristics; (2) black and white preferences for neighborhoods of varying racial composition; and (3) individual and collective acts of discrimination against black home seekers, or what is frequently termed exclusion.

The socio-economic differences hypothesis is easy to test empirically and several authors have done so (Taeuber 1968; Taeuber and Taeuber 1965; Kain 1976 and 1986; Massey and Denton 1993). One approach uses information on the incomes and other socio-economic characteristics of black and white households to predict the residence locations of black households. Taeuber and Taeuber (1965), using rents and house values, found that black–white differences in these measures explained little of the pattern of racial residential segregation in American cities. In a subsequent article, Taeuber (1968) used census tract data on black and white incomes to predict the racial composition of each Cleveland tract in 1960. Using the predicted and actual data for each tract, he found his predicted black–white index of dissimilarity was only 5.3 while the actual index was 89.7.

Persons unsympathetic to, or unconvinced by, Taeuber's analysis might argue that income is insufficient to predict the residential location of black households, since housing choices depend on many household characteristics besides income. In a subsequent analysis for Cleveland in 1970, Kain (1976, 1986) used metropolitan-wide black shares of 384 types of households to predict the percentage of black households for each Cleveland census tract.[6] The effect of housing market discrimination or other factors besides socio-economic differences on black residence patterns is evident from Table 26.2, which shows the actual and predicted number of tracts by percentage blacks in 1970. The actual numbers of tracts are concentrated in the tails; 46 tracts were 90 per cent or more black and 77 tracts were 50 per cent or more black in 1970. In contrast, only one of the 448 Cleveland census tracts in 1970 had a predicted percentage black as high as 50 per cent. Similarly, while 313 tracts had fewer than 5 per cent black persons in 1970, no census tracts had a predicted percentage below 5 per cent.

The last two columns in Table 26.2 are for a complementary analysis that examines the 'ethnic analogy' hypothesis, which argues that there is nothing unusual about the racial segregation of blacks in American cities since ethnic enclaves have long been commonplace in US cities. Kain (1976), using the same data and procedures, predicted the percentage of both total foreign stock and of eight specific ethnic/nationality groups for each tract. The actual distribution of tracts by percentage of total foreign stock, and similar data for individual ethnic

[6] These 314 household types were defined by the interaction of family type (husband and wife, other families, and primary individuals), age of head (less than 30 years of age, 30–44 years of age, 45–64 years of age, and more than 65 years of age), family size (1, 2, 3, 4, 5, and 6 or more), and household income (less than \$2,000, \$2,000–2,999, \$3,000–4,999, \$5,000–6,999, \$7,000–9,999, \$10,000–14,999, \$15,000–24,999, and \$25,000–99,999).

Table 26.2. Frequency distribution of Cleveland SMSA census tracts by actual and predicted percentage black and foreign stock

Black percentage of tract	Black		Total foreign stock		
	Actual	Predicted	Actual	Predicted	
				Model I	Model II
90–100	46	—	—	—	—
80–9	15	—	1	—	—
70–9	3	—	1	—	—
60–9	6	—	2	—	—
50–9	7	1	7	—	—
40–9	7	13	46	1	2
35–9	3	6	49	3	23
30–4	4	21	54	40	160
25–9	6	29	58	187	134
20–4	5	46	61	178	38
15–19	6	109	57	30	11
10–14	5	193	33	1	8
5–9	14	22	24	—	15
0–4	313	—	44	—	49

Source: Kain (1976).

groups, reveal that neither the total foreign stock, nor individual ethnic groups, tend to live in neighborhoods where they are a majority. This finding, of course, is entirely consistent with the fact that the segregation levels of African-Americans, whether measured by indexes of dissimilarity or any other method, are unprecedented (Lieberson 1963; Massey and Denton 1993; Taeuber and Taeuber 1974; White 1987).

Predicted tract distributions of the individual ethnic groups, like their actual distributions, cluster rather tightly around the area-wide mean percentage of each group (Kain 1976). This reflects the fact that while there are recognizable concentrations of persons of German, Polish, Czech, Hungarian, Yugoslavian, Italian, and Russian origin in Cleveland, as in every other metropolitan area, only a small fraction of these groups live in these enclaves. Most live throughout the metropolitan area at rates that closely approximate their share of the total population of the region. The predictions labeled Model I are unconstrained assignments. Those labeled Model II, in contrast, take account of the fact that intense racial segregation, high ghetto housing prices, and crowding out discourage white households from moving to ghetto neighborhoods. When the dwellings occupied by black households are removed from the choice set for each ethnic/national group, the model's assignments of both total foreign born and individual nationality groups are much closer to the actual distributions.

Housing Market Discrimination/Exclusion

Two or three decades ago it was not difficult to find clear-cut examples of collective action to prevent black households from moving into white neighborhoods and communities (Helper 1969; Jackson 1980; Kusmer 1976; Massey and Denton 1993; Cutler *et al.* 1999). If all else failed, the white residents of some neighborhoods would resort to violence to keep blacks out of 'their' neighborhoods. Farley and Frey (1993: 4), for example, refer to a report of the Chicago Commission of Race Relations (1922: 122–35) that describes 58 fire bombing episodes that occurred on that city's south side between 1917 and 1921. These explosions killed two blacks, and one prosperous black businessman had his home bombed six times.

Cutler *et al.* (1999: 457) agree that before 1970, racial residential segregation is best explained by exclusion, that is 'collective actions on the part of whites to limit the access of blacks to white neighborhoods'. By 1990, however, they argue that racial residential segregation is maintained by white preferences and willingness to pay not to live with blacks. The principal evidence they offer to support this claim is analyses that suggest that during the recent period white renters paid more for equivalent units than blacks in more segregated areas. This result leads them to conclude that 'decentralized racism has replaced centralized racism as the factor influencing residential location' (ibid. 457–8). The evidence is unconvincing. The regression analyses they rely on for this conclusion include no neighborhood quality or amenity variables. Since ghetto schools are inferior to schools in all white areas and crime rates and other bads tend to be higher in ghetto neighborhoods than in all white neighborhoods, their procedure overstates the rental premium paid by whites. This problem exists for both the earlier and later periods.

The declines in housing market discrimination discussed previously and the appearance of growing numbers of black households in previously all white suburbs give indirect testimony to the fact that individual and collective acts of discrimination are becoming less common and less effective (Kain 1985). None the less, discriminatory practices remain a barrier. Department of Housing and Urban Development (DHUD) housing audits in large numbers of metropolitan areas in 1977 and 1989 provide the most extensive evidence of continued discrimination by real estate sales and rental agents (Turner *et al.* 1991; Yinger 1993). Munnell *et al.* (1992) is the best of several studies that document differences in treatment in mortgage lending.

Yinger (1995: 48) provides a detailed assessment of the evidence from the two DHUD studies and at least 72 other audit studies conducted during the late 1970s or 1980s. Using estimates obtained from the DHUD 1989 housing discrimination (audit) study and from Munnell *et al.* (1992), he extends the Courant (1978) search model and uses it to quantify the cost to minorities of the discriminatory practices of real estate brokers and lenders. He finds that over a three-year period, the direct cost of current discrimination in housing and mortgage markets is at least $7.4 billion for black households and $4.2 billion for Hispanic households (Yinger 1995: 101).

Black and White Preferences as Explanations of Housing Market Segregation

The black and white preferences 'explanation' of racial residential segregation takes at least two forms. The first is that black–white residential segregation is caused by the preferences of black households to live in all- or predominantly black neighborhoods. Advocates of this position frequently point to the concentrations of various ethnic and nationality groups in American cities as evidence of the normality of these preferences and behavior. The previous discussion of Kain's (1976) Cleveland analyses and comparisons of segregation levels of several race/ethnic groups by Lieberson (1963), however, demonstrate that the experience of blacks and other ethnic/nationality groups in this respect could not be more different.

Another reason that it is difficult to give too much credence to, at least, the more primitive versions of the black preferences hypothesis is that attitudinal studies for many years have found that most blacks have expressed a preference for integrated communities (Schuman *et al.* 1985). Seventy-four per cent of black Americans interviewed in a 1969 *Newsweek* poll, for example, responded that they would rather live in a neighborhood that had both whites and Negroes than in a neighborhood with all-Negro families; only 16 per cent chose an all-black neighborhood (Pettigrew 1973).

Home-interview surveys conducted in Detroit in 1976 and 1992 provide especially valuable evidence on black and white preferences for neighborhoods of varying composition and other housing and neighborhood characteristics (Farley *et al.* 1993; Farley *et al.* 1978). Black and white residents were asked to rank their preferences for living in, moving into, or remaining in neighborhoods with the racial compositions indicated in Table 26.3. The data shown in the top panel indicate that 68 per cent of black respondents in 1976 identified the 71 per cent black neighborhood as their first or second choice; by 1992 this fraction had increased to 82 per cent. Similarly, the fraction that gave the zero or 14 per cent black neighborhoods as their first or second choice decreased between 1976 and 1992. An equally notable feature of these results is willingness of black households to move into neighborhoods of widely varying racial compositions in both years. In 1992, 87 per cent of black respondents indicated they would be willing to move into a neighborhood that was only 14 per cent black and the fraction was even larger in 1976. Similarly, the percentages that indicated they would be willing to move into an all-white neighborhood was 31 per cent in 1992 and 38 per cent in 1976. The importance of this difference between 'preference' and 'willingness' cannot be overemphasized, particularly since it is consistent with other evidence that indicates that blacks are less interested in integration *per se* than they are in the better housing, safer neighborhoods, and higher quality schools that are to be found in predominantly white, middle class, and suburban communities.

The second position, credited to Bailey (1959), Becker (1957), and Muth (1969), is that black–white residential segregation is caused by the unwillingness of whites to live near blacks and by their willingness to pay a premium to live in segregated living patterns. Consequently, the so-called Bailey–Muth model predicts that the price of comparable housing will be lower in all-black areas than in all-white areas. Courant and Yinger (1977), as well as others, have published effective theoretical critiques of the Bailey–Muth model. In addition, a large number of empirical studies considered whether the price of standard housing was higher in the ghetto than in white neighborhoods and the higher quality studies generally indicate the opposite.[7] As noted previously, Cutler *et al.* (1999) resurrect this argument in explaining the persistence of black–white segregation in the past decade or so.

The lower panel in Table 26.3 provides strong evidence that white households in Detroit have become more comfortable with the idea of living in integrated settings. More than one-third in 1992 indicated they would feel comfortable living in a neighborhood that was 57 per cent black and 56 per cent indicated they would feel comfortable living in a neighborhood that was 36 per cent black. Both percentages increased between 1976 and 1992. During the same period, the fraction of white households indicating they would try to move out of a 57 per cent black neighborhood declined from 64 per cent to 53 per cent and the fraction indicating they would be willing to move into a 36 per cent black neighborhood increased from 27 per cent to 41 per cent. The significance of this result cannot be overstated. Research on racial transition clearly indicates that it is the decline of white demand, following, or in anticipation of, the entry of black families into communities located in the path of ghetto expansion, rather than white flight, that produces the seemingly inevitable transition of previously all-white neighborhoods to all-black neighborhoods (Kain and Quigley 1975; Karlen 1968; Phares 1971; and McKenna and Werner 1970).[8]

[7] This is a large, complex, and contentious literature that cannot be adequately treated here. A survey of the pre-1975 evidence is provided by Kain and Quigley (1975). More recent analyses by Berry (1976), Schnare and Struyk (1977), Schafer (1979), Yinger (1978), Chambers (1992), and Cutler *et al.* (1999) demonstrate that there remains considerable disagreement on the facts. Methodological flaws, particularly the complete absence or inadequacy of neighborhood quality variables, and the failure to deal with differences in appreciation, credit availability, and price, and differences in the availability and cost of insurance make the results of studies of owner-occupied housing particularly difficult to assess.

[8] Analyses by Lee and Wood (1991) of 1970–80 changes in the racial composition of tracts that

Table 26.3. Preferences of Detroit black and white households for neighborhoods of varying racial composition in 1976 and 1992

(1) Preferences of black households

	Year	Neighborhood percentage black				
		100%	71%	50%	14%	0%
Percentage neighborhood						
First or second choice	1992	20	82	77	18	4
First or second choice	1976	17	68	82	24	5
Percentage						
Willing to move in	1992	75	98	98	87	31
Willing to move in	1976	69	99	99	95	38

(2) Preferences of white households

	Year	Neighborhood percentage black				
		100%	57%	36%	21%	7%
Percentage of households who						
feel comfortable	1992	n.a.	35	56	70	84
feel comfortable	1976	n.a.	28	43	58	76
would try to move out	1992	n.a.	53	29	15	4
would try to move out	1976	n.a.	64	41	24	7
are willing to move in	1992	n.a.	27	41	69	87
are willing to move in	1976	n.a.	16	27	50	73

Source: Farley *et al.* (1993, figs. 7 and 10).

While the Detroit data on black and white stated preferences are valuable indicators of the likely response of white residents to black entry into their neighborhoods and of their willingness to move into, or remain in, neighborhoods of varying racial composition, they do not tell us enough about the motivations behind, or basis of, these attitudes. Are white households who indicate they would be unwilling to move into a neighborhood that is 36 or 57 per cent black simply racist, or is there something else going on? Undoubtedly some are racists and are expressing deeply ingrained racial prejudice. Many of those who are unwilling to move into a neighborhood that is 36 or 57 per cent black have other concerns. In particular, they may see the entry of one or a few black house-

were between 15 and 80% black in 1970 indicate that racial transition is not as automatic as is commonly believed. In particular, they found stability was closer to the norm in western metropolitan areas. These results are consistent with Kain's (1985) analyses of black suburbanization in the San Francisco–Oakland metropolitan area during 1970–80. None the less, the widely held belief that integrated neighborhoods generally become all-black neighborhoods is a powerful force for maintaining existing patterns of black–white segregation, even if careful analyses indicate the patterns are in fact much less automatic or certain than the conventional wisdom suggests.

holds into a particular neighborhood as the first stage of a process that they anticipate will very soon produce a neighborhood that is predominantly or entirely black. This is a reasonable expectation in many situations, and particularly for neighborhoods adjacent to the ghetto or in the path of ghetto expansion.

Even whites who might prefer living in an integrated community may be dissuaded by fears about the inevitable deterioration in services, school quality, and property values that are widely believed to accompany black entry. Studies by Laurenti (1960), Karlen (1968), Phares (1971), McKenna and Werner (1970), and others do not support the notion that the entry of blacks into previously all-white neighborhoods causes property values to decline. None the less, many whites believe otherwise. The actual impact of black entry on property values is both somewhat different and more complex. Unfortunately, what matters is what potential white residents believe. These beliefs, particularly about declines in neighborhood and school quality, have just enough basis in fact to make even unprejudiced whites worry about the consequences of racial transition.

Schelling (1969, 1972*a*, 1972*b*) provided a highly influential analysis of the way in which differences in black and white preferences could affect residence patterns. His highly stylized models have been interpreted (Clark 1986, 1991) as demonstrating that the massive and persistent patterns of racial segregation in American cities are primarily due to an inconsistency between black and white preferences for neighborhoods of varying racial composition.[9] Schelling was much more circumspect. He emphasized that his models consider only black and white preferences for neighborhood racial composition and do *not* consider intra-metropolitan variations in housing prices, differences in dwelling unit size and quality, in the quality of public schools and other local government services, in household incomes, or the impact of different employment locations on the choice of neighborhood.

Ellen (1996) does the best job of combining Schelling-type models and empirical data on residential location decisions of black and white households in an analysis of neighborhood racial change. She begins with the following observations: (1) that 'nearly one fifth of all neighborhoods in the U.S. were racially mixed in 1990', (2) that 'over three quarters of neighborhoods that were integrated in 1980 remained integrated in 1990', and (3) that 'both the number of racially mixed communities and their degree of stability has increased markedly with time' (ibid. 10). Finally, she used her econometric results in a

[9] Clark (1991) presents survey data from a number of other metropolitan areas collected by defendants in civil rights actions in those areas. In many respects, these data are broadly consistent with the Detroit survey data. There are important differences, however. First, they were telephone rather than home-interview surveys and thus could not use the cards with hypothetical neighborhoods of varying racial concentration that were an important feature of the Detroit surveys. Secondly, and perhaps more importantly, black households were asked about their preferences for neighborhoods of varying racial composition, but apparently were not asked about their willingness to move into all- or predominantly white neighborhoods. This is a serious omission.

simulation framework to predict changes in neighborhood racial composition. In discussing her simulation results, Ellen (1996: 293) observes 'they do not suggest great hope for integration in the very long-run, though they predict considerable stability in mixed areas over the course of ten or twenty years'. At the same time, she emphasizes that 'different kinds of mixed neighborhoods may be considerably more stable than the average'. Finally, echoing earlier analyses by Karlen (1968), Taub *et al.* (1984), McKenna and Werner (1970: 131–3), and Kain and Quigley (1975: 72–82), she adds that the simulations provide strong support for the view that entry rather than exit is the driving force behind neighborhood racial change.

Economic Segregation in US Metropolitan Areas

Residential segregation by income and other measures of socio-economic status has received much less attention by social scientists than segregation by race. The few studies of this question that have been completed, moreover, have generally concluded that, given the very high levels of racial segregation, economic segregation must be examined within racial/ethnic groups. Much of the research on economic segregation, moreover, has dealt with the extent of and trends in concentrated poverty. Of these studies, Wilson's (1987) research on changes in the geographic concentration of poverty in Chicago and Jargowsky's (1994, 1996*a*, 1996*b*) research on concentrated poverty in US metropolitan areas during the period 1970 to 1990 are the most influential.

Using Chicago data, Wilson (1987) showed that the number of poverty areas increased sharply and the fraction of the total poor population living in them rose during the 1970s. He attributed these changes to the simultaneous loss of central city manufacturing jobs and reductions in racial discrimination in suburban housing markets that permitted middle-class blacks to leave inner city ghetto communities. A serious consequence of these trends, he argued, was the loss or weakening of role models and crucial social institutions in the ghetto.

Massey and Eggers (1990: 1170), using Census data for the 50 largest SMSAs plus 10 others with large numbers of Hispanics to calculate measures of interclass segregation for whites, blacks, Hispanics, and Asians, generally confirmed Wilson's hypothesis that black segregation by income increased between 1970 and 1980. They also concluded, however, that the increase in income segregation for black households was the exception that proved the rule. They found that while the index of black income segregation increased by 0.029 over the decade, income segregation among whites, Hispanics, and Asians fell by 0.013, 0.054, and 0.138. The corresponding 1990 levels were 0.495 for blacks, 0.700 for Asians, 0.614 for Hispanics, and 0.391 for whites. Neither the changes or levels account for the pronounced differences in concentration/clustering of these groups.

Massey and Eggers (1990: 1160) used the mean of pairwise indexes of dissimilarity obtained for four income categories as their measure of interclass segregation for each race/ethnic group. Jargowsky (1996*b*: 987), after providing a detailed critique of this methodology, argues for the use of the 'correlation' ratio. This measure, which is also referred to as eta-squared or the segregation statistic, had been previously used by several other authors to measure segregation (Bell 1954; Farley 1977; Schnare 1980). According to Jargowsky, the principal advantage of the correlation ratio, which he terms the *Neighborhood Sorting Index* or NSI, is that income can be treated as a continuous variable. NSI is simply the ratio of the weighted standard deviation of household income for all neighborhoods in an SMSA and the standard deviation of household income for all households living in the SMSA.

Jargowsky finds the NSI increased between 1970 and 1980 and again between 1980 and 1990 for whites, blacks, and Hispanics. He did not calculate NSI for Asians. This result holds whether he uses a variable number of metropolitan areas or a constant set of 228 areas for whites, 76 for blacks, and 30 for Hispanics. While the NSIs for both whites and blacks increased in both decades, those for whites are smaller than those for blacks and Hispanics. Jargowsky (1996*b*: 989–90) contends that the values of NSI for all three groups 'are relatively modest though increasing' and that his results agree with previous studies that 'found relatively low levels of economic segregation, regardless of the measures employed' (Farley 1977; Massey and Eggers 1990; White 1987). He concludes that his 'results show *a pronounced trend toward increasing economic segregation*' for all three groups during the period 1970 to 1990 (Jargowsky 1996*b*: 990).

The preceding discussion of economic segregation by race/ethnic group is closely related to the continuing debate about the extent and trends in concentrated poverty. Two sociologists, Wilson (1987) and Kasarda (1988, 1989), resurrected the dormant field of research on the link between racial discrimination in urban housing markets and urban poverty. Encouraged by Wilson and Kasarda's example, research on these issues, and particularly spatial mismatch, which had previously been an active area of social science research, grew rapidly (Cutler and Glaeser 1997; Holzer 1991; Ihlanfeldt and Sjoquist 1991; Jencks and Mayer 1990; Kain 1968, 1992; Zax and Kain 1996).

While Wilson and Kasarda deserve credit for reopening the debate, Jargowsky has completed the most extensive and best research on the extent and trends in concentrated poverty. As Wilson notes in his foreword to *Poverty and Place: Ghettos, Barrios, and the American City*, Jargowsky uses tract data for a panel of 239 metropolitan areas in 1970, 1980, and 1990 to complete 'the most comprehensive analysis of changes in neighborhood poverty nationwide'. Jargowsky (1996*b*: 38) defines high-poverty neighborhoods as census tracts where more than 40 per cent of their population have incomes below the poverty level. Using this defintion, he finds that the metropolitan area population living in high-poverty neighborhoods grew by 25 per cent between 1970 and 1980 and by 54 per cent between 1980 and 1990, while total metropolitan area populations grew by only 13 per cent in both periods.

By 1990, Jargowsky (1996*b*: 16) finds there were nearly 3,000 high-poverty tracts with about 8.5 million residents in the 239 metropolitan areas he used for his analysis. The term ghetto refers to tracts that meet the 40 per cent poverty threshold and are predominantly (more than two-thirds) black, while the terms barrio and slums refer to high-poverty neighborhoods that are predominantly Hispanic or white. Using these criteria, black ghettos in 1990 were about half of all high-poverty neighborhoods, 14 per cent of high-poverty tracts were white slums, 17 per cent were barrios, and 27 per cent were mixed slums (no group accounted for more than two-thirds of the tract's residents). Nearly one-quarter of blacks living in high-poverty tracts lived in barrios, white slums, or mixed slums. Black ghettos accounted for 42 per cent of the residents of all high-poverty neighborhoods in 1990. Combining all types of high-poverty tracts, 34 per cent of all poor blacks living in metropolitan areas lived in high-poverty tracts, as contrasted to 22 per cent of poor Hispanics and only 6 per cent of poor whites.

Conclusions

This survey has examined the findings of social science research on racial/ethnic and economic segregation in US metropolitan areas. The most important is that the very high levels of black–white segregation that have long characterized US cities, after several decades of little or no change, have exhibited unmistakable declines in nearly all metropolitan areas. The largest declines have occurred in rapidly growing southern and western metropolitan areas. None the less, current levels of black–white segregation in all parts of the country remain higher than those of any other racial/ethnic group, either currently or in the past. While consensus about the precise reasons for these declines remains elusive, reductions in white prejudice, fair housing laws and their increased enforcement, declines in exclusionary practices, and the growth of the black middle class have clearly made important contributions.

It would be surprising if estimates of segregation indexes, similar to those described in this chapter, for the 2000 Census do not demonstrate a continued decline in the levels of black–white segregation. While these analyses will be important, there is a clear need for more extensive analyses of individual preferences and behavior. Ellen's (1996) analyses are an obvious starting point for this line of research. The role of high levels of Asian and Hispanic immigration in a growing number of metropolitan areas is also a fruitful area of study.

Finally, additional careful surveys of black and white preferences, similar to those by Farley and his associates (1978, 1993), could prove of great value. Such surveys could greatly improve our understanding of the role of expectations and preferences for local public goods and neighborhood amenities, as contrasted to neighborhood racial composition *per se*, in determining the residence decisions of individual black and white households. Ellen's (1996) research is again a useful starting point.

Persistent high levels of black–white segregation over several decades have had a major impact on the spatial structure of US metropolitan areas. Without the nation's long history of racial discrimination and the resulting rapid growth of concentrations of low income minorities in central cities, America's cities would be very different places. Suburban areas with their preponderance of single family homes and safe streets would still have attracted large numbers of higher income families with children. But without racial discrimination a significantly larger fraction of suburban residents would have been African-Americans. With a slower growth of central city ghettos, central city residential neighborhoods would have been more attractive to middle and higher income whites, particularly those employed at central locations. In the absence of racial discrimination, central cities would have been more diverse, both whiter and richer, and both central cities and the rest of the metropolitan area would have been much less segregated by income and social status.

In a growing number of large American cities, there has emerged surprisingly extensive construction of middle and high income housing near downtown, both new construction and conversions of loft and other commercial space. Neither the quantitative importance nor the reasons for these developments have been determined. Research on these questions could have large societal benefits.

In contrast to the declines in black–white segregation during the past decade, Hispanics and Asians became somewhat more segregated from non-Hispanics and non-Asians, trends that reflect high immigration levels for these groups. The resulting rapid growth of these populations in a few large metropolitan areas may also have contributed to the declines in black–white segregation, although black–white segregation declined in areas with small Asian and Hispanic populations and those with large ones. In spite of recent increases in Hispanic–non-Hispanic and Asian–non-Asian segregation and decreases in black–white segregation, the levels of Hispanic and Asian segregation remain far lower than those of blacks. Data from the 1990 Census will be useful in determining the extent to which the increased income segregation of Asians and Hispanics is a transitional phenomenon that is related to language differences or a more permanent change.

While black–white segregation declined in nearly all metropolitan areas during the 1980–90 period, income segregation increased for blacks, whites, and Hispanics. More than one observer has suggested that the same forces that contributed to the declines in black–white segregation and the rapid growth of black suburban populations played a role in the increased income segregation of blacks.

In spite of the welcome declines in racial residential segregation and a rapid growth in black suburban populations during the past two decades, African-Americans remain heavily concentrated in massive low income, central city ghettos. In 1990, 34 per cent of all blacks living in metropolitan areas lived in high-poverty areas. The comparable figures for Hispanics and whites were 22 and 6 per cent. This remains a dangerous situation. Research on programs and policies that contribute to a decrease in these high levels of concentrated poverty could yield very large benefits.

References

Bailey, Martin J. 1959. Note on the economics of residential zoning and urban renewal. *Land Economics* (Aug.): 288–90.

Becker, Gary 1957. *The Economics of Discrimination*. Chicago: University of Chicago Press.

Bell, Wendell 1954. A probability model for the measurement of ecological segregation. *Social Forces*, 32: 357–64.

Berry, Brian 1976. Ghetto expansion and single-family houses prices: Chicago, 1968–72. *Journal of Urban Economics*, 3/4 (Oct.), 397–423.

Chambers, Daniel N. 1992. The racial housing price differential and racially transitional neighborhoods. *Journal of Urban Economics*, 32: 214–32.

Clark, William A. V. 1986. Residential segregation in American cities. *Population Research and Policy Review*, 5: 95–127.

—— 1991. Residential preferences and neighborhood racial segregation: a test of the Schelling segregation model. *Demography*, 28/1: 1–19.

Courant, Paul N. 1978. Racial prejudice in a search model of the urban housing market. *Journal of Urban Economics*, 5/3 (July), 329–45.

—— and Yinger, John 1977. On models of racial prejudice and urban residential structure. *Journal of Urban Economics*, 4: 272–91.

Cutler, David M., and Glaeser, Edward L. 1997. Are ghettos good or bad? *Quarterly Journal of Economics*, 112/3 (Aug.), 827–72.

—— —— and Vigdor, Jacob L. 1999. The rise and decline of the American ghetto. *Journal of Political Economy*, 112/3.

Ellen, Ingrid Gould 1996. Sharing America's neighborhoods: the changing prospects for stable racial integration. Ph.D. in Public Policy. Harvard University, July.

Farley, Reynolds 1977. Residential segregation in urban areas of the United States in 1970: an analysis of social class and racial differences. *Demography*, 14: 497–517.

—— Bianchi, S., and Colasanto, D. 1978. Chocolate city, vanilla suburbs: will the trend toward racially separate communities continue? *Social Science Research*, 7 (Dec.), 319–44.

—— Steek, Charlotte, Jackson, Tara, Krysan, Maria, and Reeves, Keith 1993. Continued racial residential segregation in Detroit: chocolate city, vanilla suburbs revisited. *Journal of Housing Research*, 4/1: 1–38.

——and FREY, WILLIAM 1993. Changes in the segregation of whites from blacks during the 1980s: small steps toward a more integrated society, *American Sociological Review*, 59: 23–45.

HARRISON, RODERICK J., and WEINBERG, DANIEL H. 1992*a*. Racial and ethnic residential segregation in 1990. Washington: US Bureau of the Census, 13 Apr.

————1992*b*. Changes in racial and ethnic residential segregation, 1980–1990. Washington: US Bureau of the Census, 29 July.

HELPER, ROSE 1969. *Racial Policies and Practices of Real Estate Brokers*. Minneapolis: University of Minnesota Press.

HOLZER, HARRY J. 1991. The spatial mismatch hypothesis: what has the evidence shown? *Urban Studies*, 28/1: 105–22.

IHLANFELDT, KEITH R. 1991. The effect of job access on black and white youth employment: a cross section analysis. *Urban Studies*, 28: 255–65.

——and SJOQUIST, DAVID L. 1990. Job accessibility and racial differences in youth employment rates. *American Economic Review*, 80: 267–76.

JACKSON, KENNETH T. 1980. Race, ethnicity, and real estate appraisal: the home owners loan corporation and the federal housing administration. *Journal of Urban History* 6/4 (Aug.), 419–52.

JARGOWSKY, PAUL A. 1994. Ghetto poverty among blacks in the 1980s. *Journal of Policy Analysis and Management*, 13/2: 288–310.

——1996*a*. *Poverty and Place: Ghettos, Barrios and the American City*. New York: Russell Sage Foundation.

——1996*b*. Take the money and run: economic segregation in U.S. metropolitan areas. *American Sociological Review*, 61 (Dec.), 984–98.

JENCKS, CHRISTOPHER, and MAYER, SUSAN 1990. Residential segregation, job proximity, and black opportunities. In *Inner-City Poverty in the United States*, ed. Lawrence E. Lynn, Jr. and Michael G. H. McGeary. Washington: National Academy Press.

KAIN, JOHN F. 1968. Housing segregation, negro employment, and metropolitan decentralization. *Quarterly Journal of Economics*, 82/2 (May), 175–97.

——1976. Race, ethnicity, and residential location. In *Public and Urban Economics: Essays in Honor of William S. Vickrey*, ed. Ronald E. Grieson. Lexington, Mass.: Lexington Books.

——1985. Black suburbanization in the eighties: a new beginning or a false hope? In *American Domestic Priorities: An Economic Appraisal*, ed. John M. Quigley and Daniel L. Rubinfeld. Berkeley and Los Angeles: University of California Press.

——1986. The influence of race and income on racial segregation and policy. In *Housing Desegregation, Race, and Federal Policies*, ed. John M. Goering. Chapel Hill, NC: University of North Carolina Press.

——1987. Housing market discrimination and black suburbanization in the 1980s. In *Divided Neighborhoods: Changing Patterns of Racial Segregation, Vol. 32, Urban Affairs Annual Review*, ed. Gary A. Tobin. Newbury Park, Calif.: Sage Publications.

——1992. The spatial mismatch hypothesis: three decades later. *Housing Policy Debate*, 3/2: 371–460.

——and QUIGLEY, JOHN M. 1975. *Housing Markets and Racial Discrimination: A Microeconomics Analysis*. New York: National Bureau of Economic Research.

KARLEN, DAVID H. 1968. Racial integration and property values in Chicago. Urban Economics Report No. 7, University of Chicago, Apr.

KASARDA, JOHN. 1988. Jobs, migration, and emerging urban mismatches. In *Urban Change and Poverty*, ed. Laurence E. Lynn, Jr. and Michael G. H. McGeary. Washington: National Academy Press.

—— 1989. Urban industrial transition and the urban underclass. *Annals of the American Academy of Political and Social Sciences*, 501: 26–47.

KUSMER, KENNETH L. 1976. *A Ghetto Takes Shape: Black Cleveland, 1870–1930*. Urbana, Ill.: University of Illinois Press.

LAURENTI, LUIGI 1960. *Property Values and Race: Studies in Seven Cities*. Berkeley and Los Angeles: University of California Press.

LEE, BARRETT A., and WOOD, PETER B. 1991. Is neighborhood racial succession place-specific? *Demography*, 28/1 (Feb.), 21–40.

LIEBERSON, STANLEY 1963. *Ethnic Patterns in American Cities*. Glencoe: Free Press of Glencoe.

MCKENNA, JOSEPH P., and WERNER, HERBERT D. 1970. The housing market in integrating areas. *Annals of Regional Science* (Dec.).

MASSEY, DOUGLAS S., and DENTON, NANCY A. 1987. Trends in the residential segregation of blacks, Hispanics, and Asians. *American Sociological Review*, 52: 802–25.

—— —— 1993. *American Apartheid: Segregation and the Making of the Underclass*. Cambridge, Mass.: Harvard University Press.

—— and EGGERS, MITCHELL L. 1990. The ecology of inequality: minorities and the concentration of poverty, 1970–1980. *American Journal of Sociology*, 95/5 (Mar.), 1153–88.

—— and GROSS, ANDREW B. 1991. Explaining trends in racial segregation, 1970–1980. *Urban Affairs Quarterly*, 27/1 (Sept.), 13–35.

MUNNELL, ALICIA H., BROWNE, LYNN E., MCENEANEY, JAMES, and TOOTELL, GEOFFREY M. B. 1992. Mortgage lending in Boston: interpreting HMDA data. Federal Reserve Bank of Boston, Working Paper, Series No. 92–7 (Oct.).

MUTH, RICHARD 1969. *Cities and Housing*. Chicago: University of Chicago Press.

PETTIGREW, THOMAS 1973. Attitudes on race and housing: a socio-psychological view. In *Segregation in Residential Areas*, ed. A. M. Hawley and Vincent P. Rock. Washington: National Academy of Sciences.

PHARES, DONALD 1971. Racial change and housing values: transition in an inner suburb. *Social Science Quarterly* (Dec.).

SCHAFER, ROBERT. 1979. Racial discrimination in the Boston housing market. *Journal of Urban Economics*, 6: 176–96.

SCHELLING, THOMAS C. 1969. Models of segregation. Santa Monica: RAND Corporation Memorandum, RM-6014-RC, May.

—— 1972*a*. Dynamic models of segregation. *Journal of Mathematical Sociology*, 1: 148–86.

—— 1972*b*. A process of residential segregation: neighborhood tipping. In *Racial Discrimination in Economic Life*, ed. Anthony H. Pascal. Lexington, Mass.: Lexington Books, D.C. Heath and Co., 157–84.

SCHNARE, ANN B. 1980. Trends in residential segregation by race: 1960–1970. *Journal of Urban Economics*, 7: 293–301.

—— and STRUYK, RAYMOND J. 1977. An analysis of ghetto housing pricing over time. In *Residential Location and Urban Housing Markets*, ed. Gregory K. Ingram. Cambridge, Mass.: Ballinger Publishing Co.

SCHUMAN, HOWARD, STEEH, CHARLOTTE, and BOBO, LAWRENCE 1985. *Racial Attitudes in America: Trends and Interpretations*. Cambridge, Mass.: Harvard University Press.

SØRENSEN, ANNEMETTE, TAEUBER, KARL E., and HOLLINGSWORTH, LESLIE J., JR. 1975. Indexes of racial segregation for 109 cities in the United States, 1940–1970. *Sociological Focus*, 8: 128–30.

TAEUBER, KARL 1968. The effect of income redistribution on racial residential segregation. *Urban Affairs Quarterly*, 4: 5–15.

——and TAEUBER, ALMA F. 1965. *Negroes in Cities: Residential Segregation and Neighborhood Change*. Chicago: Aldine.

———— 1974. The negro as an immigrant group. *American Journal of Sociology*, 64/4 (Jan.).

TAUB, RICHARD, GARTH TAYLOR, D., and DUNHAM, JAY 1984. *Paths of Neighborhood Change*. Chicago: University of Chicago Press.

TURNER, MARGERY AUSTIN, STRUYK, RAYMOND J., and YINGER, JOHN 1991. Housing discrimination study: synthesis. The Urban Institute and Syracuse University, Aug.

VAN VALLEY, T. L., ROOF, W. C., and WILCOX, J. E. 1977. Trends in residential segregation, 1960–70. *American Journal of Sociology*, 82/2: 824–44.

WHITE, MICHAEL J. 1987. *American Neighborhoods and Residential Differentiation*. New York: Russell Sage Foundation.

WILSON, WILLIAM JULIUS 1987. *The Truly Disadvantaged: The Inner City, The Underclass, and Public Policy*. Chicago: University of Chicago Press.

YINGER, JOHN 1978. The black-white price differential in housing: some further evidence. *Land Economics*, 44: 185–206.

——1993. Access denied, access constrained: results and implications of the 1989 housing discrimination study. In *Clear and Convincing Evidence: Testing for Discrimination in America*, ed. M. Fix and R. Struyk. Washington: The Urban Institute.

——1995. *Closed Doors, Opportunities Lost: The Continuing Costs of Housing Discrimination*. New York: Russell Sage Foundation.

ZAX, JEFFREY, and KAIN, JOHN F. 1996. Moving to the suburbs: do relocating companies leave their black employees behind? *Journal of Labor Economics* (July).

Section 12

Communities, Politics, and Power

Chapter **27**

Elite Power, Global Forces, and the Political Economy of 'Glocal' Development

Erik Swyngedouw

> At the beginning . . . , there is a capitalism within the confines of a Nation-State, with the accompanying international trade . . . , what follows is the relationship of colonization in which the colonizing country subordinates and exploits . . . the colonized country; the final moment of this process is the paradox of colonization in which there are only colonies, no colonizing countries—the colonizing power is no longer the Nation-State but directly the global company. In the long term, we shall not only wear Banana Republic shirts but also live in banana republics.
>
> (Zizek 1997: 44)

My purpose in this contribution is to explore two interrelated themes. First, the emergence of a new space economy in the context of rapidly altering global economic conditions will be discussed. I shall argue that the 're-scaling' of the economy and the emergence of a new dynamic articulation between local/regional economies and global economic flows and processes is paralleled by the formation of new forms of governance at both sub-national and super-national scales. This new 'scalar gestalt' of both economy and governance, in turn, complements, alters, and redefines the national State which, until recently, played a pivotal role in regulating national economic spaces. In a second part, I shall consider the rise to prominence of regional growth complexes and the central role of local or regional institutions in shaping processes of dynamic, innovative, and competitive economic development. The importance of the political armature in structuring processes of urban and regional political-economic change under conditions of prolonged economic stress and intensifying competition will be assessed. The argument will then turn to considering the role of hegemonic political formations in fostering development and the relationships between changing socio-economic conditions and reconfigurations of political power lines.

It is my contention that excavating the role of the institutional-political framework is central to permit a better understanding of the political economic dynamics of spatial change and restructuring (Sadler 1992; Cooke 1995; Moulaert 1996; Benko and Lipietz 1992, 1995; Baeten *et al.* 1999). In addition, I wish to highlight the importance of a political-economic analysis in geographical economic studies (Dunford 1990; Amin and Thrift 1994). Such a perspective concentrates on the ways in which social and political power geometries (Massey 1996), and the shifting alliances of and between political and economic elites interconnect with economic processes. The choreographies of elite power strategies, whether political or economic, produce a restless landscape of changing institutions, actors, and socio-economic processes that, taken together, give form, coherence, and trajectory to 'the urban' or to 'the region'.

In recent years, institutional theory (Hodgson 1988; Storper 1997), evolutionary perspectives (Altvater 1993; Hodgson 1993), the regulation approach (Boyer 1989; Lipietz 1987), and other related views have insisted on the interaction between social and institutional processes on the one hand and regional economic dynamics on the other (Amin 1994; Keating and Loughlin 1997). On occasion, these analyses have been related to the abundant literature on the role and importance of urban or regional 'growth coalitions' (Cox and Mair 1989, 1991; Peck 1995). Shifting power relations are central to this analysis, but always mediated by the historical-geographical trajectories through which the regional socio-economic fabric is constituted. The complex texture of these political-economic configurations that, so it seems to me, is central to come to grips with the dynamics of regional change is invariably complicated, finely grained, and subtle in its many and variegated details. These 'local' institutional and political changes and fluctuating power geometries frame the articulation with political and economic processes operating at other geographical scales (Bachtler and Michie 1993; Swyngedouw 1996*a*). This chapter is concerned, therefore, with excavating how shifting relations of power, how the spatial scales at which they operate, and how the mechanisms through which power is (re)negotiated articulate with socio-economic transformations (see Swyngedouw 1997).

The New Space Economy: A Global World?

It is of course commonplace to argue that a tumultuous reordering of socio-economic life has swept through urban and regional landscapes over the past two decades or so. In an ideological milieu in which socio-spatial ordering for and by the market has become the dogma of the day, the city and the region have, more than ever, become landscapes of socio-economic power where islands of extreme wealth are interspersed with spaces of poverty, social exclusion, and erosion of the socio-economic fabric. The process of economic, political, and cultural globalization and accompanying intensified competition is often invoked as the principal motivation for the pursuit of more openly market-led development strategies and as the main driving force leading to persistent restructuring of urban and regional economies (Kofman and Youngs 1996; Weiss 1997). This process of globalization is welcomed by a new international elite as an integral part of the establishment of a new world order that will bring universal stability, welfare, and economic growth. Others lament it as the prime cause of irreversible decline, the persistence of structural unemployment, and violent shocks that move from place to place, leaving cities and regions under profound socio-economic stress (Group of Lisbon 1994).

Of course, globalization is by no means as pervasive and new as many make it out to be. Economic globalization has been an integral part of a capitalist market economy since at least 1492. During most of the nineteenth and early twentieth centuries, many parts of the world were culturally and economically more intensely interconnected than today (Harvey 1995). In the current phase of profound shake-up of geographical processes, 'globalization' is often invoked as a short-hand term to summarize processes of de-territorialization and re-territorialization, but in a way that renders them aspatial or ageographical and, as such, profoundly disempowering (O'Brien 1992; Ohmae 1995; Kofman and Youngs 1996). As Hirst and Thompson (1996), among others, have pointed out, the process of globalization is indeed not as pervasive and total as many make it out to be. They show how—at least until 1913—international interdependence in terms of global trade and foreign direct investment was significantly higher compared with the subsequent period of national 'Fordist' development (1925–73) (see also Figs. 27.1 and 27.2).

It is only in recent years that parts of the world economy have begun to approach again (at least in relative terms) the conditions of integration that characterized the world economy at the turn of the present century. This is, of course, not to say that nothing new has happened. The essence of capitalism is, as Schumpeter (1943) showed a long time ago, about perpetual creative destruction in which 'everything that is solid melts into air' (Marx and Engels 1848/1985: 83). Some of the key changes are summarized below.

1. There has been a profound internationalization of financial markets. The DAILY turnover on international capital markets was in 1998 *circa* US$ 1.6 trillion (while the total TRADE figure for the whole of 1994 was a 'mere' US$ 4.3 trillion (Swyngedouw 1996*b*)). The greatest part of these financial transactions

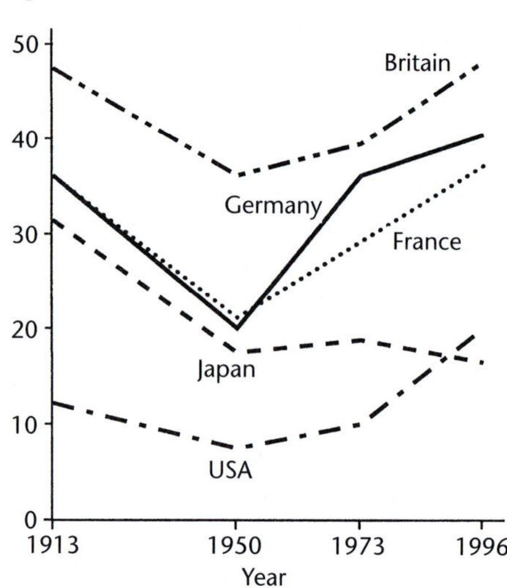

Fig. 27.1. Merchandise trade (exports and imports) as a percentage of GDP

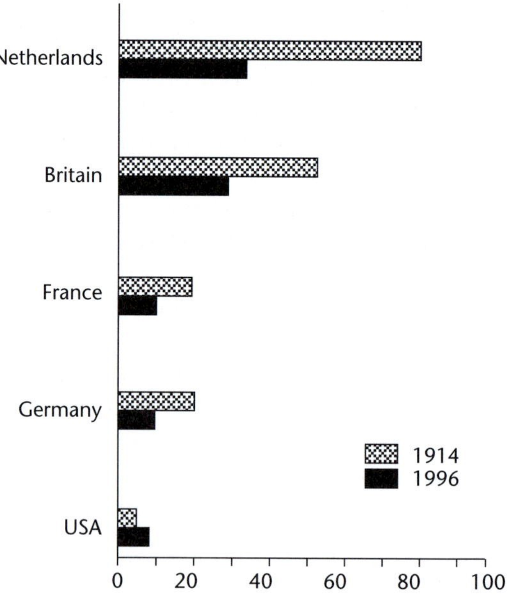

Fig. 27.2. Stocks of outward foreign direct investment (percentage of GDP)

whiz around the globe from place to place for speculative gain and moves quickly around space in search of new spaces of accumulation as the 1998 roller-coaster of geographically leapfrogging boom-bust cycles in the financial markets has demonstrated.

2. In addition, a profound geographical sectoral reshuffling has taken place. Large Fordist industries have (at the least in the West) disappeared or greatly reduced in importance (through closure, de-localization, or intense rationalization) and have been replaced by consumer and business services. This has resulted in intense disequilibriums in urban and regional economies and to serious problems in terms of aligning labor supply with demand. The 'new' service economy is highly specialized and fragmented, and is characterized by strictly segmented labor markets, a growing differentiation in terms of labor conditions, salaries, security, or flexibility (Peck 1996). Of course, industrial production continues to thrive in a number of urban and regional economies, but is also often characterized by growing polarization, segmentation, and differentiation (Sassen 1991; Fainstein *et al.* 1992).

3. The socio-economic structure of many urban and regional economies—although nodal points in the formation and management of global economic networks—testifies to a growing polarization, and often persistent processes of social and economic exclusion. While parts of the social economy are thriving, others dwell in enduring poverty, unemployment, and precarious conditions of life and work (Hamnett 1996; Mingione 1996; Castells 1998).

4. There is an accelerating process of proletarianization on a world scale in a context of growing spatial differentiation in terms of working conditions (Harvey 1995). The continuing erosion of economic systems that assured some degree of self-sufficiency (with the possible exception of parts of the former Soviet Union), combined with an extremely volatile or insufficient demand for labor, has not only intensified social conflict in many parts of the world, but also accelerated processes of mass migration. Much of this often illegal immigration is drained to the imagineered honey-pots of the world's growth regions.

5. Cities and regions, and in particular the more successful ones, have become or are rapidly becoming multi-cultural and diversified mosaics where the exotic and unexpected may turn up at the turn of every corner. Urban and regional identities become increasingly multi-layered and 'hybrid'. The contemporary social economy of cities like Brussels, London, Los Angeles, or Paris suggests how urban social economies are imbedded in a cosmopolitan identity that is often at odds with historically produced territorial and geo-political identities (Sandercock 1998).

6. Furthermore, the technological and information revolution has increased and intensified cultural globalization (Featherstone *et al.* 1995; Castells 1989). While global media flows have become more dense, the actual direct interchange in economic terms with many of the remote places that fill our television

screens on a daily basis have actually disintegrated. Of course, the speed of commodity flows has accelerated and this in itself propelled the process of deterritorialization and re-territorialization to new heights. Undoubtedly, this acceleration of the ease by which people and commodities overcome the barrier of space is unprecedented. Of course, this brings growing cultural, ethnic, gender, and other forms of differentiation among the working class, but also intensifies the geographical processes that are so central to current restructuring (see Harvey 1995).

7. It is, in this context, not surprising to find a great number of geographical tensions, conflicts, and struggles arising in many parts of the world, and many of them are certainly not even remotely emancipatory, liberating, or empowering. The labor unrest in South Korea, the first European-wide strike, and workers' action against the closure of the Brussels Renault factory (a closure which had of course everything to do with overproduction in the sector and little to do with globalization), the genocide in Central Africa, the rise of anti-internationalist and deeply regionalist struggles (exemplified by the rise of the extreme right in Europe or of the localist militia in the USA, or the regionalist struggles that are dotted on the world map), but also the recent waves of plant closures, company restructuring, bank collapses, and turmoil in the financial markets bring out the profound spatial tensions and contradictions that arise out of the maelstrom of spatial transformations wrought from recent changes in the organization of capital circulation processes.

8. In this networked economy, in which people, goods, and commodities move with greater ease (although with significant remaining barriers), it is a relatively limited number of urban and regional economic growth engines that are dotted over the maps of America, Europe, or Asia that have become nodal points in the governance and structuring of these global networks (Castells and Hall 1994; Scott 1998).

Of course, the rhetoric and partial practice of globalization has decisive ideological connotations. Invoking processes of irreversible internationalization and open competition has prompted a '*pensée unique*' in which each government at whatever geographical scale of governance inscribes itself, while pursuing policies in tune with market-led strategies (Scholte 1996). While the verbal pyrotechnics of the globalization discourse insist on the logic of an untrammeled market-Stalinism, it has become increasingly clear that the economic success of cities and regions is highly dependent on the local sectoral and institutional configuration and on the framework of governance in which regional or urban economies are embedded. As locational opportunities expand and locational capabilities increase, so does the importance of 'local' characteristics of cities and regions in maintaining or asserting their competitive advantages. Indeed, the enduring economic success of regional configurations such as Ile de France, London, Bavaria, Flanders, Randstad Holland, and others, suggests that competitive success is indebted to specific and historically created forms of territorial and socio-institutional organization (Swyngedouw 1998, 2000).

Consider for a moment how these regional economies are characterized by often highly specialized local or regional *filières* that are embedded in local institutional, political, or cultural frameworks. A fragile balance of co-operation and competition, and a very dense layering of formal or informal networks provide the anchors for powerful—but often volatile and vulnerable—urban or regional economies. A host of new terms have been suggested to capture such competitive growth complexes: 'learning regions' (Maskell and Malmberg 1995), 'competitive cities' (Kearns and Philo 1993), 'reflexive economies', '*milieux innovateurs*' (Aydalot 1986), 'associational economies' (Cooke and Morgan 1998) are among the many metaphors introduced in recent years. They all refer to the importance of local embedding, networking, flexible organization, the presence of market-sensitive institutions, learning ability, and with a strong internal connectivity among the key economic and political elites. Whether Silicon Valley, the City of London, or the engineering complexes of Baden-Württemberg are considered, the existence of dense and intense networks of relationships among private companies or between the private and the public sector seem pivotal in explaining their competitive attraction. Of course, such territorial complexes are always in a myriad of ways (organizationally, financially, trade relations, marketing, R&D, and the like) inserted in and part of the processes that operate at national, continental, or global scales.

An apparent contradiction emerges out of this new economic spatial 'gestalt'. That is, a more intense and successful global competition coincides directly with a growing power, importance, and, hence, re-enforcement of local urban and regional production milieux. Companies and economic activities are simultaneously intensely local and intensely global. Whereas the national economic configuration was the central arena to assess economic performance during the high days of capitalism's postwar success, the national scale has lost its pre-eminent position to the extent that urban and regional economic complexes have become the new centers for successful economic growth. In other words, an economic geographic rescaling has taken place over the past two decades, leading to a new economic articulation between different geographical scales. While global interdependency increased and global competitive pressures intensified, territorial urban and regional institutional-economic configurations have become pivotal in determining the economic success of individual companies. This process of economic 'glocalization' (global localization) is schematically presented in Figure 27.3 (Swyngedouw 1992*a*; 1997). A new 'scalar' gestalt of the space economy is increasingly asserting itself as a prime force in articulating and shaping the space economy of the world.

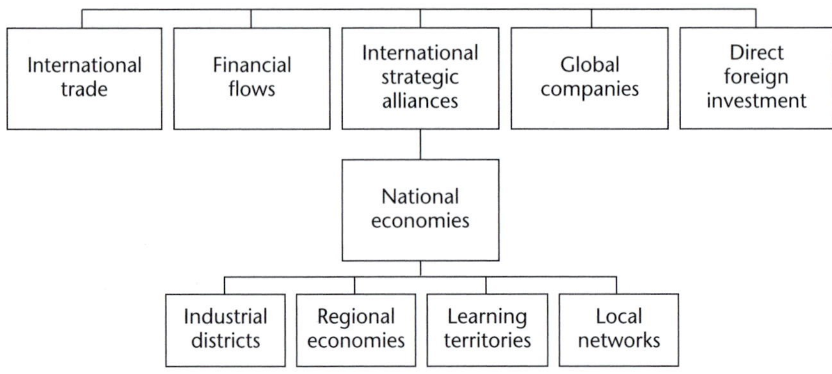

Fig. 27.3. Glocalization I: the rescaling of the economy

The Re-scaled State: From Government to Governance

Parallel to the spatial reorganization of the economic process, the institutional and political-territorial structure has also changed rather dramatically over the past twenty years or so. In particular, a significant geographical rescaling of the systems and institutional organization of governance has taken place. The national state, once the central arena for the political-economic structuring of the national territory (including citizenship rights and entitlements), has begun to transform itself, partly from within and partly from without. The Fordist and Keynesian state has not only altered its form of governing, but, perhaps most importantly, the State has to some extent 'hollowed out' as a result of a powerful process of down-scaling and up-scaling of forms of governance (Jessop 1994*a*, 1994*b*; Swyngedouw 1992*b*, 1997). In addition, the market-led reorientation of much of the state apparatus in most countries has resulted in an increasing privatization or externalization (to the market) of social and economic regulatory and organizing systems that hitherto had remained in the exclusive domain of the State. The State has set itself 'off-side' as a means to reassert the power of the market to organize the social economy (Strange 1996). Needless to say, this is having profound effects on the power and position of the citizen *vis-à-vis* the processes that shape his or her living and working environment (Cerny 1996; Hirst 1997). The pressure to create more competitive economic structures coincides with a more prominent role of local or regional forms of governance (both formally and informally organized and within a variety of institutional settings). In addition, a proliferating number of supranational forms of governance have increasingly usurped roles and powers that hitherto belonged to the exclusive domain of the State. While urban and regional institutional structures (private, public, or mixed) have asserted a much greater importance in shaping territorial development trajectories, supra-national organization, such as the International Monetary Funel (IMF), the European Union, North American Free Trade Association (NAFTA), the Group of Eight (G-8), and many others, have also risen to prominence. These new forms of governance (which are of course in many ways radically different from the classical democratic State form in terms of accountability, democratic control, or citizen's representation) and the emerging new relationships between refashioned or newly established institutional scales are often characterized by the formation of new coalitions of economic, cultural, and political elites on the one hand and by the systematic exclusion of politically and economically weaker social groups on the other. In Europe, for example, from Sweden to Greece and from the UK to the Baltic States, these new 'glocal' forms of governance are increasingly apparent. Figure 27.4 summarizes this re-articulation of the scales of governance. This new 'gestalt' of political scale that arises from this double movement of the geographies of governance results in the emergence of a growing number of often not very transparent institutions, organizational structures, competencies, political and economic agendas, and the like. The 'glocalization' of governance is often paralleled by a loss of democratic control, reduced citizenship rights, social disempowerment for some, and a growing influence and power for (inter)national or regional economic elites in the new rescaled systems of governance. These new elite coalitions are playing a central role in the promotion of a 'boosterist' climate, in perpetuating the 'ideology' of the market, and in pursuing a reliable 'business' climate (Swyngedouw 2000).

Of course, the rescaling of the State by no means implies a diminished role for the national state (Weiss 1998). On the contrary, the global-local forms of governance that are instrumental in reshaping regional social economies do so in close association with the State apparatus. They rely heavily on the State's legal,

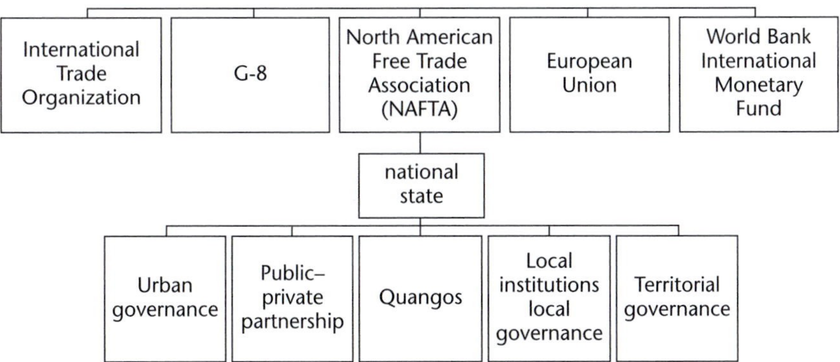

Fig. 27.4. Glocalization II: the rescaling of the State (from government to governance)

regulatory, and financial power to push through their development vision. The 'hollowed out' State is characterized by a double authoritarian touch, both at the super-national and the local level. The production of a post-Fordist socio-economic space is paralleled by a far-reaching political-institutional organization and by a more limited and rather new type of citizenship rights and powers (Swyngedouw 1996*a*).

Needless to say, the 'glocalization' of both the economy and governance has a decisive effect on the competitive structure of cities and regions in the new international division of labor. This is the theme I shall turn to in the next section.

Urban and Regional Development Reconsidered

The Rise of Institutional Theory: A Heterodox Approach

The rediscovery of the region in recent years as a key site to gain competitive advantage in a more open international competitive environment is of course closely associated with the changes outlined above. The enduring potential of places like Milan, Baden-Württemberg, Munich, Catalonia, and others is—so the argument goes—based on local and locational advantages related to minimizing transaction costs, innovative potential, positive externalities, and close competitive co-operation among economic actors on the one hand, and political and cultural elites on the other. Their success is explained not primarily by the economic structure, but by the particular institutional web, the informally (or formally) codified practices of exchange and encounter, and the regulatory environment.

Porter (1990) and Krugman (1995), for example, insist on the role of endogenous growth potential and the importance of historically created positive externalities that lead to increasing scale returns. The latter, in turn, are closely related to geographical clustering and specialization. The spatial proximity of related activities and the interdependencies associated with such spatial specialization in terms of labor markets and availability of a particular skill composition, the existence of particular technological pathways, and a related enterprise culture produce a set of positive external effects and economies of scale that provide crucial elements in the production of competitive environments.

In addition, institutional theory also insists on how, in addition to merely economic advantages, the social, cultural, and institutional armature contributes to the creation and the perpetuation of an economically dynamic environment. In particular, emphasis is put on internal relations, associational forms, regulatory conditions, and institutional forms. Storper (1997) and

Storper and Salais (1997), for example, insist on the importance of 'relational assets' or 'untraded interdependencies'. These are goods that are not commodified and can, therefore, not be traded or easily transferred. They cannot be substituted because they are an integral part of the social, economic, and physical characteristics of the networks in which economic agents participate. They belong to the production milieu and produce bundles of non-pecuniary externalities that are embedded in the social and institutional configuration of the regional fabric. It concerns knowledges that are not easily codified or transferred, often based on close and relatively enduring contacts and exchanges, embedded routines and rituals, habits, and norms. They refer to what Bourdieu (1977) calls 'Habitus', and which are engendered through the particular historical-geographical trajectory of the region. A myriad of forms of competitive co-operation produce an environment that—as a collective social economy—is often more robust than the sum total of the individual actors (Swyngedouw 2000). This again shows the importance of institutions and 'forms of governance' in the economic process. These forms of institutional or organizational 'embedding' (Grabher 1993) have become increasingly more important as the national scale gave way to a mosaic of regional production complexes (Scott 1998).

Of course, the creation and maintenance of such fine-grained networks is full of tensions and conflicts. They rely heavily on clusters of elites that, despite their internally heterogeneous and conflicting positions, are able to create a fairly coherent and relatively stable 'growth coalition'. The role of the elites in the institutional enframing of regional economies is often neglected by traditional institutional theory; yet they are of paramount importance to grasp the changing choreographies of power that characterize the contemporary socio-economic landscape (Zukin 1991). In other words, the rise of institutional theory requires attention to the configurations of power that are inevitably associated with such new regional economies.

Growth Coalitions and the Role of 'Glocal' Elites

To the extent that institutional configurations are central in the structuring of urban and regional economies, the social actors through which this institutional embedding of economic process is organized play a pivotal role. Comparative international research has demonstrated that the existence of a close and 'hegemonic' growth coalition that weaves together public and private elites plays a foundational role in generating and maintaining competitive spaces (Judge *et al.* 1995). The success of cities and regions as diverse as Baltimore, Silicon Valley, Emilia-Romagna, Veneto, Flanders, Berlin, Bilbao, or Barcelona suggests that a coherent and relatively homogeneous coalition of local, national, and international elites is instrumental to initiating and maintaining a 'boosterist' climate and a competitive growth trajectory (Cox and Mair

1989). Such coalitions play a pivotal role in generating and mobilizing financial means, the establishment of formal or informal institutions or networks, the co-ordination of key power brokers in the area, and the formulation and dissemination of a clear and visionary image of the city or region that is capable of mobilizing large segments of the local population while portraying an image of dynamism and success to the outside world (Zukin 1996). At the end of the day, economic growth is carried by the economic, political, and cultural elites. It is social power that creates growth. Despite the popular rhetoric of 'blaming the victim' whenever a city or region is hit by crisis or recession (the unemployed, migrants, unions, and the like), persistent socio-economic decline and failure of regeneration signal either the absence of innovative elites or a dominance of traditional elites that desperately try to hang on to rapidly eroding positions of power, while the centers of economic power migrate elsewhere. Whenever the elites do not rule, the economy is in trouble.

Theories on growth coalitions originated with the seminal work of Logan and Molotch (1987). They argue that the economic success of a city (and by extension a region) is dependent on and related to the nature and structure of its political and, in particular, economic elites. Regional or urban growth benefits and is appropriated by associations of 'local' elites. The latter are more or less loose groups of 'self-interested', profit-maximizing economic agents and institutions that are actively inserted in the local economy. Their mission, as 'place marketeers', is to maintain or attract activities from which they benefit themselves. Such 'place entrepreneurs' are both catalysts of the market and market-makers. They initiate projects and initiatives and mobilize the necessary financial and material means, and political support to implement them (Lloyd and Newlands 1988). They occupy the hazy and grey, but rapidly expanding, terrain between the institutional players in the private and public sector at a variety of interlocked spatial scales. Their strategies are not only based on a skilful mastering and manipulation of existing or available market information, but are also actively engaged in the creation of the market in ways that benefit them. They command considerable political and economic power and exercise considerable influence on policy formulation, planning documents, regulatory procedures, even appointments to key posts. Their 'insider information' is significant and used effectively. An active and coherent 'growth coalition' co-operates with local politicians, the media, leaders of public and semi-public institutions (development corporations, Chambers of Commerce, unions, employers' federations, and the like) with a view towards generating a coherent vision and strategy. The underlying rationality, of course, is that the collective promotion of the city/region and forms of co-operation benefit the individual agent (Papadopoulos 1996; Stone 1993).

Such growth coalitions are often opposed by a diffuse set of individuals and social movements for whom the organization and future of the city or the region as a 'living space' is more important than profit maximization and the productive capacity of the city/region. They often organize to contest or undermine the excesses and adventurism of the economic growth machine. Of course, to the extent that opposition groups are capable of gaining power, they might successfully resist the 'growth machine'. Alternatively, elite players often strategize to co-opt or to integrate actual or potential conflict by incorporating such groups in the formal or informal networks they command.

The increasing importance of such elite configurations in shaping the socio-economic trajectory of regions is closely associated with the processes outlined above. First, in a context of global localization, specific local conditions are playing a much more important role in the determination of the competitive position of cities and regions. This gives greater prominence to regional networks, relations, and institutions. Secondly, the shifting and less interventionist position of the national state, and hence the hollowing-out of national regulatory prescriptions, moves the center of gravity for fostering and promoting a growth-oriented political-economic framework to the sub-national scale (together with a greater role for supra-national formations). These have become the pivotal domains for launching pro-active development strategies. The often non-democratic and little transparent organization and decision-making procedures and mechanisms at these scales of governance turn them into implicit or explicit elite playing-fields that permit shaping territorial trajectories in the image of dominant or hegemonic elite coalitions. These new, elite-based and led, institutions and networks have become key forms of governance and have—at least to some extent—replaced the State (often with the State's implicit or explicit consent) as rule-making, policy-formulating and implementing, and even executive organizations with powers that influence and shape a broadening range of socio-economic aspects (Swyngedouw *et al.* 1999).

Clearly, the particular composition of elite alliances, the interests, perspectives, and strategies of individual and collective players, the sort of interactions, the institutional capacities, and the like will shape trajectories in ways that are highly variegated and differ from place to place, further accentuating an already highly uneven global mosaic of regional spaces in the world economy. Of course, all manners of conflict and tension—both internally and externally—may stall the formation of or fracture existing growth coalitions (Swyngedouw 1996*a*; Baeten *et al.* 1999). The interests of different elite fractions do not necessarily run in parallel. Moreover, political, cultural, or economic elites do not always share the same interests or their power bases might be founded on different socio-territorial configurations. Divergent interests, centrifugal forces, competitive individualism, and other fractures may lead to disintegrated, disjointed, conflicting, and heterogeneous strategies. Old (traditional) elites might feel threatened by the rise of new power centers. The rise of 'glocal' elites, in particular, has accentuated tensions between traditional regional or national elites and the rising centers of power that operate simultaneously on a series of nested, but interrelated, spatial scales. Divergent accumulation strategies and power configurations produce all sorts of conflict that may limit the power of or fragment the institutional embedding of political-economic actors in systems of governance that enable the formation of the 'relational assets' and the 'untraded interdependencies' that provide key comparative advantages in the 'regional worlds of production' of 'glocal' capitalism. In addition, if mechanisms of co-optation and legitimization fail to bring broad layers from civil society in line with the visions of the elites, conflicts between elite projects and social movements might further erode the institutional base on which successful growth rests. More importantly, the systematic exclusion of often broad layers of civil society from the elite forums many undermine cohesion in civil society, intensify tension and conflict between systems of governance and the 'public', erode an already precarious position of the (elected) state apparatus, and even produce the sort of active or latent conflicts that could jeopardize any effort to produce a cohesive and hegemonic regional socio-economic fabric. In addition, the non-accountable, but extremely influential, new forms of governance shape urban and regional trajectories that might (or might not) be better positioned to engage in successful global competition. They also customarily ignore, silence, or side-step imaginings of possible alternative urban and regional futures (Mayer 1994). In particular, visions that do not put a premium on competitiveness and market rationality or those that emerge from social groups that lack the social power of those who command are customarily neglected, ridiculed, or marginalized.

Conclusion

'Globalization' has become part of a powerful political-economic ideology and practice through which capital–labor relationships, relative class power positions, and socio-spatial configurations have shifted in profound ways. While the rhetoric of globalization insists on the pervasive penetration of a global logic of the market, locally or regionally embedded strategies are heralded as the harbinger of revived and competitive economies and of social empowerment in an environment of allegedly reduced State power and of the 'death of government'. Without ignoring the more enduring and pervasive aspects of the current round of global restructuring of capitalism, the argument developed in this chapter insisted that—rather than a generalized process of globalization—the world economy is going through a process of reconfiguration of its economic and institutional 'scalar gestalt'. A new configuration of articulated economic spaces and scales of governance is rapidly emerging. A spatial economic analysis and policy that ignores the subtleties of power relations, the new institutional configurations, and the shifting power geometries that are associated with this process of 'glocalization' will invariably fail to account for or influence regional socio-economic development trajectories. In addition, my analysis suggests how mechanisms of social and political inclusion and exclusion are an integral part of restructuring processes. The recent search for idealized policy formulae and models for the economic regeneration of regions, based on generalized economistic models—varying from 'learning regions', 'reflexive economies', industrial districts, 'networked' regions to flexibly innovative places—will not only fall short of success if stripped of a political analysis that puts the dynamics of socio-political power and the socio-spatial choreography of power alliances squarely at the heart of the analysis, but also be oblivious to urgent questions about who decides and controls the path of economic change.

References

ALTVATER, E. 1993. *The Future of the Market—An Essay on the Regulation of Money and Nature after the Collapse of Actually Existing Socialism*. London: Verso.

AMIN, A., ed. 1994. *Post-Fordism: A Reader*. Oxford: Blackwell.

—— and THRIFT, N., eds. 1994. *Globalization, Institutions and Regional Development in Europe*. Oxford: Oxford University Press.

AYDALOT, P., ed. 1986. *Milieux Innovateurs en Europe—Innovative Environments in Europe*. Groupement de Recherche sur les Milieux Innovateurs en Europe, Université de Paris I. Paris: Sorbonne.

BACHTLER, J., and MICHIE, R. 1993. The restructuring of regional policy in the European Community. *Regional Studies*, 27: 719–25.

BAETEN, G., SWYNGEDOUW, E., and ALBRECHTS, L. 1999. Politics, institutions and regional restructuring processes: from managed growth to planned fragmentation in the reconversion of Belgium's last coal mining region. *Regional Studies*, 33: 247–58.

BENKO, G., and LIPIETZ, A., eds. 1992. *Les Régions qui gagnent*. Paris: Presses Universitaires de France.

—— —— 1995. De la régulation des espaces aux espaces de régulation. In *Théorie de Régulation. L'Etat des Savoirs*, ed. R. Boyer and R. Saillard. Paris: La Découverte, 293–312.

BOURDIEU, P. 1977. *Outline of a Theory of Praxis*. Cambridge: Cambridge University Press.

BOYER, R. 1989. *Regulation Theory: A Critical Perspective*. New York: Columbia University Press.

CASTELLS, M. 1989. *The Informational Society*. Oxford: Blackwell.

—— 1998. *End of Millennium*. Oxford: Blackwell.

—— and HALL, P. 1994. *Technopoles of the World—The Making of 21st Century Industrial Complexes*. London: Routledge.

CERNY, P. G. 1996. What next for the state? In Kofman and Youngs 1996: 123–37.

COOKE, P., ed. 1995. *The Rise of the Rustbelt*. London: University College Press.

—— and MORGAN, K. 1998. *The Associational Economy*. Oxford: Oxford University Press.

Cox, K., and Mair, A. 1989. Urban growth machines and the politics of local economic development. *International Journal of Urban and Regional Research*, 13: 137–46.

—— —— 1991. From localised social structures to localities as agents. *Environment and Planning A*, 23: 197–213.

Dunford, M. 1990. Theories of regulation. *Environment and Planning D: Society and Space*, 8: 297–321.

Fainstein, S., Gordon, I., and Harloe, M., eds. 1992. *Divided Cities: New York and London in the Contemporary World*. Oxford: Blackwell.

Featherstone, M., Lash, S., and Robertson, R., eds. 1995. *Global Modernities*. London: Sage.

Grabher, G., ed. 1993. *The Embedded Firm: On the Socioeconomics of Industrial Networks*. London: Routledge.

Group of Lisbon 1994. *Limits to Competition*. Cambridge, Mass.: Harvard University Press.

Hamnett, C. 1996. Social polarisation, economic restructuring and welfare state regimes. *Urban Studies*, 33: 1407–30.

Harvey, D. 1995. Globalization in question. *Rethinking MARXISM*, 84: 1–17.

Hirst, P. 1997. *From Statism to Pluralism*. London: University College Press.

—— and Thompson, G. 1996. *Globalization in Question*. Cambridge: Polity Press.

Hodgson, G. M. 1988. *Economics and Institutions: A Manifesto for a Modern Institutional Economics*. Cambridge: Polity Press.

—— 1993. *Economics and Evolution*. Cambridge: Cambridge University Press.

Jessop, B. 1994*a*. Post-Fordism and the state. In Amin 1994: 251–79.

—— 1994*b*. The transition to Post-Fordism and the Schumpeterian workfare state. In *Towards a Post-Fordist Welfare State?* ed. R. Burrows and B. Loader. London: Routledge, 13–37.

Judge, D., Stoker, G., and Wolman, H., eds. 1995. *Theories of Urban Politics*. London: Sage.

Kearns, G., and Philo, C., eds. 1993. *Selling Places*. Oxford: Pergamon.

Keating, M., and Loughlin, J., eds. 1997. *The Political Economy of Regionalism*. London: Frank Cass.

Kofman, E., and Youngs, G., eds. 1996. *Globalization: Theory and Practice*. London: Pinter.

Krugman, P. 1995. *Development, Geography and Economic Theory*. Cambridge, Mass.: MIT Press.

Lipietz, A. 1987. *Mirages and Miracles: The Crisis of Global Fordism*. London: Verso.

Lloyd, M. G., and Newlands, D. A. 1988. The 'growth coalition' and urban economic development. *Local Economy*, 3: 31–9.

Logan, J., and Molotch, H. 1987. *Urban Fortunes: The Political Economy of Place*. Berkeley: University of California Press.

Marx, K., and Engels, F. 1848/1985. *The Communist Manifesto*. London: Penguin Books. 1st edn. 1848.

Maskell, P., and Malmberg, A. 1995. Localised learning and industrial competitiveness. Mimeographed paper, presented at the Regional Studies Association Conference on 'Regional Futures', Gothenburg, Sweden, 6–9 May.

Massey, D. 1996. Space/power, identity/difference: tensions in the city. In Merrifield and Swyngedouw 1996: 100–16.

Mayer, M. 1994. Post-Fordist city politics. In Amin 1994: 316–37.

Merrifield, A., and Swyngedouw, E., eds. 1996. *The Urbanisation of Injustice*. London: Lawrence and Wishart.

Mingione, E., ed. 1996. *Urban Poverty and the Underclass: A Reader*. Oxford: Blackwell.

Moulaert, F. 1996. Rediscovering spatial inequality in Europe: building blocks for an appropriate 'regulationist' analytical framework. *Environment and Planning D: Society and Space*, 14: 327–45.

O'Brien, R. 1992. *Global Financial Integration: The End of Geography*. London: Pinter.

Ohmae, K. 1995. *The End of the Nation State—The Rise of Regional Economies*. London: HarperCollins.

Papadopoulos, A. 1996. *Urban Regimes and Strategies—Building Europe's Central Executive District in Brussels*. Chicago: University of Chicago Press.

Peck, J. 1995. Moving and shaking: business elites, state localism and urban privatism. *Progress in Human Geography*, 19: 16–46.

—— 1996. *Work Place*. New York: Guilford Press.

Porter, M. 1990. *The Competitive Advantage of Nations*. London: Macmillan.

Sadler, D. 1992. *The Global Region*. Oxford: Pergamon Press.

Sandercock, L. 1998. *Towards Cosmopolis: Planning for Multicultural Cities*. Chicester: J. Wiles and Sons.

Sassen, S. 1991. *The Global City: New York, London, Tokyo*. Princeton: Princeton University Press.

Scholte, J. A. 1996. Beyond the buzzword: towards a critical theory of globalization. In Kofman and Youngs 1996: 43–57.

Schumpeter, J. A. 1943. *Capitalism, Socialism, Democracy*. New York: Harper and Row.

Scott, A. 1998. *Regions and the World Economy*. Oxford: Oxford University Press.

Stone, C. N. 1993. Urban regimes and the capacity to govern: a political economy approach. *Journal of Urban Affairs*, 15: 1–28.

Storper, M. 1997. *The Regional World*. New York: Guilford Press.

—— and Salais, R. 1997. *Worlds of Production*. Cambridge, Mass.: Harvard University Press.

Strange, S. 1996. *The Retreat of the State—The Diffusion of Power in the World Economy*. Cambridge: Cambridge University Press.

Swyngedouw, E. 1992*a*. Territorial organization and the space/technology nexus. *Transactions Institute of British Geographers*, NS, 17: 417–33.

—— 1992*b*. The mammon quest: 'glocalization', interspatial competition and the monetary order: the construction of new scales. In *Cities and Regions in the New Europe: The Global-Local Interplay and Spatial Development Strategies*, ed. M. Dunford and G. Kafkalas. London: Belhaven Press, 39–67.

—— 1996*a*. Reconstructing citizenship, the re-scaling of the state and the new authoritarianism: closing the Belgian mines. *Urban Studies*, 33: 1499–1521.

—— 1996*b*. Producing futures: international finance as a geographical project. In *The Global Economy in Transition*, ed. P. Daniels and W. Lever. Harlow: Longman, 135–63.

—— 1997. Neither global nor local: 'glocalisation' and the politics of scale. In *Spaces of Globalization: Reasserting the Power of the Local*, ed. K. Cox. New York and London: Guilford and Longman, 137–66.

—— 1998. Homing in and spacing out: re-configuring scale. In *Europa im Glo-*

balisieringsprozess von Wirtschaft und Gesellschaft, ed. H. Gebhardt, G. Heinritz, and R. Weissner. Stuttgart: Franz Steiner Verlag, 81–100.

—— 2000. Authoritarian governance, power and the politics of rescaling. *Environment and Planning D: Society and Space*, 17.

—— Moulaert, F., and Rodriguez, A. 1999. Large scale urban development projects: a challenge to urban policy in European cities. In *Urban Redevelopment and Social Polarisation in the City*, i, ed. F. Moulaert, E. Swyngedouw, and A. Rodriguez. Report to the European Commission, DGXII, Framework IV Programme, Brussels, 1–33.

Weiss, L. 1997. Globalization and the myth of the powerless state. *New Left Review*, 225: 3–27.

—— 1998. *The Myth of the Powerless State—Governing the Economy in a Global Era*. Cambridge: Polity Press.

Zizek, S. 1997. Multiculturalism, or, the cultural logic of multinational capitalism. *New Left Review*, 225: 28–51.

Zukin, S. 1991. *Landscapes of Power*. Berkeley: University of California Press.

—— 1996. Cultural strategies of economic development and the hegemony of vision. In Merrifield and Swyngedouw 1996: 223–43.

Chapter 28

Economic Geography in Practice: Local Economic Development Policy

Amy K. Glasmeier

ECONOMIC distress is not new, nor is public policy designed to contend with recent state and regional differences in economic development. In the USA, waves of program development began with efforts in the 1920s to alter the economic circumstances of urban and rural areas (Nivola 1999). Such efforts have transformed the economic landscape of the nation, its cities, and rural areas—yet expressed targets of public policy, such as uneven development and poverty, have proved far more difficult to change (Nyden and Wiewel 1991).

In urban areas, federal and state economic development programs have had little effect on the loss of population and industrial employment and have failed to stem the inexorable decline of retail and consumer service sectors (Bingham and Meir 1997). In rural areas, economic distress arises from the decline in the price of commodities, international competition for natural resource-based products, changes in the use of raw materials, the legacy of external ownership of land and resources, and the historic impact of native lands appropriation, slavery, and the plantation economy. History bears witness to the complex origins of uneven development and persistent poverty. This may explain why policy has been largely deficient and ineffective in managing these long-standing problems in the USA. Economic development theory has provided surprisingly little practical or pragmatic guidance and insight into the search for resolutions of these types of overarching concerns.

Economic and urban development policy in the USA is the focus of this chapter. At first blush, the US emphasis may seem misplaced and lacking in generalizability; however, there is considerable convergence of policy prescriptions among the developed nations and, increasingly, among developing nations as well. In reciting the recent experience of development policy in the USA, Cox (1997), Peck and Tickell (1994, 1995); Peck *et al.* (1997), and others suggest that neoliberal economic development prescriptions are becoming increasingly pervasive. Nations and regions, strapped for resources, uncritically adopt US practices in order to contend with processes of globalization and economic change. Beneath such programs is a surprising convergence of policy efforts aimed primarily at reducing the cost of doing business in localities as a stimulus for change. This stands in stark contrast with programs of the 1960s and 1970s, which were explicitly aimed at redistributing opportunities for wealth creation and enhanced economic well-being. The problem of uneven development and unequal standards of living remains a challenge in most developed countries despite long-standing efforts to bring about regional convergence.

In this chapter, the economic development policy experience is reviewed at two geographic scales: the region and the city. In both cases, the discussion focuses on policy interventions and discourses on the resolution of uneven development. In the first part of the chapter, I review the standard economic development policy and practice of the last thirty years. After looking at the broad realm of economic development policy, recent developments in urban economic development policy are discussed, emphasizing the role played by public sector programs in addressing inner-city decay and persistent poverty. In taking this two-level approach, I explore how economic geographic concepts are embedded in policy prescriptions, often with little regard for the weak links between conventional theories of economic development and the underlying development problems found in inner cities and troubled rural areas (Dewar 1997).

In the early 1980s, debates about the failure of policy to eradicate poverty and bring about more even development placed blame largely on bad macroeconomic policy and the lack of dynamism in the national economy. The extraordinary US economic resurgence in the last ten years has done little to transform deep pockets of urban poverty or protect communities ravaged by technological change and increasing economic globalization (Tu 1999; Wyly and Hammel 1999). In the 1990s it could be said that macroeconomic policies have actually made things worse by privileging increased trade and low inflation twinned with limited government expenditures for economic adjustment (Braun 1991). As the economy moves toward a world of high skills based on advanced education, big swaths of American society, and by implication many places, are being left behind. Market-based palliatives are simply unable to address the deep-seated nature of many contemporary development problems. Unless government is willing to re-open a dialogue about the need to redistribute resources and to provide access to those failing to achieve economic well-being, we will begin the next century as a society of those with access and those without—certainly an ominous prospect.

Evolving Paradigms in State and Local Economic Development: Three Waves (and Perhaps a Fourth)

The First Wave

State and local economic development policy in the USA evolved since the end of World War II in a cumulative succession of 'waves', or paradigms. Prior to World War II, the first wave of development policy consisted of industrial recruitment by state and local development officials and politicians. Businesses were lured from one region to another, usually from a high-cost to a low-cost region, with the promise of cheap labor, a hospitable business climate, and lax regulations. The South's program of replacing agriculture with industry rested on a fundamental belief in industrial attraction (Cobb 1984; Glasmeier and Leichenko 1996). In the late 1970s when job decline in the Northeast and Midwest went from relative to absolute losses, the search for a new source of economic development became a matter of survival (Johnson 1988; Rosenfeld 1986; Shulman 1991). Although states' recognition that 'not all jobs were created equal' dates at least to the early postwar years, by the late 1970s with Silicon Valley and Route 128 as a backdrop of successful high-tech development, state development officials began to recognize that to either build or attract such investments required a new set of strategies (Glasmeier 1987).

Second Wave

The second wave of development policy consisted of a set of programmatic interventions devised to augment local conditions through a combination of supply-and-demand-side inducements. Supply-side inducements took the form of efforts to improve the local business environment through investments in infrastructure, capacity building, and technology transfer between public institutions, such as government laboratories and universities. Demand-side inducements attempted to create new markets for existing businesses by establishing export processing zones, export assistance programs, and public procurement programs. A large component of state-led supply-side programs shied away from more developmental efforts such as labor force develpment and focused solely on reducing the cost of doing business by providing direct business subsidies in the form of cash grants, in-kind services, or tax abatements.

Broadening the emphasis beyond simple recruitment, governments of predominantly industrial states, faced with economies racked by job loss and a lack of new start-ups, also emphasized retention of existing business and incubation of new start-ups, especially in high-tech sectors. Quite aware of the zero-sum nature of this interjurisdictional competition for 'new rateables' and jobs, and by the low odds of success, a new generation of elected leaders, particularly those in the Northeast and Midwest, were, by the late 1970s and early 1980s, ready for a more sophisticated strategic approach to state and local economic development. Thus the emphasis switched toward the creation of new jobs through the stimulation of small businesses and technology-based firms (Eisinger 1995). States became entrepreneurs investing in business activities that were presumed to pay off in new jobs and wealth creation.

The new policy instruments attempted to copy what was then thought to underlie successful high-tech development experiences. These more developmental policies were relatively short-lived as states and localities grew weary of the calls for patient capital and the need to create new business cultures. By the late 1980s, there was much disillusionment with these state and local entrepreneurial (or, as they were sometimes more accurately called, 'local industrial policy') approaches (Eisinger 1995). The fate of second-wave programs fell at the hands of political expediency.

Riding the Third Wave

So-called 'third wave policy development' attempted to redeem developmental policy efforts that were perceived to be intrusive of market processes, by putting a private sector face on public sector programs. Government would no longer provide business development services, but instead would act as a broker for private firms providing similar types of services. In addition, the third wave was characterized by some as emphasizing activities such as education and training and industrial modernization where market failures were considered prevalent. Third-wave prognosis regarding the previous generation of policy was that it was hard to use, cumbersome, and bureaucratic. Like business in general, state economic development policy had forgotten (or may never have known) who the 'customer' was. Programs were rigid in portraying business problems as uniform and hence prescribed one-size-fits-all solutions. They also missed the point that the short-lived political cycles require a more immediate payoff through market-based solutions. Third-wave thinking greatly influenced then Governor, soon to be President, Bill Clinton, and became an integral part of the Clinton administration's strategy when Robert Reich (another third-wave advocate) was designated US Secretary of Labor in late 1992.

Eisinger's survey of state economic development officials (1995) led him to conclude that by the mid-1990s, there was less diffusion of third-wave models among the states than might have been expected. In the early 1990s, close examination of expenditures for state economic development still reflected a bias toward industrial plant attraction. Funds expended to lure businesses dwarfed other initiatives by a large margin (see Bob Wilson's work in the early 1990s for figures; Schmandt and Wilson 1990). In the late 1990s, governors openly boasted of their hunting expeditions once again, hearkening back to the early days of branch plant attraction of the 1920s. Indeed, state officials seemed, to Eisinger, to be 'ambivalent' about economic development policy as a whole (1995: 149).

What seems to have happened in the last half of the 1990s is a consolidation of existing state approaches—what Eisinger calls 'a defensive posture having more to do with political survival than with effective economic development' (1995: 154). As part of this consolidation, Eisinger, Bartik, and other scholarly observers see a resurgence of first-wave thinking: a new round of competitive attraction policies (including both 'smokestack' and 'chip chasing'). In this round, the targets are often foreign companies looking for attractive production sites inside the USA. These big ticket items are proving to be quite costly as exemplified by Alabama's estimated $168,000 per job pledge to Mercedes Benz (Bartik 1995), which won Birmingham a new auto assembly plant in 1996; that city's incentive package holds the record to date (Eisinger 1995: 151). Given the rising stakes associated with the resurgence of smokestack and chip chasing, economic development consultants and progressive policy makers have been provoked into calling for 'claw back' provisions requiring companies to return public funds if their economic benefits failed to materialize (Schweke 1999).

Until recently, most empirical evidence documenting the effect of recruitment and business incentive programs suggests that incentives matter as 'tie breakers', when companies are choosing between two similar site locations (Glickman and Woodward 1989). In many cases firms do not change their initial decisions when offered more incentives at one site than another. In the aggregate, the cost of incentives offered to firms that stay the course with their initial decision exceed the tax revenues generated from firms that do change their decisions. There is also no evidence that incentives diminish the disadvantages of high-cost locations. Incentives may in fact serve to reinforce uneven development. Fisher and Peters's results show that the top twenty and bottom twenty location positions are not altered by incentive packages. Winning locations are winners regardless of tax incentives, while losing locations lose regardless of how much they provide in the way of benefits (Bartik 1995; Fisher and Peters 1998).

The Emergence of a Fourth Wave? The Revitalization of the Cluster Concept

At the end of the 1990s, another round of policy innovation appears to be emerging with the encouragement of industry clusters. The origins of the renewed interest in clusters can be traced to three key academic treatises of the early 1980s and 1990s: Allen Scott's 1980s work on transactions costs and the formation of the Los Angeles conurbation (1988); Michael Piore and Charles Sabel's influential chronicle of the growth and development of the industrial districts of Central Italy (1984); and the 1990 publication of Michael Porter's widely cited book, *The Competitive Advantage of Nations* (1990). Building on insights that date back to the early part of this century and the work of Alfred Marshall and other more recent theorists of the 1960s, the three different perspectives converged on one core insight: economic activity tends to be sectorally concentrated and geographically clustered in space.

Gazing out at the Los Angeles economy teeming with activity, Allen Scott saw a landscape composed of a multitude of small firms interacting and participating in the same sector, filling niches in the supply base of larger and more diversified firms (Scott 1988). Arguing the existence of niche players that emerge in response to highly contingent demand too small in scale to warrant internalization by bigger firms or too difficult to specify with the exactness of contracts, these producers comprised nets of transactions held together by sectoral specialization and geographic proximity.

Coming to the problem of industrial development from an institutional economics perspective, Piore and Sabel argued that small, highly innovative, and sectorally focused firms offered a way out of the Fordist dilemma of mass production and dependence on big firms (Piore and Sabel 1984; Sabel 1989). Whereas Scott's and Piore and Sabel's work provided the theoretical basis of small firm cluster development from a spatial and microeconomic perspective, Porter built on his earlier work on business strategy with the publication of his book, *The Competitive Advantage of Nations*, arguing that a nation's wealth and opportunity were tied to the success of the sectors in which it had a competitive advantage. Almost overnight a new policy domain had been charted as local and state governments quickly latched on to the new buzz words of networks, clusters, external economies, and so on.

The growing pervasiveness of this new development strategy was further deepened by the independent efforts of economic development consulting groups proselytizing the benefits of sectorally based development plans (Rosenfeld 1995; Sabel 1992). Providing further legitimacy to the cluster idea, states such as Minnesota, Oregon, and New York set up authorities and programs to nurture and encourage the growth of existing industry concentrations. Many state programs drew on the institutional program design of business services practised in Central Italy and Denmark.

Opinion varies considerably about whether this additional wave of policy innovation offers much new to the field of development. In the last five years both the major development agency of Emilia-Romagna, known as ERVET, and the Danish Technology Institute have fallen on hard times (Glasmeier 1999). Today they provide fewer services to the firms they were set up to help in their own areas, spending more of their time selling themselves as models of development to other agencies of government. In the USA, the equivalent policy response, the Manufacturing Extension Partnership (MEP) program, has as yet been unable to do more than help firms reduce the cost of doing business. The hoped-for transformation of the nation's businesses toward high-road strategies that value workers, build skills, and compete on quality rather than solely on price have so far eluded policy (Luria 1997).

Why the emphasis on clusters now? Isn't this just revisiting old ground? Wassily Leontief, Hollis Chenery, Francois Perroux, Walter Isard, Gunnar Myrdal, Benjamin Chinitz, William Alonso, Brian Berry, and, especially, Albert Hirschman are some of the leading architects of this body of theory whose writings have been fixtures on the reading lists of students of development planning in the USA, Europe, Latin America, and South Asia for many years. These theoretical perspectives are complemented by a large number of empirical statistical studies done in the 1960s and 1970s to suggest the extent to which firms found in space actually transact business locally. Bennett Harrison pointed out in a classic article that what distinguishes present from past discussions of industrial clusters is the contemporary emphasis on non-market forms of interaction, including trust and non-traded interdependencies (Harrison 1992). These presumed interactions are employed with great frequency in the theoretical development literature to explain spatial behavior, but are not matched by comparable studies that actually measure such non-market forms of interchange (see Fuellhart 1998 and Fuellhart and Glasmeier 1999 for exceptions).

Since the late 1980s, numerous studies tested the efficacy of cluster strategies (Harrison *et al.* 1992; Harrison *et al.* 1995; Kelley and Helper 1997). The underlying assumption is that the tendency of firms to cluster geographically is sufficiently general to warrant all of this strategic policy intervention that starts from the fact of such agglomeration (Doeringer and Terkla 1995). But just how important, how common, is this 'fact' and to what extent is clustering something other than a reflection of the evolutionary cycle of industrial development? Do firms or individual plants within particular sectors always agglomerate? To the extent they are found in space together, do they transact business and hence benefit from or create external economies?

Empirical research shows that some do more than others, and that history matters. That is, firms in dynamic, 'young', information-intensive sectors such as biotechnology certainly tend to concentrate in a few locations at first. Over time, ageing firms expand locally, branch out to other places, 'reinvent' themselves through restructuring and strategic alliances, or disappear, while new firms are born into the original and/or newer sites. The result over time is 'diffuse development'.

For policy purposes, it is necessary to determine why many industrial (and, for that matter, service) sectors tend to agglomerate to at least some extent or in certain stages of their evolution. Theory offers two possible explanations for this observed pattern, each suggesting its own set of policy directions. Some companies seem to benefit by clustering with others that make similar or closely related families of products. Thus we have steel-making districts, places whose firms specialize in producing computers, and complexes devoted to optics. This is known as 'localization'. For other companies, however, when it comes to innovation, the most important aspects of a successful location have to do with proximity to a broad mix of economic activities—firms from many different sectors, research labs, and trade associations—as well as a dense fabric of social and cultural institutions. Economists, planners, and geographers call this 'urbanization'.

Urbanization and localization need not be mutually exclusive. Los Angeles, for example, has a rich mix of civic and commercial institutions along with a population speaking a dozen languages and practicing thousands of occupational skills: that's urbanization. But Los Angeles is also home to at least three highly concentrated industrial districts focusing on entertainment, aerospace, and garment making. Similarly, central New Jersey—site of the greatest concentration of pharmaceutical companies in the USA—also boasts rich ethnic and cultural diversity and an array of businesses in scores of unrelated industries. Most regions tend not to be so balanced.

There is now considerable evidence that innovation and economic growth derive unambiguously from a locale's urbanization, and (in some settings) from a sectorally narrower industrial specialization (Glaeser *et al.* 1992; Glasmeier 1987; Harrison *et al.* 1992; Harrison *et al.* 1995; Kelley and Helper 1997; Kelley and Arora 1998). Diversity of information, institutions, and workers' skills—rather than concentration of companies in a particular industry—appears to be key among cities that grow faster and periodically reinvent themselves.

Embedded in discussions of sectorally specific spatial clusters is the presumption that ease of learning by firms is heightened by spatial proximity. Hence learning is seen as an outgrowth of clustering, which is presumed to facilitate change and lead to new technological development. One key to long-term survival and adaptability is the availability, circulation, and absorption of new information by firms. And yet, by itself, firm learning is history based and draws explicitly from a firm's previous successes. It is precisely the reinforcing nature of spatial clustering of like firms that tends to deepen relations within, as opposed to between, firms in other domains. Firms found in space together have no greater advantage in identifying, acquiring, and acting on new non-regular information than firms separated in space. In fact, history demonstrates that clustering of firms in the same industry often leads to a strong sense of self-satisfaction and self-administered evaluation of the basis for success that often leads to myopia and rigidity. Levitt and March, two distinguished scholars of organizational theory, argue that the conventional behavior of an organization in the process of learning is based around:

> three classical observations drawn from behavioral studies of organizations. The first is that behavior in an organization is based on routines. Action stems from a logic of appropriateness or legitimacy more than from a logic of consequentiality or intention. The second observation is that organizational actions are history-dependent. Routines

are based on interpretations of the past more than anticipations of the future. The third observation is that organizations are oriented at targets. Their behavior depends on the relationship between outcomes they observe and the aspirations they have of those outcomes. (Levitt and March 1988: 322)

This passage reveals a significant divergence between how firms actually act in the process of learning and how the archetypical learning organization is described in contemporary management literature. There is a significant divergence between the normative vision and the actual behavior of firms. It is obviously important to keep in mind how organizations actually learn as opposed to how we might hope or wish they would learn, if we are to avoid reading into an organization's behavior actions that are not commonplace occurrences. Learning is built upon routines and tends to reinforce rather than depart from the status quo. Thus, rather than being amenable to explicit intervention, the antecedents of successful industrial concentrations are long in formation and subject to path dependence (Glasmeier and Fuellhart 1996).

Even Porter's own work on present-day complexes points to the perplexing problem that 'success often breeds failure'. As former collaborator Michael Enright points out, while Porter's work provides an *ex ante* explanation of cluster composition, it lacks the ability to isolate characteristics that predict the creative forces which lay behind the formation of successful, integrated regional economies (Enright 1993, 1995).

Perhaps the more serious shortcoming of the renewed interest in industrial clusters and complexes as it relates to economic development is proponents' failure to appreciate the unique circumstances under which such descriptions apply. From Perroux's seminal writings in the 1950s onward it has been recognized (but largely ignored) that cluster/complex models of development only apply to locations where a substantial accumulation of diverse economic activity already exists. Scott's work on Los Angeles chronicles a complex that *is*, not one that is becoming. The project is an attempt to tease out of an existing agglomeration a new form of economic activity, but the seeds of potential future development are already there. Los Angeles is not an isolated plain. A far more vexing problem, for which clusters as a development strategy may not apply, are those locations lacking the economic mass necessary to support specialization. We may wish cluster development to be, but it only occurs where there are sufficient levels of economic activity to support the creation of new markets and to warrant the formation of industrial linkages.

At this point it is important to ask what, if anything, has been accomplished by standard economic development practice to ameliorate the problems of inner cities and rural areas and to lessen the economic uncertainty faced by the nation's most vulnerable citizens. Clearly the economic development policies just described are responsive mainly to short-run problems of labor market adjustment and the perceived shortcomings of contemporary business practices. Most are spatially indiscriminate, allowing interested firms to make location selections based on their own competitive calculus. Very few are designed to confront structural problems of enduring importance. Although reducing poverty and uneven development and providing jobs for disadvantaged citizens are often invoked as the rationale behind development policies, in fact these policies are not designed to reconcile problems of deep poverty and economic abandonment. Most contemporary policy, rhetoric aside, relies upon a model of development diffusion based on the principle of benefits trickling down to troubled targets. Conventional policy has yet to find the key that unlocks the fates of truly troubled locales. In this next section I explicitly examine recent policy developments that focus on resolving and if possible avoiding the old policy problems that attend uneven development.

Urban Policy Context

Although long considered a problem primarily of aging industrial belt states and of the nation's largest cities, evidence recently compiled by the US Department of Housing and Urban Development (HUD) suggests that no region, no city of even small size is immune to urban decline. Similar conditions can be found around the country, including both Sunbelt and Frostbelt regions as well as smaller and medium-sized cities and inner suburbs. HUD's recent report, aptly titled *Now is the Time: Places Left Behind in the New Economy*, demonstrates that the conditions of urban America are far more varied and more troubling than characterizations of the late 1970s and 1980s would imply (HUD 1999). The problems of big cities were thought to be uniform in content and selective in geography. Urban abandonment arose largely in response to deindustrialization and the massive job losses occurring in the nation's older industrial areas.

In contrast, a new phenomenon seems to be emerging in cities in the West and South where inner-city areas suffer from an absence of enough jobs to provide for their burgeoning populations swelled by immigration. Many smaller cities of the Southwest and Western USA, long dependent on limited sources of income such as a single manufacturing plant or a community economic base dependent on natural resource exploitation, also find themselves with rising unemployment, a limited skill base, and growing poverty populations. It seems that no urban location is immune to the effects of economic change and in many instances they face the specter of longer-term absolute decline (Miller 1999; Pack 1998).

The problem, though perhaps exaggerated in the USA, is evident in other developed countries including Japan and Great Britain, and in city regions such as the Ruhr in Germany. The sources of decline are summed up in deindustrialization, movement of population and industry to the suburbs facilitated by federal highway expenditures and mortgage interest and property tax deductions, and a reconcentration of immigrant populations in aging housing stock within the confines of older inner suburbs and central city areas. Vacant buildings, boarded-up storefronts, decaying infrastructure, and deserted streets are all grim reminders of the decline of urban areas.

How have states and localities come to grips with such issues? Over the past ten years a number of new initiatives reflect the need to incorporate all relevant actors and institutions in the process of community development. This stands in sharp contrast with programs of the 1970s and 1980s, which tended to be topdown and bureaucratically driven, demonstrating striking parallels with the one-size-fits-all form of program design found in economic development practice of the same era. As in the broad economic development arena, new calls for more integrated programming have begun to make inroads in the design of new policies. Especially in the field of urban and community economic development, old disciplinary, functional, and areal boundaries that, in the past, sharply marked off one subject—and place—from another are becoming blurred. These new developments stand in sharp contrast with those of conventional economic development practice which still by and large resists intergovernmental collaboration and regionalization of activities.

Enterprise Zones Come of Age with Uncertain Results

To contend with inner-city decline, the idea of enterprise zones and programs designed to respond to the special disadvantages of inner-city urban areas reached new heights of acceptance when the Clinton administration created the Empowerment Zones and Enterprise Communities (EZEC) program. According to President Clinton, the EZEC program was a community investment strategy 'which would empower people to determine their own future' (Clinton 1994). Federal funds would be provided to lucky communities that proposed development plans which emphasized economic opportunity; were built around notions of sustainable community development; operated through and developed community-based partnerships; and were guided by a strategic vision for change (Thomas 1995). Whatever else their accomplishments may turn out to be, these new HUD initiatives are clearly committed to an integrative spatially specific vision (Boyle 1995; Gibson 1998; Riposa 1996; Snow 1995; Sridhar 1996; Wright 1999). That alone represents a vast improvement over such superficially similar initiatives of a generation ago, like the Model Cities Program. In the nine federally designated Empowerment Zones and the ninety-five (less amply funded) Enterprise Communities, projects are transacting across the borders of the zones, reaching out to the wider region. An example would be a training program or a business loan program established over an entire labor market area rather than a single neighborhood or all within a single county. This contrasts with the past tendency of programs to be too spatially specific while ignoring the structure and extent of labor markets. And within the zones, human service, housing, education, skill training, transportation, and business development activities are frequently integrated through inter-agency task forces and committees. These programs aim to incorporate the most vulnerable citizens in new efforts toward change. The recent extension of the Community Reinvestment Act's coverage of small business loans as well as mortgage lending, and the explicit eligibility of community development activities for loans to satisfy banks' legal obligation for fair lending within poor geographic areas, will further reinforce this functional and spatial integration.

Michael Porter's Proposals for Inner-City Economic Development

Michael Porter is also becoming well known in economic development circles for his Institute for Competitive Inner Cities (ICIC) (Porter 1995). There is genuine excitement in the urban economic development policy community that Porter has turned his attention to the problems of the inner city. Porter is convinced that his strategic approach to development through the promotion of clusters of companies and activities is as applicable to inner-city communities as it has proven to be to whole nations. Thus, if locations (and the events of history) give rise to clusters, it is clusters that drive economic development. They create new capabilities, new companies, and new industry (Porter 1995: 57).

In 'The Competitive Advantage of the Inner City' (Porter 1995) (by which Porter means largely black, Latino, and immigrant-intensive low-income urban neighborhoods or enclaves), he begins by remarking on the surprising potential viability, even attractiveness, of such places. Location itself constitutes their most important potential competitive advantage. Why? Because these areas are often situated close to major business districts, accessible to shoppers from many directions, and generally near to major transportation and communications nodes. (Indeed, the southern segment of Los Angeles's South Central community, Watts, was once itself a major node in a region-wide trolley system.)

Of particular significance to urban development practitioners, many of Porter's themes have been sounded before. For three decades, community development activists have recognized that some of the poorest neighborhoods in our biggest cities are among the best situated in terms of access to the rest of their proximate region. It was commonplace in the research and policy literature of the 1960s and 1970s to remark on the paradox of high poverty rates for individuals and families co-existing with the substantial aggregate purchasing power of the community as a whole.

Why has Porter's call to arms struck such a responsive chord in the economic development community now, given that community-based development practitioners have long sung the same song? They are doing so for many of the same reasons that the Fortune 500, along with new high-technology start-ups, form boundary-spanning strategic alliances and other networks with one another, foreign companies and government laboratories, key suppliers, major hospitals, and other institutions. Networking gives them access to resources and information 'impacted' within other organizations and locations (Harrison and Glasmeier 1997).

Porter's strongest contribution to the new wave of thinking about inner-city economic development lies in the extension of his influential advocacy of planning for interdependent 'clusters' or sectors, rather than focusing on individual companies or occupations. He proposes that inner-city businesses exploit their potential linkages to other firms located outside their immediate neighborhoods by becoming suppliers or co-venturers. He even employs this idea as a framework for thinking about upgrading the skills of inner-city youth and other workers, suggesting that training, too, might usefully be organized by and around the region's most important or promising clusters, for example, under the governance of key trade associations.

While the importance of Porter's intervention cannot be underestimated, it still glosses over many critical, underlying problems that thwart or impede inner-city development. Problems of deep and intractable poverty will not be addressed by increasing the effectiveness of the local business sector in the absence of more interventionist and people-based programs.

Using Untapped Markets to Build Inner-City Economies

Of major and new significance is Porter's recent effort to highlight the potential of the inner-city market as a locus of demand (Initiative for a Competitive Inner City and the Boston Consulting Group 1998). Piggy-backing on this idea, a parallel effort has recently been launched by HUD Secretary Andrew Cuomo, to recognize the value of inner-city markets. Teamed with one of the nation's well-known accounting firms, Porter's ICIC undertook an empirical effort to measure the size of inner-city unmet demand. The results are quite impressive and suggest that weakness in the retail sector inhibits the formation of establishments to serve inner-city residents. Fear of crime, loss of merchandise, and unsteady cash flow are cited justifications for the underservicing of inner-city markets. Porter's work identifies a number of successful cases in which investments in inner-city areas to serve local residents have paid off abundantly.

The identification of urban inner cities as sites of untapped demand is an important restatement of the potential of urban areas; however, its focus on consumption draws attention away from the far more deep-seated problem of inner-city areas—the absence of job opportunities for its residents. This idea, too, has much earlier origins and points up many of the continuing challenges facing urban economic development.

Targeted Employment Programs

In response to the perceived failure of conventional policy to deliver jobs and economic opportunity to poor inner-city residents, a new set of initiatives more directly tied to the eradication of poverty has made an appearance in the last few years. Labeled as 'asset-based' programs, these largely non-governmental organization (NGO) and foundation-based programs emphasize the need to increase the wealth and enhance the access of the poor to the formal economy by directly intervening in the labor market and targeting job opportunities on a sectoral basis (Giloth 1995). These initiatives are incorporated under a broader umbrella of targeted economic development, job-centered, or employer-linked development efforts, funded largely by foundations and, to a growing extent, state governments. These new efforts directly engage the labor market by building organizations that target the labor market needs of firms in specific sectors such as the machine shop training program of Jane Adams Resource Corporation in Chicago or the hospital technician training program of Project Quest in San Antonio, Texas. Both of these programs identify growth sectors in their surrounding area and tailor their training programs to the specific needs of local business. Other programs work through existing intermediaries, including progressive Private Industry Councils, which are business-based organizations funded by the federal government to set local labor market program policy and to provide assistance to the hard core unemployed.

The impetus behind direct labor market engagement lies in several spheres. Perhaps most prominent is the effect of welfare reform and the requirement that the unemployed seek employment first as a prerequisite for maintaining some form of public support. The second is a realization that the labor market is not homogeneous, but rather is comprised of pockets of employment not easily accessed by blanket employment readiness or even training programs. Accessing such circumscribed sources of employment presents serious challenges due to significant market failures in information, institutional capacity, and biases based on class, race, and gender. Direct intervention in the form of sector programs and sheltered work programs are thus seen as necessary gestures simply to increase the number of jobs available to hard-to-place citizens long locked out of the labor market, and to overcome institutional failures that sequester available jobs, thereby limiting their access to all but the best-connected, job-ready workers.

Welfare-to-Work Stimulates Need for New Policies

Welfare-to-work programs are abundant and the subject of intensive investigation and evaluation. The decline of welfare rolls around the country has been striking. In some states the decline has been as much as 80 per cent. In states such as Wisconsin, the decline has been met with documented success in placing former welfare recipients in jobs paying living wages. State officials readily acknowledge, however, that their initial expectations of the need for ancillary services to make the transition to work had led them to seriously underestimate the resources required to support successful transitions of welfare families to work (Daskal and Sard 1998). Existing evidence points to the fact that while some families make the transition with success, there remains a core of people who will have special difficulty engaging the labor market. States such as West Virginia readily admit to not having solved the problems of the truly poor, and may never get the formula right to help many in greatest need (*New York Times*, 23 Aug. 1999).

President Clinton's fascination with locally grown development is clearly seen in his support for programs aimed at taking welfare recipients and turning them into entrepreneurs. The microenterprise development movement speaks directly to this interest. The growth in programs providing financial credit to would-be entrepreneurs has been meteoric. In less than ten years, microenterprise activities have gone from fewer than 100 or so programs providing guidance and resources for fledgling businesses, to more than 400 programs nationwide (Langer 1999). Modeled after the Grameen Bank in Bangladesh, these financing programs can now be found throughout the country in large and small cities and in rural areas.

Success stories are easily found among the many innovative programs (Servon 1997). Less conspicuous are systematic evaluations of the long-term success of businesses started and operated by the poor. The vast majority of projects provide business development training, a standard service of economic development agencies for the last twenty years. Could it be that the rise in the number of new microenterprise programs simply reflects a shift in the rhetoric of existing small business programs to an emphasis on microenterprise as a way to access new federal and state funds for business development? In an era in which other sources of economic development funding are declining, such a gesture makes sense. Indeed, one of the criticisms of the community development corporations and other foundation-funded organizations that provide economic development services is that they have grown increasingly unwieldy in size and distant from their original target of helping to eradicate poverty. No longer small and nimble, many community-based organizations now resemble a *mélange* of activities that have been grafted on as funding mandates and interests have changed.

Summary and Conclusions

More than forty years of policy have yielded many changes, and yet the most complex problems with the largest distributional implications have proved largely immune to transformation. Policy emphasis has almost completely abandoned as a goal the direct amelioration of long-standing problems of poverty and economic exclusion through programs specifically targeted at redistributing wealth. Distributional concerns have been replaced by a focus on policies that rely on trickle-down processes, limited government intervention, and market forces to bring about economic convergence. Much of contemporary policy programming has moved into the private or not-for-profit sectors with little regard for how to work with and effectively address the problems of groups in society who may be permanently unemployed. Faced with the requirement to prove quick 'success', many of these programs have been encouraged to 'cream' the participant pool for those individuals easy to place, train, and move into jobs. But what about members of society who prove difficult to place? The problem of labor market access is made ever more complex by the current period of continuous industrial restructuring which is leaving many people without hope of permanent labor market attachment. The older worker, the worker with very low levels of education, and single mothers are all increasingly finding access to only the lowest paying jobs, those that fail to provide a living wage. Initiatives like Porter's to bring consumption possibilities to inner cities are important steps, but these efforts, too, see the development problem as one of simple and correctable market failure; thus the goal of policy should be to make the economy conform to some behavioral standard. But the problems of inner cities and remote rural areas are not just the result of market failure. These are places that have literally had the foundations knocked out from underneath them and have been left to rot. Providing better inner-city consumption opportunities is a meritorious cause, but serving poor people better, far too many of whom are without work or lack the skills needed to hold a job, is not likely to lead to serious or meaningful revitalization. Unless there are concerted efforts to bring work and training opportunities to people set adrift in a world in which jobs are suburban in location and increasing in skill content, inner cities and remote rural areas will continue to stagnate. Sector-based programs sponsored by foundations and non-governmental organizations are far more realistic about the problems facing the nation's poorest citizens, but these interventions, too, fall short; they are few in number, small in scale, and their success remains highly dependent upon key individuals, thus raising questions about their replicability. Where does this leave us? What role do and can academics play in policy discussions about economic and urban development?

Across the eras of development policy, economic geographic theory has played more and less of a role in guiding programmatic undertakings. In some policy contexts, academics have warned decision makers of the limited likelihood of policy success given the initial conditions associated with uneven development. Despite warnings, policy makers have persisted and contemporary conditions verify the futility of these gestures. Renewed attempts by academics and practitioners to indiscriminately promote refashioned policy frameworks such as the contemporary fascination with clusters have been surprisingly silent on the limited applicability of such ideas to the problems of uneven regional development. Why, we might ask, have policy academics been so uncritical of attempts to use economic geographic theory to promote political development agendas? In part the problem may rest with the suspicion with which many academics view the policy process. Given its highly political and contingent nature, local development debates prove unsavory to all but the most strong-willed, thick-skinned, and opinionated. Most academics refuse to engage in the policy process. Another reason for the academic research community's failure to shape policy discourse may have to do with the disdain within its own ranks toward quantitative analysis, including hypothesis testing and model building, methods that might otherwise provide some systematic review of policy agendas. If we do not attempt to represent our theoretical hunches systematically, then we cannot be blamed for their misapplications in a policy context. Part of the problem also may be with academics' naïvety about politicians' use of their work, which is often for personal political gain. Numerous examples exist of academic research findings being taken out of context and fashioned into programmatic interventions that support dubious policy goals. A case in point is contemporary welfare reform. The shape of the existing program resembles in name only the design proposed by the concept's original architects. At the core, in the absence of discussion on the goals and purposes of economic development policy, we will remain in a period of policy formulation which favors interventions targeted toward either reducing the costs of doing business or improving the competency of firms. Such emphases will ensure that theory is invoked to justify current practice, further diverting attention from the deeper underlying bases of economic deprivation.

Acknowledgements

Had things turned out differently, this chapter probably would have been written either in conjunction with or with oversight from and commentary by Bennett Harrison. His untimely death prevented this possibility. The material in this chapter was formulated over a long period of time; elements were originally conceived as part of a larger report on American economic and urban development policy by Bennett Harrison, Karen Polenske, and me, for the Economic Development Administration. Karen Polenske was a co-author on the larger report and provided important commentary on and content to the original report. She also read this chapter and again offered her very reasoned and thoughtful insights. An earlier iteration of arguments made in this chapter was in an article Bennett and I published in the *Economic Development Quarterly*, which is cited in the text (Harrison and Glasmeier 1997). Neither Bennett nor Karen can be held accountable for the final chapter's central argument. I wish to warmly thank Meric Gertler for his very helpful and detailed comments on earlier drafts of this chapter. He went far beyond the call of duty as editor to see this chapter to fruition. Through dialogue the chapter became more focused and therefore, I hope, more helpful. While he was instrumental in attempting to ensure that the chapter is clear, he has no responsibility for its final form.

References

Bartik, T. 1995. *Economic Development Incentive Wars.* Kalamazoo, Mich.: Upjohn Institute, spring.

——1997. *Jobs for Welfare Recipients.* Kalamazoo, MI: Upjohn Institute for Employment Research. Spring.

Bingham, R., and Meir, R. 1997. *Dilemmas of Urban Economic Development: Issues in Theory and Practice.* Thousand Oaks, Calif.: Sage Publications.

Boyle, R. 1995. Empowerment zones: picking the winners. *Economic Development Quarterly*, 9/3: 207–11.

Braun, D. 1991. *The Rich Get Richer: The Rise of Income Inequality in the United States and the World.* Chicago: Nelson-Hall.

Clinton, W. 1994. Remarks on empowerment zones and enterprise communities. Transcript, *Weekly Compilation of Presidential Documents*, 30: 101.

Cobb, J. 1984. *The Selling of the South.* Knoxville, Tenn.: University of Tennessee.

Cox, K. 1997. *Spaces of Globalization: Reasserting the Power of the Local.* New York: Guilford Press.

Daskal, J., and Sard, B. 1998. *Welfare-to-Work Vouchers: Making Welfare Work.* Washington: Center for Budget and Policy Priorities.

Dewar, M. 1997. Why state and local economic development policy doesn't work. *Economic Development Quarterly*, 11/2: 113–32.

Doeringer, P., and Terkla, D. 1995. Business strategies and cross-industry clusters. *Economic Development Quarterly*, 9/2: 225–37.

Enright, M. 1993. Regional clusters and economic development: a research agenda. Revised paper originally presented at the Conference on Regional Clusters and Business Networks, Frederickton, New Brunswick.

——1995. Organization and coordination in geographically concentrated industries. In *Coordination and Information: Historical Perspectives on the Organization of Enterprise*, ed. N. Lamoreaux and D. Raff. Chicago: Chicago University Press.

Eisinger, P. 1995. State economic development in the 1990s. *Economic Development Quarterly*, 9/2: 146–58.

Fisher, P., and Peters, A. 1998. *Industrial Incentives: Competition among American States and Cities.* Kalamazoo, Mich.: Upjohn Institute.

Fuellhart, K. 1998. Networks, location and information acquisition: an analysis of small manufacturing establishments. Unpublished dissertation. Department of Geography, The Pennsylvania State University.

——and Glasmeier, A. 1999. The geography of learning, knowledge, and information acquisition of small- and medium-sized businesses. Submitted in 1999 to *Annals of The Association of American Geographers.*

GIBSON, G. 1998. Empowerment zones areas of serious doubt numbers on anti-poverty project raise questions about progress. *Lexington Herald-Leader,* A1.

GILOTH, R. 1995. Foundation perspectives on targeted economic development. *Economic Development Quarterly,* 9/3: 279–89.

GLAESER, E., KALLAL, H., SCHEINKMAN, J., and SHLEIFER, A. 1992. Growth in cities. *Journal of Political Economy,* 100/6: 1126–52.

GLASMEIER, A. 1987. Factors governing the development of high technology clusters: a tale of three cities. *Regional Studies,* 22: 287–301.

—— 1999. Territory-based regional development policy and planning in a learning economy: the case of 'real service centers' in industrial districts. *European Urban and Regional Studies,* 6/1: 48–68.

—— and FEULLHART, K. 1996. What do we know about how firms learn? EBIA International. Business Academy Annual Conference. Peer-reviewed Proceedings. Stockholm School of Economics (winter).

—— and LEICHENKO, R. 1996. From free market rhetoric to free market reality: the future of the U.S. south in an era of globalization. *International Journal of Urban and Regional Research,* 20: 601–15.

GLICKMAN, N., and WOODWARD, D. 1989. *The New Competitors.* New York: Basic Books.

HARRISON, B. 1992. Industrial districts: old wine in new bottles? *Regional Studies,* 26: 469–83.

—— and GLASMEIER, A. 1997. Why business alone won't redevelop the inner city: a friendly critique of Michael Porter's approach to urban revitalization. *Economic Development Quarterly,* 11/1 (Feb.): 28–38.

—— KELLEY, M., and APPOLD, S. 1992. *Production Networks and Locational Context: A Research Prospectus.* Pittsburgh. Working Paper Series, School of Urban and Public Affairs. Carnegie Mellon University.

—— —— and GANT, J. 1995. *Innovative Behavior and Local Milieu: Exploring the Intersection of Agglomeration, Firm Effects, and Technological Change.* Cambridge, Mass.: John F. Kennedy School of Government, Harvard University.

Initiative for a Competitive Inner City and the Boston Consulting Group 1998. *The Business Case for Pursuing Retail Opportunities in the Inner City.* June.

JOHNSON, M. 1988. *High-Technology Branch Plants as Labor-Oriented Industries in the United States South.* Report for US Department of Commerce, Economic Development Administration.

KELLEY, M., and ARORA, A. 1996. The role of institution-building in U.S. Industrial Modernization Programs. *Research Policy,* 25: 360–80.

—— and HELPER, S. 1997. Firm size and capabilities, regional agglomeration, and the adoption of new technology. *Economics of Innovation and New Technology,* 8: 79–103.

LANGER, J. 1999. Investing in entrepreneurship: a learning dialogue for microenterprise in the United States. Unpublished master's thesis. Department of Urban Studies and Planning, Massachusetts Institute of Technology.

LEVITT, B., and MARCH, J. G. 1988. Organizational Learning. *Annual Review of Sociology,* 14: 319–40.

LURIA, D. 1997. Toward lean or rich? What performance benchmarking tells us about

SME performance and some implications for extension centers services and mission. In *Manufacturing Modernization: Learning from Evaluation Practices and Results*, ed. P. Shapira and J. Youtie. Washington: National Institute of Standards and Technology.

Miller, W. 1999. Sick cities—healthy regions. *Industry Week*, 1 (Apr.) Cleveland.

Mueller, E., and Schwartz, A. 1998. Leaving poverty through work. Review. *Economic Development Quarterly*, 12/2: 166–80.

Nivola, P. 1999. *Laws of the Landscape: How Policies Shape Cities in Europe and America*. Washington: The Brookings Institution.

Nyden, P., and Wiewel, W. 1991. *Challenging Uneven Development: An Urban Agenda for the 1990s*. New Brunswick, NJ: Rutgers University Press.

Pack, J. R. 1998. Metropolitan areas: regional differences. *Brookings Review* (fall), 26–30.

Peck, J., Dicken, P., and Tickell, A. 1997. Unpacking the global. In *Geographies of Economies*, ed. R. Lee and J. Wills. London: Arnold, 158–66.

—— and Tickell, A. 1994. Searching for a new institutional fix: the *after* Fordist crisis and global-local disorder. In *Post-Fordism: A Reader*, ed. A. Amin. Oxford: Blackwell, 280–316.

—— —— 1995. Social regulation *after* Fordism: regulation theory, neo-liberalism and the global-local nexus. *Economy and Society*, 24/3: 357–86.

Piore, M., and Sabel, C. 1984. *The Second Industrial Divide: Possibilities for Prosperity*. New York: Basic Books.

Porter, M. 1990. *The Competitive Advantage of Nations*. New York: Free Press.

—— 1995. The competitive advantage of the inner city. *Harvard Business Review*, 73 (May/June), 55–71.

—— 1997. New strategies for inner-city economic development. *Economic Development Quarterly*, 11/1: 11–27.

Reich, R. 1991. *The Work of Nations: Preparing Ourselves for 21st Century Capitalism*. New York: A. A. Knopf.

Riposa, G. 1996. From enterprise to empowerment zones: the community context of urban economic development. *American Behavioral Scientist*, 39/5: 536–51.

Rosenfeld, S. 1986. *Halfway Home and a Long Way To Go*. A Report to the Southern Growth Policies Board. Durham, NC.

—— 1995. *Industrial Strength Strategies: Regional Business Clusters and Public Policy*. Washington: The Aspen Institute Rural Economic Policy Program.

Sabel, C. 1989. Flexible specialization and the re-emergence of regional economics. In *Reversing Industrial Decline*, ed. P. Hirst and J. Zeitlin. Oxford: Oxford University Press, 133–76.

—— 1992. Studied trust: building new forms of cooperation in a volatile economy. In *Industrial Districts and Local Economic Regeneration*, ed. F. Pyke and W. Sengenberger. Geneva: International Institute for Labour Studies, 78–104.

Schmandt, J., and Wilson, R. 1990. *Growth Policy in the Age of High Technology: The Role of Regions and States*. New Brunswick, NJ: Rutgers University Press.

Schulman, B. J. 1991. *From Cotton Belt to Sunbelt: Federal Policy, Economic Development, and the Transformation of the South, 1938–1980*. New York: Oxford University Press.

Schweke, B. 1999. Linking incentives and employment programs. *Accountability: The Newsletter of the Business Incentives Clearinghouse*, 1/3: 1–8.

Scott, A. 1988. *New Industrial Spaces: Flexible Production Organization and Regional Development in North America and Western Europe.* London: Pion Press.

Servon, L. 1997. Microenterprise programs in US inner cities: economic development or social welfare? *Economic Development Quarterly*, 11/2: 166–80.

Snow, L. 1995. Community-building, place targeting, and empowerment zones. *Economic Development Quarterly*, 9/2: 85–198.

Sridhar, K. S. 1996. Tax costs and employment benefits of enterprise zones. *Economic Development Quarterly*, 10/1: 69–90.

Thomas, J. 1995. Applying for empowerment zone designation: a tale of woe and triumph. *Economic Development Quarterly*, 9/3: 17–28.

Tu, J. 1999. Prosperity in Washington often ends at city limits. *Wall Street Journal*, 1.

US Department of Housing and Urban Development (HUD) 1999. *Now is the Time: Places Left Behind in the New Economy.* Apr.

US General Accounting Office 1998. *Community Development: Progress on Economic Development Activities Varies among the Empowerment Zones.* Nov.

Wright, D. 1999. *Empowerment Zones/Enterprise Communities: Rolling out a New Program.* New York: The Rockefeller Institute.

Wyly, E., and Hammel, D. 1999. *Islands of Decay in Seas of Renewal: Urban Policy and the Resurgence of Gentrification.* Working Papers. Center for Urban Policy Research, Rutgers University. No. 148.

Part **VI**

Global Transformations

Section 13

Environment and Regulation

Chapter **29**

Markets and Environmental Quality

R. Kerry Turner

Introduction

EXPERIENCE shows that markets do not seem to have been invented, they just happen (Roodman 1998). The basic argument set out in this chapter is that while market forces are powerful engines of economic growth and technological change, their extensive impacts are far from benign. To a greater or lesser extent all markets need to be regulated and markets for environmental assets in particular require quite sophisticated management if future development is to be sustainable.

Having defeated socialist central planning philosophy and practice, market capitalism in the twenty-first century will need to meet the challenges posed by environmentalism (O'Riordan 1981), while still retaining a capacity to generate and secure material wealth creation. In 1982, for example, global income (gross domestic product) stood at approximately US$ 11,000 billion and by 1997 this had increased to US$ 29,000 billion. But is this process, or something like it, sustainable over the long run? This conundrum is made more difficult when it is further realized that between 1960 and 1991 the richest 20 per cent of all nations had their share of world income rise from 70 per cent to 83 per cent, while the poorest 20 per cent of countries suffered a fall from 2.4 per cent to 1.4 per cent (UNDP 1992 and 1994).

The trend towards an ever-widening gap between the richest countries and the poorest has been reinforced by a number of factors that in combination are ensuring that the disparity will persist into the future. Only the rich countries have the capacity to invest in more technological innovations, while the poorest countries have to rely on 'trickle down' technology transfers which often prove to be ill suited to local environmental and labour market conditions. Savings rates are low in poor countries that inhibit the investment and growth process. Debts burdens mean that too great a proportion of what is generated (usually via the export of income-inelastic goods) in poor countries is transferred out in the form of interest payments. Many poor countries are plagued by political instability and strife that inhibit inward investment and divert scarce domestic resources away from community wealth creation activities. Finally, population growth in some countries is so rapid that infrastructure investment is a permanent diversion from more direct income generation (Sandler 1998).

In summary, the economic history of the last one hundred years or so and contemporary economic growth theory confirm that the rate of technological change needs to continue to exceed the rate of population growth. If it does not, capital stocks per capita (the combination of reproducible capital, i.e. machinery, roads, factories, and so on; human capital, i.e. the stock of skills and knowledge embodied in people; natural capital, i.e. environmental assets; and social capital, i.e. value and belief systems in a society) will decline and the development path will be unsustainable (Pearce and Turner 1990).

Sustainable Development

The preliminary condition for sustainable development is that the stock of capital assets should be at least constant (if not increasing) over time. If this rule is breached, the next generation will be left with fewer opportunities for 'development' than the current generation enjoys (Pearce *et al.* 1989; Turner 1993). More strictly, it is not the stocks that need to be held constant but the flow of services that can be produced with the stocks. Technological innovation can result in the capital stock becoming more productive and so some elements of the aggregate capital stock may be diminished without necessarily violating the conditions for sustainable development.

The 'constant capital' rule has been interpreted in two main ways. The first is that it is the overall stock of capital that matters, not the status of any individual form of capital. This is known as 'weak sustainability' and requires the assumption that substitution possibilities exist and are feasible between the different forms of capital. On the other hand, strong sustainability assumes well-defined limits to substitution. Under strong sustainability a minimum necessary condition for sustainability is that separate stocks of aggregate natural capital and aggregate 'other' capital must be maintained. Keeping the natural capital base intact over time has been interpreted to mean conserving all 'critical' natural capital (e.g. life-support functions and services and supporting environmental attributes) that by definition is subject to irreversible loss. There are no plausible technological substitutes for climatic stability, stratospheric ozone, and topsoil or species diversity. Technological optimism, in this regard, is simply misguided (Ayres 1993).

Markets are a significant component in the capital accumulation process and therefore in sustainable development. Unfortunately, when it comes to environmental capital assets and their sustainable utilization, the role that free markets can play is not a straightforward issue. In many environmental contexts markets are missing altogether, in others the power of the market needs to be heavily regulated in order to safeguard natural resource bases and human communities. Further, the form of market management that is adopted is also a complex problem in its own right. Constant vigilance (national and international) is required to ensure that markets are not manipulated by the few, or are not indifferent to environmental and social degradation and inequities.

In the succeeding sections of this chapter a more detailed account of the market model will be presented together with the real world complications that inhibit its operation. The related issues of environmental assets valuation and the institutional contexts in which markets might operate will also be addressed. Finally, the different forms of market management to better protect the environment—regulations, incentive instruments, and voluntary agreements—are reviewed and evaluated.

Prices, Markets, and Sustainable Welfare

The classical economists of the eighteenth and early nineteenth centuries formulated the theoretical argument in favour of a system of freely operating market prices, under naturally competitive conditions (Mathias 1971). In principle, such an economic system would guarantee the lowest effective prices to the consumer and yield the most efficient allocation of resources between the different sectors of the economy. The ultimate test of efficiency and economic welfare was therefore a freely moving price level not distorted by government intervention. Parallel arguments applied the same sort of analysis of the operation of competition within a national economy to its operation between nations in the international economy. The model clearly contained some very strong assumptions about employment, strategic weaknesses, industrial competition trends, and anti-social and anti-environmental activities of various sorts. So even the classical writers themselves suggested qualifications in terms of protective legislation and subsidies to selected stakeholders in society. Later schools of economics have subsequently refined the theory of competitive markets thought to eventually emerge as what is known as the neo-classical liberal model of the economy. In its final form the model contains a formidable set of assumptions and required operational conditions.

Prices are traditionally associated with free markets and private enterprise. They play the role of essential value signals for decentralized decision-making within an economy. Markets are situations in which two or more economic agents (producers or consumers) have an interest in the same thing and enter an exchange transaction that results in all parties being better off (increased economic welfare) than they were before the transaction. Perfect competition exists when the 'things' being exchanged, a good or factor service (e.g. labour) is homogeneous; large numbers of producers and consumers are active in the market and all take the market price as given; and there is no current or near future uncertainty in the market place. To get competition to work, each producer has to operate with rising marginal costs as output is expanded, each consumer's subjective demand price falls (all other factors held constant); and markets need to be stable and free of price rigidities.

To guarantee efficiency in the allocation of resources, all spillover effects between economic agents, such as, for example, pollution generated by a production process that is emitted/discharged into the surrounding atmosphere or watercourse and impacts negatively on the activities or health of other producers or consumers, must be included in the relevant cost/price calculations. This is known technically as the internalization of all marginal externalities. For competitive equilibrium to be 'socially optional' in welfare terms, the resulting distribution of income and resources must be judged to be fair in contemporary society and across generational time (intragenerational and intergenerational equity); and the preferences of individuals (consumer sovereignty) must be the accepted basis for evaluation of resource allocations (Collard 1972; Varian 1987).

But real world competition is not perfect and therefore not efficient, let alone optimal. A policy based on unfettered market forces cannot be recommended because of the absence of automatic and stable transitions from disequilibrium situations. It is also not politically feasible to make a clear-cut partition between efficiency and redistributional equity criteria. What is at issue is the extent to which the market can operate as a decentralized investment allocation mechanism, bounded by pre-emptive political decisions on the general path of consumption over time. The market model's restrictive assumptions need careful re-appraisal once the complexity of the interrelationships between a growing socio-economic system, driven by rapid technological progress, and the supporting ecosystem processes, functions, and goods and services are realized.

Actual markets will be operating in contexts where marginal private cost (paid by the economic agent) may not be equal to marginal social cost (paid by society); the difference is an 'externality'. The competitive mechanism cannot be relied upon in these circumstances to deliver an efficient solution. The contemporary globalization process however is now generating systemic externalities (positive and negative, e.g. genetically modified organisms, new chemicals, super drugs, zero emissions vehicles, and so on, and their consequences) as endogenous technological innovation proceeds. *Ex post* environmental protection policy responses may not have much effect on the *ex ante* choices of alternative technological paradigms and trajectories, unless they are used together with pre-emptive environmental quality standards. Technical change within a paradigm is biased in certain directions, relies heavily on learning-by-doing, and is a cumulative process (Skea 1995). Thus the more extensive the market is, the greater the requirement may be to regulate it (Vatn and Bromley 1997).

Environmental Markets

For many environmental goods and services (waste assimilation/treatment, climate regulation, nutrient cycling, and so on) markets and prices are missing completely (Costanza *et al.* 1997). These types of 'public goods' provide non-rival and non-excludable benefits for society at large over varying geographical areas up to and including the global scale. The absence or excessive cost of exclusion mechanisms means that the discipline of the market is not available to control the efficient provision of such benefits and there is the danger that individuals, groups, or nations will free ride on the actions of others and levels of environmental protection and maintenance will be sub-optimal.

A 'free market' is then often a biased competition between marketed goods and services and 'environmental conservation' goods and services that are not marketed. Take the case of a coastal wetland which in a 'healthy' state with its ecological integrity and resilience capacity kept intact, provides a host of ecosystem goods and services, for example, maintenance of biodiversity, storm buffering service, pollution sink service, and so on. Under environmental change pressure a conflict may arise between stakeholders wishing to partially drain and convert the wetland for tourism and local recreation purposes and nature conservation interests. The wetland and conversion option appears to be financially profitable but the nature conservation option does not. Government intervention is required in order to 'level the playing field' so that a more comprehensive evaluation can be made of the options available. Such intervention can be a mix of regulation and the creation of markets in environmental functions. While free markets can emerge in which the various stakeholders bargain over the harm done by the environmental change, in practice managed markets (subject to government intervention) are likely to be more prevalent.

In the next section we return to the nature and characteristics of the interrelationships including the economic transformation possibilities that exist between an expanding economy and its underpinning ecological systems.

Non-convexities, Dynamic Externality, and Ecosystem Resilience

Standard economic theory adopts a somewhat simplistic (and narrow in temporal and spatial terms) approach to the interrelationships between socio-economic systems and the supporting ecosystems. The assumption that many commodities have adequate substitutes available at a price underpins the linear model of economic transformation (production and consumption) possibilities. Thus the standard economic efficiency approach to pollution control is illustrated in Figure 29.1.

The theory assumes that the marginal (per unit of pollution) benefit and cost

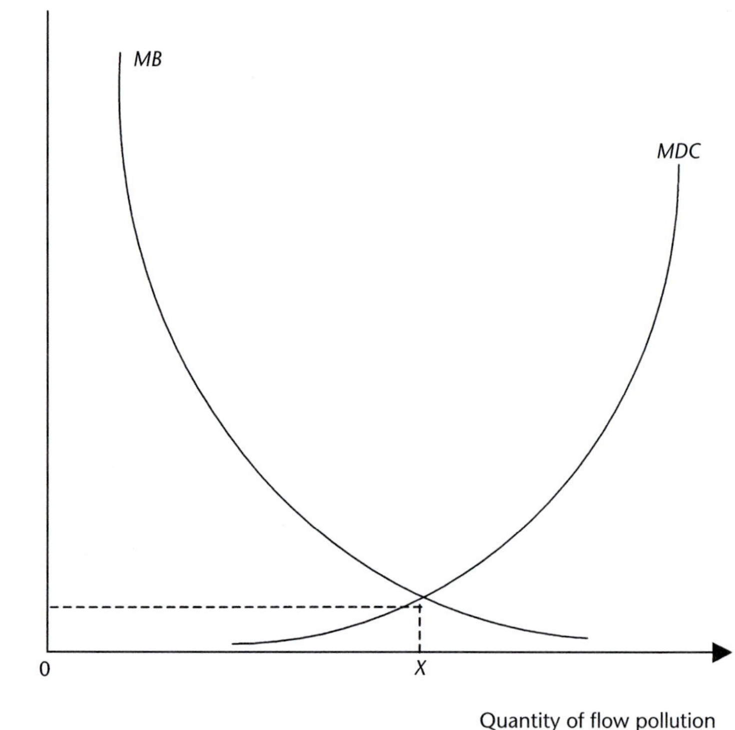

Fig. 29.1. Standard economic efficiency model of pollution

Notes: 0*X* = economically efficient level of pollution, where
MB = *MDC*;
MB = marginal benefits per unit of pollution;
MDC = marginal damage costs per unit of pollution.

functions associated with increased pollution are well behaved and that therefore the equivalent total cost curves are convex to the horizontal axis of the graph. Marginal benefits are assumed to be always decreasing while marginal costs are increasing. These well-behaved curves guarantee that if an equilibrium level of pollution exists it is unique. Therefore, if a set of complete markets exists, for example, for clean water or air or pollution control, the market will send the correct signal about the efficient level of pollution.

Discussion and analysis of policy relating to pollution is often conducted in terms of the amount of pollution control or abatement that is implied by efficiency considerations. Figure 29.2 illustrates the efficient level of pollution and pollution abatement analysis. Again convexity is assumed. As functions of pollution, marginal damages are continuously increasing and marginal costs of abatement are continuously declining.

However, for many biogeochemical systems the marginal benefit or cost

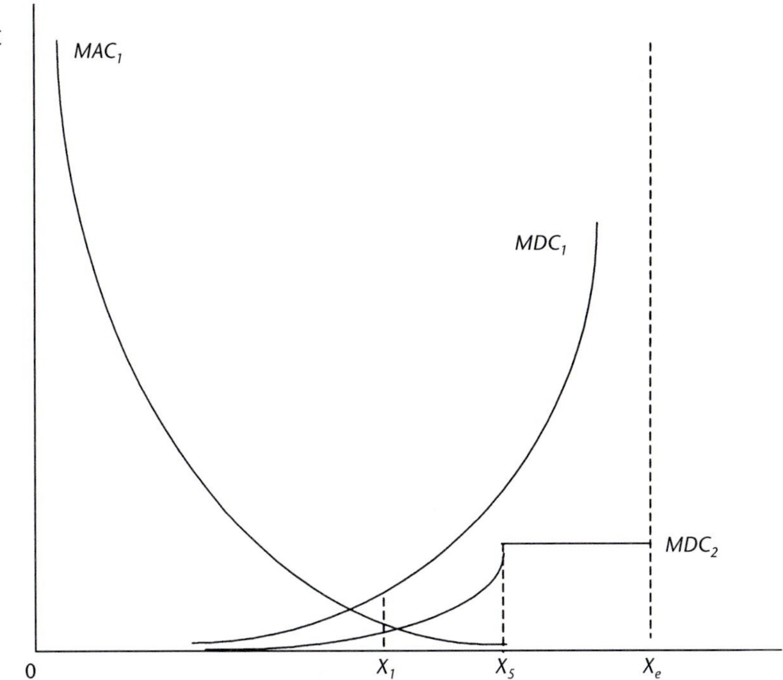

Fig. 29.2. Standard economic efficiency model of pollution control

Notes: X_e = level of pollution in an unregulated market economy;
X_1 = economically efficient level of pollution, minimizing the sum of abatement and damage costs;
X_s = threshold level.

Source: Adapted from Perman *et al.* (1996).

curve need not be well behaved and the total cost curves may not be strictly convex (U-shaped when viewed from the horizontal axis). If this is the case, the pollution level at which marginal costs of damage and abatement are equal is not unique. It may be, for example, that in the case of acid rain pollution, receiving water bodies reach saturation point when the acidity of the water reaches a threshold beyond which it fails to support aquatic plants and animals. So the marginal damage function is not continuously increasing, since beyond the threshold level no further damage is done as acidity continues to increase (see curve MDC_2 in Fig. 29.2). But the mere demonstration of non-convexity is not sufficient ground for concluding that this policy is relevant, in other words, that it has serious consequences for the design of pollution control policies (Burrows 1995).

The careful reader will have noted that the pollution illustrated in Figures 29.1 and 29.2 was labelled as flow pollution. Non-convexity is more policy relevant when another type of pollution, stock pollution, is considered and also when the pollution damage impacts threaten environmental state change at an ecosystem-wide level. In these more complex situations both temporal and spatial scale issues become important. Stock pollutants have been continually introduced into the ambient environment as economic growth has accelerated. Simplifying matters, flow pollutants tend to impose impacts, which are usually felt over relatively 'local' spatial areas and for short periods of time. By contrast, stock pollutants, including the release of contaminants, which are entirely artificial and persistent substances, once in the environment tend to bioaccumulate to a greater or lesser extent. Their damage effects can last for prolonged periods of time and can impact on large areas up to the global scale. In the most difficult case such as highly radioactive substances, their effect is virtually irreversible.

Figure 29.3 portrays the case of stock pollutants in the usual damage and abatement cost analysis. Movements along *MD* can take place only in a rightwards direction. There is almost no option to move down *MD* because of the accumulated stock of pollution in the environment, trapped in sinks such as sediments, wetlands, and other temporary traps. The removal of the stock is

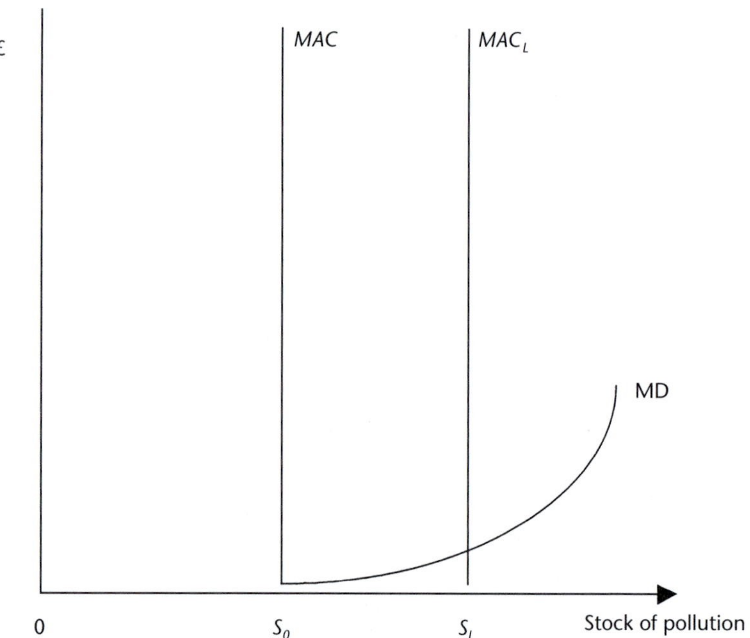

Fig. 29.3. Stock pollution damage and abatement costs

Notes: *MAC* = marginal abatement costs;
MD = marginal damage costs.

Source: Adapted from Pearce (1976).

typically not a practicable proposition. But critical to the standard economic approach to pollution is the requirement that the pollution variable be controllable in any direction. Since the stock of pollution is non-reducible, *MAC* must be vertical. If the stock level is S_0 and then increases to S_L, the *MAC* curve merely shifts to the right and no efficient level can be determined unless the initial stock is treated as a forgone cost (Pearce 1998). Concentrating only on subsequent releases, that is, the rate at which we move up the *MD* curve, economic efficiency analysis will justify additions to the stock. Given a positive discount rate (i.e. future costs are valued less than current and near term costs), the costs of pollution are shifted forward in time to future generations. Pearce (1976) has highlighted the risks posed in what he has called a 'dynamic externality' situation, when the emission/discharge of a pollutant exceeds the ambient environment's assimilative capacity and leads to a permanent and continual reduction in that capacity.

'Landscape' Scale Change

Where the weight of environmental pressures begins to impact on the functioning of ecosystems on a large scale, there is a risk posed to the integrity and resilience of such systems. Resilience is the capacity of the system to absorb disturbances without suffering significant changes in its functional characteristics. If a system loses its resilience, it can flip to a new state when subjected to even a small degree of stress or shock (non-convexities in ecological processes). Ecosystems often fail to signal the long-term consequences of loss of resilience and will seemingly continue to function normally in the short run. Because many ecosystems' goods and services are not marketed, the market mechanism cannot be expected to generate appropriate signals to warn society of impending instability in ecosystems. The societal response to environmental feedbacks is further inhibited by interrelated market and institutional failure phenomena (Turner 1991; Turner *et al.* 1997).

A range of factors such as high transactions costs can cause these 'failures'. These are costs related to establishing a 'market' in certain environmental or other contexts, and are increased wherever temporal and spatial distances become problematic. Market failure is also caused by missing, ill-defined, or unprotected property rights and inadequate and/or difficult-to-perceive information about environmental change effects. Environmental loss and degradation can equally well be caused by government (institutional) failure such as inefficient or uncoordinated resource management policies and inappropriate tax exemptions or subsidies of various sorts (Pearce and Warford 1993).

Increasing Returns to Scale

Another non-convexity problem is posed in situations where firms may experience increasing returns to scale, that is, new technologies are adopted which allow an increased set of inputs into production to deliver a more than proportionate increase in total output. The firms concerned can experience lower average costs of production, which then puts them in an advantageous position *vis-à-vis* competitors and encourages merger or take-over behaviour. Competitive markets are at risk and the prospect of oligoplistic (few large firms) conditions is raised. A number of commentators argue that multinational corporations have for some considerable time been engaged in a process of merger, cost-cutting, job-shedding, and strategic alliances. This poses a major threat to efficient decentralized resource allocation and the environment. Historically, the regulatory power of nation states was the prime restraint on the expansion of corporate power to influence markets. The processes of deregulation and globalization have effectively removed the constraint by placing corporations and finance beyond the reach of national public accountability. We return to the issue of local versus international economic power and the consequences for the environment in a later sub-section of this chapter.

The current and future environmental challenge for resource allocation mechanisms therefore includes the requirement to effectively assimilate dispersed information; to be adaptable in order to deal with coevolutionary interrelationships between socio-economic and ecological systems; and to avoid excessive myopia and gross power and income inequality. The market model utilizes a monetary metric as a common basis for the comparison of all relevant cost and benefits. The problem of environmental valuation has been the cause of extensive controversy and debate in both academic and policy circles.

Valuing Environmental Assets

In environmental economics, an individual preference-based value system operates in which the benefits of environmental gain (or the damages from environmental loss) are measured by social opportunity cost (i.e. cost of forgone options) or total economic value (Turner 1999*a*). The assumption is that the functioning of ecosystems provides society with a vast number of environmental goods and services that are of instrumental value to the extent that some individual is willing to pay for the satisfaction of a preference. It is taken as axiomatic that individuals almost always make choices (express their preferences), subject to an income budget constraint, which benefit (directly or indirectly) themselves or enhance their welfare. Households are assumed to maximize well-being deriving from different sources of value subject to an income constraint. Their private willingness-to-pay (their valuation) is a function of prices, income, and household tasks (including environmental attitudes) together with conditioning variables such as household size. The social value of an environmental resource committed to some use is then defined as the aggregation of private values. Nature conservation benefits should be valued and compared with the relevant costs. Conservation measures should only be adopted if it can be demonstrated that they generate net economic benefits.

Other environmental analysts, on the other hand, either claim that nature has non-anthropocentric intrinsic value and non-human species possess moral interests or rights, or that while all values are anthropocentric and usually (but not always) instrumental, the economic approach to valuation is only a partial approach. These environmentalist positions lead to the advocacy of environmental sustainability standards or constraints, which to some extent obviate the need for valuation of specific components of the environment. It is still necessary, however, to quantify the opportunity costs of such standards; or to quantify the costs of current, and prospective, environmental protection and maintenance measures (Ayres 1998). Nevertheless, for some people it is feasible and desirable to manage the environment without prices. According to O'Neil (1997), for example, conflicts of values in forestry and biodiversity management issues in the UK are resolved through pragmatic methods of argument between botanists, ornithologists, zoologists, landscape managers, members of a local community, farmers, and so on.

There is a growing body of evidence to suggest that humans in controlled experiments and in their everyday life systematically violate some of the conventional economic axioms. To take just one issue, it seems likely that individuals do recognize the 'social interest' and hold social preferences separate from self-interested private preferences. The origin of social interest may be explained by theories of reciprocal altruism, or mutual coercism, or by sociobiological factors (Sen 1977; Elster 1989; and Wilson 1987, respectively). The distinction between the individual as a citizen and as a consumer is not an either/or issue, but is more properly interpreted to mean that humans play a multidimensional role.

As citizens, individuals are influenced by held values, attitudes, and beliefs about public-type goods and their provision. In this context, property rights (actual and/or perceived), social choices, and moral concerns can all be involved in nature conservation versus development conflict. The polar opposite view to the conventional economic approach would hold that the very treatment of ecological assets such as biodiversity in terms of commercial norms is itself part of the environmental crisis. The argument becomes one of the 'proper' extents of market influences and commodification (O'Neil 1997). Market boundaries should not from this perspective be extended to cover as many environmental assets as is possible. Instead society should give greater consideration to the nature of deliberative institutions for resolving environmental problems and of the social and economic framework that will sustain them (O'Neil 1997). The counterbalancing argument would be that some environmental goods/services which have a mixed public/private good set of characteristics (e.g. forests watersheds, areas with ecotourism potential, and some aspects of biodiversity services) could be privatized or securitized (shares issued). In this way self-interest and the profit motive can be made to work in favour of environmental conservation (Chichilnisky and Heal 1998). Figure 29.4 summarizes three highly simplified and probably overlapping worldviews about the valuation and assessment of environmental quality (Turner and Pearce 1993; Gren *et al.* 1994; Garrod and Willis 1999; Bateman and Willis 1999; Turner *et al.* 1998).

Economic valuation data can play an important heuristic role in an extended cost-benefit analysis process, alongside other quantified but non-monetary data and more qualitative information derived from a number of possible deliberative process methods. At the 'sharp' end of policy/decision-making, politicians are required to satisfy multiple (often conflicting) policy objectives, under constrained budget conditions. The inevitable trade-offs involved require the setting of relative values either implicitly or explicitly, through an appreciation of the economic (opportunity costs) realities of life in a market-based economy and society, together with recognition of the moral issues and dilemmas present.

Institutional Contexts, Political Economy, and Global/Regional Public Goods

The institutional setting in which economic transactions take place conditions the form and the magnitude of the costs involved in such arrangements. Thus environmental externalities and their costs are related to the internal structure of the actual transaction arrangement in operation—markets or other arrangements. The clear distinction in environmental economic theory between polluter and sufferer and the presumption of value-neutral policy appraisal are both in practice highly questionable (Vatn and Bromley 1997).

Contemporary externality theory's two main doctrines—the Pigovian School and the Coasean School—are both open to critique on these grounds. The Pigovian approach makes the polluter liable and imposes an emissions/discharge tax on the polluter to internalize the externality and establish an efficient level of pollution. The Coasean approach focuses on the presumptive entitlement of one economic agent versus another. It is assumed that externalities are reciprocal, and in a world of zero transactions costs, the efficient 'bargaining' solution is determined on the basis of which agent can change behaviour most cheaply. In both approaches the rights and duties involved in a given pollution problem are assumed to be determined a priori.

In the real world, externalities appear outside the sphere of defined property rights and are often not recognized until long after the initial emission/discharge of the pollutants. Rights and duties concerning victims of pollution and compensation must therefore be established *ex post* by government. The greater the separation in space and time between pollution emission/discharge and a recognized impact on a receptor, the lower the coincidence between the cause of the pollutant release and the cause of the realized damage impact. The 'rights'

Simplified Typology

Mainstream position	Extended CBA position	Environmental management without prices
• individualism	• environmental systems, functions	• preferences not appropriate basis for valuation
• exogenous preferences	• individualism vs. collectivism—consumer and citizen motivations	• rights-based approaches environmental 'trump' cards
• fixed preferences	• endogenous preferences—psychosocial and cultural theory variables	• citizen motivations as a distinct and separate category
• rational self-interest	• expressed and revealed preferences	• keep 'markets' out of the environment
• marginal/discrete environmental changes	• focus group testing	• expert opinion
• revealed preferences via markets; household production functions	• benefits transfer	• contingent valuation as opinion polls
• positive rates of discount	• non-use values	• deliberative processes
• efficiency criterion	• validity/reliability testing protocols	
• social welfare	• equity criterion, policy trade-offs, economic welfare ≠ social welfare	
	• standards/regulations, cost effectiveness	

Fig. 29.4. Approaches to valuation

and 'wrongs' of the situation are laid down by societal norms and enacted through established institutions (determining what is internal and what is external). Vatn and Bromley (1997) have concluded that the very rules of market allocation requiring atomistic individual economic agents (protected by tailored private property rights) only serve to ensure that the potential for externality generation is always present. The market's operation increases the number of borders of interaction among economic agents, pushing up transactions costs and the risk of externality effects. It is also the case that not all externalities are necessarily either pure unintended by-products of economic activity, or intentional cost-shifting tactics by producers. But the latter motivation may become even more apparent in the future as new cost-shifting possibilities appear with the intensification of global industrial and financial competition.

Global and National Capitalism

Given their ability to transfer capital quickly around the globe, transnational corporations have assumed a key role in the globalization and environmental change process. It is now clear that corporate strategies will be pivotal to the success or otherwise of national sustainable development policies that have been promulgated during the 1990s. Analysts are divided over whether on balance transnationals serve to facilitate the international adoption of improved pollution abatement and environmental management practices; or serve to accentuate disparities in the distribution of the environmental costs and benefits, via 'pollution havens' in some developing countries, as change occurs.

On the pessimistic side, globalization may make it more difficult in the future to organize techniques at a local level to regulate access to common property resources such as grazing lands, forests, fisheries, and water resources. According to Korten (1995), there is a war going on between global and community forces of development. He draws a distinction between the global capitalism that empowers stateless corporations and the local capitalism that empowers people and communities. Corporations are potentially huge cost externalization engines, privatizing the gains from economic activity while socializing the costs by passing them on to the wider community. Activities such as strip mining forests, fisheries, and mineral deposits and hazardous waste dumping all serve to deplete the global natural capital stock and inhibit sustainable development.

But the relationship between corporate activities and the environment is neither simple nor unidirectional. Corporations have been put under increasing environmental pressure in many industrialized countries. There is a tendency for them to adopt the environmental standards of their original 'home base' nation and these are often much more stringent than environmental protection standards generally—the 'compliance plus' approach. Firms which can anticipate changes in environmental regulations may benefit from 'first-mover' advantage (Porter 1990), gaining internal cost reductions, new markets, and enhanced public image (Arora and Cason 1996). Properly designed environmental regulations can trigger innovation that may partially or more than fully offset the costs of complying with them. Relatively lax environmental regulations have stimulated 'end-of-pipe' or secondary waste treatment investment responses. Tougher regulations could force firms to take a new look at their processes and products, with the result that overall resource productivity (ecoefficiency) may improve dramatically (Porter and van der Linde 1995; Von Weizsäcker *et al.* 1997).

Large firms can also play a positive role in the promotion of sustainable development as they speed up the process of diffusing best environmental management practices (environmental audits, life cycle assessments, and so on) to firms in their own supply chain and beyond. The scope and magnitude of this 'ecoefficiency' revolution has been the subject of intense debate in the literature (Oates *et al.* 1994; Schmalensee 1993; Jaffe *et al.* 1995). The empirical evidence does not, however, support the 'pollution havens/industrial flights' hypothesis. There has not been a significant relocation of 'dirty' basic industries to developing countries. Environmental compliance costs have not been onerous enough or sufficiently differentiated country to country, to trigger corporate relocation. Labour cost differentials have been a far more powerful stimulus in this context (Jänicke *et al.* 1997).

Global and Regional Environmental Public Goods

At the international level not all global and regional public goods problems necessarily lead to inactivity and loss of environmental capital, as witnessed by the successful international cooperation that has seen significant reductions in sulphur emissions in Europe and in CFCs under the Montreal Protocol globally. Sandler (1998) has concluded that there is a need to better differentiate among global and regional public good problems in order to direct scarce policy-making resources to where they are most effective. In cases where each nation's contribution to the public good, for example, reductions in greenhouse gas emissions and global warming, adds to the overall level of the good (known as 'summation supply technology'), the outcome is often underprovision. If the benefit derived from an agent's contribution to the public good is less than the provision cost per unit, the dominant strategy is to provide none of the public good. An adequate provision would then require the intervention of some supranational structure.

Nevertheless, not all environmental pollution scenarios are necessarily linked to summation technology cases. In the case of the acid rain problem, for example, a 'weighted sum' technology applies and the 'do nothing' strategy need not dominate. For sulphur emissions a significant share of a given country's public good provision (impact of sulphur emissions reduction) is enjoyed by the country itself. This is because the wind and weather disperses the sulphur over relatively short distances, unlike nitrogen oxide, which is transferred long distances via atmospheric deposition. It is not surprising then that since 1985 significant cutbacks have been achieved in sulphur emissions, which is not the case for nitrogen oxides. The safe storage/containment of very hazardous wastes such as highly radioactive waste would be an example of a 'best-shot' public good supply technology. The overall level of the public good is equated to the largest individual provision level as the nation that makes the innovation determines the public good level of containment for all nations.

Income distribution can have a significant effect on the provision of the public good. Sandler (1998) believes that richer countries are becoming prone to 'foreign aid fatigue'. If the trend toward income inequality continues, these rich countries may have little choice but to provide global and regional environmental public goods, because of the 'best-shot' or 'summation' technologies involved. Rich countries will be forced to provide 'free rides' for the world community, by either subsidizing the poorest countries' provision, or providing it all. Supranational structures will be increasingly required to deal with pending environmental public good crises. Transactions costs can be very high when these structures are in operation and cost sharing or refund arrangements will have to be deployed to ease enforcement problems and costs. Market transactions such as, for example, pollution emissions trading can prove effective cost-saving devices when linked to the supranational structures.

The transition to a more sustainable path will require intervention policy in order to regulate and manage markets. The response will need to include modification of property rights structures, environmental pollution and resource taxes/charges, tradable permits, securitization schemes, regulations, local community control measures, and other devices to change individual and group incentives and to foster levels of trust and moral commitment. A suite of policy instruments will therefore have to be deployed in order to steer technological advances and mitigate environmental impacts. Flexible national and international institutions and regulations, together with so-called market-based incentive instruments, will form a combined enabling strategy. An element of precaution will also be necessary given the problems of ignorance through novelty. New technologies, for example, carry with them the potential for 'surprise'. They can lead to a cascade of impacts, with the secondary and tertiary effects being both large and unanticipated (Faber *et al.* 1996; Turner 1999*b*).

Policy Instruments

Until recently, environmental policy in most countries was dominated by direct regulatory measures, that is, legal instruments by which governing institutions, at all levels of government, impose obligations or constraints on the actions and behaviour of private firms and consumers, in order to protect the environment. Over the last fifteen years or so these direct 'command and control' measures have been slowly supplemented by market-based economic incentive instruments such as eco-taxes (e.g. the UK now has a tax on waste disposal at landfill sites). It is possible to categorize the main types of environmental regulation into three categories: command and control instruments, economic incentive instruments, and other instruments (see Table 29.1).

The political economy of regulation, public finances, and fiscal regimes is

Table 29.1. Categories and sub-categories of environmental regulatory instruments in OECD countries

1. Command and control instruments

These directly regulate behaviour affecting the environment, typically through permit and authorization procedures relating to the following:

(*a*) the products produced and distributed;
(*b*) the materials used in production and distribution;
(*c*) the technologies by which goods and materials are produced;
(*d*) the residuals which are released into the environment;
(*e*) the locations at which production and other economic activities take place.

2. Economic incentive instruments

These modify behaviour, using financial incentives and disincentives, to improve environmental performance through:

(*a*) charges and taxes;
(*b*) grants and subsidies;
(*c*) fines etc. for non-compliance;
(*d*) market creation mechanisms, such as emission permit trading schemes, and securitization schemes.

3. Other instruments

These, often containing a non-mandatory element, aim to improve environmental performance by (i) improving the supply of information relating to environmental problems and the ways of reducing them, and (ii) raising the level of voluntary commitment, both at an individual organization and collective level, to modify practices to reduce these problems. Elements of this approach are to be found in the following examples (although they also often contain elements of the other approaches):

(*a*) environmental planning, environmental impact assessment, life cycle assessment and related extended producer responsibility procedures: voluntary individual and association agreements to promote environmental policy objectives through industry covenants, negotiated agreements, self-regulation, codes of conduct and eco-audits;
(*b*) information disclosure schemes (voluntary or compulsory);
(*c*) environmental management systems and environmental audit procedures to improve cost-effective compliance with agreed environmental quality targets.

Source: Adapted from OECD (1997).

complex and mirrors the various stakeholders and political interests present in contemporary societies (Turner *et al.* 1998). In principle, market-based incentive instruments offer efficiency gains over direct regulation measures, although the magnitude of the efficiency advantage is conditioned by real world context and application. Moreover, economic efficiency is only one of at least six, not necessarily complementary, 'principles' that are thought to be relevant in any policy instrument choice situation (see Table 29.2).

The economic efficiency of a given instrument is, however, a useful starting point for any overall assessment of the political economy of environmental protection policy. A Pigovian economic perspective would focus on the introduction of prices, in the form of pollution emission charges and environmental taxes, for the use of the environment's goods and services. Increased scarcity value is assumed to result in reduced consumption. The government would take *de facto* ownership of the environmental assets concerned and their scarcity

Table 29.2. Political economy and green taxes

Economic efficiency principle	The instrument should interfere as little as possible with well-informed private resources allocation decisions in competitive markets; and should provide a continuous incentive for seeking least-cost solutions.
Environmental effectiveness principle	The instrument should be appropriately linked to the pollution and resource usage impacts problem so that effective mitigation results (in particular the minimization of health impacts and risks).
Fairness principle	The instrument should not be significantly regressive, i.e. should not impose a disproportionate cost burden on the least well-off in society.
Administration cost-effectiveness principle	The instrument should involve low administrative and compliance costs.
Institutional concordance principle	The instrument should be compatible with existing national regulations/legislation, and with European Union Directives; the industries affected should also be present in a majority of member countries in order that the rules of the single market are not seriously compromised.
Revenue raising principle	The instrument should be able to raise appropriate amounts of finance for given expenditures.

Source: See Russell and Powell (1999) for a more detailed and comprehensive taxonomy.

value would be internalized in the price charged for their use. There is extensive practical experience of this approach in Europe (OECD 1997).

The adoption of a Coasean approach would favour the encouragement of voluntary trading arrangements such as permit trading in fishing quotas or pollution emissions. Once the total allowable number of permits has been fixed, holders are allowed to trade permits in whatever market forms. In theory, firms with relatively high pollution control costs can continue to emit by buying additional permits, whereas firms enjoying lower control costs can continue to invest in clean up and sell their surplus permits for a profit. This flexibility should result in the minimization of overall pollution control costs. In the real world of imperfect competition, firms will have less than full information about permit trading opportunities and the trading process itself will not be free of transactions costs. The initial allocation of permits and the precise mechanism chosen for the allocation will influence the spatial and temporal pattern of emissions and abatement, as well as the economic fortunes of the individual firms. If permits were auctioned off, emitters would be required to pay for their individual pollution damage. But this procedure may be politically unacceptable in contexts where historic rights to emit have been entrenched in an existing regulatory regime and where substantial revenue transfers would be stimulated. The more pragmatic alternative is to 'grandfather' the permit, that is, allocating them free on the basis of historic emissions or previous regulatory controls (Sorrell and Skea 1999).

Another market-extending idea has recently been put forward by Chichilnisky and Heal (1998). They propose to 'privatize' natural capital and environmental goods and services, enlisting the support of market forces in nature conservation. The idea is to assign to corporations (or private–public corporate partnerships) the obligation of managing and conserving natural capital in exchange for the right to sell the services provided. Possible candidates are watershed services and ecotourism. In the watershed case, New York City was faced in 1996 with an investment choice between new sewage treatment plants, or restoration measures in the Catskill Mountains watershed. It turned out that the watershed restoration costs were $1–1.5 billion, as against capital costs alone of $6–8 billion for treatment plants. The city floated an 'environmental bond issue' and will use the proceeds to restore the functioning of the ecosystem in the Catskill watershed that provides for water purification and flow management. The cost of the bond issue and the interest payable on the bonds will be met by the savings from the avoided $6–8 billion sewage treatment plant capital, costs, and their running costs. Their cost savings could also have been 'securitized' via a 'watershed savings account' which would have received annual payments from the funds that would otherwise have to build and service the treatment plants. The account would then pay investors for the use of their capital. Given certain characteristics, namely that some of the ecosystem functioning results in goods/services which have commercial value that can also be appropriated by a producer, privatization or securitization is a feasible possibility for some environmental services. Services that fit this bill seem to include watershed services, preservation of flora and fauna as a basis for ecotourism, and, more problematically, biodiversity as a source of genetic knowledge.

Conclusions

Market forces are powerful engines of economic growth and technological change, but they also have extensive impacts. Local environmental damage and degradation are particular risks as the process of globalization and financial markets integration proceeds. The transition to an environmentally sustainable economy and society can be facilitated by the judicious use of market mechanisms and the selective extension of such transactions arrangements to environmental services previously not subject to such influences. Unfettered markets, however, are not likely to sustain the natural capital stock and flow of goods and services for future generations. Markets for environmental assets need to be regulated. Many environmental goods/services are close to being pure public goods and their optimal provision will require local, national, and supranational institutional arrangements, with the latter put in place and paid for by rich countries.

The eco-industrial transformation that is necessary to sustain future wealth creation opportunities and maintain an acceptable quality of life is likely to be too complex a process for rigid government planning. A flexible indicative planning strategy buttressed by managed markets can stimulate systematic change. A key component of such an approach is the application of the 'polluter pays principle' enabled via environmental fiscal reform and other policy instruments. The yet to be fully resolved trade-off is whether *ex ante* market regulations and precautionary environmental standards should be dominant, or less restrained market forces tempered *ex post* by taxes and changes, as and when externalities are recognized.

References

Arora, S., and Cason, T. N. 1996. Why do firms volunteer to exceed environmental regulations. *Land Economics*, 7: 413–32.

Ayres, R. U. 1993. Cowboys, cornucopians and long-run sustainability. *Ecological Economics*, 8: 189–207.

—— 1998. The price-value paradox. *Ecological Economics*, 25: 17–19.

Bateman, I. J., and Willis, K. G., eds. 1999. *Valuing Environmental Preferences.* Oxford: Oxford University Press.

Brouwer, R., Powe, N., Turner, R. K., Langford, I., and Bateman, I. J. 1999. Public preferences for environmental values. *Environmental Values*, 8: 325–47.

Burrows, P. 1995. Nonconvexities and the theory of external costs. In *The Handbook of Environmental Economics*, ed. D. W. Bromley. Oxford: Blackwell.

Chichilnisky, G., and Heal, G. 1998. Economic returns from the biosphere. *Nature*, 391: 629–30.

Collard, D. 1972. *Prices, Markets and Welfare*. London: Faber and Faber.

Costanza, R., *et al.* 1997. The value of the world's ecosystem services and natural capital. *Nature*, 387: 253–60.

Elster, J. 1989. Social norms and economic theory. *Journal of Economic Perspectives*, 3: 99–117.

Faber, M., Manstetten, R., and Proops, J. 1996. *Ecological Economics: Concepts and Methods*. Cheltenham: Edward Elgar.

Garrod, G., and Willis, K. G., eds. 1999. *Economic Valuation of the Environment: Methods and Case Studies*. Cheltenham: Edward Elgar.

Gren, I.-M., Folke, C., Turner, R. K., and Bateman, I. 1994. Primary and secondary values of wetland ecosystems. *Environmental and Resources Economics*, 4: 55–74.

Jaffe, A. B., Peterson, S. R., Portney, P. R., and Stavins, R. N. 1995. Environmental regulation and the competitiveness of U.S. manufacturing: what does the evidence tell us? *Journal of Economic Literature*, 33: 132–63.

Jänicke, M., Binder, M., and Mönch, I. 1997. Dirty industries: patterns of change in industrial countries. *Environmental and Resource Economics*, 9: 467–91.

Korten, D. C. 1995. *When Corporations Rule the World*. London: Earthscan.

Mathias, P. 1971. *The First Industrial Nation*. London: Methuen.

Oates, W. E., Palmer, K., and Portney, P. R. 1994. Environmental regulation and international competitiveness: thinking about the Porter hypothesis. Resources for the Future Working Paper, 94-02, Washington.

OECD 1997. *Reforming Environmental Regulation in OECD Countries*. Paris: Organization for Economic Cooperation and Development.

O'Neil, J. 1997. Managing without prices: the monetary valuation of biodiversity. *Ambio*, 26: 546–50.

O'Riordan, T. 1981. *Environmentalism*. London: Pion Press.

Pearce, D. W. 1976. The limits of cost-benefit analysis as a guide to environmental policy. *Kyklos*, 29, fasc. 1.

—— 1998. *Economics and Environment*. Cheltenham: Edward Elgar.

—— Markendya, A., and Barbier, E. B. 1989. *Blueprint for a Green Economy*. London: Earthscan.

—— and Turner, R. K. 1990. *Economics of Natural Resources and the Environment*. Hemel Hempstead: Harvester Wheatsheaf.

—— and Warford, J. 1993. *World Without End: Economics, Environment and Sustainable Development*. Oxford: Oxford University Press.

Perman, R., Ma, Y., and McGilvray, J. 1996. *Natural Resource and Environmental Economics*. Harlow: Longman.

Porter, M. E. 1990. *The Competitive Advantage of Nations*. London: Macmillan.

—— and van der Linde, C. 1995. Towards a new conception of the environment—competitiveness relationship. *Journal of Economic Perspectives*, 9: 97–118.

Roodman, D. 1998. *The Natural Wealth of Nations*. London: W. W. Norton.

Russell, C. S., and Powell, P. T. 1999. Practical guidelines and comparisons of instruments of environmental policy. In *Handbook of Environmental and Resource Economics*, ed. J. van den Bergh. Cheltenham: Edward Elgar, 307–28.

Sandler, T. 1998. Global and regional public goods: a prognosis for collective action. *Fiscal Studies*, 19: 221–47.

Schmalensee, R. 1993. The costs of environmental regulation. Massachusetts Institute of Technology, Centre for Energy and Environmental Policy Research Working Paper, 93-015, Cambridge, Massachusetts.

Sen, A. K. 1977. Rational fools: a critique of the behaviour foundations of economic theory. *Philosophy and Public Affairs*, 16: 317–44.

Skea, J. 1995. Environmental technology. In *Principles of Environmental and Resource Economics*, ed. H. Folmer, H. Landis-Gabel, and I. B. Opschoor. Cheltenham: Edward Elgar.

Sorrell, S., and Skea, J., eds. 1999. *Pollution for Sale: Emissions Trading and Joint Implementation*. Cheltenham: Edward Elgar.

Turner, R. K. 1991. Economics and wetland management. *Ambio*, 20: 59–63.

——ed. 1993. *Sustainable Environmental Economics and Management: Principles*. London: Belhaven Press.

——1999*a*. The place of economic values in environmental valuation. In Bateman and Willis 1999, 17–41.

——1999*b*. Environmental economics perspectives. In *Handbook of Environmental and Resource Economics*, ed. J. van den Bergh. Cheltenham: Edward Elgar, 1001–33.

——Adger, W. N., and Brouwer, R. 1998. Ecosystem services value, research needs, and policy relevance: a commentary. *Ecological Economics*, 25: 61–5.

——and Pearce, D. W. 1993. Sustainable economic development: economic and ethical principles. In *Economics and Ecology*, ed. E. B. Barbier. London: Chapman and Hall.

——Perrings, C., and Folke, C. 1997. Ecological economics: paradigm or perspective. In *Economy and Ecosystems in Change*, ed. J. van den Bergh and J. van der Straaten. Cheltenham: Edward Elgar, 25–49.

——Salmons, R., Power, J., and Craighill, A. 1998. Green taxes, waste management and political economy. *Journal of Environmental Management*, 53: 121–36.

United Nations Development Programme (UNDP) 1992. *Human Development Report 1992*. Oxford: Oxford University Press.

——1994. *Human Development Report 1994*. Oxford: Oxford University Press.

Varian, H. R. 1987. *Intermediate Microeconomics*. New York: W. W. Norton.

Vatn, A., and Bromley, D. 1997. Externalities—a market model failure. *Environmental and Resource Economics*, 9: 135–51.

Von Weizsäcker, A., Lovins, A. B., and Lovins, L. H. 1997. *Factor Four: Doubling Wealth, Halving Resource Use*. London: Earthscan.

Wilson, E. O. 1987. *On Human Nature*. Cambridge, Mass.: Harvard University Press.

Chapter **30**

Environmental Innovation and Regulation

David P. Angel

Introduction

EFFORTS to substantially improve the environmental performance of economic activity is emerging as a critical transformative challenge for firms, industries, communities, and policy makers in coming decades. Any analysis of such transformative dynamics will necessarily be inter-disciplinary in scope, drawing upon a wide body of scholarship in the human and physical sciences. This chapter lays out the contribution that economic geography might make to such an inter-disciplinary endeavor. The kinds of theoretical frameworks and analytical approaches that have emerged in economic geography in recent decades, building upon various forms of political economy, provide an important entry point to the analysis of economy–environment relations. At the same time, the increasing focus on economy–environment relations will undoubtedly yield further theoretical and empirical advances within the sub-discipline of economic geography itself.

The relation of economies to nature, or more accurately to the environment, is a growing concern both for economic geographers, and for the patterns of urban and industrial development that they study. Arguably, environmental performance has emerged as a driver of economic systems in ways and to a degree that has not occurred in the recent past. The roots of this upswelling in environmental concern are reasonably clear (for a recent review of the roots of US environmental policy see Andrews 1999). During the 1960s and 1970s a growing body of scientific evidence emerged documenting significant public health risks deriving from current patterns of economic activity, especially in the areas of air and water quality and exposure to toxic chemicals. At the same time, public awareness and concern over environmental issues grew rapidly in the 1970s (in the USA the timing of this upsurge is usually linked to the publication in 1962 of Rachel Carson's study *Silent Spring*). Particular events, such as the toxic waste site at Love Canal in the USA, the Chernobyl nuclear accident, and declining water quality in the American Great Lakes, had major impacts on public awareness of environmental risk and degradation. Public health concerns, consensus within the scientific community around industrial activity as a source of significant environmental problems, and a build-up in community pressure triggered a wave of intensified environmental regulation of industry within OECD economies. Industry itself began to initiate new, potentially significant, environmental programs from the late 1970s onwards.

Of course regulation of industry in response to environmental, health, and safety concerns is not new (consider, for example, the development of zoning and building code requirements during the early twentieth century). Five dimensions distinguish the current period and help to explain the growing interest in economy–environment linkages within economic geography. First, the long history of transformative impacts of economic activity on the natural environment notwithstanding (Turner *et al.* 1990), the worldwide expansion of production and consumption associated with the current phase of globalized capitalist commodity production is characterized by a substantial intensification of environmental impacts from economic activity. Rapid urban-industrial growth in East Asia, Latin America, and elsewhere has extended the spatial scope of energy- and materials-intensive industrial activity. Secondly, there is growing evidence that the environmental impacts of current and past economic activity go beyond localized environmental problems to degradation of the planet's life support systems (most notably in the areas of biodiversity and climate change). In other words, the emerging environmental challenge is less one of localized environmental quality than the biophysical sustainability of the current trajectory of energy and materials-intensive economic activity. There is now consensus within the science community that the escalation of greenhouse gas emissions into the atmosphere is a product of human economic activity and that these emissions result in a process of global atmospheric warming and associated climate change. There is at least anticipation on the part of many firms and industries that substantial change in the structure of economic activity will be required in response to climate change and efforts to abate greenhouse gas emissions. Thirdly, the development of information technologies has rendered more visible the international environmental effects of global production systems, reconnecting consumers in advanced industrial economies to environmental degradation deriving from extractive and processing activities dispersed to peripheral locations, and highlighting the kinds of environmental degradation accompanying economic marginalization within low income economies, from sub-Saharan Africa to the Amazonian rain forest. Fourthly, the emergence of civil society organizations as an influential international force and the growing capacity of local and regional non-governmental organizations (NGOs) around the world, have increased the pressure on industry to address environmental problems and on governments to implement and enforce environmental policies (Matthews 1997). Fifthly, in most advanced industrial economies firms are now subject to comprehensive national (and increasingly international) environmental regulation that shapes many aspects of economic activity, from technology choices to industrial location. Debate over the effectiveness and appropriateness of different approaches to environmental regulation has drawn further attention both to the environmental impacts of economic development, and to the economic effects of environmental regulation (Jaffe *et al.* 1995; Jorgensen and Wilcoxen 1990).

It is this set of processes that underlie widespread calls for 'changing course', for a shift to patterns of economic activity (both production and consumption) that are substantially less energy, materials, and waste intensive; in short, for a sustainability transition in the relation of economic activity to nature. Much of the research addressing issues of economy and the environment is inter-disciplinary in character, linking the analysis of biophysical processes to that of organizations and of societal change. With geography's rich history of research on various aspects of human–environment relations, the discipline is well placed to participate in this inter-disciplinary endeavor. Economic geography in particular has much to contribute through the extension of existing conceptual and empirical research on the dynamics of economic change to the particular problem of constraints and opportunities surrounding changes in the environmental performance of industry. The remainder of this chapter examines the contribution that economic geographers have made to our understanding of these issues of economy and the environment, beginning with a review of key conceptual approaches and research questions. The chapter continues with a historical review of the emergence of the environment as a concern within economic geography, a discussion of contemporary debates within the field, and an agenda for future research.

Conceptual Approaches and Research Questions

In this context of renewed interest in economy–environment relations, what are the critical research questions? Most research within the field shares the common conceptual starting point that economic activity is a material process taking resources and transforming them into products and services through which human needs and preferences are met. Through this process, nature is transformed and new geographies are produced, sometimes in ways that undermine or limit the capacity for future production, and of social reproduction. From this modest starting point, there is much divergence of theoretical approach and much disagreement over the causes and extent of the environmental challenge. Information on the historical pattern of energy and materials use, and associated waste and pollution, on a global scale is uneven. Numerous country-based studies have documented a trend toward reductions in the energy intensity of economic activity per unit of GDP within the OECD, or what has been called the 'decarbonization' of the economy (Schipper *et al.* 1996). While a similar trend toward dematerialization has been claimed for selected materials, such as steel, lead, and timber (Considine 1991; Malenbaum 1978; Tilton 1990; Wernick *et al.* 1996), recent reviews suggest these claims be treated with considerable caution as they are fraught with problems of data comparability and other analytical problems (see e.g. Cleveland and Ruth 1999). Further, given the international scope of production systems, country-based studies inevitably miss the effects of global shifts in economic activity, such as the dependence of OECD economies on resource extraction and materials processing in developing economies. Whatever the trend in energy and materials intensity of economic activity, the total volume of materials and energy use is in most cases increasing. And it is this absolute volume, rather than relative intensity of use, that is the critical concern from an ecological standpoint (Bunker 1996).

If our understanding of current trends in energy and materials use is uneven, there is little consensus about the causes of the current environmental challenge, and the capacity for significant reductions in energy and materials use within existing institutions, and political-economic relations. As Harvey (1974) and Watts (1983), among others, have argued, environmental problems are often constructed as a problem of nature rather than of the structural relations of societies to nature. In broadest terms, the critical research questions revolve around the capacity for, and determinants of, reforms of existing production systems and modes of social regulation to bring about substantial improvements in the environmental performance of economic activity (both production and consumption), and to do so in ways that support other societal goals, such as improvements in social welfare.

Two broad schools of thought have emerged in this regard. The first is now typically labeled ecological modernization (Gouldson and Murphy 1996; Hajer 1996; Simonis 1989). The central thesis of this work is that substantial improvements in the environmental performance of economic activity can be achieved within the context of existing institutions and social structures. The challenge is to reconfigure incentives, regulatory structures, and management systems to the goal of enhanced environmental performance. A key element of this restructuring is the accelerated development, deployment, and use of products and production processes that are ever less energy, materials, and waste intensive. While much of the early work was technocratic in orientation, subsequent writings focused more on issues of institutional and cultural change (for the latter, see Hajer 1995; Mol 1996), drawing on concepts of reflexive modernization by Beck (1992) and others (Beck *et al.* 1994). In this view, improved environmental performance is consistent with the structural characteristics of capitalist production. What is needed are corrections in markets and institutions, such as elimination of *de facto* subsidies on energy- and materials-intensive activity, full environmental cost pricing, state intervention to overcome market failures in the development and deployment of clean technologies and in the development of markets for reuse and recycling, new approaches to environmental regulation, supply chain management, introduction of environmental concerns into international regulation of trade and investment (such as the World Trade Organization (WTO) and the Multilateral Agreement on Investment), and so on. Much of this is consistent with mainstream economic and policy analysis with its focus on property rights, incentives, and institutional innovation. It also draws upon themes from industrial ecology that suggest environmental improvement will in many cases reduce cost and enhance the competitiveness of industry (Graedel and Allenby 1995). In 'strong' versions of ecological modernization, calls for greater information disclosure, democracy in goal setting, and public participation in decision making accompany these themes (Christoff 1996).

A second broad body of research argues that the scale of improvement in environmental performance of economic activity will not be achieved without fundamental transformation in social structures, modes of economic development, ethics, and values (see e.g. Welford 1995). Much of this critique has its roots in Marxist political economy and in an analysis of the structural relations within society that shape the relation of economic systems to the environment (Harvey 1996). In this regard, perhaps the most influential theoretical approach within economic geography today is that of regulation theory. In recent years, several authors have applied regulation theory to the problem of economy–environment relations (Gibbs and Healey 1997; Lipietz 1992). By this account, the environmental degradation associated with energy and materials-intensive economic development has created both a material crisis of production and a legitimization crisis for capital. The strengthening of environmental regulation within the OECD economies from the 1970s onwards constitutes a remaking of the existing mode of social regulation of industry in an attempt to address the supply crisis and to bound the potential challenge to capital in terms of issues of compliance with environmental statutes (Bridge 1998). The important point from a regulationist perspective is that such regulatory responses, whether in the form of 'real' regulation or in the discursive and political construction of environment–economy relations, do not address the underlying contradiction of nature–society relations implied by an expansionist regime of capitalist accumulation. Research in this political-economy tradition, as well as the burgeoning field of political ecology (Escobar 1995; Peet and Watts 1996), calls into question the drivers of ecological modernization (what processes will drive forward the proposed restructuring of production and regulatory systems?), and draws attention to the ongoing discursive construction of current economy–environment relations as an issue of 'environment' rather than political economy.

The primary contribution of economic geographers to these questions continues to derive from an analysis of space and place. In general terms, economic geography seeks to understand how the spatiality of economic life structures economy–environment relations, and how in turn political economy produces particular environmental and geographical outcomes. As indicated above, the current environmental challenge has quite distinctive geographical dimensions. Three themes are of particular importance. The first theme concerns the contribution of the globalization of economic, social, and political processes to the dynamic of energy- and materials-intensive capitalist accumulation. Of critical concern here is whether globalization necessarily involves a deepening and broadening of the environment/development crisis, or whether the processes of globalization themselves can be harnessed to a goal of improved environmental performance, for example by the development of international civil society (Matthews 1997) and of international regulatory regimes (Esty 1997). A second core geographical concern is the significance of political, economic, and social context for regulatory response. Currently, there are strong forces supporting a convergence of environmental policy around a kind of global regulatory 'best practice', typically modeled on the export of regulatory approaches of the USA and other OECD economies. Such transfers of regulatory policy models are increasingly reinforced by the growing importance of regional and international environmental regulatory standards, by the actions of large multinational and trans-national corporations, whose internal environmental management systems apply standardized practices to multiple corporate facilities around the world, and by the growing international significance of private-business standards, such as ISO 14001.[1] A countervailing argument suggests that regulatory approaches do not transfer well, and that policy approaches need to be tailored to political, social, economic, and cultural context. Thirdly, economic geographers have been at the forefront in analyzing the significance of local scale processes for economy–environment relations (see e.g. Angel *et al.* 1998). A particular interest here is the opportunity for local scale, bottom-up approaches to improve upon the dominant model of top-down national and international policy making.

How Did We Get Here?

As Gibbs and Healey (1997) have noted, until quite recently economic geography largely ignored the relation of economic systems to the natural environment. Even as the field experienced profound shifts in methodological approach and theoretical and epistemological framework in the mid- and late twentieth century, the key problems and questions of economic geography con-

[1] ISO 14001 is an environmental management system certification program carried out under the auspices of the International Organization of Standardization (ISO), a coalition of standards setting organizations from countries around the world.

tinued to be framed in terms of space and place, and the complex and varied geographies produced through economic change. The failure of economic geography to engage with the natural environment in anything more than limited terms is hardly a historical accident. It broadly follows the discursive construction of the natural environment within the capitalist accumulation process itself, namely, as a resource factor input to production to be managed through market process, innovation, and technology change. As service sectors replaced agriculture and mining, and then manufacturing, as the dominant sources of employment within advanced industrial economies, and as knowledge and technology-intensive industries became the leading-edge of high value-added industrialization, so the relation of advanced industrial economies to nature became further attenuated during the twentieth century in a discourse of post-industrial, post-material, economies. And it was above all this experience of the postwar advanced industrial economies that provided the context for the development of the field of economic geography as we know it today (Lee and Wills 1997).

The lack of attention to nature within economic geography is perhaps less of an anomaly for economists and other social scientists, the bulk of whom consider modern geography as a science of space, than for geographers themselves. For the latter, it surely stands at odds with the long-standing tradition of nature–society research within the discipline of geography as a whole. In Chisholm's early economic text, the environment was first and foremost a geography of material resources, a locational inventory of factor inputs to the production of wealth (Chisholm 1889). In Alfred Weber's classic locational theory, the environment defines the fixed location of resource inputs for consideration in the calculation of an optimal least-cost location for sites of production (Weber 1929). Changes in factor inputs brought about through technology change and factor substitution were of course an important part of the locational calculus. Thus in his classic study of locational dynamics of the iron and steel industry, Walter Isard (1948) traces out the significance of increased material and energy efficiency for the location of the industry (Bunker 1996). But the energy and material demands of iron and steel production were an exogenous input to the locational calculus, rather than a concern in their own right. The emergence of regional science during the 1960s and beyond if anything further weakened the connection of economic geography to the environment. The abstract analytical models of regional science served to distance economic geography from the material environment, both conceptually and physically.

The tendency to abstract away from the relation of economies to nature was reinforced to some degree by a dominant focus in modern economic geography on industrial systems, especially manufacturing and services, and on advanced industrial economies. Agrarian and pastoral systems, where cultural ecology and other nature–society traditions within geography remained quite vibrant, received much less attention within economic geography. And this was especially the case with respect to theoretical development where it was above all the economic restructuring of advanced industrial economies that provided the context for conceptual and theoretical advance in economic geography. The appearance of individual papers on industry–environment issues, such as Stafford (1985) and Walker *et al.* (1979), only underscored the dominant empirical and theoretical focus on the location of industry. Of course some aspects of economy–environment interface were pursued within other sub-disciplinary niches within geography, such as energy studies, resource geography, and risk-hazards research. But just as the ability of economic geography to understand the dynamics of contemporary economic change was undermined by a failure to theorize effectively nature–society relations, so research within resource geography and other sub-disciplines was hampered by the limited engagement with the kinds of vibrant theoretical and empirical political economy pursued within economic geography over the past three decades.

Given this disciplinary history, it is not surprising that issues of the environment entered modern economic geography in the first instance through a process of re-engagement among sub-disciplinary specializations. Of particular importance in this regard were a series of political economic critiques of the behavioral and cultural ecology traditions that dominated resource geography and the analysis of natural hazards within geography (examples of these critiques include Emel and Peet 1989; Susman *et al.* 1983; and Watts 1983). Out of this critique emerged an important body of work on political ecology that brought together the structural analysis of political economy with detailed studies of land use within developing economies (Blaikie 1985; Blaikie and Brookfield 1987). To date this work has remained principally focused on agrarian economies; the application of political ecology approaches to advanced industrial economies has been slower in developing. As a consequence, the impact of political ecology upon economic geography has been modest, enriching but as yet not transforming the core theoretical and empirical concerns. More recently, political ecology has served as a platform for a post-structuralist critique of contemporary environment and development policy, focusing on the discursive construction of the environment within mainstream policy and within the public at large (Escobar 1996).

A second line of engagement between economic geography and the environment can be traced back to efforts within Marxist political economy to re-examine the so-called second contradiction of capitalism, namely, its relation to nature (Benton 1989; Benton and Redclift 1994; Leff 1994; O'Connor 1988). Important work in this regard within geography includes Smith (1984) and Fitzsimmons (1991). Among the themes developed within this Marxist political economy are the idea of 'second nature' (that is to say that the environment is itself produced within economic systems), and analysis of the commodification of nature.

With the rapid emergence of regulation theory as an influential conceptual framework within economic geography, this theoretical approach has in turn begun to be applied to economy–environment relations. Several characteristics of the regulationist approach suggest that it will likely be the most significant platform through which the environment is brought into economic geography. First, the historical character of regulation theory, based around a periodization of capitalist production, will likely prove helpful in understanding the character of the contemporary environmental challenge. Disentangling the material constraints that the environment now places upon economic systems (e.g. through resource depletion and degradation) from the political challenge to the legitimacy of capital resulting from the pollution and health and safety effects is an important line of research. At the same time, regulation theory provides an effective framework within which to examine processes of environmental regulation, paralleling important work already under way on such issues as employment and welfare policy, and the linkages between production and consumption within economic systems. Perhaps the critical challenge will be to go beyond the application of regulation theory to economy–environment relations, to an analysis of how the dynamics of economy–environment relations requires a rethinking of regulation theory itself. For example, it is far from clear that the current periodization of economic transformation proposed by regulation theory matches up to the changing patterns of economy–environment relations within advanced industrial economies.

As in economics, sociology, and other social science disciplines, it was largely the external pressure of environmental problems that forced environment on to the agenda of economic geography. As firms and industries began to devote resources to environmental management and regulation, so the environment became a more visible aspect of economic geography. In this regard, analysis of global environmental change has been an important arena within which economic geographers have sought to engage with environmental concerns. But much of this emerging analysis of economy–environment relations does not fit easily into disciplinary boundaries. Alongside the growing interest of economic geography in the environment, there has been a proliferation of interdisciplinary initiatives under such rubrics as the greening of industry (Fischer and Schot 1993; Roome 1998), industrial ecology (Socolow *et al.* 1994), environmental policy, sustainable cities, and others.

Contemporary Debates within the Discipline

Analysis of economy–environment relations remains in its infancy within economic geography. As with firms and industries, the engagement with the environment remains tightly circumscribed. Thus within most firms issues of the environment are addressed within the specialized domain of environmental management (and largely as an issue of regulatory compliance), rather than as a pervasive issue of market opportunity, innovation, profitability, cost control, and investment. This compartmentalization is reproduced within public policy through such chaotic concepts as green technology, suggesting that environmental performance should be addressed through a designated set of clean technologies, rather than through improvements in the environmental performance of all products and production processes (for an alternative view see Heaton 1997). Some breakdown in this compartmentalization is beginning to occur, as for example, in the search for so-called 'win-win' opportunities in innovation and production, and in the examination of how such practices as flexible manufacturing and just-in-time production can yield improvements in both production quality and environmental performance (Florida 1996). If the pressure on firms and industries to improve environmental performance intensifies in coming years (in response for example to commitments made under the Framework convention on climate change), then we can anticipate a further mainstreaming of environmental concerns within processes of innovation, investment, and market demand. In this context, the analysis in economic geography of such meso-level dynamics of the territoriality of technology development and change, and the geography of inter-firm linkages, will be as relevant to the issue of the environment as to any other aspect of economic performance.

But currently the analysis of the environment within economic geography remains more narrowly defined. Three main lines of research are currently of particular importance. The first concerns the character and significance of contemporary processes of globalization. There is of course a healthy debate within geography and other disciplines concerning the conceptualization of globalization (Dicken 1998; Hirst and Thompson 1996; Held *et al.* 1999). Building upon this work, there is an important opportunity for economic geography to examine the significance of the intensification and extensification of global linkages for the environmental performance of industry. Among the more important aspects of this problem are the environmental character of global investment and technology flows, and the attendant transfer of production practices worldwide; the implications of increasing international market interlinkage for industrial environmental performance; the role of emerging industrial standards, such as ISO 14001, as well as international regulation through such organizations as the WTO; the extent of market failures in the development and transfer of clean production systems; and the potential significance of international networks of NGOs and the growing importance of civil society as a driver of the environmental performance of industry. There is to date surprisingly little systematic analysis of these and other important aspects of globalization as they relate to the environmental performance of industry, and economic activity as a whole.

Nowhere are these issues of global economic development of greater significance than in the rapidly industrializing economies of Asia, Latin America, and elsewhere. It is above all within these developing economies that the vast majority of new urban and industrial growth will take place over the next thirty years, and it is imperative that the practice of economic geography reflects this global development dynamic. Most of Asia, for example, is in the midst, not at the end, of a process of urban-industrial transformation unprecedented in its scale and intensity. A (pre-crisis) World Bank (1994) study of the Indonesian economy predicted that 85 per cent of the urban and industrial capital stock that will be in place in 2020 is not on the ground today. Influencing the pattern of new urban and industrial investment is a critical environmental policy challenge. By one estimate the urban population of the East Asian newly industrializing countries (NICs), including China, will increase from 550 million in 1995 to 1.2 billion in 2025 (World Resources Institute 1997). Asia's share of global output, which was roughly 10 per cent in 1950 and 30 per cent in 1995, is expected to reach 55 to 60 per cent by 2025 (Radelet and Sachs 1997). The rate of growth may be in doubt; the direction of change is not. The likely environmental impacts of such large-scale urban development are also reasonably predictable. Even with a substantial strengthening of environmental regulation in developing Asia, the Asia Development Bank (Lohani 1998) predicts significant declines in environmental quality within the lower income economies of South and South-East Asia. Understanding the character of this global development process, and identifying opportunities for turning the trajectory of industrial development toward less energy and materials-intensive patterns of development, is a critical research and policy concern. And clearly this is a concern that has to be addressed in the global context of structural north–south relations, patterns of unsustainable consumption within the OECD, and the geography of investment and technology flows.

A second significant line of research is the examination of alternative approaches to the environmental regulation of economic activity. There is now a widely ranging debate within OECD economies about the effectiveness of command and control regulation, market-based regulation, so-called private-law models of environmental regulation, as well as various 'third wave' regulatory approaches based on information disclosure and greater public participation in environmental policy making (DeWitt 1994; OECD 1997). Traditional command and control-based regulation, with its dependence upon a set of ambient media-based standards and associated facility-level emissions permits, is criticized for the high costs of implementation and enforcement, and for constraining impacts upon technology innovation. Implicit in this policy debate is the question of the likely importance of different drivers of the environmental performance of industry, from traditional regulatory drivers, to end-user demand, supplier chain requirements, international environmental agreements, as well as public and community pressure. The policy debate also calls into question the character of recent environmental initiatives by industry, such as voluntary performance agreements, and environmental reports of one form or another.

The primary contribution of economic geography to these research and policy debates centers around two broad questions, namely, the significance of political, economic, and social context for successful regulatory policy, and the contribution of local, bottom-up, initiatives as a policy response. In the midst of the ongoing debate within the OECD concerning environmental policy, significant development assistance is being committed to the transfer of these same policy approaches to developing economies, and to economies in transition. This policy transfer raises an important question about the significance of a match between policy approach and political, social, and economic context for the success of regulatory policy. What works in Thailand may not be appropriate for Brazil. In addition, economic geography is in a good position to examine the issue of scale in environmental regulation. This issue is often raised with respect to the potential disjuncture between global production systems and country-based systems of regulation. But equally important are the conditions under which local and regional-based policy, developed from the bottom up, might provide preferred outcomes to those achieved through top-down national and international regulation.

The third broad area of research revolves around the meso-level analytics of the economy and environment interface. A recent research assessment by the International Human Dimension Programme, Industrial Transformation (IHDP-IT) emphasizes two critical research needs (IHDP-IT 1999). The first concerns the re-connection of the analysis of production and consumption processes (see also Stern *et al.* 1997). Economic geography for the most part has focused on the dynamics of production and has paid less attention to the processes of consumption, and the ways in which patterns of consumption are structured and produced. Regulation theory provides an entry point for the re-connection of these twin dynamics, and for an examination of how the full environmental effects of economic activity—from production to consumption—might be examined analytically. The IHDP-IT report also voices a continuing interest in the development of theoretical and analytical frameworks that effectively link processes operating at the macro-scale (such as investment flows), meso-level (such as policy formation), and micro-scale (such as technology choices made by individual firms), especially in such areas as technological and institutional change.

Given the quite preliminary status of work around these core research themes—within economic geography and in other disciplines—the three areas of scholarship identified above (globalization and the environmental performance of industry, the significance of social and geographical context for environmental regulation, and the linking of analysis across different spatial scales) continue to provide an important agenda for future research. Researchers entering the field also have the opportunity to draw upon several recent efforts

to develop international research agendas on such issues as global change (Committee on Global Change Research 1999), and environmentally significant consumption (Stern *et al.* 1997). In broadest terms, perhaps the most significant issue for both theory and practice concerns the capacity for innovation and change within existing institutions to generate significant improvement in the environmental performance of economic activity worldwide. The vast majority of current public policy is predicated on this claim. And much of our shared environmental future depends upon the result of this policy innovation.

References

ANDREWS, R. 1999. *Managing the Environment, Managing Ourselves: A History of American Environmental Policy*. New Haven: Yale University Press.

ANGEL, D., ATTOH, S., KROMM, D., DEHART, J., SLOCUM, R., and WHITE, S. 1998. The drivers of greenhouse gas emissions: what do we learn from local case studies. *Local Environment*, 3: 263–77.

BECK, U. 1992. *Risk Society: Toward a New Modernity*. London: Sage Publications.

——GIDDENS, A., and LASH, S. 1994. *Reflexive Modernization: Politics, Tradition and Aesthetics in the Modern Social Order*. Cambridge: Polity Press.

BENNETT, P. 1999. Governing environmental risk: regulation, insurance and moral economy. *Progress in Human Geography*, 23: 189–208.

BENTON, T. 1989. Marxism and natural limits: an ecological critique and reconstruction. *New Left Review*, 194: 55–74.

——and REDCLIFT, M., eds. 1994. *Social Theory and the Global Environment*. London: Routledge.

BLAIKIE, P. 1985. *The Political Economy of Social Erosion*. London: Methuen.

——and BROOKFIELD, H. 1987. *Land Degradation and Society*. London: Methuen.

BRIDGE, G. 1998. Excavating nature: environmental narratives and discursive regulation in the mining industry. In *Unruly World? Globalization, Governance, and Geography*, ed. A. Herod, G. Otuathail, and S. Roberts. London: Routledge.

BUNKER, S. 1996. Raw material and the global economy: oversights and distortions in industrial ecology. Mimeo.

CARSON, R. 1962. *Silent Spring*. Boston: Houghton Mifflin.

CHISHOLM, G. 1889. *Handbook of Commercial Geography*. London: Longman, Green, and Co.

CHRISTOFF, P. 1996. Ecological modernization, ecological modernities. *Environmental Politics*, 5: 476–500.

CLEVELAND, C., and RUTH, M. 1999. Indicators of dematerialization and the materials intensity of use. *Journal of Industrial Ecology*, 2: 15–50.

Committee on Global Change Research, US National Research Council 1999. *Global Environmental Change: Research Pathways for the Next Decade*. Washington: National Academy Press.

CONSIDINE, T. J. 1991. Economic and technological determinants of the materials intensity of use. *Land Economics*, 67: 99–115.

Davies, T., and Mazurek, J. 1998. *Regulating Pollution: Does the U.S. System Work?* Washington: Resources for the Future.
DeWitt, J. 1994. *Civic Environmentalism: Alternatives to Regulation in States and Communities.* Washington: Congressional Quarterly.
Dicken, P. 1998. *Global Shift: Industrial Change in a Turbulent World.* 3rd edn. New York: Guilford Press.
Emel, J., and Peet, R. 1989. Resource management and natural hazards. In *New Models in Geography*, ed. R. Peet and N. Thrift. London: Unwin Hyman.
Escobar, A. 1995. *Encountering Development.* Princeton: Princeton University Press.
—— 1996. Constructing nature: elements of a post-structural political ecology. In Peet and Watts 1996.
Esty, D. 1997. Foreign investment, globalization and the environment. In *Globalization and the Environment*, ed. T. Jones. Paris: OECD.
Fischer, K., and Schot, J., eds. 1993. *Environmental Strategies for Industry.* Washington: Island Press.
Fitzsimmons, M. 1991. The matter of nature. *Antipode*, 21: 106–20.
Florida, R. 1996. Lean and green: the move to environmentally conscious manufacturing. *California Management Review*, 39: 80–105.
Gibbs, D., and Healey, M. 1997. Industrial geography and the environment. *Applied Geography*, 17: 193–201.
Graedel, T. E., and Allenby, B. R. 1995. *Industrial Ecology.* Upper Saddle River, NJ: Prentice-Hall.
Gouldson, A., and Murphy, J. 1996. Ecological modernization and the European Union. *Geoforum*, 27: 11–21.
Hajer, M. 1995. *The Politics of Environmental Discourse: Ecological Modernization and the Policy Process.* Oxford: Clarendon.
—— 1996. Ecological modernization as cultural politics. In *Risk, Environment and Modernity: Towards a New Ecology*, ed. S. Lash, B. Szerszynski, and B. Wynne. London: Sage.
Harvey, D. 1974. Population, resources, and the ideology of science. *Economic Geography*, 50: 256–77.
—— 1996. *Justice, Nature, and the Geography of Difference.* London: Blackwell.
Heaton, G. 1997. Toward a new generation of environmental technology. *Journal of Industrial Ecology*, 1: 23–32.
Held, D., McGrew, A., Goldblatt, D., and Perraton, J. 1999. *Global Transformations.* Stanford, Calif.: Stanford University Press.
Hirst, P., and Thompson, G. 1996. *Globalization in Question: The International Economy and the Possibility of Governance.* Cambridge: Polity.
International Human Dimension Programme, Industrial Transformation (IHDP-IT) 1999. Science Plan. IHDP Report No. 12. Bonn: IHDP.
Isard, W. 1948. Some locational factors in the iron and steel industry since the early nineteenth century. *Journal of Political Economy*, 65: 203–17.
Jaffe, A., Peterson, S., Portney, P., and Stavins, R. 1995. Environmental regulation and the competitiveness of U.S. manufacturing: what does the evidence tell us? *Journal of Economic Literature*, 33: 132–63.
Jorgenson, D., and Wilcoxen, P. 1990. Environmental regulation and U.S. economic growth. *Rand Journal of Economics*, 21: 314–40.

Lee, R., and Wills, J. 1997. *Geographies of Economies*. London: Arnold.

Leff, E. 1994. *Green Production: Toward an Environmental Rationality*. New York: Guilford Press.

Lipietz, A. 1992. *Towards a New Economic Order: Postfordism, Ecology and Democracy*. Cambridge: Polity Press.

Lohani, B. 1998. *Environmental Challenges in Asia in the 21st Century*. Manila: Asian Development Bank.

Malenbaum, W. 1978. *World Demand for Raw Materials in 1985 and 2000*. New York: McGraw-Hill.

Matthews, J. T. 1997. Power shift. *Foreign Affairs*, 76: 50–66.

Mol, A. 1996. Ecological modernization and institutional reflexivity: environmental reform in the late modern age. *Environmental Politics*, 5: 302–23.

O'Connor, D. 1994. *Managing the Environment with Rapid Industrialization*. Paris: OECD.

O'Connor, J. 1988. The second contradiction of capitalism. *Capitalism Nature Socialism*, 1: 1–15.

OECD 1997. *Reforming Industrial Regulation in OECD Countries*. Paris: OECD.

Peet, R., and Watts, M., eds. 1996. *Liberation Ecologies: Environment, Development, and Social Movements*. London: Routledge.

Porter, M. E., and Van der Linde, C. 1995. Toward a new conception of the environment-competitiveness relationship. *Journal of Economic Perspectives*, 9: 97–118.

Radelet, S., and Sachs, J. 1997. Asia's reemergence. *Foreign Affairs*, 76.

Roome, N., ed. 1998. *Sustainable Strategies for Industry*. Washington: Island Press.

Schipper, L., Ting, M., Khrushch, M., Unander, F., Monahan, P., and Golove, W. 1996. *The Evolution of Carbon Dioxide Emissions from Energy Use in Industrialized Countries: An End Use Analysis*. Berkeley: Lawrence Berkeley National Laboratory.

Simonis, U. 1989. Ecological modernization of industrial society: three strategic elements. *International Social Science Journal*, 121: 347–61.

Smith, N. 1984. *Uneven Development: Nature, Capital and the Production of Space*. Oxford: Blackwell.

Socolow, R., Andrews, C., Berkhout, F., and Thomas, V., eds. 1994. *Industrial Ecology and Global Change*. New York: Cambridge University Press.

Stafford, H. 1985. Environmental protection and industrial location. *Annals of the Association of American Geographers*, 75: 227–40.

Stern, P., Dietz, T., Ruttan, V., Socolow, R., and Sweeney, J. L. 1997. *Environmentally Significant Consumption: Research Directions*. Washington: National Academy Press.

Susman, P., O'Keefe, P., and Wisner, B. 1983. Global disasters, a radical interpretation. In *Interpretations of Calamity*, ed. K. Hewitt. Boston: Allen Unwin.

Tilton, J. E. 1990. *World Metal Demand, Trends and Prospects*. Washington: Resources for the Future.

Turner, B. L. II, Clark, W. C., Kates, R. W., Richards, J. F., Mathews, J. T., and Meyer, W. T. 1990. *The Earth as Transformed by Human Action*. Cambridge: Cambridge University Press.

Walker, R., Storper, M., and Gersch, E. 1979. The limits of environmental control: the saga of Dow in the delta. *Antipode*, 11: 48–60.

WATTS, M. 1983. *Silent Violence: Food, Famine, and Peasantry in Northern Nigeria.* Berkeley and Los Angeles: University of California Press.

WEBER, A. 1929. *Alfred Weber's Theory of the Location of Industries* (translation). Chicago: University of Chicago Press.

WELFORD, R. 1995. *Environmental Strategy and Sustainable Development.* London: Routledge.

WERNICK, I. K., HERMAN, R., GOVIND, S., and AUSUBEL, J. 1996. Materialization and dematerialization: measures and trends. *Daedalus*, 125: 171–98.

World Bank 1994. *Indonesia: Environment and Development.* Washington: The World Bank.

World Resources Institute 1997. *World Development Report.* New York: Oxford University Press.

Section 14

Trade and Investment Blocs

Chapter **31**

Spontaneous Integration in Japan and East Asia: Development, Crisis, and Beyond

Tetsuo Abo

Introduction: Theoretical Focal Points and Framework

ECONOMICS has not explicitly incorporated an important aspect of geography into its dominant theoretical framework. Of course, geographical distance has been incorporated as an abstract dimension of economic theory. But socio-cultural variation between regions and countries is not easily dealt with in the theoretical framework of mainstream economics. Though not a specialist of geography, this author believes that cultural differences, which are closely connected to the differences in geographical locations and their historical contexts, form an essential factor in the competitive advantage of industries or nations (see Abo 1994; Porter 1990).

The 'miracle' of economic growth in the East Asian region in the 1980s up until the mid-1990s was led primarily by foreign direct investment (FDI). In particular, Japanese manufacturing firms, through FDI, implemented the transfer of their management systems and production technologies to local economies throughout East Asia, producing a unique form of region-based economic development which has variously been referred to as 'flying geese', 'tandem', 'staged', and so forth. A principal factor in the successful transplantation of Japanese-style production systems into these local economies was the similarity of the socio-cultural backgrounds (and underlying institutions) in

Japan and the other countries of the East Asian region, compared with those in other regions such as North America and Europe.

This process of economic development generated a 'spontaneous' and 'defensive' pattern of economic integration and regionalism, which represents a 'third way' of economic transformation quite distinct from the other two types—EU (European Union), and NAFTA (North American Free Trade Agreement). However, since the summer of 1997, financial and economic crisis befell almost all of the East Asian economies including Japan. Does this mean a wholesale collapse of the above pattern of economic growth? What do these recent developments hold in store for the future of the region? These are the main points addressed in this chapter.

Foreign Direct Investment-Led Economic Growth

Figure 31.1 highlights the fact that economic growth rates of East Asian countries since the 1980s, especially since the mid-1980s, were significantly higher than both the world average and the industrial countries as a group. Equally impressive is the fact that foreign direct investment (FDI) into the East Asian countries surged even more sharply alongside economic growth in the region. As will be explained later, this pattern may be described as FDI-led economic

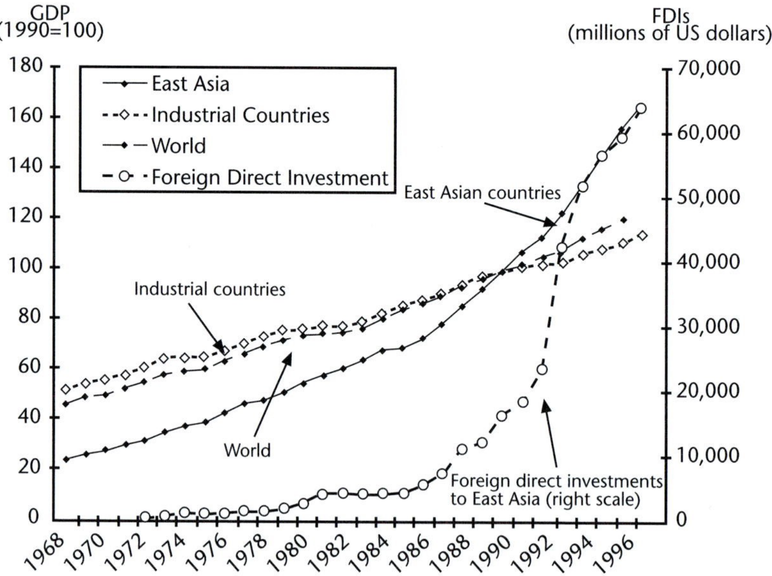

Fig. 31.1. GDP of, and foreign direct investments to, East Asia

Source: IMF, *International Financial Statistics, Yearbook*, 1998.

growth. It may be characterized as a relatively endogenous type of economic development, in the sense that it has unfolded without the assistance of any deliberate institutional apparatus such as trade and economic blocs which have accompanied supranational integration in other world regions. Instead, the principal mechanism underlying this development has been market-based FDI originating from within East Asia itself.

Indeed, Japanese firms have played the principal and leading role in this process of FDI-led economic growth. As shown in Figure 31.2, at the end of 1993 the cumulative total of US$ 65 billion of FDI by Japanese firms into East Asia was a little larger than the combined total of $61 (38 + 23) billion of foreign direct investment into East Asia by US and EU-based firms.

One also needs to take into account another important group of new investors within East Asia. Firms based in the newly industrializing economies, or NIEs (Hong Kong, Taiwan, Singapore, and Korea) have generated an increasing amount of FDI in the region over the 1990s. An exact comparison is difficult to make because of the differences in data sources (JETRO 1996: 19–20, 171).

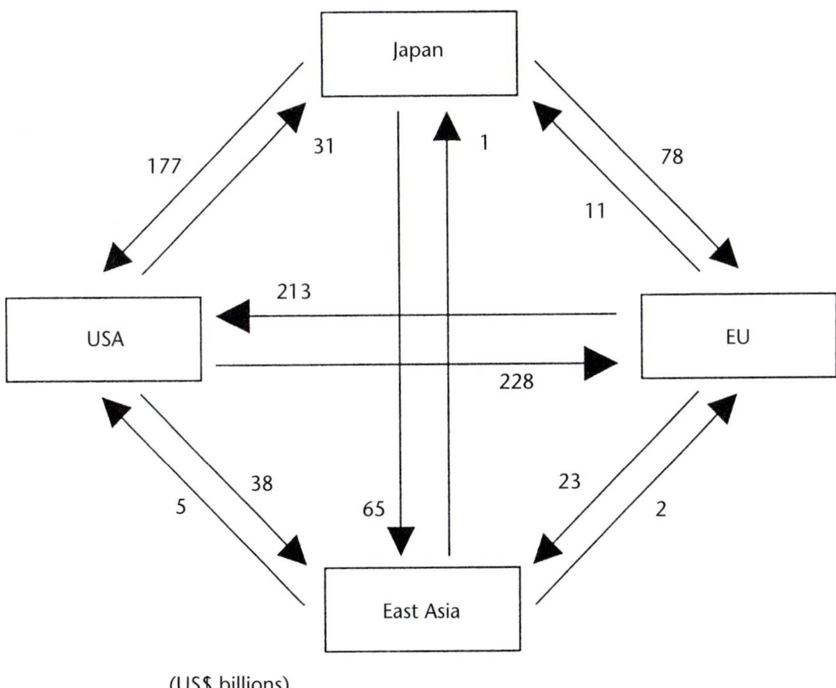

Fig. 31.2. Cumulative totals of foreign direct investments between Japan, USA, EU, and East Asia

Source: Ministry of International Trade and industry, *White Paper of International Trade*, 1996 (in Japanese).

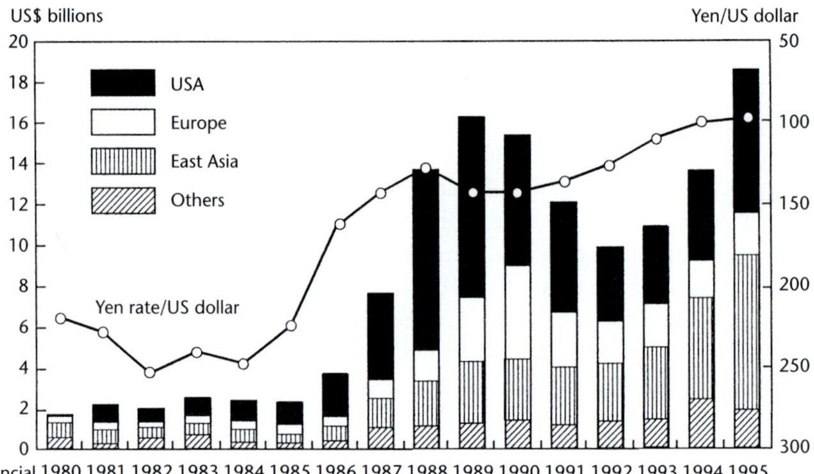

Fig. 31.3. Japanese manufacturing foreign direct investments and foreign exchange rates

Source: JETRO (1997: 26) (in Japanese).

Still, based on calculations by the respective governments (which may be somewhat overestimated compared to Figure 31.1 which is based on OECD and IMF data), in 1994 the NIEs invested $46 billion ($10 billion in 1989). In contrast, Japan invested $17 billion and the USA invested $23 billion ($34 and 11 billion for each in 1989). Besides the problem of overestimation, the comparison is also vitiated by the fact that more than half of the FDI of two big NIE investors, Hong Kong and Taiwan, was comprised of investments into industries other than manufacturing, such as real estate and infrastructure including apartments, hotels, and shopping centres. In contrast, more than half of the Japanese FDI to East Asia was in manufacturing industry. Further, FDI from the NIEs into East Asia included a considerable amount of money reinvested by subsidiaries of Japanese firms in the NIEs, especially Hong Kong and Taiwan, to nearby third countries (see also JETRO 1997: 35 ff.).

Figure 31.3 also reveals that Japanese manufacturing FDI into East Asia grew fairly steadily beginning in the late 1980s. By 1995, the East Asian component of Japanese FDI had grown to rival the US share, with the European component having shrunk to a very low proportion of worldwide Japanese FDI.

Though the role of foreign direct investment was a leading dynamic factor in the 'miracle' of East Asian economic growth, it was still only a necessary condition since there was an additional need to secure markets for the products produced by such investments. Twu's (1997) Asian 'growth triangle' (or GT) model

(A) China

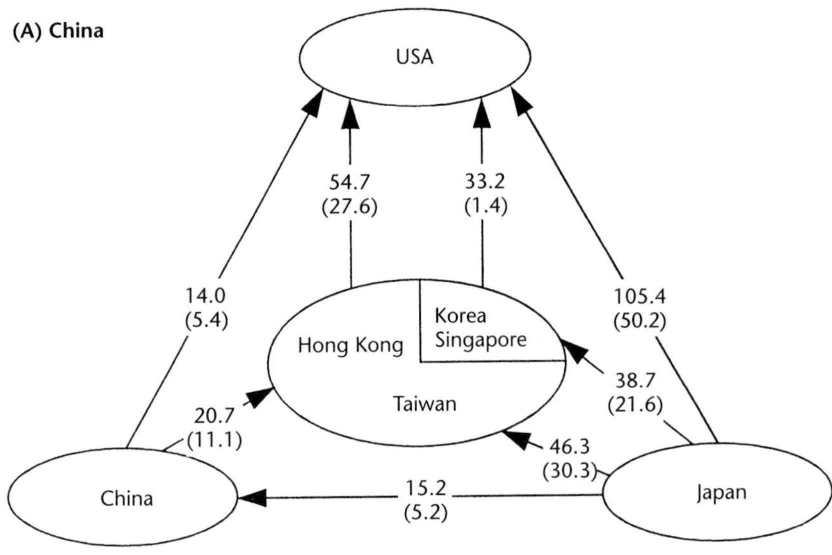

(B) ASEAN countries

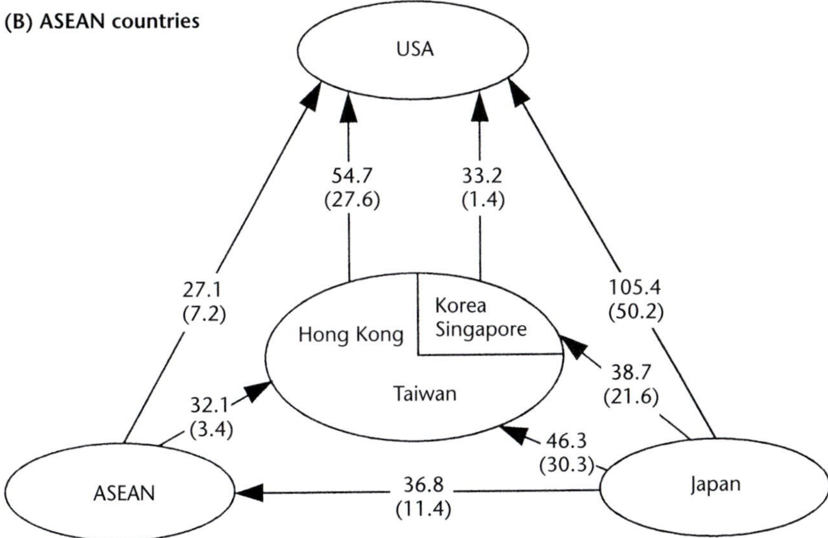

Fig. 31.4. Multi-structure on triangle trade, 1993, US$ billion (per cent)

Notes:

1. Sign indicates the export direction, figure in parentheses indicates trade surplus.
2. Japan–NIEs–USA figures indicate total trade of NIEs.
3. Trade from NIEs, ASEAN, and China is indicated.
4. Chinese exports via Hong Kong equivalent to 61.2 billion.

Source: Twu (1997: 103), based on Economic Planning Agency, *Overseas Economic Data*, July 1995: 88–100 (in Japanese).

is extremely useful in explaining the market structure that complemented the above dynamic development of FDI within the East Asian region. In Figure 31.4 this triangle relationship is elucidated clearly in the form of the two triangular trade structures, the first among Japan, the NIEs, China, and the USA, and the second among Japan, the NIEs, the ASEAN, countries and the USA.

With the NIEs at the centre and with Japan, the USA, and ASEAN or China surrounding the NIEs, there emerges a multiple triangle structure. Thus, (1) each triangle shows an interdependent trade relationship necessarily via the NIEs; (2) the location and role of the USA, which is the only country generating a large export surplus for all other countries and regions, is the key force enabling and sustaining this 'compound GT'; (3) Japan is the only country generating large export surpluses from all other countries and regions; and (4) the location and role of the NIE countries and regions is also crucial, since the NIEs enable Japan and ASEAN countries or China to make both 'indirect exports' to the USA via the NIEs as well as direct exports; (5) the intermediating roles of Hong Kong and Taiwan in supporting the newly emerging economies such as the ASEAN countries and China is also notable. In short, the USA has played a major role as a market of final demand for the FDI-led economic growth process in East Asia. As a result, the USA has accumulated substantial trade and current account deficits and huge foreign debts (about $1.3 trillion in 1997), every year to date since the early 1980s. However, the importance of such a role for the USA has been decreasing to some extent for the Asian countries, given a rising share of the Japanese market in the region, as will be discussed later.

It is also notable that a sizeable part of the exports to the USA from the countries and regions in the NIEs, ASEAN, and China has been carried out by the local Japanese or Japanese-affiliated firms in East Asia. Since this is an important aspect of Japanese FDI-led economic development in the region, the next section discusses the main topic of this chapter: local production activities by Japanese firms.

The Local Production by Japanese Multinational Enterprises and Staged Economic Development

Global Diffusion of the Subsidiaries of Japanese Companies

Table 31.1 presents a range of indicators documenting the international diffusion of Japanese companies at the end of 1996. For all industries, more than 20,000 local subsidiaries of Japanese companies, with around 3.1 million employees, were operating in 138 countries. In manufacturing industries more than 7,700 subsidiaries, with around 2.34 million employees, were present in 128 countries. The most noticeable patterns evident in the figures in Table 31.1 are as follows.

Table 31.1. Numbers of Japanese subsidiaries and their employees by country

	All industry					Manufacturing				
	Country (A)	Subsidiary (B)	Employee (C)	Expatriate (D)	(D)/(C) %	Country (A′)	Subsidiary (B′)	Employee (C′)	Expatriate (D′)	(D′)/(C′) %
Total	138	20,455	3,086,260	52,820	1.71	128	7,739	2,343,948	23,612	1.01
Asia	24	8,684	1,763,667	24,031	1.36	14	4,709	1,508,878	14,327	0.95
Korea		533	137,920	478	0.35		422	120,494	343	0.28
China		1,532	366,187	3,730	1.02		1,138	323,739	2,897	0.89
Taiwan		1,016	130,957	1,927	1.47		644	108,215	1,230	1.14
Hong Kong		1,287	120,264	3,807	3.17		278	86,764	1,204	1.39
Thailand		1,138	332,324	4,563	1.37		651	291,790	3,063	1.05
Singapore		1,159	93,338	3,729	4.00		338	63,856	1,303	2.04
Malaysia		841	224,510	2,531	1.13		502	197,959	1,911	0.97
Philippines		340	98,924	794	0.80		190	82,042	563	0.69
Indonesia		574	193,415	2,107	1.09		373	174,020	1,563	0.90
India		95	38,133	139	0.36		75	36,428	101	0.28
Others	14	169	27,695	226	0.82	4	98	23,571	149	0.63
Middle East	10	131	9,779	275	2.81	10	32	4,546	43	0.95
Europe	33	3,956	313,079	8,419	2.69	33	813	204,209	1,975	0.97
UK		1,062	131,437	3,109	2.37		236	86,835	750	0.86
The Netherlands		478	17,077	824	4.83		49	10,052	128	1.27
Belgium		197	26,428	606	2.29		52	22,275	149	0.67
Luxembourg		65	870	56	6.44		5	499	7	1.40
France		421	21,940	643	2.93		111	11,814	210	1.78
Germany		742	47,797	2,048	4.28		121	26,634	360	1.35
Switzerland		129	2,899	178	6.14		7	6	1	16.67

Table 31.1. Continued

	All industry					Manufacturing				
	Country (A)	Subsidiary (B)	Employee (C)	Expatriate (D)	(D)/(C) %	Country (A′)	Subsidiary (B′)	Employee (C′)	Expatriate (D′)	(D′)/(C′) %
Spain		181	16,240	223	1.37		60	12,257	101	0.82
Italy		213	12,589	320	2.54		61	8,206	72	0.88
Others	24	468	35,802	412	1.15	24	111	25,631	197	0.77
North America	2	5,200	670,048	16,937	2.53	2	1,593	454,497	6,206	1.37
Canada		424	38,067	709	1.86		118	22,211	296	1.33
USA		4,776	631,981	16,228	2.57		1,475	432,286	5,910	1.37
Mid-S. America	30	1,277	251,004	1,688	0.67	30	396	128,715	765	0.59
Mexico		175	50,218	464	0.92		104	48,225	308	0.64
Panama		235	1,011	64	6.33		4	6	1	16.67
Brazil		415	175,156	697	0.40		194	64,323	358	0.56
Others	27	452	24,619	463	1.88	27	94	16,161	98	0.61
Africa	26	299	15,040	189	1.26	26	47	11,395	55	0.48
Liberia		181	24	17	70.83		0	0	0	
Others	25	118	15,016	172	1.15	25	47	11,395	55	0.48
Oceania	13	908	63,643	1,281	2.01	13	149	31,708	241	0.76
Australia		645	43,044	870	2.02		116	21,508	164	0.76
New Zealand		121	7,585	119	1.57		24	4,957	39	0.79
Guam		76	3,464	150	4.33		1	11	2	18.18
Others	10	66	9,550	142	1.49	10	8	5,232	36	0.69

Source: Toyo Keizai Inc., Kaigai Shinshutsu Kigyo Soran (Directory of the Japanese Subsidiaries and Affiliates Abroad) by company (1996) and country (1997).
Notes: (A), (A′), (B), (B′) as at the end of 1995; (C), (C′), (D), (D′) as at the end of 1996.

The greatest number of manufacturing plants are concentrated in Asia, followed by North America and Europe, though there is a considerable number of plants in Latin America, Oceania, and even in Africa and the Middle East. The Asian region is conspicuous in several respects. Asia has the highest concentration of transplants (4,709 out of 7,739 or 61% of all manufacturing subsidiaries) and the greatest proportion of manufacturing subsidiaries as a percentage of all Japanese subsidiaries (4,709 out of 8,684 or 54% of the all-industry total). In each of nine Asian countries from the Philippines to China, between 190 and 1,138 Japanese plants exist, which are operated with much smaller percentages of Japanese expatriates, compared with those in Western countries, excepting the UK. The percentages are 0.28 per cent for Korea, 0.89 per cent for China, 1.14 per cent for Taiwan, 1.05 per cent for Thailand, compared with 1.37 per cent for the USA, 0.86 per cent for the UK, 1.35 per cent in Germany, and 1.78 per cent in France. Part of the explanation for this difference lies in the fact that in Asian countries, joint ventures with local firms are a prominent form of ownership among transplants. Yet, as described later, there is also need to consider the more important issue of managerial challenges in the cross-cultural transfer of technologies and work methods.

Technology Transfer by Japanese Auto and Electronics Firms in East Asia, the USA, and Europe: 'Application-Adaptation' Evaluations of Japanese 'Hybrid Factories'

The following analysis uses the 'Application-Adaptation (A-A)' or 'Hybrid' model developed by the Japanese Multinational Enterprise Study Group (JMNESG)[1] to investigate, in a systematic and detailed way, how Japanese transplants have been transferring production systems to local settings in the three regions.

Analytical Framework

The A-A model seeks to determine the extent to which the Japanese-style production system, summarized in terms of 23 elements and 6 groups (see Table 31.2), has been introduced and applied in the foreign subsidiaries of Japanese manufacturing firms (Abo 1994, chs. 1 and 2; Itagaki 1997, ch. 1). This model emphasizes those specific aspects of the production system which are vital for achieving high product quality and efficient production over a wide range of operations. The focus is on the degree to which a strong sense of identity with

[1] The Japanese Multinational Enterprise Study Group, under my direction, has undertaken field studies many times in North America (1986, 1989, and 1993), the NIEs (1992), the ASEAN countries (1993, directed by Professor H. Itagaki), the UK (1997), and continental Europe (1998, directed by H. Kumon and T. Abo), in addition to numerous supplemental research projects. Its work has led to the publication of a great number of books and articles in Japanese and English. For collections of this work in English, see Abo (1994) and Itagaki (1997).

the company on the part of employees has been established, and on the extent of flexibility deriving from 'work site-oriented operations'. The model was completed around the latter half of the 1980s just before the onset of the bubble economy in Japan. Though there have been some changes in the Japanese system since the crash, we think it is still appropriate to use the model as a prototype against which to measure the degree of conformity to (or deviation from) it, in both foreign and home plants. The focal point of the model is the human factor which underlies and provides strength to the Japanese system, a factor not only intimately related to the historical and cultural background of Japanese society but also strongly based on in-house education and training. Our hypothesis is that, when Japanese firms 'apply' their successful technological systems to settings in foreign countries, they will face problems in adapting to the local managerial and regulatory environment. This is a 'dilemma model' in the sense that it exposes difficulties or even trade-offs that exist in the application-adaptation aspects of the transplanted production system. However, various applications and adaptations generate different patterns of 'hybrids' blending Japanese elements and local influences within the subsidiary plants. The precise character of these hybrids largely depends on the socio-cultural background of the host setting, which is itself influenced to a considerable extent by the historical and geographical context of each society.

We use a five-point scale ('hybrid ratio') to determine where the overseas plants of Japanese firms are to be positioned relative to these opposing models. A score of 5 indicates the highest possible degree of application (and consequently, the lowest level of adaptation: this score would be given to a Japanese plant operating in Japan). Conversely, a score of 1 represents the highest degree of adaptation (which would be given to a non-Japanese plant operating in its domestic environment).

Six-Group and Twenty-Three-Item Evaluations

Table 31.2 summarizes the results from applying the A-A model based on field research in 50 auto assembly, auto parts, and consumer electronics plants in the USA, the NIEs (Taiwan, Korea), ASEAN region (Thailand, Malaysia, and Singapore), and Europe (UK and Germany) over the period 1989–94. (Precise breakdowns of factories by industry and country are given in the second note of Table 31.2). The figures shown in Table 31.2 are average scores for each of the three chosen industries as calculated by the members of the research team or by me alone in the case of Europe.

Overall Evaluation. The overall average application score of Japanese plants for all three industries in the four regions is 3.2. This indicates a slight tendency towards the application side. In other words, although Japanese elements predominate somewhat, Japanese and 'other' (mostly 'local') elements are mixed in nearly equal portions. The Japanese local plants as a whole thus operate with a

Table 31.2. The hybrid ratios (six groups–twenty-three items) of Japanese auto and electronics plants in North America, NIES, ASEAN, and Europe, 1989–1993

	USA				NIEs				ASEAN				Europe				Total			
	AA	AP	CE	av.	AA	AP	CE	av.	AA	AP	CE	av.	AA	AP	CE	av.	AA	AP	CE	av.
G1 Work organization/ administration	3.3	3.1	2.3	2.7	4.0	4.1	3.7	3.9	3.5	2.8	3.1	3.2	4.0	4.2	2.7	3.6	3.7	3.4	2.9	3.3
1. Job classification	4.8	3.5	2.6	3.4	5.0	5.0	4.8	4.9	5.0	4.3	4.1	4.4	4.3	4.0	3.5	4.0	4.8	4.2	3.7	4.2
2. Job rotation	3.3	2.5	1.9	2.4	3.8	4.5	2.2	3.2	3.0	2.3	2.4	2.5	4.3	5.0	2.0	3.7	3.5	3.4	2.1	2.8
3. Training	3.3	2.5	2.0	2.5	3.8	4.0	3.2	3.5	3.3	2.5	2.9	2.9	3.7	4.0	2.5	3.3	3.5	3.1	2.6	3.0
4. Wage	2.3	3.0	2.1	2.3	4.5	3.5	3.8	4.0	3.5	3.0	3.0	3.2	4.0	4.0	2.5	3.5	3.5	3.3	2.9	3.2
5. Promotion	3.3	4.0	2.6	3.0	3.5	4.0	4.2	3.9	3.1	2.5	3.4	3.2	4.0	4.0	2.8	3.6	3.4	3.6	3.2	3.4
6. Supervisor	3.0	3.0	2.4	2.7	3.5	3.5	3.8	3.6	3.0	2.5	3.1	3.0	3.3	4.0	3.0	3.3	3.2	3.1	3.0	3.1
G2 Production control	3.6	3.8	2.9	3.2	3.7	3.7	3.6	3.7	3.0	3.3	3.4	3.3	3.7	3.5	3.0	3.4	3.5	3.6	3.3	3.4
7. Equipment	4.3	4.5	3.7	4.0	3.3	3.5	3.4	3.4	3.5	4.0	3.7	3.7	3.7	2.0	4.0	3.5	3.7	3.7	3.7	3.7
8. Maintenannce	3.0	3.5	1.9	2.5	3.5	4.0	3.8	3.7	2.8	2.8	3.2	3.0	3.7	4.0	2.8	3.4	3.2	3.5	2.9	3.1
9. Quality control	4.0	3.5	2.9	3.3	4.0	3.5	3.6	3.7	2.8	3.5	3.5	3.3	3.7	4.0	2.5	3.3	3.6	3.6	3.2	3.4
10. Operation management	3.0	3.5	3.1	3.2	4.0	3.5	3.6	3.7	2.9	3.0	3.2	3.1	3.7	4.0	2.8	3.4	3.4	3.4	3.2	3.3
G3 Parts procurement	2.8	2.7	2.5	2.6	3.0	2.7	3.2	3.0	3.0	3.2	3.0	3.0	2.0	2.0	2.8	2.3	2.8	2.7	2.9	2.8
11. Local content	2.0	2.0	2.0	2.0	2.3	2.5	3.0	2.6	2.9	3.8	2.8	3.0	1.3	1.0	2.8	1.8	2.2	2.5	2.6	2.4
12. Suppliers	3.5	3.5	3.4	3.5	3.0	3.0	3.2	3.1	3.6	3.8	3.7	3.7	1.7	2.0	3.3	2.3	3.0	3.2	3.5	3.3
13. Methods	3.0	2.5	2.0	2.4	3.8	2.5	3.4	3.4	2.5	2.0	2.6	2.5	3.0	3.0	2.5	2.8	3.1	2.4	2.6	2.7

Table 31.2. Continued

	USA				NIEs				ASEAN				Europe				Total			
	AA	AP	CE	av.	AA	AP	CE	av.	AA	AP	CE	av.	AA	AP	CE	av.	AA	AP	CE	av.
G4 Team sense	3.9	4.3	2.2	3.1	4.0	4.0	3.3	3.7	2.9	2.9	3.5	3.2	3.6	3.7	2.8	3.3	3.6	3.7	3.0	3.3
14. Small group	2.8	3.5	2.1	2.5	4.0	4.0	2.8	3.5	3.0	1.8	3.2	2.9	2.7	4.0	1.5	2.5	3.1	3.2	2.6	2.9
15. Information	4.5	5.0	2.3	3.4	3.8	3.5	3.4	3.5	3.3	3.3.	3.5	3.4	4.0	3.0	3.0	3.5	3.9	3.8	3.0	3.4
16. Unity	4.5	4.5	2.1	3.2	4.3	4.5	3.8	4.1	2.4	3.8	3.9	3.4	4.0	4.0	3.8	3.9	3.8	4.2	3.3	3.6
G5 Labor Relations	4.3	4.1	2.5	3.3	3.8	3.4	3.7	3.7	3.3	2.7	3.2	3.1	4.2	4.0	2.9	3.7	3.9	3.5	3.1	3.4
17. Employment policy	4.5	3.5	2.1	3.1	3.3	3.0	3.4	3.3	3.0	2.8	3.0	3.0	4.3	3.0	3.3	3.8	3.7	3.1	2.8	3.2
18. Employment security	5.0	4.0	2.0	3.2	4.0	3.5	3.6	3.7	3.4	3.0	3.1	3.2	3.7	4.0	2.8	3.4	4.0	3.6	2.8	3.4
19. Union	4.5	5.0	3.3	3.9	4.3	4.0	4.4	4.3	3.8	2.3	3.3	3.3	4.7	5.0	3.0	4.2	4.3	3.9	3.5	3.8
20. Grievance	3.3	4.0	2.7	3.1	3.5	3.0	3.4	3.4	3.0	2.5	3.1	3.0	4.0	4.0	2.5	3.5	3.4	3.3	3.0	3.2
G6 Parent/subsidiary	3.0	4.0	3.1	3.2	1.8	2.8	2.3	2.2	2.5	2.8	2.7	2.7	3.1	1.7	2.8	2.8	2.6	3.0	2.7	2.7
21. JPN ratio	3.0	4.5	2.9	3.2	1.3	2.5	1.2	1.5	1.3	1.8	1.4	1.4	3.7	1.0	2.3	2.8	2.2	2.6	1.9	2.1
22. Power delegation	3.0	3.5	3.3	3.2	1.8	3.0	3.0	2.5	2.8	2.5	2.9	2.8	2.7	3.0	3.0	2.8	2.5	3.0	3.0	2.9
23. Local managers	3.0	4.0	3.1	3.2	2.3	3.0	2.6	2.5	3.4	4.0	4.1	3.8	3.0	1.0	3.0	2.7	2.9	3.3	3.3	3.2
Total average	3.5	3.6	2.5	3.0	3.5	3.6	3.4	3.5	3.1	2.9	3.2	3.1	3.5	3.3	2.9	3.3	3.4	3.3	3.0	3.2

Notes:

1. AA: auto assembly, AP: auto parts, CE: consumer electronics.
2. USA (1989): 13 plants (AA—4, AP—2 and CE—7), NIEs (1992): 11 plants (AA—4 Taiwan, AP—2 Taiwan and CE—4 Taiwan/1 Korea), ASEAN (1993); 18 plants (AA—4 Thailand and 1 Malaysia, AP—2 Thailand and 1 Malaysia, and CE—2 Thailand, 6 Malaysia, and 2 Singapore), Europe (1989–93): 8 plants (AA—3 UK, AP—1 UK, and CE—2 UK and 2 Germany).

mixture of Japanese and local elements, which is why we call them 'hybrid factories'. The overall hybrid ratios for four regions are located between 3.0 and 3.4, and many countries and companies also have similar overall hybrid ratios, though the combinations of items and groups differ. In descending order, the average application scores for all 23 items are Taiwan/Korea (3.4), Europe (3.2), ASEAN (3.1), and the USA (3.0).

A-A Evaluation by Groups and Items. In Table 31.2 (6 groups and 23 items) and in Figure 31.5 (6 groups), total average hybrid ratios for the NIEs and ASEAN transplants show several noticeable differences compared with average ratios for the USA alone (the average US hybrid ratio represents a sort of 'standard Japanese transplant' in our research).

1. In Figure 31.5, the most significant difference in the degree of application of groups is between the NIEs and the USA. There are two sets of reverse combinations of groups. On the one hand, for the NIE transplants we find a higher application score (3.9) for Group 1 (work organization and administration),

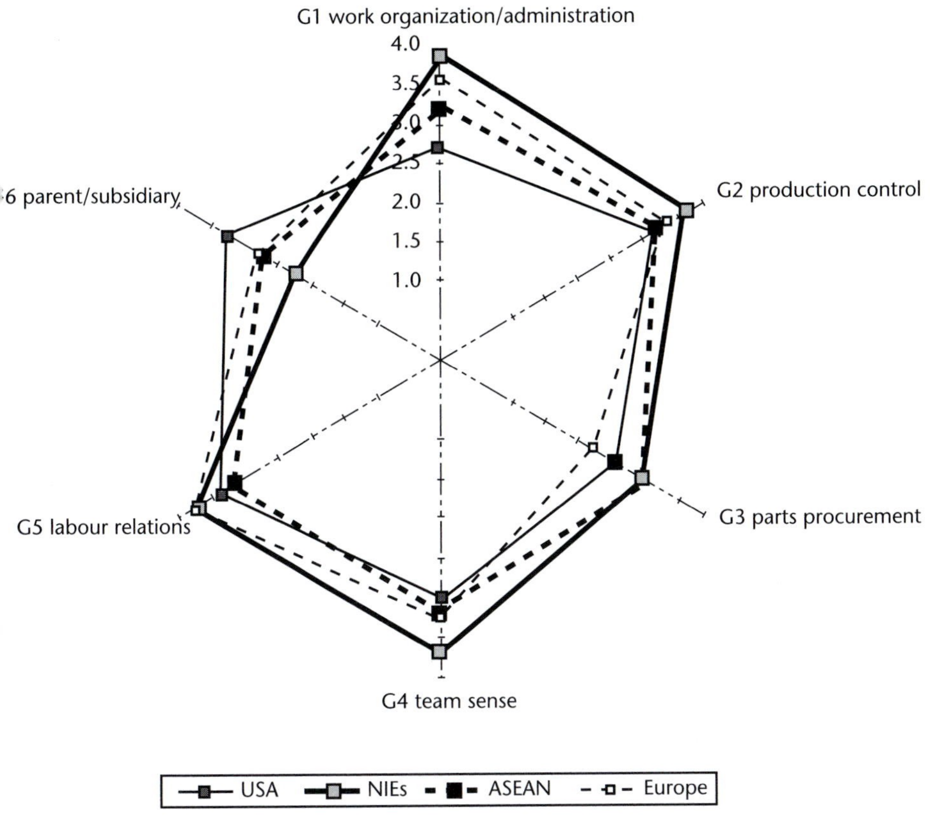

Fig. 31.5. Hybrid ratios of six groups

which is the core of the human-related methods of Japanese production system, and a lower score (2.2) for Group 6 (parent–subsidiary relations), indicating extensive delegation of decision-making power to non-Japanese managers. On the other hand, there is a much lower Group 1 score (2.7) and a relatively higher Group 6 score (3.2) in the USA. Thus, the human-related methods of the Japanese system were more fully and easily transferred to the Japanese plants in the NIEs, and to a certain extent in ASEAN, with more complete delegation of power to local managers compared with plants in the USA. Further, the application scores for Europe (UK and Germany) are closer to Asia than to the USA. These contrasts between the NIEs and the USA are seen even more sharply when the differences in the specific items included in Groups 1 and 6 are examined (see Table 31.2 and Abo 1998*a*).

2. In Group 2, for production control, which plays a critical role in the competitive edge of each transplant, the average application scores for the USA (3.2) and for the NIEs (3.7), ASEAN (3.3), and Europe (3.4) are quite similar. Within the group, the differences in application scores vary widely (compare scores for Group 7 equipment in the USA and NIEs with those for Group 8 maintenance), reflecting especially the difficulty of in-house skill training in the USA (for a more complete evaluation on other groups and items, also see Abo 1998*a* or *b*).

Regional and Industry Comparison. Based on the above, we can draw a more distinct comparative picture of the four regions and three industries, using Figure 31.5.

1. NIEs–ASEAN versus USA–Europe: two major regional patterns emerge. In terms of regional comparison, two sets of reverse combinations of groups are between NIEs–ASEAN and USA–Europe. The NIEs–ASEAN pattern has higher scores for Group 3 (3.0 and 3.0 for NIEs and ASEAN) and lower scores for Group 6 (2.2 and 2.7). The USA–Europe pattern has lower application scores in Group 3 (parts procurement) (2.6 and 2.3 for USA and Europe) and higher application scores in Group 6 (parent/subsidiary) (3.2 and 2.8), indicating a more prominent role for Japanese managers in their transplant operations. In the USA, the UK, and Germany, compared to the NIEs and ASEAN, Japanese plants tend to procure a greater proportion of their inputs from local suppliers, who have both higher technological capabilities and stronger political power to exert on transplant firms. Under such circumstances, the transplants themselves have to maintain a much higher ratio of Japanese expatriates in order to manage their local operations effectively.

As shown in Table 31.2, these regional patterns are closely related to the differences in the application scores of industries between USA–Europe and NIEs–ASEAN. In NIEs–ASEAN the application scores are balanced between industries, ranging from highest to lowest across consumer electronics (CE), auto assembly (AA), and auto parts (AP). But in the USA–Europe there is a very sharp contrast between the scores for different industries: higher levels for AA and AP versus lower scores for CE. In short, in the Asian region, consumer electronics transplants, and in the USA and Europe, auto transplants, are operated at differing scales in terms of size, application level, and performance.

2. NIEs versus ASEAN: although Japanese plants in Asian countries share features different from those in the Western countries, there are notable differences even among Asian countries. This chapter discusses only two significant differences between the NIEs and ASEAN countries. Most application scores (except for Groups 3 and 6) are much higher in the NIEs than those in ASEAN transplants. The much higher application level for Group 1 (work organization) in NIEs (3.9 versus 3.2 in ASEAN) is remarkable, considering that both have comparable low scores for Group 6 (parent/subsidiary) (2.2 for NIEs and 2.7 for ASEAN). Strikingly, with less Japanese delegation, a more Japanese style of organizational management has been implemented in the NIE transplants than in the ASEAN ones. Further, the difference in the application scores for Group 2 (production control) (3.7 and 3.3 respectively for NIEs and ASEAN) is not so great and scores for Group 3 (parts procurement) are the same (3.0). In light of the above comparisons, we can conclude that the pattern of 'hybridization' in Japanese plants in the NIEs is the most desirable variant of those found in any of the four regions, in the sense that the Japanese human-resources-based approaches and methods of work organization have been much more fully transferred, and with a considerable degree of participation by local (non-Japanese) managerial personnel. In other words, these methods have been transferred in the most fundamental way, with local managers and workers developing a deep understanding of their application. We call this the 'East Asian pattern of the Japanese hybrid factory'.

3. Japanese Electronics Assembly Factories in East Asia: based on the above, it would be appropriate to analyse the Japanese electronics industry further to illuminate concrete activities and significant characteristics of management and technology transfer by Japanese companies in East Asia (for further details, see Abo 1997*a*). As will become evident, this industry has played a leading role in not only disseminating Japanese production methods to nearby countries, but also more generally in the integration of the individual economies of East Asia through investment and trade linkages.

The overseas production activities of the Japanese electronics industry in East Asia occurred in two major waves. During the first wave from the 1960s up until the early 1970s Japanese electronics firms set up local plants in the region. Typically these operations were export oriented, located in Free Trade Zones (FTZs), and often 'mini-Matsushita' ('mini-M') in type. Small volumes of almost all the electric and electronic product lines of Matsushita in Japan were produced for each closed local market such as Taiwan, Thailand, Malaysia, and Korea. The second wave emerged during the drastic appreciation of the yen after the Plaza Agreement of 1985. In this phase, the 'mini-M' type of organization lost its effectiveness. Instead, 'new-Matsushita' ('new-M') types of operation prospered in Malaysia, Thailand, and other nations. The organizational characteristics of this new form of operation represented a major discontinuity from the previous generation of transplants in these countries.

The 'new-M' operations relied for the most part on the transfer of 'ready-made' elements of the Japanese production system, sometimes referred to as the transfer of 'results' rather than 'methods' (for a fuller discussion of this distinction within the context of the 'Four Perspective Evaluation Method', see Abo 1994: 21–2, 54–6). The 'method' transfer required a substantial transfer of the fundamental logic, know-how, and methods of work organization at the heart of the Japanese system, as embodied in elements G1 to G4 of the hybrid model (work organization, production control, parts procurement methods, and team concepts). In contrast, the 'result' transfer relied on high degrees of production automation based on the latest machinery and equipment technology and high-quality parts. Indeed, the 'new-M' plants, which were largely built to provide new export bases for Japanese firms, incorporated production technologies that had leapfrogged one or two levels past the 'mini-M' plants. These production systems, which were very close to state of the art, and indeed measured up well even against the Japanese parent plants, required relatively large numbers of Japanese expatriate managers in order to achieve the necessary levels of quality, cost, and on-time delivery required to be competitive in world markets.

Across almost all product lines, which incorporated the large-scale deployment of logistics for parts and material procurement, the electronics products sector led the development of the East Asian region, helping it to become one of the major centres of world economic growth. This process generated an impressive sequential pattern of staged development which has been associated with the term 'flying geese' (see above), and which helped set up the trade dynamics of the 'growth triangle' described earlier.

In terms of plant size, the average number of employees in East Asia (1,394) is almost double that of the average figure (749) for the nine Japanese consumer electronics plants studied in the USA (Abo 1994: 152). It is also a little larger than that found in the nine similar plants in the UK (1,140, according to UK research in the spring of 1997). This is an important indicator of the significant position of the electronics assembly industry in East Asia. In terms of the ratio of Japanese expatriates to total employees, the difference between East Asia and the USA is even clearer: 0.73 per cent versus 1.99 per cent. The variety of product lines in the East Asian plants, from colour televisions, video cassette recorders, and various other consumer home appliances to office information and communication appliances and electronic parts and components, is much higher than in the US plants, where usually only a couple of sizes of colour TVs, and sometimes microwave ovens, are produced.

However, East Asian economic development and interregional relations characteristic of the second phase since the latter half of 1980s are now entering a period of transition. First, in countries such as Taiwan and Korea, priorities have shifted towards greater specialization of product lines in the direction of new higher value-added products, more local R&D activity, and providing support for local production in the ASEAN region and mainland China. In Taiwan, the 1990s have also seen another direction of dynamic development in the electronics industry: OEM (original equipment manufacturing) assembly of computers, semiconductors, and electronic parts for foreign producers. Secondly, production methods in the ASEAN countries have undergone a transformation from the typical 'mini-M' form to a mixture of both 'mini' and 'new-M' types. Thirdly, the financial crisis experienced in many East Asian countries is a very recent and destabilizing phenomenon which has produced rising current account deficits (see below). Fourthly and finally, a major issue looming on the horizon that will have serious effects on the cost structure of Asian economies is the problem of pollution. Here, the development of abatement strategies in the Asian countries has been long delayed.

Against the backdrop of these developments, one can now summarize the 'A-A' evaluation of the Japanese electronics assembly plants in the NIEs and ASEAN countries in comparison with those in the USA. In Figure 31.6 the most

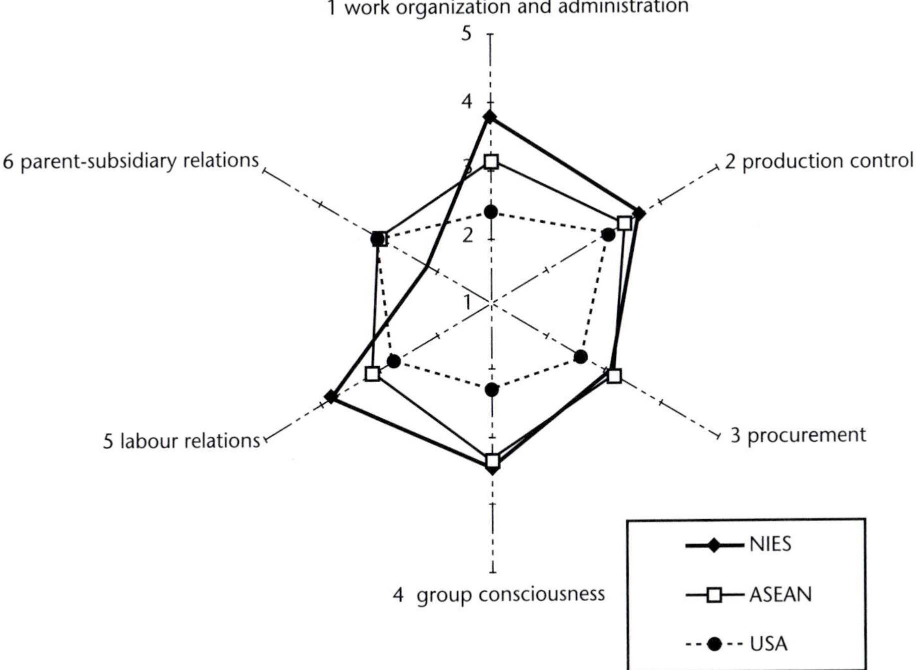

Fig. 31.6. Hybrid evaluation in electronic assembly plants: six groups

salient feature of the Japanese electronics 'hybrid factories' is that the application scores from G1 to G5 for the NIE and ASEAN plants are *much* higher than those in the US plants. Only for the G6 element does a different pattern emerge (indicating a higher dependence on Japanese expatriate managers in the US and ASEAN plants). These patterns are similar to the average across all three industries, where the same conspicuous differences between East Asia and the USA are also evident.

The ASEAN plants represent an especially interesting case at this stage in the industry's development. While the ASEAN electronics plants occupy a position which is, for the most part intermediate between the NIEs and US plants (in terms of the degree and type of 'hybrid factory'), a recent transition towards the 'new-M' type of operation (with its characteristic emphasis on the transfer of 'ready-made' or 'results' aspects of the Japanese production model) is also now visible in this region. It is by no means a foregone conclusion that the ASEAN plants can successfully move to a new stage of highly automated, upgraded production technologies, in which Japanese expatriates lead local production from new export bases which is sent to the world market. To achieve this new stage without first progressing through the continuous stages of learning the 'methods' which are the foundations of the Japanese techniques, such as the logic and know-how underlying work organization, quality control (QC), and parts procurement systems, will be a tall order. Thus far, it is too early to reach any definitive conclusions about the viability of this strategy. However, this remains an important area for current and future research.

Staged Economic Growth and 'Spontaneous' Regional Integration

'Flying Geese', 'Tandem Growth', and Staged Economic Development in East Asia

As mentioned in the earlier analysis of the growth triangle and the Japanese electronics industry, we can see a sequential pattern of staged development in many industries in East Asia, where the diffusion and development of industries and technologies has progressed in steps from lower to higher levels. There are corresponding shifts in the location of production functions from countries at higher stages of this process to those at lower stages: from Japan to the NIEs, and from the NIEs to the ASEAN countries. Several explanations for this phenomenon have been advanced from different perspectives. Given the present context, the discussions of Ozawa (1995) and Cho (1994) are particularly interesting and useful.[2]

[2] On the subjects of 'flying geese' and staged development, the main references are Akamatsu (1960), Kojima (1978), Ozawa (1995), and Cho (1994). Notwithstanding their remarkable contribution to our understanding of East Asian development, these theoretical frameworks share a common weak point: while they have succeeded in illuminating the pattern of staged and sequen-

The well-known thesis of Kojima (1978) and Ozawa (1995, 1996) is concerned primarily with an industry-level sequential process of economic development, from advanced countries to underdeveloped countries in Asia, based on the theory of comparative advantage. This approach is referred to as the 'flying geese' or 'tandem growth' paradigm. According to this argument, shifts in the location of industries follow shifting comparative advantages. The typical sequence is from a sector such as textiles to electrical products, electronics, automotive, and so forth. This same sequence is followed first in Japan and then subsequently in the NIEs (Korea, Taiwan, and Singapore), and then the ASEAN countries (Thailand, Malaysia, and so forth). Moreover, the focus here is on changing levels of development among countries with relatively similar socio-economic structures.

Another notable theoretical approach focuses on the staged, *intra-firm* technology transfer within East Asia (Cho 1994). This thesis illuminates the relationship between (1) the tiered nature of technologies accumulated sequentially within a multinational firm, and (2) the sequential cross-border transfer of each tier of technologies, usually from a simpler level to a more advanced level, between a parent company in a technology-exporting country (Japan) and its subsidiary in a technology-receiving country (e.g. Korea). This is then followed by a subsequent transfer from the first subsidiary, after being upgraded to the next tier, to a second subsidiary in a third country (e.g. Thailand), and so on. This approach stresses the continuous and sequential nature of technology transfer, the different degrees of difficulty of technology transfer depending on the levels and nature of the technology tiers involved, and the different levels of technologies already present at the different subsidiaries (which is itself strongly influenced by the broader socio-cultural and managerial environment prevailing at those subsidiaries).

The above two research models are particularly useful for analysing dynamic economic growth in the East Asian region in the 1980s up until the mid-1990s as led by Japanese FDI. Ozawa's model is perhaps more effective for explaining the macroscopic aspects of such a pattern, while Cho's approach focuses on the more microscopic aspects of development and thus is methodologically closer to the field research results for the Japanese manufacturing transplants described earlier. Many case studies support the model, as, for example, a case study of Murata Manufacturing (see Hao and Abo 1997).

'Spontaneous' Regional Integration

Economic growth within East Asia since the early 1980s represents a form of regional integration which is quite distinct from the experiences of Europe or

tial economic growth (i.e. following an orderly sequence from lower to higher levels of industrial or technological development), they have almost completely neglected to consider any possibility of skipped development—for example, Japanese and Korean type industrial development and the 'new-M' type of technology transfer described above.

North America, in that it has been accomplished without the formation of specific supranational trade and investment-regulating institutions for regional integration such as the EU or NAFTA. The above analysis clarifies the actual processes and structures for the progression of such a development pattern, and the reasons why such a distinct pattern has been possible in this region. Given the absence of such supranational institutions, and the leading role of market-mediated private investment, this East Asian process may be termed a 'spontaneous' approach to regional economic integration.

It is interesting to consider the political background underlying this integration process. According to Twu's insightful inquiry (1997: 104), one of the most important reasons why East Asia has been able to maintain free trade and investment flows is that ASEAN, a cornerstone in determining the final direction of trade balances within the 'growth triangle', was established (in 1967) and has been sustained to promote political co-operation within the member nations in order to cope with the Vietnam War and Kampuchean civil war. In other words, if the main purpose of the creation of ASEAN had been economic co-operation it would have been difficult for the organization to maintain such a free trade regime, or to survive for such a long period. Thus, only after having created a strong political basis for substantial economic co-operation among ASEAN countries, is AFTA (the ASEAN Free Trade Area) going to set up a common tariff of less than 5 per cent by 2003. This development, while driven by its own endogenous dynamic, may also be seen as a response to external pressures—especially the protectionist threats emerging from the EU and NAFTA.

In contrast, APEC's establishment was motivated more by political reasons and cannot be said to be a true economic zone with interdependent development relations. So long as the USA continues to play a crucial role in the trade pattern in the Pacific Rim, geopolitics suggest that any Asian nation would have to follow US leadership in APEC. The US role in the region's economic progress is still very important, especially in the 1990s when the strength of the Japanese economy in Asia has been hampered by the crash of its 'bubble economy' and the severe damage inflicted by the financial crisis throughout the Asian region since the autumn of 1997. However, the lead role of the USA may itself become less certain due to the possible emergence of its own 'bubble economy' phenomena in the late 1990s (Abo 1998*b*).

The Financial Crisis and Prospects for East Asian Regional Integration

The Asian financial crisis presented a major challenge to the dynamic development pattern described above. However, as of September 1999, foreign exchange rates and stock prices in almost all the East Asian countries have recovered and regained stability at a level of around 20 to 30 per cent lower than the peak levels reached in the summer of 1997. Foreign exchange rates have generally been stable since the spring of 1998, having rebounded from the low points reached in early 1998. Stock prices have recovered sharply from the severe setbacks encountered in the summer of 1998. Agencies such as the IMF, the Japan Economic Planning Agency, and the Asian Development Bank now forecast that growth rates for real GDP in the region will improve dramatically from around minus 10 per cent in 1998 to 2 to 3 per cent in 1999 and much higher in the next few years. The critical factors for the sustainability of this recovery process and the return of lasting stability are the revitalization of the Japanese economy and the future of the booming US economy. Subject to these factors, the East Asian economies still have the potential to retain their characteristic pattern of dynamic development, though they may have reached a turning point in which growth rates will decline from around 10 per cent to around 5 per cent.

The first reason for optimism is the fact that the primary causes of the crises in East Asian countries were limited mostly to the financial sector, especially the over-borrowing of short-term loans from foreign financial organizations including the notorious 'hedge-funds'. In this sense the nature of the recession was basically cyclical not structural. However, since this is the first serious economic setback experienced by the Asian countries since they fully embraced the capitalist system, it will take them some time to recover from the damage and confusion that these events have caused.

Secondly, the region still retains considerable potential to resume its familiar pattern of development, in at least a couple of specific ways. The most important consideration is that human resource systems and institutions throughout many East Asian countries retain a special affinity to the Japanese-style management systems which have enabled the preceding rapid growth.[3] The supply of human resources, as well as land, is still relatively abundant in many East Asian countries. This is particularly so if we take into account the adjustment effects (i.e. wage and price reductions) which resulted from the late 1990s economic crisis.

Differences in the stage of development, another source of growth through the 1980s and 1990s, still persist between the countries in the region, despite some important changes: (1) the leading position of Japanese industries in the region has been weakened; (2) the financial and economic damage in Korea has

[3] Judging from the above analyses, especially of the Japanese electronics assembly industry, we would take issue with Krugman's pessimistic evaluation of the potential inherent in technological development in East Asia. His analysis is principally based on the use of analytical models such as total factor productivity, which is built on a distinctly American conception of technology now dominant in Western society. On the contrary, it should be pointed out that the 'methods'-oriented characteristics, in particular the training orientation, of the Japanese system or company, and its more fundamental affinity with the character of East Asian societies, have produced a course of industrial development which is very distinctive from that followed in Russia or the other non-Asian developing regions on which Krugman's argument depends (see Krugman 1994).

been relatively large, forcing the country to implement significant reforms of its traditional socio-economic structure such as the 'chaebol'; (3) the influence of the crisis on the Taiwanese economy has been much lighter, partly because of the already mature nature of its economy as a forerunner in the region, partly due to its development of intermediary roles as a parts supplier in the relations between Japan and China and between Japan and the ASEAN countries, and partly because of industrial development having taken a new direction led by computer-related micro-electronics industries primarily in the form of OEM contracts.

In contrast to the above optimism concerning the future growth potential in East Asian countries, the prospects associated with two key preconditions which underlay the early prosperity—the substantial demand for imports into the growing economies of the USA in particular and Japan—are less certain now. It would be too optimistic for Asian countries to expect the consumption and asset market-led boom of the American economy to remain sustainable indefinitely. Limitations to the expansion of its 'real' economy (i.e. supply bottlenecks) have accelerated 'asset inflation' in securities and land markets, a situation that was exacerbated by successive reductions in interest rates by the Federal Reserve Board from October to December in 1998. Subsequently, the Fed has pursued a policy of monetary tightening in order to 'rein in' a possibly 'overheated' US economy. Since the summer of 1999, the position of the US economy has become considerably more delicate and uncertain. The apparent weakening of stock prices in New York has been triggered by the decline of the US dollar's value against the Japanese yen and, to some extent, the EU currencies, following more optimistic projections for a Japanese recovery and European growth.

As for the Japanese economy, its management and production systems remain fundamentally strong, particularly in its major manufacturing industries such as auto and electronics. This is underscored by the continuously large magnitude of the export and current account surplus, except for finance and some service sectors. Yet, at the same time, it is also true that the Japanese economy remained vulnerable until late 1998, due to the loss of business and consumer confidence. This loss derived from the lasting psychological effects of the shock of the bubble crash. The excessive loss of self-confidence in the Japanese system, further amplified by the uncertain framework of the world economy and its floating foreign exchange rate system, fed a vicious circle of a weak psychological outlook and a weaker economy. Thus, only if the Japanese people regain their confidence in the future will Japan's economic recovery proceed smoothly. Some of the signs for this recovery have already appeared: the first three-quarters of 1999 saw a consumption-led increase in sales and production activities, which has further spurred business confidence, encouraged a subsequent recovery of price levels for key assets such as stocks and land, and thereby led to an improvement in the quality of assets held by banks. Should these conditions hold, we can expect businesses to resume their investment in new, innovative production capacity and to create new employment opportunities. Finally, imports into Japan, which dropped sharply after the crash of the bubble economy, should recover enough to support region-wide growth in the next phase of Asian economic recovery, compensating for any future decline in US imports.

To sum up, over the next couple of years the Japanese and East Asian countries will be challenged by several difficult problems which will render them vulnerable in the near future. However, if these kinds of problems are resolved in line with the scenario suggested above, there is a very good possibility that a second phase of Asian economic growth will be realized. Furthermore, we can expect this new phase to be characterized by a fundamentally similar pattern of FDI-led, sequential staged development, but producing somewhat lower growth rates with some modifications in the transitional period. We can also expect to see a continuation of the 'East Asian pattern' of the Japanese hybrid factory, pursued most actively by the automotive and electronics industries, and not only by Japanese firms but also by European and American or local firms operating in the region.

Secondly, in the coming new phase, East Asia will and must move towards a stronger economic regionalism or regional integration in order to meet the challenges presented by the earlier large-scale regional integration in Europe and North America. This need not translate necessarily into a stronger AFTA (Asean Free Trade Area) or APEC (Asia–Pacific Economic Co-operation Conference). In this regard, one of the most urgent regional integration policies should be to establish a more stable regional currency system in East Asia. In the wake of the recent hardship arising from unstable and risky foreign exchange rate fluctuations in the spring of 1995 in Japan, and since the summer of 1997 in East Asia, major countries such as Malaysia, Korea, Thailand, and the Philippines, as well as Japan, have now found common ground on which they can seriously discuss the creation of a framework to adjust and stabilize Asian currency fluctuations. Of course, if more comprehensive regional integration is the goal, East Asia cannot be expected to bypass the long and difficult process followed by the member states of the EU. Although the starting point is a long way from that in Europe, if the East Asian countries could adopt a currency band system in which foreign exchange rate fluctuations were restricted to a range of, say, 15 per cent around current levels, this would be a very significant start. East Asia's long-term economic stability may well depend on it.

References

Abo, T., ed. 1994. *Hybrid Factory: Japanese Production System in the United States.* New York: Oxford University Press.

Abo, T., ed. 1995. A comparison of Japanese 'hybrid factories' in U.S., Europe and Asia. *Management International Review*, Gabler Verlag, 1995/1.

—— 1996. The Japanese production system: the process of adaptation to national settings. In *States against Markets: The Limits of Globalization*, ed. R. Boyer and D. Drache. London: Routledge.

—— 1997*a*. Electronics assembly industry. In Itagaki 1997.

—— 1997*b*. Changes in Japanese automobile and electronic transplants in the USA, 1989–1993. In Hasegawa and Hook 1997.

—— 1998*a*. Hybridization of the Japanese production system in North America, newly industrializing economies, South-East Asia, and Europe: contrasted configurations. In *Between Imitation and Innovation*, ed. R. Boyer, E. Charron, U. Jurgens, and S. Tolliday. New York: Oxford University Press.

—— 1998*b*. Changing impacts of the Japanese economy on America: pessimistic and optimistic aspects in mid-1998. *Journal of American Studies* (American Studies Association of Korea), 30/2 (winter): 413–34.

Akamatsu, K. 1960. A theory of unbalanced growth in the world economy. *Weltwirtschaftliches Archive*, 86/2.

Cho, D.-S. 1994. Nihon Kigyo no Takokusekika to Kigyo-nai Gijutsu Iten. (In Japanese. Multinationalization of Japanese firms and intrafirm technology transfer.) *Soshiki Kagaku*, 27/3.

Hao, Y., and Abo, T. 1997. Murata Manufacturing Co. Ltd. In Itagaki 1997, ch. 5.

Hasegawa, H., and Hook, G. D., eds. 1997. *Japanese Business Management: Restructuring for Low Growth and Globalization*. London: Routledge.

Itagaki, H., ed. 1997. *The Japanese Production System: Hybrid Factories in East Asia*. London: Macmillan.

Japanese External Trade Organization (JETRO) 1996 and 1997. *Foreign Direct Investments of the World and Japan.* (In Japanese.) Tokyo: JETRO.

Kojima, K. 1978. *Direct Foreign Investment*. London: Croom Helm.

Krugman, P. 1994. The myth of Asia's miracle. *Foreign Affairs*, 73/6: 62–78.

Ozawa, T. 1995. Structural upgrading and concatenated integration: the vicissitudes of the Pax Americana in tandem industrialization of the Pacific Rim. In *Corporate Strategies in the Pacific Rim: Global versus Regional Trends*, ed. D. Simon. London: Routledge.

—— 1996. Professor Kojima's 'trade augmentation' principle and the 'flying geese' paradigm of tandem growth. *Surugadai Economics Studies*, 5/2: 269–96.

Porter, M. 1990. *The Competitive Advantage of Nations*. New York: The Free Press.

Trevor, M. 1983. *Japan's Reluctant Multinationals*. London: Frances Pinter.

Twu, J.-Y. 1997. The Asian growth triangle: structure, change and perspective. In Itagaki 1997.

Yamashita, S. 1997. Japanese investment strategy and technology transfer in East Asia. In Hasegawa and Hook 1997.

Chapter 32

Regional Economic Integration in North America

John Holmes

Introduction

MULTILATERAL trade liberalization in the postwar period has been paralleled by a process of integration through regional trade agreements. In fact, one of the most striking and surprising features of the international trading system at the end of the twentieth century is the extent to which world trade is covered by such regional integration agreements (Hoekman and Kostecki 1995; OECD 1995; Frankel 1998). Over the last three decades, the liberalization of domestic economies, the strengthening of liberal regimes in international trade and finance, and the transnationalization of corporate structures have all contributed to the accelerated growth of globally integrated production and market structures. Thus, it seems somewhat ironic that just when international economic relations have become increasingly global in character, the multilateral trading system has faltered and regionalism has been in the ascendancy. In North America, this trend towards increased regionalization in the international trading system is manifested in the negotiation of the 1989 Canada–US Free Trade Agreement (CUSTA) and the 1994 North American Free Trade Agreement (NAFTA) between the USA, Mexico, and Canada.

The most favoured nation (MFN) clause became the cornerstone of the post-1945 international trading system and was incorporated into the various rounds of tariff reductions negotiated under the General Agreement on Tariffs and Trade (GATT), and more recently the World Trade Organization (WTO). This non-discriminatory approach to tariff reductions resulted in significant progress towards liberalized global trade. Paralleling this long-term postwar trend towards trade liberalization, however, were two periods which saw a surge in regional integration agreements (Bhagwati 1993: 24; De Melo and

Panagariya 1993). The first period, the 1960s, saw the establishment of the rival European Economic Community and European Free Trade Association (EFTA). In the context of the broader international economy, however, the USA was then the undisputed global hegemon and a staunch supporter of multilateralism. As a consequence, and although proposals were touted for a number of other regional free trade areas in the 1960s, 'regionalism had virtually died by the end of the decade [of the 1960s], except for the original European Community and EFTA' (Bhagwati 1993: 29).

The second wave of regional trade agreements began in the mid-1980s and this time the USA was a major participant, negotiating both the CUSTA and NAFTA.[1] During the same period, European economic integration widened and deepened and other regional trading arrangements emerged in Asia (ASEAN and APEC) and Latin America (MERCOSUR). Regionalization is now so widespread that on the eve of the establishment of the WTO nearly all of its members were parties to at least one regional trade agreement (WTO 1995: 27).

Intra-regional trade in North America and Western Europe was already substantial and influenced heavily by geographical proximity even prior to the second wave of regional integration agreements. In large measure, this is a result of the postwar evolution of production systems driven by the increasing segmentation and vertical disintegration of many production processes, the increasingly sophisticated elaboration of complex regional and international divisions of labour, and the concomitant growth in specialization and intra-industry and intra-firm trade across national boundaries. The fact that this process of specialization and trade in intermediate products is facilitated by geographical proximity which reduces transportation and related costs provides a strong rationale for regional integration. Besides increasing the overall level of trade between partners, regional trade agreements have facilitated the process of economic rationalization, restructuring, and integration. Countries have sought to enter into regional economic integration agreements to maximize the competitive position of their key industries.[2] Thus, there is a very intricate relationship between the process of trade regionalization and the shift in the paradigm of international competition at the level of the firm towards what some writers have labelled a glocalization strategy (Ruigrok and van Tulder 1995: 178).

A wide range of motivations and factors shape the negotiation of regional integration agreements and existing arrangements around the world differ con-

[1] For a comprehensive chronology of the growth of regionalism in the postwar trading system and its acceleration in recent years, see Whalley (1998).

[2] While the growth of specialization and co-production and trade in intermediate products can be understood in efficiency and competitive terms, at the same time it lies at the heart of the unease that surrounds NAFTA on the part of labour unions concerned over the movement of production to Mexico to take advantage of less costly labour (Weintraub 1997: 38).

siderably in their specifics (Anderson and Blackhurst 1993; Atkinson 1998; Gamble and Payne 1996; Gibb and Michalak 1994; Whalley 1998). Here, we will focus exclusively on regional trade arrangements and economic integration in North America and not attempt to draw comparisons with arrangements in other parts of the world. One of the most striking features that distinguishes the NAFTA from many other regional trade agreements is that it involves the integration of a developing economy (Mexico) with two of the world's most highly developed economies and, thus, has the potential to 'change the economic map of North America quite radically' (Dicken 1998: 109).

The aim of this chapter is to examine the development of regional economic integration within North America. The chapter is divided into two main sections. The first provides an overview of the development of economic integration within North America leading up to and including the negotiation of NAFTA. The second section examines some of the recent trends in North American trade and investment and speculates on the impact that NAFTA might have on the economic geography of North America.

From the Auto Pact to NAFTA: The Development of the North American Trade Bloc

Debates in Canada over nationalist versus continentalist economic development projects date back to the nineteenth century. The first real impetus towards continental integration, however, came in the mid-1960s with the signing of the Canada–United States Automotive Products Trade Agreement (the Auto Pact). The Auto Pact is a managed trade agreement which permits the duty-free movement of automotive parts and assembled vehicles between the two countries subject to certain production safeguards (Holmes 1992).[3] The Auto Pact enabled the large American-based automakers (GM, Ford, and Chrysler) to rationalize and rapidly integrate their production of both parts and assembled vehicles into *one industry* supplying the combined US and Canadian market. One result was the development of significant intra-industry trade and trade in intermediate products between the two countries. At the time, the Auto Pact was viewed by some in Canada as the prototype for what it was hoped would become a series of bilateral sectoral trade agreements between the USA and Canada. However, despite the very obvious success of the Auto Pact, especially from Canada's perspective, the USA's strong commitment to the GATT principle of multilateralism and the resurgence of Canadian economic nationalism blocked further development in that direction.

[3] Although the Auto Pact has remained intact through the negotiation of both the CUSTA and NAFTA, it is likely that the Auto Pact will be struck down in the face of a recent challenge brought before the WTO by Japan and the European Community.

In the mid-1980s the USA reversed its long-standing opposition to bilateral or regional free trade agreements and this paved the way for the negotiation of the CUSTA in 1989 and NAFTA in 1994 between the USA, Mexico, and Canada. The development of regional agreements in North America has been driven by the following factors:

- the search for safe haven trade agreements by the two smaller countries, Canada and Mexico, who now more than ever before wish to secure access to the US market because of the fear of higher trade barriers in the future or of getting side-swiped by trade wars between the USA, Japan, and Europe. Traditionally, small countries have been the main proponents of multilateralism and perhaps the most remarkable feature of the regional agreements in North America is that it has been the smaller countries who have been the initiators; Canada in the case of CUSTA and Mexico in the case of NAFTA;[4]
- frustration on the part of the USA in the mid-1980s with progress towards new multilateral liberalization under the GATT and their belief that threatening to negotiate or actually negotiating regional arrangements on their part might force other reluctant larger powers to make concessions multilaterally;
- the desire of the USA to enlarge its sphere of trade policy influence for subsequent bargaining with other large blocs. While the USA received limited direct trade creation benefits, the agreements allowed it either to discipline annoying domestic policies (e.g. in the case of CUSTA with regard to Canada's foreign investment review and national energy policies) or achieve exclusionary arrangements to keep third parties out of smaller country markets (as in the case of Mexico through regional content rules incorporated into the NAFTA). The USA also hoped that extending the free trade area to Mexico would help ensure continued peaceful and smooth political and economic transition in Mexico and help address the increasingly vexatious cross-border issues of immigration, illegal drug importation, and environmental degradation;
- economic integration was already well under way between the three countries in a number of key manufacturing sectors such as motor vehicles and electronics as a result of the glocalization investment and production strategies of large transnational firms. Such strategies had produced significant growth in both intra-industry and intra-firm trade across the continent with intra-regional trade growth outstripping growth in global trade. As a result, CUSTA and NAFTA were strongly supported by transnational corporations who

[4] The NAFTA negotiations were initiated and largely driven by the Mexican desire to achieve a trade agreement with the USA following Mexico's unilateral liberalization of its domestic economy launched in 1983 and its entry into the GATT in 1986 (Whalley 1993).

viewed the agreements as facilitating the further restructuring, rationalization, and integration of their North American production systems (Kelly 1997: 502; Weintraub 1997: 36).

There was a marked contrast between the two agreements with regard to both the reception they received in the USA and their projected and actual impacts on cross-border trade and investment flows. Although CUSTA represented a ground-breaking step for US trade policy, at its core it was still traditional, in the sense that it was an agreement between two highly developed economies. As such, and although highly controversial in Canada, it attracted very little public debate in the USA and sailed through the congressional approval process. By contrast, NAFTA, involving as it did trade integration with a developing country sharing a common border with the USA, represented something very new and led to 'the most contentious national and congressional trade debate since the Smoot-Hawley tariff measures of 1930' in the USA (Weintraub 1997: 3). The debate in both the USA and Canada has continued and remained contentious but now focuses on the impact of NAFTA.[5]

CUSTA was negotiated against a backdrop of academic studies and government claims showing large trade and welfare gains to follow from its implementation. In Canada, free trade advocates such as the Macdonald Commission and the C. D. Howe Institute saw free trade as a central part of a broader agenda of market liberalization, deregulation, and privatization. They argued that the CUSTA would lead to a more efficient economy via economies of scale, higher productivity, and higher rates of innovation. Opponents of free trade feared downward pressures on Canadian wages and labour standards, deindustrialization, and the massive loss of Canadian manufacturing jobs. They argued that the world was now one in which absolute advantage rather than comparative advantage was predominant. As a consequence, competition in regions integrated through trade and investment agreements will tend to shift production, investment, and jobs to those locales which offer the lowest combination of wage and other costs in relation to productivity.

In reality, CUSTA was never likely to change US–Canada trade flows dramatically since prior to the agreement the average tariff on Canadian exports to the USA was 1 per cent and nearly 80 per cent of Canadian trade with the USA was already duty free. Furthermore, trade barriers in key sectoral areas such as textiles, steel, agriculture, and energy remained largely untouched by the agreement. In the first three years following its implementation, growth in

[5] Recent assessments of NAFTA range from defining it as an unqualified success (USTR 1997; DFAIT 1999) to defining it as a clear failure (EPI 1997). Among other studies there seems to be a consensus that though NAFTA has had some effect on trade it has had remarkably small net effects on output and employment, except in a few specific sectors such as apparel and electronics (ITC 1997; Weintraub 1997; Jackson 1999).

US–Canada trade actually slowed, increases in net inward foreign investment did not occur to the degree expected, and the agreement became mired in disputes over alleged job losses and out-of-country plant relocations.

In contrast, over the five years immediately prior to NAFTA coming into force, US–Mexico trade had doubled and there had been a sharp increase in net foreign direct investment into Mexico. During the 1990s both Mexico and Canada have experienced significant increases both in trade with the USA and in their dependence on such trade. The huge disparity in size between the US economy on the one hand and the Canadian and Mexican economies on the other means that the economic consequences and impacts of NAFTA are likely to be far greater for Mexico and Canada than for the USA. While the three NAFTA countries have a combined population of 391 million people and a combined GDP of $8 trillion, the USA accounts for 68 per cent of the population, 84 per cent of GDP, 73 per cent of the labour force, and 49 per cent of the trade in goods (Cremeans 1998: 8).

Many commentators argue that the NAFTA is simply an improved and expanded version of the CUSTA. In large part the agreement involves commitments by Mexico to implement the degree of trade and investment liberalization promised between its northern neighbours in the CUSTA. However, the NAFTA went further by addressing unfinished business from the CUSTA, including protection of intellectual property rights, rules against distortions to investment (local content and export performance requirements), and coverage of transportation services. The NAFTA provides for the phased elimination of tariff and most non-tariff barriers on regional trade within ten years, although a few import-sensitive products will have a fifteen-year transition period. The innovative dispute settlement procedures of the CUSTA were extended to Mexico and precedent-setting rights and obligations were established with regard to services and investment. The investment obligations of NAFTA accord national treatment to NAFTA investors. For capital, this means that the locale of production and investment within North America can be determined solely according to the logic of profit maximization rather than political criteria and that Canada, Mexico, and the USA can be viewed as a single market.[6] Unlike Europe, the North American integration process has deregulated the market by limiting the scope for national government intervention without creating new trilateral institutions which pool sovereignty.[7]

[6] Despite greatly liberalizing trade and investment, NAFTA continues to provide protection to a number of key sectors: notably, primary energy and Canadian cultural industries and, through complex 'rules of origin', to automotive products and textiles.

[7] The North American environmental and labour commissions, created as supplementary or 'side' agreements to NAFTA, stand as minor weak exceptions. For example, the North American Agreement on Labor Cooperation (NAALC) was created to ensure the effective enforcement of *domestic* labour law in each of the three countries. NAALC does not establish common laws or labour standards across the three countries.

CUSTA at Ten and NAFTA at Five: Changing Patterns of Trade, Investment, and Labour Market Conditions

> This marks the fifth anniversary of the North American Free Trade Agreement (NAFTA) between Canada, Mexico and the United States. By any measure, [NAFTA] has been an unqualified success for Canada and our NAFTA partners. . . . the numbers speak for themselves . . . Indeed, trade and investment flows between all three NAFTA partners have increased substantially as a result of the Agreement.
>
> (Sergio Marchi, Canadian Minister for International Trade (DFAIT 1999: 3))

> The Canada-US Free Trade Agreement (FTA) has now been in effect for ten years. Media commentators used the occasion to proclaim the FTA a great success, one-sidedly highlighting the rapid growth of exports . . . Those ten years of recession and anemic recovery, however, mark easily the worst period since the 1930s for Canadian workers.
>
> (Jackson 1999: 141)

It will probably be at least another decade before the full impacts of North American regional integration on patterns of trade, investment, and employment and the geography of production become apparent. Furthermore, any analysis of impacts at the present is complicated by three events which have had a significant impact on trilateral trade during the 1990s; the prolonged recession in Canada during the first half of the 1990s, the long and strong economic recovery in the USA which has also meant that total employment growth in the USA has swamped any negative employment effects that NAFTA might have generated, and the severe monetary crisis in Mexico in 1995 (Cremeans 1998: 9). Bearing in mind that any analysis must, at best, be tentative and that at the sectoral level the impacts vary significantly between industries, this section provides a preliminary assessment of the more general effects of CUSTA and NAFTA on trade flows, investment flows, and labour market adjustments.[8]

Trade and Specialization

Both trade and economic interdependence within North America increased significantly during the 1990s. By 1998 *total* three-way trade among Canada, Mexico, and the USA reached $489 billion and the dependence of both Canada and Mexico on trade with the USA had deepened. However, there is a striking asymmetry to the trade dependencies between the three countries (Table 32.1).

[8] For detailed cross-sectoral analyses of the USA, see ITC (1997) and for Canada Schwanen (1996). For a detailed trinational analysis of the impacts of NAFTA on the automotive industry see the essays in Weintraub and Sands (1998).

Table 32.1. Trade indicators, NAFTA countries, 1997

Trade indicator	USA	Canada	Mexico
Billions of US$			
GDP	8,111	610	386
Global exports	965	242	117
Global imports	1,059	231	117
Exports as % of GDP	11.9	39.7	30.2
Imports as % of GDP	13.1	37.9	30.2
Trade in goods			
Percentage of total goods Exports:			
Exports to USA	—	80.6	84.2
Exports to Canada	22.1	—	9.4
Exports to Mexico	10.3	0.7	—
Percentage of Total Imports:			
Imports from USA	—	77.9	77.4
Imports from Canada	19.3	—	1.5
Imports from Mexico	9.8	5.0	—
Percentage of GDP:			
Exports to USA	—	28.0	22.4
Exports to Canada	1.9	—	2.5
Exports to Mexico	0.9	0.2	—

Source: Extracted from Cremeans (1999: 3; table 1).

In 1997, Canada sent over 80 per cent of its total goods exports to the USA and Mexico sent over 84 per cent. Similarly, Canada and Mexico both received approximately 77 per cent of their total goods imports from the USA. Although Canada and Mexico are both highly dependent on the USA for both exports and imports, the US trade dependency is much lower; total US exports account for only around 12 per cent of GDP (compared to 40% for Canada and 30% for Mexico) and the other two NAFTA countries account for only 32 per cent of US goods exports and 29 per cent of imports to the USA. While growing, trade between Canada and Mexico remains almost minuscule in comparison with the level of each country's trade with the USA (Table 32.1).

Tables 32.2 and 32.3 document the annual value and growth rates of bilateral and total trade in goods between the three NAFTA countries over the last ten years. Several points are worth highlighting:

- both Canada and Mexico have seen their merchandise trade surplus with the USA increase under free trade. Conversely, the US trade deficit within NAFTA, which had been diminishing in the pre-NAFTA period, rose from near balance at $2.7 billion in 1992 to $56 billion in 1996;

Table 32.2. Bilateral trade in goods among USA, Canada, and Mexico, 1989–1998 (millions of US dollars)

Trade flow	1989	1990	1991	1992	1993	1994	1995	1996	1997	1998
Bilateral trade										
US exports to Canada	78,809	83,674	85,150	90,594	100,444	104,307	113,261	120,738	134,794	137,768
Canadian exports to USA	87,953	91,380	91,064	98,630	111,216	128,406	144,370	155,893	168,051	174,844
US exports to Mexico	24,982	28,279	33,277	40,592	41,581	49,139	44,881	54,707	68,393	75,369
Mexican exports to USA	27,162	30,157	31,130	35,211	39,917	49,494	62,101	74,297	85,872	94,709
Canadian exports to Mexico	524	551	492	662	619	772	819	894	881	936
Mexican exports to Canada	1,442	1,498	2,251	2,294	2,876	3,313	3,899	4,426	5,070	5,176
Trade balances within NAFTA										
Canada	8,225	6,759	4,155	6,404	8,515	21,558	28,029	31,623	29,068	32,836
Mexico	3,099	2,825	(388)	(3,749)	593	2,896	20,300	23,122	21,668	23,580
USA	(11,324)	(9,584)	(3,767)	(2,655)	(9,108)	(24,454)	(48,329)	(54,795)	(50,736)	(56,416)

Sources: For 1989–93 Cremeans (1999: 17; table 1). For 1993–8 Strategis On-line Trade Data (Statistics Canada, US Department of Commerce).

Table 32.3. Growth in bilateral and total goods trade before and after NAFTA (compound annual growth rate)

Trade flow	1989–93	1993–8	Percentage difference
US exports to Canada	6.3	6.5	0.2
Canadian exports to USA	6.0	9.5	3.5
US exports to Mexico	13.6	12.6	(1.0)
Mexican exports to USA	10.1	18.9	8.8
Canadian exports to Mexico	4.3	8.6	4.3
Mexican exports to Canada	18.8	12.5	(6.3)
Total NAFTA Trade	7.7	10.5	2.8

Source: Calculated by the author from trade data in Table 32.2.

- Weintraub (1997: 10) argues that in assessing the impact of NAFTA on trade, attention should not focus on particular bilateral trade balances but rather on whether total trade is increasing and is mutually beneficial. Although total trade between the three NAFTA countries was already growing at a substantial compound annual growth rate of 7.7 per cent prior to NAFTA, it increased to 10.5 per cent in the five years following NAFTA. In both the pre- and post-NAFTA periods growth was particularly strong with regard to bilateral Mexico–US trade and Mexican exports to Canada;
- it can be conjectured that the growth in exports to the USA were a strong factor in helping both Canada and Mexico weather problems in their domestic economies during the 1990s. Although the implementation of NAFTA brought few significant changes to the regulation of Canada–US trade, which had already been liberalized under the CUSTA, after 1992 the decline in value of the Canadian dollar against the US dollar and the strong economic recovery in the USA combined to boost Canadian exports to the USA.[9] In turn, this compensated for the prolonged recession and slow economic recovery in Canada which saw unemployment average 10 per cent from 1990 to 1997 (Cremeans 1999: 17). In Mexico's case, goods exports to the USA have grown at an 18.9 per cent annual rate since the implementation of NAFTA. Although in the year following the December 1994 peso crisis, real GDP fell by over 6 per cent and domestic demand by over 15 per cent, exports continued to grow

[9] Price cuts resulting from reduced tariffs under CUSTA and NAFTA have been minuscule in comparison to the price cuts brought about by movements in the rates of exchange; the import-purchasing power of the US dollar has risen 19.1% for Mexican imported goods since the implementation of NAFTA and 20.6% for Canadian goods and has fuelled the surge in imports to the USA from its two NAFTA partners (Cremeans 1999: 32).

throughout the crisis and according to many observers were crucial to the economic recovery and continuing political and economic stability in Mexico (Weintraub 1997; Campbell 1999).[10]

- although NAFTA direct trade between Canada and Mexico has almost doubled in value, it continues to be extremely modest; representing only 3 per cent of Canada–US trade. The annual rate of growth of Mexican exports to Canada has actually been lower in the post-NAFTA period and although the rate of growth in Canadian exports to Mexico has increased, they still represent less than 1 per cent of total Canadian exports.

A key stated purpose of NAFTA is to facilitate economic integration in North America and one measure of whether this is being achieved would be evidence of an increase in specialization and intra-industry trade. Much of the trade between the three NAFTA countries is conducted by a relatively small number of large US-based transnational companies (TNCs) that produce and market in all three countries and it is estimated that between 60 and 70 per cent of this trade is not in final products but in their components. According to Rugman (1994) just fifty large corporations account for 70 per cent of US–Canada trade. Certainly, the most explosive growth in US–Mexico trade in recent years has been not only intra-industry but also intra-firm; Weintraub (1997: 35) estimates that close to 50 per cent of Mexican exports are intra-firm. The intra-firm trade stems mostly from US-based TNCs' investment in the automobile, computer, electronics, apparel, pharmaceutical, and other industries in Mexico and the automobile industry in Canada.

North American regional economic integration is probably most advanced in the automobile industry which presently accounts for approximately 30 per cent of total annual trade under NAFTA. While US–Canada trade in automotive products has been virtually barrier free since the Auto Pact came into force in 1965, prior to NAFTA the majority of automotive product exports from the USA and Canada to Mexico faced restrictive trade balancing and local content requirements as well as tariffs of 20 per cent. By contrast, and with the notable exception of duties on light trucks, Mexico's automotive exports enjoyed largely open access to the US and Canadian markets. On implementation of NAFTA, Mexico lowered the trade balancing requirement and local content requirements, eliminated import quotas on new cars and light trucks, and liberalized foreign investment in the automotive components sector. Thus, while automotive trade patterns between Canada and the USA have not changed significantly

[10] A key structural change associated with the trade and investment liberalization-driven transformation of the Mexican economy during the 1980s was the growth in manufactured exports to the USA using imported inputs or intermediate goods from the USA. By 1995 a full 80% of Mexican imports were intermediate goods. The demand for Mexican exports (i.e. US demand) is now the key determinant of Mexican imports rather than changes in domestic demand (Campbell 1999: 38).

as a result of NAFTA, there has been a surge in two-way automotive trade between the USA and Mexico.[11]

NAFTA also established strong North American rules of origin for preferential trade to ensure that automotive products benefiting from trade liberalization are substantially manufactured within the region. This prevents Asian or European manufacturers gaining preferred entry to the North American market for their final product by simply setting up establishments in Mexico to assemble vehicles from components imported from overseas. The rules of origin also serve to exclude from Mexican markets Japanese transplant production originating in the USA or Canada.

In the wake of the 1965 Auto Pact, a very high level of intra-industry trade and specialization in automotive products developed between Canada and the USA. Similar integration is now under way between the USA, Canada, and Mexico. There is convincing evidence that intra-industry trade within the North American auto industry increased significantly over the last four years (Kumar and Holmes 1998). There is increasing specialization between the three NAFTA countries in the production of different types of motor vehicles which are then supplied to all three national markets. Specialization and cross-border trade is also of growing importance with regard to major components such as engines, transmissions, and stampings (Kumar and Holmes 1998). Given the past history of integration in the industry, the emerging geography of the integrated North American auto industry—with one major regional production complex centred in the Midwest/Upper South/Ontario and a second, but at present much smaller, complex emerging in northern Mexico—and the relative sizes of the three national markets, in the coming years intra-industry trade in the auto industry will likely grow most rapidly between the USA and Mexico.

In summary, with regard to trade, the post-NAFTA period has seen a continuation and acceleration of trends begun long before its inception. Trilateral trade, industrial specialization, and intra-industry trade have all continued to increase. A detailed analysis of changes in the pattern of trade by Schwanen (1997) concluded that the CUSTA and NAFTA contributed to the increase in Canada–US trade 'over and above what could have been expected from macro-economic factors or past industry trends'. It showed that growth has been particularly strong in sectors liberalized by the agreements. However, the changes in relative currency exchange rates and the strength of the US domestic econ-

[11] US vehicle exports to Mexico grew from 16,530 in 1993 to 140,652 in 1997 and the total value of US automotive exports to Mexico increased from $5.3 billion in 1994 to $7.9 billion in 1998. Imports of automotive products from Mexico to the USA grew from $7.8 billion in 1994 to $18.1 billion in 1998. In comparison, over the same time period Mexican automotive exports to Canada only increased from just under $2.0 billion to $2.6 billion and Canadian exports to Mexico at $169 million remained almost insignificant relative to other intra-regional automotive trade flows.

omy as compared with Canada and Mexico probably account for a larger share of the increase in trade flows between the three countries in the 1990s than the trade agreements *per se.*

Investment Flows and Capital Relocation

Another of the stated objectives of NAFTA was to liberalize cross-border flows of investment capital in order to facilitate and enhance the integration of the three member countries' economies. Although not adjusted for inflation, flows of direct investment between the three countries show substantial increases in US direct investment in both Canada and Mexico and in Canadian direct investment in the USA since the advent of NAFTA (Table 32.4). Cremeans (1999: 27) notes that whereas 'prior to the agreement slightly more than two-thirds of US investment [in Canada] was in manufacturing, after the agreement more than half of US investment (54 per cent) was in nonmanufacturing'. Canadian investments in Mexico and Mexican investments in the other two countries are relatively insignificant by comparison. One striking feature of these data is that between 1994 and 1997 Canadian investment in the USA grew at a faster rate than US investment in Canada. When it is considered that Canada's GNP is only 8 per cent that of the USA, the relative size of Canadian direct investments in the USA is quite remarkable.

When the picture is broadened to examine total inward foreign direct investment to the North American bloc as a whole, Mexico's share of *new FDI inflows*

Table 32.4. Foreign direct investment flows between NAFTA countries, 1987–1997 (millions of US dollars)

Year	US direct investment in		Canada direct investment in		Mexican direct investment in	
	Canada	Mexico	USA	Mexico	USA	Canada[1]
1987	6,099	310	4,336	125	22	—
1988	2,653	670	1,852	71	38	—
1989	1,268	1,652	1,793	87	107	—
1990	3,902	1,926	1,821	54	224	—
1991	1,337	2,321	103	148	167	—
1992	2,068	1,320	1,335	114	730	—
1993	3,584	2,516	3,753	200	(110)	—
1994	6,247	4,457	4,584	490	1,058	—
1995	8,602	2,983	4,824	393	(263)	—
1996	7,260	2,713	8,235	718	38	—
1997	10,734	5,933	9,411	—	145	—

Note: [1] Foreign direct investment flows from Mexico to Canada not available but are known to be very small; total stock of Mexican FDI in Canada in 1997 was only Can. $317 million.

Source: OECD (1998).

to North America increased significantly during the 1990s and in many years exceeded Canada's share (Table 32.5). The USA continued to attract over 75 per cent of FDI inflows in the region. As a consequence, the Canadian share of *inward FDI stock* in North America fell from 24.1 per cent in 1985 to under 14.5 per cent in 1997 while the shares for the USA and Mexico increased from 68.9 per cent to 76.3 per cent and from 7.0 per cent to 9.2 per cent respectively. Such data have led Jackson (1999: 154) to conclude that the CUSTA and NAFTA 'have not resulted in a significant inflow of net new foreign direct investment to Canada to expand and positively restructure the old "branch plant" economy as promised by the advocates of free trade'.

In the months leading up to the signing of the NAFTA, a major fear articulated by labour unions and other groups in the USA and Canada was that the agreement would encourage the accelerated relocation of US and Canadian companies to Mexico. To date, the evidence seems to suggest that the impact has not been as dramatic as once feared and that, as with trade flows, the post-NAFTA period has simply seen the continuation of pre-NAFTA trends. The incentive for US firms to move south did not begin with NAFTA but much earlier in the 1960s with the introduction of the US Customs 806–807 programme and the establishment of the maquiladora programme by the Mexican government.

The US Customs programme permitted the duty-free reimportation of US intermediate goods which had not been transformed in the course of off-shore assembly. Under the maquiladora programme, components and raw materials are imported into Mexico from abroad without duty and held in bond by the manufacturer while further processing takes place. The resulting products

Table 32.5. Shares of foreign direct investment inflows to North America: 1987–1997

Year	USA		Canada		Mexico		North America	
	$US m.	% of NA	$US m.	% of NA	$US m.	% of NA	$US m.	% of NA
1987	58,140	88.7	4,198	6.4	3,246	4.9	65,584	100.0
1988	58,571	90.2	3,795	5.8	2,594	4.0	64,960	100.0
1989	67,736	89.2	5,018	6.6	3,174	4.2	75,928	100.0
1990	47,918	82.2	7,855	13.5	2,549	4.4	58,322	100.0
1991	22,799	75.2	2,740	9.0	4,762	15.7	30,301	100.0
1992	18,885	67.3	4,777	17.0	4,393	15.7	28,055	100.0
1993	43,534	82.6	4,768	9.0	4,389	8.3	52,691	100.0
1994	45,095	69.9	8,476	13.1	10,973	17.0	64,544	100.0
1995	58,772	74.3	10,824	13.7	9,526	12.0	79,122	100.0
1996	76,453	84.0	6,398	7.0	8,169	9.0	91,020	100.0
1997	90,748	81.7	8,246	7.4	12,101	10.9	111,095	100.0

Note: NA: North America.

Source: UNCTAD, various years.

are then re-exported with only the value added in Mexico subject to Mexican taxes. A large number of US, Asian, and other foreign companies took advantage of these programmes to open plants in Mexico for the assembly of products for export. On the eve of NAFTA's implementation, over half-a-million workers were employed in over two thousand maquiladora plants, the vast majority of which were located along Mexico's northern frontier with the USA. Since 1994 the growth of the maquiladora sector has continued and in 1997 there were over 3,500 plants employing more than three-quarters of a million workers, concentrated in the electric and electronic, automotive equipment, and apparel industries. When fully implemented and after all tariffs are eliminated, NAFTA will make the maquiladora exemption unnecessary for Canada and the USA, although plants belonging to non-NAFTA countries will continue to benefit.

Over the last two decades the economic integration of North America has had a far larger impact on the geography of production in Mexico than in either of the other two countries. With the move towards an export-oriented development strategy in Mexico there was a very pronounced shift in the centre of gravity of manufacturing production towards the northern states of Mexico and away from the central region around Mexico City. Cobos (1996) conjectures that NAFTA will promote further growth in the maquiladora industries located primarily in northern Mexico and the expansion of certain industries in centres such as Hermosillo, Saltillo, Aguascalientes, Chihuahua, Monterey, and Guadalajara. At the same time it will lead to the decline of less-competitive small and medium-sized industries and the partial deindustrialization of some of these same cities, thus generally deepening inequality in territorial development.

There are few signs of NAFTA leading to a significant shift in the geography of production within Canada or the USA; in the case of Canada the centres of commerce and industry have always been located very close to the border with the USA and in the USA the sheer size of the domestic-oriented economy swamps any marginal shifts in production. However, there is debate in Canada with regard to the impact that the realignment of continental trade flows might have on the national political economy. For example, Courchene (1998) argues that we are seeing the beginnings of a fundamental realignment of Canadian trade flows away from the historical interprovincial east–west orientation which arose out of the protectionist National Policy at the end of the last century towards a new cross-border north–south alignment linking Canadian provinces with their neighbouring US states. As a consequence, he sees Ontario's role being transformed from that of the heartland of the Canadian political economy to one of a competitive North American region state. Conversely, Helliwell (1998: 3), extending earlier work by McCallum (1995), demonstrates empirically that 'even after accounting for the expansion of trade between the USA and Canada in the wake of the Free Trade Agreement that came into force in 1989 [CUSTA], interprovincial trade linkages are still twelve times tighter than those between provinces and states'. In other words, borders and history still seem to matter to a surprising degree.

Labour Market Adjustments

In Canada and the USA, much of the debate and controversy around NAFTA turned on the effects on employment, wages, and benefits. According to prevailing economic orthodoxy, while trade and investment liberalization may produce short-term transitional dislocation for some workers and communities, in the longer term it will have positive impacts on efficiency and growth which, in turn, will lead to an improvement in wages and labour and social standards. On the other side of the debate are those who argue that in the 'real world' (as opposed to the idealized world of neoclassical economics) it cannot simply be assumed that there will be mutual gains from increased trade since investment and jobs in countries integrated through trade and investment agreements will tend to shift to those locales which are most cost competitive; that is, those that provide the best combination of wage and other costs in relation to productivity. A common perception is that large wage differentials between Mexico and its NAFTA partners reflect the fact that productivity in Mexico is much lower. While this is true for the economy as a whole, it is not true for the manufacturing export sector. Between 1980 and 1996 average manufacturing unit labour costs in Mexico fell 64 per cent against US labour costs as a result of rising Mexican productivity and falling real wages. Thus, many commentators feared that with the advent of NAFTA there would be a significant loss of jobs in the USA and Canada as companies moved production to Mexico.[12]

The domestic economies of the three NAFTA partners performed quite differently during the 1990s although, in general, the experience of workers with respect to wages and working conditions has been similar and negative. While the USA has experienced a prolonged economic expansion, the early and mid-1990s were years of recession and low growth for Canada and, especially, Mexico. Between 1990 and 1995 GDP per capita fell in both Canada and Mexico. While employment levels rose steadily in the USA, in Canada the absolute number of full-time jobs in 1990 was not regained until 1997. Canada saw a contraction of 255,000 (12.8%) manufacturing jobs between 1988 and 1996; proportionately more than three times the decline in the USA. Much of this loss occurred between 1989 and 1992 as shifts in trade in response to the CUSTA and highly restrictive domestic macroeconomic policy led to a massive restructuring of Canada's manufacturing sector. Job losses were often in US-

[12] Despite the large differential in labour costs, recent estimates of production costs in the automotive industry suggest that the overall cost of production in Mexico is only 1–2% lower than in the USA due to the higher cost of transportation, power, and an inefficient infrastructure.

owned companies which decided to close their Canadian operations and shift production to their larger and more efficient plants in the USA and industries such as apparel and food processing, which previously had enjoyed significant tariff protection, were particularly hard hit (Jackson 1999: 146). Although total employment in the Mexican manufacturing sector as a whole declined only slightly between 1988 and 1996, maquiladora sector employment more than doubled while the non-maquiladora sector lost over 40 per cent of its workforce (Campbell 1999: 40). In Canada, and to a lesser extent in the USA, job creation in the 1990s has been dominated by the growth of self-employment and involuntary part-time employment, as well as increased work hours and a significant intensification of work for most full-time, permanent workers. Unemployment in Canada soared from a 1980s low of 7.5 per cent in 1989 to more than 11 per cent in the early 1990s and remains above 8 per cent. While labour productivity has increased in all three countries, it has outpaced wage gains; the delinking of productivity and wages has been greatest in Mexico. As a consequence, average real wages have stagnated in both Canada and the USA, despite the strong growth in jobs in the latter country, and have fallen significantly in Mexico. Wage inequality has deepened in both the USA and Canada.

In Canada, many of the long-time opponents of free trade argue that the weak economic performance of Canada in the 1990s results directly from the FTA and NAFTA. Furthermore, many on the left continue to equate free trade with massive job losses and deindustrialization. However, a leading economist in the Canadian labour movement (Jackson 1999: 142) argues persuasively that while the CUSTA and NAFTA certainly intensified the pressures of international competition on workers with negative effects on wages and social standards, the direct negative impacts have been more modest than many of the critics of free trade predicted. Rather, domestic macroeconomic policy was the major cause of Canada's weak economic performance in the 1990s. According to the best estimates available, NAFTA's effects on labour in the USA overall appear to have been negative and moderate in size (Larudee 1999). However, the strong growth performance and job-creating ability of the domestic US economy during the 1990s meant that in most sectors the employment effects of NAFTA were experienced as a slower rate of job or wage growth than is normal during such a boom rather than as net US job loss.[13]

The influence on labour market conditions of regional integration agreements such as CUSTA and NAFTA goes beyond the direct impact on jobs of shifts in investment and production. They also have an important symbolic

[13] Note that in a few sectors such as apparel (323,000 jobs or 17% lost between 1988 and 1996) the loss of jobs has been quite substantial (ITC 1997). As of mid-August 1998 the NAFTA Trade Adjustment Assistance (NAFTA-TAA) programme had certified 192,034 US workers who had lost their jobs as a result of NAFTA (Cremeans 1999: 29). To put this number in perspective, over the same period (Jan. 1994 to Aug. 1998) US total employment grew by about 9.7 million and manufacturing jobs by 565,000.

impact by adding fuel to the ideological discourse of market liberalism, globalization, and 'competitiveness'. Thus, in both Canada and the USA, they have strengthened the bargaining power exercised by capital in the labour market and contributed to slower increases in wages, downward pressure on employment standards, and increased resistance to unionization on the part of employers (Holmes and Kumar 1999). On the eve of NAFTA, Gunderson (1993: 18) conjectured that under NAFTA 'the threat of capital mobility and plant location decisions will put pressure on different jurisdictions to harmonize their labour law and regulations . . . harmonization will be towards the lowest common denominator since jurisdictions with more costly regulations will be subject to pressures from investment flight and business relocations'. There is a growing consensus that this has indeed come to pass. For example, Jackson (1999: 149) notes that

> Canadian employers have extensively used the argument of international competition vis-à-vis the U.S. and Mexico to press not just workers on wages and working conditions but also to press governments for changes in labour laws and regulations and social programs . . . the recent trend, notably in Ontario, Alberta and Manitoba, has been to severely limit the effective right of workers to organize, and to roll back even basic employment standards.

A detailed study conducted by NAALC (1997) on the effect of plant closure or threat of plant closure on the right of workers to organize in the USA concluded that 'NAFTA has created a climate that has emboldened employers to more aggressively threaten to close or actually close their plants to avoid unionization'.

Conclusions

The process of deepening economic integration within North America did not begin with NAFTA, or even with the CUSTA. Most factors that underlie trilateral trade and investment were established well before the free trade agreements were signed. In general, tariffs on goods entering the USA and Canada from Mexico were already very low and opportunities for US and Canadian firms to move south date back to the introduction of the Mexican maquiladora programme in the 1960s. By the mid-1980s, in sectors such as the automotive industry, an emerging integrated North American regional production and marketing bloc had already become 'a centerpoint of many firms' strategic outlooks' (Blank and Haar 1998: 2). In a very real sense CUSTA and NAFTA have only formalized trade and investment trends that were already well established while removing, in the case of NAFTA, the remaining barriers to liberalized trade and investment in Mexico.

While the free trade agreements clearly have had some impact on trade, investment, and employment, these effects have been swamped by more dramatic macroeconomic events; the prolonged boom in the USA, the 1994 peso crisis in Mexico, and, in Canada, the very slow recovery from the recession of the early 1990s. Intra-regional trade within NAFTA has grown faster than external trade but the trade flows between the three NAFTA countries are very asymmetric; the volumes of trade between Canada and Mexico are still very small in comparison to the existing large flow of both exports and imports between Canada and the USA and the rapidly growing trade between Mexico and the USA.[14] A very large proportion of this intra-regional trade is also both intra-industry and intra-firm, reflecting the strategic thrust towards specialization and continentally integrated production networks on the part of large corporations.

The fear of large-scale job losses in the USA as a result of a shift of investment to Mexico has turned out to be largely unfounded. There has certainly been some significant job dislocation in both the USA and Canada in sectors such as apparel and electrical products but strong overall job growth in the USA has swamped any negative impact on job numbers. However, it is clear that regional economic integration has strengthened the hand of employers at the labour bargaining table and in lobbying government for changes in labour regulations and social programmes by adding to the rhetoric of international competition and threats of capital mobility. The increased bargaining power of capital has been reflected in significant downward pressure on real wages, labour standards, and working conditions in both the USA and Canada. Despite significant increases in investment and labour productivity, Mexican workers have experienced a fall in real wages and large-scale dislocation in both agricultural and manufacturing sectors. As a whole, while CUSTA and NAFTA have liberalized trade and investment to the advantage of large North American-based corporations, they have not produced the prosperity for workers promised by the advocates of free trade.

Perhaps, it is with respect to its relationship to the broader process of globalization that the true significance of North American regional economic integration can best be understood (Blank and Haar 1998). Continental economic integration is precisely the form that globalization has taken in North America. By providing a legal framework which embodies the principles of market supremacy and international competitiveness, NAFTA in its broadest sense is an agreement which advances and consolidates the restructuring and integration of national economies in North America along neo-liberal lines. From this perspective, the trade deals are a central component of a neo-liberal policy agenda which since the late 1970s has been transforming national economies and restructuring the roles and relationships among governments, markets,

[14] The academic and governmental writing on NAFTA also tends to mirror this asymmetry. In reading many American-authored reports on the impact of NAFTA, the reader might be forgiven for believing that the agreement is simply a bilateral agreement between the USA and Mexico!

and citizens in the march towards an integrated market-centred global economy. The agreements were strongly supported by large North American-based TNCs who viewed them as facilitating the process of economic rationalization, restructuring, and integration necessary in order to maintain their 'international competitiveness'. NAFTA has certainly intensified the pressures of international competition on workers with negative effects on wages and social standards. It has made it easier for Canadian and Mexican policy makers to promote structural adjustment of their social and labour market institutions in order to bring them into line with the dominant US model. As Campbell (1999) argues, while it might well have helped enhance the competitiveness of North American based capital, 'NAFTA is pulling apart the social and economic fabric of North American societies. By weakening public policy instruments and labour power at the bargaining table, it increases the pressure to level down employment conditions, wages and employment and social standards; changes that are being observed globally as central elements of the process of globalization'.

References

Anderson, K., and Blackhurst, R., eds. 1993. *Regional Integration and the Global Trading System.* New York: Harvester Wheatsheaf.

Atkinson, G. 1998. Regional integration in the emerging global economy: the case of NAFTA. *The Social Science Journal*, 35/2: 159–68.

Bhagwati, J. 1993. Regionalism and multilateralism: an overview. In Melo and Panagariya 1993: 22–51.

Blank, S., and Haar, J. 1998. *Making NAFTA Work: U.S. Firms and the New North American Business Environment.* Miami: North-South Center Press, University of Miami.

Campbell, B. 1999. CUFTA/NAFTA and North American labour markets. In Campbell *et al.* 1999.

——Gutierrez Haces, M. T., Jackson, A., and Larudee, M. 1999. *Pulling Apart: The Deterioration of Employment and Income in North America Under Free Trade.* Ottawa: Canadian Centre for Policy Alternatives.

Cobos, E. P. 1996. NAFTA and territorial integration in Mexico. In *Economic Integration in the Americas*, ed. C. C. Paraskevopoulos, R. Grinspun, and G. E. Eaton. Cheltenham: Edward Elgar, 43–54.

Courchene, T. J. with Telmer, C. R. 1998. *From Heartland to North American Region State: The Social, Fiscal and Federal Evolution of Ontario.* Toronto: University of Toronto, Faculty of Management, Centre for Public Management.

Cremeans, J. E., ed. 1998. *Handbook of North American Industry.* Lanham, Md.: Bernan Press.

——ed. 1999. *Handbook of North American Industry*, 2nd edn. Lanham, Md.: Bernan Press.

De Melo, J., and Panagariya, A., eds. 1993. *New Dimensions in Regional Integration.* Cambridge: Cambridge University Press.

DFAIT (Canada, Department of Foreign Affairs and International Trade) 1999. *The NAFTA at Five Years: A Partnership at Work*. Ottawa: DFAIT.

Dicken, P. 1998. *Global Shift: Transforming the World Economy*, 3rd edn. New York: Guilford Press.

EPI (Economic Policy Institute) 1997. *The Failed Experiment: NAFTA at Three Years*. Washington: Economic Policy Institute.

Frankel, J. A. 1997. *Regional Trading Blocs in the World Economic System*. Washington: Institute for International Economics.

—— ed. 1998. *The Regionalization of the World Economy*. Chicago: University of Chicago Press.

Gamble, A., and Payne, A., eds. 1996. *Regionlism and World Order*. London: Macmillan.

Gibb, R., and Michalak, W., eds. 1994. *Continental Trading Blocs: The Growth of Regionalism in the World Economy*. Chichester: John Wiley & Sons.

Gunderson, M. 1993. *Efficient Instruments for Labour Market Regulation*. Kingston, Ont.: IRC Press.

Helliwell, J. F. 1998. *How Much Do National Borders Matter?* Washington: Brookings Institution Press.

Hoekman, B., and Kostecki, M. 1995. *The Political Economy of the World Trading System: From GATT to WTO*. Oxford: Oxford University Press.

Holmes, J. 1992. The continental integration of the North American auto industry: from the Auto Pact to the FTA and beyond. *Environment and Planning A*, 24: 95–119.

—— and Kumar, P. 1999. NAFTA, lean production and autoworkers' unions. *Les Actes du Gerpisa*, 21.

ITC (United States International Trade Commission) 1997. *The Impact of the North American Free Trade Agreement on the U.S. Economy and Industries: A Three-Year Review*. Investigation No. 332–381. Publication 3045. Washington: USITC.

Jackson, A. 1999. The Free Trade Agreement—a decade later. *Studies in Political Economy*, 58: 141–60.

Kelly, W. P. 1997. Restructuring under NAFTA. *Canada–United States Law Journal*, 23: 497–506.

Kumar, P., and Holmes, J. 1998. The impact of NAFTA on the auto industry in Canada. In Weintraub and Sands 1998.

Larudee, M. 1999. NAFTA's impact on U.S. labour markets, 1994–97. In Campbell *et al.* 1999.

McCallum, J. 1995. National borders matter: Canada–U.S. regional trade patterns. *American Economic Review*, 85: 615–23.

NAALC (Commission on Labor Cooperation, North American Agreement on Labor Cooperation) 1997. *Plant Closings and Labor Rights*. Dallas: Commission for Labor Cooperation and Bernan Press.

OECD 1995. *Regional Integration and the Multilateral Trading System: Synergy and Divergence*. Paris: OECD.

—— 1998. *International Direct Investment Statistics Yearbook*. Paris: OECD.

Rugman, A. 1994. *Foreign Investment and NAFTA*. Columbia, SC: University of South Carolina Press.

Ruigrok, W., and van Tulder, R. 1995. *The Logic of International Restructuring*. London: Routledge.

SCHWANEN, D. 1997. *Trading Up*. Toronto: C. D. Howe Institute.

UNCTAD (United Nations Conference on Trade and Development) various years. *World Investment Reports*. Geneva: UNCTAD.

USTR (United States Trade Representative) 1997. *Study on the Operation and Effects of the North American Free Trade Agreement*. Washington: USTR.

WEINTRAUB, S. 1997. *NAFTA at Three: A Progress Report*. Washington: CSIS Press.

—— and SANDS, C., eds. 1998. *The North American Auto Industry under NAFTA*. Washington: CSIS Press.

WHALLEY, J. 1993. Regional trade arrangements in North America: CUSTA and NAFTA. In De Melo and Panagariya 1993: 352–82.

—— 1998. Why do countries seek regional trade arrangements. In Frankel 1998: 63–90.

WTO (World Trade Organization) 1995. *Regionalism and the World Trading System*. Geneva: WTO.

Chapter 33

The European Union as more than a Triad Market for National Economic Spaces

Ash Amin

Introduction

THE debate on the implications of transnational economic arrangements such as continental trade blocs or global-scale corporate structures remains solidly framed in territorial terms. The discussion of trading blocs, for example, is couched in terms of supra-national regulatory or trade spheres pitted against each other, to protect or erode the nation as a basic unit of economic organization and regulation. Similarly, the debate on globalization has been dominated by analysis of whether the rise of global firms and banks, international regulatory institutions and consumption norms, threatens or preserves local and national economic specificity and integrity. Opposing camps, from those who see the erosion of national and local influence under the advance of global capitalism, to those who prefer the language of interdependency and division of labour between nations, share the common assumption that the basic unit of economic organization remains the sequestered territorial unit—city, region, nation, continental bloc, world system. The central dispute, thus, is over the shifting balance between these basic territorial units.

Economists, political scientists, and geographers studying different aspects of economic integration tend to share this territorial ontology. It is common among not only geographers whose professional instinct is to think in terms of the spatial and territorial co-ordinates of economic activity, but also political scientists whose traditional concern is with issues of state-craft and associated levels of governance, from local and regional government to national and supra-national government. Economists too, once they extend their gaze beyond abstract universal economic laws and individuals as the basic economic unit, instinctively aggregate economic activity into territorial containers of varying size, from the regional economy to the national economy and continental blocs. Indeed, the structure and organization of this very *Handbook* around the 'local', 'regional', 'urban', 'national', 'international', and 'global' as meaningful spatial containers of the economy is symptomatic of the pervasive influence of the territorial ontology.

My aim in this chapter is not to be so arrogant as to claim that the territorial ontology is wrong. Certainly in matters of governance and regulation, the administrative units as we have them remain crucially the key sites of intervention, even if their relative powers might be changing. In the economy, while international integration unquestionably challenges any notion of the national or sub-national as self-contained circuits of economic activity, the institutions which shape and influence economic behaviour and opportunity—from industrial and innovation support systems to entrepreneurial traditions and business conventions—remain squarely rooted in local and national traditions. My aim, instead, is to argue that an important consequence of global economic integration is the breakdown of sequestered territorial boundaries owing to the rise of economic flows and organizational networks which cut across these boundaries. Thus, notably in terms of the regulatory challenges posed, integration might not involve a shift or division of economic action and responsibility from one spatial scale to another. Instead, it might result in overlapping organizational fields which are partly territorial and partly relational (e.g. global communities of professionals linked by internet, or the production networks of transnational corporations). These fields of organization of varying geographies require overlapping regulatory arrangements mobilized *across* different spatial scales.

The chapter advances its aterritorial logic through a discussion of the changing nature of the EU (European Union) as production system. The first section focuses on the idea of the EU as a trade bloc, in order to develop a critique of the territorial ontology in studies of international economic integration. The second section reviews currently fashionable accounts which stress the localized sources of competitiveness within the EU, to argue that the case tends to be based on a failure to consider the trans-territorial sources of competitiveness locked into the networks of transnational corporations (TNCs). The third section picks up on some of the implications of envisioning the EU economy as a mosaic of overlapping organizational and territorial fields.

The EU as a Trade Bloc Preserving National Interests?

It has become commonplace to argue that the rise of the three major continental trading blocs—NAFTA, EU, and ASEAN—can be explained in terms of the attempts of national governments in each bloc to get together to advance the interests of their own economies by removing internal trade barriers and by resisting trade imbalances with the other blocs. Each continental area, thus, is seen as a regulatory field, composed of inter-governmental agreements or supra-national regulations and as a trading arena in which, by implication, production and economic organization in general lies at a lower territorial scale.

A chapter by Richard Gibb (1998), in a recent collection of essays by geographers on economy, society, and environment in the new Europe (Pinder 1998), perfectly illustrates the thesis on the EU as a trade bloc that preserves national economic interests. Gibb shows that 67 per cent of global trade involves the EU, NAFTA, and the ASEAN bloc, with the EU as the largest among the three in terms of intra-regional trade, accounting for 40 per cent of world exports (including intra-EU trade). On the basis of such trade statistics, he concludes that the EU can be seen as the model trade bloc, providing considerable trade security for the majority of its member states.

Gibb interprets the economic policies of the EU—ranging from those designed to complete European economic integration, to negotiations with the World Trade Organization, GATT, and dominant trading nations such as the USA and Japan—as a new form of international regulation, a new continental regionalism, through which states cope with globalization (defined as tendencies in the economy for the factors of production to become increasingly mobile). He claims (1998: 48):

> Regionalism—in the form of groupings of nations states—may therefore offer a solution to the weakening of national powers associated with the globalisation process . . . as a response designed to defend the territorial integrity of the EU and its member states. . . . regionalism can be seen as a new form of international regulation designed to accommodate the contradictory requirements of flexibility; that is, to preserve and intensify mobility in the factors of production (by eliminating barriers to trade within) while at the same time limiting the external threat (by reducing foreign competition).

The logic of the argument is clear. The nation as an economic unit is under threat, but its integrity is being preserved by the regulation of trade at the continental level, because the terms of regulation provide export opportunities for nationally based firms. I do not wish to dispute that the EU can be seen as a trade bloc, or that part of the political game of the European Commission is to nurture European champions, through the offer of scale opportunities, against giant US and East Asian giant corporations. Nor do I wish to dwell on the question of whether the trade blocs work to the advantage of all member states and regions. I have argued elsewhere (Amin and Tomaney 1995), echoing other political economists, that market and monetary harmonization and union in the EU has tended to work against the weaker national and regional economies by diverting trade opportunities to bigger and more competitive firms located in the more prosperous and supply-rich regions and nations. On this point it is interesting to note that Gibb does not provide figures for individual member states on import penetration or trade balance over a twenty to thirty-year period in order to monitor the effects of the EU integration process on their trade performance.

The question I do wish to ask is whether it is useful to read the European economy as a sequestered territorial space, in which the EU can claim 'integrity' as a sealed trade bloc and as a grouping of more or less powerful national economies (Charrié 1998). The moment we begin to think of the EU largely as a trading bloc competing with NAFTA and the ASEAN bloc, and of the EU as a regulatory unit seeking to preserve national interests, we tend to assume that trade within and beyond the EU is a matter of imports and exports generated by locally owned and controlled firms based in their respective national economies. In other words, the national economy is seen as a production space, while the EU and the rest of the world are seen as a trading space.

The EU as a Transnational Corporate Space

The key question, as Robert Reich has posed in the context of the USA (Reich 1992), is who is 'us' and who is 'them' within the EU, and how far can we continue to think of production as a process confined to the national territorial space? My thesis—by no means a novel one—is that increasingly the EU is replacing the nation as an integrated production space and sphere of exchange in the hands of transnational corporations, as a result of growing cross-border investment between EU and non-EU countries. As such, the EU cannot be seen as a trade-regulating bloc serving to protect the interests of national economies and national firms.

As a first step in making sense of who is 'us' in the EU and its member states, consider the fact that the EU is a very significant source and recipient of world foreign direct investment (FDI), largely in the hands of TNCs. In 1997 the fifteen EU member states received 27 per cent of world inward FDI and originated 42 per cent of world outward FDI (UNCTAD 1998), with over half of EU outflow occurring between member states. The EU, thus, is a major arena of cross-border investment. Fifty per cent of this intra-EU FDI since the mid-1980s has been based on mergers and acquisitions of existing assets and this is also the preferred mode of entry into the EU for non-EU investors (as opposed to new green-field investment). The last two decades have been a period of considerable global cross-penetration of corporate investment, with FDI growth rates far outstripping GDP growth rates since the mid-1980s: since 1986, while global GDP has grown annually between 5 and 12 per cent, FDI inflows have grown annually by over 20 per cent, as have FDI outflows (UNCTAD 1998). Thus, steadily, the proportion of EU production in the hands of TNCs has been rising. In 1980, the stock of inward FDI amounted to 5.5 per cent of EU GDP, but rose to 13.2 per cent in 1995, and the ratio of outward FDI stock to EU GDP rose from 6.3 per cent to 14.6 per cent in the same period (UNCTAD 1997). The EU remains the most significant holder of FDI stock among the developed and developing markets, accounting for 45.1 per cent of world outward FDI stock and 34.6 per cent of world inward FDI stock in 1997.

In the main FDI is controlled by TNCs, which is why FDI figures are a reasonable proxy for measuring the reach of TNCs. For example, according to the United Nations Conference on Trade and Development (UNCTAD), the world's top 50 TNCs control 60 per cent of outward FDI stock in France, 52 per cent in Germany, 76 per cent in Sweden, 71 per cent in the UK, and 63 per cent in the USA (UNCTAD 1997). It claims that there are 44,000 TNCs with almost 280,000 foreign affiliates active today. Over half of these TNCs are EU owned, with 54,862 foreign affiliates based in the EU. Of the world's top 100 TNCs, which employ nearly 6 million people worldwide and which raise the equivalent of 7 per cent of global GDP through their foreign affiliates, 40 are EU registered, accounting for 37 per cent of the assets, 38 per cent of the sales, and 46 per cent of the employment of these 100 TNCs (UNCTAD 1997). The EU is a major source of the headquarters and affiliates of many of the world's TNCs, and, as already implied in the discussion of inward FDI flows and stock, it hosts a very large number of the affiliates of non-EU TNCs (some 55,000 according to UNCTAD 1998).

The EU can be seen as a gigantic international production complex made up of the networks of TNCs which straddle across national boundaries and form trade networks in their own right. Intra-firm trade accounts for a substantial proportion of cross-border imports and exports—a sobering thought for observers who continue to think of international trade as the exclusive realm of goods produced nationally and then traded in the open market. The 1997 *World Investment Report* by UNCTAD (1997: 18) succinctly captures the phenomenon:

> Complex integration strategies pursued by TNCs and the proliferation and deepening of regional integration schemes have facilitated trade among affiliates of the same TNC system . . . All in all, around one-third of world trade takes place within transnational corporate networks . . . about two-thirds of international transactions are associated with the international production of TNCs.

The European Commission does not provide consolidated figures which measure the proportion of intra-firm trade within total inter-state and international trade. Thus, while it is well known that intra-firm trade accounts for 45 per cent of total US imports and 32 per cent of US exports, differences in data collection methods among EU member states do not allow a similar measure. However, the available patchy evidence, together with the legitimate assumption that the degree of domination of the US economy by TNCs is not dissimilar to that of the EU, would imply that the situation is likely to be similar to the

USA. UNCTAD (1997), for example, estimates that since 1982, 50 per cent of the exports of foreign affiliates based in the EU are destined for other affiliated firms, while research in France has shown that 34 per cent of manufacturing exports and 18 per cent of manufacturing imports are intra-firm (European Commission 1995). In the absence of more accurate data on intra-firm trade trends in the EU, it might be legitimately claimed that a substantial volume of continental trade does not occur between national firms as implied in the literature on trade triads, but within transnational firm production complexes stretching across the EU's internal and external boundaries.

Large corporations, of varying national origin and with global reach, have come to increasingly dominate the economies of the EU member states. Up to date evidence is not available to illustrate the degree of control of TNCs of EU output, employment, investment, and sales (market concentration ratios). It is revealing, perhaps, of the EU's own reluctance to confront head-on the anti-competitiveness implications of increasing activity in the hands of the TNCs, that the most recent data it quotes on market concentration is for manufacturing industry in 1993 for the then twelve member states, based on figures generated by outside researchers (European Commission 1998). It reveals that in a typical industry, the top five firms accounted for 25 per cent of the market. It also shows, interestingly, that such concentration rose from 29 per cent in 1987 to 34 per cent in 1993 among industries sensitive to the Single European Market (i.e. those benefiting from integration of markets), and from 40 per cent to nearly 42 per cent in industries of high R&D and advertising sensitivity. We can be relatively sure that the situation today is no different as the dynamic or expanding industries of Europe attract greater interest from the largest corporations. This said, it would be wrong to assume that concentration has increased only as a result of recent EU integration policies. As Table 33.1 shows, the top firms in a variety of sectors have dominated production at an EU scale for well before the 1990s.

Local Geographies of Production?

Once we begin to consider firm or industry characteristics we are forced to recognize that TNCs vary enormously in terms of how they organize their production and exchange across national boundaries. Thus, to assert their rising power and influence across these boundaries—the aim of the preceding section—is not to assume a uniform organizational trend towards dislocation from national production sites and markets. Producer concentration in continuous process industries such as chemicals or high-scale economy sectors such as standardized foodstuffs, might make it most efficient to focus production in large sites, serviced from plants around the world, with the output exported to different markets. On the other hand, growing concentration in volatile or

Table 33.1. Percentage share of top five European Community (12) firms in total value added of each sector (C5 ratio)

Sector	1986	1991	Change %
Tobacco	58.39	59.16	0.76
Textiles	7.71	8.24	0.54
Chemicals	42.25	41.48	–0.77
Rubber and plastic products	14.78	21.71	6.93
Construction materials	28.39	24.29	–4.11
Iron and steel	47.21	82.31	35.10
Metal goods	9.79	11.69	1.90
Electronics	33.92	31.48	–2.44
Motor vehicles and parts	55.45	56.49	1.05
Aerospace	51.24	71.97	20.72
Pharmaceuticals	19.28	27.66	8.38
Computers	34.08	33.17	–0.91
Industrial machinery	20.07	21.10	0.03
Drink	39.73	43.24	3.50
Food	16.92	20.37	3.45
Printing and publishing	19.20	19.34	0.14

Source: European Commission (1994).

knowledge-intensive industries in which markets and technologies are constantly shifting and unpredictable, might favour local production customized for local markets and drawing on unique local knowledge and supply infrastructures. But, here too, some TNCs might continue to source inputs within local branches from expertise across the corporation, while others, less troubled by local autonomy, might display a higher level of local embeddedness by sourcing inputs from external suppliers. All kinds of local–global organizational permutations are possible, depending on industry and corporate tradition (Watts 1998).

The implication of the above observation is that commentators such as Richard Gibb who assume national production for triad markets might not be entirely wrong to the extent that the production arrangements of TNCs remain somehow 'locally contained'. Many economists and economic geographers working on the sources of competitiveness, indeed, make much of the locally or nationally bounded nature of production systems, against wilder accounts of globalization stressing the end of geography.

Conceptually, their case draws, in part, upon insights offered within endogenous growth economics and strategic trade theory (see earlier chapters in this volume) which acknowledge the externalities and increasing returns to scale associated with the spatial clustering of firms and local specialization in particular industries (Krugman 1995; Porter 1994; Martin and Sunley 1996). The economic advantages include reduced transaction costs due to proximity, scale economies of agglomeration, and technological or skill advantages associated with specialization. These advantages, said to accrue on a cumulative basis, serve to reinforce a local supply base that firms depend upon in order to gain international competitiveness.

More recently, a 'new regionalism' (Lovering 1999) has emerged, drawing upon insights offered by institutional and evolutionary economics, to stress proximity and local ties of association as a source of economic knowledge and learning (Amin and Thrift 1995; Storper 1997; Sunley 1996). For example, Michael Storper (1997) suggests that a distinctive feature of those fortunate places in which globalization is consistent with the localization of economic activity is the strength of their 'untraded interdependencies'. These include commonly shared industrial conventions and business practices, and a culture of co-operation between economic agents, which are considered to be sources of dynamic efficiency, notably economic learning. According to Anders Malmberg (1996), high levels of inter-firm interaction, shared know-how, and strong enterprise support systems are sources of learning, enabled through reduced opportunism and enhanced mutuality within networks of interdependence; the spillover of knowledge into the wider local economic system; and the exchange of information and know-how, underpinned by local technological infrastructures (see also Scott 1995).

Other observers who emphasize the difference between formal and informal knowledge in economic competitiveness (e.g. Maskell *et al.* 1998; Asheim 1997; Nooteboom 1999; Blanc and Sierra 1999) have suggested that proximity plays a unique role in supplying *informally constituted* assets. Maskell *et al.* (1998) argue that tacit forms of information and knowledge are better consolidated through face-to-face contact, not only due to the transactional advantages of proximity, but also because of their dependence upon a high degree of mutual trust and understanding, often constructed around shared values and cultures. Similarly, Nooteboom and Asheim distinguish between codified knowledge as a feature of trans-local networks (e.g. R&D laboratories or training courses of large corporations) and formally constituted institutions (e.g. business journals and courses, education and training institutions, printed scientific knowledge), and non-codified knowledge (e.g. workplace skills and practical conventions) as aspects locked into the 'industrial atmosphere' of individual places.

Both conceptual strands—endogenous growth theory and the new regionalism—reassert the powers of place in economic competitiveness. To this literature, we might add another strand that continues to emphasize the role of national and local institutions—from technology policy and technology transfer agencies to business service centres and industrial policies of various sorts—serving to underpin the competitiveness of firms and business networks.

Partly influenced by such a grounded understanding of economic life, commentators interested in the changing geography of production in the EU, from its new centres of competitiveness to its patterns of spatial inequality, continue to offer highly territorialized accounts of the European production system, implying the local boundedness of production processes. The worst example comes from those who see localized production complexes everywhere—a 'Europe of the regions' composed of a multitude of product specialist local agglomerations or learning regions; a Europe of industrial districts and technopoles. These accounts simply fail to recognize both the presence of trans-territorial networks in the hands of TNCs as well as the marked persistence of declining and lagging regions in the EU.

But the assumption of territoriality is also present in more differentiated accounts which are sensitive to the persistence of sharp regional economic inequalities in the EU. For example, in an otherwise excellent recent summary of increasing regional inequality in Europe, Michael Dunford and Adrian Smith (1998: 213) identify five sets of growth areas:

> The first and most studied group comprises strong industrial economies and industrial districts in Switzerland, Germany and northern Italy. The second is made up of global cities. To these groups it is important to add a number of areas that have had quite high rates of growth, including regions where expansion was closely related to large inflows of inward investment, areas (other than global cities) whose growth is related to increases in output and employment in services, and localities that have developed around tourist-related activities.

The authors do not dissent with the conceptualization above, stressing the qualities of the local supply base (ibid. 213):

> To explain the relative success of different areas, most attention is paid to supply-side factors such as the transformation of the productive system, the creation of a framework of co-operative industrial relations, the development of transport and telecommunications infrastructures, the establishment of synergies between public research and industry, the implementation of strategies for technology transfer and investment in education and skills.

Against the success of global cities, metropolitan growth, industrial districts, and technopoles, Dunford and Smith pose the difficulties of the old industrial areas suffering from capital flight and jobless growth, as well as other lagging regions held back by unemployment and social exclusion, lack of mobilization of human resources, specialization in low-value-added goods, and poor productivity in general.

The economic geography presented is a Europe of regional and urban economies. In fairness, since the aim of Dunford and Smith is to discuss regional inequalities in Europe, a territorial focus is to be expected. However, their account of success and failure draws on a territorial reasoning which emphasizes the quality of local assets. In other words both the object and explanation of study become territorial, and we are left with a sense of the European economic space as a mosaic of locally bounded production systems—a Europe of regional containers.

There are alternative economic accounts which recognize the corporate production spaces stretching across and beyond European regional and national boundaries. This geography of production does not readily fit into the confines of territorial containers. For example, Ray Hudson (1998) has argued that with every example of high-value-added production by TNCs drawing upon local sources of competitiveness within relatively autonomous plants, can be matched a corporate network of low-value-added production that includes local plants which are poorly integrated into their local economies. More pessimistically, in a study of the local embeddedness of the plants of high performance (or high-valued-added) firms across a spectrum of EU less favoured regions, we found local integration at point of entry to be universally low and only subject to improvement over a ten to twenty-year period after considerable effort on the part of local managers and local development agencies to bid in intra-corporate tournaments for further investment (Amin *et al.* 1994). As argued by Watts (1998), these local production sites, locked into wider corporate networks stretching across Europe, need to be considered alongside accounts based on the resurgence of localized networks such as industrial districts.

Similarly, despite all talk of an alliance capitalism set to replace hierarchically controlled global corporate geographies by decentred heterarchies composed of alliances, partnerships, and local branch autonomies, no convincing evidence exists to show an accompanying increase in the local orientation of individual plants and affiliates. Corporate decentralization and the formation of network linkages between firms does not automatically favour a re-territorialization of production. Indeed a number of studies of corporate and locational restructuring within different European industries tend to show that local plant upgrading and autonomy resulting from a shift towards alliance networking by corporations has not necessarily resulted in greater local sourcing of inputs or local spin-off. Thus even plants which have managed to upgrade tasks, improve local managerial autonomy, achieve a product mandate, or develop local research and development capabilities, find themselves scanning the globe for inputs and other resources, including know-how, information, and learning opportunities (Dicken 1998; Nilsson *et al.* 1996). Heterarchy, thus, might raise the potential for local sourcing, but it also situates local units into a wider network of intra-corporate and inter-corporate inter-dependencies and relationships, with the balance between the two (local versus global linkage) centrally dependent on the quality of the local supply base.

If we are to look for a meeting point between the position that claims localized production systems everywhere it looks and the position that asserts the primacy of global networks, it is likely to be found in issues concerning the quality of the local supply base. Where a locality offers little more than a supply of cheap labour or resources, the chances of local asset building will be slight. On the other hand, where a locality offers a range of assets such as high quality skills, advanced infrastructure, embedded or learnt knowledge environments, the chances of attracting high performance-oriented investments will be much higher, and therefore also the scope for inward investors sustaining a localized production system. According to UNCTAD (1998: p. xxxi), *laissez-faire* investment regimes around the world may ironically speed up the pace towards local asset building for competitive advantage:

> One of the peculiar consequences of recent development in the FDI area is that, by becoming commonplace, liberal national policy frameworks have lost some of their traditional power to attract foreign investment. What is more likely to be critical in the years to come is the distinctive combination of locational advantages—including human resources, infrastructure, market access and the created assets of technology and innovative capacity—that a country or region can offer potential investors.

One consequence of such asset building may well be that those best equipped will attract the most investments promising local spin-offs. But, this is not a pregiven, and is subject to many other factors influencing the relationship between investors and their host location, from the position of the investment in the wider division of labour, corporate philosophy, and the attitudes and strategies of local institutional actors.

Conclusion: Negotiating Territorial and Trans-territorial Production Spaces

The European Union is more than a triad market serviced by regionally or nationally contained production systems. The trans-territorial geography of TNCs in Europe has become far too pervasive and influential to allow perpetuation of the myth of a territorial European economy. This is not to say that a cross-European geography of production is replacing the latter. Instead, the new corporate geography is being superimposed upon the old territorial geography and, as a consequence, altering meanings and possibilities at the national and local level.

Importantly, the transnationalization of production does question the assumption held by endogenous growth theory and the new regionalism that the sources of competitiveness are purely local or national. Increasingly, the sources of competitiveness are situated across corporate hierarchies and networks spanning across national boundaries. For example, a revealing study by John Dunning (1997) of the sources of competitive advantage in 131 TNCs (110 of which were ranked among the *Fortune* 500 in 1993) shows that across a range of indicators, corporations claim to derive competitive advantage outside of the home base, and that this foreign reliance is becoming more important. The study considered four groups of advantages which broadly correspond to Michael Porter's (1990) fourfold diamond of the competitive advantage of nations (access to resources, consumer demand, inter-firm competition/rivalry, linkages with firms and institutions). Dunning (1997: 286) concludes:

> The data . . . taken as a whole . . . suggest that sample firms derive an important part of their competitive advantages—on average between 40 and 50 per cent—from their presence in foreign countries, either by way of FDI or by strategic alliances. The access provided by a foreign location (cf. a domestic location) to natural resources (including unskilled labour), linkages with suppliers, industrial competitors and other foreign producers, and the benefits of larger markets and more stringent consumer demands, were all ranked particularly high . . . By contrast, and in line with perceived theory and the data on innovatory activity, the sample firms perceived that their domestic operations and/or the indigenous resources and capabilities of their home countries continued to provide the main source of competitiveness—and especially so in the case of technological capacity and of skilled and professional labour.

Interestingly, however, contra the claims of 'perceived theory', the results also show that medium to high technology firms, those with a high degree of multinational presence, and firms with investments in the EU, relied in quite central ways upon the foreign locations to source strategic assets such as managerial expertise and innovatory capacity. The EU, possibly with the exception of its less favoured regions, is replete with such corporations, increasingly relying on different countries for both their strategic and non-strategic sources of competitive advantage.

Why is it important to highlight the rise of an increasingly integrated European corporate production system? First, following the arguments of the first part of this chapter, it brings to attention that a substantial part of employment, investment, output, and trade is of an intra-firm or inter-firm nature and driven by the rules of the trans-European corporate systems to which they are accountable. The production and exchange of value in Europe is going beyond the domain of the 'home base'. The EU is no longer solely an economy of regions and nations with clearly separable territorial boundaries. As such, it is not only trade that integrates the European economy.

Secondly, and as a consequence, there lies a potential clash of interests between regional and national economic needs and the needs of major corporate players. Two geographies of production—one global and the other more localized—are at work, with no easy fit between the two. If, as Dunning argues (1997), alliance capitalism is leading to the formation of complex intra-firm and inter-firm networks spread across the globe, with increasing relative autonomy at the local level (operational, managerial, and strategic), even this corporate geography does not guarantee the conditions for self-sustaining local economic development. For all the autonomy gained by local plants and affiliates, it is global corporate profitability and competitiveness that ultimately matters, with local supply linkages decisively locked into the logic of global value chain imperatives, rather than the developmental needs of local and national economies. Some local plants and affiliates may now provide better stimuli for local embedding than in the past, but the dependency of regions and nations on TNC strategies has not lessened.

Thirdly, and finally, the economic policy community in Europe has to abandon any lingering illusion of the viability of autarkic territorially based economic development policies. At one level, this means an acceptance that the regulation of triad trade alone will not serve to safeguard the economic interests of the member states and their regions. At another level, it means that there is nothing like a wholesale shift towards the micro-foundations of competitiveness, favouring the organization of economic activity in bounded territorial spaces such as industrial districts and national economic systems. Instead, the growing articulation of corporate and territorial economic spaces in Europe necessitates attention being paid to corporate policy as a *sine qua non* for national and regional policies. For the EU, such attention may require effective monitoring of the national and regional consequences of currently light controls over cross-border mergers, takeovers, and inter-firm alliances, aimed towards preventing the erosion of local competitors and supply chains. Within member states it almost certainly requires the closer alignment of industrial and spatial policies with corporate policy. For example, it is no longer sustainable for member states to keep policies to attract inward investment—with locational tournaments now escalating to ruinous proportions despite EU efforts to impose restrictions on wayward states (UNCTAD 1997)—separate from national competition policies (regulating uncompetitive practices) as well as infrastructural policies designed to upgrade the national supply base (from transport and telecommunications to education and training). Every effort needs to be made to maximize the local advantages of growing external dependency on TNCs and the insertion of the national productive base into global value chains. The policy community needs seriously to acknowledge that the EU has become more than an agglomeration of national and regional economies.

Acknowledgement

I am grateful to Meric Gertler for his helpful comments on an earlier draft.

References

Amin, A., Bradley, D., Howells, J., Tomaney, J., and Gentle, C. 1994. Regional incentivies and the quality of mobile investment in the less favoured regions of the EC. *Progress in Planning*, 41: 1–106. Oxford: Pergamon.

——and Thrift, N. 1995. Institutional issues for the European regions: from markets and plans to socioeconomics and powers of association. *Economy and Society*, 24/1: 41–66.

——and Tomaney, J., eds. 1995. *Behind the Myth of European Union*. London: Routledge.

Asheim, B. 1997. 'Learning regions' in a globalised world economy: towards a new competitive advantage of industrial districts? In *Interdependent and Uneven Development: Global-Local Perspectives*, ed. S. Conti and M. Taylor. London: Avebury.

Blanc, H., and Sierra, C. 1999. The geography and organisation of TNC R&D: benefiting from external and internal proximities. *Cambridge Journal of Economics*, 23/2: 187–206.

Charrié, J. P. 1998. Trade, European integration and territorial cohesion. In Unwin 1998.

Dicken, P. 1998. *Global Shift*. London: Paul Chapman.

Dunning, J. 1997. *Alliance Capitalism and Global Business*. London: Routledge.

Dunford, M., and Smith, A. 1998. Uneven development in Europe. In Pinder 1998.

European Commission 1994. *European Economy: Competition and Integration*, No. 57. Brussels: CEC.

—— 1995. *The Globalization Newsletter*, No. 2 (Oct.). Brussels: CEC.

—— 1998. *The Competitiveness of European Industry, 1998 Report*. Brussels: CEC.

Gibb, R. 1998. Europe in the world economy. In Pinder 1998.

Hudson, R. 1998. Industrial restructuring in Europe: recent tendencies in the organization and geography of production. In Unwin 1998.

Krugman, P. 1995. *Development, Geography and Economic Theory*. Cambridge, Mass.: MIT Press.

Lovering, J. 1999. Theory led by policy? The inadequacies of 'the New Regionalism' in economic geography. *International Journal of Urban and Regional Research*, 23/2: 379–95.

Malmberg, A. 1996. Industrial geography: agglomeration and local milieu. *Progress in Human Geography*, 20/3: 392–403.

Martin, R., and Sunley, P. 1996. Slow convergence? Post-neoclassical endogenous growth theory and regional development. *Working Paper 44*, ESRC Centre for Business Research. Cambridge: University of Cambridge.

Maskell, P., Eskelinen, H., Hannibalsson, I., Malmberg, A., and Vatne, E. 1998. *Competitiveness, Localised Learning and Regional Development*. London: Routledge.

Nooteboom, B. 1999. Globalization, learning and strategy. *Cambridge Journal of Economics*, 23/2: 127–50.

Nilsson, J.-E., Diken, P., and Peck, J. 1996. *The Internationalisation Process: European Firms in Global Competition*. London: Paul Chapman.

Pinder, D., ed. 1998. *The New Europe: Economy, Society and Environment*. Chichester: Wiley.

Porter, M. 1990. *The Competitive Advantage of Nations*. New York: Free Press.

—— 1994. The role of location in competition. *Journal of the Economics of Business*, 1/1: 35–9.

Reich, R. 1992. *The Work of Nations: Preparing Ourselves for 21st Century Capitalism*. New York: Vintage Books.

Scott, A. J. 1995. The geographic foundations of industrial performance. *Competition and Change*, 1/1: 51–66.

Storper, M. 1997. *The Regional World: Territorial Development in a Global Economy*. New York: Guilford Press.

Sunley, P. 1996. Context in economic geography: the relevance of pragmatism. *Progress in Human Geography*, 20/3: 338–55.

UNCTAD (United Nations Conference on Trade and Development) 1997. *World Investment Report 1997*. Geneva: United Nations.

—— 1998. *World Investment Report 1998*. Geneva: United Nations.

UNWIN, T., ed. 1998. *A European Geography*. Harlow: Longman.

WATTS, H. D. 1998. Restructuring of the western European manufacturing sector. In Pinder 1998.

Part VII

Coda

Chapter 34

Pandora's Box? Cultural Geographies of Economies

Nigel Thrift

Introduction

THIS chapter serves as a coda to this volume and therefore, appropriately enough, I want to consider some quite fundamental issues, issues which arise out of the so-called cultural turn in economic geography but which apply equally to all those many subjects currently wrestling with the problem of how to study the economic as a cultural formation. The chief problem, of course, is that the turn to culture both destabilizes what is conventionally regarded as 'the economic' and, at the same time, produces an almost bewilderingly large research agenda. Many writers are uncomfortable with this state of affairs; it seems to produce a diffuse state of uncertainty in which almost anything goes. But, I will argue that, to the contrary, what is demanded is actually more rather than less rigour since it is no longer possible to shelter behind old disciplinary boundaries and certainties. It is as though an effort was being made to construct a body of international law which would, in the end, supersede the old national legal systems: not surprisingly, there would be a certain amount of resistance!

In the chapter that follows, I will therefore begin by pointing to the rise of the cultural dimension as a legitimate arena of economic concern and the economic dimension as a legitimate area of cultural concern. I will then move to considering the cultural turn that has taken place in economic geography, probably the most important event to impact on the sub-discipline in the last ten or fifteen years. I will show what this turn has added through specific examples—namely the study of the geography of financial markets and consumption. Then, finally, I will enumerate some of the ways in which the cultural turn is beginning to have effects on the conduct of the economy and what is defined as economics. I will argue that Pandora's box has been opened and it cannot now be closed again.

The Rise of Culture

The practice of economic geography has become more difficult. In the 1960s, there seemed to be a self-evident object of study—the economy. This economy was populated by actors which themselves were undeniably 'economic'—firms, workers, and the like. These actors made things which consumers bought via markets. Those bits of the economy which didn't fit into this Janet and John picture—financial systems, governments, and the like—were generally consigned to economics proper, or simply ignored.[1] The labour of division was, like the division of labour, self-evident.

But, now, this picture no longer holds. The reasons are of four main kinds. First, critiques of economics have become more common. To begin with, the logical consistency of the neo-classical model is now consistently and continually questioned. Indeed, in certain senses, the question that now needs answering is why this model has been able to retain such a tenacious hold on the discipline of economics, a point to which I will return. Then, secondly, the economy is itself increasingly constructed as a discursive phenomenon, that is as a law-abiding system of commerce closely related to the creation of a rule-governed general mode of writing about that system, and to the accompanying constitution of a body of economic 'expertise' (e.g. Foucault 1970; Agnew 1986; Poovey 1998) and moral attitudes (Hausman 1992, 1994; Hausman and McPherson 1996). In turn, that means that economics can itself be seen as a form of rhetoric (which does not mean that it therefore offers no knowledge about the world) (Mirowski 1991; McCloskey 1990, 1997; Mäki 1995). Thirdly, many well-known models of the economy now stress social and cultural dimensions. In particular, there is all the work which stresses the social and cultural 'embeddedness' of economies and the economic virtues of this embeddness. There is, for example, Marshall's work on industrial atmosphere which, in turn, has spawned a mass of work on 'industrial districts' (see Chs. 21, 22, and 13 in this volume). There is Granovetter's (1985) work on embeddedness (adapted from Polanyi), which though it comes from economic sociology, has been widely influential. Then, there is the work on trust, convention, and habit which is certainly prominent in analytical economic history (e.g. North 1990; Williamson 1985) and is becoming more important in some parts of economics. And there is the concerted work on the economics of innovation and

[1] Inevitably, this statement is something of a caricature. One thinks only of the remarkable work by Sargent Florence in the 1940s, or Estall and Buchanan's work on the financial system in the 1960s.

learning (e.g. Dosi 1988; Lundvall 1992). Finally, the world of business has turned to cultural issues *en masse*. The key to the 'new economy' is knowledge and learning. There is a general emphasis on boosting innovation and creativity, on fostering skills—especially tacit knowledge—and on worker involvement. Whilst some of the work in this area is heavily, even tediously, rhetorical, the fact remains that it is also influential, especially in those service and consumer industries which retail intangibles based upon skill and knowledge (cf. Thrift 1997, 1998).

Under these circumstances, it is no surprise that economics has changed. The core of the discipline—neo-classical economics—remains tightly policed, bound into place by a tight publishing hierarchy unknown elsewhere in the social sciences. But even in the core, things have changed rather more than certain, critical commentators seem to have realized. Not only has neo-classical economics become more pragmatic and less ideological, willing to accept the existence of market imperfections and 'stylized facts', but it has also continued to undergo rapid change because of its need for constant innovation in order to feed the publication process.[2] In other words, neo-classical economics has not stood still, as attested by work on, for example, information economics (Stiglitz 1997), quasi-rational and heterogeneous beliefs (Thaler 1994), and sunk costs, as well as the explosion of work on endogenous growth, including the so-called new economic geography (Krugman 1991; Krugman and Venables 1995; Ottaviano and Puga 1998; Brülhart 1998).

In turn, a whole array of new kinds of economics have also arisen—for example, institutional economics, evolutionary economics, feminist economics, new political economy—which, though tangential to the mainstream, actually support very large numbers of economists and, as importantly, have brought economists into interaction with those from other disciplines.[3]

In turn, disciplines which have traditionally fought shy of the economic and economics are now becoming very interested in economic issues. For example, in cultural studies, the next boom area will most likely be the economy, spurred on by the work of cultural theorists like Bataille and Goux whose chief interest is in economies of excess and in notions of value based on speculation (e.g. Goux 1998). Similarly, in the highly influential sociology of science, there is a wholesale shift into considering economic and commercial issues, based especially upon careful anthropological study of the interaction of technological networks as found in financial markets (see Callon 1998). More generally, in social theory, issues of risk and uncertainty have loomed large (e.g. Beck 1990).

[2] Even econometrics changes quite rapidly. For example, one thinks of the rise of vector autoregressive models in recent years; and their subsequent decline.

[3] Accountancy provides an interesting half-way house in this process, as a discipline often included within or alongside economics departments but which has taken something of a cultural turn of late (e.g. Power 1995).

Though much of this larger-scale theory might seem to contain a good deal of bluster, it raises important issues.

The Cultural Turn in Economic Geography

Against this general background, it is no surprise that there has been a cultural turn in economic geography: it was in the general intellectual atmosphere. Indeed, it is possible to argue that economic geographers have become some of the leading exponents of cultural geography.

In certain senses, there is no doubt that the cultural turn saved economic geography from what might otherwise have been a musty oblivion. By the 1980s, economic geography was in a pretty moribund state, at risk of boring its audience to death.[4] The work being done, though often on very important topics, had lost any sparkle of innovation. But there were other reasons as well. To begin with, human geography is a profoundly trendy subject, in part because it still tends to import most of its ideas from outside the discipline. New generations of postgraduates therefore tend, rather more than in other larger and more fragmented disciplines, to follow new trends. The discipline is therefore characterized by generational cycles which leave little room for work outside the norm. Then, for many of the new generation of cultural geographers, the economy figured as what they were *not* about: it represented capitalism (bad), money (bad), rationality (bad), industrial landscapes (bad), and so on. Culture was culture because it had been purified of the taint of the economic. Then again, for the many more women coming into the discipline, the economy and economic geography sometimes seemed a male domain better avoided in favour of studies of landscape and other more obviously cultural topics.

These judgements were deeply ironic, of course, in at least three ways. First, it is difficult to see how it is possible to ignore economic issues in writing about culture. From the influence of patrons on art through to the influence of economics on rural landscapes, there is no escape. The market is so pervasive in modern societies that there is no way to ignore it, or go around it, or find some pristine space where it doesn't exist. Secondly, much of the cultural variation in the world is now of a determinedly economic character. One has only to think of the growth around the world of all kinds of 'cultural capitalisms', and the range of variation represented by the overseas Chinese and the marginal capitalisms growing up in certain former client states of the Soviet Union. Thirdly, much of the best work done in the cultural turn in economic geography has in

[4] Of course, economic geography had already been de-stabilized by Marxist incursions but by the 1980s these were coming to an end, their influence already spent, and many of the leading proponents looking for more subtle accounts (as in regulation theory) or chasing explanations with cultural overtones (as in much of the work on conventions).

fact been carried out by women, from research on the gendering of labour markets, to work on consumption, through to work on the cultural construction of the firm (e.g. Schoenberger 1996).

Indeed, I would argue that some of the most interesting work carried out in human geography recently, and in cultural geography, if one really still believes in these kinds of fruitless distinctions, has been on the cultural geography of economies. I will mention just four areas of work which are quite clearly of a standard as good as that found in the rest of the social sciences, and will then move on to the examination of two more detailed case studies. The first area of work is on the experience of labour in the service sector. Crang's (1994, 1998) work on performativity in restaurants and the tourist industry has proved particularly enlightening. A second area of work has been on the differential transmission of skills and practices in modern industry. For example, Gertler's work on the different structure of expectations in the German and North American machine tool industry has proved seminal (Gertler and Di Giovanna 1997). A third area of work has considered the growth of the overseas Chinese in the Pacific Basin. Work on the transnational business practices of this diverse ethnic group has proved utterly fascinating (e.g. Olds 1995; Mitchell 1996; Thrift and Olds 1996). Then, as one last area of work, consider the growing interest in high value agricultural products as a transnational phenomenon, all the way from exotic fruit (Cook and Crang 1996) to cut flowers (Maier 1999). Here, then, is a list of examples that are both innovative and seamlessly blend the economic and the cultural. In the next two sections, I will expand on these examples, by taking just two case studies which show that the cultural geography of economies has now become an affair which is producing knowledge across existing disciplinary boundaries, but in which economic geographers have played an important role.

Case Study 1: The Economic Geography of Trading in Financial Markets

Around the world, financial markets have become a potent force in the everyday lives of people. Not only are their impacts felt in the wallet—in the ups and downs of interest rates, in pension bonuses, and the like—but also in the imagination. Popular culture pursues a kind of romance with the financial markets, even if it is sometimes a condemnatory one, born out of their capacity to break national economies, firms, and people. Yet, what is startling is how little these markets are understood. Though the increasing financial literacy of many Western populations is evident (Leyshon *et al.* 1997), still explanations are often bracketed in the 'forces of nature' category. Markets run out of control; there are panics, stampedes, switchback rides, booms and busts, storms, breakdowns.

Of course, financial markets aren't quite like this (though they have to be liquid and volatile to make money). First, markets are mainly humdrum. There are many different kinds of markets but commentators tend to fix only on the most spectacular (chiefly the foreign exchange markets, stock markets, and options markets). Secondly, many of the practices of markets are old and venerable. Though the late twentieth century has seen a massive growth in new markets, many are still modelled on practices which in embryo date from the seventeenth century. Thirdly, the markets thrive on information. Much of this information must necessarily be privileged if it is to be of much use. Therefore most markets are highly social in character, even when the social interaction is at a distance, since social interaction produces competitive advantage. However, fourthly, markets are increasingly based on virtual information as well, and on techniques of analysis and representation that winnow this information. Increasingly, these technical figures are taking on a life of their own, becoming constitutive, not just reflective: the model of the world becomes the world of the model (see e.g. Merton 1994 and Mandelbrot 1997).

Over the last twenty years, there has been a massive interdisciplinary effort to understand trading in these markets. In economics, this has meant a gradual relaxation of assumptions of rationality. For example, the notion of rational beliefs has been introduced (Kurz 1997), which suggests that divergent but still rational beliefs arising when the same information is held can induce heterogeneity in market participants' expectations. In turn, this relaxed assumption can be used to suggest why certain well-observed effects exist—for example, foreign exchange markets exhibit higher volatility than equity markets, even though the relevant fundamental information is more symmetrically distributed. In other disciplines which do not have the burden of the assumption of rationality, the emphasis has also become more and more heterogeneous. In certain kinds of economic sociology, for example, a wide range of human motivations, such as face, prestige, peer-pressure, moral conviction, and cognitive dissonance are added in (Adler and Adler 1984). Then, more generally again, in fully social and anthropological accounts, it is possible to look beyond the economic and sociological factors to issues of power, culture, and history and thereby to query the whole mode of practice upon which the markets are predicated. Calling on writers like Marx, Weber, Simmel, and Mauss, this mode of analysis tends to interpret the markets as based on the interpretation of signs and value. Myriad bits of information have to be read, giving rise to new forms of semiotic expertise. There is a 'mythology of circulation' which plays indefinitely with the fluctuations of prices, thereby producing tokens of value.

Whatever the interpretation of these markets, their geography is crucial to them. Notwithstanding the widespread adoption of information and communication technologies (indeed, in certain senses, because of this adoption), geography is a constructive factor. Thus, in economics, the geographical location of traders may induce heterogeneity. For example, traders are likely to have a locally selective memory of events in their own geographical markets and time zones and react accordingly, traders located in different countries are likely to display different degrees of sensitivity to local information (for example, a trader in London is likely to give more attention to events affecting the UK than a trader located in Japan), and traders are likely to react differently to announcements about stock prices, inflation, and so on, according to the local structure of news supply (see e.g. Taylor 1995; Frankel *et al.* 1996; Cabrales and Hoshi 1996; De Long *et al.* 1990; Kandel and Pearson 1995; O'Hara 1995; Peters 1997; Goodhart 1985; Fischer 1993; Joyce and Read 1999). At a more general sociological level, market traders clearly act in different ways in different places and the 'trading crowds' found in markets at particular times therefore vary quite strongly in composition and outlook. Further, it is precisely this difference in practices which is an important element of the markets themselves. After all,

> the trading crowd is a community not of intention but of effects. And, it produces these effects not through the mobilisation of sameness but through the realisation of difference. It is these differences in the financial situations among investors and their evaluations of different shares which allow for a trade, and it is the accumulation of these differences which allows us to speak as if the market is moving in one direction or another. (Hertz 1998: 190)

Then, more generally again, precisely because financial markets tend to be complex places born out of difference, they need centres of interpretation. Though these are increasingly virtual sites, the fact remains that a series of centres in which people can meet face to face become *more* rather than less important as the amount of virtual information increases (Amin and Thrift 1992; Thrift 1994; Thrift and Leyshon 1994; Leyshon and Thrift 1997). Even the most powerful analytical model (and it is worth remembering what happened to the Black–Scholes–Merton model—and who Merton's father was) cannot substitute for informed dialogical interaction and coming to judgement (which may well produce narratives which did not exist before) (Allen and Pryke 1994, 1999).

In turn this means that the nature of face-to-face interaction is still important and seminal research by McDowell (1998) has shown the degree to which this interaction is still highly gendered and ethnically specific. Thus who gets to know about and do finance is still a matter of quite traditional social networks which are, now, however, having to change to accommodate new kinds of actor, with interesting consequences in terms of the patterns and institutions of sociality in financial centres. Some economists might retort that these kinds of social and cultural changes would have no impact on economic fundamentals: the answer currently is that no one really knows—which is why this is now such an interesting research area.

Whatever the case, geography is quite clearly an important determinant of trading in financial markets, to the understanding of which economic geographers have made modest but important contributions. In another area of work, this contribution has been even greater. Indeed, in the area of consumption, the work of human geographers has clearly been key.

Case Study 2: Economic Geography of Consumption

An interest in consumption has flowered across the social sciences since the 1980s with the publication of a series of classic texts (e.g. Miller 1987; Appadurai 1986; Campbell 1987), and the rising tide of consumer objects washing around the world. Yet the problem has been that the consumer, both individually and collectively, has been more often spoken for than spoken to, forced into a mould he or she is expected to fit. This contention is true in both of the major literatures on consumption. In neo-classical economics, the consumer is assumed to be a rational actor choosing between preferences with a known information structure. In social and cultural theory, the consumer is a cipher lost in the abstract imaginings of sociological categorizations and oppressed by commodity fetishism. For example, in theories of the post-modern, the consumer becomes a kind of semiotic connoisseur, vacuuming up illusions in a world in which consumption has replaced production. Miller (1998*a*: 209) puts the case for a more knowing consumer in a typically trenchant fashion.

> I am not convinced that the contemporary world is post-modern at all, because I am sceptical about the foundations of poststructuralist ideals in anthropology and particularly because I am sceptical about the representation of consumption in this literature. In my own ethnographic work on consumption in Trinidad and Britain, I have seen no real evidence that most people's relationship with consumption is less attenuated or more superficial than their relationship to production. (Indeed in Trinidad, there is much to suggest the reverse). Pleasure is of limited relevance to real consumption; the core factors that determine desire and purchase have surprisingly little to do with capitalism, points that are invisible to academics who simply read off their view of consumption from their model of capitalism. Very few of the people I encountered in my research on consumption appear to be particularly superficial . . . What postmodernity produced was not an empathetic understanding of consumption as a complex human practice that is part of the struggle for human welfare within capitalism. Instead, they produced a rhetoric based on the homogenising 'consumer society' and 'consumer culture', that simply stood for the consumer who in turn was reduced to a symbol of superficial difference.

Luckily this kind of theoretical hegemony is now changing. In line with Strathern's (1996: 44) argument for 'a certain brand of empiricism, making the data so presented apparently outrun the theoretical effort to comprehend it', a whole host of ethnographic and quasi-ethnographic studies have been carried out by human geographers and others which give the lie to these kinds of easy depictions. I will just consider three of these studies, each of which provides evidence of the extraordinary effects of culture on economy and, just as importantly, the extraordinary (and increasing) difficulty of separating out something called 'the economic' from something called 'the cultural'.

The place to start is with economic history. For it is fair to say that the economic history of consumption is still very much in its infancy. But already, work by a series of authors has queried the standard account of consumption retailed across so many different disciplines—that modern consumption started in Paris with the invention of the department store and then took on the world. Now we know that this is an exaggeration and a simplification. Work by researchers in economic and social history, geography, and cultural studies has shown that the history of consumption before the nineteenth century is both extensive and already shows many of the trademarks associated with modernity before the supposed onset of modernity. For example, in Britain, in the seventeenth and eighteenth centuries, shops were extensive, selling practices were sophisticated, and shoppers showed much of the knowledge we would expect of ourselves (Glennie 1998; Glennie and Thrift 1992, 1996*a*, 1996*b*). Thus,

> earlier changes in shop forms and layout from the late-17th century involved a reshaping of consumption spaces incorporating some of the features [later] central to department stores and made earlier shops important sites for the acquisition of consuming skills and experience . . . Shopping for most female consumers was elaborated and refined rather than 'invented' during the 19th century. (Glennie 1998: 936)

So conglomerations of shops rather like department stores and shopping malls existed from a quite early date in history, which brings us to the second more contemporary form of study of consumption: the shopping mall.

The modern equivalent of the department store is often considered to be the shopping mall. In purely monetary terms, shopping malls are of extraordinary importance to modern economies. They rule the retail roost, generating very large amounts of profit per unit of retail floorspace. Yet early studies of shopping malls conformed to easy, reductive depictions. Either, malls were simply shadows of the neo-classical system, temples to choice between preferences, or they were shadows of a new post-modern age, temples to a slavish semiotic consumerism (e.g. Goss 1999). Both depictions reduced consumers to robots, in one case pre-programmed by their own on-board economic computer, in the other by a new form of capitalism. But a concerted effort by anthropologists, sociologists, social psychologists, and geographers to actually study what consumers are doing has shown that both of these depictions are mistaken (see Miller 1995). Consumers are a highly diverse set of actors who react in grounded and contextual ways and consumption in malls is similarly heterogeneous. Thus different malls actively represent quite different consumer economies, based chiefly upon cultural dimensions. That said, what is clear is that consumers are remarkably rarely superficial or passive. For example, work by anthropologists and geographers on shopping malls in London showed consumers were using consumption as a means of constructing key social relationships, even objectifying devotional love (Miller 1998; Jackson *et al.* 1998). In other words, what seemed to be simple economic acts of exchange could often only be explained by vast penumbra of social relationships of obligation.

One more example shows this conclusion in an even stronger light. This is the rapid growth of 'alternative' forms of exchange, especially second-hand. The second-hand market has been a crucial form of exchange through history and this is no less the case now (think only of the enormous value of the second-hand car market). What is interesting is the increasing number of new outlets for (chiefly) second-hand goods which have grown up in many Western countries over the last twenty years, especially car-boot sales, charity shops, and the like. Geographers have worked extensively on these outlets and the consumers who use them. Once again, what is interesting is the sheer diversity of motive of the shoppers. For example, in Gregson *et al.*'s (1997) study of car-boot sales,

> the car boot sale is understood by the majority of participants as a game in which the rules of the formal retail environment are impeded; in which one can choose to be buyer, vendor, stroller, to look, to gaze, to laugh at and with the spectacle; and in which the risks are evidently understood and mediated by accumulated knowledge and by the possession of particular skills, for example the ability to repair defective electrical equipment. (Gregson *et al.* 1997: 1725)

These two case studies show the importance of both a geographical approach and the work of geographers to the study of the 'economic'. Geography is a crucial element of how financial markets function and how consumers consume. But economic geographers cannot just be tied to the locational dimension as under-labourers for economists, noting down the 'wheres' whilst economists do the 'whys'. As these case studies also show, as economic geographers have turned to the cultural dimension so they have been able to do two inter-related things. First, they have been able to demostrate the very great importance of the 'how' of the economy, the often mundane practices—nearly all of them involving various means of producing new spaces and times—which allow an economy to run on and which have too often been neglected by economists. In a period in which e-business may be about to transform value chains and business organizations, it is these rude mechanics—from market bidding behaviours to logistics to consumption—which are in desperate need of more such study. Secondly, they have become a part of a community which wants to broaden out what counts as the economic in economic theory. Membership of this community should not be subject to over-interpretation. It is clearly not an attempt to trivialize the importance of economic forces—who, after all would claim that either financial markets or consumers are insignificant actors? Nor is it an attempt to relegate the work of economists—who would want to turn their back on each and every one of the formal insights forged by economists? Rather it is the sign of an attempt to produce more generous accounts of the economic, accounts which will, in turn, allow us to see and do more, and more different, things. In the final part of the chapter, I want to conclude by considering how the new research agendas now being written out can be connected back to economics, for the logical end point of this chapter, given its content so far, must surely be the practices of economics itself.

Conclusions

What the cultural turn in the social sciences and humanities, including human geography, has done is to open up a Pandora's box, one which, as in the Greek myth, cannot now be slammed shut again. What was in the box was the practice of economics itself. That practice is now open to inspection as a cultural entity. In the past, studies of the economy tended to take place on economics' terms, using economic procedures and concepts. When the economy has been studied by other disciplines, it has often been through recourse to these same practices and concepts, even if sometimes to criticize them. Various forms of economic anthropology and economic history are cases in point. But, aided by a growing crisis in some parts of economics, as potential students turn away from curricula which stress highly abstract models (see Becker 1997),[5] many in the social sciences and humanities are no longer willing to make the procedures and concepts of economics into the Rosetta Stone of economic practice. Instead, what is happening is that slowly but surely an alternative body of economic knowledge is being generated which sometimes takes remarkably little (perhaps too little) note of economics. For example, there is the enormous raft of research coming out of business and management schools, the growth of work on material culture and consumption (see e.g. the *Journal of Material Culture*), and so on. And this is to ignore the growth of new areas of economics like evolutionary political economy which often have precious little to do with economics as traditionally formulated, as well as all the practical knowledge currently being gleaned from attempts to construct alternative economic institutions, for example, those based on ecologically sound principles, or on new, alternative means of finance (Leyshon and Thrift 1997).

So the logical extension of the cultural turn in the study of economics may well turn out to be an examination of the culture of economics itself. Not surprisingly, this is beginning to happen. There is the much greater attention being paid to matters of economic methodology (as in the *Journal of Economic Methodology*). There is the voluminous source material that is to hand, in the

[5] Though in a general picture of decline in many countries, financial economics and accountancy carry on as strongly as ever.

shape of histories, memoirs and letters, numerous biographies and autobiographies, interviews, and so on. And there are a battery of cultural approaches which are now being tested for size (e.g. Breit and Spencer 1995; Colander and Coats 1993; Reder 1999; Szenberg 1999). This tentative movement is, in many ways, an economics equivalent of the sociology of science, a movement which has attracted heavy criticism from some scientists for daring to intrude on their domain and for daring to question the exact status of scientific knowledge. For those economists who regard what they do as a science, no doubt much the same reaction is likely, but, for other economists, such a move might begin to tell us a lot about how modern economics has been and is being constructed. Already therefore, this nascent examination of economics—like the sociology of science before it—has moved beyond the relatively trivial observation that the economic sphere is socially and culturally constructed—after all, what is not socially and culturally constructed—to much more concrete observation and theorization. In particular, this examination has shown that the gradual construction and validation of economic 'facts' about the world emerged through the creation of a space of public writing. Nearly all the early economic innovations—double entry book-keeping, the naming of a market system, the notion of number were aimed at creating a basis for claiming impartial and certain knowledge which effaced the stain of politics. Petty's *Political Arithmetic*, for example, was aimed at appealing to 'Visible Foundations in Nature' and most certainly not to 'mutable minds, opinions, appetites and passions' (Petty, cited in Poovey 1998: 132).[6] In turn, this new form of immutable knowledge was backed up by a formidable array of scientific instruments and metrics which helped to legitimize this knowledge. It is perhaps less far than might be thought from these early efforts to produce new 'economic' knowledges to the rigours of neo-classical economics, and the heavy emphasis on numerical representation, computing, and the like. The mutable stability of the discipline is the result of foundations laid down over hundreds of years. Economists form perhaps one of the best examples of a continuously functioning community of practice: a 'culture' if you like. None of this is to suggest that economists have *no* worthwhile knowledge to offer about the world. However, it is to suggest that their view of the world, heavily shaped by continuous interaction with many powerful institutions (Miller 1997), deserves more *cultural* study than it currently receives since it is clear that *economic knowledge is itself a powerful actor in the world*, and not just a representation of it. Which brings me to my final point. Miller (1998) and others have argued that, in a sense, the world has become more theoretical, more and more based upon virtual models which the world is measured against, found wanting in terms of, and made to conform to. For Miller (1998:

[6] The nascent 'economics' early on allied itself to rhetoric, precisely because of that subject's respectability. This is a delicious irony, considering the controversial nature of the current study of economics as rhetoric.

198), economic models are the best example of this tendency towards theoretical conformity; 'even though it purports to model capitalism, economics is actually an abstract modelling procedure . . . that sometimes acts entirely against the interests of transnational capitalism and the major states'. If economics is this powerful a cultural institution, it certainly demands that economic geographers look not only at what economists purport to study but also at the institution of economics itself. A cultural geography of economics and economists? Now there's a thought.

Acknowledgements

I would like to thank Uskali Mäki and Gordon Clark for discussions about the current state of economics and economic methodology.

References

Adler, P. A., and Adler, P., eds. 1984. *The Social Dynamics of Financial Markets*. Greenwich, Conn.: JAI Press.

Agnew, J. C. 1986. *Worlds Apart: The Market and the Theatre in Anglo-American Thought*. Cambridge: Cambridge University Press.

Allen, J., and Pryke, M. 1994. The production of service space. *Environment and Planning D: Society and Space*, 12: 453–77.

—— —— 1999. Money cultures after Georg Simmel: mobility, movement and identity. *Environment and Planning D: Society and Space*, 17: 51–68.

Amin, A., and Thrift, N. J. 1992. Neo-marshallian nodes in global networks. *International Journal of Urban and Regional Research*, 16: 571–87.

Appadurai, A., ed. 1986. *The Social Life of Things*. Cambridge: Cambridge University Press.

Beck, U. 1990. *Risk Society*. London: Sage.

Becker, W. E. 1997. Teaching economics to undergraduates. *Journal of Economic Literature*, 43: 1347–62.

Breit, W., and Spencer, R. W. 1995. *Lives of the Laureates: Thirteen Nobel Economists*. Cambridge, Mass.: MIT Press.

Brülhart, M. 1998. Economic geography, industry location and trade: the evidence. *The World Economy*, 21: 775–801.

Cabrales, A., and Hoshi, T. 1996. Heterogeneous beliefs, wealth accumulation and asset price dynamics. *Journal of Economic Dynamics and Control*, 20: 1073–100.

Callon, M., ed. 1998. *The Laws of the Markets*. Oxford: Blackwell.

Campbell, C. 1987. *The Romantic Ethic and the Spirit of Consumerism*. Oxford: Blackwell.

Carrier, J. G., and Miller, D., eds. 1998. *Virtualism: A New Political Economy*. Oxford: Berg.

Colander, D., and Coats, A. W. 1993. *The Spread of Economic Ideas*. Cambridge: Cambridge University Press.

Cook, I., and Crang, P. 1996. The world on a plate: culinary culture, displacement and geographical knowledges. *Journal of Material Culture*, 1: 131–53.

Crang, P. 1994. Its showtime: on the workplace geographies of display in a restaurant in south-east England. *Environment and Planning D: Society and Space*, 12: 675–704.

—— 1998. Performing the tourist product. In *Touring Cultures*, ed. C. Rojek and J. Urry. London: Routledge.

De Long, B., Shleifer, A., Summers, A., and Waldmann, R. 1990. Noise trader risk in financial markets. *Journal of Political Economy*, 98: 703–30.

Dosi, G. 1988. Institutions and markets in a dynamic world. *The Manchester School*, 56: 119–46.

Fischer, A. M. 1993. Canadian CPI announcements over the disinflationary cycle: evidence from the foreign exchange rate market. *Applied Economics*, 25: 1045–51.

Foucault, M. 1970. *The Order of Things: An Archaeology of the Human Sciences*. London: Tavistock.

Frankel, J. A., Galli, G., and Giovanni, L. 1996. *The Microstructure of Foreign Exchange Markets*. Chicago: University of Chicago Press.

Gertler, M., and Di Giovanna, S. 1997. In search of the new social economy: collaborative relations between users and producers of advanced manufacturing technologies. *Environment and Planning A*, 29: 1585–1602.

Glennie, P. 1998. Consumption, consumerism and urban force: historical perspectives. *Urban Studies*, 35: 927–51.

Glennie, P., and Thrift, N. J. 1992. Modernity, urbanism and modern consumption. *Environment and Planning D: Society and Space*, 10: 423–43.

—— —— 1996*a*. Consumers, identities and consumption spaces in early-modern England. *Environment and Planning A*, 28: 25–45.

—— —— 1996*b*. Consumption, shopping and gender. In *Retailing, Consumption and Capital. Towards the New Retail Geography*, ed. N. Wrigley and M. Lowe. Harlow: Longman, 221–37.

Goodhart, C. A. E. 1985. The impact of news on financial markets in the United Kingdom. *Journal of Money, Credit and Banking*, 17: 507–11.

Goss, J. 1999. Once upon a time in the commodity world: an unofficial guide to the mall of America. *Annals of the Association of American Geographers*, 89: 45–75.

Goux, J. 1998. Values and speculations: the stock exchange paradigm. *Cultural Values*, 1: 159–77.

Granovetter, M. 1985. Economic action and social structure: the problem of embeddedness. *American Journal of Sociology*, 91: 481–510.

Gregson, N., and Crewe, L. 1997. The bargain, the knowledge and the spectacle: making sense of consumption in the space of the car-boot sale. *Environment and Planning D: Society and Space*, 15: 87–112.

—— —— and Longstaff, B. 1997. Excluded spaces of regulation: car boot sales as an enterprise culture out of control? *Environment and Planning A*, 129: 1711–900.

Hausman, D. M. 1992. *Essays on Philosophical and Economic Methodology*. Cambridge: Cambridge University Press.

—— ed. 1994. *The Philosophy of Economics: An Anthology*. Cambridge: Cambridge University Press.

—— and McPherson, M. S. 1996. *Economic Analysis and Moral Philosophy*. Cambridge: Cambridge University Press.

Hertz, E. 1998. *The Trading Crowd: An Ethnography of the Shanghai Stock Market.* Cambridge: Cambridge University Press.

Jackson, P., Miller, P., Holbrook, B., Thrift, N. J., and Rowlands, M. 1998. *Consumption, Place and Identity*. London: Routledge.

Joyce, M., and Read, V. 1999. Asset price reactions to RPI announcements. *Bank of England Working Paper*, 94.

Kandel, E., and Pearson, N. D. 1995. Differential interpretation of price signals and trade in speculative markets. *Journal of Political Economy*, 4: 831–72.

Krugman, P. 1991. Increasing returns and economic geography. *Journal of Political Economy*, 99: 483–99.

—— and Venables, A. J. 1995. Globalisation and the inequality of nations. *Quarterly Journal of Economics*, 110: 857–80.

Kurz, M., ed. 1997. *Endogenous Economic Fluctuations: Studies in the Theory of Rational Beliefs*. Berlin: Springer Verlag.

Leyshon, A., and Thrift, N. J. 1997. *Money/Space: Geographies of Monetary Transformation*. London: Routledge.

———— and Pratt, J. 1998. Reading Financial Services: Texts, Consumers, and Financial Literacy. *Environment and Planning D: Society and Space*, 16: 29–55.

Lundvall, B. A., ed. 1992. *National Systems of Innovation*. London: Frances Pinter.

McCloskey, D. 1990. *If You're So Smart: The Narrative of Economic Expertise*. Chicago: Chicago University Press.

—— 1997. *The Rhetoric of Economics*. Madison: University of Wisconsin Press.

McDowell, L. 1998. *Capital Culture: Gender at Work in the City*. Oxford: Blackwell.

Mäki, U. 1995. Diagnosing McCloskey. *Journal of Economic Literature*, 33/3 (Sept.): 1300–18.

—— 1998*a*. Against Posner, against Coase, against theory. *Cambridge Journal of Economics* 22/5 (Sept.): 587–95.

—— 1998*b*. Is Coase a realist? *Philosophy of the Social Sciences*, 28/1 (March): 5–31.

Mandelbrot, B. B. 1997. *Fractals and Scaling in Finance: Discontinuity, Concentration, Risk*. Berlin: Springer-Verlag.

Maier, V. 1999. Cut flower production in Colombia—a major success story for women. *Environment and Planning A*, 31: 273–90.

Merton, R. 1994. Influence of mathematical models in finance on practice: past, present and future. *Philosophical Transactions of the Royal Society*, 347: 451–63.

Miller, D. 1987. *Material Culture and Mass Consumption*. Oxford: Blackwell.

—— ed. 1995. *Acknowledging Consumption*. London: Routledge.

—— 1998*a*. A theory of virtualism. In Carrier and Miller 1998: 187–216.

—— 1998*b*. *A Theory of Shopping*. Cambridge: Polity Press.

Miller, G. J. 1997. The impact of economics on contemporary political institutions. *Journal of Economic Literature*, 43: 1173–204.

Mirowski, P. 1991. The when, the how and the why of mathematical expression in the history of economic analysis. *Journal of Economic Perspectives*, 5: 145–57.

Mitchell, K. 1996. Transnational subjects: constituting the cultural citizen in the era of Pacific Rim capital. In *Ungrounded Empires: The Cultural Politics of Chinese Transnationalism*, ed. W. Ong and D. Nonini. New York: Routledge.

North, D. 1990. *Institutions, Institutional Change and Economic Performance.* Cambridge: Cambridge University Press.

O'Hara, M. 1995. *Market Microstructure Theory.* Oxford: Blackwell.

Olds, K. 1995. Globalisation and the production of new urban spaces in Pacific Rim megaprojects in the late twentieth century. *Environment and Planning A*, 27: 1713–44.

Ottaviano, G. I. P., and Puga, P. 1998. Agglomeration in the global economy: a survey of the 'new economic geography'. *The World Economy*, 21: 231–52.

Peters, B. 1997. Informed traders, intervention and price leadership: a deeper view of the microstructure of the foreign exchange market. *Journal of Finance*, 52: 63–87.

Poovey, M. 1998. *The History of the Fact: Problems of Knowledge in the Sciences of Wealth and Society.* Chicago: Chicago University Press.

Power, M. 1995. *Accounting and Science: Natural Inquiry and Commercial Reason.* Cambridge: Cambridge University Press.

Reder, M. W. 1999. *Economics: The Culture of a Controversial Science.* Chicago: University of Chicago Press.

Schoenberger, E. 1996. *The Cultural Crisis of the Firm.* Oxford: Blackwell.

Stiglitz, J. 1997. *Economics.* New York: W. W. Norton.

Strathern, M. 1996. Cutting the network. *Journal of the Royal Anthropological Institute*, NS 2: 517–35.

Szenberg, M. 1999. *Passion and Craft: Economists at Work.* Ann Arbor: University of Michigan Press.

Taylor, M. 1995. The economics of exchange rate. *Journal of Economic Literature*, 33: 13–47.

Thaler, R. 1994. *Quasi-Rational Economics.* New York: Russell Sage Foundation.

Thrift, N. J. 1994. On the social and cultural determinants of international financial centres: the case of the City of London. In *Money, Power and Space*, ed. S. Corbridge, N. J. Thrift, and R. L. Martin. Oxford: Blackwell, 327–55.

—— 1997. The rise of soft capitalism. *Cultural Values*, 1: 21–57.

—— 1998. Virtual Capitalism: the globalisation of reflexive business knowledge. In Carrier and Miller 1998: 161–86.

—— and Leyshon, A. 1994. A phantom state? The de-traditionalisation of money, the international financial system and international financial centres. *Political Geography*, 13: 299–327.

—— and Olds, K. 1996. Refiguring the economic in economic geography. *Progress in Human Geography*, 20: 311–37.

Williamson, O. E. 1985. *The Economic Institutions of Capitalism: Firms, Markets, Relational Contracting.* New York: Free Press.

Index of Names

ABN–AMRO 304, 307, 308, 310
Abo, Tetsuo 281, 625, 625–47, 633 n., 640, 643
Abraham, F. 481
Acemoglu, D. 479
Ackerman, E. A. 20
Adams, J. D. 260 n., 376, 377 n., 457
Adelman, Irma 366 n.
Ades, A. 96, 488, 490
Adkins, L. 504
Adler, P. A. 694
Aero, A. 32
Aglietta, M. 112
Agnew, J. C. 32, 690
Aitken, B. 486
Ajo, R. 20
Akamatsu, K. 642 n.
Albin, P. 108
Albion, R. 50
Alexander, J. W. 20
Allassandrini, P. 232, 234
Allen, J. 231, 236, 456, 468, 695
Allen, Robert C. 403
Allenby, B. R. 611
Almeida, P. 380, 381
Alonso, William 3, 7, 21, 85, 318, 565
Alston, P. 204
Altvater, E. 67, 542
Amin, Ash 30, 31, 62, 70, 72, 73, 74, 100, 236, 276, 284, 414, 419, 422, 542, 671–83, 673, 678, 680, 695
Amin, S. 26
Amos, O. M. 232 n.
Andersen, Esben S. 356, 359 n.
Anderson, K. 651
Anderson, P. 101, 107
Andrews, R. 607
Angel, David P. 30, 258 n., 607–19, 612
Anselin, L. 378
Antonelli, Cristiano 9, 389, 395–408, 397, 401, 402, 403
Appadurai, A. 696
Archibugi, D. 362
Arnold, David 199 n.
Arora, A. 566
Arora, S. 599
Arthur, W. B. 32, 101, 107, 115
Asheim, Bjørn T. 413–28, 415, 418, 419, 420, 421, 427, 678
Asian Development Bank 645
Atkinson, D. 467
Atkinson, G. 651
Audretsch, David B. 8, 89, 96, 133, 149, 262 n., 333–44, 375, 376, 377, 378, 381, 383, 385, 387, 388, 404, 437, 487
Autant-Bernard, C. 389
Autler, Gerald 317 n.
Axon, A. E. 232
Axtell, R. 108
Aydalot, P. 30, 547
Ayres, R. U. 586, 595

Bachtler, J. 542
Baddeley, M. 466
Baeten, G. 542, 553
Bagchi-Sen, S. 232 n.
Bagguley, P. 506
Bagnasco, A. 419
Bailey, Martin J. 527
Bailly, A. 21, 29

Bairoch, P. 363 n., 478
Baldwin, Richard E. 139
Ball, George 277
Bania, Neil 404
Bardhan, P. 198
Barff, R. 293
Barnes, B. 18
Barnes, Trevor J. 6, 19, 26, 33, 61 n., 62, 63, 66, 109, 111, 112 n., 276, 499
Barnet, R. J. 277
Barone, Larry 317 n.
Barrell, Ray 138 n., 139
Barrett, M. 503
Barro, Robert 4, 96, 106, 162, 171
Barry, Frank 141
Bartik, T. J. 485 n., 563
Bartlett, C. A. 284, 285, 441, 443
Bateman, I. J. 596
Baumol, W. 161
Baxter, C. I. 240
Becattini, Giacomo 29, 403, 414, 415, 417, 420
Beck, U. 610, 691
Becker, Gary 499 n., 506, 527
Becker, W. E. 699
Beechey, V. 506
Beeson, P. E. 96, 376, 385, 482
Beise, M. 389
Bell, Wendell 531
Bellandi, M. 415, 416, 417, 420, 421
Bellon, B. 444
Benabou, R. 457
Benko, G. 23, 542
Benton, T. 614
Berger, S. 288
Berman, E. 338
Bernis, G. D. de 356
Berry, Brian J. L. 3, 15, 21, 527 n., 565
Best, M. 233
Bhagwati, J. 649, 650
Bianchi, P. 421, 424, 425
Bianchi, S. 511
Biasiotto, M. 309
Biggart, N. W. 280, 357
Billinge, M. 19
Bingham, R. 559
Birch, D. 269 n.
Birkinshaw, J. M. 285
Black, D. 477, 478, 479, 483, 491
Blackhurst, R. 651
Blaikie, P. 614
Blanc, H. 154, 678
Blanchard, O. J. 89, 95, 457, 477, 478, 481, 490 n.
Blanchflower, D. G. 457, 466
Blank, S. 666, 667
Blau, F. 505
Blaut, J. M. 25
Block, F. 71
Blomström, Magnus 126, 342
Blonigen, Bruce A. 138 n.
Bloom, David 170, 193
Bluestone, B. 25, 320 n.
Bobbio, N. 210
Boden, D. 151, 237
Bohle, H. G. 199, 201, 206
Bordo, S. 501
Borges, Jorge Luis 195
Borjas, G. J. 483
Borts, G. H. 106
Bothwell, J. L. 233
Bouba-Olga, O. 162
Boudeville, J. R. 22
Bourdieu, P. 326, 365, 551
Bowles, P. 234
Boyer, R. 30, 63, 64, 66, 67, 259 n., 288, 458, 542
Boyle, R. 569
Bradley, H. 505
Bradley, John 141
Brainard, S. Lael 135
Branstetter, L. 382, 382 n.
Braun, D. 560
Braunerhjelm, Pontus 140 n.
Breit, W. 700
Breschi, S. 362
Bridge, G. 611
Bromley, D. 588, 596, 598
Brookfield, H. C. 32, 356, 614
Brown, L. A. 375
Brülhart, M. 691
Brusco, S. 144, 414, 415, 420, 421, 423

Brush, J. E. 20
Bryson, J. 6
Buckley, Peter J. 341
Budd, L. 215, 237
Bunge, W. 22
Bunker, S. 610, 613
Burmeister, E. 105 n.
Burrows, P. 591
Burt, R. S. 365
Burton, I. 22

Caballero, R. J. 386
Cabrales, A. 695
Cairncross, F. 253
Callon, M. 691
Camagni, R. 422–3
Campbell, B. 659, 659 n., 665, 668
Campbell, C. 696
Cantwell, J. A. 341, 342, 443
Capecchi, V. 424
Caplen, B. 219
Capron, H. 389
Carlton, D. W. 83, 485
Carnevali, F. 234
Carney, J. 25
Carrincazeaux, C. 389
Carson, Rachel 607
Case, A. 264 n.
Casey, C. 509
Caskey, J. P. 239
Cason, T. N. 599
Cassis, Y. 236
Casson, M. 341
Castells, Manuel 31, 152, 275, 293, 403, 545, 546
Catalano, A. 25
Cavendish, R. 505
Caves, Richard E. 126 n., 138, 138 n., 263 n., 318
Cawson, A. 286
Cerny, P. G. 548
Chagall, Marc 282
Chamberlin, Edward H. 100
Chambers, Daniel N. 527 n.
Chandler, Alfred D. 283, 319, 333, 334
Charrié, J. P. 674
Chaterjee, L. 231 n.
Chen, Y.-C. 158
Chenery, Hollis 565
Chichilnisky, G. 596
Chinitz, Benjamin 92, 565
Chisholm, G. 613
Cho, D.-S. 642, 642 n., 643
Chodorow, N. 501
Chorley, R. J. 23
Christaller, W. 22, 58, 154
Christoff, P. 611
Christopherson, S. 29
Ciccone, A. 483
Cincera, M. 389
Clark, Gordon L. 3–15, 4, 7, 9, 12, 13, 26, 32, 62, 62 n., 100, 101, 109, 112, 230, 235, 293, 320 n., 325, 326, 456, 464
Clark, K. B. 340, 358 n.
Clark, William A. V. 529, 529 n.
Claval, P. 19, 23
Cleveland, C. 610
Clinton, Bill 562, 569, 573
Cloke, P. 19
Coase, R. H. 264 n., 320
Coats, A. W. 700
Cobb, J. 561
Cobos, E. P. 663
Cochrane, A. 62 n., 75
Cockburn, C. 509
Coe, D. T. 157, 382
Cohen, B. J. 237
Cohen, Wesley M. 387, 388, 402
Colander, D. 700
Coleman, J. 365
Collard, D. 588
Committee on Global Change Research 619
Conejos, J. 265 n.
Considine, T. J. 610
Cook, I. 693
Cook, P. 159
Cooke, P. 5, 28, 264 n., 424, 542, 547
Corbridge, S. 32, 231
Corina, J. 457
Cornwall, A. 509
Cossentino, F. 423

Costanza, R. 589
Cotterill, R. W. 302
Courant, Paul N. 525, 527
Courchene, T. J. 663
Cournot, A. A. 100
Covill, L. 217
Cowan, R. 152
Cox, J. C. 216, 232 n., 234 n.
Cox, K. R. 24, 28, 542, 551, 560
Crang, P. 33, 99, 693
Cremeans, J. E. 654, 655, 656, 657, 658, 661, 665 n.
Crevosier, O. 420, 421
Crewe, L. 33
Cromwell, B. A. 232 n.
Crouch, C. 5 n.
Cullen, I. G. 24
Cuomo, Andrew 571
Curry, L. 22, 103
Cusunano, M. 329
Cutler, David M. 519, 519 n., 520, 527, 527 n., 531

Dacey, M. F. 21, 22
Dahmén, E. 356
Dale, A. 509
Dalle, J.-M. 9
Daniels, P. W. 29, 232
Darby, M. R. 377, 380, 382, 387, 388
Daskal, J. 573
David, Paul A. 9, 32, 403
Davies, C. 509
Davis, D. R. 488
Davis, S. J. 468, 470
de Gaay Fortmann, B. 204, 204 n.
de la Fuente, A. 162
de la Mothe, J. 445
De Long, B. 695
De Melo, J. 649
de Palma, A. 103
De Vault, M. L. 504
de Waal, A. 198, 198 n., 199 n., 202, 205, 206
De Witt, J. 617
Dear, M. 25
Decressin, J. 457
Dei Ottati, G. 425, 426
DeLong, B. 94
Demsetz, H. 320
Denis, D. J. 302
Denton, Nancy A. 519, 520, 521, 523, 524, 525
Department of Foreign Affairs and International Trade (DFAIT) (Canada) 655
Deseran, E. 509, 512
Devereux, S. 198
Dewar, M. 560
Di Giovanna, S. 68, 693
Dicken, Peter 31, 69, 70, 275, 275–88, 276, 278, 279, 283, 284, 292, 293, 294, 455, 616, 651, 680
Dickenson, R. E. 20
Dimou, P. 416, 419
Dixit, Avinash 51, 103, 110, 397
Dobkins, L. H. 478, 491
Doeringer, P. 565
Donaghu, M. T. 293
Dore, R. 288, 360
Doremus, P. N. 11, 280, 281
Dosi, G. 108, 359, 691
Dow, Sheila C. 62, 233, 234
Doyal, L. 209
Drake, Tracey A. 138, 138 n.
Dreze, J. 198, 199 n., 200, 201, 207
Dumais, G. 84, 89, 92, 478, 485, 487, 488, 489
Duncan, S. S. 28
Dunford, M. F. 26, 109, 542
Dunford, Michael 679
Dunning, John H. 126, 136, 156, 162, 275, 280, 284, 336, 337, 343, 439, 443, 448, 681, 682
Dymski, G. A. 239, 240

East Asia Analytical Unit 281
Eaton, J. 95, 96, 157, 479, 483, 490
Eberts, R. 482
Eckstein, Z. 94, 95, 479, 483, 490
Edquist, C. 359 n., 360, 437
Edwards, R. 470
Eggers, Mitchell L. 530, 531

Ehrenreich, A. 505
Eichengreen, B. 457
Eisinger, P. 562, 563
Ekholm, Karolina 140, 140 n.
Ellen, Ingrid G. 529–30, 532, 533
Elliot, L. 467
Ellis, M. 509, 512
Ellison, G. 6, 480
Elster, J. 595
Emel, J. 614
Emmanuel, A. 26
Engelbrecht, Hans-Jurgen 402
Engels, Friedrich 543
England, K. 503, 504, 509
Enloe, C. 503
Ennals, R. 427
Enright, M. 254, 263 n., 266 n., 567
Epstein, J. M. 108
Escobar, A. 611, 614
Esping-Andersen, G. 209
Esslezbichler, J. 111
Esty, D. 612
European Commission 139, 460, 468, 676
Evans, P. 457
Evans, Peter 206

Faber, M. 600
Fainstein, S. 545
Farley, Reynolds 520, 520 n., 521, 521 n., 522, 525, 526, 531, 532, 533
Fatas, A. 457
Featherstone, M. 545
Feenstra, Robert C. 136
Feis, H. 363 n.
Feldman, Maryann P. 3–15, 8, 31, 89, 96, 149, 262 n., 373–89, 375, 375 n., 376, 377, 378, 383, 385, 386, 387, 388, 395 n., 403, 404, 437, 487
Feldstein, M. 485 n.
Feller, Irwin 343
Fellmann, J. D. 19
Ferber, M. 505
Ferner, A. 470
Fernie, J. 306, 311
Ferrucci, L. 421
Fields, Gary 317 n.
Fine, Ben 197, 198, 198 n., 199 n., 200, 202, 209, 457, 458, 461
Fine, G. 509
Fischer, A. M. 695
Fischer, K. 615
Fisher, P. 563
Fitzsimmons, M. 614
Florence, Sargent 690 n.
Florida, R. 376, 385, 486, 616
Folbre, N. 502 n., 503, 504
Foley, D. K. 108
Folkerts-Landau, D. 220, 221
Fontagné, L. 157
Foray, Dominique 9, 152, 403
Forbes, D. 26, 32
Ford, Henry 324
Foucault, Michel 18, 197, 500, 690
Frank, A. G. 26
Frank, R. 159
Frankel, J. A. 13, 649, 695
Franks, J. 217, 219
Fransman, M. 358 n.
Fraser, Nancy 198, 208, 511
Freeman, Christopher 354, 355 n., 358 n., 360, 362, 363, 366, 366 n., 402, 403, 407
Freeman, R. B. 457, 466
Frey, William 520, 520 n., 521, 521 n., 522, 525
Friedmann, J. 21, 283
Fröbel, F. 31, 320 n.
Froot, Kenneth A. 138 n.
Fruin, W. M. 329
Fua, G. 417
Fuelhart, K. 565, 567
Fuentes, A. 505
Fujimoto, T. 358 n.
Fujita, Mashisa 4, 51, 53, 57, 101, 133 n., 479, 480
Fukuyama, F. 365

Gabaix, X. 95
Gabor, A. 263 n.
Gallup, John L. 169–93, 170, 171, 191, 192, 193
Gamble, A. 651

Garcia-Mila, T. 92 n.
Garcia-Ramon, D. 509
Gardiner, Jean 503, 504
Garofoli, G. 418, 419, 420, 421
Garrison, William L. 21
Garrod, G. 596
Garvin, D. 341
Gasper, D. 198
Gassmann, O. 441
Geiger, R. 174
Gentle, C. J. S. 232
George, P. 20
Gereffi, G. 292, 311
Gerlach, M. L. 280
Gertler, Meric S. 3–15, 5, 30, 31, 68, 234, 253, 259 n., 276, 281, 308, 576, 683, 693
Ghoshal, S. 284, 285, 441, 443
Gibb, Richard 651, 673, 674, 677
Gibbons, M. 365
Gibbs, D. 611, 612
Gibson, G. 569
Gibson-Graham, J.-K. 9, 63, 510, 510 n.
Giddens, A. 27, 28, 29, 113
Gilligan, C. 501
Giloth, R. 572
Giordani, M. G. 421
Gittelman, Michelle 136
Glaeser, Edward L. 6, 83–96, 84, 86, 88, 89, 90, 91, 92, 93, 94, 95, 258 n., 376, 380 n., 382, 383, 384, 477, 478, 480, 481, 483, 486, 488, 490, 519 n., 531, 566
Glasmeier, Amy K. 262 n., 422, 559–76, 561, 564, 565, 566, 567, 571
Glendon, S. 89, 91
Glenn, E. 504
Glennie, P. 697
Glucksmann, M. 503
Godlund, S. 20
Goldberg, M. A. 232 n.
Golledge, R. G. 24
Goodhart, C. A. E. 695
Goodman, D. 199 n., 209
Goodman, E. 414
Goodwin, M. 68
Goodwin, R. M. 113
Gordon, D. M. 70
Gordon, P. 509
Gore, Charles 203
Goss, J. 697
Gough, I. 209
Gould, P. 22, 24
Gouldson, A. 610
Goux, J. 691
Grabher, G. 276, 551
Graedel, T. E. 611
Graham, F. D. 56
Graham, G. 220
Graham, J. 34, 67
Gram, H. 105
Granovetter, Mark 279, 320, 321, 417, 464, 690
Gray, H. Peter 343
Greenaway, D. 158
Greenhut, M. L. 101, 103
Gregory, D. 24, 26
Gregson, N. 504, 698
Gren, I.-M. 596
Griliches, Z. 375 n., 377
Grilli, V. 106
Gross, Andrew B. 520, 521 n.
Grossberg, M. 509
Grotz, E. 501
Group of Lisbon 543
Groupe de reflexion pour les strategies industrielles (GRESI) 356
Groupement de Recherche Européenne sur les Milieux Innovateurs (GREMI) 422
Gruber, W. H. 337
Guerrieri, P. 362, 438
Gustavsen, B. 427
Gyourko, J. 482

Haar, J. 666, 667
Hägerstrand, T. 20, 24
Haggett, P. 23
Haining, R. 9
Hajer, M. 610
Hakim, C. 506
Halford, S. 504, 508, 509
Hall, P. 29, 546
Hall, R. 483

Hamilton, G. G. 280, 281, 357
Hammel, D. 560
Hamnett, C. 545
Hamoudi, Amar 192
Hannan, T. H. 238
Hanson, Gordon H. 136, 477–91, 484, 488, 489, 490
Hanson, P. 27
Hanson, S. 27, 68, 114, 456, 505, 506, 510
Hao, Y. 643
Harcourt, G. C. 101, 105
Harding, S. 501
Harris, C. D. 20, 58, 484
Harrison, Bennett 25, 258 n., 262 n., 284, 320 n., 417, 418, 419, 434, 447, 565, 566, 571, 575
Harrison, Roderick J. 521, 522
Hart, O. 264 n.
Hartmann, H. 503, 510
Hartshorne, R. 20
Harvey, David 22, 25, 26, 102, 104, 111, 231, 231 n., 238, 322 n., 324 n., 458, 471, 505 n., 543, 545, 546, 610, 611
Hatzichronoglou, T. 364
Hausman, D. M. 690
Head, C. K. 376, 377, 384
Head, K. 486
Heal, G. 596
Healey, M. 611, 612
Heaton, G. 616
Hecht, S. B. 32
Heery, E. 467
Held, D. 70, 292, 616
Helleiner, E. 237
Heller, P. 204
Helliwell, J. F. 663
Helper, Rose 525
Helper, S. 374 n., 565, 566
Helpman, Elhanan 106, 131, 146, 147 n., 150, 157, 382
Henderson, J. V. 31, 89, 92, 376, 383, 384, 387, 479, 479 n., 485, 486
Henderson, R. 388
Henderson, V. 477, 478, 479, 483, 491
Henry, N. 456, 468
Herod, A. 68, 112, 456, 464, 471
Hertz, E. 695
Herzenberg, S. A. 471
Hines, J. R. 485, 490
Hirschman, Albert O. 26, 356, 565
Hirst, Paul 32, 66, 70, 209, 543, 548, 616
Hobsbawm, E. J. 355 n.
Hochschild, A. 504
Hodgson, G. M. 32, 62, 416, 416 n., 464, 542
Hoekman, B. 649
Holland, J. H. 108
Hollingsworth, J. R. 68, 288
Holly, B. P. 232 n., 238
Holmes, John 649–68, 651, 666
Holmes, T. J. 93–4, 485 n., 488, 490
Holt-Jensen, A. 19
Holzer, Harry J. 519 n., 531
Hoover, E. M. 22, 59, 83
Hopt, K. J. 10
Horstmann, Ignatius 130
Hoshi, T. 695
Hotelling, H. 103, 318–19
Hotz-Hart, Beat 432–49
Hounshell, D. 327
House, R. 218, 220
Hout, T. 324 n.
Houthakker, H. 13
Hu, Y.-S. 278–9, 281
Hudson, Ray 69, 465, 680
Hughes, S. 281
Humphries, J. 498, 499, 505, 506, 512 n.
Hutchinson, R. W. 234
Hutton, W. 468
Hyman, R. 470
Hymer, Stephen 283, 284, 319, 320 n., 335–6

Iansiti, M. 340
Ihlanfeldt, Keith R. 519 n., 531
Illeris, S. 233
Immergluck, D. 240
Imrie, R. 74
Ingham, Veronica H. 253
International Monetary Fund (IMF) 626, 628, 645
Ioannides, Y. 478, 491

Irvine, S. 225
Irwin, D. A. 377
Isard, Walter 21, 22, 318, 353, 565, 613
Isserman, A. 23
Itagaki, H. 633 n.
Ito, T. 226, 227

Jackson, A. 653, 655, 662, 665, 666
Jackson, C. 505
Jackson, Kenneth T. 525
Jackson, P. 226
Jacobs, Jane 84, 91, 384, 385
Jacobsen, J. P. 498, 505, 506
Jacoby, S. M. 470
Jaeger, K. 512
Jaffe, A. B. 96, 260 n., 262 n., 375, 376, 377, 377 n., 378, 379, 380, 384, 386, 387, 389, 404, 487, 599, 609
Jänicke, M. 599
Japan Economic Planning Agency 645
Japanese External Trade Organization (JETRO) 627, 628
Jargowsky, Paul A. 521, 530, 531–2
Jencks, Christopher 519 n., 531
Jensen, M. C. 304
Jessop, B. 64, 65, 68, 71, 72, 74–5, 76, 239, 470, 548
Jessop, R. 205, 209
Johnson, B. 155, 360, 365, 425
Johnson, M. 561
Johnston, R. J. 19
Jonas, A. 464
Jones, D. 470
Jones, K. 309
Jones, M. 74
Jorgensen, D. 609
Joyce, M. 695
JP Morgan 306
Judge, D. 551
Justman, M. 385, 488

Kain, John F. 83, 518–34, 519 n., 523, 524, 525, 526, 527, 527 n., 530, 531
Kaldor, N. 108
Kalecki, M. 101, 109
Kaminski, Bartlomiej 141
Kandel, E. 695
Kanter, R. M. 439, 443, 509
Kargon, R. 373
Karlen, David H. 527, 529, 530
Kasarda, John 531
Katz, L. F. 89, 95, 457, 477, 478, 481, 490 n.
Katzenstein, P. J. 354
Kearns, G. 547
Keating, M. 32, 542
Keeble, D. 154
Keene, D. 202
Keller, Catherine 501
Keller, W. 382
Kelley, M. 565, 566
Kelley, W. P. 653
Kelly, Jim 222
Kerfoot, D. 506
Kerr, C. 458
Keynes, M. 101
Killick, J. R. 232
Kim, S. 484–5
Kimura, Fukunari 138
Kindleberger, Charles 231, 232, 319
King, L. J. 22
Kinnaird, V. 503, 509
Kirman, A. 108
Klein, B. 264 n.
Klenow, P. J. 377
Kline, S. J. 360, 375
Knickerbocker, F. 319
Knights, D. 506
Knudsen, D. C. 458
Kobayashi, A. 505, 509
Kofman, E. 543
Kogut, Bruce 340, 380, 381
Kojima, Kiyoshi 139, 642 n., 643
Kokko, Ari O. 126, 342
Kondo, D. 509
Köppen, Wladmir 174
Korten, D. C. 598
Kortum, S. 157, 338
Korzeniewicz, M. 293
Kostecki, M. 649
Kotz, M. 67
Kozul-Wright, R. 335, 336

Krätke, S. 68
Kravis, Irving B. 135 n.
Krugman, Paul 3, 4, 11, 23, 49–58, 51, 53, 54, 56, 57, 63, 84, 99, 100, 101, 103, 104, 105 n., 106, 107, 107 n., 131, 146, 147 n., 150, 152, 258 n., 276, 373 n., 378, 379, 402, 403, 437, 457, 466, 479, 484, 487, 488, 490, 550, 645 n., 677, 691
Kuemmerle, W. 443
Kuhn, T. S. 34
Kumar, A. 217, 218, 223, 224, 666
Kumon, H. 633 n.
Kunda, G. 509
Kurz, H. 106, 106 n.
Kurz, M. 694
Kusmer, Kenneth L. 525
Kuznets, S. 353, 365
Kynaston, D. 236

La Porta, R. 13
Lamberton, Don 402
Lane, D. 232
Langer, J. 573
Langton, C. G. 108
Lansbury, Melanie 139
Larudee, M. 665
Latour, B. 18, 34
Laulajainen, Risto I. 215–28, 227
Laurenti, Luigi 529
Lawless, P. 456, 457, 461
Lawrence, R. Z. 466
Lazonick, W. 426, 427, 447, 447 n.
Leamer, Edward E. 133, 336
Leborgne, D. 31, 67
Lee, Barrett A. 527 n.
Lee, Roger 6, 62, 235, 241, 242, 276, 500 n., 613
Lefebvre, Henri 236, 322 n.
Leff, E. 614
Leichenko, R. 561
Leidner, R. 504
Leontief, Wassily 147 n., 565
Lerner, J. 338, 377, 388
Leslie, D. 311
Leslie, S. 373
Lever, W. F. 31
Levin, R. C. 385
Levinsohn, James 133
Levinthal, Daniel A. 388, 402
Levitt, B. 566–7
Levy, F. 161
Leyshon, A. 32, 230, 231 n., 236, 239, 240, 242, 693, 695, 699
Lichtenberg, F. R. 376, 386
Lichter, D. 512
Lieberson, Stanley 524, 526
Liebeskind, J. P. 387
Limao, Nuno 132
Lincoln, J. R. 280
Lindisfarne, N. 59
Liossatos, P. 109
Lipietz, A. 25, 30, 31, 65, 67, 542, 611
Lipsey, Robert E. 135 n.
Lipton, Michael 196
List, Friedrich 354–5, 355 n.
Livas, R. 488
Livingstone, D. N. 19, 33
Lloyd, M. G. 552
Lloyd, P. 455
Locke, R. 471
Loesch, A. 383
Logan, J. 552
Lohani, B. 617
Lord, D. 232 n.
Lösch, August 22, 58, 101, 103, 154, 231
Loughlin, J. 542
Loveman, G. 338
Loveridge, R. 460
Lovering, J. 30, 70, 73, 74, 678
Lowe, M. 33, 301, 504
Lucas, R. E. 83, 84, 373 n., 382, 479, 479 n., 482, 483
Luce, C. 471
Lukermann, F. 20, 102
Lundvall, Bengt-Åke 152 n., 155, 264 n., 353–67, 354, 356, 359, 359 n., 360, 362, 365, 402, 403, 413, 425, 691
Lung, Y. 389
Luria, D. 565
Lynch, Merrill 309–10, 311

McCall, J. 258 n.
McCarty, H. H. 20
McCloskey, D. 690
McCormick, B. 457
McCullum, J. 663
McDowell, J. M. 238
McDowell, Linda 4, 27, 31, 33, 62 n., 68, 276, 456, 467, 497–513, 498, 500 n., 504, 505, 506, 508, 695
McGovern, S. 106
McGuire, T. 92 n.
Mackay, R. R. 234, 235
McKelvey, M. 359
McKenna, Joseph P. 527, 529, 530
Mackenzie, S. 498
McKillop, D. G. 234
MacLeod, G. 67, 68
McNally, Rand 177
McPherson, M. S. 690
Madanipour, A. 457, 461
Maddison, A. 363 n.
Magee, S. P. 338
Maier, A. 28, 325, 542, 551, 693
Maillat, D. 423
Malecki, E. J. 29, 375
Malenbaum, W. 610
Malerba, F. 362
Malmberg, Anders 31, 365, 547, 678
Mandelbrot, B. B. 694
Mannheim, K. 19
Mansfield, Edwin 157, 385, 404
Marble, D. F. 21
March, J. G. 566–7
Marchak, M. P. 238
Marcus, C. E. 239, 240
Maré, D. C. 258 n., 481
Marelli, E. 109
Markusen, A. 29, 320 n.
Markusen, James R. 126, 130, 131
Marshall, Alfred 59, 364, 385, 389, 414, 415, 416, 416 n., 418, 420–1, 422, 426 n., 479, 564, 690
Marshall, J. N. 232, 233
Marston, S. T. 457
Martin, P. 107
Martin, Ronald L. 3, 4, 23, 26, 62, 62 n., 63, 66, 100, 106, 231, 232, 233, 234, 235, 237, 417, 455–71, 456, 457, 464, 468, 470, 471, 677
Marx, Karl 101, 105 n., 109, 111, 197, 324 n., 543
Maskell, Peter 353–67, 354, 362, 364, 365, 547, 678
Massard, N. 389
Massey, Doreen 25, 26, 27, 61 n., 76, 276, 283, 319, 320 n., 455, 498, 507, 507 n., 542
Massey, Douglas S. 519, 519 n., 520, 521, 521 n., 523, 524, 525, 530, 531
Mathias, P. 587
Matthews, J. T. 609, 612
Maurice, M. 357
Mayer, Susan 519 n., 531, 554
Meegan, R. 25, 27, 61 n., 320 n.
Meir, R. 559
Mellinger, Andrew C. 169–93
Menzel, U. 354
Merlin, P. 23
Merton, R. 694
Metcalfe, S. 437
Michalak, W. 651
Michie, R. 542
Mies, M. 505, 510
Miller, G. J. 696, 697, 700
Miller, W. 568
Mingione, E. 545
Ministry of International Trade and Industry (MITI) (Japan) 627
Minns, R. 234
Miracky, W. 92, 93
Mirowski, P. 690
Mishel, L. 161, 466
Mitchell, K. 693
Mitter, S. 505
Miyamachi, Y. 67
Mody, Ashoka 90, 135, 135 n., 138, 485
Mok, A. L. 460
Mol, A. 610
Molho, I. I. 509
Molotch, H. L. 151, 552
Molyneux, P. 234, 235
Momsen, J. 503, 509
Monk, J. 509
Montgomery, E. 376, 385

Mooij, J. 204, 207, 207 n.
Moomaw, R. L. 384, 484
Moore, Barrington 203
Moore, Henrietta 498
Moore, P. 216
Moran, M. 236
Morgan, G. 506
Morgan, K. 5, 264 n., 424, 547
Mori, T. 57
Morishima, M. 109
Morrill, R. L. 21
Morris, L. 503
Morrison, A. J. 285
Moses, L. N. 22
Moulaert, F. 62 n., 66, 68, 69, 542
Mowery, D. C. 361
Mueller, W. F. 302
Muller, Larissa 317 n.
Muller, R. E. 277
Munnell, Alicia H. 525
Murphy, J. 610
Murphy, L. 233
Murray, G. 471
Muth, Richard 527
Myrdal, Gunnar 26, 446 n., 565

Nadvi, K. 32
Nagurney, A. 100 n.
Nakamura, R. 384, 485
Nardinelli, C. 91
Neidercorn, D. 83
Nell, E. 110
Nelson, Julie 499, 500, 501, 502, 512
Nelson, Richard R. 32, 108, 340, 341, 359 n., 402, 403, 407
Newlands, D. A. 552
Nilsson, J.-E. 680
Niosi, J. 444
Nivola, P. 559
Nohria, N. 284
Nolan, P. 202
Nonaka, K. 365
Noonan, C. 342
Nooteboom, B. 678
Norman, G. 101, 103
North, D. 318, 320, 690
Noyelle, T. 232 n.
Nyden, P. 559
Nystuen, J. D. 21

Oates, W. E. 599
Oberhauser, A. 503, 509
O'Brien, Richard 31, 215, 230, 543
O'Connor, J. 614
O'Connor, K. 32, 235
Odell, K. A. 232
Odland, J. 509, 512
Office of National Statistics (UK) 502, 503 n.
Office of Technology Assessment 284
O'Hara, M. 695
Ohmae, K. 276, 277, 282, 543
Olds, K. 33, 62 n., 235, 693
O'Neil, J. 595
O'Neill, P. M. 71
Organization for Economic Cooperation and Development (OECD) 433–4, 435, 436, 437, 444, 447, 457, 469, 601, 603, 617, 628, 649, 661
O'Riordan, T. 585
Orru, M. 281
Osmani, S. 198, 199, 202 n.
Oswald, A. J. 457, 466
Ottaviano, G. I. P. 107, 480, 691
Overby, A. B. 240
Oxley, J. E. 361
Ozawa, T. 642, 642 n., 643

Pacione, M. 241
Pack, J. R. 568
Pain, Nigel 138 n., 139
Palander, T. 22
Panagariya, A. 650
Papadopoulos, A. 552
Paquet, G. 445
Park, W. G. 382
Parpart, J. 505
Pascal, A. 258 n.
Pasinetti, L. L. 101, 105, 105 n.
Patchell, J. 426
Patel, P. 284, 438
Pateman, C. 501
Paterson, T. W. 302
Pauly, L. W. 233, 281, 282

Pavitt, K. 284, 438
Payne, A. 651
Pearce, D. W. 586, 593, 596
Pearson, N. D. 695
Pearson, R. 505
Peck, Jamie 31, 32, 61–75, 63, 65, 67, 68, 74, 76, 233, 276, 456, 464, 469, 542, 545, 560
Peet, R. 19, 25, 31, 611, 614
Penrose, E. 357
Peri, G. 483
Perloff, H. S. 477
Perrons, D. 26
Perroux, François 22, 418, 435, 446 n., 565, 567
Peters, A. 563
Peters, B. 695
Pettigrew, Thomas 526
Petty, Sir William 700
Phares, Donald 527, 529
Philo, C. 547
Philpott, J. 466, 469
Pianti, M. 362
Pinder, D. 673
Piore, Michael J. 30, 321, 334, 339 n., 420, 426, 435, 563, 564
Pisano, Gary 339
Piscitello, L. 341
Plummer, P. S. 9, 100, 110, 113
Pohl, W. 174
Polanyi, Karl 197
Polanyi, M. 260 n., 361, 690
Polenske, Karen 575
Pollard, J. S. 238, 239
Pollert, A. 30, 465, 505
Pollin, R. 471
Ponsard, C. 22
Poovey, M. 690, 700
Porteous, D. 235
Porter, Michael E. 8, 31, 56, 93, 253–72, 254, 256, 256 n., 257 n., 259 n., 263 n., 264 n., 265 n., 266 n., 268 n., 279, 280, 284, 359 n., 426, 426 n., 435, 436, 443, 447, 447 n., 550, 564, 570–1, 574, 599, 625, 677, 681
Pouder, R. 262 n.
Powell, P. T. 602
Power, M. 691 n.
Pratt, A. C. 62
Pratt, G. 68, 456, 503, 505, 506, 510
Pratt, J. 239
Pred, A. 24, 29, 53, 102
Preston, V. 509
Preteceille, E. 25
Pringle, R. 505, 509
Pryke, M. 235, 236, 695
Puga, D. 53, 56, 480 n., 691
Putnam, R. D. 365, 427
Pyke, F. 417, 423

Quah, D. 87, 490
Quigley, John M. 484, 519 n., 527, 527 n., 530

Radelet, Steven 132, 192, 617
Rappaport, J. 86, 87, 88, 90, 94
Rauch, J. 91, 94, 258 n.
Read, V. 695
Redclift, M. 614
Redding, S. G. 281
Reder, M. W. 700
Rees, J. 29
Reger, G. 442
Regional Studies 456, 464
Reich, Robert B. 466, 562, 674
Reich, S. 281, 282
Reimer, S. 311, 467, 468
Reinertsen, D. 324 n.
Rhoades, S. 239
Riboud, Michelle 141
Ricardo, David 101, 146
Richards, P. 201 n., 203
Richardson, G. B. 357
Richardson, R. 233
Rifkin, J. 12
Rigby, David L. 9, 26, 101, 109, 111, 112, 113
Riposa, G. 569
Rivera-Batiz, F. L. 480
Roback, J. 482
Robbins, Lionel 195
Robins, K. 30, 31

Roebuck, Sears 295
Roemer, J. 109, 111 n.
Rogers, E. 264 n.
Romeo, A. 157
Romer, Paul M. 83, 104, 106, 373 n.
Romero, G. 503
Roodman, D. 585
Roome, N. 615
Rorty, R. 18, 19
Rose, G. 498
Rosen, S. 482
Rosenberg, N. 360, 375
Rosenfeld, S. 561, 564
Rothwell, R. 360
Roweis, S. T. 25
Rowthorn, R. 335, 336
Rowthorne, B. 25
Rubery, J. 506, 512 n.
Rugman, A. 659
Ruigrok, W. 278, 650
Russell, C. S. 602
Ruth, M. 610

Sabel, Charles, F. 30, 321, 334, 339 n., 420, 426, 435, 563, 564
Sachs, Jeffrey, D. 132, 169–93, 170, 191, 192, 193, 195, 196–7, 617
Sadler, D. 542
St John, C. 262 n.
Sako, M. 360
Sala-i-Martin, X. 4, 94, 162
Salais, R. 4, 11, 31, 209, 321, 551
Sally, R. 276, 280
Salvadori, N. 106, 106 n.
Salzinger, L. 504
Samuelson, Paul A. 52, 104, 466
Sandercock, L. 545
Sandler, T. 586, 599, 600
Sands, C. 655
Sapsford, D. 457
Sard, B. 573
Sartre, Jorge Luis 195
Sassen, S. 283, 545
Savage, M. 28
Saxenian, Anno 5, 31, 68, 151, 260 n., 282, 317 n., 373 n., 435
Sayer, Andrew 28, 29, 33, 61 n., 62 n., 100, 465
Schaefer, F. K. 20
Schaefer, S. 217, 219
Schafer, Robert 527 n.
Schelling, Thomas C. 529
Scherer, F. M. 335
Schhoenberger, E. 693
Schipper, L. 610
Schmalensee, R. 599
Schmandt, J. 562
Schmitt, J. 466
Schmitz, H. 32
Schnare, Ann B. 527 n., 531
Schoenberger, Erica 30, 62 n., 276, 286, 317–30, 320 n., 324 n., 329
Scholte, J. A. 546
Schot, J. 615
Schuman, Howard 526
Schumpeter, J. A. 444, 543
Schwanen, D. 655
Schweitzer, F. 108
Schweke, B. 563
Scott, Allen J. 4, 11, 18–35, 22, 25, 26, 30, 31, 62, 68, 101, 109, 150, 152 n., 233, 256 n., 264 n., 319, 321, 546, 551, 563, 564, 567, 678
Scott, H. S. 222
Seccombe, W. 503
Seeborg, M. 512
Sen, Amartya, K. 198, 199, 199 n., 200, 201, 202, 202 n., 203, 205, 206, 207, 209, 210, 504, 595
Sengenberger, W. 339, 417, 423
Senghaas, D. 354
Sergio, Marchi 655
Servon, L. 573
Shatz, Howard J. 125–42, 135, 135 n.
Shear, W. B. 241
Sheppard, Eric S. 6, 9, 26, 62, 99, 99–114, 109, 110, 111, 112 n.
Shirreff, D. 221
Shleifer, A. 94
Shulman, B. J. 561
Siebert, H. 106
Siegal, Abby 317 n.

Sierra, C. 154, 678
Silverberg, G. 107, 108
Simmie, J. 31
Simon, C. 91
Simonian, H. 282
Simonis, U. 610
Sinclair, T. 237
Sjoquist, David L. 519 n., 531
Skea, J. 588
Slater, S. 25, 26
Smelser, N. 279
Smith, Adam 170, 177, 354, 355
Smith, Adrian 679
Smith, Alasdair 130
Smith, C. 220
Smith, D. 4, 376, 385, 455
Smith, D. F. 486
Smith, D. L. G. 306
Smith, K. 433
Smith, N. 26, 28, 322 n., 324 n., 614
Smith, P. 324 n.
Smith, Y. 461
Snow, L. 569
Socolow, R. 615
Soja, E. W. 25, 26
Sokoloff, K. L. 382
Solow, R. 456
Sölvell, Ö 256 n.
Sørenson, Annemette 520
Sparks, L. 306
Spencer, R. W. 700
Spender, J.-C. 260 n., 365
Sraffa, P. 101, 102 n., 109
Sridhar, K. S. 569
Stafford, H. 29, 614
Stahl, H. 389
Stalk, G. 324 n.
Standing, G. 465
Stanley, C. 237
Steedman, I. 105
Stein, Jeremy C. 138 n.
Stein, J. L. 106
Steinmetz, G. 64
Stephan, P. E. 373 n., 381, 387, 388, 404
Stern, P. 618, 619
Sternberg, R. 343
Stevens, B. H. 21
Stewart, F. 356
Stichter, S. 505
Stiell, B. 503, 504
Stigler, G. 258 n.
Stiglitz, Joseph E. 51, 103, 110, 407, 691
Stoakes, C. 227
Stone, C. N. 552
Stopford, J. 446
Storper, Michael 4, 11, 26, 29, 31, 62, 68, 102, 146–63, 149, 152 n., 158, 160, 209, 264 n., 276, 319, 320 n., 321, 414, 424, 455, 542, 550, 551, 678
Strahler, Alan H. 174, 175
Strahler, Arthur N. 174, 175
Strange, Susan 5 n., 235, 548
Strathern, M. 696
Streeck, W. 5 n.
Struyk, Raymond J. 527 n.
Sunley, P. 3, 23, 33, 106, 416, 464, 468, 677, 678
Susman, P. 614
Sutton, John 397
Sveikauskas, L. 484
Svennilson, I. 366
Swedberg, R. 279, 464
Swedenborg, Birgitta 140 n.
Swidler, G. M. 238
Swift, J. 201, 203, 206
Swyngedouw, E. 31, 32, 62 n., 68, 276, 541–55, 542, 543, 547, 548, 549, 550, 551, 553
Szenberg, M. 700

Taeuber, Alma F. 519, 519 n., 520, 523, 524
Taeuber, Karl 519, 519 n., 520, 523, 524
Taibi, A. D. 240, 241
Tait, N. 282
Takeuchi, Kenji 138
Taub, Richard 530
Taylor, M. J. 31, 695
Taylor, P. J. 19
Teece, David J. 339, 341
Terkla, D. 565

Tett, G. 217
Thaler, R. 691
Theodore, N. 76, 469
Thisse, J.-F. 3, 23, 101, 479, 480
Thomas, E. N. 22
Thomas, H. 74
Thomas, J. 569
Thomas, W. A. 232
Thompson, E. P. 26
Thompson, G. 32, 70, 543, 616
Thompson, W. R. 375
Thorne, L. 241
Thrift, Nigel J. 26, 31, 32, 33, 62, 62 n., 70, 72, 73, 74, 231, 232, 235, 236, 237, 239, 240, 242, 276, 284, 414, 419, 420, 542, 678, 689–701, 691, 695, 697, 699
Tickell, Adam 31, 32, 63, 65, 68, 230, 230–43, 233, 235, 236, 237, 238, 560
Tilton, J. E. 610
Tobler, Waldo 174, 176, 177, 182
Tomaney, A. 673
Topalov, C. 25
Topel, R. H. 457, 481, 490 n.
Tracy, J. 482
Trajtenberg, M. 375, 379, 380, 387
Tronto, J. 504
Tu, J. 560
Turing, A. 57
Turner, B. L. 608
Turner, Margery 525
Turner, R. Kerry 585–604, 586, 593, 594, 596, 600, 602
Turok, I. 470
Twu, J.-Y. 628, 629
Tylecote, A. 358 n., 362, 438
Tzannatos, Z. 457

Ullman, E. L. 20
United Nations Conference on Trade and Development (UNCTAD) 125, 126 n., 278, 278 n., 286, 287, 662, 674, 675, 676, 681, 683
United Nations Development Programme (UNDP) 585
Urry, J. 28
Utterback, James M. 156, 402, 403

van der Linde, C. 599
van Dijk, M. P. 339
van Parijs, P. 209
van Tulder, R. 278, 650
Van Valley, T. L. 520
Varaldo, R. 421
Varian, H. R. 588
Vatn, A. 588, 596, 598
Veitch, J. M. 239, 240
Veltz, P. 32, 155
Venables, Anthony J. 51, 53, 55, 56, 125–42, 130, 131, 132 n., 158, 276, 480, 484, 488, 490, 691
Vickery, G. 439
Vigdor, J. 94
Vivarelli, M. 149, 376
von Braun, J. 196, 199, 202, 203
von Hayek, F. A. 109
von Hippel, Eric 264 n., 386, 402, 403, 443
Von Thünen, J. H. 22, 50, 57
Von Weizsacker, A. 599
von Zedtwitz, M. 441

Walby, S. 505, 506, 510, 511
Walker, M. 306
Walker, R. 25, 26, 102, 319, 320 n., 455, 465, 614
Walker, R. A. 13
Walker, R. L. 231
Walliser, B. 3
Walsh, J. 471
Walsh, V. 105
Wang, F. 90
Ward, C. 509
Warf, B. 216, 232 n., 234 n., 238
Warford, J. 593
Waring, M. 502
Warntz, W. 21
Waters, R. 228
Watts, H. D. 677, 680
Watts, Michael J. 32, 195–210, 198, 199 n., 201, 201 n., 203, 204, 206, 207 n., 209, 610, 611, 614
Webb, P. 203
Webber, Michael, J. 9, 26, 101, 109, 112, 113, 318

Weber, Alfred 22, 197, 283, 613
Webster, D. 470
Weidenbaum, M. 281
Weinberg, Daniel H. 521, 522
Weinstein, D. E. 488
Weintraub, S. 650 n., 653, 653 n., 655 n., 658, 659
Weiss, L. 543, 549
Weitzman, M. 91
Welford, R. 611
Werner, Herbert D. 527, 529, 530
Wernick, I. K. 610
Whalley, J. 650 n., 651, 652 n.
Wheeler, David 135, 135 n., 485
Wheeler, J. O. 232 n.
Whitaker, J. K. 415
White, Michael J. 531
Whitley, R. D. 279, 280, 281, 288, 357
Wiewel, W. 559
Wilcoxen, P. 609
Wilkinson, F. 154, 426, 426 n.
Williams, C. C. 241
Williamson, J. 478
Williamson, O. E. 264 n., 320, 690
Williamson, P. J. 13
Willis, K. G. 596
Wills, Jane 6, 62, 235, 276, 471, 500, 613
Wilson, A. G. 22
Wilson, E. O. 595
Wilson, R. 562
Wilson, William J. 530, 531
Windebank, J. 241
Winter, S. G. 32, 340, 341
Wise, M. 20
Wittfogel, Karl 172
Wojtkiewicz, R. 509
Wolf, H. C. 488
Wolkowitz, Carol 504–5
Wolpert, J. 24
Women and Geography Study Group (WGSG) 498
Wong, K.-Y. 106
Wood, A. 466
Wood, Peter B. 527 n.
Wood, P. R. 215, 217, 220, 221, 222, 225
Woolcock, M. 365, 366 n.
World Resources Institute 617
Wright, D. 569
Wright, E. O. 109 n.
Wrigley, N. 112, 301, 302, 305
Wrigley, Neil 292–311
Wyly, E. 560

Xenos, Nicholas 197

Yamada, T. 67
Yeung, H. W.-C. 276, 280
Yinger, John 519, 525, 526, 527, 527 n.
You, J.-I. 426, 426 n.
Youngs, G. 543

Zander, Udo 340
Zax, Jeffrey 519 n., 531
Zazzaro, A. 232
Zeitlin, J. 66
Zucker, L. G. 157, 376, 377, 380, 381, 381 n., 382, 387, 388
Zuker, L. 237
Zukin, S. 551, 552
Zunz, O. 64

Subject Index

Aalborg group 362
absorptive capacity:
innovation systems 444
research and development (R&D) 341
accumulation, regimes of 63–7
acid rain 599
acquisition, and merger: globalization 301–4
Africa:
development: climate and coastal proximity 192–3
famine 199
sub-Saharan: foreign direct investment 129
trade with USA 136
see also under individual countries
agglomeration 12, 54, 101, 258
and concentration 55–6
firms and workers 477–91
foreign direct investment 132–3
trade and industrial linkages 487–9
and urban growth 84–5
workers 481–4
see also clusters; enterprise zones; industrial districts; location; regional development
agglomeration economies 383–6
and industrial districts 415–16, 418, 420–2
and innovation 420–2, 486–7
productivity 485–6
and regional growth 486–7
universities 385
see also clusters; industrial districts; location; regional development
Alabama, development policy 563
Anglo-Saxon countries, and Japan compared: innovation 360, 361
anthropology, and feminism 498
APEC 650
Application–Adaptation model, Japanese subsidiaries 633–42
areal differentiation 20
Asda 296
Asia:
development and the environment 617
Japanese subsidiaries 631
see also East Asia; individual countries
Asian Development Bank 617, 645
Association for the Advancement of Women (AAW) (USA) 502 n.
Association of South-East Asian Nations (ASEAN) 650
electronics industry 641–2
Japanese production system in subsidiaries 633–42
trade 629, 630
associational democracy 209
associational economies 547
Auto Pact (Automotive Products Trade Agreement) 651, 651 n., 659
automobile industries:
Japanese investment in 385
Japanese subsidiaries 635–6

Bailey–Muth model, race and housing prices 527
Bank of England 232, 235, 237
Bank for International Settlements (BIS) 225, 226, 237
banking:
  Barings 235, 237
  British Gas 238
  and gender 507–8
  General Motors 238
  liquidity 221
  regional development 234
  regulation 218, 220–2
  technological change 238–9
  UK 238, 239, 507–8
  USA: weakening of social contract 239–40
  Virgin 238
Barings Bank 235, 237
Basle Accord, regulation of international finance 225–6
BCCI, and financial regulation 227
behavioural geography 23–4
Benetton 293
Bengal, famine 200
Big Bang, and financial regulation 217
biotechnology 380–1, 387
Black–Scholes–Merton model 695
Blue Arrow, and financial regulation 227
bodywork, caring work 504–5
bounded rationality 24, 340–1
Bretton Woods agreement 10
Britain, *see* UK
British Gas, banking 238
built environment, and production of wealth 323
business system approach 357–8

California School 29–30
Canada:
  Canada–US Free Trade Agreement 649, 652–8
  trade with USA 136
  see also North America
Canada–US Free Trade Agreement (CUSTA) 649, 652–8
capital:
  laws of motion and institutions 65
  mobility 10–11
  people as 380–2
  political economy 109
capital accumulation, laws of 66
Capital Adequacy Directives (CAD) 226
capital relocation, and investment flows: NAFTA 661–4
capitalism:
  critique of 25
  spatial dynamics 101
car-boot sales 698
caring, domestic labour 504
Carrefour/Promodès 293, 294, 304, 305
caveat emptor 217
C.D. Howe Institute (Canada) 653
Central and Eastern Europe (CEE), foreign direct investment 141
Central Europe, globalization of retail 297, 298
chain-linked model 360
'Changing Urban and Regional Systems in the UK' (CURS) 28
Chicago Commission of Race Relations 525
China 617
  foreign direct investment and GDP 128–9
  trade 629, 630
  see also East Asia
cities *see* urban development
civil rights movement (USA) 24
class relations 25, 325
  and institutional forms 65
  political economy 109, 110–13
  see also social relations
class structure, poverty and hunger 201–2
Cleveland (USA), racial segregation 523–4
climate:
  economic development: Africa 192
  effect on economic performance 170–1, 172–3

and gross domestic product 181, 184–8
and income 184–6, 197
and income: map 183
Köppen–Geiger climate zones: map 175
and land area 180
and population density 181, 184, 189–91
and poverty 197
see also environment
clusters:
and competition 254–65
and competitiveness 259–63, 265–6, 436
complementarities 260–1
corporate role in upgrading 269–71
development policy in USA 563–8
forces that generate proximity 150–6
incentives 261
information 260
innovation 261–3, 395–6, 436
inter-organizational forms 263–5
and knowledge as input 338–9
productivity 259–60
see also agglomeration; agglomeration economies; concentration; enterprise zones; location; regional development
Coase–Demsetz–Alchian–Williamson–North (CDAWN) school 198
Coasean School, pollution control 596, 603
coastal proximity:
and economic development 170, 177, 192–3
and sea-navigable rivers: map 178
see also rivers
Committee on Global Change Research 619
communication processes 402–8
see also knowledge spillovers
Community Reinvestment Act (CRA) (USA) 240–1, 570
comparative advantage 643
knowledge 337–42
political economy 112–13
see also competition; competitiveness; economic development; innovation
compensation principle 216
competition 253–4
classical view of 587
and clusters 254–65
and cooperation in USA 447 n.
and disequilibrium dynamics 104–5
entrepreneurship 93
and location 256–9
and location theory 318
see also competitiveness; economic development, comparative advantage
competitive assets, and globalization 70
competitive cities 547
competitiveness 8
clusters 259–63, 265–6, 436
and cooperation 433, 436–7, 447 n.
and cooperation: industrial districts 423–8
and culture 625
foreign direct investment 682
globalization 364
and knowledge: European Union 678
location 265–6
nations and multinational corporations 280
retail business in emerging markets 304–8
see also comparative advantage; competition; economic development; regional development
complementarities, clusters 260–1
complexity theory 108
see also evolution and complexity school
concentration:
and agglomeration 55–6
and diversity 91–2
firms and workers 477–91

concentration (*cont*):
  see also agglomeration; clusters; location
Consolidated Metropolitan Statistical Areas (CMSA) 377
constant capital 586
constant returns to scale 150–1
consumption:
  case study 696–9
  and post-modernism 696
  see also retail
convergence, and globalization 445
convergence debate 94–5
cooperation:
  and competitiveness 433, 436–7, 447 n.
  industrial districts 423–6, 427–8
  and innovation 423–6, 433–4
  see also clusters; knowledge spillovers; regional development
core competency 388
core-periphery model 53–5
corporate strategy
  and clusters 265–72
  innovation and stability 326–9
  see also competition; competitiveness; entrepreneurship; firms; foreign direct investment; innovation; multinational corporations
corporation, emergence of 334–5
cultural geography 33, 689–701
cultural globalization 545–6
cultural practice 99
culture:
  and competitive advantage 625
  entrepreneurship 92–3
  globalization of and information revolution 545–6

debt relief 196
decentralized industrial creativity (DIC) 421
deindustrialization 568–9
Dell 268
demand-linkage hypothesis 484
democracy, and famine 198, 208, 210
Denmark, Technology Institute 564
density:
  and transport costs 84
  see also agglomeration; clusters; industrial districts; location
Department of Foreign Affairs and International Trade (DFAIT) (Canada) 655
Department of Housing and Urban Development (DHUD) (USA) 525, 568
department stores 697
  see also consumption; retail
deregulation 71
  and the environment 594
  see also banking; Big Bang; financial regulation; foreign direct investment; globalization; international finance
Detroit, racial segregation 526, 527–8
developing countries:
  financial regulation 218
  see also newly industrializing economies; uneven development
development policy:
  USA 559–76
  see also economic development
difference, and differentiation 4–5
discrimination, *see* gender; racial discrimination
disease, and economic development 191–3
disequilibrium dynamics 104
distance 102, 103
  as commodity; political economy 110–13
  see also clusters; location; spatial theory; transportation
distribution, globalization of 292–4
diversity, and concentration 91–2
Dixit–Stiglitz 51
DIY, value of 502
domestic labour 502–4
Dutch Flower Council 271

dynamic capabilities 339–42
dynamic externality 593

e-commerce, global retailing 308–11
E-mapping 199–206
East Asia:
economic growth and foreign direct investment 626–30
economic growth and regional integration 642–4
electronics industry 640–1
exports to USA 646
financial crisis 645
foreign direct investment 625, 626–30
gross domestic product 645
growth after financial crisis 644–7
Japanese production system in subsidiaries 633–42
tandem growth 642–3
triangle trade 629
see also individual countries
East Asia Analytical Unit 281
ecological modernization school 610–11
ecology, *see* environment
economic density, and population density 180–90
economic development:
Asia: environment 617
coastal proximity 170, 177, 192–3
East Asia 626–30, 642–4
effect of climate 170–1, 172–3
effect of rivers 177–8
foreign direct investment: East Asia 626–30
geography 172–3
impact of disease 191–3
and knowledge 362
location 477–91
national states 353–67
patterns 152–6
policy (local/regional) 559–75
tropics 171
urban and regional 550–4
USA: clusters 563–8
see also competition; competitiveness; foreign direct investment; regional development economic segregation, and racial segregation in USA 518–34
economics 49–50
definition 497–8, 512
and economic geography 61
and gender 497–513
see also political economy
ecosystems, resilience 593
ecotourism 603
education:
and innovation 437
and labour productivity 483–4
see also intellectual capital; intellectual spillovers; knowledge; knowledge spillovers; learning; universities
efficiency, and technological change 397–401
electronics industry:
ASEAN 641–2
Japan 639–42
Japanese subsidiaries 635–6, 639
see also e-commerce
elites, and globalization 551–4
Ellison-Glaeser agglomeration measure 149
embeddedness 279, 417
emerging markets:
globalization of retail 304–8
see also newly industrializing countries; uneven development
Emilia-Romagna 423, 424
employment programs, USA 572
Empowerment Zones and Enterprise Communities (EZEC) 569
endogenous growth:
and climate 192
monopolistic competition 106
endogenous growth economics 677–8
endowments, and entitlements 199–201, 205
Enterprise Communities (USA) 569
enterprise unionism 471
enterprise zones 569–70
see also agglomeration; clusters; industrial districts

entitlement approach, hunger and famine 198, 199–202, 209–10
entitlement networks, and modes of production 202–6
entrepreneurship:
 culture 92–3
 and location 269
environment:
 Coasean School 596, 603
 deregulation 594
 economics of environmental assets 594–6, 597
 flow pollution and stock pollution 589–93
 and foreign aid 600
 global, regional and national capitalism 598–600
 green taxes 602
 greenhouse gas emissions 608
 location theory 613
 and the markets 585–604
 multinational corporations 71–2, 275, 276
 non-governmental organizations 608, 616
 Organization for Economic Cooperation and Development 601, 618
 Pigovian School 596, 602–3
 policy instruments 600–4
 political economy 596–600, 601–2
 regulation of industry 607–19
 resilience of ecosystems 593
 role of competition 587–9
 sustainable development 586–7
 technology and increased output 593–4
 see also climate
environmental markets 589
Erie Canal 50
ERVET 564
Ethiopia, famine 200
Eurobonds 224
Europe:
 foreign direct investment 139–42
 globalization 549
 Japanese production system in subsidiaries 633–42
 Japanese subsidiaries 631
 see also European Union; individual countries
European Commission 139, 460, 468, 676
European Economic Community (EEC) 650
European Free Trade Association (EFTA) 650
European Union (EU)
 and BIS 225, 226
 breaking down of national economies 8
 competition in durable-goods manufacturing 157–8
 competitiveness 678
 foreign direct investment 139–42, 627, 674–5
 globalization and territoriality 671–83
 gross domestic product 674–5
 international knowledge flows 159
 labour market compared to USA 457, 460, 466, 469
 multinational corporations 674–6
 outward foreign direct investment 139–42
 regionalism 677–9
 research and development 676
 securities 224–5
 spatial reach of firms 10
 see also France; Germany; Ireland; Italy; Netherlands; UK
'evolution' 52
evolution and complexity school 107–9
evolutionary economics 425
exchange rates, and foreign direct investment: Japan 628
exclusion, social and economic 545
exports:
 international investment 125
 see also trade
externality theory, pollution control 596, 598

factor content 147 n.
factor endowments:
  and dynamic capabilities 339
  and foreign direct investment 131
factor prices, and foreign direct investment 132
famine:
  entitlement approach 197, 199–200
  and poverty 202–6
  see also food security; hunger; poverty
Farrell inefficiency 397
feminism:
  and anthropology 498
  gender and economics 497–513
  see also gender
feminization, labour markets 505–6
finance:
  and location 231–3
  Marxism on 231
  and regional development 233–5
  see also deregulation; foreign direct investment; globalization; international finance
financial crisis, East Asia 645
financial markets:
  internationalization of 543, 545
  trading in: case study 693–6
financial regulation 215–28
  Basle Accord 225–6
  BCCI 227
  Big Bang 217
  Blue Arrow 227
  compensation 216
  developing countries 218
  insurance 218
  Japan 217, 218–19
  Maxwell foundations 227
  securities 218, 222–5
  UK 216, 218, 220
  USA 216, 217, 219, 228
see also deregulation; foreign direct investment; globalization; international finance
financial services:
  Germany 232
  Italy 232
  UK 231–2, 234–5
  USA 232–3
Financial Services Authority (FSA) (UK) 218
firms:
  agglomeration 477–91
  business growth and location 268–9
  characteristics and location 388–9
  gender discrimination 505–10
  information: interdependence 151–2
  spatial agglomeration 484–9
  see also corporate strategy; multinational corporations
flexibilism, neoliberal models 63–9
flexibility, local labour markets 465–9
flexible specialization 30, 66, 321
  and mass-production 339
  see also specialization
flow pollution, and stock pollution 591–3
'flying geese', economic development in East Asia 642–3
Food and Agricultural Organization (FAO) 196
food availability decline (FAD) 198
food retail, merger and acquisition 303
food security:
  entitlement approach 209–10
  entitlement networks and modes of production 202–6
  Gambia 207–8
  and gender 208
  history of hunger and poverty 195–8
  and human rights 205
  India 207
  politics of 206–9
  see also famine; hunger
Ford 325, 326
Fordism:
  decline of 545
  labour markets 457–8
  and post-Fordism 29, 31, 63–4
foreign aid, and environment protection 600
foreign direct investment (FDI) 125–6
  Africa, sub-Saharan 129
  agglomeration 132–3

foreign direct investment (FDI) (*cont*):
Asia 626
China 128–9
competitiveness 682
destination 127–9
East Asia 625
economic growth in East Asia 626–30
Europe 139–42
European Union 139–42, 627, 674–5
and exchange rates: Japan 628
and exports 125
factor endowments 131
and factor prices 132
France 544
and GDP 125, 127–8, 439, 544, 626, 674–5
Germany 544
globalization 439
Group of Seven 127
growth of 335–7
Hong Kong 628
horizontal 129–31, 135
incentives by states 287
Ireland 141
Japan 136–9, 625, 627, 628
location 132
market access 129–31, 336
multinational corporations 126
NAFTA 661–2
new trade theory 130
newly industrializing economies 627, 628, 630
non-codifiability of knowledge 341
productivity spillovers 342
research and development 337
scale economies 336
sources of 126–7
Taiwan 628
UK 141, 544
USA 133–6, 141, 627, 628
vertical 129, 131, 135
see also deregulation; financial regulation; globalization; international finance; multinational corporations
Fortune 500 681
Four Perspective Evaluation Method 640
France 356
trade, foreign direct investment and GDP 544
see also European Union
Fred Meyer 302
free markets 587–8
and environment 589
functionalism 65

Gambia:
food security 207–8
see also Africa
gambling laws 216
Gap Inc. 293, 294, 296, 301
Gateway 267
gender:
and banking 507–9
discrimination in labour markets 505–10
and economics 497–513
food security 208
high-tech workplaces 507
income differentials 511
Marxism 510
see also patriarchy
General Agreement on Tariffs and Trade (GATT) 364, 649, 651
General Motors 324 n., 325
banking 238
Genzyme 271
geographic information systems (GIS) 169, 174
geography:
end of, allegedly 275
and multinational corporations 277–82
Germany 356
financial regulation 217, 218–19
financial services 232
inward direct investment 342
small firms 339
trade, foreign direct investment and GDP 544
see also European Union

Gibrat's law 95
Gini coefficients 378
global cities 679
global commodity chains 161
global localization (globalization), political economy of 541–55
globalization 31, 32, 69–75
  acquisition and merger 301–4
  competitiveness 70, 364
  cultural 545–6
  and death of geography 275
  distribution 292–4
  e-commerce 308–11
  economic connotations 546
  elites 551–4
  environment 598–9, 612
  European Union 671–83
  foreign direct investment 439
  forms of 159–62
  and governance 72–5
  historical overview 543
  ideology of 554–5
  industrial districts 419
  information revolution 545–6
  innovation 363–4
  international knowledge flows 156–9
  international trade 56
  and local economies 162–3, 238–42
  local labour markets 465–9
  and location 147–9, 149–52, 266–8
  merger and acquisition 301–4
  and nation-state 14, 70–2, 365–7
  and national economies 442
  neo-liberal strategies 72
  regional development 444–7
  research and development 438–44
  restructuring; political and institutional 71
  retail 292–311
  role of local institutions 72–4
  Small and Medium-sized Enterprises 419, 420
  and specialization 146–7, 445–6
  and standardization 446
  territoriality: European Union 671–83
  trade theory 146–7
  see also financial regulation; foreign direct investment; international finance; multinational corporations
globalization (global localization), political economy of 541–55
governance, and globalization 72–5
government intervention, business 343
Grameen Bank (Bangladesh) 573
green taxes 602
greenhouse gas emissions 608
gross domestic product (GDP)
  and climate zones 181, 185–8
  East Asia 626, 645
  European Union 674–5
  and foreign direct investment 125, 127–8, 439, 544, 626, 674–5
  France 544
  Germany 544
  and income: map 179
  Japan 544
  North America 656
  and physical geography 169
  purchasing power parity 177, 177 n.
  purchasing power parity: map 179
  and trade 543–4, 656
  UK 544
  USA 544
  value of domestic labour 502
  see also economic development; income
Group of Eight (G-8) 549
Group of Lisbon 543
Group of Seven, foreign direct investment 127
Groupe de Recherche Européen sur les Milieux Innovateurs (GREMI) 30
Groupe de reflexion pour les strategies industrielles (GRESI) 356
Groupement de Recherche Européenne sur les Milieux Innovateurs (GREMI) 422
growth:
  and human capital 90–1
  and institutions 66

growth (*cont*):
see also economic development; local growth; regional development; urban growth
growth poles 22
growth theory *see* new growth theory
growth triangle (GT), Asia 628–30

Habitus 551
Heckscher–Ohlin theory 111, 131, 336
Heckscher–Samuelson–Ohlin theory 336, 337–8
heterarchy 680
heterogeneity 5, 12
heterogeneous space, political economy 110
hierarchy:
assumptions in economics 505
and use of metaphors in economics 499
high-tech workplaces, and gender 507
Highly Indebted Poor Countries 196–7
see also famine; food security; hunger; poverty; underdevelopment; uneven development
homo economicus 499, 500–1
Hong Kong:
foreign direct investment 628
trade 629, 630
horizontal FDI 129–31, 135
household, social relations within 503
housing, racial segregation in USA 519–30
human capital, local 90–1
human rights, food security 205
humanitarian industry, privatization 206
hunger:
class structure 201–2
and poverty 195–8, 199, 201–2, 209–10
UK 196
USA 196
see also famine
hybrid factories, Japan 633–42

'iceberg' model 52, 104
idiographic approaches 20
income:
and climate zones 184–6
and climate zones: map 183
differentials: women 511
gross domestic product and purchasing power parity: map 179
and racial segregation 523, 530–2
see also gross domestic product; pay; wages
increasing returns approach 100
see also monopolistic competition
India 204
famine 200
food security 207
individual, economists' conception of 500
Indonesia 617
see also ASEAN
industrial districts 29, 31, 100, 413–28
competitiveness and cooperation 423–8
division of labour 418
and globalization 419
information 418
innovation 420–3
learning economies 423–8
post-Fordism 422
Third Italy 417–19
see also agglomeration; clusters; location; regional development
industrial linkages, and agglomeration 487–9
industrial organization 320–1
industrial space 321–2
industry, concentration 56
information:
availability 24
clusters 260
collecting and exchanging 101
incomplete: political economy 110
interdependencies among firms 151–2
network in industrial districts 418

see also intellectual spillovers; knowledge; knowledge spillovers
information revolution, and cultural globalization 545–6
informational economies 70
initial public offering (IPO) 387–8
inner-city, development 569–72, 574
innovation 359–63
agglomeration economies 420–2, 486–7
and authority 361
capacity: industrial districts 419–23
clusters 261–3, 395–6, 436
and cooperation 433–4
and cooperation: industrial districts 423–6
definition 374–6
and education 437
and globalization 363–4
industrial districts 420–3
influence of professional traditions 437
localized technological change 395–408
and location 373–89
regional labour market 437
and restructuring 395–408
and stability: corporate strategy 326–9
see also competition; competitiveness; economic development; intellectual spillovers; knowledge; knowledge spillovers
innovation networks 432–49
see also National Innovation System approach
innovation systems 359–61, 365–7
absorptive capacity 444
and globalization 363–4, 438–49
research and development 438–44
specialization 361–2
and structure 362–3
insolvency, banking regulation 221–2
Institute for Competitive Inner Cities (ICIC) 570
institutional field, knowledge sharing 157
institutional forms, and social struggles 65
institutional theory, urban and regional development 550–1
institutional thickness 422
institutions:
causal effects and liabilities 68
change 67
and the economy 62
and globalization 72–4
and growth 66
and structure 363
insurance, financial regulation 218
Intel 268
intellectual capital 380–2
intellectual spillovers 83–4
see also education; knowledge spillovers; universities
inter-organizational forms, clusters 263–5
inter-sectoral interdependence, political economy 110–13
inter-sectoral relationships 105–7
international finance:
location 235–42
regulation 215–19; banking 218, 220–2; costs and benefits of 219–20; efficacy 227–8; international cooperation 225–7; Organization for Economic Cooperation and Development 226, 227; securities 222–5
see also deregulation; foreign direct investment; globalization
International Food Policy Research Institute (IFPRI) 196, 199
International Human Dimension Programme, Industrial Transformation (IHDP-IT) 618
international investment:
and exports 125
see also deregulation; foreign direct investment; international finance
International Monetary Fund (IMF) 549, 626, 628, 645
poverty 196

International Organization of Securities Commissions (IOSCO) 226–7
International Organization for Standardization (ISO) 612, 612 n., 616
international trade 49
  and globalization 70
international trade theory 56
  see also trade theory
internationalization, financial markets 543, 545
investment flows, and capital relocation: NAFTA 661–4
Ireland:
  foreign direct investment 141
  see also Europe; European Union
irreversibility, and location 396
'isolated state' 57
Italian School 29
Italy:
  financial services 232
  small firms 339
  Third Italy: industrial districts 417–19, 423–4
  see also Europe; European Union

Jane Adams Resource Corporation (USA) 572
Japan:
  and Anglo-Saxon countries compared: innovation 360, 361
  Application-Adaptation model 633–42
  auto plants 635–6
  economy after financial crisis 646–7
  electronics industry 635–6, 639–42
  exchange rates 628
  financial regulation 217, 218–19
  foreign direct investment 136–9, 625, 626–30
  growth 626–30
  hybrid factories 633–42
  investment in automobile industries 385
  investment in USA: localization economies 384
  labour costs and foreign direct investment 139
  Latin America: subsidiaries 632
  location of plants in USA 486
  manufacturing foreign direct investment 628
  mass production 328–9
  multinational enterprises 630–42
  and newly industrializing economies 633–42
  outward foreign direct investment 136–9
  subsidiaries: production systems 631, 633–42
  trade 629
  trade and GDP 544
  triangle trade 629
  see also East Asia
Japan Economic Planning Agency 645
Japanese External Trade Organization (JETRO) 627, 628
Japanese Multinational Enterprise Study Group (JMNESG) 633, 633 n.
jobs, *see* labour markets
just in time 324

Keynesian welfare state (KWS) 27, 63–4, 71
knowledge 34
  appropriability 386–8
  clusters 338–9
  as comparative advantage 337–42
  and competitiveness: European Union 678
  dynamic capabilities 339–42
  economic performance 362
  flows and globalization 156–9
  industrial districts 421
  sharing 157
  tacit and articulable 386, 421
  see also education; information; innovation; intellectual spillovers; knowledge spillovers; universities
knowledge spillovers 83–4, 342–4, 438
  location 156–9, 377–9
  new trade theory 158 n.

paper trails 379–80
research and development 157, 382–3
trade 382–3
see also competition; competitiveness; information; innovation; knowledge
Köppen-Geiger climate zones, map 175
Köppen-Geiger-Pohl classification 174
Korea:
financial crisis 645–6
trade 629
see also Asia; East Asia
Kroger 302

labour:
division of: industrial districts 418
division of: multinational corporations' use of 283
division of: product cycles 319–20
spatial division of 37–8, 455
turnover 468
labour costs:
Japanese foreign direct investment 139
NAFTA 664
US foreign direct investment 135
labour markets:
European Union and USA compared 457, 460, 466, 469
feminization 505–6
flexibility 465–9
gender discrimination 505–10
globalization 465–9
local 455–71
NAFTA 664–6
regulation 455–71
social reproduction 464
tertiarization 467
labour productivity 483–4
land area, and climate zone 180
Latin America, Japanese subsidiaries 632
learning:
source of dynamic capabilities 341
see also education; innovation; intellectual spillovers; knowledge; knowledge spillovers; universities
learning economies, industrial districts 423–8
learning regions 547
Leontief Paradox 338
linkages, backward and forward 55
liquidity, banking regulation 221
local economic development policy, USA 559–76
local economies:
evolution of 162–3
and globalization 162–3, 238–42
growth 85–90
localities debate 27–9
localization economies 383–4
localized technological change, and restructuring 395–408
location:
business growth 268–9
and competition 256–9
and competitiveness 265–6
concentration of economic activity 477–91
entrepreneurial management 269
finance 231–3
forces that generate proximity 149–56
foreign direct investment 132
global strategy 266–8
globalization 147–9, 149–52, 266–8
and innovation 373–89
international finance 235–42
irreversibility 396
knowledge spillovers 377–9
and money 231–3
patents 378
and practice of management 321–5
productivity 256–7, 485–6
research and development 377–9
technological change 397–401
trade and international knowledge flows 156–9
see also agglomeration; clusters; concentration; industrial districts; regional development
location theory 22, 103–4, 318–19
and competition 318

location theory (*cont*):
 environment 613
 multinational corporations 129–33
lock-in 4
Los Angeles 566, 567

Macdonald Commission (Canada) 653
macroeconomics, and development of economic geography 7
management:
 emergence of the corporation 334–5
 innovation and stability 326–9
 and location 321–2
 multi-locational corporation 319–20
 spatial and temporal processes 323–5
 as strategic activity 325–6, 340
 see also corporate strategy; firms
manufacturing, European Union 157–8
Manufacturing Extension Partnership (MEP) (USA) 564
maps:
 ice-free coasts and sea-navigable rivers 178
 income density in temperate climate zones 183
 income per person (1995) 179
 Köppen-Geiger climate zones 175
 population density (1994) 176
maquiladora industries (Mexico) 662–3
market access, and foreign direct investment 129–31, 336
markets 694
 and the environment 585–604
 and prices 587–9
 see also financial markets
Marshallian approach:
 industrial districts 413–28
 see also industrial districts
Marxism 25, 26
 and gender 510
 money and finance 231
 and regulationists 66
masculinity, *see* gender; patriarchy
mass-production:
 emergence of 334
 and flexible specialization 339
 USA 328
 see also Fordism; post-Fordism; production
Massachusetts Miracle 385 n.
Maxwell foundations, and financial regulation 227
Memoranda of Understanding (MoU) 226–7
Mercedes Benz 563
merchant banks, and gender 508
MERCOSUR 650
merger and acquisition (M&A) 301–4
metagovernance 74
metaphor, use of 499
metropolitan areas, racial discrimination: USA 518–34
Metropolitan Statistical Areas (MSA) 377
Mexico:
 maquiladora industries 662–3
 trade policy and location 489
 trade with USA 136
 wages compared to USA 484
 see also North America
milieux innovateurs 547
mini-Matsushita (mini-M) 639–40
minimum efficient scale (MES) 334, 339
Ministry of International Trade and Industry (MITI) (Japan) 627
mode of social regulation (MSR) 64
 and laws of capital accumulation 66
Model Cities Program (USA) 569
modes of production:
 and entitlement networks 202–6
 see also mass-production; production
monasteries, science parks as 507
monetary regulation *see* financial regulation
money, and location 231–3
monopolistic competition 51–2, 100–1, 103–7
 agency 107
 endogenous growth 106
 inter-sectoral relationships 105–7
 neo-classical theory 691
 spatiality 103–4

time 104–5
trade theory 106
Monte-Carlo simulation 382
Montreal Protocol 599
Moody's 236
most favoured nation (MFN) 649
multi-locational corporations, product cycles and division of labour 319–20
Multilateral Agreement on Investment 611
multinational corporations (MNCs) 71–2, 275, 276
country of origin 277–82
division of labour 283
and the environment 594, 598–9
European Union 674–6
foreign direct investment 126
and geography 277–82
Japanese 630–42
location: empirical studies 133–42
location: theory 129–33
motivations for establishing 335–7
nationality 277–82
nations and competitiveness 280
organizational hierarchy 284
power structures 285–6
as relational network 282–7
research and development 438–44
strategic options 440–1
trade within NAFTA 659
and uneven development 283
see also foreign direct investment; globalization

nation-states:
business systems 357–8
comparative advantage 9–10
compete for multinational corporations 287
development policy in USA 561–3
economic development 353–67
and globalization 14, 70–2, 365–7, 673
governance and globalization 72–5
incentives for foreign direct investment 287
innovation systems 359–64
market-led reorientation 548–50
systems of production 354–7
National Business System approach 357–8
national economies:
breaking down of in European Union 8
and development of economic geography 7
and globalization 442
National Innovation System (NIS) approach 359–67, 432–49
globalization of research and development 438–44
regional base 434–8
National Production System approach 354–7
Neighbourhood Sorting Index (NSI) 531
neo-classical theory 691
monopolistic competition 105
questioning of 690
neo-liberal models, flexibilism 63–9
neo-liberal strategies:
and globalization 72
as response to crisis 65
neo-Marshallian approach 417–19
Nestlé 268
Netherlands:
Dutch Flower Council 271
see also European Union
network intensity, and spatial structure 8
networks of social entitlements 202–6
New Biotech Entities (NBEs) 376, 381
New Deal, UK 469
new economic geography 49–51, 58–9, 99, 373–4
agglomeration and concentration 55–7, 383–6
core-periphery model 53–5
Dixit-Stiglitz model 51–3
innovation 374–6
knowledge spillovers 377–83
and location 376–7, 383–9
and spatial structure 57–8

new growth theory 51, 83–96
new institutionalism 320
New International Division of Labor (NIDL) 319–20
New Jersey 566
new trade theory 46–50
 and foreign direct investment 130
 international flows of knowledge 158 n.
 scale economies 150–1
New York City 50, 58
 watershed services 603
new-Matsushita (new-M) 640
newly industrializing economies (NIEs)
 foreign direct investment 627, 628, 630
 Japanese production system in subsidiaries 633–42
 see also developing countries; uneven development
Nigeria 204
 see also Africa
Nike 293
nitrogen oxide emissions 600
non-bank financial institutions (NBFI), securities 222–5
non-governmental organizations (NGOs), and environmental problems 608, 616
North America:
 Auto Pact 651, 651 n., 659
 Canada–US Free Trade Agreement 649, 652–8
 gross domestic product and trade 656
 Japanese production system in subsidiaries 633–42
 Japanese subsidiaries 632
 North American Free Trade Agreement 649–68
 specialization and trade 655–61
 see also Canada; Mexico; USA
North American Agreement on Labor Cooperation (NAALC) 654 n., 666
North American Free Trade Agreement (NAFTA) 549, 649, 652–68
 capital relocation 661–4
 foreign direct investment 661–2
 labour costs 664
 labour markets 664–6
 multinational corporations and trade within NAFTA 659
North-South divide, and international trade 56
Northern Telecom 268

Oceania, Japanese subsidiaries 632
Office of National Statistics (UK) 502, 503 n.
Office of Technology Assessment (USA) 284
Organization for Economic Cooperation and Development (OECD) 10, 127, 433–4, 435, 436, 437, 444, 447, 457, 469, 601, 603, 617, 628, 649, 661
 environmental policy 601, 618
 regulation of international finance 226, 227
 Technology/Economy Programme 432
organizational hierarchy, multinational corporations 284

paper trails, knowledge spillovers 379–80
patents:
 location 378
 paper trails 379–80
 universities 380
patriarchy:
 banking 508–9
 see also gender
pay, and gender 506
pensions, regulations 224
people, as capital 380–2
performance measurement, clusters 261
periphery, and core 53–5
persistence (of systems) 4
physical geography, effect on economic performance 169–93
Pigovian School, pollution control 596, 602–3

Pinault Printemps-Redoute 296
Plaza Agreement 639
Political Arithmetic (Petty) 700
political economy 24–7
 comparative advantage 112–13
 and the environment 596–600, 601–2
 food and poverty 195–210
 glocalization (global localization) 541–55
 heterogeneous space 110
 information 110
 inter-sectoral interdependence 110–13
 profits 111–12
 regional 100, 101, 109–13
 social class 109, 110–13
politics, and food security 206–9
pollution control, *see* environment
population:
 1994: map 176
 and climate zones 181, 184, 189–91
 and economic density 180–90
post-Fordism:
 and Fordism 29, 31, 63–4
 and Fordism: labour markets 457–8, 459
 and industrial districts 422
 and regulation approach 66–7
 workfare state 470
post-modernism, and consumption 696
postwar boom 21
poverty:
 class structure 201–2
 and famine 202–6
 and hunger 195–8, 199, 201–2, 209–10
 prevalence of 195–8
 UK 196
 see also income; pay; wages
power structures, multinational corporations 285–6
pre-capitalist structures, modern economies 413–14, 416
prices, and markets 587–9
privatization, humanitarian industry 206
product cycles, and international division of labour 319–20
production:
 European Union 674
 modes of: entitlement networks 202–6
 organization of and location 147–8
 systems of 354–7
 systems of: Japanese subsidiaries 633–42
 see also mass-production; modes of production
productive factors, and trade structure 336–7
productive forces, theory of 355
productivity:
 agglomeration economies 485–6
 and clusters 259–60
 and location 256–7, 485–6
 spillovers: foreign direct investment 342
 see also competitiveness; innovation
professional traditions, localized innovation 437
profits, political economy 111–12
Project Quest (USA) 572
proletarianization, process of 545
protectionism 355 n.
purchasing power parity (PPP):
 and gross domestic product 177, 177 n.
 and gross domestic product: map 179

Qualified Institutional Buyers (USA), securities 223
quantitative approach, economics 100
quantitative geography 22

racial discrimination:
 and Bailey–Muth model on housing prices 527
 Cleveland (USA) 523–4
 Detroit (USA) 526, 527–8
 US metropolitan areas 518–34
rationality 694
 economists claim to 499

realist epistemology 28
redistribution, government policy 93–4
regimes of accumulation 63–7
regional development 29–32, 73
  East Asia 643–4
  Europe 677–9
  finance 233–5
  and globalization 444–7
  innovation and agglomeration economies 486–7
  institutional theory 550–1
  labour market 437
  Marshallian local external economies 108
  North America 649–68
  restructuring and innovation 395–408
  and urban development 90–5, 550–4
  see also agglomeration; clusters; industrial districts; location
regional growth theory 106
regional political economy approach 100, 101, 109–13
regional science, and spatial analysis 21–3, 24
regional synthetic approach 20
regulation:
  banking 218, 220–2
  costs and benefits of 219–20
  efficacy 227–8
  international cooperation 225–7
  international finance 215–19
  labour market 455–71
  securities 222–5
  see also deregulation; financial regulation
regulation approach:
  environment 611
  flexibilism 63–9
  and Marxism 66
  and post-Fordism 66–7
  social relations 63
regulation theory 67–8
relational network, multinational corporations as 282–7
rent differentials 482–3
research and development (R&D) 375
  absorptive capacity 341
  European Union 676
  foreign direct investment 337
  globalization 438–44
  localized innovation 437
  location 377–9
  multinational corporations 438–44
  spillovers 157
  tacit knowledge 386
  trade and knowledge spillovers 382–3
  universities 378–9
  see also innovation; knowledge spillovers
residential segregation, USA 519–20
resilience, ecosystem 593
resources, mobile and immobile 53–4
restructuring:
  gender issues in banking 508–9
  and globalization: political and institutional 71
  technological change 395–408
  UK 28
retail:
  department stores 697
  emerging markets 304–8
  globalization 292–311
  see also consumption
retail banking, and gender 508–9
rigidity, impediment to technological change 397
rivers:
  and development 177–8
  income density in temperate climate zones 183
  sea navigable: map 178
  see also coastal proximity
Route 128, Massachusetts 435, 561
routinization:
  and bounded rationality 340–1
  as organizational knowledge 340
Royal Ahold 293, 294, 297–300, 304, 306, 307

St Lawrence Seaway 177, 177 n.
scalar gestalt 541
scale economies, motivation for foreign direct investment 150–1, 161, 336
scarcity, and liberal governance 197
science parks, as monastries 507
sea-navigable rivers:
  map 178
  see also coastal proximity
'second nature' 614
securities:
  European Union 224–5
  regulation 218, 222–5
  USA 223–4
segregation:
  gender and the labour market 506
  racial and economic in USA 518–34
Serious Fraud Office (SFO) (UK) 227–8
service industries 467
shopping malls 697–8
shrimp packing industry 486
Silicon Valley 58, 373, 435, 482, 561
Singapore:
  trade 629
  see also ASEAN; South East Asia
Small Business Innovation Research (SBIR) 388
Small and Medium-sized Enterprises (SMEs) 419, 420
  and globalization 443
social capital 365–6
social relations:
  and consumption 698
  regulation approach 63
  within the household 503
  see also class relations
social reproduction, and labour markets 464
socio-spatial dialectic 25
sociology 27
solvency, banking regulation 221
South Africa 129
  see also Africa
South East Asia, globalization of retail 299
Southern Common Market (MERCOSUR) 650
space 33, 102
  social construction of 322–3
  and time: corporate strategy 317–31
space economy 101, 542–7
spatial agglomeration 100
  economic activity 477–91
spatial allocation, economic activity 11–14
spatial analysis, and regional science 21–3
spatial division of labour 27–8, 455
spatial economy:
  approaches to 100–2
  as evolving complex system 107–9
  monopolistic competition 103–4
spatial equilibrium 85
spatial structure, and network intensity 8
spatial system 57–8
spatial theory 57–8
  dynamics of capitalism 101
  labour markets 455–71
  monopolistic competition 103–4
  von Thünen isolated state 57
  see also location
specialization:
  and globalization 146–7, 445–6
  industrial districts 418
  and trade in North America 655–61
  see also flexible specialization
stability, and innovation: corporate strategy 326–9
Standard Metropolitan Statistical Areas (SMSA) (USA), and racial segregation 520, 524, 531
Standard and Poor's 236
standardization, and globalization 446
star scientists 380–1
state *see* nation-states
stock pollution, and flow pollution 591–3
structural competitiveness 72
structuralist economists, French 356

structure-agency theory 28
structures:
  and institutions 363
  multinational corporations 285–6
sub-national regions 13
sulphur emissions 599–600
sunk costs 4, 308
superfixed production factors 397–400, 406
supranational systems 444 n.
sustainable development 586–7
sustainable welfare 587–9
systems of innovation 433–4

Taiwan:
  electronics industry 641
  financial crisis 646
  foreign direct investment 628
  trade 629, 630
  see also Asia; East Asia
'tandem growth', economic development in East Asia 642–3
tariffs *see* trade agreements
technological change:
  banking 238–9
  efficiency 397–401
  localized and innovation 395–408
  location 397–401
  and restructuring 395–408
Technology Institute (Denmark) 564
technology transfer, Japanese firms 633–4
Technology/Economy Programme (TEP), OECD 432
territoriality, and globalization: European Union 671–83
tertiarization, labour markets 467
Tesco 297
Third Italy, industrial districts 417–19, 423–4
time 104–5
  corporate strategy 317–31
  and space 102
Toyota 325
trade 467
  agglomeration 487–9
  China 629, 630
  electronics 629, 630
  France 544
  GDP 543–4
  Germany 544
  Hong Kong 629, 630
  international knowledge flows 156–9
  Japan 544, 629
  knowledge spillovers 382–3
  Korea 629
  location 156–9
  Mexico 136, 489
  North-South divide 56
  and productive factors 336–7
  Taiwan 629, 630
  UK 544
  USA foreign direct investment 133, 135–6, 544
trade agreements:
  European Union (EU) 672–4
  North America 649–68
trade theory 52, 104, 353
  and globalization 146–7
  monopolistic competition 106
  see also international trade theory
trading, financial markets: case study 693–6
training, and wages 466–7
transnational corporations (TNCs) *see* multinational corporations
transportation:
  costs and density 84
  foreign direct investment 132
  globalization 148
  political economy 111
  US foreign direct investment 135
  see also distance
triad market, European Union 671–83
triangle trade, East Asia and Japan 629
tropics:
  and economic development 191–2
  income levels 171
Tuscany 423

uberrimae fidei 217
UK:
  Bank of England 232, 235, 237
  banking 238, 239

Big Bang 217
City of London as financial centre 236, 237
concentration of financial services 231–2, 234–5
domestic labour 502, 503 n.
economic decline and restructuring 28
financial regulation 216, 218, 220
foreign direct investment 141
hunger 196
income differentials: women 511
labour turnover 468
merchant banks and gender 507–8
poverty 196
Serious Fraud Office 227–8
small firms 339
trade, foreign direct investment and GDP 544
urban regeneration and local training initiatives 74
see also European Union
underdevelopment 196
see also developing countries; famine; Highly Indebted Poor Countries; hunger
uneven development 26, 31, 559
exploited by multinational corporations 283
see also developing countries; Highly Indebted Poor Countries; newly industrializing countries
unions, local labour markets 470–1
United Nations Conference on Trade and Development (UNCTAD) 125, 126 n., 278, 278 n., 286, 287, 674, 675, 676, 681, 683
United Nations Development Programme (UNDP) 585
universities:
agglomeration economies 385
patents 380
research and development 378–9
urban development:
and agglomeration economics 84–5
institutional theory 550–1
and regional development 90–5, 550–4
UK 74
USA 568–73
see also agglomeration; clusters; location
urban economy, and whole economy 50–1
urban space 25
urbanization economies 383–4
USA 356
and Africa: trade 136
agglomeration 488
banking: weakening of social contract 239–40
Canada: trade 136
Canada–US Free Trade Agreement 649, 652–8
civil rights movement 24
Cleveland: racial segregation 523–4
clusters: development policy 563–8
Community Reinvestment Act 240–1, 570
competition and cooperation 447 n.
concentration of economic activity 477–8
Department of Housing and Urban Development 525, 568
Detroit: racial segregation 526, 527–8
development policy 559–76
e-commerce 309
East Asian exports 646
financial regulation 216, 217, 219, 228
financial services 232–3
foreign direct investment 133–6, 141, 544, 627, 628
globalization of retail 300
gross domestic product 544
hunger 196
Japanese investment: localization economies 384
knowledge and economic performance 362
labour costs: foreign direct investment 135
labour market compared to Europe 457, 460, 466, 469

USA (*cont*):
labour turnover 468
location of Japanese plants 486
mass production 328
Massachusetts 435, 561
medical devices cluster 255
multinational corporations in UK 282
New Jersey 566
New York City and watershed services 603
outward FDI 133–6, 141
Project Quest 572
Qualified Institutional Buyers 223
racial and economic segregation 518–34
securities 223–4
skilled labour as comparative advantage 338
trade 133, 135–6, 488, 544, 629, 630
urban development 568–73
wages compared to Mexico 484
women in labour market 511–12
see also North America
usury 216

valuation, environmental assets 594–6, 597
value, theory of 355
value-at-risk (VaR) models 226
Veneto 423
vertical foreign direct investment 129, 131, 135
Vietnam War 24
Virgin, banking 238

wages:
flexibility 466
Mexico and USA compared 484
regional differences 482–3
and training 466–7
see also income; labour costs; labour market; pay
Wal-Mart 293, 296–7, 301, 305, 311
Wall Street 482
war, and famine 202
watershed services 603
weak sustainability 586
wealth production, built environment 323
welfare, prices and markets 587–9
welfare-to-work (USA) 572–3
women *see* gender
Women and Geography Study Group (WGSG) 498
work 503
workers:
firms: agglomeration 477–91
geographic concentration 481–4
workfare system (USA) 469, 470
World Bank, poverty 196, 617
World Investment Report (UNCTAD) 675
World Resources Institute 617
World Trade Organization (WTO) 10, 237, 364, 611, 616, 649, 650

Zipf's law 95